COSTA RICA

Where to Stay and Eat
for All Budgets

Must See Sights
and Local Secrets

Ratings You Can Trust

Fodor's Travel Publications   New York, Toronto, London, Sydney, Auckland
www.fodors.com

FODOR'S COSTA RICA 2004

Editor: Shannon M. Kelly

Editorial Contributors: Gregory Benchwick, David Dudenhoefer, Dorothy MacKinnon, Jeffrey Van Fleet, Carol Weir

Maps: David Lindroth *cartographer;* Bob Blake and Rebecca Baer, *map editors*

Design: Fabrizio La Rocca, *creative director;* Guido Caroti, *art director;* Melanie Marin, *senior picture editor*

Production/Manufacturing: Lisa Montebello

Cover Photo (Monteverde Cloud Forest Biological Reserve): Steve Dunwell/The Image Bank

COPYRIGHT

ISBN 1–4000–1255–4

ISSN 1522–6131

SPECIAL SALES

Fodor's Travel Publications are available at special discounts for bulk purchases for sales promotions or premiums. Special editions, including personalized covers, excerpts of existing guides, and corporate imprints, can be created in large quantities for special needs. For more information, contact your local bookseller or write to Special Markets, Fodor's Travel Publications, 1745 Broadway, New York, NY 10019. Inquiries from Canada should be directed to your local Canadian bookseller or sent to Random House of Canada, Ltd., Marketing Department, 2775 Matheson Boulevard East, Mississauga, Ontario L4W 4P7. Inquiries from the United Kingdom should be sent to Fodor's Travel Publications, 20 Vauxhall Bridge Road, London SW1V 2SA, England.

AN IMPORTANT TIP & AN INVITATION

Although all prices, opening times, and other details in this book are based on information supplied to us at press time, changes occur all the time in the travel world, and Fodor's cannot accept responsibility for facts that become outdated or for inadvertent errors or omissions. So **always confirm information when it matters,** especially if you're making a detour to visit a specific place. Your experiences—positive and negative—matter to us. If we have missed or misstated something, **please write to us.** We follow up on all suggestions. Contact the Costa Rica editor at editors@fodors.com or c/o Fodor's at 1745 Broadway, New York, NY 10019.

PRINTED IN THE UNITED STATES OF AMERICA

10 9 8 7 6 5 4 3 2 1

DESTINATION COSTA RICA

Costa Rica's beauty would flatter a land ten times as large. The sheer plenty of flora and fauna packed into this tiny nation, combined with a wild variety of climates and landscapes, can make the senses reel. And for all the enchanting ecozones, beach resorts and surf sites dot both shores, mixing revelry and relaxation. Almost every trip begins and ends in Costa Rica's urban hub, the feisty capital of San José, where dining and nightlife abound. Within day tripping distance are volcanoes and rivers prime for white-water adventures. For some serious rest and relaxation, experience the Pacific side of the country, with untouched nature and massive Volcán Arenal in the north, and heading south, unspoiled beaches, world-class surfing, abundant wildlife, and virgin rain forests. Or set out for Costa Rica's eastern coast, where life marches more to Caribbean drummers than to the Central American rhythms of the rest of the country. Riding horseback toward simmering volcanoes, tramping through the rain forest, or surfing the long waves you'll discover why Costa Rica has become one of the hottest destinations in the western hemisphere. Have a fabulous trip!

Karen Cure, Editorial Director

CONTENTS

ABOUT THIS BOOK

There's no doubt that the best source for travel advice is a like-minded friend who's just been where you're headed. But with or without that friend, you'll have a better trip with a Fodor's guide in hand. Once you've learned to find your way around its pages, you'll be in great shape to find your way around your destination.

SELECTION

Our goal is to cover the best properties, sights, and activities in their category, as well as the most interesting communities to visit. We make a point of including local food-lovers' hot spots as well as neighborhood options, and we avoid all that's touristy unless it's really worth your time. You can go on the assumption that everything you read about in this book is recommended wholeheartedly by our writers and editors. Flip to On the Road with Fodor's to learn more about who they are. It goes without saying that no property mentioned in the book has paid to be included.

RATINGS

Orange stars ★ denote sights and properties that our editors and writers consider the very best in the area covered by the entire book. These, the best of the best, are listed in the Fodor's Choice section in the front of the book. Black stars ★ highlight the sights and properties we deem Highly Recommended, the don't-miss sights within any region. Fodor's Choice and Highly Recommended options in each region are usually listed on the title page of the chapter covering that region. Use the index to find complete descriptions. In cities, sights pinpointed with numbered map bullets ❶ in the margins tend to be more important than those without bullets.

SPECIAL SPOTS

Pleasures & Pastimes focuses on types of experiences that reveal the spirit of the destination. Watch for Off the Beaten Path sights. Some are out of the way, some are quirky, and all are worth your while. If the munchies hit while you're exploring, look for Need a Break? suggestions.

TIME IT RIGHT

Wondering when to go? Check chapters' Timing sections for weather and crowd overviews and best days and times to visit.

SEE IT ALL

Use Fodor's exclusive Great Itineraries as a model for your trip. (For a good overview of the entire destination, follow those that begin the book, or mix regional itineraries from several chapters.) In cities, Good Walks guide you to important sights in each neighborhood; ☞ indicates the starting points of walks and itineraries in the text and on the map.

BUDGET WELL

Hotel and restaurant price categories from ¢ to $$$$ are defined in the opening pages of each chapter—expect to find a balanced selection for every budget. For attractions, we always give standard adult admission fees; reductions are usually available for children, students, and senior citizens. Look in Discounts & Deals in Smart Travel Tips for information on destination-wide ticket schemes.

BASIC INFO

Smart Travel Tips lists travel essentials for the entire area covered by the book; city- and region-specific basics end each chapter. To find the best way to get around, see the transportation section; see individual modes of travel ("By Car," "By Train") for details. We assume you'll check Web sites or call for particulars.

ON THE MAPS	Maps throughout the book show you what's where and help you find your way around. Black and orange numbered bullets ❶ ❶ in the text correlate to bullets on maps.
BACKGROUND	In general, we give background information within the chapters in the course of explaining sights as well as in CloseUp boxes and in Understanding Costa Rica at the end of the book. To get in the mood, review the suggestions in Books & Movies. The glossary can be invaluable.
FIND IT FAST	Within the book, chapters are arranged in a roughly counterclockwise direction starting with San José, in the center of the country. Chapters are divided into small regions, within which towns are covered in logical geographical order; attractive routes and interesting places between towns are flagged as En Route. Heads at the top of each page help you find what you need within a chapter.
DON'T FORGET	Restaurants are open for lunch and dinner daily unless we state otherwise; we mention dress only when there's a specific requirement and reservations only when they're essential or not accepted—it's always best to book ahead. Hotels have private baths, phone, TVs, and air-conditioning and operate on the European Plan (a.k.a. EP, meaning without meals). We always list facilities but not whether you'll be charged extra to use them, so when pricing accommodations, find out what's included.
SYMBOLS	

Many Listings

★ Fodor's Choice

★ Highly recommended

⊠ Physical address

✢ Directions

🗐 Mailing address

☎ Telephone

🖷 Fax

⊕ On the Web

✍ E-mail

🎫 Admission fee

☉ Open/closed times

► Start of walk/itinerary

▭ Credit cards

Outdoors

🏌 Golf

⛺ Camping

Hotels & Restaurants

🏨 Hotel

🛏 Number of rooms

⌂ Facilities

🍽 Meal plans

✕ Restaurant

⚑ Reservations

🎩 Dress code

⚲ Smoking

🍷 BYOB

✕🏨 Hotel with restaurant that warrants a visit

Other

☺ Family-friendly

🔳 Contact information

⇨ See also

⊠ Branch address

☞ Take note

ON THE ROAD WITH FODOR'S

A trip takes you out of yourself. Concerns of life at home completely disappear, driven away by more immediate thoughts—about, say, what marvels will beguile the next day, or where you'll have dinner. That's where Fodor's comes in. We make sure that you know all your options, so that you don't miss something that's around the next bend just because you didn't know it was there. Because the best memories of your trip might well have nothing to do with what you came to Costa Rica to see, we guide you to sights large and small all over the country. You might set out to relax on the beaches at Manuel Antonio, but back at home you find yourself unable to forget spotting your first Blue Morpho as it flitted past your screened-in cabana and hiking the perimeter of Volcán Arenal. With Fodor's at your side, serendipitous discoveries are never far away.

Our success in showing you every corner of Costa Rica is a credit to our extraordinary writers. Although there's no substitute for travel advice from a good friend who knows your style, our contributors are the next best thing—the kind of people you would poll for travel advice if you knew them.

A frequent Fodor's contributor, **Gregory Benchwick** loves traveling and exploring the less-seen areas of Latin America. His zest for exploration has led him to the mining outposts of Chile's Atacama Desert, the remote jungles of Costa Rica's Osa Peninsula, and to Bolivia, where he worked as the managing editor of the *Bolivian Times*. Gregory updated the San José and the Central Valley chapters for this edition.

Writer and photographer **David Dudenhoefer** spent most of the 1990s based in San José and traveling much of Central and South America. A biologist by training, as a writer he specializes in the environment and travel. David has worked in 20 countries on three continents and has written about everything from migratory birds to intransigent politicians. He has written and updated material for Fodor's guides to Cuba, Panama, Colombia, Ecuador, Belize, and Guatemala, and for five editions of *Fodor's Costa Rica*. David updated the Central Pacific Coast chapter for this

edition and wrote the essay *A Biological Superpower*.

Seasoned traveler and journalist **Dorothy MacKinnon** took up a post in San José, from which to contribute to the *Tico Times* on ecotourism, restaurants, and nonprofit development stories—and to update the Nicoya Peninsula and Southern Pacific Coast chapters of this guide. She has written on travel and other topics for several North American newspapers, including *The Washington Post*.

San José–based freelance writer **Jeffrey Van Fleet** has spent the better part of the last decade enjoying Costa Rica's long rainy seasons and Wisconsin's winters. (Most people would try to do it the other way around.) He saw his first Resplendent Quetzal, that bird-watcher's Holy Grail, while researching this guide. Jeff is a regular contributor to Costa Rica's English-language *Tico Times* and has written for Fodor's guides to Chile, Argentina, Peru, and Central and South America.

Carol Weir divides her time between San José, Costa Rica, and Hilton Head Island, South Carolina. She has worked as an investigative reporter for a daily newspaper, as a teacher in Costa Rica and in the U.S., and as an editor at the *Tico Times*, Costa Rica's English-language newspaper. Carol updated Smart Travel Tips and Understanding Costa Rica for this edition.

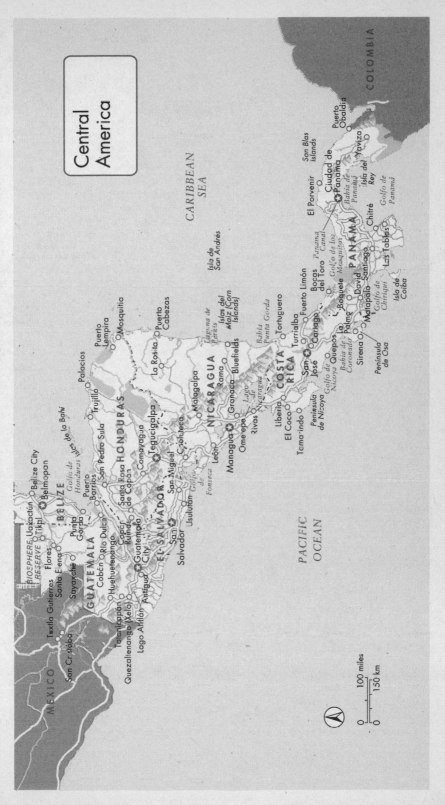

Central America

PACIFIC
OCEAN

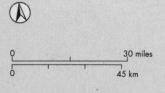

0 _____ 30 miles
0 _____ 45 km

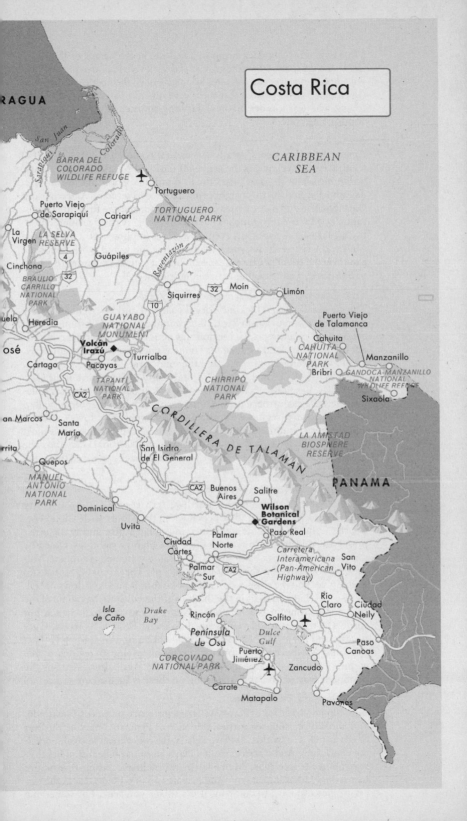

Costa Rica

WHAT'S WHERE

Most trips to Costa Rica begin in San José, at the center of the country. Day trips to the surrounding Central Valley yield coffee plantations, volcanoes, and river canyons. An hour's flight to the north, east, or west transports you to pristine beaches, verdant rain forest, sleepy surfing towns, active volcanoes, and exhilarating snorkeling, scuba diving, or windsurfing waters.

① San José

Ringed by mountains, Costa Rica's capital is more than 914 m (3,000 ft) above sea level and is the center of national political, cultural, and economic life. A third of Costa Rica's 4 million people live in San José, its suburbs, and in the neighboring cities of Heredia, Alajuela, and Cartago. The city has a varied cultural calendar, some first-rate restaurants, good museums, raucous bars, and discos. A stroll around downtown plazas and parks, an evening at the symphony, or a visit to the Mercado Central shows you how Ticos live, play, and work. Since the capital is the country's transportation hub, it's often necessary to return to San José when traveling between destinations.

② The Central Valley: Around San José

The Central Valley, which includes the capital and is the most densely populated region of Costa Rica, is surrounded by a ring of stunning volcanoes and mountains. The region has active volcanic craters, luxuriant cloud forests, and some of the country's best hotels and restaurants. The upscale suburb of Escazú, and the small cities of Heredia, Alajuela, and Cartago, the former colonial capital until 1823, are part of the Central Valley. Costa Rica's most accessible volcanoes, Poás and Irazú, define the valley's northern edge. To the east lies the smaller Orosi Valley, a coffee-growing region with historic monuments and lovely scenery, and the agricultural community of Turrialba, near the country's most important archaeological site, the Monumento Nacional Guayabo. The golden (coffee) bean is the country's economic backbone, and this is the heart of the industry.

③ Northern Guanacaste & Alajuela

In the country's untrammeled northwestern corner, nature is pretty much untouched. Birds and birders flock to the Monteverde Cloud Forest, the Caño Negro Wildlife Refuge in the far north, and many other preserves and parks, allowing for once-in-a-lifetime sightings. Down by the sea, at Santa Rosa National Park, wildlife watching is sublime. Volcanoes loom large on the ethereal landscape. The Arenal Observatory Lodge gives you the closest views of smoke spirals and lava flows of Volcán Arenal. Lake Arenal, in the shadow of the volcano, has some of the best windsurfing in the Americas. Nearby, you can soak in the hot springs at the beautifully landscaped Tabacón Resort. Northern Guanacaste and Alajuela—with some notable exceptions including La Fortuna and Monteverde—is one of the least developed regions of the country, and thus one of the most authentic. Agriculture remains the dominant way of life, and what tourism there is focuses on nature.

④ The Nicoya Peninsula

With top-notch surfing at Playa Avellanas, the beach resorts of Tamarindo, and scads of nesting sea turtles, the Nicoya Peninsula may be the best of all Costa Rican worlds. At Playa Pelada, the rocks create surreal snorkeling landscapes. And whoever named Playa Hermosa—Beautiful Beach— was telling it like it is. Many large, all-inclusive beach resorts are increasingly focusing on golf. And private cabanas concealed in the forest are not too hard to come by, if it's solace you seek. For something a little more wild, visit the party town of Montezuma, near the private reserve Curú National Wildlife Refuge and Cabo Blanco Nature Reserve, Costa Rica's first protected area. Whether you surf, turtle-watch, or sightsee, Nicoya keeps you breezily occupied.

5 The Central Pacific Coast

Some of the country's most popular destinations are in this region—from the surfing town of Jacó to gorgeous Manuel Antonio National Park, home to endangered squirrel monkeys, sloths, iguanas, many birds, and three white-sand beaches. The glowing sunsets and sparkling water are reason enough to visit the coast, but there are also private reserves, dolphin-watching tours, swaying bridges suspended high in the forest canopy, and other nature-based attractions. Sea-kayaking, hiking, rafting, and horseback riding are all first-rate. The area is known for its seafood. Quepos, a town adjacent to Manuel Antonio, lives off tourism, and has several discos, decent restaurants, and cheaper hotels. Just north, the overdeveloped surf town of Jacó has plenty of activity day and night—it's funky, fun, and unabashedly tacky, with casinos, discos, and bars.

6 The Southern Pacific Coast

Even by local standards, the sheer number of plant and animal species in the Southern Pacific is astonishing. In the lush and enormous Corcovado National Park, hikers scamper past swamplands, jungle-thick riverbanks, unspoiled beaches, and heavenly primary rain forest. Lodges in the heart of the Osa Peninsula accommodate those who want to bond with nature but aren't ready to sleep outdoors in it. A boat ride in Drake Bay shows you the rugged coastline that Sir Francis saw when he paid a call, and some of the country's most beautiful underwater scenery is at Isla del Caño. Luxurious lodges in Drake Bay cater to amateur naturalists, anglers, and scuba divers. Puerto Jiménez and Golfito are air transportation hubs, with a few hotels and restaurants and some good fishing. South of Golfito lie some of Costa Rica's most remote beaches and best surfing destinations, with a few less hedonistic lodges.

7 The Atlantic Lowlands & the Caribbean Coast

The Caribbean influence is apparent on Costa Rica's Atlantic side. You find reggae, johnnycakes, and fluent English-speakers in Limón. Natural sights explode here, both above and below sea level; experience both at Cahuita National Park, where you can snorkel the coral reef or stroll the snowy-white, forest-edged beach. At Tortuguero National Park, majestic green sea turtles come ashore to nest; the park also hides crocodiles, manatees, and more. Rustic Barra del Colorado welcomes avid anglers. Inland and up in the clouds, the sprawling Braulio Carrillo National Park is the lush, comfortable home of still more plants and animals, and you can soar above them all in the Rain Forest Aerial Tram. While visitors to Costa Rica tend to favor the Pacific Coast, partly because the Atlantic has fewer luxury accommodations and more rain, many of Costa Rica's most beautiful spots—and true bargains—are found here.

Costa Rica Classic
5 to 7 days.

Rugged topography and uneven road conditions mean destinations that look close on the map in Costa Rica are actually a half day's drive apart. To avoid the frustration of packing too much in, follow this itinerary that hits the highlights, from spectacular volcanoes and misty cloud forests to golden beaches, leaving you time to relax and enjoy each region in the process.

THE CENTRAL VALLEY 1 day. Don't spend much time in San José. Go straight to one of the small or large luxury hotels in Alajuela or Heredia. Xandari Plantation, near Alajuela, and the Marriott Hotel and Resort in San Antonio de Belén, are luxurious, attractive, and close to the Juan Santamaría International Airport.

ARENAL 1 day. In the morning, drive to La Fortuna, visit Arenal Volcano and soak in Tabacón hot springs. Spend the night at one of the nature lodges near the volcano. Arenal Observatory Lodge affords the best view, while Tilajari Resort Hotel, in Muelle de San Carlos, has quiet rooms beside a river and its own large forest preserve. In the morning, go for a horseback ride through this charming agricultural region.

MONTEVERDE CLOUD FOREST 3 days. Make the daylong drive to Monteverde via Lake Arenal. Stop for lunch at one of the restaurants that ring the lake; most are inside hotels. In Monteverde, check into an inn near the private cloud forest reserve. After a casual dinner at Johnny's Pizza or other local eateries, turn in early—unless you're up for a night of salsa dancing at La Catarata, a lively night spot that draws locals and visitors. In the morning, get to the reserve as early as possible, and hire a local guide to hike with you. Spend two days in Monteverde visiting the town's butterfly and orchid gardens, seeing a slide show of spectacular nature photography by Michael and Patricia Fogden, and for the adventurous—zipping through the forest on a canopy tour.

THE NICOYA COAST 2 days. If you have a couple more days, drive to Tamarindo or other beaches along the coast of the Nicoya Peninsula and spend the rest of your time in the sun.

A Walk in the Clouds
5 to 8 days

This itinerary takes you from an impressive active volcano to the Osa Penninsula—the country's most remote region—and back to warm sands and rolling waves.

THE CENTRAL VALLEY 1 or 2 days. When you arrive, check in to one of the Central Valley inns for a night or two to acclimatize to Costa's Rica's *pura vida*—the good life—philosophy. After you've rested, get up early and drive to the Poás Volcano. If you go too late in the day the crater will be foggy. There is a hot sulfur lake at the bottom of the volcano with active fumaroles. Warm up with a steaming cup of hot chocolate or coffee at the park's café. Then head to nearby La Paz Waterfall Gardens. After hiking to the pounding waterfalls and visiting the butterfly and hummingbird gardens, eat lunch at the open air restaurant. The typical Costa Rican meal tastes even better in the mountain air. Resplendent Quetzals nest here between December and February, and wild orchids bloom along the property's many kilometers of well-kept trails. Spend the night close to the airport.

THE OSA PENINSULA 2 to 5 days. The next day, fly to the gorgeous and remote Osa Peninsula for jungle living. Choose a lodge such as Lapa

Ríos or Corcovado Lodge Tent Camp, which include meals, bird watching, and guided nature walks. End your trip here or head north for a relaxing stint on a Nicoya beach.

NICOYA BEACHES 2 to 3 days. From the Osa Peninsula, fly back to San José and then to the upscale beach areas of Tamarindo, or Manuel Antonio National Park, or one of the less-touristed areas along the northern Pacific.

A Caribbean Caper
7 to 9 days

On the Caribbean coast, living is easy and the ocean is crystal-clear and warm. Prices are lower than on the Pacific side of the country, and the culture—shaped by descendants of mainly Jamaican immigrants—has a distinctly Afro-Caribbean flavor.

THE NORTHERN LOWLANDS 2 to 3 days. After your first night at a Central Valley inn, drive east on the Braulio Carrillo highway, passing through the majestic cloud forest in the national park by the same name. Stop at the Rain Forest Aerial Tram for a breathtaking tram ride through the treetops, lunch and a short guided hike. Continue another hour to Puerto Viejo de Sarapiquí, and check into the comfortable Selva Verde Lodge. Raft on the beautiful, gently rolling Sarapiquí River, go bird-watching with one of the Selva Verde's expert local guides, and visit the La Selva Biological Station. Also in the area, and worth a visit, are the Jewels of the Rainforest insect museum housed at La Quinta de Sarapiquí Country Inn, and Centro Neotrópico Sarapiquís, which includes ornamental and tropical fruit gardens and a replica 15th century pre-Columbian village.

COASTAL TALAMANCA 2 days. Leave this lush lowland region and continue on to Puerto Viejo de Talamanca, where you check into one of the small nature lodges tucked behind the palm trees along the road to Manzanillo, or at one of the small hotels in town. Spend your days snorkeling, biking down the dirt road to Manzanillo Beach, and sampling jerk chicken, johnnycake, coconut-flavored rice and beans and other Caribbean treats. At night, check out a reggae bar. Cahuita National Park, about an hour north of Puerto Viejo by bus or car, is definitely worth a visit for its excellent snorkeling and shady trails in the forest beside the beach.

SAN JOSÉ 1 day. Return to San José and spend a night at the Hotel Grano de Oro or other historic hotel. Visit one of the capital's many museums— the Jade, Gold and National museums are all within walking distance of each other. In the evening, attend the symphony or other productions at the Teatro Nacional, a national monument built in 1894.

TORTUGUERO 2 to 3 days. The next morning, having made reservations at Mawamba Lodge or another jungle lodge in Tortuguero, journey to this remote natural paradise in a motorized pontoon boat driven by a local guide. Along the way, you might see sloths, caimans, iguanas, White-faced and Howler Monkeys, and maybe a boa constrictor sleeping on the banks of the canals. Tortuguero is the largest nesting area in the western hemisphere for the Green Sea Turtle. Leatherbacks also nest there, and a turtle walk by a local guide is a must. Rent a dugout canoe and explore the canals yourself. From Tortuguero, fly back to the capital. Depending on your time and interests, visit Monteverde, Volcan Arenal or a Central Pacific or Guanacaste beach before you head home.

The dry season on the Pacific coast runs from mid-December through April. From mid-December until early February, you have the combined advantages of good weather and lush vegetation. Some areas, especially Guanacaste, are dry and dusty by April. The Caribbean coast is always unpredictable when it comes to rain, but enjoys a short "dry" season in September and October. Both coasts get some sunny weather in July, August, and early September. Hotels are most likely to be full during dry seasons, so plan several months in advance. To avoid crowds and high prices, visit in the rainy season, when vegetation is lush and gorgeous, but some roads are washed out, and beaches are often wet in the afternoon but sunny and dry in the morning. You can find deals in July or August, when the storms let up a bit, or mid-December, when rains are tapering off. September and October are a quiet time to visit—some hotels are virtually empty, and you might have the beaches to yourself.

Climate

Costa Rica's climate varies greatly between the lowlands and the mountains. Tropical temperatures generally hover between 20°C (70°F) and 30°C (85°F). High humidity, especially in the dense jungle of the Caribbean coast, is the true culprit in any discomfort. Guanacaste, on the more arid Pacific coast, is Costa Rica's hottest region, with frequent temperatures in the 90s during the dry season.

⏰ Forecasts Weather Channel Connection ☎ 900/932–8437, 95¢ per minute from a Touch-Tone phone ⊕ www.weather.com.

The following are the average daily maximum and minimum temperatures for San José, whose weather is typical of other highland towns, and Golfito, which has a climate similar to that of most coastal and lowland towns.

SAN JOSÉ

Jan.	75F	24C	May	80F	27C	Sept.	79F	26C
	58	14		62	17		61	16
Feb.	76F	24C	June	79F	26C	Oct.	77F	25C
	58	14		62	17		60	16
Mar.	79F	26C	July	77F	25C	Nov.	77F	25C
	59	15		62	17		60	16
Apr.	79F	26C	Aug.	78F	26C	Dec.	75F	24C
	62	17		61	16		58	14

GOLFITO

Jan.	91F	33C	May	91F	33C	Sept.	91F	33C
	72	22		73	23		72	22
Feb.	91F	33C	June	90F	32C	Oct.	90F	32C
	72	22		73	23		72	22
Mar.	91F	33C	July	90F	32C	Nov.	91F	32C
	73	23		72	22		72	22
Apr.	91F	33C	Aug.	90F	32C	Dec.	91F	33C
	73	23		72	22		72	22

PLEASURES & PASTIMES

Bird-watching
Many of Costa Rica's creatures are named after their homes: for example, the wild turkey (Highland Tinamou), the melodious Riverside Wren, or the Volcano Hummingbird. You may be surprised to encounter a Canadian Warbler, Baltimore Oriole, or Kentucky Warbler—some of the 200 North American birds found in Costa Rica. Some of these species stay year-round and others come and go during the winter migration. In addition to the tourist species, Costa Rica also has the requisite tropical birds, including 6 kinds of toucans, 16 parrots and parakeets, and more than 50 hummingbirds. Other tropical groups, such as ant birds, are well represented. The birds of Costa Rica represent close to 10 percent of the total bird species in the world.

Fishing
Costa Rica is a freshwater and saltwater angler's dream. Marlin, sailfish, tuna, and dorado abound in the Pacific and fishing folk fill Golfito-area lodges all the way up the coast. Experienced captains, small and medium sized marinas, and charter fishing companies compete for business, so prices remain reasonable. Fishing-and-lodging packages are common. Tarpon and snook are the highlights of the Caribbean. The Barra del Colorado River, in the heart of the rain forest, gets more than 200 inches of annual rainfall and has its best fishing from December to early May, and late July to late August. *Guapote* (sea bass), catfish, and *gaspar* (Alligator Gar) can also be caught here. Lake Arenal has many rainbow bass and gaspar, and several mountain lodges offer trout fishing in tumbling streams. Good fishing is also found in the Río Frío, which passes through Los Chiles near Nicaragua. Tarpon, snook, White Drum, gar, and more bite here. You can fish from the municipal dock in Los Chiles or rent a *panga* (small boat) driven by a local guide.

Rain Forests
The lowland rain forests of Costa Rica and the rest of the New World tropics are the most complex biological communities that exist. A typical hectare (2½ acres) of Costa Rican rain forest might be home to nearly 100 species of trees, whereas 30 is typical in the richest forests of the United States. In addition to trees, you'll see epiphytes and giant rain forest versions of orchids, as well as sloths, monkeys, copious birds, and more. Good places for hiking are Braulio Carrillo National Park, near San José which contains rain forest and cloud forest, and the hot and humid rain forest in La Selva Biological Station. On the Pacific coast, Corcovado National Park and Marenco Wildlife Refuge have well-maintained—but often muddy and steep—trails where you can meander for hours through impressive primary forests. Filled with giant strangler figs and dripping with moss, Monteverde's private reserve is a good place to hike through primeval cloud forests. Even a quick walk through forest trails on the way to the beach in Manuel Antonio National Park can reveal squirrel monkeys, White-faced Coatis, and iguanas. For a closer look at the canopy, ride the Rain Forest Aerial Tram, near the Guápiles Highway or, for an adventurous angle, take a canopy tour. It's best to walk or hike with a local guide—a good one points out plants and animals you would surely miss on your own.

Shopping
Many of the colorful goods sold in Costa Rica are actually made in Guatemala, Nicaragua, or Panama, but some local crafts are still practiced.

The oxcart is the national symbol of Ticos' hardworking, self-reliant character and rural roots. Brightly painted carts come in all dimensions—from the size of a matchbook to life-size. In Sarchí, in the Western Central Valley, the art of making oxcarts has been passed down through generations. Sarchí's artisans also work native hardwoods into bowls, boxes, toys, platters, and jewelry. In the capital, art and crafts galleries near the Parque Morazón and the northern suburb of Moravia have the best shopping. Wood-framed mirrors in the shape of forest creatures, bamboo mobiles of tropical fish, and leather rocking chairs are good buys. The outdoor crafts market beside the Museo Nacional is a fun place to browse, although most items are overpriced. A good place to buy anything from local music recordings to hand-painted ceramic tiles is the Annemarie Souvenir shop inside the Hotel Don Carlos, near the National Library. Coffee and rum make good gifts, too. Most tourists buy Café Britt, but Volio and Café Rey Tarrazú are much cheaper, available at supermarkets, and almost as good. As for rum, look for Ron Centenario or better still, the Nicaraguan brand, Flor de Caña.

Snorkeling & Scuba Diving
Along the Caribbean coast, the areas from Puerto Viejo de Talamanca to Gandoca-Manzanillo Wildlife Refuge and from Limón to Isla Uvita are good for snorkeling or diving. The Caribbean is clearest in October and November, when visibility can reach 30 m (100 ft). The country's largest reef, which has been severely damaged but still has plenty to admire, is protected within the Parque Nacional Cahuita. Pacific excursions depart from the southern zone's Drake Bay, and Flamingo, Ocotal, and Playa del Coco in the northern province of Guanacaste. The Pacific Coast has less colorful coral but more big animals, such as manta rays, sea turtles, and even Whale Sharks. The best Pacific coast diving spot is Isla del Caño, near Drake Bay. The snorkeling is excellent around the rocky points that flank Bajo del Diablo and Paraíso, where you are guaranteed to encounter thousands of big fish. In the northwest, there are dozens of dive spots around Santa Catalina. Costa Rica's best dive spot, Cocos Island, must be visited on 9- or 10-day scuba trips aboard either the *Okeanos Aggressor* or the *Undersea Hunter*. For experienced divers only, this remote destination 600 km (375 mi) southwest of the mainland has waters teeming with manta rays and eight shark species including Hammerhead and Whale Sharks. Dive schools in San José offer PADI open-water diving courses and some beach hotels allow noncertified divers to use scuba equipment for shallow dives of 15 m (49 ft) or less.

Surfing
Costa Rica is one of the world's most popular surfing destinations, but the waves—from the radical, experts-only reef break at Puerto Viejo de Talamanca to the mellower waves off Tamarindo on the Pacific—remain relatively uncrowded. The water is deliciously warm on both coasts and there are good waves year-round. The Central Pacific is the most popular surfing destination because it's close to San José and has plenty of diversity. The party town of Jacó has a fun beach break and is home to some of Costa Rica's best surfers and surfing facilities. It's an ideal base for trips to nearby Playa Hermosa, with a long beach and surfing competitions, and less-crowded Playa Panama. Near Puntarenas, the sand spit at the mouth of the Barranca River produces one of the world's longest left-breaking waves, although the water is polluted.

About a dozen popular surf spots are scattered along the coast south of Tamarindo, and because of its excellent surf shop and many hotels and restaurants, it is a base for trips to Playas Langosta, Avellanas, and Negra. Playa Avellanas has eight surf spots ranging from beach breaks to rock-reef breaks to river-mouth sandbar breaks. A spectacular and well-known break is Witches Rock at Playa Naranjo, inside Parque Nacional Santa Rosa. Those willing to make the journey to Pavones and Matapalo, on Costa Rica's southern Pacific coast, can ride some of the world's longest waves. Dominical has also long drawn surfers to its consistent beach breaks, and a surf shop here rents, sells, and repairs surfboards. Puerto Viejo de Talamanca's Salsa Brava is one of the country's best breaks and one of the Atlantic coast's few surf spots. The water starts deep and runs quickly onto a shallow reef, forming seriously huge waves.

Volcanoes

Costa Rica has 100 or so volcanoes, seven of which are active today. Near San José, paved roads run right to the summit of Poás and Irazú Volcanos. Volcán Irazú, Costa Rica's highest at 3,753 m (12,313 ft), last erupted on the day of U.S. President John F. Kennedy's visit in 1963. Ash showers followed by rain left the Central Valley covered in black soot and sludge for months. Dormant Volcán Barva, north of San José and cloaked in cloud forest, has two crater lakes and spectacular scenic overlooks as rewards for a steep all-day hike to the summit. A tough hike to the steaming crater at Rincón de la Vieja National Park, in the country's northern zone, reveals steaming fumaroles bubble on the ground, and a cold river that collides with a warm sulfur spring. However, nothing in Costa Rica rivals the sheer mass and power of Volcán Arenal. By day, it is veiled by an ominous haze, but at night, red hot molten lava can be seen oozing from the cone, a flirtatious dance with disaster. In August 2000, an eruption sent poisonous gases spilling down the eastern side of the mountain, killing three people who were watching from a supposedly safe distance. Geologists later found the popular Tabacón Hot Springs Resort and a campground to be in a high-risk zone. The government has since posted warning signs at the hot springs and various other points around the volcano.

White-Water Rafting

Half a dozen Olympic kayak teams spend the winter on the wild rivers of Costa Rica. Single and multiday trips are marked by gorgeous scenery, various difficulty levels, and year-round warm water. The country's rafting center is Turrialba, a hospitable, medium-size town on the banks of the Reventazón River and home to some of the country's best guides. The Reventazón and nearby Pacuare rivers are popular for their exciting runs and proximity to San José. Outfitters in La Fortuna, near Volcán Arenal, lead Class III and IV white-water trips on the narrow Río Peñas Blanca and Río Toro. Nearby, you can take half-day trips on the tamer but gorgeous Sarapiquí River, through verdant rain forest and tranquil towns. Near Quepos, rafting companies run three white rivers during rainy season—the Parrita, Naranjo, and Savegre. The country's longest white-water run is the Río General, a rousing raft or kayak trip that has long stretches of flat water and starts in San Isidro.

Wildlife

Costa Rica covers less than 0.03% of the earth's surface but contains nearly 4% of the planet's animal species. The country has 4 species of monkeys, 6 types of wild cats, and 876 bird species, which is more than are found in the United States and Canada combined. About half of the country's mammals are bats; Costa Rica has 103 bat species, including White Bats—with a wingspan of ½ m (2 ft)—and 2 species of vampire bats, 1 that favors birds and 1 that prefers mammals. This abundance of wildlife is due in part to the country's geographical position on a land bridge between North America and South America. Flitting around Costa Rica are more than 2,000 species of butterflies, including the huge and incandescent Blue Morpho. Five of the world's 7 species of sea turtles nest in Costa Rica, including the Green, Leatherback, Loggerhead, Olive Ridley, and Hawksbill. More than 30 of the world's 80 species of dolphins, whales, and porpoises inhabit Costa Rican waters, and tour companies in Quepos and near the Gandoca-Manzanillo National Wildlife Refuge lead dolphin- and whale-watching excursions.

If you expect a National Geographic–style safari, you will be disappointed. Forests with dense foliage combined with the animals' skittish nature and excellent camouflage make them hard to see. Realistically, you can expect to see coatis, monkeys, and perhaps a sloth or agouti. Sightings of large mammals like wildcats and tapirs are extremely rare. You probably won't see any of Costa Rica's 18 species of poisonous snakes either. (Snakes try to flee unless cornered or protecting a nest.) As you move through the country, you have continuous opportunities to see wildlife. It's mostly a matter of luck and patience, although talking with locals and hiring local guides increases your chances of being at the right place at the right time.

Windsurfing

Champion windsurfers have called Costa Rica's Lake Arenal one of the world's top five windsurfing spots. The man-made lake, which has spectacular views of the country's most active volcano, is 35 km (22 mi) long and the water temperature averages 23°C (73°F) from December to April. Unusually stable winds average 40 kph (25 mph); windsurfers can typically sail one sail all day. The best windsurfing is on the north and northwest sides of the lake. Coto Lake, a small, remote lake north of Arenal, has excellent conditions during the same months. Bolaños Bay, in Guanacaste near the border with Nicaragua, is the place for ocean windsurfing, with winds as strong and consistent as Arenal's. The closed bay combined with side-onshore winds makes it very safe. Conditions are best from November to April. Also near the border with Nicaragua, the waters off the beautiful beaches Cuajiniquil and Puerto Soley are tranquil, with direct offshore winds during the December-to-April dry season. Farther south, Tamarindo and Playa Flamingo also have good windsurfing conditions. Ocean windsurfing is not very popular in Costa Rica, so bring your own equipment unless you're staying at Bolaños Bay Resort, which rents everything you need.

FODOR'S CHOICE

The sights, restaurants, hotels, and other travel experiences on these pages are our editors' top picks—our Fodor's Choices. They're the best of their type in Costa Rica—not to be missed and always worth your time. In the destination chapters that follow, you will find all the details.

LODGING

$$$$ **Bosque del Cabo**, Cabo Matapalo. The rustic and yet world-class bungalows (love the garden showers) afford breathtaking views of the ocean, and the lodge's nonstop activities in and around the private nature reserve make a hum-drum vacation unlikely.

$$$$ **Hotel Punta Islita**, Punta Islita. Overlooking the Pacific, this secluded resort offers luxurious rooms, splendid views, sybaritic spa treatments, and abundant peace and quiet.

$$$$ **Lapa Ríos**, Cabo Matapalo. Perched on a ridge in a private rain forest reserve, with views of the surrounding jungle and the ocean beyond, Lapa Ríos is a small hotel that brings you close to nature without skimping on the amenities.

$$$$ **Makanda By the Sea**, Manuel Antonio. This Central Pacific gem is a gorgeous retreat whose sprawling and private villas have every convenience and are shrouded by pristine jungle.

$$$–$$$$ **Xandari**, Alajuela. Whether you fix your vision on the clever design of the spacious villas or just watch birds and butterflies flit through the surrounding tropical gardens, its hard not to be enchanted by this unique inn and spa.

$$$ **Club del Mar**, Jacó. Spacious one- and two-story condominiums at this luxury resort are just steps from the beach in a quiet cove surrounded by huge tropical trees.

$$$ **Finca Rosa Blanca Country Inn**, Volcán Barva. An exciting mix of Gaudíesque architecture, Tico hardwoods, and incredible attention to detail make this the Central Valley's nicest bed-and-breakfast. You have to see it to believe it.

$$$ **Hotel Capitán Suizo**, Tamarindo. Many consider this Swiss-run gem the finest beachfront lodging in Guanacaste. Its lush gardens provide a wonderful sense of seclusion not far from Tamarindo's resort-town amusements and gorgeous beach.

$$$ **Sueño del Mar**, Playa Langosta. A sweet little Mexican-style B&B, with Balinese outdoor showers, fantastic breakfasts, charming gardens, and a perfect beach, sleeps just a handful for an intimate getaway. It can also accommodate a larger gathering of family or friends.

$$ **Aviarios del Caribe**, Limón. See hundreds of bird species before breakfast at this nature-heavy B&B and wildlife refuge, where injured animals are nursed back to health. Highly personalized service is icing on the cake.

$$ **Fonda Vela**, Monteverde. Built with local hardwoods, these spacious rooms have plenty of windows, the better to enjoy the surrounding forest and distant Gulf of Nicoya. The restaurant serves food to match the view.

$$ **Le Bergerac**, San José. Deluxe rooms and extensive gardens have long kept this quiet, friendly hotel a notch above the competition, and the presence of L'Ile de France, one of the city's best restaurants, makes it that much more compelling.

BUDGET LODGING

$ **Cariblue Bungalows**, Puerto Viejo de Talamanca. Lovely wooden bungalows with thatched roofs near a palm-lined white-sand beach are designed to slow your internal clock to Caribbean time.

$ **El Encanto Bed & Breakfast**, Cahuita. An ultimate relaxation destination that realizes the owners' Zen Buddhist ideals, El Encanto has a serene tropical garden, yoga classes, and large healthful breakfasts.

¢–$ **Hotel Aranjuez**, San José. Lush gardens, abundant common areas, hearty breakfasts, and low prices make this little B&B in the quiet Barrio Aranjuez a real bargain.

¢ **Corcovado Lodge Tent Camp**, Corcovado National Park. Truly isolated from civilization, this collection of rustic tents facing the sea is literally steps from the beach and the rain forest. It's a fabulous place to end your Costa Rican adventure.

RESTAURANTS

$–$$$ **El Gran Escape**, Quepos. Succulent and fresh seafood—from sashimi and ceviche to surf and turf—is the reason to visit this restaurant and bar. Bring in your own catch of the day to be prepared any way you like.

$$ **L'Ile de France**, San José. Costa Rica is not known for its fine dining, but this elegant spot, with its brilliant French cuisine, is a notable exception to the rule.

$–$$ **Ambrosia**, San José. Fifteen minutes from downtown, this eclectic restaurant has long been popular among local epicureans thanks to its delicious inventions.

$–$$ **El Camarón Dorado**, Brasilito. Beachside seating, plentiful portions of fresh seafood, and spectacular sunset vistas make this an excellent choice for a romantic evening or a relaxing end to your day.

$–$$ **Café Mundo**, San José. From its lovely old wooden house in historic Barrio Amón, this popular café serves pastas, salads, meat and seafood dishes at reasonable prices. The pastries are to die for.

BUDGET RESTAURANTS

$ **Chubascos**, Volcán Poás. It's a winning combination: brisk mountain air, delicious refrescos, green surroundings, and platters packed with traditional Costa Rican taste treats.

$ **Cha Cha Cha**, Cahuita. Simple but masterful international and eclectic cuisine is expertly prepared at this low-key place in the center of town.

$ **Lazy Wave Food Company,** Tamarindo. Don't miss these irresistible lunches, dinners, and desserts at prices that are just as irresistible.

ARCHAEOLOGY

Guayabo National Monument, Turrialba. Costa Rica's only ruins, this partially excavated ancient city was once home to 20,000 people. Abandoned in the 15th century, it lay undiscovered until 1968.

NATURE

Jungle rivers. Slip into the rain forest the old-fashioned way. Adventures range from heart-stopping paddles down the hair-raising rapids of the Pacuare to lazy navigation of Caribbean canals or Pacific estuaries. With luck you'll spot a roseate spoonbill, purple gallinule, howler monkey, crocodile, or caiman along the way.

Pacific sunsets. There's something about the cloud formations, colors, and settings that makes these exemplary crepuscular productions. Flocks of diving pelicans scarfing up sardines often add foreground action.

Volcán Arenal erupting at night. Arenal's perfectly conical profile dominates the southern end of a lake, and thrills onlookers with regular incendiary performances. (Check safety conditions at this active volcano before going.)

OUTDOOR ACTIVITIES

Bird-watching on the Osa Peninsula. If you already own a few field guides, then you've probably planned your trip with our feathered friends in mind. If you don't, sign up for a tour, borrow some binoculars, and get up at dawn—you won't regret your search for a Baird's Trogon or a Scarlet Macaw.

Monkeying around on an Original Canopy Tour, Monteverde. Do as the monkeys, and swing from tree to tree on a canopy tour, with locations in Monteverde and around the country. With mountain climbing gear fastening you in, you'll have a perspective of the Costa Rican rain forest from the top down.

Riding the Rain Forest Aerial Tram, near Braulio Carrillo National Park. Fly through the the various levels of rain-forest canopy in an open gondola on this thrilling tour. This is one of the best ways to reach the rain forest canopy and this tour has an excellent safety record.

Soaking in the Tabacón hot springs. From the Tabacón Resort's gorgeously landscaped hot-springs streams, you can soak away your cares and take in views of magnificent and rumbling Volcán Arenal. Check safety conditions at this active volcano before going.

SMART TRAVEL TIPS

Finding out about your destination before you leave home means you won't squander time organizing everyday minutiae once you've arrived. You'll be more streetwise when you hit the ground as well, better prepared to explore the aspects of Costa Rica that drew you here in the first place. The organizations in this section can provide information to supplement this guide; contact them for up-to-the-minute details, and consult the A to Z sections that end each chapter for facts on the various topics as they relate to Costa Rica's many regions. Happy landings!

ADDRESSES

In Costa Rica, addresses are usually given in terms of how many meters the place is from a landmark. Street names and building numbers are not commonly used. Churches, stores, even large trees that no longer exist—almost anything can be a landmark, as long as everyone knows where it is, or where it used to be. A typical address in San José is *100 metros este y 100 metros sur de Mas x Menos* (100 meters east and 100 meters south from the Mas x Menos supermarket).

Street numbers are used in downtown San José, where streets are laid out in a logical system, with odd-numbered streets east of Calle Central and even-numbered avenues south of this main thoroughfare. In other parts of the city, a business may have an "official" address with a street number, and an "unofficial" address like the one for Mas x Menos, above. Ticos, as Costa Ricans call themselves, spend a lot of time asking people to describe where things are and are usually happy to help lost visitors.

AIR TRAVEL

Most people who come to Costa Rica fly to San José. Most U.S. visitors fly via Miami, though some other major cities have direct flights. Note that heavy rains in the afternoons and evenings during the May–November green, or rainy, season sometimes cause flights coming into San José to be rerouted to Panama City, where passengers may be forced to spend the night. In the rainy season, always take the earliest departure available.

BOOKING

When you book, **remember that "direct" flights stop at least once.** Two airlines may operate a connecting flight jointly, so ask whether your airline operates every segment of the trip; you may find that the carrier you prefer flies you only part of the way. To find more booking tips and to check prices and make on-line flight reservations, log on to www.fodors.com.

CARRIERS

Continental flies twice daily from Houston and once from Newark. American flies daily from Miami and Dallas. Delta flies nonstop from Atlanta daily. United flies from Chicago and Los Angeles. You can also fly from Los Angeles via Mexico City on Mexicana.

Central American airline Grupo TACA has flights from San Francisco, Los Angeles, Dallas, Houston, New Orleans, Miami, Washington, D.C., New York's JFK, Montréal, and Toronto. Some flights are direct. Martinair flies nonstop from Orlando, Florida, to and from San José every Monday.

American Airlines flies from Heathrow to Miami, and Virgin Atlantic flies from Gatwick to Miami, where you can connect with flights to San José. You can fly from London to San José on Iberia, but you have to change planes in Madrid and Miami. United Airlines flies from Heathrow to Washington, D.C., connecting to Costa Rica via Mexico. From New Zealand and Australia, consult a travel agent, who will probably send you first to Los Angeles and then on one of the flights mentioned above to Costa Rica.

Given Central America's often difficult driving conditions, distances that appear short on a map can represent hours of driving on dirt roads pocked with craters, so **consider domestic flights.** Because car-rental rates are so steep, flying can often be actually cheaper than driving.

Costa Rica has two domestic airlines, SANSA and NatureAir. SANSA flies from Juan Santamaría International Airport to Barra del Colorado, Coto 47, Golfito, Liberia, Nosara, Palmar Sur, Puerto Jiménez, Punta Islita, Quepos, Samara, Tamarindo, Tambor, and Tortuguero. SANSA also flies between Quepos and Palmar Sur.

NatureAir has daily flights from Tobias Bolaños Airport, in the San José suburb of Pavas, to Barra del Colorado, Carrillo, Drake Bay, Golfito, Puerto Jiménez, Liberia, Nosara, Palmar Sur, Punta Islita, Quepos, Tamarindo, Tambor, and Tortuguero. More than a dozen flights also run between those destinations, saving you the trouble of returning to San José.

Note that domestic flights on both SANSA and NatureAir technically impose a luggage weight limit of 13.6 kilograms (30 pounds)—*including* carry-ons—on their domestic flights, as the planes are tiny. Excess weight, if safety permits, is charged by the pound. Copa, and Grupo TACA airlines have flights to Panama City, Panama, and Managua, Nicaragua.

✈ **Major Airlines American** ☎ 000/433-7300 in the U.S., 0208/222-8900 in the U.K. ⊕ www.aa.com. **Continental** ☎ 800/231-0856 in the U.S. ⊕ www.continental.com. **Delta** ☎ 800/221-1212 in the U.S. ⊕ www.delta.com. **Iberia** ☎ 0208/222-8900 in the U.K. ⊕ www.iberia.com. **United Airlines** ☎ 800/241-6522 in the U.S., 0845/844-4777 in the U.K. **Virgin Atlantic** ☎ 0208/897-5040 in the U.K. ⊕ www.virgin-atlantic.com.

✈ **Regional Airlines Copa** ☎ 506/222-6640 ⊕ www.copaair.com. **Grupo TACA** ☎ 506/296-9353, 800/535-8780 in the U.S. ⊕ www.grupotaca.com. **NatureAir** ☎ 506/220-3054 ⊕ www.natureair.com. **SANSA** ☎ 506/221-9414 or 506/442-9385 ⊕ www.flysansa.com.

CHARTER FLIGHTS

Several charter companies in San José, NatureAir included, offer flights to places not served by scheduled flights. Helinorte provides helicopter service. During the dry season, weekly charter flights serve Costa Rica from half a dozen American and Canadian cities, most landing in Liberia, Guanacaste. These flights are sold as part of packages that include hotel stays. Departure cities for charters include Miami, Detroit, Philadelphia, Minneapolis, Atlanta, Dallas, and others. Ask a travel agent about charter options.

✈ **Charter Companies Aero Costa Sol** ☎ 506/440-1444. **Aerolineas Turisticas** ☎ 506/232-1125. **Aeronaves** ☎ 506/282-4033 in San José; 506/775-0278 in Golfito. **Helinorte** ☎ 506/232-7534.

CHECK-IN & BOARDING

Always **ask your carrier about its check-in policy.** Plan to arrive at the airport about 2 hours before your scheduled departure time for domestic flights and 2½ to 3 hours before international flights. You may need to arrive earlier if you're flying from one of the busier airports or during peak air-traffic times. Allow at least a half hour for domestic flights within Costa Rica. Note that when you fly out of Costa Rica, you'll have to pay a $17 airport departure tax at Juan Santamaría Airport. To avoid delays at airport-security checkpoints, try not to wear any metal. Jewelry, belt and other buckles, steel-toe shoes, and barrettes are among the items that can set off detectors.

Assuming that not everyone with a ticket will show up, airlines routinely overbook planes. When everyone does, airlines ask for volunteers to give up their seats. In return, these volunteers usually get a several-hundred-dollar flight voucher, which can be used toward the purchase of another ticket, and are rebooked on the next flight out. If there are not enough volunteers, the airline must choose who will be denied boarding. The first to get bumped are passengers who checked in late and those flying on discounted tickets, so **get to the gate and check in as early as possible,** especially during peak periods.

Always **bring a government-issued photo ID to the airport**; even when it's not required, a passport is best.

CUTTING COSTS

Depending on the time of year and what airline specials are available, the cheapest way to arrive may be to combine a round-trip ticket from Miami with a separate round-trip ticket from your departure city in the United States or elsewhere. Airlines run specials throughout the year, but you can usually get the best deals from May–November, the rainy season in most of Costa Rica. Fares from Canada typically cost 25- to 50-percent more than those from the U.S.

The least expensive airfares to Costa Rica are priced for round-trip travel and must usually be purchased in advance. Airlines generally allow you to change your return date for a fee; most low-fare tickets, however, are nonrefundable. It's smart to **call a number of airlines and check the Internet**; when you are quoted a good price, **book it on the spot**—the same fare may not be available the next day, or even the next hour. Always **check different routings** and look into using alternate airports. Also, price off-peak flights, which may be signif-

icantly less expensive than others. Travel agents, especially low-fare specialists (⇨ Discounts & Deals), are helpful.

Consolidators are another good source. They buy tickets for scheduled flights at reduced rates from the airlines, then sell them at prices that beat the best fare available directly from the airlines. Sometimes you can even get your money back if you need to return the ticket. Carefully read the fine print detailing penalties for changes and cancellations, purchase the ticket with a credit card, and **confirm your consolidator reservation with the airline.**

🚩 Consolidators AirlineConsolidator.com ☎ 888/468-5385 ⊕ www.airlineconsolidator.com; for international tickets. Best Fares ☎ 800/576-8255 or 800/576-1600 in the U.S. ⊕ www.bestfares.com; $59.90 annual membership. Cheap Tickets ☎ 800/377-1000 or 888/922-8849 in the U.S. ⊕ www.cheaptickets.com. Expedia ☎ 404/728-8787, 800/397-3342 in the U.S. ⊕ www.expedia.com. Hotwire ☎ 920/330-9418 or 866/468-9473 ⊕ www.hotwire.com. Now Voyager Travel ✉ 45 W. 21st St., 5th Floor Arcade, New York, NY 10010 ☎ 212/459-1616 📠 212/243-2711 ⊕ www.nowvoyagertravel.com. Onetravel.com ⊕ www.onetravel.com. Orbitz ☎ 888/656-4546 ⊕ www.orbitz.com. Priceline.com ⊕ www.priceline.com. Tico Travel ☎ 800/493-8426 in the U.S. Travelocity ☎ 888/709-5983 in the U.S., 877/282-2925 in Canada, 0870/876-3876 in the U.K. ⊕ www.travelocity.com.

FLYING TIMES

From New York, flights to San José are 5½ hours nonstop or 6–7 hours via Miami. From Los Angeles, flights are 8½ hours via Mexico; from Houston, 3½ hours nonstop; from Miami, 3 hours. Flying times to San José from Chicago, Toronto, London, and Sydney vary widely depending on the routing, and the number of connections.

RECONFIRMING

Before leaving Costa Rica it's a good idea to **reconfirm your flight by phone within 72 hours of departure.** Check the status of your flight before you leave for the airport. You can do this on your carrier's Web site, by linking to a flight-status checker (many Web booking services offer these), or by calling your carrier or travel agent. Always confirm international flights at least 72 hours ahead of the scheduled departure time.

AIRPORTS

Juan Santamaría International Airport (SJO) is Costa Rica's main airport. It's about 30 minutes north of downtown San José, in Alajuela. The SANSA terminal for domestic flights is located here. The country's other international airport is the Daniel Oduber International Airport, a small airport near Liberia used by charter companies. This airport is about five hours by car from San José. The tiny Tobias Bolaños airport, in the San José suburb of Pavas, serves domestic airline NatureAir and domestic charter companies.

Besides the larger airports listed here, other places where planes land aren't exactly airports. They more resemble a carport with a landing strip, at which a SANSA or NatureAir representative arrives just minutes before a plane is due to land or take off. The informality of domestic air service means you might want to **purchase your domestic airplane tickets in advance,** although you can buy them once you're in the country. You can buy tickets from both airlines via their Web sites.

🔁 Airport Information Aeropuerto Internacional Daniel Oduber ☎ 506/668-1032. **Aeropuerto Internacional Juan Santamaría** ☎ 506/443-2622 or 506/443-2942. **Aeropuerto Internacional Tobias Bolaños** ✉ 3 km (2 mi) west of San José, Pavas ☎ 506/232-2820.

AIRPORT TRANSFERS & TRANSPORTATION

At Juan Santamaría Airport, all international passengers are funneled out one tiny doorway to an underground fume-filled parking area, which is flanked with hordes of tour operators waiting for arriving visitors and cab drivers calling out "Taxi?" If you're with a tour, you need only look for a representative of your tour company with a sign that bears your name. Others should **take an orange cab,** called *taxi unidos,* which work only from the airport; avoid *collectivos,* or minivans—they're almost the same price as a taxi, but the van is almost always crammed with other passengers, and you'll have to make stops at their hotels, which in San José traffic can really make your transfer another journey in itself. It's also safe to take any red or orange cab identified with a number and that has a meter. Avoid *piratas* (pirates), or unregulated cabs.

More than 90% of travelers spend the night in San José and leave for their domestic destination the first thing the next morning out of the SANSA terminal next to the international airport or out of tiny Tobias Bolaños airport. Rarely does an international flight get into San José early enough to make a domestic connection, as the weather for flying is typically clear until about noon only. When given a choice, **always take the earliest morning flight.** Also, domestic flights to the far south may not be direct. You might stop in Golfito first, then continue on to Puerto Jiménez, for example.

BOAT & FERRY TRAVEL WITHIN COSTA RICA

Regular passenger and car ferries connect Puntarenas with Playa Naranjo, Tambor, and Paquera, on the south end of the Nicoya Peninsula. These ferries take you to the southern and mid-Nicoya Peninsula. Ferries are also an important part of the transportation in the Southern Pacific zone. The Taiwan Friendship Bridge (also called the Río Tempisque Bridge), which at this writing is scheduled to open at the end of 2003, should eliminate the wait of up to three hours that is common for the ferry that crosses the Tempisque River. The bridge will span the section of the river near Puerto Nípero, crossing the mouth of the river, and end near Barra Honda National Park, making it the preferred travel route to Guanacaste.

FARES & SCHEDULES

Cash is the only method of payment accepted by ferries. Ferries cost $1–$2 for passengers and $8–$12 for cars. Printed schedules are usually posted at the ticket offices on the docks where ferries embark. No other printed schedules are available. The Zancudo passenger ferry, which runs from Golfito to Zancudo, leaves from the municipal dock in Golfito daily at 11:30 AM and returns from Zancudo daily at 6:30 AM. The Puntarenas–Playa Naranjo Ferry leaves from Puntarenas at 3:15 AM, 7 AM, 2:50 PM, and 7 PM and returns from Naranjo at 5:10 AM, 8:50 AM, 12:50 PM, and 5 PM. Two ferries leave Puntarenas for Pacquera, on the southern tip of the Nicoya Peninsula: the Tambor Ferry leaves Puntarenas daily at 12:30 PM and 5 PM, plus 5 AM weekends, and returns at 2:30 PM and 8:30 PM weekdays with an additional return at 8:30 AM weekends; the larger Ferry Peninsular leaves Puntarenas at 5 AM, 8:45 AM, 12:30 PM, 3:30 PM, 5:30 PM, and 8:30 PM.

Boat & Ferry Information Ferry Peninsular ☎ 506/641–0118. Puntarenas–Playa Naranjo Ferry ☎ 506/641–0118. Tambor Ferry ☎ 506/661–2084. Zancudo Ferry ☎ 506/776–0012.

BUSINESS HOURS

Business hours are about the same from region to region and don't differ much from cities to rural areas and resorts. Most shops and offices are open 8–6. Government offices, except for the Tourism Institute, close at 4 PM. In rural areas and smaller cities, some shops and offices close at lunch for an hour or more. This practice is going out of fashion in San José. Businesses usually close only on legal holidays, some of which are religious holidays. In small towns and rural areas, nothing is open on Sunday. In San José and resorts, supermarkets and some restaurants are open Sunday. Most of Costa Rica's public museums are closed Monday.

BANKS & OFFICES

Most state banks are open weekdays 9–3, and some are open Saturday morning. Several branches of Banco Nacional are open until 6. Private banks—Scotia, Banco Banex, and Banco de San José—tend to keep longer hours and are usually the best places to change U.S. dollars and traveler's checks. At Juan Santamaría International Airport, a branch of the Banco de San José is open every day from 5 AM to 10 PM.

GAS STATIONS

There are 24-hour gas stations near most cities, especially along the Pan-American Highway. Most other stations are open from about 7 to 7, sometimes until midnight.

PHARMACIES

Pharmacies throughout the country are generally open from 8 to 8, though it's best to consult with your hotel's staff to be sure. Some pharmacies in San José affiliated with clinics stay open 24 hours. In the Central Valley, the Fischel Pharmacy (⇨ Emergencies, below) stays open until midnight.

BUS TRAVEL WITHIN COSTA RICA

Reliable, inexpensive bus service covers much of the country. Most Costa Ricans don't have cars, so buses go almost everywhere. Several private companies leave San José from a variety of departure points—there is no main bus station. Buses range from huge, modern, air-conditioned beasts with lead-foot drivers, bathrooms, and an occasional movie to something a little less new and a whole lot more sweaty and crowded. Tall people may be uncomfortable, because there isn't much leg room; some of the vehicles are converted school buses. Buses usually leave and arrive on time and sometimes even leave a few minutes early, so get to your stop early. Buses are inexpensive and usually well maintained. Fares on long-distance routes on public buses are usually $5–$10 one way. For schedules and departure locations for your destination, *see* Bus Travel *in* the A to Z section of the appropriate chapter.

Bus routes to popular beach destinations sell out quickly, so buy your ticket in advance. In rural areas and on city bus routes in San José, standing in the aisles is permitted, but on long-distance routes from San José, everyone must have a seat. Sometimes tickets include seat numbers, which are usually printed on the tops of the chairs. Smoking is not permitted on buses.

Watch your luggage on the bus. Don't put your belongings in the overhead bin unless you have to, and if you do, keep your eyes on them. If someone—even a person who looks like an employee of the bus line—offers to put your luggage on the bus or in the luggage compartment underneath for you, politely decline. If you put your luggage underneath the bus, try to get off the bus quickly when you arrive at your destination and go around to retrieve it. The main inconvenience of buses is that you usually have to return to San José to bus between outlying regions. For example, if you want to take public buses between Quepos/Manuel Antonio and Playa Tamarindo, you have to connect in San José, which is significantly out of the way. Two private bus companies, Gray Line Tours Fantasy Bus and Interbus, offer an alternative to traveling through the capital. These buses, which are much more expensive than public buses, cost about $15–$55 one-way but can take hours off your trip. Within San José, taxis are inexpensive and much faster than city buses. City buses are crowded and uncomfortable if you have a lot of luggage.

FARES & SCHEDULES

Bus companies don't have printed bus schedules, but hotels usually know where bus stops are, when buses leave, and how much they cost. Otherwise, visit or call the bus company's office. Be prepared for bus-company employees and bus drivers to speak Spanish only.

Buses to popular beach and mountain destinations often sell out on the weekends and the day before and after a holiday. It's also difficult to get tickets back to San José on Sunday afternoon. Some bus companies take reservations over the phone, but others require you to buy a ticket in person. Tickets are sold at bus stations and on the buses themselves; you must pay with cash. Buy your ticket at the ticket window if there is one. The only way to reserve a seat is to buy your ticket ahead of time. On longer routes, buses stop midway at modest restaurants. Near the ends of their runs many nonexpress buses turn into large taxis, dropping passengers off one by one at their destinations; to save time, take a *directo* (express) bus.

🚌 **Central Valley Bus Companies Empresarios Unidos** ☎ 506/222-0064. **Sacsa** ☎ 506/223-5350. **Transtusa** ☎ 506/222-4464. **Tuasa** ☎ 506/222-5325.

🚌 **Northern Guanacaste & Alajuela Bus Companies Tralapa** ☎ 506/221-7202. **Transportes La Cañera** ☎ 506/223-4242. **Transportes Tilarán** ☎ 506/460-3554.

🚌 **Nicoya Peninsula Bus Companies Empresa Alfaro** ☎ 506/685-5032. **Empresarios Unidos** ☎ 506/222-0064. **Pulmitan** ☎ 506/222-1650.

🚌 **Central Pacific Bus Companies Transportes Delio Morales** ☎ 506/223-5567. **Transportes Jacó** ☎ 506/223-1109.

🚌 **Southern Pacific Bus Companies Tracopa-Alfaro** ☎ 506/222-2666. **Musoc** ☎ 506/222-2422. **Transportes Blanco Lobo** ☎ 506/257-4121.

🚌 **Atlantic Lowlands & Pacific Coast Bus Companies Autotransportes Sarapiquí** ☎ 506/259-8571. **Empresarios Guapilenos** ☎ 506/710-7780. **Transportes Caribeños** ☎ 506/221-2596. **Transportes Mepe** ☎ 506/257-8129.

🚌 **Private Bus Companies Gray Line Tours Fantasy Bus** ☎ 506/220-2126. **Interbus** ☎ 506/283-5573 ⊕ www.interbusonline.com.

CAMERAS & PHOTOGRAPHY

Photographic opportunities abound in Costa Rica, but don't expect to take pictures of jaguars or tapirs. Large animals are very elusive; you could live your whole life in Costa Rica and not see them. Consider bringing a macro lens, because some of the best shots are of insects, leaves, flowers, and other tiny wonders. You should be able to find monkeys and toucans willing to appear in your photos. Sunsets off Pacific beaches, panoramas of the forest canopy, and pictures of people are obligatory shots. Always ask permission before taking pictures of locals. You will not be allowed to take pictures when watching turtles nest, as any light can deter them from nesting. The *Kodak Guide to Shooting Great Travel Pictures* (available at bookstores everywhere) is loaded with tips.

🖪 **Photo Help Kodak Information Center** ☎ 800/242-2424 ⊕ www.kodak.com.

EQUIPMENT PRECAUTIONS

Humidity and rain are the biggest problems facing photographers in Costa Rica. Take plenty of resealable plastic bags for lenses, etc., and consider buying a dry bag, sold in outdoors stores, for your camera. **Don't pack film and equipment in checked luggage,** where it is much more susceptible to damage. X-ray machines used to view checked luggage are extremely powerful and therefore are likely to ruin your film. Try to **ask for hand inspection of film,** which becomes clouded after repeated exposure to airport X-ray machines, and **keep videotapes and computer disks away from metal detectors.** Always **keep film, tape, and computer disks out of the sun.** Carry an extra supply of batteries, and **be prepared to turn on your camera, camcorder, or laptop** to prove to airport security personnel that the device is real.

FILM & DEVELOPING

Although travelers are technically only allowed to bring six rolls of film into the country, customs agents almost never check. Kodak, Fuji, Mitsubishi, and AGFA film is widely available. In rural areas and smaller shops, check the expiration date of film. Most film costs at least 20% more in Costa Rica than in the United States, so try to **bring along enough film for your trip.** Plenty of shops in San José develop film, usually the same day, but they tend to change the chemicals less often than they should, so you risk getting prints of poor quality.

🄵 Local Labs **Dima Color** ✉ 325 yards east of U.S. Embassy, Pavas ☎ 506/231-4130. **Rapi Foto** ✉ C. Central at Avda. 5, Centro Colón, San José ☎ 506/223-7640.

CAR RENTAL

Most rental car companies use late-model imported economy cars such as Hyundai Excel and four-wheel-drive vehicles including Gran Vitara and Suzuki Samurai. Midsize and luxury sedans are not usually available. Most cars in Costa Rica have manual transmissions; you should specify when making the reservation if you want an automatic transmission. Many travelers shy away from renting a car in Costa Rica, if only for fear of the road conditions. Indeed, this is not an ideal place to drive: in San José, traffic is bad and car theft is rampant (look for guarded parking lots or hotels with lots); in rural areas, roads are often unpaved or potholed. The greatest deterrent of all might be the extremely high rental rates.

Still, having your own wheels gives you more control over your itinerary and the pace of your trip. If you decide to go for it, you'll have to choose which type of vessel to rent: a standard vehicle, fine for most destinations, or a *doble-tracción* (four-wheel drive), often essential to reach the more remote parts of the country, especially during the rainy season. These can cost roughly twice as much as an economy car and should be booked well in advance. If you plan to rent any kind of vehicle between December 15 and January 3, or during Holy Week, **reserve several months ahead of time.**

Costa Rica has around 50 international and local car-rental firms, the larger of which have several offices around San José. At least a dozen rental offices line San José's Paseo Colón, and most large hotels have representatives. For a complete listing, look in the local phone directory once you arrive, under *alquiler de automóviles.*

It is not common for travelers to hire a car with a driver, but at $75 per day plus the driver's food, it is almost the same price as renting a four-wheel drive. Some drivers are also knowledgeable guides; others just drive. To find a list of these services, check the the *Tico Times* classified ads. The *Tico Times* is published on Friday and is available at supermarkets, souvenir shops, bookstores, and hotels.

CUTTING COSTS

Most car rental firms are located in San José and at the Juan Santamaría International Airport. It is easier to pick up and return rental cars at the airport, and the price is the same. You may be able to save money by renting cars from private individuals who advertise in classified ads in the *Tico Times,* but there are no guarantees on the condition of the cars. Most local firms are affiliated with international car rental chains and offer the same guarantees and services as their branches abroad. Check cars thoroughly for damage before you sign the rental contract. Even tough-looking four-wheel-drive vehicles should be coddled. For a good deal, **call directly to Costa Rica or book through a travel agent who will shop around.**

Do **look into wholesalers,** companies that do not own fleets but rent in bulk from those that do and often offer better rates than traditional car-rental operations. Prices are best during off-peak periods. Rentals booked through wholesalers often must be paid for before you leave home.

🄵 Rental Agencies **Alamo** ☎ 506/233-7733, 800/522-9696 in the U.S. ⊕ www.alamo.com. **American** ☎ 506/221-5353. **Avis** ☎ 506/293-2222, 800/331-1084 in the U.S., 800/879-2847 in Canada, 0870/606-0100 in the U.K., 02/9353-9000 in Australia, 09/526-2847 in New Zealand ⊕ www.avis.com. **Budget** ☎ 506/255-4750, 800/527-0700 in the U.S., 0870/156-5656 in the U.K. ⊕ www.budget.com. **Dollar** ☎ 506/257-1585, 800/800-6000 in the U.S., 0124/622-0111 in the U.K. (where it's affiliated with Sixt), 02/9223-1444 in Australia ⊕ www.dollar.com. **Economy** ☎ 506/231-5410. **Elegante** ☎ 506/257-0026. **Hertz** ☎ 506/221-1818, 800/654-3001 in the U.S., 800/263-0600 in Canada, 0870/844-8844 in the U.K., 02/9669-2444 in Australia, 09/256-8690 in New Zealand ⊕ www.hertz.com. **Hola** ☎ 506/231-5666. **National** ☎ 506/290-8787, 800/227-7368 in the U.S., 0870/600-6666 in the U.K. ⊕ www.nationalcar.com.

🄵 Wholesalers **Auto Europe** ☎ 207/842-2000, 800/223-5555 in the U.S. 🖷 207/842-2222 ⊕ www.autoeurope.com.

INSURANCE

When driving a rented car you are generally responsible for any damage to or loss of the vehicle as well as for any property damage or personal injury that you may cause. Insurance issued by car-rental agencies in Costa Rica usually has a very high deductible. Before you rent, see what coverage your personal auto-insurance policy and credit cards provide.

RATES

High-season rates in San José begin at $45 a day and $290 a week for an economy car with air-conditioning, manual transmission, unlimited mileage, and obligatory insurance; but rates fluctuate considerably according to demand, season, and company. Rates for a four-wheel-drive vehicle during high season are $80 a day and $500 per week. When renting a car, **ask whether the rate includes the mandatory $15 daily fee for collision insurance.** Some firms don't charge the fee for economy cars but do for four-wheel-drive vehicles. Often companies will also require a $1,000 deposit, payable by credit card.

REQUIREMENTS & RESTRICTIONS

Car seats are compulsory for children under four years old, but many Costa Rican drivers don't use them. Make sure you specify that you need a car seat when booking a rental car. Rental cars may not be driven to Nicaragua and Panama. Seatbelt use is compulsory in the front seat. To rent a car with an international agency you need a driver's license, a valid passport, and a credit card; you must also be at least 25 years of age. If you use a local company, you must be 21.

SURCHARGES

Before you pick up a car in one city and leave it in another, **ask about drop-off charges or one-way service fees,** which can be substantial. Note, too, that some rental agencies charge extra if you return the car before the time specified in your contract. To avoid a hefty refueling fee, **fill the tank just before you turn in the car,** but be aware that gas stations near the rental outlet may overcharge. It's almost never a deal to buy the tank of gas that's in the car when you rent it; the understanding is that you'll return it empty, but some fuel usually remains. Car seats cost about $3–$5 per day. Additional drivers are about $5–$10 per day.

CAR TRAVEL

You can use your own driver's license in Costa Rica, but you must carry your passport showing that you entered the country less than 90 days ago. Driving can be a challenge, but it's a great way to explore certain regions, especially Guanacaste, the Atlantic Lowlands, and the Caribbean coast (apart from Tortuguero and Barra del Colorado). Keep in mind that mountains and poor road conditions make most trips longer than you'd normally expect. If you want to visit a few different far-flung areas and have a short amount of time, domestic flights are a better option.

In the rainy season, you must have a four-wheel-drive vehicle to reach Monteverde and some destinations in Guanacaste. Car trips to Northern Guanacaste from San José can take an entire day, so flying is probably better if you don't have long to spend in the country. Flying is definitely better than driving for visiting the Southern Pacific zone of Puerto Jiménez, Golfito, Drake Bay, and so on.

When visiting the Atlantic coast by car, remember that fog often covers the Braulio Carrillo mountains after noon, making driving hazardous. Don't plan to cross this area in the afternoon. The same holds true for trips to the Southern Zone, where the Cerro de la Muerte mountain is often covered with fog in the afternoons. Driving to the Central Pacific beaches, Arenal Volcano, and destinations in the Central Valley is pleasant, but be alert, because roads are in poor condition and winding, and drivers tend to pass on blind curves. Driving at night throughout the country is not recommended, because roads are poorly lit and many don't have painted center lines or shoulder lines.

AUTO CLUBS

7 In Australia **Australian Automobile Association** ☎ 02/6247-7311.

7 In Canada **Canadian Automobile Association (CAA)** ☎ 613/247-0117.

7 In New Zealand **New Zealand Automobile Association** ☎ 09/377-4660.

7 In the U.K. **Automobile Association (AA)** ☎ 0870/600-0371. **Royal Automobile Club (RAC)** ☎ 0800/015-4435.

7 In the U.S. **American Automobile Association (AAA)** ☎ 800/564-6222.

EMERGENCY SERVICES

Costa Rica has no highway emergency service organization. In Costa Rica, 911 is the nationwide number for accidents. Traffic police are scattered around the country, but Costa Ricans are very good about stopping for people with car trouble. Local car-rental agencies can give you a list of numbers to call in case of accidents or car trouble.

GASOLINE

Gas is more expensive in rural areas, and gas stations can be few and far between. Try to fill your tank in cities. Major credit cards are widely accepted. There are no self-service pumps or pumps that accept credit cards. It is customary to tip the attendant 100 colónes. Ask the attendant if you want a receipt, which is called a *factura*. Regular unleaded gasoline is called *regular* and high-octane unleaded is called *super*. Gas is sold by the liter. Cost at this writing is 58¢ per liter ($2.20 per gallon) for regular and 61¢ per liter ($2.31 per gallon) for super.

PARKING

A parking lot is always better than street parking. If you must park on the street, try to park where you can see your car. Always lock your car and don't leave valuables in sight. Accept the services of local men or boys who offer to watch your car, and pay them the equivalent of $1 per hour when you return. There are very few parking meters, almost none outside San José. They take 50 and 100 colón coins. Parking lots are easy to find in San José and other cities. Parking costs about $1 per hour. Most lots close between 9 and 11 PM, so always inquire about closing times before leaving your car.

Parking regulations are strictly enforced in San José, and police may tow your car or give you a ticket for up to $30. In rural areas, parking regulations are less strictly enforced. If you get a ticket in a rental car, always give the ticket to the company. **Park overnight in a locked garage or guarded lot,** as Central American insurance may hold you liable if your rental car is stolen. Most hotels, barring the least expensive, offer secure parking with a guard or locked gates, as car theft is rife.

ROAD CONDITIONS

San José is terribly congested during the week during morning and afternoon rush hours (7–9 AM and 4–6 PM). Avoid returning to the city on Sunday evening, when traffic to San José from the Pacific-coast beaches backs up for hours. In San José, roads are generally in good condition, but in the countryside conditions vary. During the rainy season, roads are in much worse shape throughout the city.

San José has many one-way streets and traffic circles. Streets in the capital are narrow. Pedestrians are supposed to have the right of way but do not in reality, so be alert when walking. The local driving style is erratic and aggressive but not fast, because road conditions don't permit too much speed. Frequent fender benders tie up traffic. Keep your windows rolled up in the center of the city, because thieves will reach into your car at stoplights and snatch your purse, jewelry, etc.

Outside of San José, you'll run into long stretches of unpaved road. Frequent hazards in the countryside are potholes, landslides during the rainy season, and cattle on the roads. Drunk drivers are a hazard throughout the country on weekend nights.

ROAD MAPS

Local road maps are available at gas stations and tourist information offices for about $10. Bookstores in San José that sell maps include Librería Universal, Librería Lehmann, and Seventh Street Books (⇨ Shopping *in* chapter 1.)

RULES OF THE ROAD

The highway speed limit in Costa Rica is usually 90 kph (54 mph), which drops to 60 kph (36 mph) in residential areas. Speed limits are rigorously enforced in all regions of the country. Seat belts are required, though this is not rigorously enforced. *Alto* means stop and *Ceda* means yield. Right turns on red are permitted except where signs indicate otherwise, but in San José this is usually not possible due to one-way streets and pedestrian crossings.

Local drunk driving laws are strict. Policemen who stop drivers for speeding and drunk driving are often looking for payment on the spot—essentially a bribe. Whether you're guilty or not, if you don't give in you'll get a ticket. Ask for a ticket instead of paying the bribe. It discourages corruption and if you bring the ticket to your car rental company, they might pay it on your behalf. If you feel it's in your best interest to pay the bribe, $20 is usually enough to get out of a speeding ticket and $50 is usually acceptable for a drunk driving charge.

Car seats are required for children ages 4 and under, but car-seat laws are not rigorously enforced. Many Tico babies and children ride on their parents' laps. Children are allowed in the front seat.

There are plenty of questionable drivers on Costa Rican highways; **be prepared for harebrained passing on blind corners, tailgating, and failing to signal.** Watch, too, for two-lane roads that feed into one-lane bridges with specified rights of way. Look out for potholes, even in the smoothest sections of the best roads.

You can drive over Costa Rica's borders into Panama and Nicaragua, but not in a rental car—vehicles rented in one country cannot be taken into the next.

CHILDREN IN COSTA RICA

Costa Ricans are very fond of children and are tolerant of them at restaurants, museums, and other attraction. Thanks to high safety and health standards, Costa Rica is popular with traveling families. Most of the health problems you might associate with the tropics are rare or nonexistent in Costa Rica (though they do exist in neighboring Nicaragua), and the country's most popular destinations have plenty to offer kids. Beware of dangerous currents at many popular beaches when the surf is up.

The *Tico Times*, published (in English) on Friday, lists activities for children in the "Weekend" section. The daily Spanish-language newspaper, *La Nación,* publishes a section called "Viva" on Friday and Sunday listing events and activities for families.

If you are renting a car, don't forget to **arrange for a car seat** when you reserve. For general advice about traveling with children, consult *Fodor's FYI: Travel with Your Baby* (available in bookstores everywhere).

Sights and attractions that are especially appealing to children are indicated by a rubber-duckie icon (🦆) in the margin.

FLYING

If your children are 2 or older, **ask about children's airfares.** As a general rule, infants under 2 not occupying a seat fly at greatly reduced fares or even for free. But if you want to guarantee a seat for an infant, you have to pay full fare. Consider flying during off-peak days and times; most airlines will grant an infant a seat without a ticket if there are available seats. When booking, **confirm carry-on allowances** if you're traveling with infants. In general, for babies charged 10%–50% of the adult fare you are allowed one carry-on bag and a collapsible stroller; if the flight is full, the stroller may have to be checked or you may be limited to less.

Experts agree that it's a good idea to use safety seats aloft for children weighing less than 40 pounds. Airlines set their own policies: If you use a safety seat, U.S. carriers usually require that the child be ticketed, even if he or she is young enough to ride free, because the seats must be strapped into regular seats. And even if you pay the full adult fare for the seat, it may be worth it, especially on longer trips. Do **check your airline's policy about using safety seats during takeoff and landing.** Safety seats are not allowed everywhere in the plane, so get your seat assignments as early as possible.

When reserving, **request children's meals or a freestanding bassinet** (not available at all airlines) if you need them. But note that bulkhead seats, where you must sit to use the bassinet, may lack an overhead bin or storage space on the floor.

LODGING

Most mid-price and higher-price hotels offer cribs; some offer cots. For cheaper hotels, ask in advance but be prepared to share a bed with your child or have him or her sleep in a regular single bed. Baby-sitters and children's programs are available only in the largest resorts, and usually only in the December–April high season.

Hotels that are especially good for children include Selva Verde in the Atlantic lowlands, Mawamba Lodge in Tortuguero, Sapo Dorado in Monteverde, Hotel Grano de Oro in San José, and Sí Como No in Manuel Antonio. The high-end Marriott, Melía, and Barceló hotel chains are also good for children because they have cots, cribs, and children's discounts. Most hotels in Costa Rica allow children under a certain age to stay in their parents' room at no extra charge, but others charge for them as extra adults; be sure to **find out the cutoff age for children's discounts.**

🛈 Best Choices **Mawamba Lodge** ⊠ Tortuguero ☎ 506/223-242. **Hotel Sapo Dorado** ⊠ Monteverde ☎ 506/645-5010. **Hotel Grano de Oro** ⊠ Calle 30, between Avdas. 2 and 4 ☎ 506/255-3322 **Sí Como No** ⊠ Manuel Antonio ☎ 506/777-0777. **Best Western Jacó Beach Hotel** ⊠ Playa Jacó ☎ 506/643-1000. **Hotel Costa Rica Marriott** ⊠ Alajaulea ☎ 506/298-0000. **Selva Verde Lodge** ⊠ Puerto Viejo de Sarapiquí ☎ 506/776-6800.

PRECAUTIONS

Sunburn and dehydration are problems commonly experienced by children. Slather on the sunscreen and make sure they swim in T-shirts and wear hats. Give them plenty to drink, and try to take bus trips, which can be very hot, early in the morning or late in the afternoon. Never let a child swim unattended in the ocean or go deeper than his or her waist.

SUPPLIES & EQUIPMENT

Baby formula and disposable diapers are widely available in supermarkets and pharmacies around the country. Usually only powder formula is available, and speciality types of formula (i.e., lactose-free) are available only in pharmacies. Major U.S. brands of disposable diapers are sold. Prices are about the same as or slightly higher than in the United States.

CONSUMER PROTECTION

Get receipts for your purchases, and check that the correct amount has been written in on credit-card receipts. When paying with a credit card in restaurants, make sure the slip is totaled, whether or not you are leaving a tip. It is helpful to carry a pocket calculator so you can convert to your home currency when checking prices. Whether you're shopping for gifts or purchasing travel services, **pay with a major credit card** whenever possible, so you can cancel payment or get reimbursed if there's a problem (and you can provide documentation). If you're doing business with a particular company for the first time, **contact your local Better Business Bureau and the attorney general's offices** in your state and (for U.S. businesses) the company's home state as well. Have any complaints

been filed? Finally, if you're buying a package or tour, always **consider travel insurance** that includes default coverage (⇨ Insurance).

🛈 BBBs **Council of Better Business Bureaus** ⊠ 4200 Wilson Blvd., Suite 800, Arlington, VA 22203 ☎ 703/276-0100 🖷 703/525-8277 ⊕ www. bbb.org.

CRUISE TRAVEL

Large cruise ships usually spend only one day in Costa Rica. To spend more time cruising the waters of Costa Rica and visiting destinations within the country by ship, consider Lindblad Expeditions and Cruisewest, two smaller lines that offer weeklong cruises around the country.

The U.S.–Costa Rica cruise season runs September–May, with trips lasting from three days to a week. A travel agent can explain prices, which range from $1,000 to $5,000. Luxury liners equipped with pools and gyms sail from Fort Lauderdale, Florida, to Limón, or through the Panama Canal to Caldera, south of Puntarenas. Some cruises sail from Los Angeles to Caldera, continuing to the canal. On board the ship you can sign up for shore excursions and tours. Cruise packages include the cost of flying to the appropriate port.

To learn how to plan, choose, and book a cruise-ship voyage, consult *Fodor's FYI: Plan & Enjoy Your Cruise* (available in bookstores everywhere).

🛈 Cruise Lines **Carnival** ☎ 800/327-9501 in the U.S. **Cruisewest** ☎ 800/580-0072 in the U.S. **Cunard** ☎ 800/221-4770 in the U.S. **Holland America** ☎ 800/426-0327 in the U.S. **Lindblad Expeditions** ☎ 212/765-7740, 800/397-3348 in the U.S. **Ocean Cruise** ☎ 800/556-8850 in the U.S. **Royal Viking** ☎ 800/422-8000 in the U.S. **Seabourn** ☎ 800/351-9595 in the U.S. **Sitmar Cruise** ☎ 305/523-1219.

CUSTOMS & DUTIES

When shopping abroad, **keep receipts** for all purchases. Upon reentering the country, **be ready to show customs officials what you've bought.** Pack purchases together in an easily accessible place. If you think a duty is incorrect, appeal the assessment. If you object to the way your clearance was handled, note the inspector's badge number. In either case, first ask to see a supervisor. If the problem isn't resolved, write to the appropriate authorities, beginning with the port director at your point of entry.

IN COSTA RICA

It usually takes about 10–30 minutes to clear customs when arriving in Costa Rica. When you arrive at customs, you will be asked to press a button that indicates whether your bags will be searched. Visitors entering Costa Rica may bring in 500 grams of tobacco, 3 liters of wine or spirits, 2 kilograms of sweets and chocolates, and the equivalent of $100 worth of merchandise. Two cameras, six rolls of film, binoculars, and electrical items for personal use only are also allowed. Customs officials at San José's international airport rarely examine tourists' luggage, but if you enter by land, they'll probably look through your bags.

Pets are not quarantined if you bring a health certificate obtained from a Costa Rican consulate in your home country and filled out by a veterinarian before you arrive. Contact a Costa Rican consulate for more information about bringing pets to the country.

IN AUSTRALIA

Australian residents who are 18 or older may bring home A$400 worth of souvenirs and gifts (including jewelry), 250 cigarettes or 250 grams of cigars or other tobacco products, and 1,125 ml of alcohol (including wine, beer, and spirits). Residents under 18 may bring back A$200 worth of goods. Members of the same family traveling together may pool their allowances. Prohibited items include meat products. Seeds, plants, and fruits need to be declared upon arrival.

Australian Customs Service Regional Director, Box 8, Sydney, NSW 2001 02/9213-2000 or 1300/363263, 02/9364-7222 or 1800/803-006 quarantine-inquiry line 02/9213-4043 www.customs.gov.au.

IN CANADA

Canadian residents who have been out of Canada for at least seven days may bring in C$750 worth of goods duty-free. If you've been away fewer than seven days but more than 48 hours, the duty-free allowance drops to C$200. If your trip lasts 24 to 48 hours, the allowance is C$50. You may not pool allowances with family members. Goods claimed under the C$750 exemption may follow you by mail; those claimed under the lesser exemptions must accompany you. Alcohol and tobacco products may be included in the seven-day and 48-hour exemptions but not in the 24-hour exemption. If you meet the age requirements of the province or territory through which you reenter Canada, you may bring in, duty-free, 1.5 liters of wine or 1.14 liters (40 imperial ounces) of liquor or 24 12-ounce cans or bottles of beer or ale. Also, if you meet the local age requirement for tobacco products, you may bring in, duty-free, 200 cigarettes and 50 cigars. Check ahead of time with the Canada Customs and Revenue Agency or the Department of Agriculture for policies regarding meat products, seeds, plants, and fruits.

You may send an unlimited number of gifts (only one gift per recipient, however) worth up to C$60 each duty-free to Canada. Label the package UNSOLICITED GIFT—VALUE UNDER $60. Alcohol and tobacco are excluded.

Canada Customs and Revenue Agency 2265 St. Laurent Blvd., Ottawa, Ontario K1G 4K3 204/983-3500, 506/636-5064, or 800/461-9999 www.ccra.gc.ca.

IN NEW ZEALAND

All homeward-bound residents may bring back NZ$700 worth of souvenirs and gifts; passengers may not pool their allowances, and children can claim only the concession on goods intended for their own use. For those 17 or older, the duty-free allowance also includes 4.5 liters of wine or beer; one 1,125-ml bottle of spirits; and either 200 cigarettes, 250 grams of tobacco, 50 cigars, or a combination of the three up to 250 grams. Meat products, seeds, plants, and fruits must be declared upon arrival to the Agricultural Services Department.

New Zealand Customs Head office: The Customhouse, 17–21 Whitmore St., Box 2218, Wellington 09/300-5399 or 0800/428-786 www.customs.govt.nz.

IN THE U.K.

From countries outside the European Union, including Costa Rica, you may bring home, duty-free, 200 cigarettes or 50 cigars; 1 liter of spirits or 2 liters of fortified or sparkling wine or liqueurs; 2 liters of still table wine; 60 ml of perfume; 250 ml of toilet water; plus £145 worth of other goods, including gifts and souvenirs.

Prohibited items include meat products, seeds, plants, and fruits.

HM Customs and Excise ⊠ Portcullis House, 21 Cowbridge Rd. E, Cardiff CF11 9SS ☎ 0845/010-9000 or 0208/929-0152; 0208/929-6731 or 0208/910-3602 complaints ⊕ www.hmce.gov.uk.

IN THE U.S.

U.S. residents who have been out of the country for at least 48 hours may bring home, for personal use, $800 worth of foreign goods duty-free, as long as they haven't used the $800 allowance or any part of it in the past 30 days. This exemption may include 1 liter of alcohol (for travelers 21 and older), 200 cigarettes, and 100 non-Cuban cigars. Family members from the same household who are traveling together may pool their $800 personal exemptions. For fewer than 48 hours, the duty-free allowance drops to $200, which may include 50 cigarettes, 10 non-Cuban cigars, and 150 ml of alcohol (or 150 ml of perfume containing alcohol). The $200 allowance cannot be combined with other individuals' exemptions, and if you exceed it, the full value of all the goods will be taxed. Antiques, which the U.S. Bureau of Customs and Border Protection defines as objects more than 100 years old, enter duty-free, as do original works of art done entirely by hand, including paintings, drawings, and sculptures. This doesn't apply to folk art or handicrafts, which are in general dutiable.

You may also send packages home duty-free, with a limit of one parcel per addressee per day (except alcohol or tobacco products or perfume worth more than $5). You can mail up to $200 worth of goods for personal use; label the package PERSONAL USE and attach a list of its contents and their retail value. If the package contains your used personal belongings, mark it AMERICAN GOODS RETURNED to avoid paying duties. You may send up to $100 worth of goods as a gift; mark the package UNSOLICITED GIFT. Mailed items do not affect your duty-free allowance on your return.

To avoid paying duty on foreign-made high-ticket items you already own and will take on your trip, register them with customs before you leave the country. Consider filing a Certificate of Registration for laptops, cameras, watches, and other digital devices identified with serial numbers or other permanent markings; you can keep the certificate for other trips. Otherwise, bring a sales receipt or insurance form to show that you owned the item before you left the United States.

U.S. Bureau of Customs and Border Protection ⊠ for inquiries and equipment registration, 1300 Pennsylvania Ave. NW, Washington, DC 20229 ⊕ www.customs.gov ☎ 202/354-1000 ⊠ for complaints, Customer Satisfaction Unit, 1300 Pennsylvania Ave. NW, Room 5.5D, Washington, DC 20229.

DISABILITIES & ACCESSIBILITY

Accessibility in Central America is extremely limited. Wheelchair ramps are practically nonexistent, and streets are often unpaved outside major cities, making wheelchair travel difficult. Exploring most attractions involves walking down cobblestone streets, steep trails, or muddy paths. Buses are not equipped to carry wheelchairs, so people using wheelchairs should hire a van to get around and bring someone along to help out. There is some growing awareness of the needs of people with disabilities, and some hotels and attractions in Costa Rica have made the necessary provisions; the Costa Rican Tourist Institute, known locally as the ICT, has more information.

Local Resources Costa Rican Tourist Institute ⊠ Avda. 4, between Cs. 5 and 7, 11th floor, Centro Colón, San José, Costa Rica ☎ 506/223-1733.

International Resources Access Adventures ⊠ 206 Chestnut Ridge Rd., Scottsville, NY 14624 ☎ 585/889-9096 ⊘ dltravel@prodigy.net, run by a former physical-rehabilitation counselor. **CareVacations** ⊠ No. 5, 5110-50 Ave., Leduc, Alberta, Canada T9E 6V4 ☎ 780/986-6404 or 877/478-7827 📠 780/986-8332 ⊕ www.carevacations.com, for group tours and cruise vacations. **Flying Wheels Travel** ⊠ 143 W. Bridge St., Box 382, Owatonna, MN 55060 ☎ 507/451-5005 📠 507/451-1685 ⊕ www.flyingwheelstravel.com.

LODGING

Very few hotels in Costa Rica are equipped for travelers in wheelchairs. In San José, the Hampton Inn, near the international airport, has some wheelchair accommodations; and Wilson Botanical Gardens, in San Vito (Southern Pacific), has one room equipped for a wheelchair.

Best Choices Hampton Inn ☎ 506/443-0043, 800/426-7866 in the U.S. 📠 506/442-9532. **Wilson Botanical Garden** ☎ 506/240-6696 📠 506/240-6783 ⊕ www.ots.duke.edu.

RESERVATIONS

When discussing accessibility with an operator or reservations agent, **ask hard questions.** Are there any stairs, inside *or* out? Are there grab bars next to the toilet *and* in the shower/tub? How wide is the doorway to the room? To the bathroom? For the most extensive facilities meeting the latest legal specifications, **opt for newer accommodations.** If you reserve through a toll-free number, consider also calling the hotel's local number to confirm the information from the central reservations office. Get confirmation in writing when you can.

SIGHTS & ATTRACTIONS

Most Costa Rican attractions are inaccessible for travelers with wheelchairs, as are restaurant bathrooms. Volcán Poás National Park is probably the most wheelchair-friendly site, with Volcán Irazú the runner-up. INBioparque, on the road leading from San José to Santo Domingo de Heredia, is a good choice for people in wheelchairs. It has ramps to exhibits, plenty of room for wheelchairs to maneuver, and wheelchair-accessible bathrooms and trails. The Orosi Valley and Sarchí also have limited exploring options for travelers using wheelchairs. The Rain Forest Aerial Tram and its coffee shop are wheelchair accessible, but the facility's rest rooms, trails, and main restaurant are not.

TRANSPORTATION

There are no wheelchair facilities on public buses. Call a taxi to pick you up instead. Juan Santamaría International Airport has wheelchair ramps. Developed areas, especially San José and the Central Valley, can be managed in a wheelchair more easily than rural areas. The tour company **Vaya con Silla de Ruedas** (Go with Wheelchairs) provides transportation and guided tours.

🚩 **Vaya con Silla de Ruedas** ☎ 506/391-5045 ⊕ www.gowithwheelchairs.com.

🚩 Complaints **Aviation Consumer Protection Division** ✉ U.S. Department of Transportation, C-75, Room 4107, 400 7th St. NW, Washington, DC 20590 ☎ 202/366-2220 ⊕ www.dot.gov/airconsumer. **Departmental Office of Civil Rights** ✉ for general inquiries, U.S. Department of Transportation, S-30, 400 7th St. SW, Washington, DC 20590 ☎ 202/366-4648 🖷 202/366-9371 ⊕ www.dot.gov/ost/docr/index.htm. **Disability Rights Section** ✉ NYAV, U.S. Department of Justice, Civil Rights Division, 950 Pennsylvania Ave. NW, Washington, DC 20530 ☎ ADA information line 202/514-0301, 800/514-0301, 202/514-0383 TTY, 800/514-0383 TTY ⊕ www.ada.gov. **U.S. Department of Transportation Hotline** ☎ for disability-related air-travel problems, 800/778-4838 or 800/455-9880 TTY.

DISCOUNTS & DEALS

Some local tour companies offer one-day tours to multiple attractions, usually for about $80 per person for up to five stops. These tours may sound like great deals, but be aware that you won't stay very long at any of the attractions and that your day may be very long and tiring.

Be a smart shopper and **compare all your options** before making decisions. A plane ticket bought with a promotional coupon from travel clubs, coupon books, and direct-mail offers or purchased on the Internet may not be cheaper than the least expensive fare from a discount ticket agency. And always keep in mind that what you get is just as important as what you save.

DISCOUNT RESERVATIONS

To save money, **look into discount reservations services** with Web sites and toll-free numbers, which use their buying power to get a better price on hotels, airline tickets (⇨ Air Travel), even car rentals. When booking a room, always **call the hotel's local toll-free number** (if one is available) rather than the central reservations number—you'll often get a better price. Always ask about special packages or corporate rates.

When shopping for the best deal on hotels and car rentals, **look for guaranteed exchange rates,** which protect you against a falling dollar. With your rate locked in, you won't pay more, even if the price goes up in the local currency.

🚩 Airline Tickets **Air 4 Less** ☎ 800/AIR4LESS in the U.S.; low-fare specialist.

🚩 Hotel Rooms **Accommodations Express** ☎ 800/444-7666 or 800/277-1064 in the U.S. ⊕ www.accommodationsexpress.com. **Hotels.com** ☎ 214/369-1246, 800/246-8357 in the U.S. ⊕ www.hotels.com. **Turbotrip.com** ☎ 800/473-7829 in the U.S. ⊕ www.turbotrip.com.

PACKAGE DEALS

Don't confuse packages and guided tours. When you buy a package, you travel on your own, just as though you had planned the trip yourself. Fly-drive packages, which combine airfare and car rental, are often a good deal. In cities, ask the local visitor's bureau about hotel packages that include tickets to major museum exhibits or other special events.

EATING & DRINKING

The restaurants we list are the cream of the crop in each price category. Properties indicated by a ✕🖾 are lodging establishments whose restaurant warrants a special trip.

WHAT IT COSTS (at dinner)	
$$$$	over $25
$$$	$20–$25
$$	$10–$20
$	$5–$10
¢	under $5

Prices are per-person for a main course.

MEALS & SPECIALTIES

Desayuno (breakfast) is served at *sodas* (informal café-type restaurants serving Costa Rican cuisine) and hotels. Eggs are prevalent, as is *gallo pinto* ("spotted rooster," a mix of black beans and rice), often topped with a dollop of *natilla* (sour cream), and squeezed juices from carrot to fresh-picked star fruit. Always at *almuerzo* (lunch), and sometimes at *cena* (dinner), you can depend on a casado, the *típico* Costa Rican meal. Salads with *aguacate* (avocado) and *palmito* (heart of palm) are also common. Note that lettuce is almost always served shredded.

MEALTIMES

In San José and surrounding cities, *sodas* (informal eateries) are usually open daily 7 AM to 7 or 9 PM, though some close on Sunday. Other restaurants are usually open 11 AM–9 PM. In rural areas, restaurants are usually closed on Sunday, except around resorts. In resort areas, some restaurants may be open late. The only all-night restaurants are in downtown San José casinos. Normal dining hours in Costa Rica are noon–3 and 6–9. Unless otherwise noted, the restaurants listed in this guide are open daily for lunch and dinner.

PAYING

Credit cards are not accepted at most sodas or restaurants in rural areas. Always ask before you order to find out if your credit card will be accepted. Visa and MasterCard are the most commonly accepted cards; American Express and Diners Club are less widely accepted. In Costa Rica, 23% is added to all menu prices— 13% for tax and 10% for service. An additional tip is not expected, but always appreciated.

RESERVATIONS & DRESS

Reservations are always a good idea; we mention them only when they're essential or not accepted. Book as far ahead as you can, and reconfirm as soon as you arrive. (Large parties should always call ahead to check the reservations policy.) We mention dress only when men are required to wear a jacket or a jacket and tie.

WINE, BEER & SPIRITS

Costa Rica's one brewery makes half a dozen brands of beer, including the popular Imperial, a dark brew called Steinbrau, and a local version of Heineken. All wine is imported; the best deals are usually from Chile and Argentina, particularly the Chilean Castillero del Diablo and Sangre de Toro. Costa Rica's best rum is Centenario, but most Ticos drink a rot-gut rum called *guaro*. All of the above is served at restaurants and bars and sold in supermarkets and liquor stores. Café Britt makes a refined coffee liqueur that is sold at supermarkets and liquor stores, as well as the airport.

ECOTOURISM

Ecotourism, green tourism, environmental tourism: the buzzwords have been flying around Costa Rica for more than a decade. Many tour companies have incorporated a high level of environmental awareness into their business practices. **Find out whether or not your prospective tour company has "eco-friendly" policies,** such as hiring and training locals as guides, drivers, managers, and office workers; teaching people as much as possible about the plant and animal life, geography, and history that surrounds them; controlling the numbers of people allowed daily onto a given site; restoring watersheds and anything else damaged by trail-building, visiting, or general overuse; and discouraging wildlife feeding or any other unnatural or disruptive behavior (i.e., making loud noises to scare birds into flight). All these practices can mitigate the effects of intense tourism.

After all, it's better to have a hundred people walking through a forest than to cut the forest down.

Whether you travel on your own or with a tour group, try to make your visit beneficial to those who live near protected areas: **use local guides or services,** eat in local restaurants, and buy local crafts or produce. To ensure land preservation for future generations, you can donate to local conservation groups or a few foreign environmental organizations—including Conservation International, the Nature Conservancy, and the World Wide Fund for Nature—that aid ecological efforts in Costa Rica.

Don't remove plants, rocks, shells, or animals from their natural environment. Take only pictures; leave only footprints. It's illegal to take anything, alive or dead, out of a national park or any other protected area. To see turtles nesting, go with a guide. If you go on your own you will disrupt them. Most national parks have trash cans, but pack out your trash when doing backcountry camping. Do not feed wildlife, even when animals appear tame. Do not stray from the trails for any reason.
🔳 Local Conservation Groups ANAI ☎ 506/224-3570. APREFLOFAS ☎ 506/240-6087. Monteverde Institute ☎ 506/645-5053. Neotropica Foundation ☎ 506/253-2130.
🔳 International Conservation Groups Conservation International ✉ 2501 M St. NW, Suite 200, Washington, DC 20037 ☎ 202/973-2227 or 800/429-5660 ⊕ www.conservation.org. Nature Conservancy ✉ 4245 Fairfax Dr., Arlington, VA 22203 📠 703/841-5300 ⊕ www.tnc.org. World Wide Fund for Nature ✉ Av. du Mont-Blanc, CH 1196 Gland, Switzerland ☎ 4122/364-9111 ⊕ www.panda.org.

NATIONAL PARKS

For specific information on Costa Rican parks and protected areas, call the regional offices (➪ chapters 1–7) or the national-park information line at the Ministry of Environment and Energy. For specific requests, such as reserving camping or cabin space, call the regional office of the park in question. Practical information on parks, including limited literature, is available at the Fundación de Parques Nacionales. The price of admission to Costa Rica's national parks is $6 per day.
🔳 Costa Rica Park Contacts Fundación de Parques Nacionales ✉ 300 m (328 yards) north and

300 m (328 yards) east of Church of Santa Teresita, San José ☎ 506/257-2239. Ministry of Environment and Energy (MINAE) ☎ 506/233-4533; 192 in Costa Rica.

TOURS

If you park yourself at a beach hotel or an all-inclusive you'll miss what Costa Rica does best: nature. To get the most out of your trip, **pair up with a professional bilingual nature guide,** who knows the country's diverse landscapes, birds, animals, and where you'll see them. Costa Rica Expeditions, known for its commitment to conservation, has high-quality tours led by knowledgeable, professional guides. Horizontes is also a top-notch natural-history tour operator with some of the country's best guides. Aventuras Naturales runs terrific adventure tours (including whitewater rafting and bicycling) either as a one-day trip or multiday package. Sun Tours trips are well organized and guides are informative and friendly; they do a superb job of planning trips that hit all the country's highlights. There are many tour companies and guides out there (and many lodges staff their own naturalist).

"Soft adventure" travelers are well catered to aboard the 185-ft M.V. *Pacific Explorer,* run by Cruise West, with multiday natural-history cruises along the Southern Pacific coast. Lindblad Expeditions runs cruises aboard the larger *Sea Voyager.*
🔳 Costa Rica Aventuras Naturales ✈ Box 10736-1000, San José ☎ 506/225-3939, 800/514-0411 in the U.S. 📠 506/253-6934 ⊕ www.toenjoynature.com. Costa Rica Expeditions ☎ 506/222-0333 📠 506/257-1665 ⊕ www.costaricaexpeditions.com. Horizontes ☎ 506/222-2022 📠 506/255-4513 ⊕ www.horizontes.com. Lindblad Expeditions ☎ 212/765-7740, 800/397-3348 in the U.S. ⊕ www.lindblad.com. Sun Tours ☎ 506/296-7757 📠 506/290-2723 ⊕ www.crsuntours.com. Temptress Adventure Cruises ✈ Cruise West, 2401 4th Ave., Suite 700, Seattle, WA 98121-1438 ☎ 800/580-0072 in the U.S. 📠 206/441-4757 ⊕ www.cruisewest.com.

WILDLIFE

Travelers are often surprised by how hard it can be to see animals in the rain forest. Despite their frequent appearances in advertisements and brochures, many endangered species are practically impossible to spot. Between the low density of mammals, their shyness, and the fact that thick vegetation often obstructs your view, you must **be patient and stay attentive.** Because the tropical dry forest is less overgrown than the rain forest, it's one of the best life zones for animal observation; river trips, too, can make for great viewing. **Don't give up hope:** if you take the time to explore a few protected areas, you're almost certain to spy dozens of interesting critters.

ELECTRICITY

The electrical current in Central America is 110 volts (AC). Costa Rica has standard North American two-prong outlets. Adapters are required for three-prong plugs, which are not common in Costa Rica. If your appliances are dual-voltage, you'll need only an adapter. If they aren't, use a 220-volt to 110-volt transformer. Don't use 110-volt outlets marked FOR SHAVERS ONLY for high-wattage appliances such as blow-dryers unless you use a transformer. Most laptops operate equally well on 110 and 220 volts and so require only an adapter, but you should bring a surge protector for your computer. Blackouts are common in some rural areas.

EMBASSIES

Citizens of Australia and New Zealand should contact the British Embassy.
🚩 In Canada **Embassy of Costa Rica** ✉ 208-135 York St. Ottawa, ON KIN 5T4 ☎ 613/562-2855.
🚩 In Costa Rica **British Embassy** (Embajada Británica) ✉ Centro Colón, between Cs. 38 and 40, Paseo Colón, San José ☎ 506/258-2025 ⊕ www.embajadabritanica.com. **Canadian Embassy** (Embajada Canadiense) ✉ next to tennis club, Sabana Sur, San José ☎ 506/296-4149. **United States Embassy** (Embajada de los Estados Unidos) ✉ C. 120 and Avda. 0, Pavas, San José ☎ 506/220-3939 ⊕ usembassy.or.cr.
🚩 In the U.K. **Costa Rican Embassy** ✉ Flat 1, 14 Lancaster Gate London W2 3LH ☎ 020/7706-8844.
🚩 In the U.S. **Embassy of Costa Rica** ✉ 2114 S St. NW, Washington, DC 20008 ☎ 202/234-2945 or 202/234-2946 ⊕ costarica-embassy.org.

EMERGENCIES

Dial ☎ 911 for an ambulance, fire department, or for the police. Costa Ricans are usually quick to respond to emergencies. In a hotel or restaurant, the staff will usually offer immediate assistance, and in a public area, passersby can be counted on to stop and help. Some of the Fischel

branches in San José and surrounding cities are open until 10 or 11 PM or midnight. The only 24-hour pharmacies are at hospitals.
🚩 ☎ 911. **Traffic Police** ☎ 222-9245.
🚩 Hospitals & Medical Clinics **CIMA Hospital** ✉ next to PriceSmart, Escazú ☎ 506/208-1000. **Clínica Biblica** ✉ Avda. 14 at C. 1, San José ☎ 506/257-5252. **Clínica Católica** ✉ San Antonio Guadalupe, San José ☎ 506/283-6616.
🚩 Late-Night Pharmacies **Fischel Pharmacy** (Farmacia Fischel) ✉ Tibás, San José ☎ 506/240-8598 ✉ San Pedro ☎ 506/253-5121 ✉ City center, Cartago ☎ 506/552-2430 ✉ Guachipilin Escazú ☎ 506/289-7212 ✉ Mall International Alajuela ☎ 506/442-1343 ✉ Automercado supermarket, Heredia ☎ 506/260-5765.

ENGLISH-LANGUAGE MEDIA

English is practically everywhere in Costa Rica, from abundant publications to the cable TV beamed into most San José hotels.

BOOKS

Several San José bookstores carry a good selection of new and used English-language books, at prices slightly higher than those in the United States. Some large hotels and other shops also sell English-language books, particularly titles on the tropical outdoors.
🚩 Bookstores **Lehmann** ✉ Avda. Central between Cs. 1 and 3, Centro Colón, San José ☎ 506/223-1212. **Librería Internacional** ✉ 328 m [300 yards] west of Taco Bell, Barrio Dent, San José ☎ 506/253-9553. **7th Street Books** ✉ C. 7 between Avdas. Central and 1, Centro Colón, San José ☎ 506/256-8251.

NEWSPAPERS & MAGAZINES

American newspapers and magazines are widely distributed at newsstands and hotels in San José and sold in some resorts outside the capital. The English-language weekly, the *Tico Times,* published every Friday, has local news and information on entertainment and travel.

ETIQUETTE & BEHAVIOR

If invited to someone's home, take a hostess gift such as flowers or a bottle of wine, or some memorabilia from your home country. If offered food at someone's home, accept it and eat it even if you aren't hungry. You will be offered coffee and should accept, although it's not necessary to finish the whole cup. Know that Costa Ricans don't like to say no and will often avoid answering a question or simply say *gracias* when they really mean no.

On the whole, Costa Ricans are extremely polite, quick to shake hands and place a kiss on the left cheek. Ticos tend to use formal Spanish, preferring, for example, *con mucho gusto* (with much pleasure) instead of *de nada* for "you're welcome." At the same time, an large portion of Costa Rican men make a habit of ogling or making gratuitous comments when young women pass on the street. Women should wear a bra at all times. Family is very important in Costa Rica. It is considered polite to ask about one's married status and family—don't confuse this with prying.

As you would anywhere, **dress and behave respectfully when visiting churches.** In churches, men and women should not wear shorts, sleeveless shirts, or sandals; women should wear skirts below the knee.

BUSINESS ETIQUETTE

Dress in San José is more formal than in the countryside. Men do not wear shorts outside of beach areas. Women do not wear short skirts during the day. Most Costa Ricans wear leather dress shoes instead of tennis shoes unless they are engaged in sports. Most men do not wear a tie to work. Northerners are bound to find business meetings friendlier and more relaxed in Costa Rica than at home. Dress is usually casual, and tardiness is common.

FLIGHTSEEING

San José–based pilot Jenner Rojas will take you anywhere in Costa Rica for flightseeing and picture-taking. The rate is $230 per hour, or less if you arrange a trip of several hours' duration.
🛦 Flightseeing Companies **Jenner Rojas** ☎ 506/385-5425.

GAY & LESBIAN TRAVEL

While harassment of gays and lesbians is infrequent in Costa Rica, so are public displays of affection. Discretion is advised. Same-sex couples won't have problems at hotel check-in desks unless they engage in public displays of affection. Ticos, for whom religion and family are very important, tend simply to assume that everyone is straight. However, as a result of its history of tolerance, Costa Rica has attracted many gay people from other Latin American nations and consequently has a large gay community. San José and Manuel Antonio are probably the most gay-friendly towns, and they have some gay-and-lesbian bars and hangouts. The beach at the northern end of Playa Espadilla in Manuel Antonio National Park is a small, secluded cove known to be a gay nude beach. There are no anti-gay laws.

GAY & LESBIAN RESOURCES

San José's 1@10 Café Internet serves as a gay and lesbian resource center. Its Web page (www.1en10.com) is a wealth of information on whom to contact and where to go. *Gente* magazine is a bimonthly gay Costa Rican magazine that has bilingual, LGBT–friendly tour and hotel listings. You can find it, and the community paper, *Gayness,* in gay-friendly hotels, bars, and bookshops. The informal on-line "Gay and Lesbian Guide to Costa Rica" has some good travel information, including hotels that are listed with the Costa Rican Gay Business Association.
🛦 Local Contacts **1@10 Café Internet** Uno@Diez ✉ Calle 1 at Avda. 9, Barrio Amón, San José ☎ 506/258-4561. **Gay and Lesbian Guide to Costa Rica** ⊕ www.hometown.aol.com/gaycrica/guide.html.
🛦 Gay- & Lesbian-Friendly Travel Agencies **Different Roads Travel** ✉ 8383 Wilshire Blvd., Suite 520, Beverly Hills, CA 90211 ☎ 323/651-5557 or 800/429-8747 (Ext. 14 for both) 🖷 323/651-3678 ✏ lgernert@tzell.com. **Kennedy Travel** ✉ 130 W. 42nd St., Suite 401, New York, NY 10036 ☎ 212/840-8659, 800/237-7433 🖷 212/730-2269 ⊕ www.kennedytravel.com. **Now, Voyager** ✉ 4406 18th St., San Francisco, CA 94114 ☎ 415/626-1169 or 800/255-6951 🖷 415/626-8626 ⊕ www.nowvoyager.com. **Skylink Travel and Tour** ✉ 1455 N. Dutton Ave., Suite A, Santa Rosa, CA 95401 ☎ 707/546-9888 or 800/225-5759 🖷 707/636-0951, serving lesbian travelers.

GUIDEBOOKS

Plan well and you won't be sorry. Guidebooks are excellent tools—and you can take them with you. You may want to check out color-photo-illustrated *Fodor's Exploring Costa Rica,* which is thorough on culture and history and is available at on-line retailers and bookstores everywhere.

HEALTH

Many of the doctors at San José's Clínica Bíblica and Clínica Católica, and Escazú's

CIMA Hospital (⇨ Emergencies) speak English well, and some studied medicine in the United States. These clinics have 24-hour pharmacies.

EATING & DRINKING

Most food and water is sanitary in Costa Rica. In rural areas, you run a mild risk of encountering drinking water, fresh fruit, and vegetables contaminated by fecal matter, which causes intestinal ailments known variously as Montezuma's Revenge (traveler's diarrhea) and leptospirosis (another disease borne in contaminated food or water that can be treated by antibiotics if detected early). Although it may not be necessary, you can stay on the safe side by avoiding ice, uncooked food, and unpasteurized milk (including milk products) and drink bottled water. Mild cases of Montezuma's Revenge may respond to Imodium (known generically as loperamide) or Pepto-Bismol (not as strong), both of which can be purchased over the counter. Drink plenty of purified water or tea; chamomile is a good folk remedy. In severe cases, rehydrate yourself with a salt-sugar solution (½ teaspoon salt and 4 tablespoons sugar per quart of water).

OVER-THE-COUNTER REMEDIES

Farmacia is Spanish for pharmacy, and the names for common drugs *aspirina,* Tylenol, and *ibuprofen* are basically the same as they are in English. Pepto-Bismol is widely available. Many drugs for which you need a prescription back home are sold over the counter in Costa Rica. Antibiotics do require a prescription.

PESTS & OTHER HAZARDS

Altitude sickness is not a problem unless you are climbing Chirripó, the country's highest peak (14,000 ft). Heat stroke and dehydration are real dangers, especially for hikers, so drink lots of water. Take at least 1 liter per person for every hour you plan to be on the trail. Sunburn is the most common traveler's health problem. Use sunscreen with SPF 30 or higher. Most pharmacies and supermarkets carry sunscreen in a wide range of SPFs, though it is relatively pricey.

Repelente (insect repellent spray) and *espirales* (mosquito coils) are sold in supermarkets and small country stores. U.S. insect repellent brands with DEET are sold in pharmacies and supermarkets.

Mosquito nets are available in some remote lodges; you can buy them in camping stores in San José. Mild insect repellents, like the ones in some skin softeners, are no match for the intense mosquito activity in the hot, humid regions of the Atlantic Lowlands, Osa Peninsula, and Southern Pacific. Moreover, perfume, aftershave, and other lotions and potions can actually attract mosquitoes. Malaria is not a problem in Costa Rica except in some remote northern Caribbean areas near the Nicaraguan border. Poisonous snakes, scorpions, and other pests pose a small (overrated) threat.

The greatest danger to your person actually lies off Costa Rica's popular beaches—riptides are common wherever there are waves, and several tourists drown in them every year. If you see waves, ask the locals where it's safe to swim; and if you're uncertain, don't go in deeper than your waist. If you get caught in a rip current, swim parallel to the beach until you're free of it, and then swim back to shore.

SHOTS & MEDICATIONS

According to the U.S. Centers for Disease Control, travel to Costa Rica poses some risk of malaria, hepatitis A and B, dengue fever, typhoid fever, rabies, Chagas' disease, and *E. coli.* The CDC recommends getting vaccines for hepatitis A and typhoid fever, especially if you are going to be in remote areas or plan stay for more than six weeks. Check with the CDC for detailed health advisories and recommended vaccinations. In areas with malaria and dengue, both of which are carried by mosquitoes, **bring mosquito nets, wear clothing that covers your body, apply repellent containing DEET** in living and sleeping areas. There are some pockets of malaria near the Nicaraguan border on the Caribbean coast. You probably won't need to take malaria pills before your trip unless you are staying for a prolonged period in the north, camping on northern coasts, or crossing the border into Nicaragua or Panama. You should discuss the option with your doctor. Children traveling to Central America should have current inoculations against measles, mumps, rubella, and polio.

🚩 Health Warnings National Centers for Disease Control and Prevention (CDC) ✉ National Center for Infectious Diseases, Division of Quarantine, Trav-

elers' Health, 1600 Clifton Rd. NE, Atlanta, GA 30333
☎ 877/394-8747 international travelers' health line,
800/311-3435 other inquiries ⊟ 888/232-3299
⊕ www.cdc.gov/travel.

MEDICAL PLANS

No one plans to get sick while traveling,
but it happens, so **consider signing up with
a medical-assistance company.** Members
get doctor referrals, emergency evacuation
or repatriation, hot lines for medical con-
sultation, cash for emergencies, and other
assistance.

🛂 Medical-Assistance Companies **International
SOS Assistance** ⊕ www.internationalsos.com ✉ 8
Neshaminy Interplex, Suite 207, Trevose, PA 19053
☎ 215/245-4707 or 800/523-6586 ⊟ 215/244-9617
✉ 12 Chemin Riantbosson, 1217 Meyrin 1, Geneva,
Switzerland ☎ 4122/785-6464 ⊟ 4122/785-6424
✉ 331 N. Bridge Rd., 17-00, Odeon Towers, Singa-
pore 188720 ☎ 65/338-7800 ⊟ 65/338-7611.

HOLIDAYS

National holidays are known as *feriados*.
On these days government offices, banks,
and post offices are closed, and public
transport is restricted. Religious festivals
are characterized by colorful processions.

Except for those in hotels, most restaurants and many attractions close between
Christmas and New Year's Day and during Holy Week (Palm Sunday to Easter
Sunday). Those that do stay open may not
sell alcohol between Holy Thursday and
Easter Sunday.

Major national holidays are New Year's
Day; Juan Santamaría Day (Apr. 11);
Good Friday–Easter Sunday (Apr. 9–11,
2004; Mar. 25–27, 2005); Labor Day
(May 1); Corpus Christi Day (May 29);
Annexation of Guanacaste (July 25); Vir-
gin of the Angels (Costa Rica's patron
saint; Aug. 2); Independence Day (Sept.
15); *Día de las Culturas* (Columbus Day;
Oct. 12); Christmas.

INSURANCE

The most useful travel-insurance plan is a
comprehensive policy that includes coverage for trip cancellation and interruption,
default, trip delay, and medical expenses
(with a waiver for preexisting conditions).

Without insurance you'll lose all or most
of your money if you cancel your trip, regardless of the reason. Default insurance

covers you if your tour operator, airline, or
cruise line goes out of business. Trip-delay
covers expenses that arise because of bad
weather or mechanical delays. Study the
fine print when comparing policies.

If you're traveling internationally, a key
component of travel insurance is coverage
for medical bills incurred if you get sick on
the road. Such expenses aren't generally
covered by Medicare or private policies. U.
K. residents can buy a travel-insurance
policy valid for most vacations taken during the year in which it's purchased (but
check preexisting-condition coverage).
British and Australian citizens need extra
medical coverage when traveling overseas.

Always **buy travel policies directly from
the insurance company;** if you buy them
from a cruise line, airline, or tour operator
that goes out of business you probably
won't be covered for the agency or operator's default, a major risk. Before making
any purchase, **review your existing health
and homeowner's policies** to find what
they cover away from home.

🛂 Travel Insurers In the U.S.: **Access America**
✉ 6600 W. Broad St., Richmond, VA 23230 ☎ 800/
284-8300 ⊟ 804/673-1491 or 800/346-9265
⊕ www.accessamerica.com. **Travel Guard International** ✉ 1145 Clark St., Stevens Point, WI 54481
☎ 715/345-0505 or 800/826-1300 ⊟ 800/955-
8785 ⊕ www.travelguard.com.
🛂 In the U.K.: **Association of British Insurers**
✉ 51 Gresham St., London EC2V 7HQ ☎ 020/
7600-3333 ⊟ 020/7696-8999 ⊕ www.abi.org.uk.
In Canada: **RBC Insurance** ✉ 6880 Financial Dr.,
Mississauga, Ontario L5N 7Y5 ☎ 800/565-3129
⊟ 905/813-4704 ⊕ www.rbcinsurance.com. In Australia: **Insurance Council of Australia** ✉ Insurance
Enquiries and Complaints, Level 3, 56 Pitt St., Sydney, NSW 2000 ☎ 1300/363683 or 02/9251-4456
⊟ 02/9251-4453 ⊕ www.iecltd.com.au. In New
Zealand: **Insurance Council of New Zealand**
✉ Level 7, 111-115 Customhouse Quay, Box 474,
Wellington ☎ 04/472-5230 ⊟ 04/473-3011
⊕ www.icnz.org.nz.

LANGUAGE

Spanish is the official language, although
many tour guides and locals in heavily
touristed areas speak English. You'll have a
better time if you learn some basic Spanish
before you go, and bring a phrase book
with you. When possible, choose the more
formal phrasing, such as *¿Cómo está usted?*
(How are you?) rather than the North
American or Mexican *¿Cómo está?*, which

is not used here. At the very least, **learn the rudiments of polite conversation**—niceties like *por favor* (please) and *gracias* (thank you) will be warmly appreciated. *See* the brief Costa Rican Spanish glossary *in* the Understanding Costa Rica chapter.

In the Caribbean province of Limón a creole English called Mekatalyu is widely spoken by older generations. English is understood by most everyone in these parts.

LANGUAGES FOR TRAVELERS

A phrase book and language-tape set, like *Fodor's Spanish for Travelers* (available at bookstores everywhere), can help get you started.

SPANISH-LANGUAGE PROGRAMS

Thousands of people travel to Costa Rica every year to study Spanish. Dozens of schools in and around San José offer professional instruction and home stays, and there are several smaller schools outside the capital.

🇫 **Conversa** ⊙ Apdo. 17-1007, Centro Colón, San José ☎ 506/221-7649, 800/354-5036 in the U.S. also has a school in Santa Ana, west of San José. **IPEE** ⊠ 23 m (25 yards) south of Pops, Curridabat ☎ 506/283-7731; 813/988-3916 in the U.S. **ILISA** ⊙ Dept. 1420, Box 25216, Miami, FL 33102 ☎ 506/280-0700. **La Escuela D'Amore** ⊙ Apdo. 67, Quepos ☎ 506/777-1143 is in beautiful Manuel Antonio.

LODGING

At Costa Rica's popular beach and mountain resorts **reserve well in advance for the dry season** (mid-December–April). You'll need to give credit-card information or send a deposit to confirm the reservation. Try to do this with the hotel and not a third-party reservations network. During the rainy season (May–mid-December) most hotels drop their rates considerably, which sometimes sends them into a lower price category than the one we indicate.

Luxury hotels are found mainly in San José, Guanacaste, and the Central Valley. Except for at the most popular Pacific beaches, lodging in outlying areas is usually in simple *cabinas* (cabins). Cabinas range from basic cement boxes with few creature comforts to flashier units with all the modern conveniences. Costa Rica also has an abundance of nature lodges (often within private biological reserves) with an emphasis on ecology; most of these are entirely rustic, but a few of the newest are

quite luxurious. About half the national parks in this region have campgrounds with facilities.

Nature lodges may be less expensive than they initially appear, as the price of a room usually includes three hearty meals a day. One or more guided hikes also may be included, but always ask about meals and hikes when making your reservation. Since many of the hotels are remote and have an eco-friendly approach (even to luxury), air-conditioning, in-room telephones, and TVs are exceptions to the rule. We mention air-conditioning and phones only when they're not offered.

The lodgings we list are the cream of the crop in each price category. We always list the facilities that are available, but we don't specify whether they cost extra; when pricing accommodations, always ask what's included and what costs extra. Properties are assigned price categories based on the range from the least-expensive standard double room at high season (excluding holidays) to the most expensive. Properties marked ✕⊡ are lodging establishments whose restaurants warrant a special trip.

Assume that hotels operate on the European Plan (EP, with no meals) unless we specify that they use the Continental Plan (CP, with a Continental breakfast), Breakfast Plan (BP, with a full breakfast), Modified American Plan (MAP, with breakfast and dinner), Full American Plan (FAP, with all meals), or are All-inclusive (AI, including all meals and most activities).

WHAT IT COSTS (for two people)	
$$$$	over $200
$$$	$125–$200
$$	$75–$125
$	$35–$75
¢	under $35

Prices are for two people in a standard double room in high season, excluding service and tax (16.4%).

APARTMENT & VILLA RENTALS

If you want a home base that's roomy enough for a family and comes with cooking facilities, **consider a furnished rental**. In addition to accommodating your crowd, these can save you money. Look through classified ads in the Real Estate section of Costa Rica's English-language weekly, the *Tico Times*. Home-exchange directories sometimes list rentals as well as exchanges. The paper is sold in Costa Rican bookstores, supermarkets, souvenir shops, and hotel gift shops. Costa Rica Rentals International has rental homes and apartments in the San José area and elsewhere. Tropical Waters arranges short-term rentals in the Dominical area. Marina Trading Post, an affiliate of Century 21, arranges house and condominium rentals near Playa Flamingo.

⚑ International Agents Hideaways International ✉ 767 Islington St., Portsmouth, NH 03802 ☎ 603/430-4433 or 800/843-4433 🖷 603/430-4444 ⊕ www.hideaways.com, membership $129. Vacation Home Rentals Worldwide ✉ 235 Kensington Ave., Norwood, NJ 07648 ☎ 201/767-9393 or 800/633-3284 🖷 201/767-5510 ⊕ www.vhrww.com. Villas and Apartments Abroad ✉ 370 Lexington Ave., Suite 1401, New York, NY 10017 ☎ 212/897-5045 or 800/433-3020 🖷 212/897-5039 ⊕ www.ideal-villas.com. Villas International ✉ 4340 Redwood Hwy., Suite D309, San Rafael, CA 94903 ☎ 415/499-9490 or 800/221-2260 🖷 415/499-9491 ⊕ www.villasintl.com.

⚑ Local Agents Costa Rica Rentals International ⌂ Apdo. 1136-1250, Escazú ☎ 506/228-6863. Marina Trading Post ✉ Suites Presidenciales, Playa Flamingo, Guanacaste ☎ 506/654-4004. Tropical Waters ✉ 3½ km (2¼ mi) north of Dominical ☎ 506/787-0031.

⚑ Rental Listings The *Tico Times* ☎ 506/233-6378 ⊕ www.ticotimes.net.

CAMPING

Is it not legal to camp outside of campgrounds, but land owners in rural areas often allow it if you ask. Do not pitch your tent without getting permission first. Many national parks have camping areas; it's best to contact the park rangers for information. Some popular beaches, including Manuel Antonio, Jacó, Sámara, Tamarindo, and Puerto Viejo, have private camping areas with bathrooms and showers. If you camp on the beach or in other unguarded areas, **don't leave belongings unattended in your tent.**

HOME EXCHANGES

If you would like to exchange your home for someone else's, **join a home-exchange organization,** which will send you its updated listings of available exchanges for a year and will include your own listing in at least one of them. It's up to you to make specific arrangements.

⚑ Exchange Clubs HomeLink International ⌂ Box 47747, Tampa, FL 33647 ☎ 813/975-9825 or 800/638-3841 🖷 813/910-8144 ⊕ www.homelink.org, $110 yearly for a listing, on-line access, and catalog, $40 without catalog. Intervac U.S. ✉ 30 Corte San Fernando, Tiburon, CA 94920 ☎ 800/756-4663 🖷 415/435-7440 ⊕ www.intervacus.com, $105 yearly for a listing, on-line access, and a catalog, $50 without catalog.

HOSTELS

No matter what your age, you can **save on lodging costs by staying at hostels.** In some 4,500 locations in more than 70 countries around the world, Hostelling International (HI), the umbrella group for a number of national youth-hostel associations, offers single-sex, dorm-style beds and, at many hostels, rooms for couples and family accommodations. In Costa Rica, information and reservations for some hostels are available at the Hostal Toruma in San José. Membership in any HI national hostel association, open to travelers of all ages, allows you to stay in HI-affiliated hostels at member rates; one-year membership is about $28 for adults (C$35 for a two-year minimum membership in Canada, £13.50 in the United Kingdom, A$52 in Australia, and NZ$40 in New Zealand); hostels charge about $10–$30 per night. Members have priority if the hostel is full; they're also eligible for discounts around the world, even on rail and bus travel in some countries.

⚑ Organizations Hostelling International–USA ✉ 8401 Colesville Rd., Suite 600, Silver Spring, MD 20910 ☎ 301/495-1240 🖷 301/495-6697 ⊕ www.hiayh.org. Hostelling International–Canada ✉ 400-205 Catherine St., Ottawa, Ontario K2P 1C3 ☎ 613/237-7884 or 800/663-5777 🖷 613/237-7868 ⊕ www.hihostels.ca. YHA England and Wales ✉ Trevelyan House, Dimple Rd., Matlock, Derbyshire DE4 3YH, U.K. ☎ 0870/870-8808 🖷 0870/770-6127 ⊕ www.yha.org.uk. YHA Australia ✉ 422 Kent St., Sydney, NSW 2001 ☎ 02/9261-1111 🖷 02/9261-1969 ⊕ www.yha.com.au. YHA New Zealand ✉ Level 3, 193 Cashel St., Box 436, Christchurch ☎ 03/379-9970 or 0800/278-299 🖷 03/365-4476 ⊕ www.yha.org.nz.

HOTELS

Aire condicionado (air-conditioning) is not standard in Costa Rica, and some hotels charge extra for rooms with air-conditioning. Almost all hotels in Costa Rica have private bathrooms, though *tinas* (bathtubs) are not available except in the most expensive large hotels. All hotels listed in this book have private bathrooms unless we indicate otherwise.

Many hotels have only *camas individuales* (single beds) and *camas matrimoniales* (double beds). At more expensive hotels, *camas queen* (queen-size beds) and *camas king* (king-size beds) may be available, but always ask about bed size.

Costa Rica also has a local environmental rating system for hotel, resorts, and beaches. Contact the ICT (⇨ Visitor Information) for details. There are a few large hotels on the outskirts of San José and on some of the more popular beaches, but most Costa Rican hotels are smaller, with more personalized service. Outside San José, rooms are in great demand between the week after Christmas and the week before Easter; reserve one to three months in advance for those times. Most hotels drop their rates during the "green season" (May to mid-December), and during this time—barring July—it's quite feasible to show up without reservations and haggle over rates, a process that can bring your hotel budget down to nearly half what it might be in the high season.

MAIL & SHIPPING

The main post office in San José is open weekdays 7:30 AM–6 PM and Saturday 8 AM–noon. Provincial post offices are open weekdays 8 AM–5:30 PM and Saturday 8 AM–noon. Mail from the United States or Europe can take two to three weeks to arrive in Costa Rica (occasionally it never arrives at all). Within the country, mail service is even less reliable. Outgoing mail is marginally quicker, with delivery in five days to two weeks, especially when sent from San José. **Always use airmail for overseas cards and letters.** Mail theft is a chronic problem, so **do not mail checks, cash, or anything else of value.**

f Main Post Office Correos ⊠ C. 2, between Avdas. 1 and 3, San José ☎ 506/223-9766.

OVERNIGHT SERVICES

If you need to send important documents, checks, or other noncash valuables, you can use an international courier service, such as UPS, DHL, or Jetex, or any of various local courier services with offices in San José. (Look in the yellow pages under "Courier," in English) If you've worked with international couriers before, you won't be surprised to hear that, for any

place farther away than Miami, "overnight" is usually a misnomer—shipments to most North American cities take two days, to Britain three, and to Australia and New Zealand four or five.

f Major Services DHL ☎ 506/210-3838. Jetex ☎ 506/293-0505. United Parcel Service (UPS) ☎ 506/290-2828.

POSTAL RATES

Letters from **Costa Rica** to the United States and Canada cost the equivalent of U.S. 25¢, postcards to the United States 18¢; to the United Kingdom, letters cost 31¢, postcards 23¢; and to Australia or New Zealand, letters cost 33¢, postcards 30¢.

RECEIVING MAIL

You can have mail sent poste restante (*lista de correos*) to any Costa Rican post office. There is no house-to-house mail service—indeed, no house numbers—in Costa Rica; most residents pick up their mail at the post office itself. In written addresses, *apartado*, abbreviated *apdo.*, indicates a post office box. Anyone with an American Express card or traveler's checks can receive mail at the American Express office in San José.

SHIPPING PARCELS

Shipping parcels through the post office is not for those in a hurry, because packages to the United States and Canada can take weeks, to the United Kingdom, Australia, and New Zealand months. Also, packages may be pilfered. If you must ship parcels, use a courier service, which is expensive but safe. Some stores offer shipping, which is usually quite expensive. It is best to carry your packages home with you. Packages can be sent from any post office, with rates spanning U.S. $6–$12 per kilogram and shipping time ranging from weeks to months, depending on the destination. Quicker, more expensive alternatives are DHL and Jetex, which have offices in Costa Rica—prices are about 10 times what you'd pay at the post office, but packages arrive in a matter of days.

MONEY MATTERS

Costa Rica is more expensive than other destinations in Central America, and prices are rising as more foreigners visit and relocate here. Food in modest restaurants and public transportation are inexpensive. A 1-mi taxi ride costs about

$1.50. Here are some sample prices to give you an idea of the cost of living in Costa Rica: 750-ml (¾-liter) bottle of Coca-Cola, U.S. 65¢–95¢; cup of coffee, 50¢–95¢; bottle of beer, $1–$1.50; sandwich, $2–$3; daily U.S. newspaper, $1.25–$2.25. Prices throughout this guide are given for adults. Substantially reduced fees are almost always available for children, students, and senior citizens.(⇨ Taxes).

ATMS

Don't count on using an ATM outside of San José. ATMs that supposedly accept Cirrus and Plus cards often don't. Get most or all of the cash you need in San José and carry some U.S. in case you run out of colónes. ATMs are sometimes out of order and sometimes run out of cash on weekends. Only four-digit PIN numbers are accepted at ATMs in Costa Rica. The term for ATM is *cajero automático*. In San José, the main Banco Popular, which accepts Plus cards, is at Avda. 2 and C. 1, near the National Theater. Cash advances are also available in the Credomatic office, on C. Central between Avdas. 3 and 5, or the Banco de San José, across the street, which also has an American Express office on the third floor. The Banco de San José has ATMs on the Cirrus system, and the bank has more than a dozen locations in San José, including the Centro Omni, one block north of the Gran Hotel Costa Rica.

CREDIT CARDS

Credit cards are accepted at most major hotels and restaurants in this book. As the phone system improves and expands, many budget hotels, restaurants, and other properties have begun to accept plastic; but plenty of properties still require payment in cash. **Don't count on using plastic all the time**—once you venture outside San José **carry enough cash or traveler's checks** to patronize the many businesses without credit card capability. Note that some hotels, restaurants, tour companies, and other businesses add a surcharge (around 5%) to the bill if you pay with a credit card, or give you a 5%–10% discount if you pay in cash.

Throughout this guide, the following abbreviations are used: **AE**, American Express; **DC**, Diners Club; **MC**, MasterCard; and **V**, Visa.

🔳 Reporting Lost Cards **American Express** 🕾 0800/012-3211 collect to the U.S. **Diners**

Club 🕾 702/797-5532 collect to the U.S. **Master-Card** 🕾 0800/011-0184 toll-free to the U.S. **Visa** 🕾 0800/011-0030 toll-free to the U.S.

CURRENCY

All prices in this book are quoted in U.S. dollars. The Costa Rican currency, the colón (plural: colones), is subject to continual, small devaluations. At this writing, the colón is 405 to the U.S. dollar, 478 to the Euro, 294 to the Canadian dollar, 663 to the pound sterling, 265 to the Australian dollar, and 235 to the New Zealand dollar.

CURRENCY EXCHANGE

For the most favorable rates, **change money through banks or use local ATMs.** Although ATM transaction fees may be higher than at home, ATM rates are excellent because they are based on wholesale rates offered only by major banks. Exchange rates are not as good at hotels, restaurants, or stores, though their hours are often more convenient than those of the banks. Costa Rican colónes are sold abroad at terrible rates, so you should wait until you arrive in Costa Rica to get local currency. There is a branch of the Banco de San José in the airport that is open daily 5 AM–10 PM where you can exchange money when you arrive, but taxi and van drivers who pick up at the airport do take U.S. dollars. Currencies other than U.S. dollars are not widely accepted and may be difficult to exchange, so bring U.S. dollars. Australian and New Zealand dollars can't be changed at all in Costa Rica, even at banks.

Avoid people on the city streets who offer to change money. San José's outdoor money-changers are notorious for short-changing people and passing counterfeit bills. The guys who change money at the airport aren't quite as shady, but they might not be above shortchanging you, and they don't offer great rates in any case.

🔳 Exchange Services **International Currency Express** ✉ 427 N. Camden Dr., Suite F, Beverly Hills, CA 90210 🕾 888/278-6628 orders 🖷 310/278-6410 🌐 www.foreignmoney.com. **Thomas Cook Currency Services** 🕾 800/287-7362 orders and retail locations 🌐 www.us.thomascook.com.

TRAVELER'S CHECKS

Do you need traveler's checks? It depends on where you're headed. If you're going to rural areas and small towns, go with cash; traveler's checks are best used in cities. Lost or stolen checks can usually be replaced within 24 hours. To ensure a speedy refund, buy your own traveler's checks—don't let someone else pay for them: irregularities like this can cause delays. The person who bought the checks should make the call to request a refund. If you have an American Express card and can draw on a U.S. checking account, you can buy dollar traveler's checks at the American Express office in San José for a 1% service charge.

THE OUTDOORS

BICYCLING

Costa Rica is a combination of mountainous terrain and cycle-friendly flatlands. A number of tour operators run bike tours. You can also rent bikes in most Costa Rican mountain and beach resorts.

Tour Operators **BiCosta Rica** ✉ Atenas ☎☎ 506/446-7585. **Coast to Coast** ✉ San José ☎ 506/280-8054. **Jungle Man Adventures** ✉ Hotel Don Fadrique, San José ☎ 506/225-8186. **Río Escondido Mountain Bikes** ✉ Rock River Lodge, Tilarán ☎ 506/695-5644.

BIRD-WATCHING

Tour Operators **Birding Club of Costa Rica** ☎ 506/239-2258. **Costa Rica Expeditions** ✉ San José, Costa Rica ☎ 506/222-0333. **Horizontes** ✉ San José, Costa Rica ☎ 506/222-2022.

CANOPY TOURS

If you not only want to see monkeys in Costa Rica but also want the perspective of one, **take a canopy tour.** Using rock-climbing equipment, you slide along cables strung between treetops in the canopy. It's a unique experience that's easier to manage than you might think—even for the slightly fearful. Heavier people should ask about weight limits ahead of time. One reputable company is the Original Canopy Tour, with branches in Monteverde, Tabacón (near Arenal), Drake Bay, and four other destinations. Its well-trained guides are bilingual and its safety record is good. **Don't go with the less-expensive competitors** unless you've acquainted yourself with their safety practices and feel comfortable; and **be prepared to walk away** if the trip doesn't look or feel professionally handled. It's still an unregu-

lated business, and many companies cut corners on safety to save a buck.

Sky Trek tours are similar to canopy tours but may include suspension bridges, cable flights across valleys, and a hilltop tower (not necessarily located in the rain or cloud forest). Sky Walk tours are for those not necessarily up for the "Me Tarzan, you Jane" routine, with less strenuous canopy exploration options. Here you can tiptoe through the treetops on a series of six suspension bridges, which provide a monkey's-eye view of the aerial garden of the cloud-forest canopy. Get here early if you're into bird-watching.

Canopy Tour Contacts **The Original Canopy Tour** ☎ 506/257-5149 ⊕ www.canopytour.com. **Sky Trek and Sky Walk** ☎ 506/645-5238 ⊕ www.skywalk.co.cr.

WATER SPORTS

Costa Rica is worth visiting for its water sports alone. Wild rivers churn plenty of white water for rafting, and Lake Arenal is one of the world's best places to windsurf. You can make skin-diving excursions from Drake Bay, Playa Flamingo, Playa Ocotal, and Playa del Coco, but Costa Rica's best dive spot, Cocos Island, can only be visited on a 10-day scuba safari on the *Okeanos Aggressor* or *Undersea Hunter*. Popular surfing beaches include Tamarindo, Jacó, Hermosa, Dominical, and Pavones. Airlines generally allow surfboards on board for a fee of around $15. Tico Travel and Costa Rica Surfing Adventures organize surfing vacations.

Dive Operators—Costa Rica **Bill Beard's Diving Safaris** ✉ Playa Hermosa ☎ 506/672-0012. **El Ocotal Diving Safaris** ✉ Playa del Ocotal ☎ 506/670-0321. *Okeanos Aggressor* ✉ Plaza Colonial, Escazú ☎ 506/257-4948. *Undersea Hunter* ✉ ½ km (650 yards) north and 200 m (220 yards) west of Rosti Pollos, San Rafael de Escazú ☎ 506/228-6535.

Surfing Outfitters **Costa Rica Surfing Adventures** ☎ 506/382-3413 **Iguana Surf Aquatic Outfitters** ✉ 25 m north of El Pescador restaurant Tamarindo ☎ 506/653-0148. **Mango Surf Shop** ✉ Mall San Pedro San Pedro ☎ 506/225-1067. **Quique** ✉ Avda. Central, between Cs. 5 and 7 San Pedro ☎ 506/253-5606. **Tico Travel** ☎ 800/493-8426 in the U.S.

White-Water Rafting Outfitters **Aventuras Naturales** ✉ San Pedro, Costa Rica ☎ 506/225-3939. **Costa Rica Expeditions** ✉ Avda. 3, 25 m east of the Oficina Central de Correos San José, Costa Rica ☎ 506/222-0333. **Ríos Tropicales** ✉ C. 38, be-

tween Avdas. Central and 2 San José, Costa Rica
☎ 506/233–6455.
🎏 **Windsurfing Outfitters Tilawa** ⊠ Lake Arenal
☎ 506/695–5050 ⊕ www.hotel-tilawa.com.

PACKING

Pack light, as you will probably end up having to carry your bag for some distance. Plus, domestic airlines have tight weight restrictions (at this writing 30 lbs [13.6 kg]) and not all buses have luggage compartments. It's a good idea to pack essentials in one bag and extras in another, so you can leave one bag at your hotel in San José or at the airport if you exceed weight restrictions. Frameless backpacks and duffel bags are good luggage choices—they can be squeezed into tight spaces and are less conspicuous than fancier luggage. Bring comfortable, hand-washable clothing. T-shirts and shorts are acceptable near the beach and in tourist areas; long-sleeve shirts and pants protect your skin from ferocious sun and, in some regions, mosquitoes. In less-touristed areas, women should avoid tops that show cleavage or part of the stomach and shorts and skirts much above the knee.

Leave your jeans behind—they take forever to dry and can't be worn out in the evenings like khakis. **Bring a large hat** to block the sun from your face and neck. **Pack a waterproof, lightweight jacket** and a light sweater for cool nights, early mornings, trips up volcanoes, and to the Atlantic coast; you'll need even warmer clothes for trips to Chirripó National Park or Volcán Baru and overnight stays in San Gerardo de Dota or La Providencia Lodge. Sturdy sneakers or hiking boots are essential for sightseeing on foot. Waterproof hiking sandals such as Tevas are good for boat rides, beach walks, streams (should you need to ford one), and light hiking trails. Bring at least one good (and wrinkle-free) outfit for going out at night. Costa Ricans tend to dress up a bit more than Americans. Remember to bring a small day-trip backpack or bag.

Insect repellent (especially if you're going to Tortuguero), sunscreen, sunglasses, and umbrellas (during the rainy season) are crucial. Women might have a tough time finding tampons, so bring your own. Other handy items—especially if you'll be roughing it—include toilet paper, facial tissues, a plastic water bottle, and a flashlight (for occasional power outages or inadequately lit walkways at lodges). Toilet paper is not usually available in public rest rooms unless there is an attendant. For almost all toilet articles including contact lens supplies, a pharmacy is your best bet. **Don't forget binoculars** and a comfortable carrying strap. Snorkelers staying at budget hotels should consider bringing their own equipment; otherwise, you can rent gear at most beach resorts. If you're surfing, consider buying your board here; Tamarindo has a good shop. Some beaches, such as Playa Grande, do not have shade trees, so if you're planning to linger at the beach you might consider investing in a sturdy tarpaulin.

In your carry-on luggage, **pack an extra pair of eyeglasses or contact lenses and enough of any medication** you take to last a few days longer than the entire trip. You may also ask your doctor to write a spare prescription using the drug's generic name, as brand names may vary from country to country. In luggage to be checked, **never pack prescription drugs, valuables, or undeveloped film.** And don't forget to carry with you the addresses of offices that handle refunds of lost traveler's checks. Check *Fodor's How to Pack* (available at on-line retailers and bookstores everywhere) for more tips.

To avoid customs and security delays, carry medications in their original packaging. Don't pack any sharp objects in your carry-on luggage, including knives of any size or material, scissors, and corkscrews, or anything else that might arouse suspicion.

To avoid having your checked luggage chosen for hand inspection, don't cram bags full. The U.S. Transportation Security Administration suggests packing shoes on top and placing personal items you don't want touched in clear plastic bags.

CHECKING LUGGAGE

The tiny, domestic passenger planes (seating about 6 to 12 people) in Costa Rica require that you pack light. A luggage weight limit of 30 pounds (13.6 kilograms), *including* carry-ons, is almost always enforced. For the same reason, two lighter bags are preferable to one heavy bag.

On international flights, you're allowed to carry aboard one bag and one personal article, such as a purse or a laptop computer. Make sure what you carry on fits under your seat or in the overhead bin. Get to the gate early, so you can board as soon as possible, before the overhead bins fill up.

Baggage allowances vary by carrier, destination, and ticket class. On international flights, you're usually allowed to check two bags weighing up to 70 pounds (32 kilograms) each, although a few airlines allow checked bags of up to 88 pounds (40 kilograms) in first class. Some international carriers don't allow more than 66 pounds (30 kilograms) per bag in business class and 44 pounds (20 kilograms) in economy. Check baggage restrictions with your carrier before you pack.

Airline liability for baggage is limited to $2,500 per person on flights within the United States. On international flights it amounts to $9.07 per pound or $20 per kilogram for checked baggage (roughly $640 per 70-pound bag) and $400 per passenger for unchecked baggage. You can buy additional coverage at check-in for about $10 per $1,000 of coverage, but it often excludes a rather extensive list of items, shown on your airline ticket.

Before departure, **itemize your bags' contents** and their worth, and label the bags with your name, address, and phone number. (If you use your home address, cover it so potential thieves can't see it readily.) Include a label inside each bag and **pack a copy of your itinerary.** At check-in, **make sure each bag is correctly tagged** with the destination airport's three-letter code. Because some checked bags will be opened for hand inspection, the U.S. Transportation Security Administration recommends that you leave luggage unlocked or use the plastic locks offered at check-in. TSA screeners place an inspection notice inside searched bags, which are re-sealed with a special lock.

If your bag has been searched and contents are missing or damaged, file a claim with the TSA Consumer Response Center as soon as possible. If your bags arrive damaged or fail to arrive at all, file a written report with the airline before leaving the airport.

F Complaints U.S. Transportation Security Administration Consumer Response Center ☎ 866/289-9673 ⊕ www.tsa.gov.

PASSPORTS & VISAS

When traveling internationally, **carry your passport** even if you don't need one (it's always the best form of ID) and **make two photocopies of the data page** (one for someone at home and another for you, carried separately from your passport). If you lose your passport, promptly call the nearest embassy or consulate and the local police.

U.S. passport applications for children under age 14 require consent from both parents or legal guardians; both parents must appear together to sign the application. If only one parent appears, he or she must submit a written statement from the other parent authorizing passport issuance for the child. A parent with sole authority must present evidence of it when applying; acceptable documentation includes the child's certified birth certificate listing only the applying parent, a court order specifically permitting this parent's travel with the child, or a death certificate for the nonapplying parent. Application forms and instructions are available on the Web site of the U.S. State Department's Bureau of Consular Affairs (⊕ www.travel.state.gov).

Citizens of Australia and New Zealand need only a valid passport to enter Costa Rica for stays of up to 30 days (and once you're here, you can go to the Migracion office in La Uruca and extend the visa to 90 days). Canadians need only a valid passport to enter Costa Rica for stays of up to 90 days. Citizens of the United Kingdom need only a valid passport to enter Costa Rica for up to 90 days. U.S. citizens need a valid passports to enter Costa Rica for up for 90 days, after which they must leave for at least 72 hours.

SAFETY

For many English-speaking tourists, standing out like a sore thumb can't be avoided in Costa Rica. But there are some precautions you can take. Don't wear a waist pack or a money belt, because thieves can cut the strap. Instead, distribute your cash and any valuables (including credit cards and passport) among a deep front pocket, an inside jacket or vest pocket, and a hidden money pouch. Carry some cash in your purse or wallet so you don't have to reach for the money pouch in public.

Violent crime is not a serious problem in Costa Rica, but thieves can easily prey on tourists, so be alert. Roll up car windows and lock car doors when you leave your car, and keep windows rolled up and doors locked all the time in cities. Crimes against property are rife in San José. In rural areas theft is on the rise. Park in designated parking lots, or if that's not possible, accept the offer of men or boys who ask if they can watch your car while you're gone. Give them the equivalent of a dollar per hour when you return. **Never leave valuables visible in a car.** Take them inside with you whenever possible, or lock them in the trunk. Talk with locals or your hotel's staff about crime whenever you arrive in a new location. They will be able to tell you if it's safe to walk around after dark and what areas to avoid.

Don't wear expensive jewelry or watches. Backpacks should be carried on your front. Likewise, wallets go in your front pocket. The incapacitating drug Rohypnol is still afoot and is used on men and women, so never leave a drink unattended in a club or bar. When on a crowded bus, keep your hand on your wallet or your eyes on your purse. Never leave your belongings unattended anywhere, including at the beach or in a tent. Many hotel rooms have safes, which should be used (even if it's an extra charge). If your room doesn't have one, ask the manager to put your valuables in the hotel safe. Ask him or her to sign a list of what you put in the safe. Do not carry expensive cameras or much cash in cities. Most importantly, **don't bring anything you can't stand to lose.**

LOCAL SCAMS

Scams are common in San José, where a drug addict may tell tales of having been recently robbed, then ask you for donations; a distraction artist might squirt you with cream or chocolate sauce, then try to clean you off while his partner steals your backpack; pickpockets and bag slashers work buses and crowds; and street money changers pass off counterfeit bills. To top it all off, car theft is rampant. Beware of anyone who seems overly friendly, aggressively helpful, or disrespectful of your personal space.

WOMEN IN COSTA RICA

If you carry a purse, choose one with a zipper and a thick strap that you can drape across your body; adjust the length so that the purse sits in front of you at or above hip level. Store only enough money in the purse to cover casual spending. Distribute the rest of your cash and any valuables among deep front pockets, inside jacket or vest pockets, and a concealed money pouch.

Lone women travelers will get a fair amount of attention from men, but in general should be safe. Women should not hitchhike alone or in pairs. Blonde women will get more grief than dark-haired ones. To avoid hassles, avoid wearing short shorts, short skirts, or sleeveless tops. On the bus, try to take a seat next to a woman. Women should not walk alone in San José at night or venture into dangerous areas of the city at all. Ask at your hotel which neighborhoods to avoid. Ignore unwanted comments. If you are being harassed on a bus, in a restaurant or other public place, tell the manager. In taxis, sit in the backseat.

SENIOR-CITIZEN TRAVEL

Older travelers flock to Costa Rica, and many businesses are making an effort to cater to the specific comforts of this demographic. Some senior citizens may encounter more challenges to mobility than they do at home—especially on those muddy jungle trails—but should otherwise find Costa Rica most hospitable.

To qualify for age-related discounts, **mention your senior-citizen status up front** when booking hotel reservations (not when checking out) and before you're seated in restaurants (not when paying the bill). Be sure to have identification on hand. When renting a car, ask about promotional car-rental discounts, which can be cheaper than senior-citizen rates.

🎓 **Educational Programs Elderhostel** ✉ 11 Ave. de Lafayette, Boston, MA 02111-1746 ☎ 077/426-8056, 978/323-4141 international callers, 877/426-2167 TTY 📠 877/426-2166 ⊕ www.elderhostel.org. **Interhostel** ✉ University of New Hampshire, 6 Garrison Ave., Durham, NH 03824 ☎ 603/862-1147 or 800/733-9753 📠 603/862-1113 ⊕ www.learn.unh.edu.

STUDENTS IN COSTA RICA

Although prices are on the rise, you can still travel on $25–$30 a day if you put your mind to it. There are youth hostels and hotels affiliated with Hostelling International all over Costa Rica, though one of the cheapest ways to spend the night in this region is to camp; as long as you have your own tent, it's easy to set up house almost anywhere. Still, don't ever leave your belongings or a campfire unattended.

🔲 IDs & Services STA Travel ✉ 10 Downing St., New York, NY 10014 ☎ 212/627-3111 or 800/777-0112 📠 212/627-3387 ⊕ www.sta.com. **Travel Cuts** ✉ 187 College St., Toronto, Ontario M5T 1P7, Canada ☎ 416/979-2406, 800/592-2887, 866/246-9762 in Canada 📠 416/979-8167 ⊕ www.travelcuts.com.

STUDYING ABROAD

The University of Costa Rica has exchange programs with at least half a dozen American universities, the oldest of which is the University of Kansas program. Many private language institutes offer Spanish courses for college credit (⇨ Language).

TAXES

When you fly out of Costa Rica, you'll have to pay a $17 airport departure tax at Juan Santamaría airport. (This fee may be going up to $21.) Although people may offer to sell it to you the moment you climb out of your taxi, it's best to **buy your exit stamp inside the airport**; look for airport-employee identification. If you buy elsewhere, you'll have no recourse if someone sells you fake stamps or gives you the wrong change or conversion rate.

VALUE-ADDED TAX

All Costa Rican businesses charge a 13% sales tax, and hotels charge an extra 4% tourist tax. Tourists do not get refunds on sales tax paid in Central American countries.

TELEPHONES

Local telephone numbers have seven digits. If your cell phone or pager company has service to Costa Rica, you theoretically can use it here, but expect reception to be impossible in many areas of this mountainous country. The Costa Rican phone system is very good by the standards of other developing countries. However, phone numbers change often and are handed out willy-nilly.

AREA & COUNTRY CODES

The country code for Costa Rica is 506. There are no area codes. Phoning home:

the country code for the United States and Canada is 001, Australia 61, New Zealand 64, and the United Kingdom 44.

DIRECTORY & OPERATOR ASSISTANCE

International information is 124. The international operator is 175. Calling cards from the United States or Canada with 800 numbers don't work in Costa Rica. In Costa Rica, dial ☎ 113 for domestic directory inquiries and ☎ 110 for domestic collect calls.

DOMESTIC CALLS

Making a local call in Costa Rica is pretty straightforward, because all telephone numbers in the country are seven digits. Using a phone card from a pay phone can be frustrating because different phones operate somewhat differently. In some you put the card in first and then dial; in the more modern phones, you don't insert the card. In these phones, you dial the number you want to reach and then will be instructed to punch in a PIN printed on the back of your card, which is revealed after scratching off a protective coating.

For long-distance calls within Costa Rica, you don't have to dial anything extra. All phone numbers in Costa Rica have seven digits, whether you are calling within the same town or to the other side of the country.

INTERNATIONAL CALLS

Costa Rica's *guía telefónica* (phone book) lists the rates for calling various countries. To call overseas directly, dial 00, then the country code, the area code, and the number. Calls to the United States and Canada are the same price at all times; calls to the United Kingdom are only discounted on weekends, from Friday at 10 PM to Monday at 7 AM.

It's cheapest to call from a pay phone using an international phone card, sold in shops; call from a pay phone using your own long-distance calling card; or call from a telephone office. Dialing directly from a hotel room is very expensive, as is recruiting an international operator to connect you.

LONG-DISTANCE SERVICES

AT&T, MCI, and Sprint access codes make calling long-distance relatively convenient, but you may find the local access number blocked in many hotel rooms. First ask the hotel operator to connect you. If the hotel operator balks, ask for an international operator, or dial the international operator yourself. One way to improve your odds of getting connected to your long-distance carrier is to travel with more than one company's calling card (a hotel may block Sprint, for example, but not MCI). If all else fails, call from a pay phone.

📱 Access Codes **AT&T Direct** ☎ 0800/011-4114. **British Telecom** ☎ 0000/044-1044. **Canada Direct** ☎ 0800/015-1161. **MCI WorldPhone** ☎ 0800/012-2222. **Sprint International Access** ☎ 0800/013-0123.

📱 Telephone Offices **Radiográfica Costarricense** ✉ Avda. 5 between Cs. 1 and 3.

PHONE CARDS

Costa Rica has three kinds of phone cards: domestic "chip" cards, which record what you spend; and domestic and international cards, which have codes that you have to punch into the telephone. All three types are sold in an array of shops, including Mas x Menos supermarkets, post offices, offices of the Costa Rican Electricity Institute (ICE), and at any business displaying the gold-and-blue TARJETAS TELEFÓNICAS sign. Phone cards can be purchased in different amounts; for domestic calls, the card denominations are 500 colónes, 1,000 colónes, and 3,000 colónes. Cards for international calls cost $10, $20, 3,000 colónes, and 10,000 colónes. International public phones that accept these cards are black and decorated with flags. The cost of calling to the U.S. is about a dollar a minute.

PUBLIC PHONES

Pay phones are abundant, though they always seem to be in use. Some older-style phones accept coins, but most accept only phone cards, which are sold in various shops. Local calls are charged by the minute. Rates are different depending on how far away in the country you are calling.

TIME

Costa Rica is six hours behind GMT, which is the Central Standard time zone in the U.S.

TIPPING

Taxi drivers aren't tipped. Tip gas station attendants 100 colónes. Do not use American change to tip, because there is no way for locals to exchange it. Chambermaids get 400–800 colónes per day. Concierges are usually not tipped. Room-service waiters should be tipped about 400 colónes, as should bell caps (more in the most expensive hotels). Restaurant bills include a 13% tax and 10% service charge—sometimes these amounts are included in prices on the menu, and sometimes they aren't. The menu should say or you should ask. Additional gratuity is not expected, especially in cheap restaurants, but people often leave something extra when service is good. Leave a tip of about 200 colónes per drink for bartenders, too.

At some point on a trip, most visitors to Costa Rica are in the care of a naturalist guide, who can show you the sloths and special hiking trails you'd never find on your own. **Give $10 (4,000 colónes) per day per person to guides,** if they've transported and guided you individually or in small groups. Give less to guides on bigger tours, or if they're affiliated with the hotel or lodge where you're staying.

TOURS & PACKAGES

Because everything is prearranged on a prepackaged tour or independent vacation, you spend less time planning—and often get it all at a good price.

BOOKING WITH AN AGENT

Travel agents are excellent resources. But it's a good idea to collect brochures from several agencies, as some agents' suggestions may be influenced by relationships with tour and package firms that reward them for volume sales. If you have a special interest, **find an agent with expertise in that area;** the American Society of Travel Agents (ASTA; ⇨ Travel Agencies) has a database of specialists worldwide.

Make sure your travel agent knows the accommodations and other services of the place being recommended. Ask about the hotel's location, room size, beds, and whether it has a pool, room service, or programs for children, if you care about these. Has your agent been there in person or sent others whom you can contact?

Do some homework on your own, too: local tourism boards can provide information about lesser-known and small-niche operators, some of which may sell only direct.

BUYER BEWARE

Each year consumers are stranded or lose their money when tour operators—even large ones with excellent reputations—go out of business. So **check out the operator.** Ask several travel agents about its reputation, and try to **book with a company that has a consumer-protection program.** (Look for information in the company's brochure.) In the United States, members of the National Tour Association and the United States Tour Operators Association are required to set aside funds to cover payments and travel arrangements in the event that the company defaults. It's also a good idea to choose a company that participates in the American Society of Travel Agents' Tour Operator Program; ASTA will act as mediator in any disputes between you and your tour operator.

Remember that the more your package or tour includes, the better you can predict the ultimate cost of your vacation. Make sure you know exactly what is covered, and **beware of hidden costs.** Are taxes, tips, and transfers included? Entertainment and excursions? These can add up.

⊡ Tour-Operator Recommendations American Society of Travel Agents (⇨ Travel Agencies). **National Tour Association (NTA)** ⊠ 546 E. Main St., Lexington, KY 40508 ☎ 859/226–4444 or 859/226–4404 ⊕ www.ntaonline.com. **United States Tour Operators Association (USTOA)** ⊠ 275 Madison Ave., Suite 2014, New York, NY 10016 ☎ 212/599–6599 or 800/468–7862 ⤵ 212/599–6744 ⊕ www. ustoa.com.

TRAIN TRAVEL

Costa Rica's countrywide train system has been defunct since 1986 due to recurring earthquakes and lack of profits. But a tour company called AmericaTravel now gives weekend day trips in 1940s passenger railcars from San José to the inland Pacific towns of Caldera and Orotina. At this writing, the company was considering starting train tours to the Atlantic side of the country.

⊡ Train Information AmericaTravel ☎ 506/233–3300 ⤵ americatravel@msn.com.

TRANSPORTATION AROUND COSTA RICA

The most common form of public transportation is the bus. All Costa Rican towns are connected by regular, inexpensive bus service. For example, tickets cost $5–$10 from the capital to Quepos and $5–$9 to Monteverde; the more expensive rates are for *directo* (express) service. Buses between major cities are modern and air-conditioned, but once you get into the rural areas, you may get the school-bus equivalent. Because buses can be a slow and uncomfortable way to travel, domestic flights are a desirable and practical option. Most major destinations are served by daily domestic flights; prices range from $40 to $90 one-way (round-trips are double the one-way fare). Renting a car gives you the most freedom, but rates can be expensive, especially since you need four-wheel drive in most parts of the country.

TRAVEL AGENCIES

A good travel agent puts your needs first. Look for an agency that has been in business at least five years, emphasizes customer service, and has someone on staff who specializes in your destination. In addition, **make sure the agency belongs to a professional trade organization.** The American Society of Travel Agents (ASTA)—the largest and most influential in the field with more than 20,000 members in some 140 countries—maintains and enforces a strict code of ethics and will step in to help mediate any agent-client disputes involving ASTA members if necessary. ASTA (whose motto is "Without a travel agent, you're on your own") also maintains a Web site that includes a directory of agents. (If a travel agency is also acting as your tour operator, *see* Buyer Beware *in* Tours & Packages.)

⊡ Local Agent Referrals American Society of Travel Agents (ASTA) ⊠ 1101 King St., Suite 200, Alexandria, VA 22314 ☎ 703/739–2782 or 800/965–2782 24-hr hot line ⤵ 703/739–3268 ⊕ www. astanet.com. **Association of British Travel Agents** ⊠ 68–71 Newman St., London W1T 3AH ☎ 020/

7637-2444 🖶 020/7637-0713 ⊕ www.abtanet.com. **Association of Canadian Travel Agents** ✉ 130 Albert St., Suite 1705, Ottawa, Ontario K1P 5G4 ☎ 613/237-3657 🖶 613/237-7052 ⊕ www.acta.ca. **Australian Federation of Travel Agents** ✉ Level 3, 309 Pitt St., Sydney, NSW 2000 ☎ 02/9264-3299 🖶 02/9264-1085 ⊕ www.afta.com.au. **Travel Agents' Association of New Zealand** ✉ Level 5, Tourism and Travel House, 79 Boulcott St., Box 1888, Wellington 6001 ☎ 04/499-0104 🖶 04/499-0786 ⊕ www.taanz.org.nz.

VISITOR INFORMATION

Instituto Costarricense de Turismo in San José staffs a tourist information office beneath the Plaza de la Cultura, next to the Museo de Oro. Pick up free maps, bus schedules, and brochures weekdays 9–12:30 and 1:30–5. The Costa Rican National Chamber of Tourism Web site is a good starting point for your trip. Visitor information is provided by the Costa Rica Tourist Board in Canada and the United States and by Costa Rica Tourist Services in the United Kingdom.

Learn more about foreign destinations by checking government-issued travel advisories and country information. For a broader picture, consider information from more than one country.

🗷 Tourist Information **Costa Rican National Chamber of Tourism** ⊕ costarica.tourism.co.cr. **Costa Rica Tourist Board** ☎ 800/343-6332 in the U.S. **Costa Rica Tourist Services** ✉ 47 Causton St., London SW1P 4AT ☎ 020/7976-5511 🖶 020/7976-6908. **Instituto Costarricense de Turismo (ICT)** ✉ C. 5 between Avdas. Central and 2, Barrio La Catedral, San José ☎ 222-1090 ⊕ www.tourism-costarica.com.

🗷 Government Advisories **U.S. Department of State** ✉ Overseas Citizens Services Office, Room 4811, 2201 C St. NW, Washington, DC 20520 ☎ 202/647-5225 interactive hot line or 888/407-4747 ⊕ www.travel.state.gov; enclose a cover letter with your request and a business-size SASE. **Consular Affairs Bureau of Canada** ☎ 613/944-6788 or 800/267-6788 ⊕ www.voyage.gc.ca. **U.K. Foreign and Commonwealth Office** ✉ Travel Advice Unit, Consular Division, Old Admiralty Building, London SW1A 2PA ☎ 020/7008-0232 or 020/7008-0233 ⊕ www.fco.gov.uk/travel. **Australian Department of Foreign Affairs and Trade** ☎ 02/6261-1299 Consular Travel Advice Faxback Service ⊕ www.dfat.gov.au. **New Zealand Ministry of Foreign Affairs and Trade** ☎ 04/439-8000 ⊕ www.mft.govt.nz.

VOLUNTEER & EDUCATIONAL TRAVEL

In recent years, more and more Costa Ricans have realized the need to preserve their country's precious biodiversity. Both Ticos and far-flung environmentalists have founded volunteer and educational concerns to this end: Caribbean Conservation Corporation (CCC) is devoted to the preservation of sea turtles. Earthwatch Institute leads science-based trips, and Talamancan Association of Ecotourism and Conservation (ATEC) designs short group and individual outings centered on Costa Rican wildlife and indigenous culture. Follow their lead, and you, too, can have an impact.

🗷 Operators **Caribbean Conservation Corporation (CCC)** ✉ 4424 N.W. 13th St., Suite A-1, Gainesville, FL 32609 ☎ 800/678-7853. **Earthwatch Institute** ✉ 3 Clock Tower Pl., Suite 100, Box 75, Maynard, MA 01754 ☎ 800/776-0188. **Talamancan Association of Ecotourism and Conservation (ATEC)** ✉ Puerto Viejo de Limón, ☎ 506/750-0191 ⊕ www.greencoast.com/atec/htm.

WEB SITES

Do check out the World Wide Web when planning your trip. You'll find everything from weather forecasts to virtual tours of famous cities. Be sure to **visit Fodors.com** (⊕ www.fodors.com), a complete travel-planning site. You can research prices and book plane tickets, hotel rooms, rental cars, vacation packages, and more. In addition, you can post your pressing questions in the Travel Talk section. Other planning tools include a currency converter and weather reports, and there are loads of links to travel resources.

Info Costa Rica (www.infocostarica.com) has a Web site with maps, photos, news articles, and chat rooms. For current events, check out English-language newspaper the *Tico Times* (www.ticotimes.net) on-line. Horizontes (www.horizontes.com) is a tour operator that offers nature vacations but also has extensive general information on its Web site. Similar is the site by competing nature tour company Costa Rica Expeditions (www.expeditions.co.cr), which offers ecologically minded trips.

CONVERSIONS

DISTANCE

KILOMETERS/MILES

To change kilometers (km) to miles (mi), multiply km by .621. To change mi to km, multiply mi by 1.61.

km to mi		mi to km	
1 =	.62	1 =	1.6
2 =	1.2	2 =	3.2
3 =	1.9	3 =	4.8
4 =	2.5	4 =	6.4
5 =	3.1	5 =	8.1
6 =	3.7	6 =	9.7
7 =	4.3	7 =	11.3
8 =	5.0	8 =	12.9

METERS/FEET

To change meters (m) to feet (ft), multiply m by 3.28. To change ft to m, multiply ft by .305.

m to ft		ft to m	
1 =	3.3	1 =	.30
2 =	6.6	2 =	.61
3 =	9.8	3 =	.92
4 =	13.1	4 =	1.2
5 =	16.4	5 =	1.5
6 =	19.7	6 =	1.8
7 =	23.0	7 =	2.1
8 =	26.2	8 =	2.4

WEIGHT

KILOGRAMS/POUNDS

To change kilograms (kg) to pounds (lb), multiply kg by 2.20. To change lb to kg, multiply lb by .455.

kg to lb		lb to kg	
1 =	2.2	1 =	.45
2 =	4.4	2 =	.91
3 =	6.6	3 =	1.4
4 =	8.8	4 =	1.8
5 =	11.0	5 =	2.3
6 =	13.2	6 =	2.7
7 =	15.4	7 =	3.2
8 =	17.6	8 =	3.6

GRAMS/OUNCES

To change grams (g) to ounces (oz), multiply g by .035. To change oz to g, multiply oz by 28.4.

g to oz		oz to g	
1 =	.04	1 =	28
2 =	.07	2 =	57
3 =	.11	3 =	85
4 =	.14	4 =	114
5 =	.18	5 =	142
6 =	.21	6 =	170
7 =	.25	7 =	199
8 =	.28	8 =	227

CLOTHING SIZE

WOMEN'S CLOTHING

US	UK	EUR
4	6	34
6	8	36
8	10	38
10	12	40
12	14	42

WOMEN'S SHOES

US	UK	EUR
5	3	36
6	4	37
7	5	38
8	6	39
9	7	40

MEN'S SUITS

US	UK	EUR
34	34	44
36	36	46
38	38	48
40	40	50
42	42	52
44	44	54
46	46	56

MEN'S SHIRTS

US	UK	EUR
14½	14½	37
15	15	38
15½	15½	39
16	16	41
16½	16½	42
17	17	43
17½	17½	44

MEN'S SHOES

US	UK	EUR
7	6	39½
8	7	41
9	8	42
10	9	43
11	10	44½
12	11	46

TEMPERATURE

METRIC CONVERSIONS

To change centigrade or Celsius (C) to Fahrenheit (F), multiply C by 1.8 and add 32. To change F to C, subtract 32 from F and multiply by .555.

°F	°C
0	-17.8
10	-12.2
20	-6.7
30	-1.1
32	0
40	+4.4
50	10.0
60	15.5
70	21.1
80	26.6
90	32.2
98.6	37.0
100	37.7

LIQUID VOLUME

LITERS/U.S. GALLONS

To change liters (L) to U.S. gallons (gal), multiply L by .264. To change U.S. gal to L, multiply gal by 3.79.

L to gal		gal to L	
1 =	.26	1 =	3.8
2 =	.53	2 =	7.6
3 =	.79	3 =	11.4
4 =	1.1	4 =	15.2
5 =	1.3	5 =	19.0
6 =	1.6	6 =	22.7
7 =	1.8	7 =	26.5
8 =	2.1	8 =	30.3

SAN JOSÉ

FODOR'S CHOICE

Ambrosia, *San Pedro*

Café Mundo, *Barrio Otoya*

Hotel Aranjuez, *Barrio Aranjuez*

Le Bergerac, *Los Yoses*

L'Ile de France, *Los Yoses*

HIGHLY RECOMMENDED

RESTAURANTS La Cocina de Leña, *Barrio Tournón*

Machu Picchu, *Paseo Colón*

Tin Jo, *Barrio La Soledad*

HOTELS Marriott Costa Rica, *San Antonio de Belén*

Casa Ridgway, *Barrio Gonzalez Laman*

Don Carlos, *Barrio Amón*

Grano de Oro, *Paseo Colón*

SIGHTS Jardín de Mariposas, *Barrio Tournón*

Museo de Jade, *Barrio Carmen*

Museo de Oro Precolombino, *Barrio La Catedral*

Parque Nacional, *Barrio Carmen*

Plaza de la Cultura, *Barrio La Catedral*

Teatro Nacional, *Barrio La Catedral*

SHOPPING Nuestra Tierra, *Barrio Amón*

ARTS Teatro Nacional, *Barrio La Catedral*

NIGHTLIFE Jazz Café, *San Pedro*

Updated by
Gregory
Benchwick

SHADY PARKS, QUIET MUSEUMS, LIVELY PLAZAS, and a cobblestone pedestrian boulevard that cuts through downtown make up for the city's less attractive attributes—its disproportionate share of potholes, traffic jams, and unimpressive gray office blocks that dominate the downtown grid. Fortunately, many of San José's older neighborhoods and its more affluent suburbs are downright charming. Some 1 million Ticos (as Costa Ricans call themselves) live and work in the greater metropolitan area, where such urban activities as fine dining and nightlife exist alongside such urban problems as petty crime and exhaust fumes.

Downtown San José is a mere 40-minute drive from verdant, tranquil countryside. The city stands in a broad, fertile bowl at an altitude of more than 914 m (2,998 ft) bordered to the southwest by the jagged Cerros de Escazú (Escazú Hills), to the north by Volcán Barva (Barva Volcano), and to the east by lofty Volcán Irazú. In the dry season (mid-December–April), these green uplands are almost never out of sight, and during rainy-season afternoons they're usually enveloped in cloudy mantles. Temperatures ranging from 15°C to 26°C (59°F to 79°F) create cool nights and pleasant days. The rainy season lasts from May to mid-December, though mornings during this time are often sunny and brilliantly clear.

San José was founded in 1737 and replaced nearby Cartago as the capital of Costa Rica in 1823, shortly after the country won independence from Spain. San José grew relatively slowly during the following century, as revenues from the coffee and banana industries financed the construction of stately homes, theaters, and a trolley system that was later abandoned. The city mushroomed after World War II, when many old buildings were razed to make room for cement monstrosities, and it eventually sprawled to the point of connection to nearby cities. Industry, agribusiness, the national government, and the international diplomatic corps are headquartered here, and all the institutions required of a capital city—good hospitals, schools, the country's main university, theaters, restaurants, and nightclubs—flourish in close quarters. Ticos come to San José to shop, take care of official business, and seek medical attention, and you should tend to those needs here as well. The rest of the country lags behind in modernity and convenience.

EXPLORING SAN JOSÉ

Numbers in the text correspond to numbers in the margin and on the San José map.

Costa Rica's capital is laid out on a grid: *avenidas* (avenues) run east–west, while *calles* (streets) run north–south. Avenidas north of the Avenida Central have odd numbers, and those to the south have even ones. On the western end of the city, Avenida Central becomes Paseo Colón; on the eastern end, at about Calle 31, it becomes an equally busy, though nameless, four-lane boulevard. Streets to the east of Calle Central have odd numbers; those to the west are even. This would be straightforward enough, except that Costa Ricans do not use street addresses. They rely instead on an archaic system of directions that makes perfect sense to them but tends to confuse foreigners. A typical Tico address could be "200 m (220 yards) north and 50 m (55 yards) east of the post office." The key to interpreting such directions is to keep track of east and west, and remember that a city block is 100 m (110 yards) long.

Beyond the block and street level, downtown San José is divided into numerous *barrios* (neighborhoods), which are also commonly cited in

San José has several interesting museums and theaters, more shops than you can shake a credit card at, and pleasant sidewalk amenities like newsstands and ice cream vendors. If you're here during the rainy season, head out to the countryside in the morning and return to the city to shop and visit museums in the afternoon.

If you have
1 day

1

Spend most of the day in Barrio La Catedral in downtown San José. Wander down the Avenida Central mall. Pop into the Teatro Nacional at the southwest corner of the Plaza de la Cultura. Then head to the neoclassic Catedral Metropolitana just east of Parque Central. Double back to take in one of three museums: the Museo de Oro Precolombino at the Plaza de la Cultura, the Museo Nacional, or the Museo de Jade in Barrio Carmen. If you're traveling with children, consider visiting the Jardín de Mariposas Spyrogyra (Butterfly Garden) north of downtown in Barrio Tournón.

If you have
3 days

After you've surveyed the sights in the one-day itinerary above, on the morning of day two you should get out of the capital. Take in nearby sights in the Central Valley (⇨ chapter 2) like the La Paz Waterfall Gardens on the road to Volcán Poás and INBio Parque near Heredia. Tour the Café Britt coffee plantation in Heredia, saving the afternoon for shopping. On day three head up a volcano, take a trip to the Rain Forest Aerial Tram near Santa Clara (⇨ chapter 7), or explore the historic Orosí Valley southeast of town. Consider a white-water rafting trip on the Class III and IV rapids of the Río Pacuare (thrilling, but not so thrilling as to induce heart failure), with swimmable warm water and spectacular scenery.

---

directions. Some barrios are worth exploring; others you should avoid. Barrio Amón and Barrio Otoya, northeast of the town center, are two of the city's oldest sections; some of their historic buildings are being transformed into charming hotels. Los Yoses and Barrio Escalante, east of downtown, are basically residential neighborhoods with some nice restaurants and galleries and a few B&Bs. San Pedro, another pleasant area even farther east, is the home of the University of Costa Rica and numerous youth-oriented bars and restaurants.

San José's northwest quarter (everything west of Calle Central and north of Avenida 3) is a very different story. Called the Zona Roja, or red-light district, it's a rough area, frequented by prostitutes and alcoholics, and is best avoided unless you're headed to one of the bus companies there, in which case you should take a taxi. Much of the city's southern half—south of Avenida 4 between Calles Central and 14—is equally undesirable. If you follow Avenida Central west to where it becomes Paseo Colón, you'll enter an affluent area, with plenty of restaurants, cinemas, and hotels. The farther west you head, the more exclusive the neighborhoods become. Escazú, in the hills west of San José, is a traditional town that has become a favorite among U.S. expatriates. Surrounding neighborhoods are packed with relatively upscale, U.S.-style restaurants and a few cozy inns.

Most museums, shops, and restaurants are within walking distance of each other. If you're headed for a far-flung spot, or need to get from one end of the city to another, grab a taxi—they're abundant and inexpensive (\$3–\$4 for most trips). On the whole, San José is a relatively safe city, but a growing influx of tourists has resulted in an increase in the number of thieves to prey on them, such as bag and backpack slitters, pickpockets, and distraction artists who usually work in pairs—one person hassles you, or sprays something on you and helps you clean it off, while his or her partner gets your purse, wallet, backpack, camera, and so on. Make sure you keep a photocopy of your passport and a list of credit-card phone numbers in your luggage, and never leave anything in an unguarded car.

Downtown San José

a good walk

Start at the eastern end of the **Plaza de la Cultura** ❶ ▶, where wide stairs lead down to the **Museo de Oro Precolombino** ❷, whose gold collection deserves a good hour or two. Next to the museum entrance, pop into the Instituto Costarricense de Turismo (ICT tourist office) for a free map, bus schedule, and brochures. Wander around the bustling plaza and slip into the **Teatro Nacional** ❸ for a look at the elegant interior and perhaps a cup of coffee in the lobby café. Leaving the theater, you'll be facing west, with the city's main eastbound corridor, Avenida 2, to your left. Walk 1½ blocks west along Avenida 2 to the **Parque Central** ❹ and **Catedral Metropolitana** ❺. Cross Avenida 2 and head north one block on Calle Central to Avenida Central, where you should turn left and follow the pedestrian zone to the small plaza next to the **Banco Central** ❻. Continue west along the pedestrian zone to the **Mercado Central** ❼, and shop or browse at your leisure. Head back east two blocks on the Avenida Central pedestrian zone, then turn left on Calle 2, and walk one block north to the green-and-gray–stuccoed **Correos de San José** ❽, the central post office. From there, return to Avenida Central and walk east along the mall back to the Plaza de la Cultura.

From the eastern end of the Plaza de la Cultura, near the Museo de Oro, walk two blocks east on Avenida Central, turn left onto Calle 9, walk one block north, turn right, and slither halfway down the block to the **Serpentario** ❾, which has an interesting collection of creepy crawlers. Turn left when you leave and head 1½ blocks west on Avenida 1 and one block north to **Parque Morazán** ❿. Walk across the park—be careful crossing busy Avenida 3—and walk along the yellow metal school building to shady **Parque España** ⓫. On the north side of the park, on Avenida 7, is the modern Instituto Nacional de Seguros (INS) building, whose 11th-floor **Museo de Jade** ⓬ has an extensive American-jade collection and great city views.

From the INS building, continue east on Avenida 7 two blocks, passing the Cancillería, or Foreign Ministry, and the Embajada de México (Mexican Embassy) on your left; then turn right on Calle 15 and walk a block south to the corner of **Parque Nacional** ⓭. Take a look at the Monumento Nacional at the center of the park, and then head two blocks south to the entrance of the **Museo Nacional** ⓮, housed in the old Bellavista Fortress. On the west side of the fortress lies the terraced **Plaza de la Democracia** ⓯; from here you can walk west down Avenida Central to return to the Plaza de la Cultura.

TIMING

This walk can take an entire day if you pause to absorb each museum and monument and stop to shop here and there. You can, however, easily split the tour in half: see all the sights west of the Plaza de la Cultura (❶–❽) one day and the remaining places (❾–⓯) on another. Every stop on this tour is open from Tuesday to Friday; check the hours listed below to make sure the sights you want to see are open on Mondays or weekends.

Excursions San José's central position in the Central Valley, and its relative proximity to both the Pacific coast and the mountains, invites day trips—you can be out in the countryside in just 20 to 30 minutes. The Central Valley is a boon for quick outdoor adventures, among them treks to waterfalls and volcanoes, horseback tours on private ranches, mountain hikes, and white-knuckle rafting excursions down the Sarapiquí, Reventazón, and Pacuare rivers. Most tours will pick you up at your San José hotel and drop you off the same day.

Festivals Every other year the two-week Festival Internacional de las Artes brings dancers, theater groups, and musicians from Costa Rica and elsewhere to a dozen city venues in late March. The Festival de Coreógrafos is a dance festival held each December, and the Festival Internacional de Música enlivens July and August. A carnival parade heads down Avenida 2 every December 26, and a horse parade gets under way December 27. During Semana Universitaria (University Week), usually in April, students at the University of Costa Rica put their studies on hold to concentrate on drinking and dancing. The Día de la Virgen de Los Angeles honors Costa Rica's patron saint every August 2 with processions and a well-attended mass. On the eve of this holiday, nuns, athletes, families, and friends walk *la romaría*, a 22-km (14-mi) trek along the highway from San José to Cartago.

What to See

⑥ Banco Central (Central Bank). Ten sculpted figures of bedraggled *campesinos* (peasants) stand outside the western end of Costa Rica's unattractive modern federal reserve bank. The small, shady plaza south of the bank is popular with hawkers, money changers, and retired men and can be a good place to get a shoe shine and listen to street musicians. Beware: the money changers here are notorious for circulating counterfeit bills and using doctored calculators to shortchange unwitting tourists. It is better to change money at banks or through cash machines, where you get the best rate. ⊠ *Bordered by Avdas. Central and 1 and Cs. 2 and 4, Barrio La Merced.*

⑤ Catedral Metropolitana (Metropolitan Cathedral). Built in 1871, this neoclassic structure east of the park with a corrugated tin dome is not terribly interesting outside, but inside you find patterned floor tiles and framed polychrome bas-reliefs. The interior of the small chapel (Sagrario) on the cathedral's north side is even more ornate than the cathedral itself, but it's usually closed. Masses are held throughout the day on Sunday starting at 6 AM. ⊠ *Bordered by Avdas. 4 and 2 and Cs. Central and 1, Barrio La Catedral* ☎ *221–3820* ⊙ *Weekdays 6 AM–noon and 3–6 PM, Sun. 6 AM–9 PM.*

⑧ Correos (Central Post Office). The handsome, carved exterior of the post office, dating from 1917, is hard to miss among the bland buildings surrounding it. There's a display of first-day stamp issues upstairs, from where you can see the loading of *apartados* (post-office boxes) going on below: Ticos covet these hard-to-get boxes, as the city's lack of street addresses makes mail delivery a challenge. A small café on the first floor of the Correos overlooks the bustling pedestrian boulevard and a small park shaded by massive fig trees. Behind the park is the marble facade of the exclusive, members-only Club Unión. The large building behind the Correos is the Banco Nacional, a state-run bank. ⊠ *C. 2, between Avdas. 1 and 3, Barrio La Merced* ☉ *Weekdays 8–6:30, Sat. 8–noon.*

⑦ Mercado Central (Central Market). This block-long melting pot is a warren of dark, narrow passages flanked by stalls packed with spices (some purported to have medicinal value), fish, fruit, flowers, pets, and wood and leather crafts. There are also dozens of cheap restaurants and snack stalls, including the country's first ice cream vendor. This is a great place to stop for ceviche. Be warned: the concentration of shoppers makes this a hot spot for pickpockets, purse snatchers, and backpack slitters. ⊠ *Bordered by Avdas. Central and 1 and Cs. 6 and 8, Barrio La Merced* ☉ *Mon.–Sat. 6–6.*

> **need a break?**
>
> **Ice cream** is an art in this country, and after a long walk on crowded sidewalks, it may just save your sanity. The crème de la cream is dished out by two prolific chains, Pop's and Wall's (formerly Mönpik). At Pop's (⊠ *Avda. Central, between Cs 11 and 13*), everyone loves the mango. At Wall's (⊠ *Avda. Central, at C. 6*), beware the blue *Pitufo* (Smurf) flavor, but do try the *trits*, a chocolate-swirl sandwich with a crumbly cookie crust.

★ ⑫ Museo de Jade (Jade Museum). This is the world's largest collection of American jade—that's "American" in the hemispheric sense. Nearly all the items on display were produced in pre-Columbian times, and most of the jade dates from 300 BC to AD 700. In the spectacular Jade Room, pieces are illuminated from behind so you can appreciate their translucency. A series of drawings explains how this extremely hard stone was cut using string saws with quartz-and-sand abrasive. Jade was sometimes used in jewelry designs, but it was most often carved into oblong pendants. The museum also has other pre-Columbian artifacts, such as polychrome vases and three-legged *metates* (small stone tables for grinding corn), and a gallery of modern art. The final room on the tour has a startling display of ceramic fertility symbols. ⊠ *INS building, 11th floor, Avda. 7 between Cs. 9 and 11, Barrio Carmen* ☎ *287–6034* ⊡ *$2* ☉ *Weekdays 8:30–3:30.*

★ ② Museo de Oro Precolombino (Pre-Columbian Gold Museum). The dazzling, modern museum of gold, in a three-story underground building, contains the largest collection of pre-Columbian gold jewelry in Central America—20,000 troy ounces in more than 1,600 individual pieces—all owned by the Banco Central. Many pieces are in the form of frogs and eagles, two animals perceived by the region's pre-Columbian cultures to have great spiritual significance. Most spectacular are the varied shaman figurines, which represent the human connection to animal deities. ⊠ *Eastern end of Plaza de la Cultura, Barrio La Catedral* ☎ *243–4202* ⊡ *$5* ☉ *Tues.–Sun. 10–4:30.*

⑭ Museo Nacional (National Museum). In the whitewashed Bellavista Fortress, which dates from 1870, the National Museum gives you a quick and insightful lesson in Costa Rican culture from pre-Columbian times to the present. Glass cases display pre-Columbian artifacts, period dress, colonial furniture, and photographs. Outside are a veranda and a pleasant, manicured courtyard garden. A former army headquarters, this now-tranquil building saw fierce fighting during the 1948 revolution, as the bullet holes pocking its turrets attest. ⊠ *C. 17, between Avdas. Central and 2, Barrio La Catedral* ☎ *257–1433* ⊡ *$4* ☉ *Tues.–Sun. 9–4.*

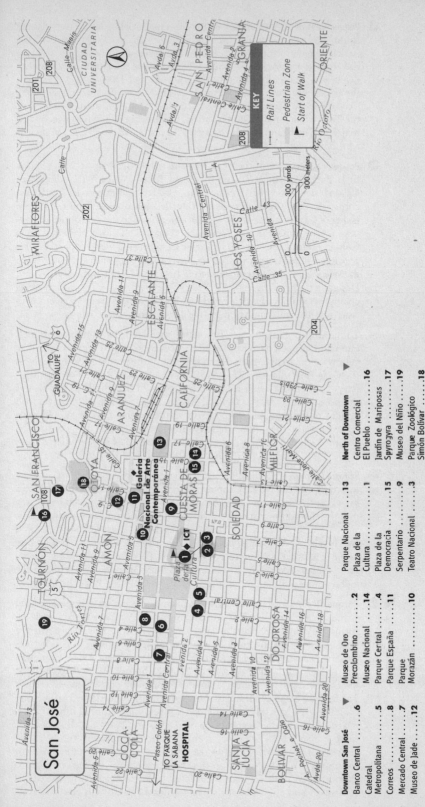

San José

KEY
Rail Lines
Pedestrian Zone
Start of Walk

④ Parque Central (Central Park). At the city's nucleus, this simple tree-planted square has a gurgling fountain and cement benches. In the center of the park is a spiderlike, mango-color gazebo donated by former Nicaraguan dictator Anastasio Somoza. Several years ago a referendum was held to decide whether to demolish the despot's gift, but Ticos voted to preserve the bandstand for posterity. Across Avenida 2, to the north, stands the **Teatro Melico Salazar,** San José's second major performance hall (after the Teatro Nacional). The fast-food outlet between the two was once a major movie theater. ⊠ *Bordered by Avdas. 2 and 4 and Cs. 2 and Central, Barrio La Catedral.*

⑪ Parque España. One of the most pleasant spots in the capital is this shady little park. A bronze statue of Costa Rica's Spanish founder, Juan Vásquez de Coronado, overlooks an elevated fountain on its southwest corner; the opposite corner has a lovely tiled guardhouse. A bust of Queen Isabel of Castile stares at the yellow compound to the east of the park— once a government liquor factory, and now the Centro Nacional de la Cultura (National Center of Culture). Covering a double block, the complex houses the Ministry of Culture, two theaters, and the extensive **Museo de Arte y Diseño Contemporáneo** (Museum of Contemporary Art and Design; ☎ 257–8702 or 257–7202 ⊕ www.madc.ac.cr), which hosts changing exhibits of work by artists and designers from all over Latin America. The museum is open Tuesday–Sunday 10–5; admission is $1.

To the west of the park is a two-story, metal-sided school made in Belgium and shipped to Costa Rica in pieces more than a century ago. The yellow colonial-style building to the east of the modern INS building is the **Casa Amarilla** (☎ 223–7555), home of Costa Rica's Foreign Ministry. The massive ceiba tree in front, planted by John F. Kennedy and the presidents of all the Central American nations in 1963, gives you an idea of how quickly things grow in the tropics. Part of the old ministry is open to the public Tuesday–Sunday 9–4. A few doors east is the elegant Mexican Embassy, once a private home. ⊠ *Bordered by Avdas. 7 and 3 and Cs. 11 and 17, Barrio Carmen* ☎ 257–7202.

⑩ Parque Morazán. Anchored by a neoclassic bandstand, the largest park in downtown San José is somewhat barren, though the tabebuia trees on its northwest corner brighten things up when they bloom in the dry months. Avoid the park late at night, when a rough crowd and occasional muggers appear. Along the southern edge are a public school and two lovely old mansions, both with beautiful facades—one is a private home, the other a prostitute pickup bar. There's a park annex with a large fountain to the northeast, across busy Avenida 3, in front of the metal school building. ⊠ *Avda. 3, between Cs. 5 and 9, Barrio Carmen.*

★ ⑬ Parque Nacional (National Park). A bronze monument commemorating Costa Rica's battle against American invader William Walker in 1856 forms the centerpiece of this large and leafy park. The park paths are made of cobblestone rescued from downtown streets, and tall trees shading concrete benches often hide colorful parakeets in their branches. The modern pink building west of the park houses the Registro Público (National Registry) and the Tribunal Supremo de Elecciones (Electoral Tribunal), which keep track of voters and oversee elections. The tall gray building to the north is the Biblioteca Nacional (National Library), beneath which, on the western side, is the **Galería Nacional de Arte Contemporánea** (☎ 257–5524), a small gallery exhibiting the work of contemporary artists, mostly Costa Rican. Quality varies, but since admission is free, it's always worth taking a peek.The walled complex to the northwest is the Centro Nacional de Cultura. Across from the park's southwest end is the Moorish **Asamblea Legislativa** (Legislative Assembly), where Costa Rica's congress meets. Next door is the Casa Rosada, a colonial-era residence now used for congressional offices, and behind that is a more modern house used by the government for parties and special events. One block northeast of the park is the former Atlantic Railway Station. The park is best avoided at night, despite ample lighting and security patrol. ✉ *Bordered by Avdas. 1 and 3 and Cs. 15 and 19, Barrio Carmen.*

★ ▶ **❶ Plaza de la Cultura.** A favored spot for local marimba bands, clowns, jugglers, and colorfully dressed South Americans playing Andean music, this somewhat sterile, large cement square is surrounded by shops and fast-food restaurants. It's a nice place to feed pigeons and buy some souvenirs. The stately Teatro Nacional dominates the plaza's southern half, and its western edge is defined by the venerable Gran Hotel Costa Rica, with its 24-hour Café Parisienne. ✉ *Bordered by Avdas. Central and 2 and Cs. 3 and 5, Barrio La Catedral.*

❶❺ Plaza de la Democracia. President Oscar Arias built this terraced open space west of the Museo Nacional to mark 100 years of democracy and to receive dignitaries during the 1989 hemispheric summit. The view west toward the dark-green Cerros de Escazú is nice in the morning and fabulous at sunset. The plaza is dominated by a statue of José "Pepe" Figueres, three-time president and leader of the 1948 revolution. Jewelry, T-shirts, and crafts from Costa Rica, Guatemala, and South America are sold in a string of stalls along the western edge. ✉ *Bordered by Avdas. Central and 2 and Cs. 13 and 15, Barrio La Catedral.*

☝ ❾ Serpentario (Serpentarium). Don't be alarmed by the absence of motion within the display cases here—the inmates are very much alive. Most notorious in this collection of snakes and lizards is the Terciopelo, responsible for more than half the poisonous snakebites in Costa Rica. The menagerie includes boa constrictors, Jesus Christ lizards, poison dart frogs, iguanas, and an aquarium full of deadly sea snakes, as well as such exotic creatures as King Cobras and Burmese Pythons. ✉ *Avda. 1, between Cs. 9 and 11, Barrio Carmen* ☎ *255–4210* ✉ *$5* ☉ *Weekdays 9–6, weekends 10–5.*

★ **❸ Teatro Nacional** (National Theater). This is easily the most enchanting building in Costa Rica. Chagrined that touring prima donna Adelina Patti bypassed San José in 1890, wealthy coffee merchants raised import taxes to hire Belgian architects to design this building, lavish with cast iron and Italian marble. The sandstone exterior is marked by Italianate arched windows, marble columns with bronze capitals, and statues of strange bedfellows Ludwig van Beethoven (1770–1827) and 17th-century Spanish golden-age playwright Pedro Calderón de la Barca (1600–81). The Muses of Dance, Music, and Fame are silhouetted in front of an iron cupola. Given the provenance of the building funds, it's not surprising that frescoes on the stairway inside depict coffee and banana production. The theater was inaugurated in 1897 with a performance of Gounod's *Faust,* featuring an international cast. The sumptuous neo-Baroque interior sparkles thanks to an ongoing restoration project. The theater is sometimes closed for rehearsals, so call before you go. The stunning Café del Teatro Nacional just off the vestibule serves upscale coffee concoctions, good sandwiches, and exquisite pastries. ✉ *Plaza de la Cultura, Barrio La Catedral* ☎ *221–1329* ✉ *$2, performance tickets $4–$40* ☉ *Mon.–Sat. 9–5.*

Universidad de Costa Rica. The University of Costa Rica, in San Pedro just east of San José, is a great place to hang out and meet people, especially if your Spanish is pretty good. The open-air gallery at the **Fac-**

ultad de Bellas Artes (College of Fine Arts), on the east side of campus, hosts free music recitals on Tuesday nights. If the Serpentario doesn't satisfy your thirst for creepy crawlers, scurry on over to the **Museo de Insectos** (✉ north of Bellas Artes, in the basement of the Artes Musicales building ☎ 207–5318 ⊕ www.insectos.ucr.ac.cr), open weekdays 1–4:45. The $2 admission buys you a good look at dead insects in recreated habitats and information in English and Spanish on everything from insect sex to the diseases these little buggers cause.

Aficionados of Spanish literature should browse around the many off-campus bookstores. Anyone who appreciates cheap grub can revel in the vast selection of inexpensive lunch places around the university. Weeknights at the university are mellow, but nearby bars are packed with students and intellectuals on weekends. To get to San Pedro, walk a few miles east along Avenida Central's strip of shops and bars or take a $2 taxi ride from downtown and get off in front of Banco Nacional, just beyond the rotunda with the fountain at its center. ✉ *Avda. Central and C. Central, Barrio Montes de Oca, San Pedro.*

North of Downtown

a good tour

Take a taxi to the **Centro Comercial El Pueblo** ⑯ ▶, in Barrio Tournón. One block east and half a block south of El Pueblo is the **Jardín de Mariposas Spyrogyra** ⑰, a butterfly garden overlooking the greenery of Costa Rica's zoo, the **Parque Zoológico Simón Bolívar** ⑱. The best way to reach the zoo, however, is to walk north from the bandstand in the Parque Morazán along Calle 7 to the bottom of the hill, then turn right. The **Museo del Niño** ⑲, a children's museum and scientific and cultural center housed in an old jail, lies several blocks to the west. It's surrounded by dubious neighborhoods, so take a taxi.

TIMING   You can visit all four of these sights in one morning.

What to See

▶ ⑯ **Centro Comercial El Pueblo** (El Pueblo Shopping Center). This shopping center was built to resemble the kind of colonial village that Costa Rica lacks. *Pueblo* means "town," and the cobbled passages, adobe walls, and tiny plazas are surprisingly convincing. Most of the commercial spaces are occupied by bars, restaurants, and discos that attract a twentysomething crowd. El Pueblo gets very busy at night, especially on weekends—but there are a few shops worth checking out during the day. ✉ *Avda. 0, Barrio Tournón* ۞ *Daily.*

★ ۩ ⑰ **Jardín de Mariposas Spyrogyra** (Butterfly Garden). An hour or two at this magical garden is entertaining and educational for nature lovers of all ages. Self-guided tours enlighten you on butterfly ecology and give you a chance to see the winged creatures close up. Following an 18-minute video introduction, you're free to wander screened-in gardens along a numbered trail. Some 30 species of colorful butterflies flutter about, accompanied by six types of hummingbirds. Try to come when it's sunny, as butterflies are most active then. A small, moderately priced café borders the garden and serves sandwiches and Tico fare. Spyrogyra abuts the northern edge of Parque Zoológico Simón Bolívar, but you enter on the outskirts of Barrio Tournón, near El Pueblo Shopping Center. ✉ *½ block east and 1½ blocks south of main entrance to El Pueblo, Barrio Tournón* ☎ *222–2937* ☒ *$5* ۞ *Daily 8–5.*

۩ ⑲ **Museo del Niño.** San José's Children's Museum is housed in a former jail, and big kids may want to check it out just to marvel at the castlelike architecture and the old cells that have been preserved in an exhibit about prison life. Three halls in the complex are filled with eye-catching seasonal exhibits for kids, ranging in subject from local ecology to outer space. The exhibits are annotated in Spanish, but most are interactive, so language shouldn't be much of a problem. The museum's **Galería Nacional,** adjoining the main building, is more popular with adults; it usually shows fine art by Costa Rican artists free of charge. Adjoining the museum is the **Auditorio Nacional,** in which the National Symphony plays morning concerts at 10 from March to November. ⊠ *North end of C. 1, Barrio Carmen* ☎ *258–4929* 🖳 *$2* ⊘ *Tues.–Fri. 8–4:30, weekends 9:30–5.*

👆 ⑱ **Parque Zoológico Simón Bolívar.** Considering Costa Rica's mind-boggling diversity of wildlife, San José's zoo is rather modest in scope. It does, however, provide an introduction to some of the animals you might see in the jungle. The park is set in a forested ravine in historical Barrio Amón, offering soothing green space in the heart of the city. ⊠ *Avda. 11 and C. 11, Barrio Amón* ☎ *233–6701* 🖳 *$2* ⊘ *Weekdays 8–3:30, weekends 9–5.*

WHERE TO EAT

Wherever you eat in San José, be it a small *soda* (café) or a sophisticated restaurant, dress is casual. Meals tend to be taken earlier than in other Latin American countries; few restaurants serve past 10 PM. Local cafés usually open for breakfast at 7 AM and remain open until 7 or 9 in the evening. Restaurants serving international cuisine are usually open from 11 AM to 9 PM. Some cafés that serve mainly San José office workers are closed Sunday. Casino restaurants in downtown San José are open 24 hours.

Note that 23% is added to all menu prices—13% for tax and 10% for service. Because a gratuity is included, there's no need to tip; but if your service is good, it's nice to add a little money to the obligatory 10%. Except for those in hotels, most restaurants close between Christmas and New Year's Day and during Holy Week (Palm Sunday to Easter Sunday). Call before heading out. Those that do stay open may not sell alcohol between Maundy Thursday and Easter Sunday. Even if you keep your base in San José, consider venturing to the Central Valley towns for a meal or two.

WHAT IT COSTS				
	$$$$	**$$$**	**$$**	**$**	**¢**
AT DINNER	over $25	$20–$25	$10–$20	$5–$10	under $5

Prices are per-person for a main course.

Downtown San José

AMERICAN/
CASUAL
$–$$
✕ **News Café.** Had your fill of rice and beans? You can get a Caesar salad and other American dishes here. Breakfasts and dinner fare are hearty, but the café is most popular at lunchtime and cocktail hour. It's one of the few eateries in the city with covered outdoor seating, and it's in the perfect place for it—right off the pedestrian boulevard's east end. Inside, the wrought-iron chairs, wood beams, and brick walls give the place an old-town tavern feel, though it's actually on the first floor of the 1960s landmark Hotel Presidente. ⊠ *C. 7 and Avda. Central, Barrio La Catedral* ☎ *222–3022* 🖃 *AE, DC, MC, V.*

CAFÉS
¢–$
✕ **Café Britt Teatro Nacional.** The country's foremost purveyor of gourmet coffee has a concession stand at Teatro Nacional. Have a cup of mocha with hazelnut and rest your weary head against cool marble while gazing at the frescoes on the ceiling. Atmosphere comes at a reasonable price

here—coffees run anywhere from $1 to $2, depending on how much alcohol or ice cream is added. Sandwiches and cakes will set you back $3 to $4. ⊠ *Teatro Nacional, Plaza de la Cultura, Barrio La Catedral* ☎ *221–3262* ⊕ *www.cafebritt.com* ⊘ *Closed Sun.*

CHINESE
¢–$
✕ **Fulusu.** Some like it hot, and this Chinese place near local landmark Hotel Presidente is one of the very few Costa Rica restaurants where you can get a spicy-food fix. The menu is full of authentic and delicious dishes, making it easy to forgive the mundane Asian prints and checkered tablecloths. Start with some *empanadas chinas* (dumplings similar to pot stickers); then move on to a main course like *vainicas con cerdo* (green beans with pork) or *carne estilo sichuan* (Szechuan beef). One entrée and two orders of rice are usually enough for two. ⊠ *C. 7 between Avdas. Central and 2, Barrio La Catedral* ☎ *223–7568* ⊟ *AE, MC, V.*

COSTA RICAN
★ $–$$
✕ **La Cocina de Leña.** La Cocina serves up traditional Costa Rican fare surrounded by old tools and straw bags hung on walls to make you feel like you're down on the farm. Popular Tico dishes such as black-bean soup, ceviche, tamales, oxtail with cassava, and plantains are served, and the restaurant has live marimba music several nights a week during high season. Although the kitchen closes at 11, you're welcome to stay as long as the band keeps playing. It is one of the few places that doesn't close during Holy Week. ⊠ *Centro Comercial El Pueblo, Barrio Tournón* ☎ *223–3704* ⊟ *AE, MC, V.*

¢–$
✕ **El Cuartel de la Boca del Monte.** Although it's one of San José's more popular late-night bars, El Cuartel is actually a nice place to have a meal, too. The restored brick walls, wood beams, and simple wood tables lend a rustic feel in one room, and you'll find a more finished room to the left of the entrance, decorated with original art. Best on the menu is arroz con pollo, but you can also order plates of delicious *bocas* (snacks), such as the *plato de gallos* (corn tortillas topped with beef, potatoes, and other fillings) and *piononos* (sweet plantains stuffed with cheese or beans and served with sour cream). ⊠ *Avda. 1, between Cs. 21 and 23, Barrio La California* ☎ *221–0327* ⊟ *AE, MC, V* ⊘ *No lunch weekends.*

¢–$
✕ **Mama's Place.** Mama's is a Costa Rican restaurant with a difference: the owners are Italian, so in addition to corvina *al ajillo* (sautéed with garlic) and other staple Tico fare, they serve homemade seafood chowder, traditional Italian pastas, and meat dishes with delicate wine sauces. The brightly decorated coffee shop opens onto busy Avenida 1; the more subdued restaurant is upstairs. At lunchtime, it's usually packed with business types drawn to the delicious and inexpensive daily specials and perhaps the macrobiotic fruit shakes, another menu item that sets this place apart. ⊠ *Avda. 1, between Cs. Central and 2, Barrio Carmen* ☎ *223–2270* ⊟ *AE, DC, MC, V* ⊘ *Closed Sun.*

¢–$
✕ **Manolo's.** This 24-hour eatery has been popular with travelers for years, both for its location on the bustling pedestrian thoroughfare and for its great sandwiches, espressos, and *churros con chocolate* (fried dough with hot fudge sauce). A few outdoor tables allow for some of the city's best people-watching. Inside, however, the place feels more like a diner than a café, down to its plastic-coated menu and its promise of breakfast food at any hour. The owner always prepares a few Spanish favorites in addition to the typical Tico fare, such as *tortilla española* (a thick potato-and-onion omelet). ⊠ *Avda. Central, between Cs. Central and 2, Barrio La Catedral* ☎ *221–2041* ⊟ *AE, MC, V.*

¢–$
✕ **Nuestra Tierra.** With its relaxed atmosphere and rough-hewn tables, Nuestra Tierra is an upscale alternative to "soda" dining. Eat in the bar area where bunches of onions and peppers dangle from the ceiling, recalling a provincial Tico ranch. In the main dining room things are a

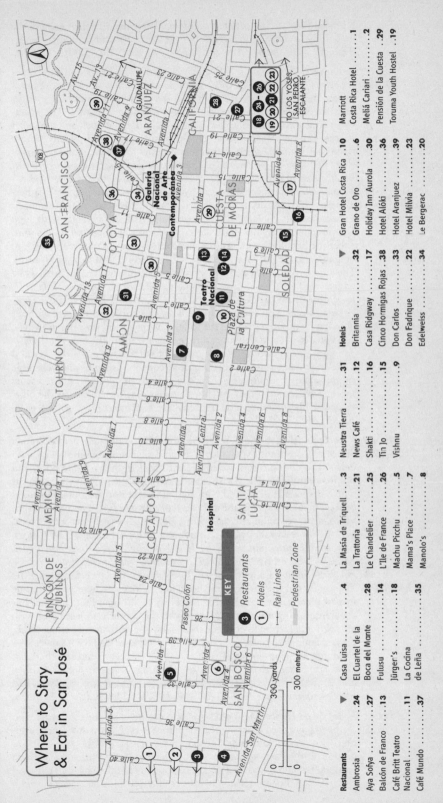

bit more formal. The generous homemade meals are delicious, and the incredibly friendly waitstaff epitomizes Costa Rican hospitality. ⊠ *Av. 9 and C. 3 Bis, Barrio Amón* ☎ *258–2983* ▤ *AE, DC, MC, V.*

ECLECTIC
$$–$$$

✕ **Jürgen's.** Decorated in gold and terra-cotta with leather and wood accents, the dining room of this contemporary restaurant feels more like a lounge than a fine restaurant. In fact, the classy bar, with a large selection of good wine and good cigars, is a prominent feature. The inventive menu, with such delicacies as medallions of roast duck and tuna fillet encrusted with sesame seeds, sets this place apart from the city's more traditional venues. Jürgen's is a common haunt for *politicos* and San José's elite. ⊠ *¾-km (½-mi) north of the Subaru dealership, on Barrio Dent Blvd., Barrio Dent* ☎ *283–2239* ▤ *AE, DC, MC, V* ☾ *Closed Sun.*

$–$$
Fodor's Choice
★

✕ **Ambrosia.** The navy-blue canopy in an open-air shopping plaza heralds this chic restaurant. The international menu draws the customers. Expect inventive salads, soups, pasta, and fish dishes. Start with *sopa Neptuna* (a creamy fish soup with tomato and bacon), and follow with either the light fettuccine Ambrosia (in a rich cream sauce with ham and oregano) or the corvina *troyana* (with a shrimp and tarragon sauce). The dining room is relaxed, with plants, subdued watercolors, crisp white tablecloths, and wood-and-cane chairs. ⊠ *Centro Comercial de la C. Real, San Pedro* ☎ *253–8012* ▤ *AE, DC, MC, V* ☾ *No dinner Sun.*

$–$$
Fodor's Choice
★

✕ **Café Mundo.** You could easily walk by this corner restaurant without noticing its tiny sign behind the foliage. Walk in and upstairs, however, and you discover an elegant eatery serving meals on the porch, on a garden patio, or in two dining rooms. Start with the soup of the day and some fresh-baked bread; then opt for penne in a shrimp and vegetable cream sauce or *lomito en salsa de vino tinto* (tenderloin in a red-wine sauce). Save room for the best chocolate cake in town, drizzled with homemade blackberry sauce. ⊠ *C. 15 and Avda. 9, Barrio Otoya* ☎ *222–6190* ▤ *AE, MC, V* ☾ *Closed Sun. No lunch Sat.*

FRENCH
$$–$$$$

✕ **Le Chandelier.** Formal service and traditional sauce-heavy French dishes are part of the experience at the city's classiest restaurant, Le Chandelier. The dining room is elegant, with wicker chairs, a tile floor, and original paintings. The Swiss chef, Claude Dubuis, might start you off with saffron ravioli stuffed with ricotta cheese and walnuts. His main courses include such unique dishes as corvina in a *pejibaye* (peach palm) sauce, hearts of palm and veal chops glazed in a sweet port-wine sauce, and the more familiar *pato a la naranja* (duck à l'orange). ⊠ *1 block west and 1 block south of the ICE building, Los Yoses, San Pedro* ☎ *225–3980* ▤ *AE, MC, V* ☾ *Closed Sun. No lunch Sat.*

$$
Fodor's Choice
★

✕ **L'Ile de France.** Long one of San José's most popular restaurants, L'Ile de France is in the Le Bergerac hotel in Los Yoses, where you can dine in a tropical garden courtyard. The fairly traditional French menu has some interesting innovations. Start with the classic onion soup or with *pâté de lapin* (rabbit liver pâté); then sink your teeth into a pepper steak, broiled lamb with seasoned potatoes, or corvina in a spinach sauce. Save room for the profiteroles filled with vanilla ice cream and smothered in chocolate sauce. ⊠ *Le Bergerac hotel, C. 35, between Avdas. Central and 2, first Los Yoses entrance, Los Yoses, San Pedro* ☎ *283–5812* ⚏ *Reservations essential* ▤ *AE, DC, MC, V* ☾ *Closed Sun. No lunch.*

ITALIAN
$–$$

✕ **Balcón de Franco.** With old sepia photos and a strolling guitarist who seems to have been working the room for years, Balcón de Franco, popularly known as Balcón de Europa, transports you to the year of its inception, 1909. Pasta specialties such as the *plato mixto* (mixed plate with lasagna, tortellini, and ravioli) are so popular that they haven't changed much, either. For something lighter, try the scrumptious heart-of-palm salad or sautéed corvina. ⊠ *Avda. Central and C. 9, Barrio La Cate-dral* ☎ *221–4841* ☰ *AE, DC, MC, V* ⊘ *Closed Sat.*

$ ✕ **La Trattoria.** Excellent homemade pasta dishes are reasonably priced at this popular lunch spot. The blond-wood tables and Tuscan yellow walls lend levity. Begin your meal with fresh bread and any number of excellent antipastis, continuing on with your favorite pasta dish. And for dessert, who can resist tiramisu? ⊠ *Behind Auto-Mercado Los Yoses, San Pedro, Barrio Dent* ☎ *224–7065* ☰ *AE, DC, MC, V.*

PAN-ASIAN ✕ **Tin Jo.** You can eat in the Japan, India, China, or Thailand room at
★ $–$$ this wide-ranging Asian restaurant with a menu to match its varied din-ing areas. Tin Jo stands apart from the two other Chinese restaurants on this block with always exceptional food and whimsical decorations that add color to this former residence. Start with a powerful Singapore Sling (brandy and fruit juices) before trying such treats as *kaeng* (Thai shrimp and pineapple curry in coconut milk), *mu shu* (a beef, chicken, or veggie stir-fry with crêpes), *samosas* (stuffed Indian pastries), and sushi rolls. The vegetarian menu is extensive. ⊠ *C. 11, between Avdas. 6 and 8, Barrio La Soledad* ☎ *257–3622* ☰ *AE, DC, MC, V.*

PERUVIAN ✕ **Machu Picchu.** A few travel posters and a fishnet holding crab and lob-
★ $–$$ ster shells are the only props used to evoke Peru, but no matter: the food is anything but plain, and the seafood is excellent. The *pique especial de mariscos* (special seafood platter), big enough for two, presents you with shrimp, conch, and squid cooked four ways. The ceviche here is quite different from, and better than, that served in the rest of the coun-try. A blazing Peruvian hot sauce served on the side adds zip to any dish, but be careful—apply it by the drop. ⊠ *C. 32, 130 m (140 yards) north of Kentucky Fried Chicken, Paseo Colón* ☎ *222–7384* ☰ *AE, DC, MC, V* ⊘ *Closed Sun.*

SPANISH ✕ **La Masía de Triquell.** San José's most traditional Spanish restaurant is
$$–$$$ appropriately housed in the Casa España, a Spanish cultural center. The dining room follows the theme with a tile floor, wood beams, white table-cloths, leather-and-wood Castilian style chairs, and red, green, and yel-low walls. *Champiñones al ajillo* (mushrooms sautéed with garlic and parsley) make a fine appetizer; *camarones Catalana* (shrimp in a tomato-and-garlic cream sauce) is a standout entrée. The long wine list is strongest in the Spanish and French departments. ⊠ *45 m (50 yards) west and 130 m (140 yards) north of Burger King, Sabana Norte* ☎296–3528 ⌸ *Reser-vations essential* ☰ *AE, DC, MC, V* ⊘ *Closed Sun.*

$–$$ ✕ **Casa Luisa.** The moment you enter this homey, upscale Catalan restau-rant, you sense you're in for a special evening. It is eclectic and artful, with wood floors, arresting artwork, soft lighting, and flamenco music in the background. Start the meal with gazpacho or eggplant pâté, ac-companied by a glass of top Spanish wine. The wonderful main dishes include rosemary lamb chops, suckling pig, and grilled lobster. Finish with a platter of nuts, dates, and figs drizzled with a wine sauce or the decadent *crema Catalana* with a *brûlée* glaze. ⊠ *Avda. 4 and C. 40, south-east of the Controlaria building, Sabana Sur* ☎ *296–1917* ☰ *AE, DC, MC, V* ⊘ *Closed Mon.*

TURKISH ✕ **Aya Sofya.** Natives of Istanbul, the chef and one of the owners have
¢–$ imported excellent recipes for red peppers stuffed with spicy beef and rice, eggplant-tomato salad, and other Mediterranean treats. The selection of vegetarian salads is good. Desserts include a scrumptious yogurt-and-honey *revani* cake and the beloved baklava. Beyond the obligatory evil-eye motif and a few wall hangings, this is a no-frills place, but good food and a friendly staff make it a find. ⊠ *Avda. Central and C. 21, Barrio La California* ☎ *221–7185* ☰ *AE, DC, MC, V* ⊘ *Closed Sun.*

VEGETARIAN   ✕ **Shakti.** Amidst the baskets of fruit and vegetables at the entrance and
¢–$ the wall of herbal teas, health food books, and fresh herbs for sale by
the register, there's no doubt you're in a vegetarian-friendly joint. The
bright and airy restaurant serves breakfast and lunch: homemade bread,
soy burgers, pita sandwiches (veggie or, for carnivorous dining companions,
chicken), macrobiotic fruit shakes, and a hearty plato del día that comes
with soup, green salad, and a fruit beverage. The *ensalada mixta* is a meal
in itself, packed with root vegetables native to Costa Rica. The restaurant closes at 8 PM daily. ⊠ *Avda. 8 between Cs. 13 and 11, Barrio Lujan*
☎ *222–4475* ⌗ *Reservations not accepted* ▤ *MC, V.*

¢   ✕ **Vishnu.** Named after the Hindu god who preserves the universe,
Vishnu has become a bit of an institution in San José. Even its dining
area looks institutional—sterile booths with Formica tables and posters
of fruit on the walls—but the attraction is the inexpensive vegetarian
food. Your best bet is usually the *plato del día* (daily special), which includes soup, beverage, and dessert, but the menu also offers soy burgers, salads, fresh fruit juices, and a yogurt smoothie called *morir soñando*
(literally, "to die dreaming"). ⊠ *Avda. 1, west of C. 3, Barrio Carmen*
☎ *233–9976* ⌗ *Reservations not accepted* ▤ *No credit cards.*

WHERE TO STAY

San José packs every kind of accommodation, from luxury to bare necessity. You can find massive hotels with all the modern conveniences
and amenities, historic buildings with traditional architecture but fewer
creature comforts, and smaller establishments with the simplicity (and
prices) beloved of backpackers. Dozens of former homes in the city's
older neighborhoods, such as Barrio Amón and Barrio Otoya, and surrounding towns such as San Pedro have been converted to moderately
priced bed-and-breakfasts. Confirm all reservations 24 hours ahead.

WHAT IT COSTS				
	$$$$	$$$	$$	$	¢
FOR 2 PEOPLE	over $200	$125–$200	$75–$125	$35–$75	under $35

Prices are for a standard double room in high season, excluding service and tax
(16.4%).

Downtown San José

Staying in the downtown area allows you to travel around the city as
most Ticos do: on foot. Stroll the city's parks, museums, and shops, and
then retire in one of many small or historic hotels that have plenty in
the way of character.

$$ ▦ **Holiday Inn Aurola.** The upper floors of this 17-story mirrored-glass
building, three blocks north of the Plaza de la Cultura, have the best
views in town. Ignoring the view of downtown San José and its sur-
roundings, however, you could just as soon be in Ohio, as the interior
decoration betrays no local influence. The high-ceiling lobby is modern
and airy, with lots of shiny marble. The good restaurant and casino are
on the top floor, making full use of their vantage points. ⊠ *Avda. 5 and
C. 5, Barrio Amón* ⌖ *Apdo. 7802–1000, San José* ☎ *222–2424, 800/
465–4329 in the U.S.* 📠 *233–0603* ⊕ *www.sanjosecr.holiday-inn.com*
⤴ *188 rooms, 12 suites* ⌂ *Restaurant, cafeteria, in-room safes, mini-
bars, cable TV, indoor pool, gym, hot tub, sauna, bar, casino, laundry
service, Internet, no-smoking floors* ▤ *AE, DC, MC, V.*

$$ ▦ **Britannia.** Except for the addition of some rooms and the conversion of the old cellar into an intimate international restaurant, this stately pink home with a tiled porch has changed little since its construction in 1910. Rooms in the newer wing are slightly small, with carpeting and hardwood furniture. Deluxe rooms and junior suites in the original house are spacious, with high ceilings and windows on the street side; they're worth the extra money but are close enough to the street that noise might be a problem if you're a light sleeper. ✉ *C. 3 and Avda. 11, Barrio Amón* ☎ *Apdo. 3742–1000, San José* ☎ *223–6667; 888/535–8832 in the U. S.* 🖷 *223–6411* ⊕ *www.centralamerica.com/cr/hotel/britania.htm* ↘ *19 rooms, 5 suites* ♦ *Restaurant, fans, in-room safes, cable TV, bar, shop, dry cleaning, laundry service, Internet, airport shuttle; no a/c in some rooms* ▭ *AE, MC, V.*

★ $$ ▦ **Grano de Oro.** Two turn-of-the-20th-century wooden houses on San José's western edge have been converted into one of the city's most charming inns. New rooms have been added to the attractive space, which is decorated with old photos of the capital and paintings by local artists. A modest restaurant, run by a French-trained chef, is surrounded by a lovely indoor patio and gardens. The old rooms are the nicest, especially the Garden Suite, with hardwood floors, high ceilings, and private garden. The hotel's sundeck has a view of both the city and the far-off volcanoes. ✉ *C. 30, between Avdas. 2 and 4, Paseo Colón* ☎ *1701 N.W. 97th Ave., Box 025216, SJO 36, Miami, FL 33102–5216* ☎ *255–3322* 🖷 *221–2782* ⊕ *www.hotelgranodeoro.com* ↘ *32 rooms, 3 suites* ♦ *Restaurant, room service, in-room safes, minibars, cable TV, outdoor hot tub, laundry service, no smoking rooms* ▭ *AE, MC, V.*

$$ ▦ **Hotel Alóki.** Guest rooms in this elegant turn-of-the-20th-century manor house surround a covered courtyard restaurant whose wicker furniture and potted tropical plants spill onto multicolored glazed tiles. The antique furniture, gilt mirrors, and old prints in the rooms make this small, quiet place one of the most tasteful in San José. The Presidential Suite has a large drawing room. ✉ *C. 13, between Avdas. 9 and 11, Barrio Otoya* ☎ *Box 02-5635 Miami, FL 33102* ☎ *222–6702* 🖷 *221–2533* ⊕ *www.tropicalcostarica.com/aloki/aloki.htm* ↘ *6 rooms, 1 suite* ♦ *Restaurant, fans, cable TV, bar; no a/c* ▭ *AE, DC, MC, V* ﴾ *BP.*

★ $ ▦ **Don Carlos.** As one of the city's first guest houses, Don Carlos has been in the same family for four generations. Most rooms in the rambling villa have ceiling fans and big windows. Those in the Colonial Wing have a bit more personality, and several newer rooms on the third floor have volcano views. Abundant public areas are adorned with orchids and pre-Columbian statues. Complimentary cocktails and breakfast are served on the garden patio; the small restaurant serves lunch and dinner. ✉ *C. 9 and Avda. 9, Barrio Amón* ☎ *Box 025216, Dept. 1686, Miami, FL 33102-5216* ☎ *221–6707* 🖷 *255–0828* ⊕ *www. doncarloshotel.com* ↘ *21 rooms, 12 suites* ♦ *Restaurant, in-room safes, outdoor hot tub, shop, laundry service, Internet, airport shuttle; no a/c in some rooms* ▭ *AE, MC, V* ﴾ *BP.*

$ ▦ **Edelweiss.** Never mind that the interior looks more European than Latin American (one of the owners is Austrian). This elegant little inn has comfortable rooms in a charming area, near the Parque España. Rooms have carved doors, custom-made furniture, and small bathrooms. Most have hardwood window frames and floors; several have bathtubs. Complimentary breakfast is served in the garden courtyard, which doubles as a bar. ✉ *Avda. 9 and C. 15, Barrio Otoya* ☎ *221–9702* 🖷 *222–1241* ⊕ *www.edelweisshotel.com* ↘ *27 rooms* ♦ *Fans, bar; no a/c* ▭ *AE, DC, MC, V* ﴾ *CP.*

$ 🏨 **Gran Hotel Costa Rica.** Opened in 1930, the grande dame of San José hotels remains a focal point of the city and is the first choice of travelers who want to be where the action is. It's a good deal for the money, but the flow of nonguests who frequent the 24-hour casino, Café Parisienne, restaurant, and bar reduces the intimacy quotient to zero. Rooms are large and somewhat lackluster, with small windows and tubs in the tiled baths. Most overlook the Plaza de la Cultura, which can be a bit noisy, and the quieter, interior rooms are pretty dark. Breakfast is complimentary. ⊠ *Avda. 2 and C. 3, Barrio La Catedral* ⅅ *Apdo. 527–1000, San José* ☎ *221–4000, 800/949–0592 in the U.S.* 🖷 *221–3501* ⊕ *www. granhotelcr.com* ➴ *106 rooms, 4 suites* ⚘ *Restaurant, café, fans, cable TV, bar, casino, shop, laundry service; no a/c* ⊟ *AE, DC, MC, V* ⎟⊘⎟ *CP.*

$ 🏨 **Pensión de la Cuesta.** Rooms in this laid-back, centrally located wooden villa in sloping Cuesta de Nuñez have hardwood floors, brightly painted walls, and original art. Rooms in back are quieter, but those in front are brighter. You can lounge and read in the sunken sitting area (also used as the breakfast room), which has a high ceiling, a wall of windows, and cable TV. You're welcome to use the kitchen for lunch and dinner. The nine rooms share four baths. A furnished apartment is also for rent. ⊠ *Avda. 1 between Cs. 11 and 15, Apdo. 1332, Barrio Cuesta de Nuñez* ☎ *256–7946* 🖷 *255–2896* ⊕ *www.suntoursandfun. com/lacuesta* ➴ *9 rooms without bath, 1 apartment* ⚘ *Fans; no a/c, no room TVs, no room phones* ⊟ *AE, MC, V* ⎟⊘⎟ *CP.*

¢–$ 🏨 **Hotel Aranjuez.** Several 1940s-era houses, with extensive gardens and
FodorśChoice cozy common areas, constitute this family-run B&B. Each room is dif-
★ ferent; some have private gardens or small sitting rooms. Aranjuez is a short walk from most San José attractions and offers such perks as discount tour service. The complimentary breakfast buffet makes lunch unthinkable. Reserve well in advance during high season. ⊠ *C. 19 between Avdas. 11 and 13, Barrio Aranjuez* ☎ *256–1825 or 877/898–8663* 🖷 *223–3528* ⊕ *www.hotelaranjuez.com* ➴ *35 rooms, 25 with bath* ⚘ *Dining room, fans, in-room safes, cable TV, Internet; no a/c* ⊟ *MC, V* ⎟⊘⎟ *BP.*

¢   🏨 **Cinco Hormigas Rojas.** The name of this whimsical little lodge translates as "five red ants." Behind the wall of vines that obscures it from the street is a wild garden that leads to an interior space filled with original artwork. Color abounds, from the bright hues on the walls right down to the toilet seats. Sure enough, the resident owner is an artist—Mayra Güell turned the house she inherited from her grandmother into San José's most original B&B–cum–art gallery. It's in the historic Barrio Otoya, one of San José's most pleasant neighborhoods. ⊠ *C. 15 between Avdas. 9 and 11, Barrio Otoya* ☎ *255–3412* 🖷🖷 *257–8581* ⊕ *www.crtimes.com/tourism/cincohormigasrojas/maincinco.htm* ➴ *6 rooms, 2 with bath* ⚘ *Fans, laundry service; no a/c, no room phones, no room TVs* ⊟ *AE, MC, V* ⎟⊘⎟ *BP.*

★ ¢   🏨 **Casa Ridgway.** Affiliated with the Quaker Peace Center next door, Casa Ridgway is the budget option for itinerants concerned with peace, the environment, and social issues in general. Set in an old villa on a quiet street, the bright, clean premises include a planted terrace, a lending reference library, and a kitchen where you can cook your own food. There are three rooms with two bunk beds each, three rooms with single beds, and one with a double bed, all of which share three bathrooms. ⊠ *Avda. 6 Bis and C. 15, Barrio Gonzalez Laman* ⅅ *Apdo. 1507–1000, San José* ☎ *222–1400.* 🖷🖷 *233–6168* ✉ *friends@racsa.co.cr* ➴ *8 shared rooms without bath* ⚘ *Library, meeting room, laundry service; no a/c, no room phones, no room TVs* ⊟ *No credit cards.*

Northeast of San José

The small properties beyond downtown, toward the university, offer personalized service and lots of peace and quiet. Plenty of restaurants and bars are within easy reach, although downtown is just a 10-minute cab ride away.

$$
Fodor'sChoice
★

✕⊞ **Le Bergerac.** Le Bergerac, surrounded by extensive green grounds, is the cream of a growing crop of small, upscale San José hotels. It occupies two former private homes and is furnished with antiques. All rooms have custom-made wood-and-stone dressers and writing tables; deluxe rooms have two beds, private garden terraces or balconies, and large bathrooms. The hotel's restaurant, L'Ile de France ($$), is one of the city's best, so dinner reservations are essential, even for guests. Breakfast is served on a garden patio. ⊠ *C. 35, between Avdas. Central and 2, first entrance to Los Yoses, Los Yoses, San Pedro* ⌖ *Apdo. 1107–1002, San José* ☎ *234–7850* 🖷 *225–9103* ⊕ *www.bergerachotel.com* ⮩ *19 rooms* ⚘ *Restaurant, fans, in-room data ports, in-room safes, cable TV, bar, laundry service, meeting room, travel services, no smoking rooms; no a/c* ▤ *AE, DC, MC, V* ⧖⧗ *BP.*

$
⊞ **Don Fadrique.** This tranquil, family-run B&B on the outskirts of San José was named after Fadrique Guttierez, an illustrious great-uncle of the owners. A collection of original Costa Rican art decorates the lobby and rooms, most of which have hardwood floors, peach walls, and pastel bedspreads. Several carpeted rooms downstairs open onto the garden. There is also an enclosed garden patio, where meals are served. ⊠ *C. 37 at Avda. 8, Los Yoses, San Pedro* ☎ *224–7583 or 888/535–8832 in the U.S.* 🖷 *224–9746* ⊕ *www.centralamerica.com/cr/hotel/fadrique. htm* ⮩ *20 rooms* ⚘ *Restaurant, fans, cable TV, laundry service, car rental; no a/c* ▤ *AE, MC, V* ⧖⧗ *BP.*

$
⊞ **Hotel Milvia.** Once a militia-arms depository, this hundred-year-old house-turned-B&B on a San Pedro back street has charming small rooms and volcano views from the second-story balcony. There is a small pond out front in the lush garden. Inside are antique pictures of old San Jose, a breakfast salon and small bar area, and classic Tico furniture. The bathrooms have lovely hand-painted tiles. Unfortunately, because of the small doors and tight corners, double beds are contrived by pushing two singles together. ⊠ *50 m (55 yards) north and 200 m (220 yards) east of Centro Comercial Muñoz y Nanne, San Pedro* ⌖ *Apdo. 1660–2050, San Pedro* ☎ *225–4543 or 283–9548* 🖷 *225–7801* ⊕ *www.novanet.co.cr/ milvia* ⮩ *9 rooms* ⚘ *Fans, in-room safes, cable TV, pond, bar, laundry service, Internet; no smoking, no a/c* ▤ *AE, DC, MC, V* ⧖⧗ *CP.*

¢
⊞ **Toruma Youth Hostel.** The headquarters of Costa Rica's expanding hostel network is housed in an elegant colonial bungalow, built around 1900, in the tranquilo Barrio La California. The tiled lobby and veranda are ideal places for backpackers to hang out and exchange travel tales. Beds on the ground floor are in little compartments with doors; rooms on the second floor have standard bunks. There are also three private rooms for couples. The on-site information center offers discounted tours. ⊠ *Avda. Central, between Cs. 29 and 31, Barrio La California* ⌖ *Apdo. 1355–1002, San José* ☎🖷 *224–4085* ⮩ *80 beds in 17 dormitory rooms with shared baths, 3 private rooms without bath* ⚘ *Dining room, Internet; no a/c, no room phones, no room TVs* ▤ *MC, V* ⧖⧗ *CP.*

Northwest of San José

The rather luxurious properties northwest of the capital cater to business travelers or those looking for something familiar or closer to the airport.

★ $$$–$$$$
⊞ **Marriott Costa Rica Hotel.** Towering over a coffee plantation west of San José, the stately Marriott evokes an unusual colonial splendor. The build-

ing's thick columns, wide arches, and central courtyard are straight out of the 17th century, and hand-painted tiles and abundant antiques complete the historic appearance. Guest rooms are more contemporary, but they're elegant enough, with hardwood furniture and sliding glass doors that open onto tiny Juliet-type balconies. ⊠ *¾-km (½-mi) west of Firestone, off Autopista General Cañas, San Antonio de Belén* ☎ *298–0000, 800/228–9290 in the U.S.* ☐ *298–0011* ⊕ *www.marriott.com* ⇨ *248 rooms, 7 suites* ⅙ *2 restaurants, café, driving range, putting green, 3 tennis courts, 2 pools, hair salon, health club, lobby lounge, business services, meeting room, car rental, travel services* ☰ *AE, DC, MC, V.*

$$$ ◫ **Meliá Cariari.** The low-rise Meliá Cariari was San José's original luxury hotel, and it remains popular for its excellent service and out-of-town location. Just off the busy General Cañas Highway, about halfway between San José and the international airport, the Cariari is surrounded by thick vegetation that buffers it from traffic noise. Spacious, carpeted guest rooms in back overlook the pool area. The relaxed poolside bar, with cane chairs and colorful tablecloths, and nearby casino are popular spots. A million-dollar renovation is underway and scheduled to finish in 2004. ⊠ *Autopista General Cañas, ½-km (¼-mi) east of intersection for San Antonio de Belén, Cariari* ✆ *Apdo. 737–1007, San José* ☎ *239–0022, 800/227–4274 in the U.S.* ☐ *239–2803* ⊕ *www.solmelia. com* ⇨ *197 rooms, 25 suites* ⅙ *3 restaurants, some in-room data ports, in-room safes, minibars, cable TV, golf course, golf privileges, 12 tennis courts, pool, gym, hot tub, 2 bars, casino, 2 shops, laundry service, business services, meeting rooms* ☰ *AE, DC, MC, V.*

NIGHTLIFE & THE ARTS

The Arts

Film

Dubbing is rare in Costa Rica; films are screened in their original language, usually English, and subtitled in Spanish. There are theaters all over downtown San José, as well as in the malls outside the city. Check the local papers *La Nación, San José Volando,* or the *Tico Times* (in English) for current listings. **Cine Variedades** (⊠ C. 5, between Avdas. Central and 1, Barrio del Carmen ☎ 222–6108) shows art movies. **Outlet Mall Cinemas** (⊠ in front of San Pedro's Catholic Church, San Pedro ☎ 234–8868) is a San José art house, near the university. **Sala Garbo and Laurence Olivier** (⊠ Avda. 2 and C. 28, Paseo Colón ☎ 222–1034) shows arty films, often in languages other than English with Spanish subtitles.

Theater & Music

The best source for play, dance, and arts information is *San José Volando,* a free monthly magazine found in most hotels. There are frequent dance performances and concerts in the **Teatro FANAL** and the **Teatro 1887,** both in the **Centro Nacional de la Cultura** (⊠ C. 13, between Avdas. 3 and 5, Barrio Otoya ☎ 257–5524). The **Eugene O'Neill Theater** (⊠ Costa Rican–North American Culture Center, Avda. 1 and C. 37, Barrio Dent, San Pedro ☎ 207–7554) has chamber concerts and plays most weekend evenings. The cultural center is a great place to meet expatriate North Americans. Dozens of theater groups (most of which perform slapstick comedies) hold forth in smaller theaters around town. An English-language troupe, the **Little Theatre Group,** performs four plays a year; check the English-language *Tico Times* for the latest. The baroque **Teatro Nacional** (⊠ Plaza de la Cultura, Barrio La Catedral ☎ 221–1329) is the home of the excellent National Symphony Orchestra, which performs on Friday evening and Sunday morning between April and December.

The theater also hosts visiting musical groups and dance companies. San José's second-most popular theater, the **Teatro Melico Salazar** (⊠ Avda. 2 between Cs. Central and 2, Barrio La Catedral ☎ 221–4952) has off-beat productions.

Nightlife

Bars

No one could accuse San José of having too few watering holes, but outside the hotels, there aren't many places to have a quiet drink—Tico bars tend to be on the lively side. For a decidedly uptown experience, head to the oh-so-chic **Café Loft** (⊠ Avda. 11 at C. 3, in front of Hotel Britannia, Barrio Amón ☎ 221–2303), a popular late-night eating spot with a modern lounge feel. It's closed Monday. The second floor of the **Casino Colonial** (⊠ Avda. 1, between Cs. 9 and 11, Barrio Carmen ☎ 258–2807) is a good place to watch a game. **Mac's Bar** (⊠ south side of Sabana Park, next to the Tennis Club, Sabana Sur ☎ 234–3145) is a quiet spot for a drink.

The **Centro Comercial El Pueblo** (⊠ Avda. 0, Barrio Tournón) has a bar for every taste, from quiet pubs to thumping discos. Several bars have live music on weekends; it's best to wander around and see what sounds good. A trendy place to see and be seen is **El Cuartel de la Boca del Monte** (⊠ Avda. 1, between Cs. 21 and 23, Barrio La California ☎ 221–0327), a large bar where young artists and professionals gather to sip San José's fanciest cocktails and share plates of tasty *bocas* (snacks). It has

★ live music Monday and Wednesday night. The **Jazz Café** (⊠ Avda. Central next to Banco Popular, San Pedro ☎ 253–8933) draws big crowds, especially for live jazz on Tuesday and Wednesday nights. University students tend to hang out on San Pedro's Calle Amargura, which has tons of bars with "binge drinking specials."

The highly recommended restaurant **Café Mundo** (⊠ C. 15 and Avda. 9, Barrio Otoya ☎ 222–6190) is also quiet spot for a drink frequented by gay and bohemian crowds. **El Bochinche** (⊠ C. 11, between Avdas. 10 and 12, Barrio La Soledad ☎ 221–0500) is a gay bar that doubles as a restaurant.

Casinos

The 24-hour **Casino Colonial** (⊠ Avda. 1, between Cs. 9 and 11, Barrio Carmen ☎ 258–2807) has a complete casino, cable TV, bar, and restaurant and a betting service for major U.S. sporting events. **Jungle Casino** (⊠ Avda. Central, between Cs. 7 and 9, Barrio La Catedral ☎ 222–5022) in the Balmoral Hotel downtown is a casino, bar, and restaurant in one. Most of the city's larger hotels have casinos, including the Aurola Holiday Inn (the view from the casino is breathtaking), Meliá Cariari, Radisson Europa, and Gran Hotel Costa Rica.

Discos

A gay and lesbian crowd frequents **La Avispa** (⊠ C. 1, between Avdas. 8 and 10, Barrio La Catedral ☎ no phone), which has two dance floors and a quieter upstairs bar with pool tables. Younger crowds fill **Club Bash** (⊠ 75 m [80 yards] north of Cine Magaly, Barrio La California ☎ 221–9978), which has a good assortment of Latin and techno rhythms. **Cocoloco** (⊠ Centro Comercial El Pueblo, Avda. 0, Barrio Tournón ☎ 222–8782) has Latin music.

Déjà Vu (⊠ C. 2, between Avdas. 14 and 16A, Barrio El Pacífico ☎ 256–6332) is a mostly gay, techno-heavy disco with two dance floors. Take a taxi to and from here; the neighborhood's sketchy. **Infinito** (⊠ Centro Comercial El Pueblo, Avda. 0, Barrio Tournón ☎ 221–9134) plays mostly techno, pop, and funk on one dance floor and Latin music on the other. For an international scene, head to **Planet Mall** (⊠ Mall San Pedro, C. 42 and Avda. 2 ☎ no phone) on the top floor of the massive San Pedro Mall. This is one of the city's most expensive dance bars.

SPORTS & THE OUTDOORS

Soccer
Professional soccer matches are usually played on Sunday morning or Wednesday night in either of two San José stadiums, one of which is the **Estadio Nacional** (⊠ western end of La Sabana park). The **Estadio Ricardo Saprissa** (⊠ next to the Clínica Interada de Tibás) hosts professional soccer matches and is in the northern suburb of Tibás. Consult the Spanish-language daily *La Nación* or ask at your hotel for details on upcoming games—you simply buy a ticket at the stadium box office. Prices range from $2 to $12. *Sombra numerado* (shaded seats) are the most expensive.

White-Water Rafting
White-water trips down the Reventazón, Pacuare, Sarapiquí, and General rivers all leave from San José. Nearly half a dozen licensed, San José–based tour companies operate similar rafting and kayaking trips of varying lengths and grades. The Reventazón's Class III and IV–V runs are day trips, as are the Sarapiquí's Class II–IV runs. You descend the General (Class III–IV) on a three-day camping trip. You can run the Pacuare (Class III–IV) in one, two, or three days.

Accommodations for overnight trips on the General or Pacuare River are usually in tents, but Aventuras Naturales, Costa Rica Sun Tours, and Ríos Tropicales have comfortable lodges on the Pacuare, making them the most popular outfitters for overnight trips on that river. The cost ranges from $75 to $95 per day, depending on the river. Two- and three-day river-rafting or kayaking packages with overnight stays are considerably more expensive.

Aventuras Naturales (⊠ 300 m [330 yards] north of Bagelmens, Barrio Escalante, San Jose ☎ 225–3939 or 224–0505 ☎ 253–6934 ⊕ www.toenjoynature.com) is a popular outfitter with high-adrenaline rafting adventures on the Pacuare and Sarapiquí Rivers. **Costa Rica Expeditions** (⊠ Avda. 3 and C. Central, Barrio Catedral ☎ 257–0766 ☎ 257–1665 ⊕ www.costaricaexpeditions.com) has been offering rafting tours to the Pacuare, Reventazón, and Sarapiquí rivers for more than 20 years. The outfitter has day trips only.

Costa Rica Sun Tours (⊠ 100 m [110 yards] south of Agromec, on the corner, Urupa ☎ 296–7757 ☎ 296–4307 ⊕ www.crsuntours.com) is a high-class operation with trips on the three major rivers. It also offers mountain-bike and horseback tours. **Ríos Tropicales** (⊠ 45 m [50 yards] south of Centro Colón, Paseo Colón ☎ 233–6455 ☎ 255–4354 ⊕ www.riostropicales.com) is the largest outfitter running white-water tours in the area.

SHOPPING

For gifts, the art and craft galleries near the Parque Morazón downtown, and the northern suburb of Moravia sell beautiful wooden bowls, mobiles, sculptures, and other items. The outdoor crafts market by the Museo Nacional is a fun place to browse.

Specialty Stores

Antiques

Antigüedades Chavo (✉ C. Central, between Avdas. Central and 1, Barrio Carmen ☎258–3966) sells mostly furniture but has some smaller antiques. **Antigüedades El Museo** (✉ Avda. 7 and C. 3 Bis, Barrio Amón ☎223–9552) sells antique paintings, ceramics, jewelry, and other small items.

Books & Maps

Lehmann (✉ Avda. Central, between Cs. 1 and 3, Barrio La Catedral ☎ 223–1212) has some books in English and a stock of large-scale topographical maps. **Librería Internacional** (✉ 300 m [330 yards] west of Taco Bell, Barrio Dent ☎ 253–9553) has English translations of Latin American literature and myriad coffee-table books on Costa Rica. **7th Street Books** (✉ C. 7, between Avdas. Central and 1, Barrio La Catedral ☎ 256–8251) has an excellent selection of new and used books in English and is particularly strong on Latin America and tropical ecology.

Coffee & Liquor

You can buy coffee in any supermarket—where you'll get the best price—or souvenir shop. The best brand is Café Rey Tarrazú; the second-best is Café Britt. Good, fresh-roasted coffee is sold at **Nuestra Tierra** (✉ Avda. 9 and C. 3 Bis, Barrio Amón ☎ 258–2983), which has a great selection of coffee souvenirs. Costa Rica's best rum is the aged Centenario—pick up a bottle for about $8. There are also several brands of coffee liqueurs, the oldest of which is Café Rica but the best of which is Britt. Buy these at any of San José's abundant supermarkets and liquor stores. **MasXMenos** (✉ 75 m [80 yards] from the Torre Mercedes on Paseo Colón ☎ 233–2437) has a wide selection of liquor.

Crafts

Atmosfera (✉ C. 5, between Avdas. 1 and 3, Barrio Carmen ☎222–4322) has three floors of crafts and local art, including wooden bowls, jewelry, and paintings and sculptures by Costa Rican artists. **Galería Namu** (✉ Avda. 7, between Cs. 5 and 7, behind Aurola Holiday Inn, Barrio Amón ☎ 256–3412) has Costa Rican folkloric art and some of the best indigenous crafts in town. Its inventory brims with colorful creations by the Guaymí, Boruca, Bribri, Chorotega, Hueter, and Maleku peoples from Costa Rica. You can also find exquisitely carved ivory nut "Tagua" figurines made by Wounan Indians from Panama's Darien region. Take note of carved balsa masks, woven cotton blankets, and hand-painted ceramics.

Souvenirs

The **Aeropuerto Internacional Juan Santamaría Gift Shop** (✉ Aeropuerto Internacional Juan Santamaría) has coffee ($5 per pound) and a terrific selection of good-quality merchandise, such as hand-carved bowls and jewelry, aromatherapy candles, banana paper stationery, and Costa Rica travel books. There's nary another store in the country carrying such a variety of desirable items all in one place. The catch is that the shop charges U.S. prices for this luxury. **Boutique Annemarie** (✉ C. 9 and Avda. 9, Barrio Amón ☎ 221–6707) in the Don Carlos hotel has a huge selection of popular souvenirs and CDs of Costa Rican musicians, including Grammy-winning Editus. The boutique carries comical figurines, cards, stationery, and standard, kitschy tourist gear.

SAN JOSÉ A TO Z

To research prices, get advice from other travelers, and book travel arrangements, visit www.fodors.com

AIRPORTS & TRANSFERS

There are two airports in the San Jose area: Aeropuerto Internacional Juan Santamaría, 16 km (10 mi) northwest of downtown San José, the destination for all international flights; and Aeropuerto Internacional Tobías Bolaños in Pavas, 3 km (2 mi) west of the city center, from which domestic NatureAir flights depart.

🛈 Airport Information **Aeropuerto Internacional Juan Santamaría** ☎443–2942. **Aeropuerto Internacional Tobías Bolaños** ☎ 232-2820.

AIRPORT TRANSFERS A taxi from the airport to downtown San José costs around $12. Drivers wait at the airport exit in a startling mass. They do not expect tips, but beware of drivers eager to take you to a particular hotel—their only motive is a hefty commission. Far cheaper (about 40¢), and almost as fast, is the bus marked RUTA 200 SAN JOSÉ, which drops you at the west end of Avenida 2, close to the heart of the city. If you rent a car at the airport, driving time to San José is about 20 minutes, 40 minutes if traffic is heavy or you get lost. Note that some hotels provide a free shuttle service—inquire when you reserve.

BUS TRAVEL TO & FROM SAN JOSE

A handful of private companies operate from San José, providing reliable, inexpensive bus service throughout much of Costa Rica from several departure points. San José has no central bus station. (⇨ For bus information and departure points from San José to other areas of the country, *see* A to Z sections *in* chapters 2–7.)

BUS TRAVEL WITHIN SAN JOSE

Bus service within San José is absurdly cheap (30¢–50¢) and easy to use. For Paseo Colón and La Sabana, take buses marked SABANA-CEMENTERIO from stops on the southern side of the Parque Morazán, or on Avenida 3 next to the Correos building. For the suburbs of Los Yoses and San Pedro near the university, take one marked SAN PEDRO, CURRIDABAT, or LOURDES from Avenida Central, between Calles 9 and 11.

CAR RENTAL

Contact any of the major agencies below to rent a car in San José. It's virtually impossible to rent a car in Costa Rica between December 20 and January 3 due to the exodus from the city for the holidays. If you want to rent a car during this time, reserve far in advance. At any other time of year, shop around for the best rate.

🛈 Major Agencies **Alamo** ⊠ Avda. 18, between Cs. 11 and 13, Barrio González-Víques ☎ 233-7733, 800/570-0671 in the U.S. **Budget** ⊠ Paseo Colón and C. 30, Paseo Colón ☎ 223-3284, 800/224-4627 in the U.S. **Dollar** ⊠ Paseo Colón and C. 32, Paseo Colón ☎ 257-1585, 800/800-4000 in the U.S. **Hertz** ⊠ Paseo Colón and C. 38, Paseo Colón ☎ 221-1818, 800/654-3001 in the U.S. **National** ⊠ 1 km [½ mi] north of Hotel Best Western Irazú, Barrio La Uruca ☎ 290-8787, 800/227-7368 in the U.S.

CAR TRAVEL

San José is the hub of the national road system. Paved roads fan out from Paseo Colón south to Escazú and northwest to the airport and Heredia. For the Pacific coast, Guanacaste, and Nicaragua, take the Carretera Interamericana (Pan-American Highway) north (CA1). Calle 3 runs east into the highway to Guápiles, Limón, and the Atlantic coast through Braulio Carrillo National Park, with a turnoff to the Sarapiquí region.

If you follow Avenida Central or 2 east through San Pedro, you'll enter the Pan-American Highway south (CA2), which has a turnoff for Cartago, Volcán Irazú, and Turrialba before it heads southeast over the mountains toward Panama.

Almost every street in downtown San José is one-way. Try to avoid driving at peak hours (8 AM–9 AM and 5 PM–6:30 PM), as traffic gets horribly congested. Parking lots, scattered throughout the city, charge around $1 an hour. Outside the city center, you can park on the street, where *cuidacarros* (car guards) usually offer to watch your car for a 100-colón tip. Even so, never leave shopping bags or valuables inside your parked car.

EMBASSIES
The British Embassy handles inquiries for citizens of Australia and New Zealand.

🚩 **British Embassy** ✉ Centro Colón, Paseo Colón between Cs. 38 and 40, 11th floor, Paseo Colón ☎ 258–2025. **Canadian Embassy** ✉ Oficentro La Sabana, Sabana Sur, Sabana Sur ☎ 296–4149. **United States Embassy** ✉ in front of Centro Comercial del Oeste, Apdo. 920–1200, Pavas ☎ 220–3939.

EMERGENCIES
You can dial ☎ 911 for just about any emergency. Your embassy can provide you with a list of recommended doctors and dentists. Hospitals open to foreigners include Clínica Bíblica, which has a 24-hour pharmacy, and Clínica Católica.

🚩 **Emergency Services Ambulance** ☎ 128. **Fire** ☎ 118. **Police** ☎ 117; 127 outside major cities. **Traffic Police** ☎ 222–9245.

🚩 **Hospitals Clínica Bíblica** ✉ Avda. 14, between Cs. Central and 1, Barrio El Pacífico ☎ 257–0466 emergencies. **Clínica Católica** ✉ Guadalupe, attached to San Antonio Church on C. Esquivel Bonilla, Barrio Guadalupe ☎ 283–6616.

MAIL & SHIPPING
It is best not to send important packages via the Tico postal system, as it is infamous for losing letters. But if you must, head to the Central Postal Office, open weekdays 8–6:30 and Saturday 8–noon. You can also post letters from large hotels. There are Internet cafés on almost every block in downtown San José.

🚩 **Post Office Correos de Costa Rica** ✉ C. 2, between Avdas. 1 and 3, Barrio La Merced.

MONEY MATTERS
Before you head out of San José, get all the cash you need. In areas outside the capital, there are few banks and ATMs and it's difficult to change money. It is virtually impossible to change currency other than U.S. dollars or traveler's checks outside of San José. You can get local currency using your MasterCard or Visa at the Juan Sanatamaría Airport; one machine accepts only MasterCard and the other only Visa—not unusual in Costa Rica. It's handy to have both types of card. Ask at your hotel for the location of the nearest bank or ATM, and specify whether you need a MasterCard- or Visa-friendly machine.

TOURS
Prescheduled half-day and full-day bus tours to waterfalls, Central Valley volcanoes, coffee plantations, botanical gardens, and San José sights can be arranged through Costa Rica Sun Tours. You can also tour San José and the surrounding area on a mountain bike, in a raft, in a sea kayak, or on horseback. Aventuras Naturales and Eclipse Tours lead rafting and mountain-biking tours. Costa Rica Expeditions is one of the country's most experienced rafting outfitters. Expediciones Tropicales arranges horseback-riding tours. Sun Tours and Horizontes customize natural-history and adventure trips with expert guides to any Costa Rican itinerary. Ríos

Tropicales offers rafting, sea-kayaking, and mountain-biking tours. The Rain Forest Aerial Tram takes you floating through the treetops on a modified ski lift. Tropical Bungee runs bungee-jump trips daily from San José to an old bridge on the way to the Central Pacific. For a day trip to the beach at Punta Coral and Isla Tortuga, try Calypso.

The popular coffee tour run by Café Britt, in Heredia, presents the history of coffee harvesting and drinking via skits, a coffee-farm tour, and a tasting. Most of San José's travel agencies can arrange one-day horseback tours to farms in the surrounding Central Valley.

Tour Companies Aventuras Naturales ⊠ 300 m [330 yards] north of Bagelmans, Barrio Escalante ☎ 225-3939 🖷 253-6934 ⊕ www.toenjoynature.com. **Café Britt** ⊠ 1 km [½-mi] north and 350 m [380 yards] west of Comandancia, Barva de Heredia, Heredia ☎ 260-2748 🖷 260-1456 ⊕ www.cafebritt.com. **Calypso** ⊠ Arcadas building, 3rd floor, next to Gran Hotel Costa Rica, Barrio La Catedral ☎ 256-2727 🖷 256-6767 ⊕ www.calypsotours.com. **Camino Travel** ⊠ C. 1 between Avdas. Central and 1 Barrio Carmen ☎ 257-0107 🖷 257-0243 ⊕ www.caminotravel.com. **Costa Rica Expeditions** ⊠ Avda. 3 at C. Central, Barrio Carmen ☎ 222-0333 🖷 257-1665 ⊕ www.costaricaexpeditions.com. **Costa Rica Sun Tours** ⊠ 100 m [110 yards] south of Agromec, on the corner, Urupa ☎ 296-7757 🖷 296-4307 ⊕ www.crsuntours.com. **Eclipse Tours** ⊠ Villa Tournón, Avda. 0, east side of traffic circle, Barrio Tournón ☎ 223-7510 🖷 233-3672. **Expediciones Tropicales** ⊠ C. 3 between Avdas. 11 and 13, Barrio Amón ☎ 257-4171 🖷 257-4124 ⊕ www.costaricainfo.com. **Horizontes** ⊠ 130 m [140 yards] north of Pizza Hut, Paseo Colón ☎ 222-2022 🖷 255-4513 ⊕ www.horizontes.com. **Rain Forest Aerial Tram** ⊠ Avda. 7, between Cs. 5 and 7, Barrio Amón ☎ 257-5961 ⊕ www.rainforestram.com. **Ríos Tropicales** ⊠ 45 m [50 yards] south of Centro Colón, Paseo Colón ☎ 233-6455 🖷 255-4354 ⊕ www.riostropicales.com. **Tropical Bungee** ⊠ Sabana Sur, 90 m [100 yards] west and 45 m [50 yards] south of Controlaria, Sabana Sur ☎ 232-3956.

TAXIS

Taxis are a good deal within the city. You can hail one on the street (all taxis are red with a gold triangle on the front door) or have your hotel or restaurant call one for you, as cabbies tend to speak only Spanish and addresses are complicated. A 3-km (2-mi) ride costs around $2, and tipping is not the custom. Taxis parked in front of expensive hotels charge about twice the normal rate. By law, all cabbies must use their meters—called *marias*—when operating within the metropolitan area; if one refuses, negotiate a price before setting off, or hail another. Cab companies include San Jorge, Coopetaxi and, if you need to go to the airport, Taxis Unidos.

Taxi Companies Alfaro ☎ 221-8466. **Coopetaxi** ☎ 235-9966. **Coopetico** ☎ 224-7979. **Taxis Unidos** ☎ 222-6865.

TRAVEL AGENCIES

Local Agent Referrals Galaxy ⊠ C. 3, between Avdas. 5 and 7, Barrio Amón ☎ 233-3240. **Intertur** ⊠ 45 m [50 yards] west of Kentucky Fried Chicken, Avda. Central, between Cs. 31 and 33, Barrio Francisco Peralta ☎ 253-7503.

VISITOR INFORMATION

The Instituto Costarricense de Turismo (ICT) staffs a tourist information office beneath the Plaza de la Cultura, next to the Museo de Oro and in the Correos building. Pick up free maps, bus schedules, and brochures weekdays 9–12:30 and 1:30–5.

Tourist Information Instituto Costarricense de Turismo (ICT) ⊠ C. 5, between Advas. Central and 2, Barrio La Catedral or ⊠ C. 2, between Avdas. 1 and 3, Barrio La Merced ☎ 222-1090

THE CENTRAL VALLEY

AROUND SAN JOSÉ

FODOR'S CHOICE

Chubascos, *Volcán Poás*

Finca Rosa Blanca Country Inn, *Volcán Barva*

Guayabo National Monument

Xandari, *Alajuela*

HIGHLY RECOMMENDED

Updated by
Gregory
Benchwick

COUNTRY ROADS WINDING UP THE HILLS of the Meseta Central, or Central Valley, lead past an abundance of charming hotels and restaurants set among cloud forests, coffee fields, and volcano villages. When skies are clear, area hotels and resorts have sweeping views.

Hovering more than 3,000 ft above sea level, the valley is Costa Rica's approximate geographic center, sandwiched between hulking mountain chains—the foothills of the Cordillera de Talamanca define the valley's southern edge, and the Cordillera Central sweeps across its northern border. Three fuming volcanoes along these chains are within easy reach: Volcán Irazú, Costa Rica's highest, towers to the east of San José; Poás, whose active crater often spews a plume of sulfuric smoke, stands to the northwest; and the older, dormant Volcán Barva looms between the two. Dramatic craters and thick cloud forests at their summits are protected within national parks, while the slopes in their shadows are coffee communities and quaint agricultural hamlets.

Though most of the region's colonial architecture has been destroyed by earthquakes and the ravages of time, several smaller cities preserve a bit more history than you'll find in San José. The central squares of Alajuela, Escazú, and Heredia, for example, are surrounded by architectural mixtures of old and new. Cartago, the country's first capital, has scattered historical structures and the impressive Basílica de Nuestra Señora de Los Angeles. Beyond these small cities lie dozens of tiny farming communities, where lovely churches and adobe farmhouses look out onto coffee fields. You can easily tackle the Central Valley's attractions on a series of half- or full-day excursions from San José, but the abundance of excellent food and lodging in the valley's other towns invites you to base yourself here for a spell.

Exploring the Central Valley

The region has an extensive network of paved roads, many of which are in relatively good shape. The Pan-American Highway runs east–west through the valley (through the center of San José) and turns south at Cartago. Dozens of roads head off of this well-marked highway, but if you stray from the main travelers' routes, you may find a lack of road signs. If you do, don't despair—locals are always happy to point you in the right direction.

About the Restaurants

Restaurants in the Central Valley range from rustic mountain lodges, where hearty meals are enhanced by the beauty of the natural surroundings, to the exceptional eateries in the hills above Escazú—fine dining with a backdrop of San José by night. Even if you keep your base in San José, consider venturing to this bedroom community for a meal or two.

About the Hotels

The accommodations scattered across this area range from rustic *cabinas* (cottages) to elegant suites. Many are family-run enterprises with unique, sometimes whimsical designs that take advantage of exceptional countryside locations. If you want to get away from it all, and be close to the transportation hub, lodgings outside the capital are a very attractive option.

Most Central Valley towns stand in the shadows of volcanoes, so try to stop in one or two towns on your way down from the summit of any volcano you visit. To reach Volcán Poás, for example, you have to drive through Alajuela; Heredia lies on the road to Volcán Barva, and Cartago sits at the foot of Irazú. From Irazú you can take the serpentine roads eastward to Volcán Turrialba, Turrialba, and Guayabo National Monument, Costa Rica's most important archaeological site. Paraíso, just southeast of Cartago, is the gateway to the Valle de Orosi (Orosi Valley), southeast of San José.

Numbers in the text correspond to numbers in the margin and on the Central Valley: Around San José map.

If you have 2 days

Drive up ⊞ **Volcán Poás** ❺ ⌐, where you can also visit nearby **La Paz Waterfall Gardens** ❻, and then settle in for a night near the summit or just have a good lunch before returning to warmer ⊞ **Alajuela** ❹ or San José. The next day, explore the Orosi Valley, stopping at the fascinating **Jardín Lankester** ⑫ on the way.

If you have 4 days

Head to ⊞ **Heredia** ❷ ⌐ and the adjacent coffee communities, continuing up the slopes of **Volcán Barva** ❸ for a picnic in the cool mountain air. The energetic can hike up to the crater lakes at the volcano's peak, or take a high-altitude horseback ride before retiring in the hills for the night. Continue exploring the western Central Valley, spending the morning at ⊞ **Volcán Poás** ❺, and the afternoon visiting the towns of ⊞ **Grecia** ❼ and **Sarchí** ❽. On day 3, head southeast for a hike in **Tapantí National Wildlife Refuge** ⑮, stopping in Cartago and spending the night in the East Valley. ⑭ Drive early the next morning to the summit of **Volcán Irazú** ⑪, and then wind your way down its slopes to **Guayabo National Monument** ⑰ and ⊞ **Turrialba** ⑯. Devote day four to white-water rafting.

WHAT IT COSTS					
	$$$$	**$$$**	**$$**	**$**	**¢**
RESTAURANTS	over $25	$20–$25	$10–$20	$5–$10	under $5
HOTELS	over $200	$125–$200	$75–$125	$35–$75	under $35

Restaurant prices are per-person for a main course at dinner. Hotel prices are for two people in a standard double room in high season, excluding service and tax (16.4%).

Timing

From January to May it tends to be sunny and breezy here. On the upper slopes of the volcanoes, January and February nights can get quite cold. Afternoon downpours are common starting mid-May, dropping off a bit between July and September; from mid-September to December, precipitation picks up again. But don't rule out travel to Costa Rica during the rainy season (May to December)—some days are spared rain, and when it does rain, it's usually during what you might call the siesta hours. Because few travelers visit in the rainy season, you probably won't need reservations. The valley is swathed in green after the rains, but come January the sun begins to beat down, and by April the countryside is parched. Costa Ricans generally take their vacations during Holy Week (the week before Easter) and the last two weeks of the year, so it's essential to reserve cars and hotel rooms in advance for these periods.

THE WESTERN CENTRAL VALLEY

As you drive north or west out of San José, the city's suburbs and industrial zones quickly give way to arable land, most of which is occupied by vast coffee plantations. Coffee has come to symbolize the prosperity of both the Central Valley and the nation as a whole; as such, this all-important cash crop has inspired a fair bit of folklore. Costa Rican artists, for example, have long venerated coffee workers, and the painted oxcart, once used to transport coffee to the coast, has become a national symbol.

Within Costa Rica's coffee heartland are plenty of tranquil agricultural towns and two provincial capitals, Alajuela and Heredia. Both cities owe their relative prosperity to the coffee beans cultivated on the fertile lower slopes of the Poás and Barva volcanoes. The upper slopes, too cold for coffee crops, are dedicated to dairy cattle, strawberries, ferns, and flowers, making for markedly different and thoroughly enchanting landscapes along the periphery of the national parks. Since the hills above these quaint valley towns hide some excellent restaurants and lodgings, rural overnights are a wonderful way to stretch out your exploration, before, after, or instead of a trip to the coast.

Escazú

❶ *5 km (3 mi) southwest of San José.*

A 15-minute drive west of San José takes you to Escazú, a traditional coffee-farming town and now a bedroom community at the foot of a small mountain range. During colonial days Escazú was dubbed the City of Good Witches, as many native healers lived in the area. Locals say that Escazú is still home to witches who will tell your fortune or concoct a love potion for a small fee, but they must be in hiding, as you'd be hard-pressed to find them anywhere near the town. Escazú's ancient church faces a small plaza, surrounded in part by weathered adobe homes. Scattered amid the coffee fields that cover the steep slopes above town are well-tended farmhouses, most painted blue and white, with tidy gardens and the occasional oxcart parked in the yard—precisely the kind of scene that captured the attention of many a Costa Rican painter in the 20th century. There are also plenty of fancy homes between the humble farmhouses, especially in the San Antonio and San Rafael neighborhoods.

High in the hills above Escazú stands the tiny community of **San Antonio de Escazú**, famous for its annual oxcart festival held the second Sunday of March. The view from here—of nearby San José and distant volcanoes—is impressive by both day and night. If you head higher than San Antonio de Escazú, brace yourself for virtually vertical roads that wind up into the mountains toward **Pico Blanco**, the highest point in the Escazú Cordillera.

Where to Stay & Eat

★ **$$–$$$$** ✕ **Restaurante Cerutti.** The diva of San José's Italian eateries is this little Italian restaurant on a busy intersection. In a lovely, century-old adobe house, its whitewashed walls are adorned with antique prints. The

2

Festivals

The Día de la Virgen de Los Angeles, which honors Costa Rica's patron saint, is celebrated in Cartago on August 2 with processions and a well-attended mass. The night before, tens of thousands of faithful worshipers walk *la romaría,* a 22-km (14-mi) trek east down the highway from San José to Cartago. April 11 is Día de Juan Santamaría in Alajuela, when a loud parade and other festivities get under way. July's Festival de los Mangoes, also in Alajuela, celebrates this tropical fruit with nine days of music, parades, markets, and general merrymaking. On the second Sunday in March, the Día del Boyero (Oxcart-Driver Day) is marked with a colorful procession of carts through San Antonio de Escazú.

Volcanoes

Some of Costa Rica's most accessible volcanoes stand on the northern edge of the Central Valley, and paved roads run right to the summits of two, Poás and Irazú. Volcán Poás is very popular, as it has an extensive visitor center, an active crater, a luxuriant forest, and a jewel-like blue-green lake. Volcán Irazú, Costa Rica's highest, is topped by a desolate landscape (the result of violent eruptions in the early 1960s), but on a clear day the view is unparalleled. Barva, in the southern section of Braulio Carrillo National Park north of San José, is cloaked in an extensive cloud forest that resounds with the songs of colorful birds, such as the Emerald Toucanet and Resplendent Quetzal. You can visit all three volcanoes on day trips from San José; Poás and Irazú require only a morning, the summit of Barva a full day.

---

menu is extensive: start with octopus and asparagus in pesto, or ravioli with mushrooms in a truffle sauce; then sink your teeth into some *cordero al horno* (rack of lamb roasted with vegetables). ⊠ *Cruce de San Rafael de Escazú* ☎ 228–4511 ▤ *AE, DC, MC, V* ⊗ *Closed Tues.*

$$–$$$$ ✕ **Le Monastère.** This former monastery turned formal restaurant high in the San Rafael hills has the best view of the Central Valley. The dining room is dressed up in antiques, with tables set for a five-course meal; waiters don friar robes. The Belgian owner prepares outstanding classic French dishes and some original Costa Rican items. La Cava, the bar beneath the dining room, has live music Monday through Saturday and is open into the wee hours. ⊠ *San Rafael de Escazú; take old road to Santa Ana, turn left at the Paco Shopping Center, and follow signs* ☎ 289–4404 ▤ *AE, DC, MC, V* ⊗ *Closed Sun. No lunch.*

¢–$ ✕ **Café de Artistas.** The Warhol's Sandwich (a bagel loaded with bacon, eggs, and cheese) and Monet's Morning (thickly sliced French toast with real maple syrup) are two breakfast dishes at this bohemian-chic café–cum art gallery. Lunch begets the veggie-based Quiche da Vinci (a vegetable and tofu dish). Walls washed in ocher create a perfect backdrop for the many whimsical paintings and antique furniture. Everything is for sale, including the nifty novelty items lying around the dining area, like hand-tooled cigar boxes from Cuba. ⊠ *San Rafael de Escazú, 90 m (100 yards) west of Rolex Plaza* ☎ 228–6045 ▤ *AE, MC, V* ⊗ *No dinner.*

★ $$$ ▦ **Alta.** The lofty location of this hotel befits the lofty price. Views from the Iberian-style hotel, which has barrel-tile roofs, ocher stuccoed walls, and hand-painted bathroom tiles, are breathtaking. A sloping stairway lined with tall columns and palms runs through the property, reminiscent of a narrow street in southern Spain. Guest rooms have beautiful terra-cotta tile floors, earth-tone fabrics and walls, colonial-style furniture, and a few paintings. The eclectic restaurant, La Luz, is popular with the expat crowd. ⊠ *Old road to Santa Ana* ⌖ *Interlink 964, Box 02–5635, Miami, FL 33102* ☎ *282–4160; 888/388–2582 in the U.S.* 🖷 *282–4162* ⊕ *www.thealtahotel.com* ➥ *18 rooms, 5 suites* ⟡ *Restaurant, in-room safes, minibar, cable TV, pool, gym, hot tub, sauna, laundry service, Internet, airport shuttle* ⊟ *AE, DC, MC, V.*

$$$ 🏨 **Tara Resort Hotel.** Modeled after the famous fictitious mansion from *Gone With the Wind* and decorated in antebellum style, this luxurious little inn is near the top of Pico Blanco. Hardwood floors are covered with patterned area rugs throughout the three-story white-and-green building. French doors in rooms open onto the public veranda. At the Atlanta Dining Gallery, try the beef tenderloin in mushroom-peppercorn sauce. After dinner, try your hand at poker in the parlor-style casino. ⊠ *½-km (¼-mi) south of the cemetery of San Antonio de Escazú* ⌖ *Interlink 345, Box 02–5635, Miami, FL 33102* ☎ *228–6992* 🖷 *228–9651* ⊕ *www.tararesort.com* ➥ *5 rooms, 8 suites, 1 bungalow* ⟡ *Restaurant, fans, in-room safes, cable TV, pool, hot tub, massage, spa; no a/c* ⊟ *AE, MC, V* ⏐◉⏐ *CP.*

$ 🏨 **Costa Verde Inn.** Rooms at this attractive B&B on the outskirts of Escazú make nice use of local hardwoods in their furniture and trim, and their white walls display traditional Peruvian art. South American art adorns the main building, where a large sitting area has comfortable chairs and a fireplace. The inn is surrounded by gardens, and at night you can see the lights of San José twinkling to the east. Breakfast is served on the shady patio. ⊠ *From southeast corner of second cemetery, 180 m (195 yards) west and 90 m (100 yards) north* ⌖ *SJO 1313, Box 025216, Miami, FL 33102-5216* ☎ *228–4080* 🖷 *289–8591* ⊕ *www.costaverdeinn.com* ➥ *15 rooms* ⟡ *Fans, cable TV, tennis court, pool, hot tub; no a/c, no room phones* ⊟ *AE, MC, V* ⏐◉⏐ *CP.*

$ 🏨 **Posada El Quijote.** At this friendly, family-run B&B perched on a hill in the Bello Horizonte neighborhood (on the San José side of Escazú), you'll find the best vantage point on the sundeck. The living room has big windows, a couch, a fireplace, and lots of modern art. "Deluxe" rooms have city views; "superior" rooms overlook the gardens. The inn is pet-friendly, so dogs, cats, and birds are often seen on the property. Breakfast is served on a covered interior patio. ⊠ *Bello Horizonte de Escazú* ⌖ *Dept. 239–SJO, Box 025216, Miami, FL 33102-5216* ☎ *289–8401* 🖷 *289–8729* ⊕ *www.quijote.co.cr* ➥ *8 rooms, 2 apartments* ⟡ *Fans, cable TV, travel services; no a/c* ⊟ *AE, DC, MC, V* ⏐◉⏐ *CP.*

Nightlife

Bars

Escazú is the Central Valley's hot spot for nightlife. Many Josefinos come into the area for Escazú's dance clubs, and tapas and sushi bars that cater to a cell-phone–toting yuppie crowd. **O Pellegrin** (⊠ San Rafael de Escazú, ½-km [¼-mi] south of El Cruce, San Rafael ☎ 288–2157) serves tapas. For sushi, a rare treat in Costa Rica, head to pricey **Samurai** (⊠ San Rafael de Escazú, ½-km [¼-mi] south of El Cruce, San Rafael ☎ 228–4124). **Sambuka** (⊠ Centro Commercial La Rambla ☎ 289–7506) is a lively discotheque with Latino and pop rhythms catering to a twentysomething crowd.

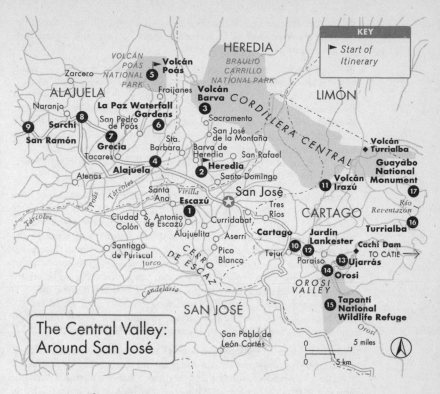

HEREDIA

BRAULIO
CARRILLO
NATIONAL PARK

KEY

▶ *Start of
Itinerary*

VOLCÁN
POÁS
NATIONAL
PARK

Zarcero

⑤ **Volcán
Poás**

ALAJUELA

Fraijanes **Volcán
Barva**

Naranjo

**La Paz Waterfall
Gardens**

③

Sacramento

LIMÓN

⑧

San Pedro
de Poás

⑨ **Sarchí**

San Ramón

⑦

Grecia

San José
de la Montaña

Sta.
Barbara

San José
de la Montaña

Barva de
Heredia

San Rafael

CORDILLERA CENTRAL

**Volcán
Turrialba**

Tacares

④

Heredia

②

Santo Domingo

**Guayabo
National
Monument**

⑰

Atenas **Alajuela**

Santa
Ana

Virilla

Escazú

①

San José

Tres
Ríos

**Volcán
Irazú**

⑪

Río
Reventazón

Tárcoles

Ciudad
Colón

S. Antonio
de Escazú

Curridabat

CARTAGO

Cartago

Turrialba **⑯**

Alajuelita

Aserri

**Jardín
Lankester**

⑩

⑫

Cachí Dam

TO CATIE →

Santiago
de Puriscal

Jorco

Pico
Blanco

Tejar

Paraíso

⑬ **Ujarrás**

CERRO
DE
ESCAZ

Candelaria

⑭ **Orosi**

OROSI
VALLEY

SAN JOSÉ

San Pablo de
León Cortés

⑮ **Tapantí
National
Wildlife Refuge**

Orosi

0 _____ 5 miles

0 _____ 5 km

**The Central Valley:
Around San José**

Shopping

El Sabor Tico (✉ Behind Plaza Colonial ☎ 289–5270) sells a hodgepodge of woodworked souvenirs. You can watch local craftsmen ply their trade at **Cerámica Las Palomas** (✉ Old road to Santa Ana, opposite Alta Hotel ☎ 282–7001). Large, glazed pots with ornate decorations that range from traditional patterns to modern motifs are the specialties here.

★

Heredia

▶ **②** *15 km (9 mi) north of Escazú, 9 km (6 mi) north of San José.*

With a population of around 30,000, Heredia is the capital of one of Costa Rica's most important coffee provinces and perhaps the country's best-preserved colonial town. It bears witness, however, to how difficult preservation can be in an earthquake-prone country: Heredia has lost many of its colonial structures over the years. Still, the city retains a historic feel, with old adobe buildings scattered throughout downtown. You can see more colonial and adobe buildings in the charming nearby villages of Barva de Heredia, Santo Domingo, and San Rafael de Heredia.

Tree-studded **Parque Central** holds some colonial appeal. The park has a cast-iron fountain imported from England in 1897 and a simple kiosk. At the eastern end of the park stands the impressive stone **Catedral de Heredia**, dating back to 1797, whose thick walls, small windows, and squat buttresses have kept it standing through countless quakes and tremors. Unfortunately, the church's stained-glass work has not fared as well. ✉ *C. Central and Avda. Central* ☎ *237–0779* ☉ *Daily 6–6.*

Surrounding Parque Central are some interesting buildings, one of which is the **Casa de la Cultura**, in an 1843 barrel-tile-roof building. Art exhibits are often displayed here. ✉ *C. Central and Avda. Central* ☎ *262–2505.*

A strange, decorative tower called the *fortín*, or small fort, stands behind the **Municipalidad** (⊠ C. Central and Avda. Central.), a brick municipal building.

Between Heredia and Barva is the **Museo de Cultura Popular** (Museum of Popular Culture), in an early-20th-century farmhouse built with an adobe-like technique called *bahareque*. Run by the National University, the museum is furnished with antiques and surrounded by a small garden and coffee fields. An inexpensive, open-air restaurant serves authentic Costa Rican lunches and can be a lively spot on weekends, when a more extensive menu is sometimes paired with marimba music and folk dancing. ⊠ *Between Heredia and Barva, follow signs for right turn* ☎ 260–1619 ☑ *$1* ⊙ *Daily 9–4, restaurant daily 11–2.*

℧ The producer of Costa Rica's most popular export-quality coffee, **Café Britt** offers a lively tour of its working coffee plantation, which highlights Costa Rica's history of coffee cultivation through a theatrical presentation. (You have to see it to believe it.) Take a short walk through the coffee farm and processing plant, and learn how professional tasters distinguish a fine cup of java in a coffee-tasting session from a not so nice one. On an additional tour ($10) you can learn how espresso beans are roasted and make your own cappuccino. ⊠ *1 km (½ mi) north and 370 m (405 yards) west of the Comandancia* ☎ 260–2748 ☐ 260–1456 ⊕ *www.cafebritt.com* ☑ *$20, with transportation and lunch $30* ⊙ *Dec.–May, tours daily at 9, 11, and 3; June–Nov., tours daily at 11.*

℧ The guided tour of **INBioparque** is an excellent introduction to three of the country's ecosystems before you head out to see them for real. After watching short videos, wander trails through climate-controlled wetlands and out to tropical dry forest. Along the way, stop at the butterfly farm, snake and insect exhibits, and a bromeliad garden. English-speaking guides end the tour with a discussion on biodiversity and INBio (Biodiversity Institute). A pleasant restaurant serves typical Costa Rican fare, and an extensive bookstore and shop has eco-friendly souvenirs. ⊠ *370 m (405 yards) north and 230 m (250 yards) west of Shell gas station in Santo Domingo* ☎ 244–4730 ☑ *$16* ⊙ *Daily 7:30–4.*

The wonderful Parque Central is at the center of **Barva de Heredia,** a small community about 2 km (1 mi) north of Heredia proper. The park is surrounded by old Spanish-tiled adobe houses on three sides and a white stucco church to the east. Flanked by royal palms, the stout, handsome church dates from the late 18th century; behind it is a lovely little garden shrine to the Virgin Mary. On a clear day you can see verdant Volcán Barva towering to the north, and if you follow the road that runs in front of the church, veering to the right, you'll reach the village of Sacramento. Here the road turns into a steep, dirt track leading to the Barva sector of Braulio Carrillo National Park.

Where to Stay

★ $$ ▦ **Hotel Bougainvillea.** You might forget that you're only 15 minutes from San José on the Bougainvillea's extensive grounds amid the coffee farms of Santo Domingo de Heredia, surrounded by tall trees and one of the country's most impressive bromeliad gardens. The spacious, carpeted guest rooms are furnished with local hardwoods and have tiled bathrooms. Original pre-Columbian works by local artists decorate the lobby and excellent restaurant. ⊠ *Road to Santo Domingo; take Guápiles Hwy. to Tibas exit* ☐ *Apdo. 69–2120, San José* ☎ *244–1414* ☐ *244–1313* ⊕ *www.bougainvillea.co.cr* ↯ *77 rooms, 4 suites* ↺ *Restaurant, fans, cable TV, tennis court, pool, sauna, bar, laundry services, Internet; no a/c* ▭ *AE, MC, V.*

COFFEE: THE GOLDEN BEAN

WHEN COSTA RICA'S first elected president, Juan Mora Fernandez, began encouraging his compatriots to cultivate coffee back in 1830, he could hardly have imagined how profound an impact the crop would have on his country. Over the last hundred years, coffee has transformed Costa Rica from a colonial backwater into a relatively affluent and cosmopolitan republic.

It was the "golden bean" that financed the construction of most of the nation's landmarks. Founding families owned the largest plantations, creating a coffee oligarchy that has produced the majority of Costa Rican presidents. The bean also provided an economic incentive for tens of thousands of immigrant families from Europe and elsewhere in the Americas, who, during the 1800s and early 1900s, were given land in exchange for cutting down the forest and planting coffee. These farmers formed the backbone of a middle-class majority that has long distinguished Costa Rica from most of the rest of Latin America. Whether you credit the power of caffeine or the socioeconomic factors surrounding the crop, the tidy homes, colorful gardens, and orderly farms of the Central Valley make Costa Ricans look like the original coffee achievers.

Thanks to its altitude and mineral-rich volcanic soil, the Central Valley is ideal for growing coffee, and the crop covers nearly every arable acre of this region. Strangely, since it dominates the Central Valley's physical and cultural landscape, coffee is not actually native to Costa Rica: biologists claim the plant evolved in the mountains of Ethiopia. Arab nations were sipping the aromatic beverage as early as the 7th century—its scientific name is Coffea arabica—but it didn't catch on in Europe until the 1600s. Coffee plants first arrived in Costa Rica from the Caribbean, probably in the early 1820s.

The coffee-growing cycle begins in May, when the arrival of annual rains makes the dark-green bushes explode into a flurry of white blossoms—as close as it comes to snowing in Costa Rica. By November, the fruit starts to ripen, turning from green to red, and the busy harvest begins as farmers race to get picked "cherries" to beneficios, processing plants where the beans—two per fruit—are removed, washed, dried by machine, and packed in burlap sacks for export. Costa Rica's crop is consistently among the world's best, and most of the high-grade exports wind up in Europe and the United States.

Traditionally, coffee bushes are grown in the shade of trees, such as citrus or the nitrogen-fixing members of the bean family. Recently, however, many farmers have switched to sun-resistant varieties, cutting down shade trees to pack more coffee bushes into each acre. Shade farms provide habitats for migratory birds and other animals, but the new, shadeless farms are practically biological deserts. Environmentalists are promoting a return to the old system by labeling shade coffee ECO-OK., and more and more fincas are returning to the old system. Not only does the coffee taste better, but the planations look more vibrant, with large trees dotting the redundant rows of coffee. Coffee prices have declined sharply since 2000, leading many coffee farmers to explore different crop options, such as tomato farming or cattle ranching. Nevertheless, coffee still remains king in the Central Valley.

Ticos are fueled by an inordinate amount of coffee. They generally filter it through cloth bags, a method that makes for a stronger cup of java than your average American brew. The mean bean is even used in a favorite local dish: chicken roasted with coffee wood. Sadly, many Ticos drink the low-grade stuff, often mixed with molasses, peanuts, or corn for bulk—and roasted too long; you're best off buying such reliable brands as Café Rey's Tarrazú, Café Britt, Américo, Volio, and Montaña.

Volcán Barva

③ *20 km (12 mi) north of Heredia, 30 km (19 mi) north of San José.*

North of Barva de Heredia, the road grows narrow and steep as it winds its way up the verdant slopes of **Barva Volcano**, whose 9,500-ft summit is the highest point in **Braulio Carrillo National Park.** To the east a similar road climbs the volcano from San Rafael de Heredia, ending atop **Monte de la Cruz,** which borders the national park. Dormant for 300 years now, Barva is massive: its lower slopes are almost completely planted with coffee fields and hold about a dozen small towns. The upper slopes consist of pastures divided by exotic pines and the occasional native oak and cedar, giving way to the botanical diversity of the cloud forest near the top. The air is usually cool at the summit. Combined with the pines and pastures, the flora here might surprise you if you've presumed that only rain-forest plants, bananas, and coffee beans can grow in Costa Rica.

Any vehicle can make the trip past San Rafael de Heredia to the Monte de la Cruz, and even buses follow the loop above Barva via **San José de la Montaña;** but it's rough going if you want to get much higher than this. From San José de la Montaña to the crater, you can, in the dry months, take a four-wheel-drive vehicle over the extremely rocky road to the park entrance; alternately, leave your car and hike up on foot, a four-hour trip.

Barva's misty, luxuriant summit is the only part of the park where camping is allowed, and it's a good place to see the rare Resplendent Quetzal if you're here early in the morning. Because it's somewhat hard to access, Barva receives a mere fraction of the crowds that flock to the summits of Poás and Irazu. A 30-minute hike in from the ranger station takes you to the main crater, which is about 180 m (200 yards) in diameter; its almost vertical sides are covered in poor man's umbrellas, a plant that thrives in the highlands, and oak trees laden with epiphytes (nonparasitic plants that grow on other plants). At the crater's lower edge is an otherworldly black lake; farther down the track into the forest lies another crater lake. Bring rain gear, boots, and a warm shirt, and stick to the trails—even experienced hikers who know the area have lost their way up here. ☎ 283–5906, 192 in Costa Rica ⊠ $7 ☾ Tues.–Sun. 7–4.

San Rafael de Heredia (⊠ 2 km [1 mi] northeast of Heredia) is a quiet, mildly affluent coffee town with a large church notable for its stained-glass windows and bright interior. The road north from the church winds its way up Volcán Barva to hotels Chalet Tirol and La Condesa and to Monte de la Cruz lookout point. **Santo Domingo** (⊠ Southeast of Heredia) is another attractive agricultural community with two churches, an abundance of adobe houses, and some traditional coffee farms on its outskirts.

Where to Stay

$$$
Fodor'sChoice
★

☷ **Finca Rosa Blanca Country Inn.** There's nothing common about this luxurious little B&B overlooking coffee farms; you need only step through the front door of the Gaudíesque main building to marvel at its soaring ceiling, white-stucco arches, and polished wood. Each guest room is different, but all have original art, local hardwoods, and colorful fabrics. The spacious, two-story suite is out of a fairy tale, with a spiral staircase leading up to a window-lined tower bedroom. Out on the grounds—planted with tropical flowers and shaded by massive fig trees—are two two-bedroom villas. Four-course dinners are optional. ⊠ *Barrio Jesus, 1 km (½ mi) east of Santa Barbara de Heredia* ⌖ *SJO*

3475, Box 025369, Miami, FL 33102-5216 ☎ 269–9392 🖷 269–9555 ⊕ *www.fincarosablanca.com* ✑ *9 rooms, 2 villas* ♨ *Restaurant, dining room, fans, in-room safes, minibars, pool, hot tub, horseback riding, airport shuttle, travel services; no a/c, no room TVs* ▤ *AE, MC, V.*

$$ ▦ Hotel La Condesa. The stone fireplace surrounded by armchairs and a small bar in the La Condesa lobby is one of the many facets of the hotel that suggest a lodge you'd expect to find in a more northern latitude. In the central courtyard, topped by a giant skylight, is one of the hotel's three restaurants. A tropical garden is similarly enclosed in the pool area. Guest rooms are carpeted and tastefully furnished, and each has a picture window. Suites have bedroom lofts, sitting areas, and the hotel's best views. Families should consider the log-cabin villas with full kitchens. ✉ *Next to Castillo Country Club, 10 km (6 mi) north of Heredia, San Rafael de Heredia* ☎ *267–6001* 🖷 *267–6200* ✑ *47 rooms, 36 suites, 4 villas* ♨ *3 restaurants, in-room safes, some kitchens, minibars, cable TV, indoor pool, hot tub, horseback riding, squash, 2 bars, meeting room, car rental, travel services, laundry service* ▤ *AE, MC, V.*

$$ ▦ Hotel Chalet Tirol. Amazingly enough, the Chalet Tirol's Austrian design doesn't seem out of place amid the pines, pastures, and cool air of Volcán Barva's upper slopes. The replica of a cobbled Tirolean town square—complete with fountain and church—may be a bit much, but the cozy, bright two-story wooden chalets are quite charming, as is the restaurant, with its ivy, wooden ceiling, and elegant murals. Quality French cuisine makes this a popular weekend destination for Costa Ricans. The suites have fireplaces and are more private than the separate chalets. ✉ *Main road, 10 km (6 mi) north of Heredia, San Rafael de Heredia* ☬ *Apdo. 7812–1000, San Jose* ☎ *267–6222* 🖷 *267–6229* ⊕ *www.chalettirol.com* ✑ *13 suites, 10 chalets* ♨ *Restaurant, cable TV, tennis court, horseback riding, bar, laundry service; no a/c* ▤ *AE, DC, MC, V* ❶ *CP.*

$ ▦ Las Ardillas. Surrounded by old pines on a country road, these unpretentious log cabins are inviting retreats for those looking to lock themselves up in front of a fireplace and tune out the world. The small on-site spa is one reason to venture from the comfortable, romantic rooms; the other is a meal at the restaurant, which specializes in meats roasted over a wood fire and has a nice selection of Spanish wines. All rooms have modest wood furniture and queen-size beds. ✉ *Main road, Guacalillo de San José de la Montaña* ☬ *Apdo. 44–309, Barva* ☎ *260–2172* 🖷 *266–1993* ✑ *15 cabins* ♨ *Restaurant, kitchenettes, hot tub, massage, sauna, spa, bar; no a/c, no room phones* ▤ *AE, MC, V* ❶ *BP.*

Nightlife

Bars

La Lluna de Valencia has live music on the weekends, and great paellas and other Valencian specialties by day. It is open from Thursday through Sunday (✉ 100 m [110 yards] north of Pulpería La Máquina, San Pedro de Barva, Heredia ☎ 269–6665).

The Outdoors

HIKING The upper slopes of **Volcán Barva** have excellent hiking conditions: cool air, vistas, and plentiful birds. The crater lakes topping the volcano can only be reached on foot, and if you haven't got a four-wheel-drive vehicle, you'll also have to trek from Sacramento up to the entrance of Braulio Carrillo National Park.

HORSEBACK Horseback-riding tours along the upper slopes of **Volcán Barva,** near
RIDING Braulio Carrillo National Park, combine views of the Central Valley with close exposure to the cloud forest and resident bird life. You can try book-

ing a horseback tour through travel agencies in San José. **Hotel Chalet Tirol** (☎ 267–6222) offers horseback tours with local guides.

Alajuela

➍ *20 km (13 mi) northwest of San José.*

Despite being Costa Rica's second-largest city (population 50,000) and a mere 30-minute bus ride from the capital, Alajuela has a decidedly provincial air. Architecturally it differs little from the bulk of Costa Rican towns: it's a grid plan of low-rise structures painted in primary colors. Royal palms and mango trees fill **Parque Central,** which also has a lovely fountain imported from Glasgow, and cement benches where locals gather to chat. Surrounding the plaza is an odd mix of charming old buildings and sterile cement boxes. ⊠ *C. Central, between Avdas. 1 and Central.*

The large, neoclassic **cathedral,** badly damaged by a 1990 earthquake, has interesting capitals decorated with local agricultural motifs and a striking red dome. The interior is spacious but rather plain, except for the ornate dome above the altar. ⊠ *C. Central, between Avdas. 1 and Central* ☎ *441–0769* ☉ *Daily 8–6.*

To the north of the park stands the **old jail,** which now houses the local offices of the Ministry of Education—an appropriate metaphor for a country that claims to have more teachers than police. ⊠ *C. Central, between Avdas. 1 and Central.*

Alajuela was the birthplace of Juan Santamaría, the national hero who lost his life in a battle against the mercenary army of U.S. adventurer William Walker (1824–60) when the latter invaded Costa Rica in 1856. The **Parque Juan Santamaría** has a statue of the youthful Santamaría. ⊠ *C. 2 and Avda. 3.*

Juan Santamaría's heroic deeds are celebrated in the **Museo Juan Santamaría,** one block north of Parque Central. The museum contains maps, compasses, weapons, and paintings, including an image of Walker's men filing past to lay down their weapons. The colonial building that houses the museum is more interesting than the displays, however. ⊠ *C. 2 and Avda. 3* ☎ *441–4775* ⊡ *Free* ☉ *Tues.–Sun. 10–6.*

℃ Spread over the lush grounds of **Zoo Ave** (Bird Zoo) is a collection of large cages holding macaws, toucans, hawks, and parrots, not to mention crocodiles, monkeys, and other interesting critters. The zoo runs a breeding project for rare and endangered birds and mammals, all of which are destined for eventual release. An impressive mural bordering part of the facility shows Costa Rica's 850 bird species painted to scale. To get here, head west from the center of Alajuela past the cemetery; then turn left after the stone church in Barrio San José. ⊠ *La Garita de Alajuela* ☎ *433–8989* ⊡ *$9* ☉ *Daily 9–5.*

℃ The **Finca de Mariposas** (Butterfly Farm), in the suburb of La Guácima, offers a regular lecture on the ecology of these delicate insects and gives you a chance to observe and photograph them up close. In addition to an apiary exhibit, the farm's several microclimates keep comfortable some 40 rare species of butterflies. Try to come here when it's sunny, as that's when butterflies are most active. ⊠ *From San José, turn south (left) at the intersection just past Cariari Hotel, then right at church of San Antonio de Belén, then left, and then follow butterfly signs* ☎ *438–0115* ⊕ *www.butterflyfarm.co.cr* ⊡ *$15, $25 with transportation from San José* ☉ *Daily 8:30–5.*

Where to Stay

$$$–$$$$
Fodor's Choice
★
🏨 **Xandari.** The tranquil and colorful Xandari is a strikingly original inn. Its bold design is the brainchild of a talented couple—he's an architect, she's an artist. Contemporary pueblo-esque villas, along a ridge overlooking Alajuela, are spacious, with plenty of windows, colorful paintings, large terraces, and secluded lanais (sunbathing patios). Some villas stand alone and some share a building. The attractive restaurant serves low-fat food, using some ingredients grown on the grounds. A trail through the hotel's forest reserve winds past five waterfalls. Villa rentals begin at $170 per night. ⊠ *3 km (2 mi) north of Alajuela, turn left after small bridge, follow signs, Apdo. 1485–4050* ☎ *443–2020, 800/686–7879 in U.S.* 🖷 *442–4847* ⊕ *www.xandari.com* 🛏 *17 villas* ⚐ *Restaurant, in-room safes, minbars, 2 pools, hot tub, spa, bar, shop, laundry service, Internet, no-smoking rooms; no a/c, no room TVs* ⊟ *AE, DC, MC, V.*

$$$
🏨 **Pura Vida Retreat Center.** Yoga classes and workshops are an integral part of your stay here. The weekly rate includes two daily yoga classes, tours, transfers, and one massage. The minimalist Japanese pagoda has a Balinese-style outdoor shower and its own hot tub and sundeck. The suites and villa have large windows and bamboo furniture, and more creature comforts than the luxury tents surrounded by tropical gardens. Staying in the carpeted tents (with night tables and a small wood desk) is meant to strengthen your connection with the outdoors, which means you're up with the sun to practice yoga. Meals are delicious and healthy, and the spa offers treatments from massage to guided meditation. ⊠ *½ km (¼ mi) south of Cantina Salón Apolo 15, Pavas de Carrizal, Apdo. 1112, 4050* ⚐ *R&R Resorts, Box 1496, Conyers, GA 30012* ☎ *392–8099; 888/767–7375 in the U.S.* 🖷 *483–0041* ⊕ *www. puravidaspa.com* 🛏 *45 tent bungalows, 3 suites, 1 villa, 1 pagoda* ⚐ *Dining room, spa, travel services; no a/c, no room phones, no room TVs* ⊟ *AE, MC, V* ⏀ *FAP.*

$$
🏨 **Orquídeas Inn.** Once the home of a coffee farmer, this Spanish-colonial residence has quirky additions that make it a lively retreat in otherwise tranquil surroundings: a bar dedicated to Marilyn Monroe and a geodesic dome that contains one of the hotel's four suites. Standard rooms have terra-cotta tile floors, Guatemalan bedspreads, and paintings by Central American artists. Rooms in a newer wing have a more tropical theme, with bamboo headboards and colorful floral bedspreads. Pet toucans, parrots, and macaws inhabit the wooded grounds, which means there's lots of squawking by the light of day. ⊠ *5 km (3 mi) west of cemetery, Apdo. 394* 🛏 *29 rooms, 4 suites* ☎ *433–9346* 🖷 *433–9740* ⊕ *www.orquideasinn.com* ⚐ *Restaurant, fans, pool, bar, shop, laundry service, travel services; no a/c in some rooms, no room phones, no room TVs* ⊟ *AE, DC, MC, V* ⏀ *BP.*

Volcán Poás

► ⑤ *37 km (23 mi) north of Alajuela, 57 km (35 mi) north of San José.*

The main crater of the Poás Volcano, at nearly 1½ km (1 mi) across and 1,000 ft deep, is one of the largest active craters in the world. The sight of this vast, multicolored pit, gurgling with smoking fumaroles and a greenish-turquoise sulfurous lake, is simply breathtaking. All sense of scale is absent here, as the crater is devoid of vegetation. A paved road leads all the way to the 8,800-ft summit: the road from Alajuela winds past coffee fields, pastures, screened-in fern plantations, and, near the summit, thick cloud forest.

The peak is frequently enshrouded in mist, and many who come here see little beyond the lip of the crater. If you're faced with pea soup, wait a while, especially if some wind is blowing—the clouds can disappear quickly. The earlier in the day you go, the better your chance of a clear view. If you're lucky, you'll see the famous geyser in action, spewing a column of gray mud high into the air. Poás last had a major eruption in 1953 and is thought to be approaching another active phase; at any sign of danger, the park is closed to visitors. It can be very cold and wet up top, so dress accordingly. If you come ill-equipped, you can duck under the poor man's umbrella plant. No one is allowed to venture onto the edge of the crater.

The 57-square-km (22-square-mi) **Parque Nacional Volcán Poás** protects the epiphyte-laden cloud forest on the volcano's slopes and the dwarf shrubs near the summit. One trail, which leads some 15 minutes off to the right of the main crater trail, winds through shrubs and dwarf trees toward the large and eerie **Laguna Botos** (Botos Lake), which occupies an extinct crater. **Sendero Escalonia** leads through a taller stretch of cloud forest from the picnic area back to the parking lot; boards along the way bear sentimental eco-poetry. Mammals are rare in this area, but you should see various birds, including insect-size hummingbirds and larger Sooty Robins. Quetzals have also been spotted in this park on occasion. Note that Volcán Poás is a popular sight and gets quite crowded, especially on Sunday. It's not a good choice if you want to commune with nature in solitude. Poás also has a modest gift shop and a cafeteria that serves hot coffee to help warm up from the high-altitude chill. ✉ *From San José, take Pan-American Hwy. to Alajuela, Rte. 130 to Poás and follow signs* ☎ *484–2424, 192 in Costa Rica* ✉ *$7* ☉ *Daily 8–4.*

★ ❻ Five magnificent rushing waterfalls are the main attractions at the **La Paz Waterfall Gardens.** To get to the waterfalls, you follow brick-lined trails through the landscaped high-elevation park. Arm yourself with a raincoat, as it's easy to get sprayed upon from the observation decks, which put the cascades within arm's reach. The main trail from the visitor center, complete with an attractive gift shop and open-air cafeteria with a view, leads first to a huge multilevel butterfly observatory and continues past a garden where hummingbird feeders attract swarms of the playful little birds. Take an alternate trail through a fern and orchid garden before winding back to the visitor center for hot tea or coffee. A free shuttle van transports you from the trail exit and back to the main building, if you'd prefer to avoid the hike back uphill. The tour takes about 1½ hours. ✉ *On the road to Poás Volcano, turn right at the sign to Poasito and continue for 1½ km (1 mi). Turn left at the sign for Vara Blanca, continue for 5 km (3 mi); it's 20 km (12 mi) from Alajuela* ☎ *482–2720* ⊕ *www.waterfallgardens.com* ✉ *$16, $25 with lunch* ☉ *Daily 8–3:45.*

Where to Stay & Eat

$ ✕ **Chubascos.** Amid tall pines and colorful flowers on the upper slopes
Fodor's Choice of Poás Volcano, this popular restaurant has a small menu of traditional
★ Tico dishes and delicious daily specials. Choose from the full selection of *casados* (plates of rice, beans, fried plantains, salad, and meat, chicken, or fish) and platters of *gallos* (homemade tortillas with meat, cheese, or potato fillings). The *refrescos* (fresh fruit drinks) are top-drawer, especially the ones made from locally grown *fresas* (strawberries) and *moras* (blackberries), blended with milk. ✉ *1 km (½ mi) north of Fraijanes* ☎ *482–2280* ▭ *AE, MC, V.*

$–$$ ▦ **Poás Volcano Lodge.** The rustic architecture of this former dairy farmhouse, with rough stone walls and pitched beam roof, fits perfectly into the rolling pastures that surround, inspired by English and Welsh country homes. The interior mixes Persian rugs with textiles from Latin America, and Guaitil Indian pottery with North American pieces. The oversize sunken fireplace may be the lodge's most alluring feature. All rooms are different, so if possible, look at a few before you decide: one has an exquisite stone bathtub. A small dairy farm and garden supply the kitchen with ingredients for the hearty breakfasts. ⊠ *6 km (4 mi) east of Chubascos Restaurant, on road to Vara Blanca* ⌂ *Apdo. 5723–1000, San José* ☎ *482–2194* ⊟ *482–2513* ⊕ *www. poasvolcanolodge.com* ↝ *9 rooms, 7 with bath* ⚘ *Dining room, billiards, Ping-Pong, laundry service, Internet; no a/c, no room phones, no room TVs* ⊟ *MC, V* ⍾ *BP.*

★ $ ▣ **La Providencia Lodge.** If you're looking for outdoor adventure, tranquillity, and close contact with nature—and you've rented a four-wheel-drive vehicle—this rustic, remote lodge perched on the northern edge of Poás Volcano National Park is just the place. The wood cabins are supplied with colorful quilts for chilly nights, but not much else in the way of creature comforts. From the lodge's 500-acre forest reserve, you can look for quetzals and dozens of other birds from horseback on the lodge's popular tour. The lodge is a great example of what ecolodges can and should be. ⊠ *2 km (1 mi) to the left, from the Poás Volcano National Park entrance* ⌂ *Apdo. 10240–1000, San José* ☎ *380–6315* ↝ *6 cabins* ⚘ *Restaurant, hiking, horseback riding; no a/c, no room phones, no room TVs* ⊟ *No credit cards.*

The Outdoors

HIKING The footpaths in Poás Volcano National Park are rather short. Nearby **La Providencia Lodge** (⊠ 2 km [1 mi] to the left, from the Poás Volcano National Park entrance ☎ 380–6315) has more extensive trails for exploring the cloud forest.

HORSEBACK RIDING **La Providencia Lodge** (⊠ 2 km [1 mi] to the left, from the Poás Volcano National Park entrance ☎ 380–6315) has three different horseback tours, one of which leads around Volcán Poás to views of waterfalls and charred forests. You don't need to be a guest to join a tour, but you do have to call a day in advance to reserve a horse.

Shopping

A number of **roadside stands** on the way up Poás sell strawberry jam, *cajeta* (a pale fudge), and corn crackers called *biscochos*. The **Neotrópica Foundation** sells nature-theme T-shirts, cards, and posters in the national park's visitor center and devotes a portion of the profits to conservation projects.

Grecia

❼ *26 km (16 mi) northwest of Alajuela, 46 km (29 mi) northwest of San José.*

Grecia's brick-red, prefabricated iron **Gothic church** overlooks a small **Parque Central**, where you might spot one of the resident sloths in the trees. The church was one of two buildings in the country imported from Belgium in the 1890s (the other is the metal schoolhouse next to San José's Parque Morazán), when some prominent Costa Ricans decided that metal structures would better withstand the periodic earthquakes that had taken their toll on so much of the country's architecture. The pieces of metal were shipped from Antwerp to Limón, then transported by train to Alajuela—from which point the church was carried, appropriately, by oxcarts. ⊠ *Avda. 1, between Cs. 1 and 3.*

☾ At the **Mundo de las Serpientes** (World of Snakes), 50 varieties of serpents are kept in large outdoor cages. If you want to take one out for petting or photographing, just ask. ⊠ *2 km (1 mi) east of Grecia, on road to Alajuela* ☎ *494–3700* ⌑ *$11* ⊙ *Daily 8–4.*

Where to Stay

★ $$$ 🏨 **Vista del Valle Plantation Inn.** Honeymooners frequent this B&B on an orange and coffee plantation outside Grecia overlooking the canyon of the Río Grande. Cottages are decorated in minimalist style with simple wooden furniture and sliding French doors that open onto small porches. Each has its own personality; the Nido is the most romantic. The hotel's forest reserve has an hour-long trail leading down to a waterfall. Breakfast is served by the pool or in the main house, where you can relax in a spacious living room. The American owners are excellent cooks who can accommodate special requests with advance notice. ⊠ *On highway, 1 km (½ mi) west of Rafael Iglesia Bridge; follow signs* ⌂ *c/o M. Bresnan, SJO–1994, Box 025216 Miami, FL 33102–5216* ☎ *450–0800* 🖷 *451–1165* ⊕ *www.vistadelvalle.com* ⇌ *2 rooms, 10 cottages* ⚒ *Restaurant, pool, hot tub, horseback riding; no a/c, no room phones, no room TVs* ⊟ *MC, V.*

Sarchí

❽ *8 km (5 mi) west of Grecia, 53 km (33 mi) northwest of San José.*

Tranquil little Sarchí is spread over a collection of hills surrounded by coffee plantations. Though many of its inhabitants are farmers, Sarchí is also one of Costa Rica's centers for crafts and carpentry. People drive here from all over the Central Valley to shop for furniture, and caravans of tour buses regularly descend upon the souvenir shops outside town. Local artisans work native hardwoods into bowls, boxes, toys, platters, and even jewelry, but the area's most famous products are its brightly colored oxcarts—replicas of those traditionally used to transport coffee. Trucks and tractors have largely replaced oxcarts on Costa Rican farms, but the little wagons retain their place in local folklore and can be spotted everywhere from small-town parades to postcards.

The vast majority of people who visit Sarchí spend all their time wandering through the **crafts bazaar** (⊠ 8 km [5 mi] northwest of Grecia, which is 53 km [33 mi] northwest of San José, just off the Pan-American Hwy.), but if you have some time, this traditional community is worth poking around. The **church** (⊠ Grecia's main road) dates only from the 1950s and is not particularly elaborate, but it is a colorful structure with several statues of angels on its facade and a simple interior with some nice woodwork. Flanked by small gardens, the church faces a multilevel park in which a brightly decorated oxcart is displayed under its own roof. The town's only real oxcart factory is **Taller Eloy Alfaro e Hijos** (Eloy Alfaro and Sons Workshop; ⊠ turn right from church, walk 2 blocks north, turn right again, and walk 1½ blocks) was founded in 1923, and its carpentry methods have changed little since then. The two-story wooden building housing the wood shop is surrounded by trees and flowers—usually orchids—and all the machinery on the ground floor is powered by a waterwheel at the back of the shop. Carts are painted in back, and although the factory's main product is a genuine oxcart—which sells for about $2,000—there are also some smaller mementos that can easily be shipped home. ⊠ *From the church, walk 2 blocks north and 1½ blocks east* ☎ *no phone* 🖾 *Donation suggested* ⊘ *Weekdays 8–4.*

Shopping

Sarchí is the best place in Costa Rica to buy miniature oxcarts, the larger of which are designed to serve as patio bars and can be broken down for easy transport or shipped to your home. Another popular item is a locally produced rocking chair with a leather seat and back. There's one store just north of town, and several larger complexes to the south. The nicest is the **Chaverri Factory** (☎ 454–4944), a little over 2 km (1 mi) south of Sarchí on the main road, and you can wander through its work shops (in back) to see the artisans in action. Chaverri is a good place to buy wooden crafts; nonwood products are cheaper in San José. Chaverri also runs a restaurant next door, Las Carretas, which serves international meals all day and has a good lunch buffet. The street behind the Taller Eloy factory comes alive on Friday for the local **farmers' market**.

San Ramón

9 *23 km (14 mi) west of Sarchí, 59 km (36 mi) northwest of San José.*

Having produced a number of minor bards, San Ramón is known locally as the City of Poets, and you may well be tempted to wax lyrical yourself as you gaze at the facade of its church or stroll through its tidy Parque Central. As pleasant a little town as it may be, however, San Ramón hides its real attractions in the countryside to the north, on the road to La Fortuna, where comfortable nature lodges offer access to private nature preserves. Aside from the poets, the massive **Iglesia de San Ramón**, built in a mixture of the Romanesque and Gothic styles, is the city's claim to fame. In 1924 an earthquake destroyed the smaller adobe church that once stood here, and the city lost no time in creating a replacement—this great gray cement structure took a quarter of a century to complete, from 1925 to 1954. To ensure that the second church would be earthquake-proof, workers poured the cement around a steel frame that was designed and forged in Germany (by Krupp). Step past the formidable facade and you'll discover a bright, elegant interior. ⊠ *Across from Parque Central* ☎ *445–5592* ⊘ *Daily 6–11:30 AM and 1:30–7 PM.*

Where to Stay & Eat

¢–$ ✕ **La Colina.** This roadside diner, with its requisite lime-green plastic chairs, offers an eclectic menu with some typical and some not-so-typical entrées. Start your meal with a delicious ceviche, moving on to the famous rice and chicken or, for the brave at heart, *lengua en salsa* (tongue in tomato sauce). Meals begin with complimentary chips and pickled vegetables. ⊠ *2 km (1 mi) west of San Ramón, Carretera a Puntarenas* ☎ *445–4956* ▭ *MC, DC, V.*

$$ ▥ **Valle Escondido.** "Hidden Valley" lies within an ornamental plant farm at the edge of a 250-acre forest preserve. You could spend days exploring the 20 km (12 mi) of trails, which wind through primary forest past waterfalls and giant trees. The spacious rooms have panoramic views and small covered porches. The restaurant serves good international fare, particularly Italian. You're welcome to hike in the preserve even if you stop in just for lunch. ⊠ *32 km (19 mi) north of San Ramón* ☐ *Apdo. 452–1150, La Uruca* ☎ *231–0906 or 460–1227* ☐ *232–9591* ⊕ *www.valleescondido.com* ↭ *31 rooms* ☖ *Restaurant, fans, pool, hot tub, hiking, horseback riding, laundry service; no a/c, no room TVs* ▭ *AE, MC, V.*

$$ ▥ **Villablanca.** Owned by former Costa Rican president Rodrigo Carazo, who is often around, this charming hotel is on a working dairy and coffee farm. The farmhouse contains the reception desk, bar, and restaurant; down the hill are lovely *casitas* (little houses), which are tiny replicas of traditional adobe farmhouses complete with whitewashed walls, tile floors, cane ceilings, and fireplaces. Resident guides lead nature walks through the adjacent cloud-forest reserve, where you can take a pulse-quickening canopy tour. Horses are available for exploring the rest of the farm. ⊠ *20 km (12 mi) north of San Ramón on road to La Fortuna* ☐ *Apdo. 247–1250, Escazú* ☎ *228–4603* ☐ *228–4004* ⊕ *www.villablanca-costarica.com* ↭ *48 casitas* ☖ *Restaurant, horseback riding, bar; no a/c, no room TVs* ▭ *AE, DC, MC, V.*

THE EASTERN CENTRAL VALLEY

East of San José are Costa Rica's highest volcano and the remains of both the country's most important archaeological site and its oldest church. Ecological attractions include a botanical garden and a protected cloud forest. Cartago, the country's first capital, has scattered historical structures and the impressive Basílica de Los Angeles.

Cartago

10 *22 km (14 mi) southeast of San José.*

Although it's a small city, Cartago was the country's first capital and held that title for almost three centuries. It's much older than San José, but earthquakes have destroyed most of its colonial structures, leaving just a few interesting buildings among the concrete boxes. Cartago became Costa Rica's second most prominent city in 1823, when the seat of government was moved to the emerging economic center of San José. You'll see some attractive old buildings as you move through town, most of them erected after the 1910 quake. The majority of the architecture in tiny Cartago is bland, with one impressive exception: the gaudy Basílica de Nuestra Señora de Los Angeles.

The devastating earthquake of 1910 prevented completion of the central Romanesque cathedral. **Las Ruinas** (the ruins) of this unfinished house of worship now stand in a pleasant central park planted with tall pines and bright bougainvillea. ⊠ *C. 1 and Avda. 2.*

The **Basílica de Nuestra Señora de Los Angeles** (Our Lady of the Angels Basilica), 10 blocks east of the central square, is a hodgepodge of architectural styles from Baroque to Byzantine, with a dash of Gothic. The interior is even more striking, with a colorful tile floor, intricately decorated wood columns, and lots of stained glass. It's also the focus of an amazing annual pilgrimage: the night of August 1 and well into the early morning hours of the 2nd, the road from San José clogs with worshipers, some of whom have traveled from as far away as Nicaragua, on their way to celebrate the 1635 appearance of La Negrita (the Black Virgin), Costa Rica's patron saint. At a spring behind the church, people fill bottles with water believed to have curative properties. Miraculous healing powers are attributed to the saint herself, and devotees have placed thousands of tiny symbolic crutches, ears, eyes, and legs next to her diminutive statue in recognition of her gifts. The constant arrival of tour buses and school groups, along with shops selling candles and bottles of holy water in the shape of La Negrita, makes the scene a bit of a circus. The statue has twice been stolen, most recently in 1950 by José León Sánchez, now one of Costa Rica's best-known novelists, who spent 20 years on the prison island of San Lucas for having purloined the Madonna. ⊠ *C. 16, between Avdas. 2 and 4* ☎ *551–0465* ☉ *Daily 6 AM–7 PM.*

Volcán Irazú

11 *31 km (19 mi) northeast of Cartago, 50 km (31 mi) east of San José.*

Volcán Irazú is Costa Rica's highest volcano, at 11,260 ft, and its summit has long been protected as a national park. The mountain looms to the north of Cartago, and its eruptions have dumped considerable ash on the city over the centuries. The most recent eruptive period lasted from 1963 to 1965, beginning the day John F. Kennedy arrived in Costa Rica for a presidential visit. Boulders and mud rained down on the countryside, damming rivers and causing serious floods. Although farmers who cultivate Irazú's slopes live in fear of the next eruption, they're also grateful for the soil's richness, a result of the volcanic deposits.

The road to the summit climbs past vegetable fields, pastures, and native oak forests. You'll pass through the villages of Potrero Cerrado and San Juan de Chicoá before reaching the summit's bleak but beautiful **crater**. Irazú is currently dormant, but the gases and steam that billow from fumaroles on the northwestern slope are sometimes visible from the peak above the crater lookouts. Head up as early in the morning as possible—before the summit is enveloped in clouds—to see the chartreuse crater lake and, if you're lucky, views of nearby mountains and either the Pacific or Caribbean in the distance. There are no trails at the summit, but a paved road leads all the way to the top, where a small coffee shop offers hot beverages to warm up intrepid visitors. Here you can also find a tiny visitor's kiosk, which is only open on occasion. Before reaching the park's main entrance, about 1 km (½ mi) from the village of Potrero Cerrado, Volcán Irazú's **Area Recreativa de Prusia** (Prusia Recreation Area) has hiking trails through oak and pine forest and picnic areas in case you've packed your own supplies. Admission at either entrance allows entry to both sectors of Volcá Irazú. Bring warm, waterproof clothing for your time on the summit. ⊠ *Signs from Cartago lead you to the park, on the Carretera a Irazú* ☎ *551–9398, 192 in Costa Rica* ✆ *$7* ⊘ *Daily 8–3:30.*

Where to Eat

¢–$ ✕ **Restaurant 1910.** Decorated with vintage photos of turn-of-the-20th-century buildings and landscapes, this restaurant documents the disastrous 1910 earthquake that rocked this area and all but destroyed the colonial capital of Cartago. The menu is decidedly Costa Rican, featuring traditional specialties like *pozol* (stew of corn and pork)—hard to find in modern Tico kitchens. ⊠ *275 m (300 yards) north of Cot–Pacayas turnoff on the way to Volcán Irazú* ☎ *536–6063* ▤ *AE, MC, V.*

THE OROSI VALLEY

Paraíso is 8 km (5 mi) east of Cartago and 1 km (¼ mi) east of Jardín Lankester.

The Orosi Valley, an area of breathtaking views and verdant landscapes 30 km (19 mi) south of San José, holds remnants of both the colonial era and the tropical forest that covered the country when the Spanish first arrived. The valley was one of the earliest parts of Costa Rica to be settled by Spanish colonists—in the 17th century, as ruins and a colonial church attest. Rich soil and proximity to San José have combined to make this an important agricultural area, with extensive plantations of coffee, chayote, and other vegetables. The valley is fed in the west by the confluence of the Navarro and Orosi Rivers and drained in the east by the ferocious Reventazón. A dam built in the 1970s to create one of the country's first hydroelectric projects formed the Lago de Cachí, or Cachí Reservoir.

Two roads descend into the valley from Paraíso, an unattractive town. Both lead to a loop around the reservoir, passing tidy patchworks of cultivated crops, small towns, and the Represa de Cachí (Cachí Dam). Find the roads by turning right just before Paraíso's shady Parque Central. If you turn left at the *bomberos* (fire station), which houses some splendid old-style fire engines, you'll be on your way to Ujarrás; if you go straight, the road will lead you toward the town of Orosi and Tapantí National Park. Whichever route you choose, you'll eventually end up back at the same intersection. As you snake down into the valley, past coffee plantations, pastures, and patches of forest, keep your eyes open for the *mirador,* or lookout point, with covered picnic tables perched on top of the canyon.

⑫ If you're into plants, especially orchids, visit the **Jardín Lankester** (Lankester Botanical Garden). Created in the 1950s by British naturalist Charles Lankester to help preserve the local flora, it's now maintained by the University of Costa Rica. The lush garden and greenhouses contain one of the largest orchid collections in the world—more than 800 native and introduced species. Orchids are mostly epiphytes, meaning they use other plants for support without damaging them in the process. Bromeliads, heliconias, and aroids also abound, along with 80 species of trees including rare palms, bamboo, torch ginger, and other ornamentals. The diversity of plant life attracts many birds. The best time to come here is January through April, when the most orchids are in bloom. To reach the gardens, drive through the center of Cartago, turn right at the Basílica, then left on the busy road to Paraíso and Orosi. After 6 km (4 mi), an orange sign on the right marks the garden's short dirt road. ✉ *Dulce Nombre, 7 km (4½ mi) east of Cartago, 57 km (35 mi) southeast of San José* ☎ *552–3247* ☎ *$5* ⊙ *Daily 8:30–4:30.*

Shopping

The nameless **gift shop** (☎ 552–3247) in Jardín Lankester is one of the few places in Costa Rica where you can buy orchids that you can take home legally: along with the endangered plants comes a CITES certificate—a sort of orchid passport—that lets you ferry them across international borders without any customs problems. These orchids come in small bottles and don't flower for four years, so you'll need some serious patience.

Ujarrás

⑬ *10 km (6 mi) southeast of Paraíso, 18 km (11 mi) southeast of Cartago.*

The ruins of Costa Rica's oldest church, **Iglesia de Ujarrás,** stand in a small park at the site of the former town of Ujarrás, on the floor of the Orosi Valley, just down the hill from Paraíso. Built between 1681 and 1693 in honor of the Virgin of Ujarrás, the church, together with the surrounding village, was abandoned in 1833 after a series of earthquakes and floods. An unlikely Spanish victory in 1666 over a superior force of invading British pirates was attributed to a prayer stop here. Today it's a pleasant monument surrounded by well-kept gardens and large trees, which often attract flocks of parakeets and parrots. ✉ *From Cartago, follow signs on Hwy. 224 to Paraíso and Cachi; ruins are 1 km (¼ mi) from Restaurante Típico Ujarrás* ⊙ *Daily 8–5.*

Where to Eat

★ $–$$ ✕ **La Casona del Cafetal.** The valley's best lunch stop is on a coffee plantation overlooking the Cachí Reservoir. The spacious brick building has a high, barrel-tile roof, with tables indoors and on a tiled portico on the lake side. Inventive twists on the local fare include *arroz tucurrique* (baked rice with cheese and heart of palm) and corvina *jacaranda* (stuffed with shrimp), as well as traditional casados. A gift shop sells locally made wood sculptures. ✉ *2 km (1 mi) south of Cachí Dam* ☎ *577–1414* ▱ *AE, MC, V* ⊙ *No dinner.*

Shopping

The unique **Casa del Soñador** (House of the Dreamer; ✉ 1 km [½ mi] south of the Cachí Dam on the main road through the valley ☎ 533–3297) was built by local wood sculptor Macedonio Quesada. Though Macedonio died years ago, his son and a former apprentice are still here, carving interesting, often comical little statues out of coffee wood. The **Casona**

del Cafetal (⊠ 2 km [1 mi] south of Cachí Dam ☎ 577–1414) sells similar sculptures to those fashioned at Casa del Soñador, which have been carved from coffee roots by yet another apprentice of Macedonio Quesada. His name is José Luís Sojo, and he also carves the huge totem poles depicting coffee harvesting that are displayed at the restaurant.

Orosi

⑭ *7 km (4½ mi) south of Paraíso, 35 km (22 mi) southeast of San José.*

The town of Orosi, in the heart of the valley, has but one major attraction: a beautifully restored **colonial church.** Built in 1743, the structure has a low-slung whitewashed facade; the roof is made of cane overlaid with terra-cotta barrel tiles. Inside are an antique wooden altar and ancient paintings of the stations of the cross and the Virgin of Guadalupe, all brought to Costa Rica from Mexico. The **museum** in the cloister annex has a small collection of old religious regalia, polychrome wood carvings, and colonial furniture. ⊠ *Across from soccer field* ☎ *no phone* ☞ *Free; museum 50¢* ☉ *Church daily 9–5; museum hrs vary (ask around for someone to open it).*

Balneario (thermal pools) fed by a hot spring are open to the public for a nominal fee. The pools are closed on Tuesday. ⊠ *South of Orosi on road to Orosi Lodge.*

Where to Stay

$ ⊡ **Orosi Lodge.** Run by a German couple who have built a warm, familiar rapport with the community, the little lodge blends in with Orosi's pretty, old-town architecture, with whitewashed walls trimmed in blue, high ceilings, and lovely use of natural wood. Local artisans provided some of the furnishings, such as the clay lamps in each room. The lodge's bright, airy coffee shop looks out onto the town's main square, and Latin music usually plays from an authentic 1960s jukebox in the foyer. The simple rooms have wood floors and wicker headboards, but common areas are colorful, with lots of painting and sculpture by local artisans. Rooms on the second floor have views of the Orosi Valley and Volcán Irazú. ⊠ *45 m (50 yards) east of the balneario (thermal pools)* ☜ *Apdo. 1122–7050, Cartago* ☎☏ *533–3578* ⊕ *www.orosilodge. com* ⇔ *6 rooms* ⚙ *Fans, minibar, mountain bikes; no a/c, no room phones, no room TVs* ▤ *AE, MC, V.*

Tapantí National Wildlife Refuge

⑮ *12 km (7 mi) south of Orosi, 28 km (17 mi) southeast of Cartago.*

Tucked into the steep southern end of the Orosi Valley, Refugio Nacional de Fauna Silvestre Tapantí encompasses a 47-square-km (18-square-mi) preserve. Drained by countless streams, this cloud forest provides refuge for more than 200 bird species, including the graceful, endangered quetzal. Quetzals are most readily visible in the dry season (mid-December to April), when they mate; ask the park rangers where to look for them. The 10-km (6-mi) track to Tapantí follows the course of the Río Grande de Orosi past coffee plantations, elegant *fincas* (farmhouses), and seasonal barracks for coffee pickers before it's hemmed in by the steep slopes of thick jungle. Stop at the rangers' office and visitor center, on the right as you enter the park, to pay the entry fee. You can leave your vehicle 1½ km (1 mi) up the road, at a parking area where trails head off into the woods on both sides. The Sendero Oropéndola trail leads to two loops. The first loop passes a picnic area and several swimming holes with brisk but inviting emerald waters. The trail on the other side of the parking lot forms a loop along a forested hillside. Farther up from the parking area, about 2½ km (1½ mi), is an entrance to the La Pava Trail on the right. This trail leads down a steep hill to the riverbank. Several miles farther up the road from La Pava is a lovely view of a long, slender cascade on the far right of the valley.

Since the park clouds up in the afternoon, it's best to get an early start. Taxis carrying up to six people make trips to the reserve from Orosi's soccer field. Camping is not permitted. ☎ 758–3996, 192 *in Costa Rica* ✉ *$7* ☉ *Daily 7–4.*

$$ 🏨 **Barcelo Rancho Rio Perlas.** This all-inclusive resort is a great place for fishing, exploring the nearby Tapantí National Wildlife Refuge, or simply relaxing in one of the 13 outdoor hot tubs. Guest rooms are in 13 two-story blocks, with covered porches overlooking flower beds frequented by legions of hummingbirds. Forested hillsides rise in the background. ⊠ *Purisil, 11 km (6 mi) east of Orosi, 2 km (1 mi) before Tapantí entrance* ☎ *533–3341* 🖷 *533–3085* ⊕ *www.barcelo.com* 🛏 *14 rooms, 35 suites* ⚲ *Restaurant, fans, in-room safes, minibars, cable TV, pool, lake, outdoor hot tubs, spa, fishing, bar, shop, laundry service; no a/c* ▭ *AE, DC, MC, V* ⋉⋈ *AI.*

TURRIALBA & THE GUAYABO RUINS

The tranquil town of Turrialba and the nearby Guayabo ruins lie considerably lower than the rest of the Central Valley, so they enjoy more tropical climates. There are two ways to reach this area, both of which pass spectacular scenery. The more direct route, accessible by heading straight through both Cartago and Paraíso, winds through coffee and sugar plantations before descending abruptly into Turrialba. For the second route, turn off the road between Cartago and the summit of Irazú near the town of Cot. That narrow route twists along the slopes of Irazú and Turrialba volcanoes, passing some stunning scenery—pollarded trees line the road to form stately avenues, and white-girder bridges cross crashing streams. From Santa Cruz a trail leads up within hiking distance of the 10,900-ft summit of Volcán Turrialba. As you begin the descent to Turrialba town, the temperature rises and neatly farmed coffee crops blanket the slopes.

Turrialba

⑯ *58 km (36 mi) east of San José.*

The relatively well-to-do agricultural center of Turrialba (population 30,000) suffered when the main San José–Puerto Limón route was diverted through Guápiles in the late 1970s. The demise of the famous Jungle Train that connected these two cities was an additional blow. But today, due to the beautiful scenery and a handful of upscale nature lodges, eco-tourism is beginning to make in-roads and has begun to revamp the stagnant economy. Though pleasant enough, Turrialba doesn't have much to offer, but the surrounding countryside hides some spectacular scenery and patches of rain forest. Turrialba is also near two of Costa Rica's best white-water rivers—the Pacuare and Reventazón—which explains why kayakers and rafters flock here. Serious water enthusiasts, including the white-water Olympic kayaking teams from a handful of countries, stay all winter.

off the beaten path

Centro Agronómico Tropical de Investigación y Enseñanza (Center for Tropical Agricultural Research and Education). Known by its acronym, CATIE is one of the leading tropical research centers in the world, drawing students and experts from all over the Americas. The

8-square-km (3-square-mi) property includes modern labs and offices, landscaped grounds, seed-conservation chambers, greenhouses, orchards, experimental agricultural projects, a large swath of rain forest, and lodging for students and teachers. A muddy trail leads down into the forest behind the administration building, where you can see some of the biggest rapids on the Reventazón River. CATIE is also a good place to bird-watch; you might even catch sight of the yellow-winged Northern Jacana or the Purple Gallinule in the lagoon near the main building. Call ahead to reserve a free tour. ⊠ *Just outside Turrialba, on the road to Siquirres* ☎ *556–6431* ⊜ *556–1533* ☽ *Daily 7–4.*

Where to Stay

$$$$ ⊡ **Rancho Naturalista.** Customized guided horseback and bird-watching tours within a 125-acre private nature reserve are the reasons to come and stay here. Three hundred species of birds and thousands of different kinds of moths and butterflies live on the reserve, and a resident ornithologist helps you see and learn as much as you want. The two-story lodge is upscale modern with rustic touches, as are its two separate cabins. Good home cooking is served in the indoor and outdoor dining rooms, both of which have beautiful views of Volcán Irazú and Turrialba Valley. Rates include guided tours. ⊠ *Southeast of Turrialba, 1½ km (1 mi) along a semi-paved road from Tuís* ☽ *Dept. SJO 1425, Box 025216, Miami, FL 33102-5216* ☎ *554–8100 or 297–4134; 888/246–8513 in the U.S.* ☎☎ *297–4135* ⊕ *www.ranchonaturalista.com* ☞ *11 rooms, 9 with bath* ☖ *Dining room, horseback riding, Internet; no smoking, no a/c, no room phones, no room TVs* ⊟ *No credit cards* ⦿ *FAP.*

$$$ ⊡ **Casa Turrire.** Standing at the edge of a sugar plantation that's bordered by an artificial lake, this timeless hotel looks like a manor house that has survived mysteriously intact from the turn of the 20th century. In fact, it's the product of more recent imaginations. From the royal palms that line the driveway to the tall columns and tile floors, Casa Turrire is an exercise in elegance and attention to detail. High-ceiling guest rooms have tropical hardwoods, small balconies, and bright bathrooms with tubs. The classy central courtyard is a civilized spot in which to relax after a day's adventure. Children are not allowed during high season. ⊠ *12 km (7 mi) north on Carretera a la Suiza from Turrialba, Apdo. 303–7150* ☎ *531–1111* ⊜ *531–1075* ⊕ *www.hotelcasaturrire.com.* ☞ *12 rooms, 4 suites* ☖ *Restaurant, fans, in-room safes, cable TV, tennis court, pool, hot tub, horseback riding, bar, shop, laundry service, Internet; no a/c in some rooms* ⊟ *AE, MC, V* ⦿ *CP.*

$$ ⊡ **Albergue Volcán Turrialba.** In the foothills of the volcano, accessible only by four-wheel-drive vehicle (which the lodge will arrange for a fee), the Volcán has comfortable rooms. You'll eat well, too: the proprietors serve healthy, Costa Rican–style meals cooked on a wood-burning stove. Even more compelling are the tours, one of which goes deep into the Turrialba crater, and another of which visits the fumaroles and thermal waters of Volcán Irazú. Mountain-biking and horseback-riding trips can be arranged, as well as a 10-hour trek from the Volcán Turrialba to Guápiles via Braulio Carrillo National Park. ⊠ *20 km (12 mi) east of Cot, turn right at Pacayas on the road to Volcán Turrialba* ☽ *Apdo. 1632–2050, San José* ☎☎ *273–4335* ⊜ *273–0703* ⊕ *www. volcanturrialbalodge.com* ☞ *19 rooms* ☖ *Dining room, bar; no a/c, no room phones, no room TVs* ⊟ *AE, DC, MC, V* ⦿ *FAP.*

$ ⊡ **Turrialtico.** From the Caribbean town of Siquirres, a hedged drive winds its way up to this dramatically positioned, open-sided hotel. The second-floor rooms, handsomely designed with wood floors and Guatemalan spreads on firm beds, might be the best bargain in Costa Rica. Ask for a room on the west side—these have dazzling views toward Turrialba and, if there are no clouds, Volcán Irazú. The restaurant serves a small selection of authentic Costa Rican cuisine cooked on a woodstove. A possible drawback is that Turrialtico is a breakfast stopover for tour and raft-trip buses. ⊠ *8 km (5 mi) south of Siquirres on road to Siquirres, Apdo. 121-7150* 🕾 *538-1111* 🖳 *538-1575* ⊕ *www.turrialtico.com* 🗬 *14 rooms* ⚒ *Restaurant, fans, shop, laundry service; no a/c, no room phones, no room TVs* 🖃 *AE, MC, V* ◎❙ *BP.*

The Outdoors

RAFTING & KAYAKING
It's no coincidence that half a dozen Olympic kayaking teams use Turrialba as their winter training ground: it lies conveniently close to two excellent white-water rivers, the Reventazón and the Pacuare. And despite their appeal to the experts, these rivers can also be sampled by neophytes. The **Río Reventazón** flows right past Turrialba and has several navigable stretches; the most popular stretch has unfortunately been cut short by the construction of a dam (the Tucurrique section, Class III). The Florida section (Class III), above Turrialba, is a rip-roaring alternative for inexperienced rafters.

Just southeast of Turrialba is the **Río Pacuare,** Costa Rica's most spectacular white-water route, which provides rafters with an unforgettable, exhilarating, adrenaline-pumping experience. The 32-km (20-mi) Pacuare run includes a series of Class III and IV rapids with evocative nicknames like Double Drop, Burial Grounds, and Magnetic Rock. The astoundingly beautiful scenery includes lush canyons where waterfalls plummet into the river and vast expanses of rain forest. Stretches of the Pacuare stood in for Africa in the otherwise forgettable 1995 film *Congo.* That riverine landscape is inhabited by toucans, kingfishers, oropéndolas, and other birds—along with Blue Morpho Butterflies, the odd river otter, and other interesting critters. The rafting outfitters Aventuras Naturales and Ríos Tropicales have their own lodges on the river, making them the best options for two- and three-day trips that include jungle hikes.

For details on rafting or kayaking both the Pacuare and Reventazón rivers, contact **Aventuras Naturales** (🕾 225–3939 or 224–0505 🖳 253–6934 ⊕ www.toenjoynature.com). **Costa Rica Sun Tours** (🕾 296–7757 🖳 296–4307 ⊕ www.crsuntours.com) is a high-class operation with trips on both rivers. White-water adventures on the Pacuare and Reventazón are also available through the San José–based **Costa Rica Whitewater** (🕾 257–0766 🖳 255–4354 ⊕ www.costaricaexpeditions.com). **Rainforest World** (🕾 556–2678) also specializes in white-knuckle trips on Turrialba's Pacuare and Reventazón Rivers. **Ríos Tropicales** (🕾 233–6455 🖳 255–4354 ⊕ www.riostropicales.com) is a San José–based operator with day tours and multiple-day rafting adventures on the Pacuare and Reventazón.

Guayabo National Monument

17 *19 km (12 mi) north of Turrialba, 72 km (45 mi) east of San José.*

Fodor'sChoice
★
On the slopes of Volcán Turrialba is Monumento Nacional Guayabo, Costa Rica's most significant archaeological site. In 1968 a local landowner was out walking her dogs when she discovered what she thought was a tomb. A friend, archaeologist Carlos Piedra, began excavating the site and unearthed the base wall of a chief's house in what eventually turned out to be the ruins of a large community (around 20,000 inhabitants) covering 49 acres. The city was abandoned in AD 1400, probably due to disease or starvation. A guided tour in Spanish takes you through the rain forest to a mirador from which you can see the layout

of the excavated circular buildings. Only the raised foundations survive, since the conical houses themselves were built of wood. As you descend into the ruins, notice the well-engineered surface and covered aqueducts leading to a trough of drinking water that still functions today. Next you'll pass the end of an 8-km (5-mi) paved walkway used to transport the massive building stones—abstract patterns carved on the stones continue to baffle archaeologists, but some clearly depict jaguars, which were revered by Indians as deities. The hillside jungle is captivating, and the trip is further enhanced by bird-watching possibilities: sacklike nests of oropéndolas hang from many of the trees. The last few miles of the road are in such bad shape that you'll need a four-wheel-drive vehicle to get here. Camping is allowed near the ranger station. ☎ 290–8202, 192 in Costa Rica ☜ $7 ⊘ Tues.–Sun. 8–4.

THE CENTRAL VALLEY A TO Z

To research prices, get advice from other travelers, and book travel arrangements, visit www.fodors.com.

AIRPORTS & TRANSFERS

The Aeropuerto Internacional Juan Santamaría is 16 km (10 mi) northwest of downtown San José.

🛈 Airport Information **Aeropuerto Internacional Juan Santamaría** ☎ 443-2622.

AIRPORT TRANSFERS You can get taxis from the airport to any point in the Central Valley for between $10 and $50. Most upscale hotels can arrange a pickup for you when you reserve your room. Buses leave the airport for Alajuela several times an hour; from Alajuela you can catch buses to Grecia, Sarchí, and San Ramón. Less-frequent buses (one to three per hour) serve Heredia. To travel between the airport and Escazú, Cartago, or Turrialba, you have to change buses in San José.

BUS TRAVEL TO & FROM THE CENTRAL VALLEY

Buses leave for Escazú from San José (Avda. 6, between Cs. 12 and 14) every 20 minutes. Buses begin the 25-minute trip to Heredia, from Calle 1 between Avenidas 7 and 9, every 10 minutes. For a 20-minute trip to Volcán Barva, take the Paso Llano bus from Heredia with the Rapidos Heredianos bus line, and get off at Sacramento crossroads; the first bus is at 6:30 AM. Note: some of these buses go only as far as San José de la Montaña, adding an hour to the hike; make sure you're on the right bus.

Departures for Alajuela, a 20-minute ride, are from Avda. 2 between Cs. 12 and 14 with TUASA bus lines, which depart daily every 10 minutes 6 AM–7 PM, and every 40 minutes 7 PM–10:30 PM. An excursion bus for Volcán Poás on TUASA departs San José daily at 8:30 AM from C. 12 between Avdas. 2 and 4 (a 90-minute ride) and returns at 2:30 PM. Departures for the 40-minute trip to Grecia, from the Coca-Cola station, C. 16 at Avda. 1, on the TUAN bus line are every 30 minutes. Direct buses to Sarchí on TUAN take 1½ hours and leave from San José's Coca-Cola station (C. 16, between Avdas. 1 and 3) at 12:15 and 5:30. Buses for the one-hour ride to San Ramón with Empresarios Unidos leave from the Puntarenas bus station (C. 16, between Avdas. 10 and 12) every hour 6 AM to 7 PM.

SACSA buses leave San José for the 45-minute trip to Cartago from C. 5 and Avda. 18 every 10 minutes daily; going from Cartago to Orosi Valley, Autotransportes Mata buses leave hourly, weekdays 8 AM–2 PM, and weekends 2 PM–7 PM, from the southern side of the Cartago Ruinas. An excursion bus, run by Metropoli, departs San José for the two-hour ride to Volcán Irazú every Saturday and Sunday at 8 AM from Avda. 2, between Cs. 1 and 3, across from the Gran Hotel Costa Rica; this bus returns at 1 PM.

TRANSTUSA buses leave for Turrialba and Guayabo National Monument, a two-hour trip, from C. 13, between Avdas. 6 and 8 hourly 8–8. **⊞ Bus Information Autotransportes Mata** ☎ 391-8268. **Empresarios Unidos** ⊠ C. 16 at Avda. 12 ☎ 222-0064. **Metropoli** ☎ 272-0651. **Rapidos Heredianos** ⊠ C. 1, between Avdas. 7 and 9 ☎ 233-8392. **SACSA** ☎ 233-5350. **TRANSTUSA** ☎ 556-0073. **TUAN** ☎ 494-2139. **TUASA** ☎ 222-5325.

BUS TRAVEL WITHIN CENTRAL VALLEY

Buses travel between Alajuela and Heredia's main bus stations every half hour. To reach Zoo Ave, take the bus to La Garita, which departs every hour from the main bus station in Alajuela. Direct buses to Sarchí depart from Alajuela (C. 8, between Avdas. 1 and 3) every 30 minutes 6 AM–9 PM; the ride takes 90 minutes. Buses traveling between San José and Grecia or San Ramón pick up passengers on the southern edge of Alajuela, at the Tuasa Bus stop (Avda. 2, between Cs. 12 and 14). Departures for Grecia leave from Naranjo, from Naranjo's Central Park, hourly 6 AM–7 PM, a 15-minute hop.

To visit Jardín Lankester, take the Paraíso bus, which leaves the south side of Cartago's Parque Central every 15 minutes daily.

Hourly Autotransportes Mata buses depart from Cartago's southern side of Las Ruinas for a loop around the Orosi Valley, stopping at Orosi and Ujarrás. To reach Tapantí, you'll have to hire a taxi in Orosi.

The bus to Guayabo National Monument, a 50-minute ride, leaves once a day from one block south of the bus station in Turrialba, Monday to Saturday at 11 AM and Sunday at 9:30 AM.

CAR RENTAL

The closest car rental agencies are in San José (⇨ San José A to Z in chapter 1).

CAR TRAVEL

Many points in Western Central Valley can be easily reached by car. To reach Escazú from San José, turn left at the western end of Paseo Colón, take the first right, get off the highway at the first exit, and turn right at the traffic light. Turn right at the bottom of the hill for San Rafael and the old road to Santa Ana. Paseo Colón ends at Parque La Sabana, on the west end of San José; turn right here for Alajuela and Heredia. For Heredia, turn right off the highway just before it heads onto an overpass, where the Hotel Irazú stands on the right; follow the road for a couple of miles and then turn left at the Universidad Nacional for the center of Heredia, or continue straight for the town and volcano of Barva. The route to Volcán Barva heads north out of Heredia through the communities of Barva, San José de la Montaña, Paso Llano, and Sacramento. At Sacramento the paved road turns to dirt, growing worse as it nears the ranger station. A four-wheel-drive vehicle can make it all the way to the ranger station in the dry season. For Alajuela, take the highway all the way out to the airport and turn right. You can reach Grecia by continuing west on the highway past the airport—the turnoff is on the right—or by heading into Alajuela and turning left just before the Alajuela cemetery. For Sarchí, take the highway well past the airport to the turnoff for Naranjo; then veer right just as you enter Naranjo. San Ramón is on the Pan-American Highway west of Grecia; head straight through town and follow the signs to reach the hotels to the north.

All the attractions in the eastern Central Valley are accessible from San José by driving east on Avda. 2 through San Pedro, then following signs from the intersection to Cartago. Shortly before Cartago, a traffic light marks the beginning of the road up Irazú, with traffic to Cartago veering right. For the Jardín Lankester head straight through Cartago (entrance on right), turning right at the Basílica and left after two blocks.

For the Orosi Valley head straight through Cartago, turn right at the Basílica de Los Angeles, and follow the signs to Paraíso. Turn right at Paraíso's central plaza. A few blocks east, at the fire station, you can either turn left for Ujarrás or continue straight for Orosi and Tapantí National Park; either way takes you into the same loop around the valley.

The road through Cartago and Paraíso continues east to Turrialba, where you pick up another road a few blocks east of that town's central plaza. Marked by signs, this road leads north to the monument.

EMERGENCIES
In case of any emergency, dial 911, or one of the numbers listed below.
🚩 Emergency Services **Ambulance** ☎ 128. **Fire** ☎ 118. **Police** ☎ 117. **Traffic Police** ☎ 222-9330.

TAXIS
Taxis parked near the central plazas in Alajuela, Cartago, and Heredia can take you to up Poás, Irazú, and Barva Volcanoes, respectively, but the trips are quite expensive (about $50) unless you can assemble a group. If you don't have a car, the only way to get to Tapantí National Park is to take a cab from Orosi. Taxis parked near San Ramón's central plaza can take you to the nature lodges north of town. Consult with your hotel's front desk manager, who can sometimes recommend private drivers who charge less, and be sure to always arrange the fee ahead of time.

TOURS
Most San José tour offices can also set you up with guided tours to the Poás and Irazú volcanoes or the Orosi Valley. Swiss Travel is one of the oldest operators in the country. Horizontes offers expertly guided adventure and natural-history tours in the Central Valley and beyond.
🚩 Tour Companies **Horizontes** ✉ Paseo Colón, 130 m [140 yards] north of Pizza Hut, San José ☎ 222-2022. **Swiss Travel** ✉ Meliá Corobicí hotel lobby, C. 42, between Avdas. 5 and 7, San José ☎ 231-4055.

VISITOR INFORMATION
Visitor Information services are based in San José (⇨ San José A to Z in Chapter 1), although Central Valley hotels are often good local sources of information.

NORTHERN GUANACASTE & ALAJUELA

3

FODOR'S CHOICE
Fonda Vela, *Monteverde*
Original Canopy Tour, *La Fortuna*
Tabacón Hot Springs, *La Fortuna*
Volcán Arenal, *La Fortuna*

HIGHLY RECOMMENDED
HOTELS Hotel San Bosco, *La Fortuna*
Los Inocentes Lodge, *Guanacaste National Park*
El Sol, *Monteverde Cloud Forest*
Tabacón Resort, *La Fortuna*

SIGHTS Monteverde Cloud Forest Biological Reserve
Ranario de Monteverde, *Monteverde*

Updated by
Jeffrey Van
Fleet

THERE AREN'T MANY PLACES ON THE GLOBE with cloud forests, miles of sun-drenched beaches, and active volcanoes. But here in the northwest, all are within proximity of each other. Beyond the myriad ecosystems of the dry coastal plain are the lush cloud and rain forests of Monteverde; waterfalls, hot springs, and estuaries bursting with life; and the volcanoes and peaks of the Cordillera de Guanacaste, the Cordillera de Tilarán, and sections of the Cordillera Central. From the wetlands of Caño Negro National Wildlife Refuge in the far north to the green farmlands and foothills around La Fortuna and San Carlos, east of Volcán Arenal, this prosperous part of the country has a magnificent landscape and array of things to do in it.

Guanacaste is bordered by Nicaragua and the Pacific Ocean. The province derives its name from the broad ear-pod trees that shade the lounging white Brahman cattle so prevalent in the region. An independent province of Spain's colonial empire until 1787, when it was ceded to Nicaragua, Guanacaste became part of Costa Rica in 1814. After their independence in 1821, both Nicaragua and Costa Rica claimed Guanacaste for their own. The Guanacastecos themselves were divided: the provincial capital, Liberia, wanted to return to Nicaragua, while rival city Nicoya favored Costa Rica. Nicoya got its way, helped by the fact that at the time the vote was taken, Nicaragua was embroiled in a civil war.

Guanacaste's far-northwestern coastline, still for the most part unblemished, offers everything the Nicoya Peninsula does and more: the dry forests and pristine sands of Santa Rosa National Park, the bird sanctuary of Isla Bolaños, the endless beaches of the Gulf of Santa Elena, and breezy Bahía Salinas. A pair of beachfront resort hotels has set up camp on this part of the coast, but the high-rise tourist-driven development common farther south on the Nicoya has yet to materialize up here.

East of the Carretera Interamericana (Pan-American Highway), Guanacaste's dry plains and forests slope upward into volcano country and the northern sector of the province of Alajuela. Marching northwest to southeast in a rough, formidable line, the volcanoes of the Cordillera de Guanacaste include Orosi, Rincón de la Vieja and its nearby sister Santa María, Tenorio, and Arenal, looming over the southeast end of man-made Laguna de Arenal. The northernmost peak in the Cordillera de Tilarán, Arenal ranks as one of the world's most active volcanoes. Coughs that sound like thunder, tufts of smoke, lava flow, and mini-avalanches are perceptible to those who come within 32 km (20 mi) of the place—and many do. Below and between these active and not-so-active craters and calderas, the terrain ranges from dry forest to impassable jungle, from agricultural plain to roadless swamp.

Parks in the province of Guanacaste protect some of the last remnants of the Mesoamerican tropical dry forest that once covered the Pacific lowlands from Costa Rica to the Mexican state of Chiapas. A few of the parks and destinations in this area are relatively accessible from San José, even for day trips. Others require grueling hours of driving over pothole-scarred roads. As you contemplate spending time in this region— or anywhere in Costa Rica, for that matter—be sure to allow plenty of time for excruciatingly slow driving. That brief hop from the smooth pavement of the Pan-American Highway up to the famous cloud forests of Monteverde, for example, looks like 30 minutes behind the wheel when measured on the map. In reality, it's two hours of bone-jarring road, although stretches of it are being repaved.

Exploring Northern Guanacaste & Alajuela

Northern Guanacaste and Alajuela encompass the volcanic mountains of the Cordillera de Guanacaste, the northern section of the Cordillera de Tilarán, and the plains stretching west to the sea and north to Nicaragua. Most destinations on the west side of the mountains, including the coastal beaches, national parks, and the northwestern end of Laguna de Arenal, lie within easy reach of the Pan-American Highway. To reach La Fortuna, Tabacón, Volcán Arenal, the east end of Laguna de Arenal, and points farther east—including Caño Negro and Upala—the easiest drive is by way of Zarcero and San Carlos (Ciudad Quesada). Several roads pass through the mountains, linking these two distinct zones. Though they're mostly paved, these roads—one follows the northern shore of Laguna de Arenal and the other skirts the volcanoes along the nation's northern edge—still have poorly surfaced stretches and are subject to washouts and other difficulties. Always get a report on road conditions before setting out on long trips.

About the Restaurants

Filling, prix-fixe lunches are standard features at most restaurants in northern Costa Rica. You have your choice of meat, with salad, beans, fruit beverage, and dessert, served *casado*-style ("married"-style, meaning that the components are joined together on the plate). Dinner begins at about 6 and is a more leisurely, à la carte affair. In this largely rural, early-to-bed, early-to-rise section of the country, most restaurants stop serving about 9.

About the Hotels

East and west of the mountains, Costa Rica's far northern zone offers a good mix of quality hotels, nature lodges, working ranches, and basic *cabinas* (cottages). In the areas of Monteverde and La Fortuna, a range of low- and mid-price hotels, cabinas, and resorts fill the demand generated by visitors to Volcán Arenal and the cloud forest. Book ahead if you're headed to the coast during the dry season (December–April), especially for weekends—and absolutely for Christmas and Easter weeks—when Ticos flock to the beach.

WHAT IT COSTS				
$$$$	**$$$**	**$$**	**$**	**¢**
RESTAURANTS over $25	$20–$25	$10–$20	$5–$10	under $5
HOTELS over $200	$125–$200	$75–$125	$35–$75	under $35

Restaurant prices are per-person for a main course at dinner. Hotel prices are for two people in a standard double room in high season, excluding service and tax (16.4%).

Timing

Given the larger numbers of tourists that visit Volcán Arenal and especially Monteverde, consider an off-season or edge-of-season trip to avoid the crowds. In terms of weather, the areas west of the Cordillera de Guanacaste are best toured in the dry season (December–April). However, during the wet season (May–November), rain generally falls for just an hour or two each day, so beyond the effect on the roads, problems with traveling are minimal. But beware September and October when it can get extremely wet. (Rainfall is about 65" per year here, the lowest in the country.) Farther inland, the northern uplands and lowlands offer a mixed climactic bag—the more easterly lowlands

As you plan your travels in this region, know that a fair amount of your time will be spent on the road. That is simply the reality of travel in Costa Rica, and particularly in these spread-out parts.

Numbers in the text correspond to numbers in the margin and on the Northern Guanacaste and Alajuela map.

3

If you have 3 days

Head northeast out of San José and through the mountains around **Zarcero ❶** ▐, en route to 🏨 **La Fortuna ❸**. The next day, hike to the La Fortuna waterfall; drive to 🏨 **Volcán Arenal ❺**, checking out the Tabacón Resort's hot springs; or take a rafting trip on the Río Sarapiquí or the Río Toro. Arrange one of the taxi–boat–taxi connections across the lake for an early trip to Monteverde. Spend the afternoon taking in the unique area attractions—the frog pond, the butterfly garden, a canopy tour—and devote the next morning to exploring the cloud-forest reserve, the earlier the better.

If you have 5 days

Start from San José with a predawn drive to the 🏨 **Monteverde Cloud Forest Biological Reserve ❽** ▐ and spend a day hiking in the cloud forest. If Monteverde is too crowded, the compelling but smaller Santa Elena Reserve is just down the road (north). After overnighting in the area, another crack-of-dawn drive will take you to 🏨 **Tilarán ❼** by way of the mountain track (four-wheel-drive vehicle only), or via the Pan-American Highway, for an active day on Laguna de Arenal. Stay in Tilarán or in one of the lodges at the lake's northwesterly end. An alternative to a direct trip to Tilarán is a taxi–boat–taxi connection from Monteverde to La Fortuna, where you can arrange a day tour of the **Caño Negro National Wildlife Refuge ❹**. Early the next day return to the highway and drive north and then inland again for a day hike in 🏨 **Rincón de la Vieja National Park ❾**. Stay at the mountain lodge, or return to the highway and head farther north for a night and a day at Hacienda Los Inocentes, the 100-year-old lodge on the northern border of 🏨 **Guanacaste National Park ⑫**. Stay a second night in the lodge, or late in the day head down to **Santa Rosa National Park ❿**. For a break from parks, your four-wheel-drive vehicle will safely deliver you to Playa Naranjo for a day at the beach.

If you have 5 days

After a pass through **Zarcero ❶** ▐, spend a day and night in the Laguna de Arenal area—🏨 **La Fortuna ❸**, 🏨 **Nuevo Arenal ❻**, or 🏨 **Tilarán ❼**—and see the volcano (and its nocturnal performance), lake, Tabacón Resort, and/or the La Fortuna waterfall. From La Fortuna, head north to spend a day touring the **Caño Negro National Wildlife Refuge ❹**. Then take the road northwest that leads through the San Rafael de Guatuso area and continues around the Volcán Orosi. Stop for a mind-expanding look at Lago de Nicaragua from the *mirador* (lookout) at La Virgen, near Santa Cecilia, and then continue down the west slope of the mountains. Spend a night at Hacienda Los Inocentes, near 🏨 **Guanacaste National Park ⑫**, then a day hiking or horseback riding before continuing on to 🏨 **La Cruz ⑬** and the resorts on the south shore of the half-moon-shape ⌖ **Bahía Salinas** ⑭. After a night (or two) here, work your way down to **Santa Rosa National Park** ⑩ for a day at the beach or take a day hike in the mixed environments of **Rincón de la Vieja National Park** ⑨. Either camp in the park or, more comfortably, tuck yourself into one of the nearby lodges or hotels.

---

share the humid Caribbean weather of the east coast, and less distinct rainy and dry seasons, while the uplands partake of the drier, cooler mountain clime.

ARENAL & THE CORDILLERA DE TILARÁN

Dense green cloud forests cloak the rugged mountains and rolling hills of the Cordillera de Tilarán extending northwest from San José. Great swaths of primary forest and jungle, including a marvelous cluster of reserves, straddle the continental divide at Monteverde. Farther north and west, Laguna de Arenal and the green hills around it pay homage to the dark heart of this region—fiery, magnificent Volcán Arenal.

Laguna de Arenal has two distinct personalities. The northwest end is windsurf central; a row of power-generating windmills, with blades awhirl on the ridge above the Hotel Tilawa, signals another use for the relentless, powerful wind. The more sheltered southeast end, closer to the dam, is popular for other water sports, especially fishing for guapote (it looks like a rainbow bass). The southeast is also a marvelous place from which to view the volcano. If you took away the volcanoes, you might mistake the green, hilly countryside for the English Lake District.

Zarcero

▶ ❶ *70 km (43 mi) northwest of San José.*

Ninety minutes from San José, the small town of Zarcero looks like it was designed by Dr. Seuss. Evangelisto Blanco, a local landscape artist, modeled cypress topiaries in fanciful animal shapes—motorcycle-riding monkeys, a lightbulb-eyed elephant—which enliven the park in front of the town church. The church interior is covered with elaborate pastel stencils and detailed religious paintings by the late Misael Solís, a well-known local artist.

Passing through Sarchí and Naranjo on your way here, you wind upward through miles of coffee plantations, with spectacular views of the mountains. There are some hair-raising roadside chasms, particularly on the east slopes, and the highway gets foggy by late afternoon, but the road is paved all the way.

Juan Castro Blanco National Park. East of Zarcero, where foothills mark the transition from the coastal lowland to the central mountains, lies this park, which spans 142 square km (88 square mi). It was created to protect large tracts of virgin forest around the headwaters of the Plantar, Toro, Aguas Zarcas, Tres Amigos, and La Vieja Rivers. Unfortunately, the park has no facilities of any kind at present, though it's possible to explore some of the park's southern trails on foot or with four-wheel-drive vehicle. ⌖ *10 km (6 mi) northeast of Zarcero* ☎ *192 in Costa Rica.*

Where to Stay

¢ ⌖ **Hotel Don Beto.** Flory Salazar, one of the country's most gracious hotel owners, opens her home on the central park to guests. The immaculate hotel is tastefully decorated with the mementos she has picked up in her travels. Rooms vary in size and all are decorated with bright, pastel drapes and bedspreads. Consummate traveler though Flory is, she's an expert on the home front, too, and is happy to advise. ⊠ *Northeast corner of Central Park* ☎ *463–3137* ➳ *8 rooms, 4 with bath* ♨ *No a/c, no room phones, no room TVs* ☰ *MC, V.*

Shopping

Zarcero is renowned for its peach preserves and mild white cheese, both of which are sold in stores around town and along the highway. Stop at **El Tiesto Souvenir Shop,** across from the park, and talk politics with owner Rafael, a native Tico who lived in New Jersey for a while. He knows everything about the area and can arrange day trips to nearby waterfalls. At the tiny café-store **Super Dos** on the main street opposite the church in Zarcero, you can get a coffee and empanada *de piña* (of pineapple) while you mull over jars of excellent local peach preserves.

Ciudad Quesada (San Carlos)

② *45 km (28 mi) northwest of Zarcero.*

Highway signs point you to Ciudad Quesada, but it's simply "San Carlos" in local parlance. This lively, if not particularly picturesque, mountain market town serves a fertile dairy region and is worth a stop for a soak in the soothing thermal waters. Choose from a variety of sources. A visit to Hotel Occidental El Tucano ($4 per day; $10 weekends) is a private resort popular with travelers on tours. Aguas Termales, just west of El Tucano's grounds but served by the same hot springs, lets you soak those tired muscles for $2 per day.

Where to Stay

$$ ⌂ **Hotel Occidental El Tucano.** You come to El Tucano for the waters: the hotel abuts a river of hot, healing, marvelously invigorating natural springs. Two large outdoor hot tubs, the Olympic-size pool, and natural sauna are all fed by the Río Aguas Caliente, the cascading river that flows through the property. The hotel itself is somewhat overscale, and its public spaces suffer from too much concrete and the impersonality of any hotel subject to tour-group bookings. The food is ordinary at best, and air-conditioning and in-room safes cost extra. Spa treatments, including mud wraps, are brusque. ⊠ *8 km (5 mi) east of San Carlos on Hwy. 140* ☎ *460–6000* 🖷 *460–1692* 🖃 *Apdo. 434-1150, San José* ☎ *221–9095* ⊕ *www.occidentaltucano.com* ➳ *87 rooms* ♨ *Restaurant, in-room safes, cable TV, 2 tennis courts, miniature golf, pool, gym, sauna, spa, horseback riding, 2 bars, shop, laundry service, meeting rooms* ☰ *AE, MC, V.*

$ ⌂ **Laguna del Lagarto Lodge.** One of Costa Rica's smaller ecolodges is a hideaway in a 1,250-acre rain forest near the Nicaraguan border. Most of the rustic cabin rooms come with single beds. Some 380 bird species and counting have been logged here, including the endangered Great Green Macaw. Buffet-style meals are served on a patio with splendid river and forest views. Rates include one guided walk and use of canoes. Recommended extras include horseback riding and a boat trip on the San Carlos River. ⊠ *7 km (4 mi) north of Boca Tapada* ☎ *289–8163* 🖷 *289–5295* ⊕ *www.lagarto-lodge-costa-rica.com* ➳ *20 rooms, 18 with bath* ♨ *Restaurant, horseback riding, bar, laundry service; no a/c, no room phones, no room TVs* ☰ *MC, V.*

La Fortuna

❸   *17 km (11 mi) east of Volcán Arenal, 50 km (30 mi) northwest of Ciudad Quesada.*

At the foot of towering, overpowering Volcán Arenal, the small farming community of La Fortuna de San Carlos (commonly called La Fortuna) attracts visitors from around the world. The town overflows with restaurants, hotels, and tour operators. Volcano viewing can be hit-and-miss during the May–November rainy season. One minute, Arenal looms menacingly over the village; the next minute, clouds shroud its cone. (Early morning is always the best time to catch a longer gaze.) La Fortuna is also the best place to arrange trips to the popular Caño Negro National Wildlife Refuge. Tours vary in price and quality, so ask around, but all provide an easier alternative than busing up north to Los Chiles and hiring a boat to take you down through the rain forest on Río Frío.

Fodor'sChoice
★ **Tabacón Hot Springs.** Besides access to a multitude of outdoor adventures, La Fortuna also provides the opportunity for some serious soaking and pampering. Where else can you lounge in a natural hot-springs waterfall with a volcano spitting fireballs overhead? Kick back at the Tabacón Resort, a busy day spa and hotel, with gorgeous gardens, waterfalls, mineral-water soaking streams (average 39°C [102F°]) complete with subtle ladders and railings, plus swimming pools, swim-up bars, and dining facilities, which mingle in a florid Latin interpretation of grand European baths. If you aren't a guest of the hotel, you can purchase a day pass. The best deal is to sign up for a zip-through-the-trees canopy tour ($45), the price of which includes access to the waters. If you're seeking an Iskandria Spa treatment, make an appointment a day in advance. The resort operates every-two-hour van shuttle service from noon until evening from the office of Sunset Tours in La Fortuna. ⊠ *Hwy. toward Nuevo Arenal, 13 km (8 mi) northwest of La Fortuna* ☎ *460–2020, 256–1500 San José* 🖷 *460–5724, 221–3075 San José* ⊕ *www.tabacon. com* 🖃 *$17, 45-min massage $40, mud-pack facial $20* ☉ *Daily noon–10* 🚍 *MC, V.*

Baldi Termae. If Tabacón is full or if you want a less expensive spa alternative, head to Baldi Termae. The complex's seven hot-springs-fed pools vary in temperature but share views of Volcán Arenal. There's also a swim-up snack bar. ⊠ *4 km (2½ mi) west of La Fortuna* ☎ *479–9651* 🖃 *$10* ☉ *Daily 10–10.*

off the beaten path

Venado Caverns. In 1945 a farmer in the mountain hamlet of Venado fell in a hole, and thus were discovered the Cavernas de Venado (Venado Caverns). The limestone caves, 45 minutes (about 35 km [21 mi]) north of La Fortuna and 20 minutes (15 km [9 mi]) southeast of San Rafael, contain a series of eight chambers with an assortment of stalactites, stalagmites, underground streams, and other subterranean formations. Sunset Tours normally runs trips from La Fortuna. The excursion is not advisable if you suffer from claustrophobia. ☎ *479–9415* 🖃 *$35* ☉ *Daily 7 AM–8 PM.*

Where to Eat

$ ✕ **Las Brasitas.** Chicken turns over wood on a rotisserie in a brick oven at this pleasant restaurant on the road heading out of town toward the volcano. Try the succulent chicken when it ends up in the tangy fajitas or any of the other amply sized Mexican dishes. You have your choice

3

Cloud Forests & Wildlife Refuges
The far north encompasses high- and low-altitude—wetland and dry forest conservation—areas. The lowland rain-forest Caño Negro National Wildlife Refuge abounds with waterfowl, crocodiles, and *caimanes* (caimans). Contrast that with Santa Rosa National Park's dry forest, crawling with ocelots, armadillos, various species of small monkeys, and the Olive Ridley Sea Turtle, which comes to nest on the park's beaches August–November. World renowned, the Quaker-administered Monteverde Cloud Forest Reserve is one of Costa Rica's top tourist draws. Expect to see an incredible variety of mammal and bird life within its confines. If you're lucky, you'll catch a glimpse of that bird-watcher's Holy Grail, the Resplendent Quetzal. Monteverde also affords you the opportunity to make like a bird and view the cloud forest via a canopy tour. With the aid of cables, secure harnesses, and platform landings, you can glide through the air with the greatest of ease.

Comida Guanacasteca
Guanacaste's traditional foods derive from dishes prepared by pre-Columbian Chorotega Indians. Typical fare includes *frito guanacasteco* (black beans, rice, vegetables, and meat), *pedre* (carob beans, pork, chicken, onions, sweet peppers, salt, and mint), *sopa de albóndigas* (meatball soup with chopped eggs and spices), and *arroz de maíz* (a kind of corn stew, sometimes made *con pollo*, with chicken). Meat lovers, rejoice: the northwest, whose plains are covered with cattle ranches, produces the country's best steak.

Hot Springs & Waterfalls
After a day of heavy-duty sightseeing, pamper yourself and soak those tired muscles in one of the region's three hot-springs complexes. The famed Tabacón Resort complex and the smaller Baldi Termae, both near La Fortuna, as well as the Hotel Occidental El Tucano, outside San Carlos, all offer chances to take the waters. You're in for a more invigorating experience with a moderately strenuous hike to the *cataratas* (waterfalls) of La Fortuna.

Volcanoes
The sheer mass and power of Volcán Arenal, often ringed with an ominous haze, dominates Laguna de Arenal (Lake Arenal). The Volcano reiterates its presence at night, when you can sometimes see red-hot molten lava oozing from the cone, a flirtatious dance with disaster. Closest looks can be had from the Arenal Observatory Lodge, which, according to those who monitor the volcano, is also thankfully out of the path of danger. It's easy to reach Arenal from the Pan-American Highway—watch for the turnoff at the town of Cañas—or from the east through La Fortuna. You may have to spend more than one day here, as the cone can be covered by clouds, especially during the rainy season. Farther northwest, experienced hikers can trek to the lip of the steaming Rincón de la Vieja crater on trails through the namesake national park; less-active travelers can check out Las Pailas, a cluster of miniature volcanoes, fumaroles, and mud pots encircled by a relatively easy trail. Among the other (inactive) volcanoes are Orosi, in Guanacaste National Park, and Tenorio, which shares its name with yet another national park. Guanacaste National Park is minimally developed for tourism, and Tenorio, though protected, as yet has no infrastructure.

Windsurfing World-champion windsurfers have called Laguna de Arenal "one of the world's top five windsurfing spots." From December through April, Caribbean trade winds sneak through a pass in the Cordillera Central, crank up to 80 kph (50 mph) or more, and blow from the east toward the northwest end of the lake, creating perfect conditions for high-wind freshwater sailing. The scenery here, too, is unmatched: watch the frequent volcanic eruptions while you glide along. The lake is somewhat choppy due to its narrow shape, but strong winds, fresh water, and hassle-free rigging and launch sites on both shores make it worthwhile. On the far northwest Pacific coast, Bahía Salinas gives Lake Arenal a run for its money in windsurfing circles. The winds aren't quite as strong, but the November–August season makes Costa Rica close to a year-round windsurfing destination.

---

of three open-air dining areas arranged around a garden. Two are secluded and intimate; the third less so, being closer to the road. ⊠ *150 m (165 yards) west of church* ☎ *479–9819* ⊟ *MC, V.*

¢–$ ✕ **La Choza de Laurel.** The tantalizing rotisserie chicken and the cloves of garlic and bunches of onions dangling from the roof always draw in passersby to this open-air Costa Rican–style restaurant near the center of town. These folks open early; it's a great place to grab a hearty breakfast on your way to the volcano. ⊠ *100 m (110 yards) northwest of church* ☎ *479–9231* ⊟ *MC, V.*

¢–$ ✕ **Rancho la Cascada.** You can't miss its tall, palm-thatch roof in the center of town. The festive upstairs contains a bar, whose large TV, neon signs, and flashing lights give it the appropriate ambience. Downstairs, the spacious dining room—decorated with foreign flags—serves basic, mid-priced Costa Rican fare as well as hearty, American-style breakfasts. ⊠ *Across from northeast corner of Parque Central* ☎ *479–9145* ⊟ *AE, MC, V.*

¢–$ ✕ **La Vaca Muca.** It isn't a posh place, but the food is good and the servings are generous. The exterior is draped with foliage, and the interior has turquoise paneling and bamboo aplenty. Try the casado heaped with chicken, beef or fish, rice, beans, fried egg, fried banana, and cabbage salad. ⊠ *2 km (1 mi) west of La Fortuna* ☎ *479–9186* ⊟ *V* ☉ *Closed Mon.*

¢ ✕ **Soda La Parada.** It's busy 24 hours a day but never crazy. Grab an open-air seat alongside the locals, under the canvas tarp (from which hangs a huge color TV), and devour fresh carrot-and-orange juice, a beef or chicken empanada, or one of the tasty casados. You and your wallet leave full. ⊠ *Across from town church and regional bus stop* ☎ *479–9547* ⊟ *No credit cards.*

Where to Stay

★ $$$ ⊡ **Tabacón Resort.** Without question, Tabacón, with its impeccably landscaped gardens and hot-springs rivers at the base of Volcán Arenal, is one of Central America's most compelling resorts. The hot springs and small but lovely spa customarily draw visitors inland from the ocean with no regrets. All rooms have tile floors, a terrace or patio, and big bathrooms. Some have volcano views; others overlook the manicured gardens. The suites are some of the country's finest lodgings, with tile floors, plants, beautiful mahogany armoires and beds, and two-person whirlpool baths. The hotel's intimacy is somewhat compromised by its scale and its popularity with day-trippers, but it has some private areas—including a dining room and pool—for overnight guests only. ⊠ *13 km (8 mi) northwest of La Fortuna on highway toward Nuevo Arenal*

☎ 460–2020 🖷 460–5724 ✒ *Apdo. 181–1007, San José* ☎ 256–1500 🖷 221–3075 ⊕ *www.tabacon.com* ↯ 73 *rooms, 9 suites* ⌂ *Restaurant, dining room, cable TV, 9 pools, outdoor hot tub, spa, 3 bars, airport shuttle* ▭ *MC, V* ⦿ *BP.*

$–$$ ▦ **Arenal Observatory Lodge.** You're as close as anyone should be to an active volcano at the end of the winding road leading to the lodge—a mere 1¾ km (1 mi) away. The isolated lodge was founded by Smithsonian researchers in 1987. It's fairly rustic, emphasizing that outdoor activities are what it's all about. Rooms are comfortable and simply furnished (comforters on beds are a cozy touch), and most have stellar views. After a hike, take a dip in the infinity-edge pool or 12-person hot tub, which face tall pines one side and the volcano on the other. The dining room, which serves tasty and hearty food, has great views of the volcano and lake. ⊠ *3 km (2 mi) east of dam on Laguna de Arenal; from La Fortuna, drive to Tabacón Resort and continue 4 km (2½ mi) past resort to turnoff at base of volcano; turn and continue for 9 km (5½ mi)* ☎🖷 695–5033 ✒ *Apdo. 13411–1000, San José* ☎ 290–7011 🖷 290–8427 ⊕ *www.arenal-observatory.co.cr* ↯ 35 *rooms, 2 suites* ⌂ *Restaurant, pool, outdoor hot tub, horseback riding, bar, laundry service; no room phones, no room TVs* ▭ *AE, MC, V* ⦿ *BP.*

$$ ▦ **Montaña de Fuego Inn.** On a manicured grassy roadside knoll, this highly recommended collection of cabins affords utterly spectacular views of Volcán Arenal. The spacious, well-made hardwood structures have large porches and rooms have rustic decor. The friendly management can arrange tours of the area. ⊠ *8 km (5 mi) west of La Fortuna* ☎ 460–1220 🖷 460–1455 ⊕ *www.montanadefuego.com* ↯ 52 *cabinas* ⌂ *Restaurant, fans, cable TV, pool, hot tub, spa, shop, laundry service* ▭ *AE, MC, V* ⦿ *BP.*

$$ ▦ **Arenal Country Inn.** It doesn't quite approximate an English country inn, although it is charming. Each brightly furnished modern room has two queen-size beds and a private patio. The lush grounds have great views of the Arenal volcano. A big breakfast is served in the restaurant, an open-air converted cattle corral. You can take lunch and dinner there as well. ⊠ *1 km (½ mi) south of church of La Fortuna, south end of town* ☎ 479–9670 🖷 479–9433 ⊕ *www.arenalcountryinn.com* ↯ 20 *rooms* ⌂ *Dining room, in-room safes, minibars, pool, bar, laundry service, meeting room, travel services; no room TVs* ▭ *AE, MC, V* ⦿ *BP.*

$$ ▦ **Chachagua Rain Forest Lodge.** At this working ranch, intersected by a sweetly babbling brook, you can see *caballeros* (horsemen) at work, take a horseback ride into the rain forest, and look for toucans from the open-air restaurant, which serves beef, milk, and cheese produced on the premises. Each cabina has a pair of double beds and a deck with a picnic table. Large, reflective windows enclosing each cabina's shower serve a marvelous purpose: birds gather outside your window to watch their own reflections while you bathe and watch them. The lodge is 3 km (2 mi) up a rough track—four-wheel drive is recommended in rainy season—on the road headed south from La Fortuna to La Tigra. ⊠ *12 km (7 mi) south of La Fortuna* ✒ *Apdo. 476–4005, Ciudad Cariari* ☎ 239–6464 🖷 290–6506 ⊕ *www.novanet.co.cr/chachagua* ↯ 22 *cabinas* ⌂ *Restaurant, tennis court, pool, sauna, horseback riding, bar, casino, meeting rooms; no room phones, no room TVs* ▭ *AE, MC, V.*

$$ ▦ **Tilajari Hotel Resort.** As a comfortable base from which to have outdoor or adventure tours, this 35-acre resort with a butterfly garden and orchard is a good choice. The hotel organizes horseback tours through its own rain-forest preserve, kayak tours in the river that nudges up against the property, as well as other area tours. "Papaya on a stick" feeders hang outside the open-air dining room, attracting an array of raucous toucans and parrots to entertain you while you sip your morning cof-

fee. The modest guest quarters have river-view balconies; family suites have lofts. Tilajari is a half hour outside of town, and there's no shuttle service. ⊠ *San Carlos Valley, just outside Muelle (follow signs), about 25 km (15 mi) east of La Fortuna* ⌂ *Apdo. 81, San Carlos, Alajuela* ☎ *469–9091* 🖷 *469–9095* ⊕ *www.tilajari.com* ⇨ *56 rooms, 16 suites* ⌂ *Restaurant, snack bar, in-room safes, cable TV, 6 tennis courts, 2 pools, outdoor hot tub, sauna, basketball, horseback riding, Ping-Pong, racquetball, bar, laundry service, meeting rooms* ▤ *AE, MC, V.*

$ 🏨 **Cabinas Los Guayabos.** A great budget alternative to the more expensive lodgings lining the road to the volcano is this group of basic but spotlessly clean cabins managed by a friendly family. The units have all the standard budget-lodging furnishings, but each comes with its own porch facing Arenal, ideal for viewing the evening spectacle. ⊠ *9 km (5½ mi) west of La Fortuna* ☎ *460–6644* ⇨ *5 cabins* ⌂ *No a/c, no room phones, no room TVs* ▤ *No credit cards.*

★ $ 🏨 **Hotel San Bosco.** Covered in blue-tile mosaics, this two-story hotel is certainly the most attractive and comfortable in the main part of town. Two kitchen-equipped cabinas (which sleep 8 or 14 people) are a good deal for families. The spotlessly clean, white rooms have polished wood furniture and firm beds and are linked by a long veranda lined with benches and potted plants. ⊠ *220 m (240 yards) north of La Fortuna's gas station* ☎ *479–9050* 🖷 *479–9109* ⊕ *www.arenal-volcano.com* ⇨ *34 rooms, 2 cabinas* ⌂ *Restaurant, pool, hot tub, laundry service; no room phones, no TV in some rooms* ▤ *AE, MC, V.*

$ 🏨 **Lomas del Volcán.** You'd think you were right on top of the volcano, but Arenal is really a reassuring 6 km (4 mi) away. You need a four-wheel-drive vehicle to get here, but once you do, you can luxuriate in the splendid isolation. The simple cabins have hot water and come with two beds and throw rugs. Each has a volcano-viewing porch. ⊠ *Road entrance 1½ km (1 mi) west of La Fortuna* ☎ *479–9000* 🖷 *479–9770* ⊕ *www.lomasdelvolcan.com* ⇨ *13 cabins* ⌂ *Fans, refrigerators, hot tub, horseback riding; no a/c, no room phones, no room TVs* ▤ *AE, MC, V* ⏍ *BP.*

$ 🏨 **Luigi's Lodge.** Every one of this hotel's rooms fronts a stunning view of the volcano; it's the only lodging in the center of town able to make that claim. Rooms also have high wooden ceilings and stenciled animal drawings. The green-and-white tiled bathrooms have bathtubs, a rarity in Costa Rica. The adjoining restaurant serves pizza. ⊠ *200 m (220 yards) west of town church* ☎ *479–9636* 🖷 *479–9898* ⊕ *www.luigislodge.com* ⇨ *30 rooms* ⌂ *Restaurant, cable TV in some rooms, pool, gym, hot tub, billiards, bar, casino, meeting room* ▤ *AE, MC, V* ⏍ *BP.*

¢–$ 🏨 **La Pradera.** "The Prairie" is a simple roadside hotel with comfortable guest rooms that have high ceilings, spacious bathrooms, and verandas. Two rooms have whirlpool tubs. Beef eaters should try the high thatched-roof restaurant next door. The steak with jalapeño sauce is a fine, spicy dish. ⊠ *About 2 km (1 mi) west of La Fortuna* ☎ *479–9597* 🖷 *479–9167* ⇨ *10 rooms* ⌂ *Restaurant, bar, hot tubs; no a/c in some rooms* ▤ *AE, MC, V.*

¢ 🏨 **Don Manuel Inn.** The folks at Sunset Tours operate this basic but good-value budget lodging near the center of town. The tile-floor rooms are simple. All contain one double and one single bed. Opt for one of the rooms with private bath. They're more secluded and a bit more removed from the commotion of the common areas. ⊠ *Across from south side of church* ☎ *479–9069* 🖷 *479–9415* ⇨ *9 rooms, 4 with bath* ⌂ *No a/c, no room phones* ▤ *MC, V* ⏍ *CP.*

Shopping

Lunática (✉ 350 m [380 yards] east of town church ☎ 479–8255) exhibits and sells vibrant, colorful works by artists, local and from around the country, established and emerging, and has become a focal point for La Fortuna's small but growing art community.

Nightlife

A soak at Tabacón or a gaze at the volcano makes up most of La Fortuna's nightlife. **Volcán Look** (✉ 5 km [3 mi] west of La Fortuna ☎ 479–9690), which bills itself as the largest Costa Rican disco outside San José, erupts with dancing and music on weekends.

The Outdoors

CANOPY TOURS
Fodor'sChoice
★

Want a bird's-eye view of the trees? Let the professionals at the **Original Canopy Tour** (✉ Tabacón Resort, 13 km [8 mi] northwest of La Fortuna on highway toward Nuevo Arenal ☎ 460–2020 or 256–1500 ⊜ 221–3075 ⊕ www.canopytour.com) show you the canopy from a new perspective. You're securely strapped into a rock-climbing harness and attached to a pulley and horizontal zip line. Well-trained guides then send you whizzing between trees that stand about 328 ft over the streams of Tabacón. (If it's a small tour, they may even be able to snap a picture of you.) The tour requires a certain amount of fearlessness, but it's not rigorous and it's certainly exhilarating and unique. Tours are at 7:30 AM, 10 AM, 1:30, and 4. The price of a tour ($45) includes admission to Tabacón Hot Springs for the day.

In line with the "bigger is better" phenomenon overtaking tourist activities in this region, **Sky Walk/Sky Trek** (☎ 645–5238 ⊕ www.skywalk.com) in Monteverde plans to open a second canopy tour–bridge walk complex near La Fortuna with alpine-style gondolas transporting clients to the site. Inauguration is scheduled for late 2003 or early 2004.

FISHING
The eastern side of **Laguna de Arenal** has the best fresh-water fishing in Costa Rica, with guapote aplenty, although it is difficult to fish from the shore. **Arenal Observatory Lodge** (☎ 695–5033) is one of many hotels and tour companies in the area offering boats and guides.

HIKING
A pleasant but steep 6-km (4-mi) day hike takes you from La Fortuna to the 177-ft **Cataratas de la Fortuna.** Look for the yellow entrance sign off the main road toward the volcano. After walking 1½ km (1 mi) and passing two bridges, turn right and continue straight ahead until you reach the river turnoff. Then walk 10 or 15 minutes down a steep but very well constructed steep trail that has a few vertiginous spots along the way. Swimming in the pool under the waterfall is fairly safe. You can work your way around into the cavelike area behind the cataract for an unusual rear view, but you have to swim in turbulent waters and/or hike over slippery rocks. A $2 fee is collected at the head of the trail, which is open daily 7–4. If you don't want to walk, several operators in La Fortuna can take you to the falls by car or on horseback.

Ecocentro Danaus (✉ 4 km [2½ mi] east of La Fortuna ☎ 460–8005), a small ecotourism project outside of town, exhibits 300 species of tropical plants, abundant animal life—including sloths and caimans—and butterfly and orchid gardens. It's also a great place to see Costa Rica's famed red venomous dart frogs up close.

HORSEBACK
RIDING
If you're interested in getting up to Monteverde from the Arenal–La Fortuna area without taking the grinding four-hour drive, there's an alternative: the ever-ingenious Suresh Krishnan, a transplant from California, has a wonderful adventure out of his tour agency, **Desafío Tours** (✉ 75 m [80 yards] west of Banco Nacional ☎ 479–9464 ⊕ www.desafiocostarica.

com). The 4½-hour guided horseback trip takes you around the southern shore of Lake Arenal and on to Monteverde. The trip involves taxi service on both ends, as well as a boat ride across Laguna de Arenal. Desafío takes your luggage and drives your car to Monteverde if need be, all for $65 per person. You leave La Fortuna at 7:30 AM and arrive in Monteverde around 2:30 PM. Note that many other agencies in La Fortuna and Monteverde lead horseback tours over a muddy, poorly maintained trail, and some riders have returned with stories of terrified horses barely able to navigate the way. Stick with Desafío.

RAFTING   Several La Fortuna operators offer Class III and IV white-water trips on the Río Toro. The narrow shape of this river requires the use of special, streamlined, U.S.-made boats that seat just four and go very fast. The easier Ríos Balsa and San Carlos have Class II and III rapids and are close enough to town that they can be worked into half-day excursions. **Desafío Expeditions** (⊠ 75 m [80 yards] west of Banco Nacional ☎ 479–9464 ⊕ www.desafiocostarica.com) has trips on the Toro, San Carlos, and Balsa Rivers for $45–$65 per person.

SPELUNKING   **Sunset Tours** (⊠ 50 m [55 yards] north of Banco Nacional ☎ 479–9415 ⊕ www.sunsettourscr.com) can take you to the Venado Caverns for $25, which includes an English-speaking guide, entrance fee, boots, and a lantern. Prepare to get wet and muddy.

Caño Negro National Wildlife Refuge

❹ *91 km (57 mi) northwest of La Fortuna.*

A lowland rain-forest reserve in the far northern reaches of Alajuela, Refugio Nacional de Vida Silvestre Caño Negro covers 62 square km (38 square mi). Caño Negro has suffered severe deforestation over the years, but most of the Río Frío is still lined with trees, and the park's vast lake is an excellent place to watch such waterfowl as Jabiru, Anhinga, and the Roseate Spoonbill, as well as a host of resident exotic animals. In the dry season, you can ride horses; but the visit here chiefly entails a wildlife-spotting boat tour. Caño Negro can be reached from the Nuevo Arenal–La Fortuna area, or you can approach via Upala (a bus from here takes 45 minutes). Visiting with a tour company is the best way to see the park. Camping is permitted, or you can stay in a couple of surprisingly nice lodgings—ones you'd never expect to find in such a far-flung corner of the country—in Caño Negro village. ⊠ $6 ⊙ *Daily 7–4.*

Sunset Tours (☎ 479–9415), in La Fortuna, runs top-notch, informative daylong tours, among the best in the country, down the Río Frío to Caño Negro for $45. Bring your jungle juice: the mosquitoes are voracious.

Where to Stay

$$ 🏨 **Caño Negro Natural Lodge.** That such an upscale property exists in this remote place might amaze you, but this Italian-designed, family-operated resort on the east side of the reserve is never pretentious. Rooms have high ceilings, colorful drapes and bedspreads, and huge showers; some rooms have bunk beds. There are two- or three-day packages available for fishers or non-fishers alike. The lodge offers a variety of meal options; most guests opt for taking all meals here, since there are few other restaurants in town. ⊠ *Caño Negro village* ☎ 265–6370 🖷 265–4561 ⊕ *www.canonegrolodge.com* ➷ *10 rooms* ⌂ *Restaurant, in-room safes, miniature golf, pool, hot tub, badminton, croquet, Ping-Pong, volleyball, laundry service, meeting room; no a/c, no room phones, no room TVs* 🗖 *AE, MC, V* 🍴 *CP.*

$ ⌷ **Fishing Club Caño Negro.** Despite the name, all are welcome here, though the lodge is best known for its tours, and equipment and boat rental for the tarpon and bass fishing to be found in the lake. Four white bungalows of high-quality wood each contain two bright, sparkling rooms, and are arranged around the wooded property. The produce from the lodge's citrus orchard ends up on your breakfast plate. ⊠ *Caño Negro village* ☎ *656–0071* 🖷 *656–0260* ⊕ *www.canonegro.com* ⌕ *8 rooms* ⚴ *Restaurant, fishing, bar; no a/c, no room phones, no room TVs* ⊟ *AE, MC, V* ⦿⦿ *CP.*

Volcán Arenal

❺   *17 km (11 mi) west of La Fortuna, 128 km (80 mi) northwest of San José.*

Fodor'sChoice   If you've never seen an active volcano, Arenal makes a spectacular first—
★   its perfect conical profile dominates the southern end of Laguna de Arenal. Night is the best time to observe it, as you can clearly see rocks spewing skyward and red-hot molten lava enveloping the top of the cone. Phases of inactivity do occur, however, so it's wise to check ahead. The volcano is also frequently hidden in cloud cover, so you may have to stay more than one day to get in a good volcano-viewing session.

Arenal lay dormant for 400 years until 1968. On July 29 of that year an earthquake shook the area, and 12 hours later Arenal blew. Pueblo Nuevo to the west bore the brunt of the shock waves, poisonous gases, and falling rocks; 80 people perished. Since then, Arenal has been in a constant state of activity—eruptions, accompanied by thunderous grumbling sounds, are sometimes as frequent as one per hour. An enormous eruption in 1998 put the fear back into the local community and led to the closure of Route 42 and the evacuation of several nearby hotels. This earth-shaking event reminded everyone what it really means to coexist with an active volcano.

Though folks here still do it, hiking is not recommended on the volcano's lower slopes; in 1988 two people were killed by fast-flowing lava when they attempted to climb it. History repeated itself in 2000 with the death of an American traveler and her guide who were hiking on the lower slopes in a supposedly safe area. The conventional wisdom in these parts is that it's still safe to approach from the south and west, within the national park. It's really best to enjoy the spectacle from no closer than any of the lodges themselves.

Nuevo Arenal

❻   *40 km (25 mi) west of La Fortuna.*

There's little reason to stop in Nuevo Arenal itself. Off the main road, the pleasant, if nondescript, *nuevo* town was created in 1973 to replace the original Arenal, flooded when the lake was created. If you're staying overnight in the area make sure you find a hotel with a view of the volcano. On the north shore, between the dam and the town of Nuevo Arenal, there's one short stretch of road still unpaved, potholed, and at times quite dangerous; beware of deep, tire-wrecking washouts at all times. This stretch adds a bone-jarring hour to an otherwise lovely drive with spectacular lake and volcano views all the way.

Jardín Botánico Arenal (Arenal Botanical Gardens). Five kilometers (3 mi) east of Nuevo Arenal, these elegantly organized botanical gardens exhibit more than 2,000 plant species from around the world. Countless orchids, bromeliads, heliconias, and roses; varieties of ferns; and a Japanese garden with a waterfall are among the many floral splendors laid out along well-marked trails. An accompanying brochure describes everything in delightful detail; well-placed benches and a fruit-and-juice stand provide resting places along the paths. ☎ 694–4305 ☞ $8 ⊙ Nov.–Apr. daily 9–5; May–Oct. Mon.–Sat. 9–5.

Where to Stay

$$–$$$ ▥ **Arenal Lodge.** Surrounded by macadamia trees and rain forest, this modern white bungalow is high above the dam, midway between La Fortuna and Nuevo Arenal. You need four-wheel drive to negotiate the steep 2-km (1-mi) road, but the hotel can ferry you from the bottom. Bedroom suites, some in a newer annex, are pleasantly furnished, with pretty green-tile baths; there are also cheaper, smaller, darker rooms without volcano views. Interiors are finished in natural wood, with walls of louvered windows. Hilltop chalets have floor-to-ceiling windows and kitchenettes. Perks include a small snooker table and a free hour of horseback riding. ⊠ *18½ km (11½ mi) west of La Fortuna, past Arenal Dam, then 2 km (1 mi) north* ☎ 383–3957 ☎ 289–6798 ☏ *Apdo. 1139–1250, Escazú* ☎ 228–3189 ⊕ *www.arenallodge.com* ☞ *6 rooms, 18 suites, 10 chalets* ⑁ *Dining room, some kitchenettes, hot tub, fishing, bicycles, hiking, horseback riding, bar, library, shop, laundry service, Internet; no a/c, no room phones, no room TVs* ☰ *AE, MC, V* ⦿ *BP.*

$ ▥ **Hotel Joya Sureña.** In the midst of a working coffee plantation, this Canadian-owned property with variously sized suites occupies a rather imposing three-story hacienda-style building surrounded by tropical gardens. It's fairly luxurious for up-country Costa Rica. Extensive trails in and around the place bring a rich diversity of plant, animal, and bird life to view. ⊠ *1½ km (1 mi) down a rocky road that leads east from Nuevo Arenal* ☎ 694–4057 ☎ 694–4059 ☞ *28 rooms* ⑁ *Restaurant, pool, health club, hot tub, massage, sauna, boating, fishing, hiking, horseback riding, laundry service* ☰ *AE, MC, V.*

$ ▥ **Lake Coter Eco-Lodge.** This ruggedly handsome mountain hideaway tucked into cloud forest offers lots to do, thanks to the setting. The lodge has canopy tours on-site, hikes on 29 km (18 mi) of trails, kayaking and sailing on Laguna de Arenal, and an extensive stable of horses for trail rides through the cloud forest. Stay in comfortable ridge-top cabinas, if they're available. Clean, basic rooms are attached to the main brick-and-hardwood reception building, which has a friendly bar and a fireplace. ⊠ *3 km (2 mi) up a rough track off north shore of Laguna de Arenal* ☎ 694–4480 or 440–6768 ☎ 694–4460 or 440–6725 ⊕ *www. ecolodgecostarica.com* ☞ *23 rooms, 14 cabinas* ⑁ *Restaurant, boating, billiards, hiking, horseback riding, bar, laundry service, meeting room; no a/c, no room phones, no room TVs* ☰ *AE, MC, V.*

Shopping

Toad Hall (⊠ road between Nuevo Arenal and La Fortuna ☎ 692–8020) sells everything from indigenous art to maps to recycled paper. The owners can give you the lowdown on every tour and tour operator in the area; they also run a deli-café with light Mexican food and stunning alfresco views of the lake and volcano. Toad Hall is open daily from 7:30 to 5.

Tilarán

❼ *22 km (14 mi) southwest of Nuevo Arenal, 62 km (38 mi) west of La Fortuna.*

Heading west around Laguna de Arenal, you pass a couple of small villages and several charming hotels ranging from the Cretan-inspired fantasy Hotel Tilawa to the rustic Rock River Lodge. The quiet white-washed town of Tilarán, on the southwest side of Laguna de Arenal, is used as a base by bronzed windsurfers.

Where to Stay & Eat

$ ▦ **Hotel Tilawa.** This knockoff of the Palace of Knossos on Crete has neoclassic murals, columns, and plant-draped arches that somehow don't seem dramatically out of place, even on the west of Laguna de Arenal. The large rooms have two queen-size beds with Guatemalan bedspreads and natural wood ceilings; the bathrooms are especially spacious. The property could use a renovation, but the sailing tours in a 39-ft catamaran, windsurfing school and shop, and skateboarding park makes this a practical place to base yourself. Packages include the use of windsurfing gear. The open-air patio restaurant dishes up steaks and seafood. ⊠ *8 km (5 mi) north of Tilarán* ☎ *695–5050* 🖷 *695–5766* ⊕ *www.hotel-tilawa. com* ✑ *Apdo. 92–5710, Tilarán* ⤴ *28 rooms* ⌂ *Restaurant, pool, windsurfing, boating, mountain bikes, hiking, horseback riding, bar, laundry service; no a/c, no room TVs* ▭ *AE, MC, V.*

$ ▦ **Rock River Lodge.** A long, handsome building on a grassy hill above the road leading from Tilarán to Nuevo Arenal houses rustic wooden cabinas. They share a shaded front porch with views of the volcano. Santa Fe–style cabinas are farther up the hill. The restaurant, bar, and lobby occupy another building closer to the road, with plenty of porch space and lounging sofas, an open kitchen, and a welcoming fireplace. The hotel rents windsurfing gear; its launching site is across the lake from that of the Hotel Tilawa. The restaurant serves well-prepared food at reasonable prices. ⊠ *Apdo. 95–5710* ☎🖷 *692–1180* ⊕ *www. rockriverlodge.com* ⤴ *6 rooms, 8 cabinas* ⌂ *Restaurant, windsurfing, fishing, mountain bikes, horseback riding, bar, laundry service; no room phones, no room TVs* ▭ *V.*

¢ ▦ **Hotel Naralit.** Spell Tilarán backward and you get the name of a great budget option in the center of town. It's very basic but comfortable, run by friendly folks, and spotlessly clean. A large glass door fronts a porch in each pleasantly furnished room, letting in lots of light. The Naralit manages a small restaurant next door. ⊠ *Opposite south side of cathedral* ☎ *695–5393* 🖷 *695–6767* ⤴ *26 rooms* ⌂ *Restaurant, some refrigerators, cable TV in some rooms* ▭ *V.*

The Outdoors

HORSEBACK RIDING Uncounted miles of good horse trails cover a marvelous mix of terrain. **Hotel Tilawa** (☎ 695–5050) and nearly every other reputable hotel can make arrangements for guided and unguided horseback treks.

MOUNTAIN BIKING For those days when the windsurfers get "skunked" (the wind fails to blow), the **Hotel Tilawa** (☎ 695–5050) rents mountain bikes for riding a network of roads and trails in the area at the north end of Laguna de Arenal.

WINDSURFING **Rock River Lodge** (☎ 692–1180) is one of several hotels that rent windsurfing equipment. The best selection of windsurfing equipment for rent or purchase can be found at **Tilawa Wind Surf** (☎ 695–5050), the lakefront shop associated with the Hotel Tilawa and the only outfitter here open year-round.

en route If your bones can take it, a very rough track leads from Tilarán via Cabeceras to Santa Elena, near the Monteverde Cloud Forest Biological Reserve, doing away with the need to cut across to the Pan-American Highway. You may well need a four-wheel-drive vehicle—inquire locally about the present condition of the road—but the views of Nicoya Peninsula, Lake Arenal, and Volcán Arenal reward those willing to bump around a bit. Note, too, that you don't really save much time—on a good day, it takes about 2½ hours as opposed to the 3 required via Cañas and Río Lagarto on the highway.

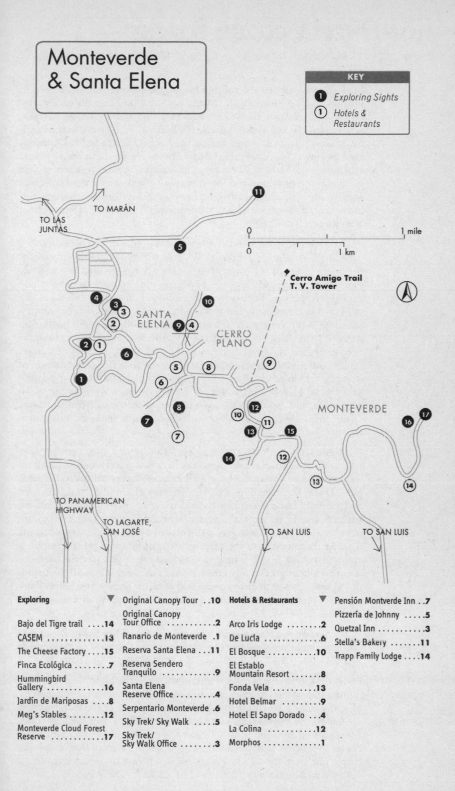

Monteverde & Santa Elena

KEY

1 *Exploring Sights*
1 *Hotels & Restaurants*

TO MARÁN

TO LAS JUNTAS

Cerro Amigo Trail
T. V. Tower

SANTA ELENA

CERRO PLANO

MONTEVERDE

TO PANAMERICAN HIGHWAY

TO LAGARTE, SAN JOSÉ

TO SAN LUIS

TO SAN LUIS

1 mile

1 km

MONTEVERDE CLOUD FOREST

★ ▶ **❽** *35 km (22 mi) southeast of Tilarán, 167 km (104 mi) northwest of San José.*

In close proximity to several fine hotels, the private Reserva Biológica Bosque Nuboso Monteverde (Monteverde Cloud Forest Biological Reserve) is one of Costa Rica's best-kept reserves, with well-marked trails, lush vegetation, and a cool climate. The area's first residents were a handful of Costa Rican families fleeing the rough-and-ready life of nearby gold-mining fields during the 1940s. They were joined in the 1950s by Quakers from Alabama who came in search of peace, tranquility, and good grazing, but the cloud forest that lay above their dairy farms was soon to attract the attention of ecologists. Educators and artisans followed, giving Monteverde and its "metropolis," the village of Santa Elena, a mystique all their own.

The collision of moist winds with the continental divide here creates a constant mist whose particles provide nutrients for plants growing at the upper layers of the forest. Giant trees are enshrouded in a cascade of orchids, bromeliads, mosses, and ferns, and, in those patches where sunlight penetrates, brilliantly colored flowers flourish. The sheer size of everything, especially the leaves of the trees, is striking. No less astounding is the variety: 2,500 plant species, 400 species of birds, 500 types of butterflies, and more than 100 different mammals have so far been cataloged at Monteverde. A damp and exotic mixture of shades, smells, and sounds, the cloud forest is also famous for its population of quetzals, which can be spotted feeding on the *aguacatillo* (like an avocado) trees; best viewing times are early mornings from January until September, and especially during the mating season of April and May. Other forest-dwelling inhabitants include hummingbirds and multicolor frogs.

For those who don't have a lucky eye, a short-stay aquarium is in the field station; captive amphibians stay here just a week before being released back into the wild. Although the reserve limits visitors to 160 people at a time, Monteverde is one of the country's most popular destinations and gets very busy, so come early and allow a generous slice of time for leisurely hiking to see the forest's flora and fauna; longer hikes are made possible by some strategically placed overnight refuges along the way. At the entrance to the reserve you can buy self-guide pamphlets and rent rubber boots; a map is provided when you pay the entrance fee. A two-hour guided night tour starts each evening at 7:30. Note that the Monteverde settlement has no real nucleus; houses and hotels flank a 6-km (4-mi) road from Santa Elena until you arrive at the reserve's entrance. ☎ *645–5122* ⊕ *www.cct.or.cr* ✉ *$12, guide $15* ⊙ *Daily 7–4.*

☾ At the **Serpentario Monteverde,** greet 30 species of live Costa Rican reptiles and amphibians. ✉ *Just outside Santa Elena on road to Monteverde* ☎ *645–6002* ✉ *$7* ⊙ *Dec.–Apr., daily 9–9; May–Nov., daily 11–8.*

Only in Monteverde would visitors groove to the nightlife at an exhibition of 20 species of frogs, toads, and other amphibians. Bilingual biologist-guides take you through a 45-minute tour of the terrariums in

★ ☾ the **Ranario de Monteverde,** just outside Santa Elena. For the best show, come around dusk and stay well into the evening, when the critters become more active and much more vocal. There's a small frog-and-toad-theme gift shop too. ✉ *½ km (¼ mi) southeast of Supermercado La Esperanza, Monteverde* ☎ *645–6320* ✉ *$8* ⊙ *Daily 9–8:30.*

Several conservation areas that have sprung up near Monteverde make attractive day trips, particularly if the Monteverde reserve is too busy. The **Reserva Santa Elena,** just west of Monteverde, has a series of trails that can be walked alone or with a guide. ⊠ *6 km (4 mi) north of Santa Elena* ☎ *645–5390* ⊕ *www.monteverdeinfo.com* ⊠ *$8* ⊙ *Daily 7–4.*

Hike 200 acres through four different stages of cloud forest at the **Reserva Sendero Tranquilo,** including one area illustrating the results of cloud-forest devastation. Tours are arranged through the El Sapo Dorado hotel and require a 2-person minimum and 10-person limit. ⊠ *3 km (2 mi) north of Monteverde park entrance, Cerro Plano* ☎ *645–5010 El Sapo Dorado* ⊠ *$20.*

Finca Ecológica is a private wildlife refuge with four trails on its 75-acre Ecological Farm, plus abundant bird life, sloths, agoutis, coatimundis, two waterfalls, and a coffee plantation. If you can't make it all the way up to the Monteverde Reserve for the evening hike, there's a top-notch guided twilight walk. ⊠ *Off main road between Santa Elena and Monteverde, on turnoff to Jardín de Mariposas* ☎ *645–5363* ⊕ *www. fincaecologicamonteverde.com* ⊠ *$6, twilight walk $14* ⊙ *Daily 7–5.*

Tropical butterflies flit about in three enclosed botanical gardens at the ☙ **Jardín de Mariposas** (Butterfly Garden)—all have stunning views of the Golfo de Nicoya. A guided tour helps you understand the stages of a butterfly's life. The private **bird farm** next door has several trails through secondary forest. More than 90 bird species have been sighted here, from the Crowned Motmot to the Resplendent Quetzal. Admission price includes a guided tour. ⊠ *Near Pensión Monteverde Inn, Monteverde; take right-hand turnoff 4 km (2½ mi) past Santa Elena on road to Monteverde, continue for 2 km (1 mi)* ☎ *645–5512* ⊠ *$7* ⊙ *Daily 9:30–4.*

Where to Stay & Eat

$–$$ ✕ **De Lucía.** Cordial Chilean owner José Belmar is the walking, talking (in five languages) menu at this elegant restaurant, always on hand to explain with enthusiasm such masterfully prepared dishes as sea bass with garlic sauce and orange chicken. All entrées are served with an impressive assortment of grilled vegetables and fried plantains. The handsome wooden restaurant with red mahogany tables is given a distinct South American flavor by an array of Andean tapestries and ceramics. An excellent dessert choice is *tres leches* (a rich cake of condensed and evaporated milk and sugar) with decaf coffee—a novelty in Costa Rica. ⊠ *Off main road between Santa Elena and Monteverde, on turnoff to Jardín de Mariposas* ☎ *645–5337* ⊟ *AE, MC, V.*

$–$$ ✕ **Pizzería de Johnny.** Everyone makes it to this stylish but informal place with candles and white tablecloths during a visit. The Monteverde pizza, with the works, is the most popular dish, and pastas, sandwiches, and a fine wine selection round out the menu. ⊠ *1½ km (1 mi) southeast of Santa Elena on road to Monteverde Reserve* ☎ *645–5066* ⊟ *V.*

$ ✕ **Morphos.** This is about as upscale as Santa Elena dining gets, but Morphos serves up a mix of meat, with quite a few vegetarian options on the menu—a rarity up here—all very casually. Inside this second-floor restaurant are stone walls, log-hewn chairs, artwork, and huge wooden light fixtures in the shape of the famed blue butterfly from which the restaurant takes its name. A large glass window lets you survey all that goes on in town. ⊠ *Across from La Esperanza Supermarket, Santa Elena* ☎ *645–5607* ⊟ *MC, V.*

¢–$ ✕ **Stella's Bakery.** An old standby that dishes up fast food, Monteverde-style, Stella's is one of the few spots that open at 6 AM, and it is a great place to get an early morning fix before heading to the reserve. Luscious pastries, rolls, muffins, natural juices, and coffee are standard break-

CloseUp

BIRD-WATCHING, FROM ARACARI TO Z

I **F YOU VISIT A COSTA RICAN** cloud forest, you'll probably have your eyes peeled for the Emerald Toucanet or the Three-wattled Bellbird, but if you're here between October and April, you'll actually be just as likely to see a Kentucky Warbler. Experienced birders shouldn't be surprised to see that some of their feathered friends from home made similar vacation plans, but many people probably don't realize that when northern birds fly south for the winter, they don't all head to Miami.

Seasonal visitors are just part—about a quarter—of the amazing avian panorama in Costa Rica. Nearly 850 bird species have been identified here, more than the United States and Canada have between them—all in an area about half the size of Kentucky. The country is consequently a mecca for amateur ornithologists, who flock here by the thousands. Though the big attractions tend to be such spectacular species as the Keel-billed Toucan and Resplendent Quetzal, it is the diversity of shape, size, coloration, and behavior that makes bird-watching in Costa Rica so fascinating.

The country's avian inhabitants range in size from the Scintillant Hummingbird, standing a mere 2½" tall and weighing just over 2 grams, to the Jabiru, a long-legged stork that reaches a height of more than 4 ft and a weight of 14 pounds. The diversity of form and color varies from such striking creatures as the showy Scarlet Macaw and the quirky Purple Gallinule to the relatively inconspicuous, and seemingly ubiquitous, Clay-colored Robin, which is, surprisingly enough, Costa Rica's national bird. These robins may look a bit plain, but their song is a melodious one, and since the males sing almost constantly toward the end of the dry season—the beginning of their mating season—local legend has it they call the rains, which play a vital role in a nation so dependent on agriculture.

Foreigners tend to ooh and aah at the sight of those birds associated with the tropics: parrots, parakeets, and macaws; toucans and toucanets; and the elusive but legendary quetzal. But there are many other, equally impressive species flitting around, such as the motmots, with their distinctive racket tails; oropendolas, which build remarkable hanging nests; and an amazing array of hawks, kites, and falcons.

On the color scale, the country's tanagers, euphonias, manakins, cotingas, and trogons are some of its loveliest plumed creatures, but none of them match the iridescence of the hummingbirds. Costa Rica hosts 51 members of the hummingbird family, compared to the just one species for all of the United States east of the Rocky Mountains. A bit of time spent near a hummingbird feeder will treat you to an unforgettable display of accelerated aerial antics and general pugnacity.

You just might find that the more you observe Costa Rica's birds, the more interesting they get. Bird-watching can be done everywhere in the country—all you need is a pair of binoculars and a copy of A Guide to the Birds of Costa Rica, the excellent field guide by Gary Stiles and Alexander Skutch. Wake up early, get out into the woods or the garden, focus those binoculars, and you'll quickly be enchanted by the beauty on the wing. For more information about Costa Rican birds, see the Wildlife Glossary in the Understanding Costa Rica chapter.

fast fare. Take them with you if you're running short of time. Lunch consists of light sandwiches, soups, and pastas. All are prepared with organic ingredients grown right here on the property. ⊠ *Across from CASEM, Monteverde* ☎ *645–5560* ⊟ *V* ⊗ *No dinner.*

$$ ✕⊞ **Hotel El Sapo Dorado.** After beginning its life as a nightclub, the "Golden Toad" became a popular restaurant and then graduated into a very pleasant hotel. Geovanny Arguedas's family arrived here to farm 10 years before the Quakers did, and he and his wife, Hannah Lowther, have built secluded hillside cabins with polished paneling, tables, fireplaces, and rocking chairs. The restaurant is renowned for its pasta, pizza, vegetarian dishes, and sailfish from Puntarenas. ⊠ *6 km (4 mi) northwest of Monteverde park entrance, Monteverde* ☎ *645–5010* 🖷 *645–5180* ⊕ *www.sapodorado.com* ⌂ *Apdo. 9–5655, Monteverde* ⇨ *30 rooms* ⇘ *Restaurant, massage, bar, laundry service; no a/c, no room phones, no room TVs* ⊟ *V.*

$$ ✕⊞ **Fonda Vela.** Owned by the Smith brothers, whose family was among
Fodor'sChoice the first American arrivals in the 1950s, these steep-roof chalets have
★ large bedrooms with white-stucco walls, wood floors, and huge windows. Some have markedly better views of the wooded grounds, so specify when booking. The most innovatively designed of Monteverde's hotels is also one of the closest to the reserve entrance. Local and international recipes, prepared with flair, are served in the dining room or on the veranda. ⊠ *1½ km (1 mi) northwest of Monteverde park entrance, Monteverde* ☎ *645–5125* 🖷 *645–5119* ⊕ *www.fondavela.com* ⌂ *Apdo. 70060–1000, San José* ☎ *257–1413* 🖷 *257–1416* ⇨ *40 rooms* ⇘ *Restaurant, refrigerator, bar, meeting room; no a/c, no TV in some rooms* ⊟ *AE, MC, V.*

$–$$ ⊞ **El Establo Mountain Resort.** Mixing old and new, "The Stable" began life as just that, a stable near the road, remodeled and apportioned into comfortable rooms with basic furnishings. A newer pink building perches on the hill above with large suites with wood-and-stone walls. Some contain lofts; all come with amenities rarely seen up here, such as bathtubs, phones, and enormous windows with views of the Golfo de Nicoya. ⊠ *3½ km (2 mi) northwest of Monteverde* ☎ *645–5110* 🖷 *645–5041* ⊕ *www. hotelestablo.com* ⇨ *50 rooms* ⇘ *Restaurant, snack bar, cable TV, pool, hot tub, massage, bar, travel services; no TV in some rooms* ⊟ *AE, DC, MC, V* ⑩ *BP.*

$–$$ ✕⊞ **Hotel Belmar.** Built into the hillside, Hotel Belmar resembles two tall Swiss chalets and commands extensive views of the Golfo de Nicoya and the hilly peninsula. The amiable Chilean owners have designed both elegant and rustic rooms, paneled with polished wood; half the rooms have balconies. In the dining room, you can count on adventurous and delicious *platos del día* (daily specials) of Costa Rican and international fare. ⊠ *4 km (2½ mi) north of Monteverde* ☎ *645–5201* 🖷 *645–5135* ⊕ *www.centralamerica.com/cr/hotel/belmar.htm* ⌂ *Apdo. 17–5655, Monteverde Puntarenas* ⇨ *34 rooms* ⇘ *Restaurant, hot tub, basketball, bar, laundry service; no a/c, no phone in some rooms, no room TVs* ⊟ *DC, V.*

★ **$–$$** ⊞ **El Sol.** A charming family, natives of the Canary Islands, tends to guests at one of those quintessential get-away-from-it-all places just 10 minutes down the mountain from—and a noticeable few degrees warmer than—Santa Elena. Two fully furnished ojoche-wood cabins perch on the mountainside on the 25-acre farm. Every vantage point in the cabins—the living area, the bed, the desk, the shower, and even the toilet—possesses stupendous views. The property has 3 km (2 mi) of trails, a stone-walled pool, and Finnish sauna. Gourmet cuisine is a mix of Spanish and German; meals can be taken in the main house or brought to your cabin. ⊠ *4 km (2½ mi southwest of Santa Elena* ☎ *645–5838* 🖷 *645–5042*

⊕ *www.geocities.com/elsolmayo* ➥ *2 cabins* ⚙ *Dining room, pool, sauna; no a/c, no room phones, no room TVs* ▤ *No credit cards.*

$ ▥ **Trapp Family Lodge.** Take a whiff in this cozy lodge and you can imagine yourself in a lumberyard. The enormous rooms, with wood paneling and ceilings, have lovely furniture marvelously crafted from—you guessed it—wood. The architectural style is appropriate, as the lodge is surrounded by trees, just a 10-minute walk from the park entrance, making it the closest lodge to the reserve. The friendly Chilean owners are always around to provide personalized service. ⊠ *Main road from Monteverde Reserve, Monteverde* ☎ *645–5858* 🖷 *645–5990* ⊕ *www. trappfam.com* ✉ *Apdo. 70–5655, Monteverde* ➥ *20 rooms* ⚙ *Restaurant, bar, laundry service; no a/c, no room TVs, no smoking* ▤ *V.*

¢–$ ▥ **Arco Iris Lodge.** You can't tell that you're in the center of town at this tranquil spot, with its cozy cabins among 4 acres of birding trails. Cabin decor ranges from rustic to more plush, but all lodgings come with porches. Start your day with a delicious breakfast buffet, including homemade bread, granola, and marmalades. A commitment to environmental sustainability is reflected throughout the lodge; many of the kitchen's ingredients come from its own organic garden. The laid-back German management can provide good advice about how to spend your time in the area. ⊠ *70 m (75 yards) south of Banco Nacional, Santa Elena* ☎ *645–5067* 🖷 *645–5022* ⊕ *www.arcoirislodge.com* ➥ *10 cabins* ⚙ *Horseback riding, laundry service; no a/c, no room phones, no room TVs* ▤ *AE, MC, V.*

¢–$ ▥ **La Colina.** This Colorado ranch–style place is a longtime Monteverde standby. Rust colors and earth tones prevail in the rooms, which are accentuated with the occasional wagon wheel and old western trunk. A hearty American-style breakfast keeps you going until your evening dinner. The friendly management gives discounts for extended stays. ⊠ *290 m (300 yards) south of Cheese Factory, Monteverde* ☎ *645–5009* 🖷 *645–5580* ⊕ *www.lacolina.com* ➥ *11 rooms, 6 with bath* ⚙ *Restaurant, hot tub; no a/c, no room phones, no room TVs* ▤ *V* ⦿ *BP.*

¢ ▥ **El Bosque.** Convenient to the Bajo del Tigre nature trail and Meg's Stables, El Bosque's quiet, simple rooms are grouped around a central camping area. A bridge crosses a stream and leads to the hotel. Brick-oven pizzas are served on the veranda. ⊠ *2½ km (1½ mi) southeast of Santa Elena on road to Monteverde Reserve* ☎ *645–5158* 🖷 *645–5129* ✉ *elbosque@racsa.co.cr* ✉ *Apdo. 5655, Santa Elena* ➥ *27 rooms* ⚙ *Restaurant, bar, laundry service; no a/c, no room phones, no room TVs* ▤ *AE, MC, V.*

¢ ▥ **Pensión Monteverde Inn.** One of the cheapest Monteverde inns is quite far from the park entrance, on a 28-acre private preserve. The bedrooms are basic, but they have stunning views of the Golfo de Nicoya and have hardwood floors, firm beds, and powerful, hot showers. Home cooking is served by the chatty David and María Savage and family. ⊠ *5 km (3 mi) past Butterfly Garden on turnoff road, Monteverde* ☎☎ *645–5156* ➥ *8 rooms* ⚙ *Dining room; no a/c, no room phones, no room TVs* ▤ *No credit cards.*

¢ ▥ **Quetzal Inn.** Three buildings ascend a hill at three levels, both in price and elevation, at the Quetzal near the center of Santa Elena. Opt for the rooms in cedar-and-guanacaste–wood cabins with balconies, in the lower-level building: they're the nicest. The lowest-priced rooms with shared bath sit overhead the main building. Highest on the hill are more spartan wood-and-plaster cabins, the medium-range rooms here. All are pleasantly furnished. This is a real budget find. ⊠ *75 m (80 yards) south of Banco Nacional, Santa Elena* ☎ *645–6076* 🖷 *645–5358* ➥ *15 rooms, 11 with bath* ⚙ *Restaurant; no a/c, no room phones, no room TVs* ▤ *No credit cards.*

Long before tourists flocked up here, dairy farming was the sole foundation of Monteverde's economy. The Quakers still operate what is locally referred to as the Cheese Factory, or **La Lechería** (✉ ½ km [¼ mi] south of CASEM, halfway between Santa Elena and Monteverde Reserve ☎ 645–2850). It's a much grander milk-processing plant today than the original settlers ever envisioned. The factory store scoops up some of the best ice cream around. Stop in for a dish or a cone when you pass by. It's open Monday–Saturday 8–5 and Sunday 10–4; it's closed Sunday April–November.

The Outdoors

CANOPY TOURS One of the most unique ways to explore the rain-forest canopy is on an exhilarating canopy tour. Though billed as a way to get up close with nature, the tours more resemble a ride—they're great fun, but don't plan on seeing the Resplendent Quetzal as you zip from platform to platform. Don't hesitate to ask questions about safety of all canopy tour companies, and be prepared to walk away if the trip doesn't look professionally handled.

You can visit the Monteverde cloud-forest treetops courtesy of the **Original Canopy Tour** (✉ across from La Esperanza Supermarket Santa Elena ☎ 645–5243; 257–5149 San José ⊕ www.canopytour.com), which has 11 platforms in the canopy—the company's longest tour. You arrive at most of the platforms using a cable-and-harness traversing system and climb 42 ft inside a strangler fig tree to reach one. Several knockoff tours, with uneven reputations, have sprung up around Costa Rica, also calling themselves "canopy tours." This one, which calls itself "the original," is top-notch. The tours last 2½ hours and are held at 7:30 AM, 10:30 AM, and 2:30 PM. The cost is $45.

Sky Walk (✉ across from Banco Nacional Santa Elena ☎ 645–5238 ⊕ www.skywalk.com) lets you walk between treetops, up to a height of 138 ft, by way of five hanging bridges connected from tree to tree. Imposing towers are also used as support, although they somewhat mar the landscape. The hour-long walk can be done anytime between 7 and 4 daily and costs $15. Tours with an English-speaking guide for $27 leave at 8 and 1—be sure to make reservations. At the same facility is the more adventurous **Sky Trek**, which uses rock-climbing gear and zip lines and has seven platforms and longer cables between them than those of the Original Canopy Tour. Tours cost $40 and leave at 7:30, 9:30, 11:30, 1:30, and 2. The company provides cheap transport to and from hotels when called a few hours in advance.

You can find it all—canopy tour, bridge walks, butterfly and hummingbird gardens—at **Selvatura** (✉ across from church Santa Elena ☎ 645–5929 ⊕ www.selvatura.com), a complex just outside the Santa Elena Reserve. Selvatura's 18-line, 20-platform canopy tour ($35) is the only such operation built entirely inside the cloud forest. If zipping from tree to tree isn't quite your thing, the operation's **Tree Top Walkways** ($15) takes you on 3 km (2 mi) of very stable bridges through the same canopy terrain. Quite frankly, if viewing nature is what you're after, the bridge walk is a more realistic way to do it. A small hummingbird garden and an enormous enclosed 25-species *mariposario* (butterfly garden) sit near the visitor center. Transportation from area hotels is included in the price.

A more sedate variation on the canopy tours is the **Natural Wonders Tram** (✉ off main road between Santa Elena and Monteverde, on turnoff to Jardín de Mariposas ☎ 645–5960), in which two-person carriages on an elevated track take you on an hour-long ride through the rain-forest canopy. You control the speed of your carriage. Alternatively, a 1½-km (1-mi) walk gives you a different ground-level perspective. The site opens for night visits, too.

HIKING   The Monteverde Conservation League's **Bajo del Tigre trail** (⊠ follow signs along highway to Monteverde ☎ 645–5003 ⊕ www.acmonteverde. com), in the Bosque Eterno de los Niños, makes for a gentle, self-guided 1½-km (1-mi) hike through secondary forest. Admission to the trail is $5, and it's open daily 8–4:30.

HORSEBACK   **Meg's Stables** (⊠ main road, halfway between Santa Elena and Mon-
RIDING   teverde ☎ 645–5419) leads horseback-riding trips for everyone from toddlers to seasoned experts. Guided rides through the Monteverde area cost $15 an hour; prices drop for longer rides. Reservations are a good idea in high season. Just outside of Santa Elena, family-operated **El Palomino** (☎ 645–5479) gives escorted half-day horseback-riding tours on farm areas around Santa Elena. El Palomino provides transportation from your hotel to the tour location.

Shopping

In Monteverde, the **Comité de Artesanas de Santa Elena y Monteverde** (CASEM; ☎ 645–5190), an artisans' cooperative next to the El Bosque hotel-restaurant, sells locally made crafts, mostly by women, and English-language books. The **Hummingbird Gallery** (⊠ just outside entrance to Monteverde Reserve ☎ 645–5030) sells books, gifts, T-shirts, great Costa Rican coffee, prints, and slides by nature specialists Michael and Patricia Fogden, as well as watercolors by nature artist Sarah Dowell.

Bromelia (⊠ 100 m [110 yards] east of CASEM, Monteverde ☎ 645–6093) sells a good selection of nature books and music and has a small downstairs café. **Chorotega** (⊠ next to gas station, Cerro Plano ☎ 645–6919) sells ceramics made by the indigenous Chorotega from the artisan community of Guaitil in northwest Costa Rica as well as Nicaraguan woodwork. Local artist and art instructor Marco Tulio Brenes exhibits and sells his wood reliefs and turning, painting, and ceramics works at **Galería Extasis** (⊠ 100 m [110 yards] west of CASEM, Monteverde ☎ 645–5548). Artists from around the country exhibit at Extasis, too. **Librería Chunches** (⊠ 25 m [30 yards] south of Banco Nacional, Santa Elena ☎ 645–5147) has books in English, as well as a good selection of Spanish-language literature and CDs from Costa Rican artists.

FAR NORTHERN GUANACASTE

The mountains, plains, and Pacific coastline north of Liberia up to the border of Nicaragua are encompassed in Far Northern Guanacaste. The capital of Guanacaste is Liberia, which is home to Costa Rica's second-largest airport. You'll most likely pass through it on your way to the beaches west of the city and on the Nicoya Peninsula or up north to the national parks of Guanacaste, Santa Rosa, or Rincón de la Vieja. Volcán Rincón de la Vieja, an active volcano that last erupted in 1991, is pocked with eerie sites such as boiling creeks, bubbling mud pools, and vapor-emitting streams—look, but don't touch!

West of Rincón de la Vieja, on the coast, Santa Rosa National Park is a former cattle ranch where Costa Ricans defeated the invading mercenary army of American William Walker in 1857. Santa Rosa is also home to Playas Naranjo and Nancite, where hundreds of thousands of Olive Ridley Sea Turtles lay their eggs between August and November. Closer still to the Nicaraguan border are Guanacaste National Park and the town of La Cruz, overlooking the pristine beaches and a pair of resorts on the lovely Golfo de Santa Elena and Bahía Salinas.

> **en route**   From Liberia, access to Rincón de la Vieja National Park is on 27 km
> (17 mi) of unpaved road. The road begins 6 km (4 mi) north of
> Liberia off the Pan-American Highway (follow signs for Albergue
> Guachipelín) or 25 km (15 mi) along the Colonia Blanca route
> northeast from Liberia, which follows the course of the Río Liberia to
> the Santa María park headquarters. A four-wheel-drive vehicle is
> recommended, though not essential, for either of these bone-rattling
> 1- to 1½-hour rides.

Rincón de la Vieja National Park

⑨ *27 km (17 mi) northeast of Liberia.*

Parque Nacional Rincón de la Vieja is Costa Rica's Yellowstone, with volcanic hot springs and boiling, bubbling mud ponds. The park protects more than 177 square km (54 square mi) of Volcán Rincón de la Vieja's upper slopes, much of which are covered by dry forest. The wildlife here is diverse: 200 species of birds, including Keel-billed Toucans and Blue-crowned Motmots, plus mammals such as brocket deer, tapirs, coatis, jaguars, sloths, and armadillos.

The mass of Volcán Rincón de la Vieja, often enveloped in a mixture of sulfurous gases and cloud, dominates the scenery to the right of the Pan-American Highway as you head north. The volcano has two peaks: **Santa María** (6,868 ft) and **Rincón de la Vieja** (6,806 ft). The latter, which is barren and has two craters, is thought unlikely to erupt violently due to the profusion of fumaroles through which it constantly lets off steam. (The last violent eruptions were between 1966 and 1970, but vulcanologists were alarmed by a temporary increase in activity in 1995.) **Las Hornillas** (The Kitchen Stoves), on the southern slope of the Rincón de la Vieja crater, is a 124-acre medley of mud cones, hot-water pools, bubbling mud pots, and vent holes most active during the rainy season. Don't get too close to the mud pots—their edges are brittle and several people have slipped in and been severely burned. To the east, **Los Azufrales** are hot sulfur springs in which you can bathe; be careful not to get sulfur in your eyes.

Bosque Encantado, where the Río Zopilote cascades into the forest to form an enticing pool, is a 2-km (1-mi) hike from Santa María. Three kilometers (2 mi) farther are Los Azufrales, and 4 km (2½ mi) beyond that are the boiling mud pots and fumaroles of Las Hornillas, near the Las Pailas entrance to the park.

The trail to the summit heads into the forest above Las Pailas, but it's a trip for serious hikers, best done in dry season with preparation for cold weather at the top. A less strenuous option is the 3-km (2-mi) loop through the park, along which you'll see fumaroles, a *volcáncito* (baby volcano), Las Pailas, and many animals including semidomesticated, raccoonlike coatis, looking for handouts (a plea you should ignore: a cardinal rule of wildlife encounters is don't feed the animals).

Trail maps and hiking information are available at the park stations by both entrance gates. If you want to explore the slopes of the volcano, go with a guide; the abundant hot springs and geysers have given unsuspecting visitors some very nasty burns. In addition, the upper slopes often receive fierce and potentially dangerous winds—before your ascent, check at either ranger station for conditions. Alternatively, head to **Rincón de la Vieja Mountain Lodge** (☎ 661–8156), which has guides for hiking or horseback riding; call ahead to check availability. ⊠ *Entrances at Hacienda Santa María on road leading northeast from Liberia, and at Las Pailas, via mostly unpaved road through Curubandé* ☎ *661–8139* 🖙 *$6* ⊙ *Daily 7–4.*

Where to Stay

$ 🏨 **Rincón de la Vieja Lodge.** On the slopes of Rincón de la Vieja are the lodge's paneled cabins, small doubles, and comfy dormitory-style rooms. The sitting room has a TV with a VCR and a few movies. Meat, fish, and vegetarian (made with homegrown produce) entrées are good, though on the pricey side. The affable staff can take you to explore the park and volcano on foot or on horseback through the woods. Trails lead to a hot-water, sulfur bathing pool and a blue lake and waterfall. The lodge provides transport up from Liberia for up to six people. ⊠ *2 km (1 mi) northeast of park entrance* ☎☎ *661–8156* ⊕ *www. rincondelaviejalodge.com* 🖂 *Apdo. 114–5000, Liberia* 🛏 *38 rooms* ♨ *Dining room, pool, horseback riding, tennis court, volleyball, bar; no room phones, no room TVs* 🖃 *AE, MC, V.*

The Outdoors

Treetop Trails (☎ 661–8156) runs four-hour canopy tours ($50) from the Rincón de la Vieja Mountain Lodge, which include a forest-floor hike and canopy observation from 16 cable-linked treetop platforms. A more elaborate seven-hour tour ($79) also includes horseback riding to the park's blue lake and waterfall.

Santa Rosa National Park

⑩ *35 km (22 mi) north of Liberia.*

With the largest swath of tropical dry forest in Central America, Parque Nacional Santa Rosa is one of Costa Rica's most impressive parks. Because of its less luxuriant, low-density foliage, the park is a good one for viewing wildlife, especially if you station yourself next to water holes during the dry season. The park might also be the country's most beloved of protected areas because of its historic significance as the sight of the 1856 triumph over American invader William Walker. Santa Rosa is also the country's first national park, so it has become a model for community involvement in preservation and conservation. As you approach the entrance from the Pan-American Highway, you can see the forested slopes of Volcán Orosí, protected within Guanacaste National Park. A few miles after you enter Santa Rosa, a scenic overlook on the right grants your first good view of the park's dry forest.

Typical dry-forest vegetation includes oak, wild cherry, mahogany, calabash, bullhorn acacia, hibiscus, and gumbo-limbo, with its distinctive reddish-brown bark. Inhabitants include Spider, White-faced, and Howler monkeys, as well as deer, armadillos, coyotes, tapirs, coatis, and ocelots. Ocelots, commonly known as *manigordos* (literally, "fat hands") on account of their large feet, are wildcats that have been brought back from the brink of extinction by the park's conservation methods. These wildlands also define the southernmost distribution of many North American species such as the Virginia Opossum and the cantil, a pit viper snake. From the ecology perspective, Santa Rosa is important because it protects and regenerates 520 square km (200 square mi) of forest land, both moist, basal-belt transition and deciduous, tropical dry forests.

Arsonists burned the park's centerpiece, the **Hacienda La Casona,** to the ground in 2001. The rambling colonial-style farmstead was the site of a famous 1856 battle in which a ragged force of ill-equipped Costa Ricans routed the superior army of the notorious William Walker. Fundraising and reconstruction, in true Costa Rican style, were slated to take several years. But awash in patriotism for the beloved monument, one of the few military historic sites in this army-less country, Costa Ricans raised funds and rebuilt La Casona in record time.

From the entrance gate, 7 km (4½ mi) of paved road leads to the **park headquarters.** A small nature trail loops through the woods, and there's a large camping area nearby. Note that Santa Rosa's **campgrounds,** which can sleep 150 people, sometimes fill up during the dry season, especially in the first week of January and during Easter week. Throughout the park it's wise to carry your own water, since water holes are none too clean.

White-sand **Playa Naranjo** (⊠ 13 km [8 mi] west of the administrative area; a two- to three-hour hike or one-hour trek with a four-wheel-drive vehicle) is popular for beachcombing thanks to its abundance of shells and for surfing because of its near-perfect break. The campsite here has washing facilities, but bring your own drinking water. The lookout at the northern tip of the beach has views over the entire park. ⊠ *Km 269, Pan-American Hwy., 13 km (8 mi) northwest of Porterillos* ☎ *666–5020* ☎ *$6* ☉ *Daily 7–5.*

Playa Nancite. A two-hour walk north from Playa Naranjo—and also accessible by four-wheel-drive vehicle—this beach is a premier place to watch turtle *arribadas* (mass nestings). It is estimated that 200,000 turtles nest here each year. Backed by dense hibiscus and button mangroves, the gray-sand beach is penned in by steep, tawny, brush-covered hills. Previously a difficult point to get to, it's now the world's only totally protected **Olive Ridley Turtle arribada.** Olive Ridleys are the smallest of the sea turtles (average carapace, or hardback shell, is 21″–29″) and the least shy. The majority arrive at night, plowing the sand as they move up the beach and sniffing for the high-tide line, beyond which they use their hind flippers to dig the holes into which they lay their eggs. They spend an average of one hour on the beach before scurrying back to the sea. Hatching also takes place at night. Because the brightest light is that of the shimmering ocean, the phototropic baby turtles naturally know to head for the sea, which is vital for their continued survival. Many of the nests are churned up during subsequent arribadas, and predators such as coatis, ghost crabs, raccoons, and coyotes lie in wait; hence just 0.2% of the eggs laid result in young turtles reaching the sea. Their nesting season is August to November, peaking in September and October. You need a permit to stay at Nancite; ask at the park's headquarters. ⊠ *7 km (4 mi) northwest of Playa Naranjo* ☎ *666–5020* ☎ *$6* ☉ *Daily 7–5.*

Camping

¢ 🏕 **La Casona.** Santa Rosa National Park has a rugged terrain and an isolated feel. The campsite, near the Hacienda La Casona, overhung by giant strangler figs, has no set sites—you choose where to set up—and provides washing facilities, rustic bathrooms, and picnic tables. Be careful of snakes. Between Playas Naranjo and Nancite, another campground at Estero Real is available with tables only. ⊠ *Santa Rosa National Park* ☎ *666–5051* ⛺ *Picnic areas* ☰ *No credit cards.*

Cuajiniquil

⑪ *10 km (6 mi) north of Santa Rosa National Park.*

North from Santa Rosa on the Pan-American Highway is the left turn to Cuajiniquil, famous for its waterfalls. If you have time and a four-wheel-drive vehicle, Cuajiniquil has lovely views. The Golfo de Santa Elena is renowned for its calm waters, which is why it's now threatened by tourist development. Playa Blanca in the extreme west has smooth white sand, as its name implies. The rough track here passes through a valley of uneven width caused, according to geologists, by the diverse granulation of the sediments formerly deposited here. To the south rise the rocky Santa Elena hills (2,548 ft), bare except for a few chigua and nancite shrubs.

Guanacaste National Park

12 *32 km (20 mi) north of Liberia.*

The 325-square km (125-square mi) Parque Nacional Guanacaste was created in 1989 to preserve rain forests around **Volcán Cacao** (5,950 ft) and **Volcán Orosi** (5,330 ft), which are seasonally inhabited by migrant wildlife from Santa Rosa. The park is a mosaic of interdependent protected areas, parks, and refuges; the goal is eventually to create a single Guanacaste megapark to accommodate the natural migratory patterns of myriad creatures, from jaguars to tapirs. Much of the park's territory is cattle pasture, which, it is hoped, will regenerate into forest. Currently, there are 300 different birds and more than 5,000 species of butterflies here. Camping is possible at each of the park's biological stations. Call the park headquarters in advance to arrange accommodations.

The **Mengo Biological Station** (📠 no phone) lies on the slopes of Volcán Cacao at an altitude of 3,946 ft. Accommodation is in rustic wood dormitories; bedding is provided but towels are not. From the Mengo Biological Station, one trail leads up Volcán Cacao, and another heads 9 km (5½ mi) north to the **Maritza Station** (📠 no phone), about a three-hour hike away at the base of Orosí, with lodging. There are meals and electricity here; conditions are a bit more luxurious than at Mengo. You can also reach Maritza by four-wheel-drive vehicle, a minimum half-hour drive from Mengo. From the Maritza Station you can trek about two hours, a 4-km (2½-mi) jaunt, to **Llano de los Indios,** a cattle pasture dotted with volcanic petroglyphs. North and a little east of Llano de los Indios is **Pitilla Station** (📠 661–8150). The station has basic lodging with electricity and very basic meals. Despite its lower elevation than other stations in the park, it has views of the coast and Lago de Nicaragua across the border. Advance reservations are essential to stay at any of the park's field stations.

✉ *From Liberia, head 32 km (20 mi) north on Pan-American Hwy. to Poterillos, then 18 km (11 mi) northwest* 📞 *666–5051* 🎫 *$6* 🕐 *Daily 7–5.*

Where to Stay

★ **$$** 🏨 **Los Inocentes Lodge.** Built more than 100 years ago, this handsome, exquisitely maintained hardwood hacienda is in a private reserve along the northern border of Guanacaste National Park. A 14-km (8½-mi) drive on a smoothly paved road east from the Pan-American Highway to Santa Cecilia takes you to the entrance of the working ranch, with horses, cattle, and numerous birds. The hardwood-finished rooms are rustic but comfortable, with hot showers in bathrooms (some shared by two rooms) across the halls. Meals are included in most packages. Experienced ranch-hand guides, friendly horses, and miles of trails get you into the forests. ✉ *15 km (9 mi) west of La Cruz* 📞 *679–9190* 📠 *679–9224* 🌐 *www.losinocenteslodge.com* 📬 *Apdo. 228–3000, Heredia* 📞 *265–5484, 888/613–2532 in the U.S.* 📠 *265–4385* 🛏 *11 rooms, 3 with bath; 12 cabins* ⚒ *Dining room, pool, horseback riding, bar; no room phones, no room TVs* ▤ *AE, MC, V* ⑩ *FAP.*

La Cruz

⓭ *56 km (35 mi) north of Liberia, 12 km (7 mi) south of the Nicaraguan border.*

Farther north on the west side of the highway is a turnoff to La Cruz, noteworthy for the stunning views of Bahía Salinas from its bluff. It also serves as a gateway to the two resorts and beaches on the south shore of Bahía Salinas, the hamlet of Puerto Soley, and the Golfo de Santa Elena.

The Nicaraguan border lies just north of La Cruz at Peñas Blancas. All travelers are stopped at two pre-border checkpoints south of La Cruz for passport and cursory vehicle inspection. You will notice heightened police vigilance in the region.

Where to Stay & Eat

$ ✕ **El Mirador Ehecatl.** Don't pass up a chance to have a drink at this two-story restaurant-bar overlooking Bahía Salinas, Isla Bolaños, and the Nicaraguan coastline. The food is delicious: try anything with seafood—the ceviche is especially well-prepared—or one of the many cheap, rice-based combination plates. *Ehecatl* means "god of the wind" in the indigenous Chorotegan language, and the name suits these windy environs. ⊠ *Turn left before the main road from the town square goes downhill toward the bay* ☎ 679–9104 ☰ *V.*

$ ✕▦ **Colinas del Norte.** On the Pan-American Highway halfway between La Cruz and the Nicaraguan border, 20 km (12 mi) north of Peñas Blancas, this rugged, two-story hardwood hotel bills itself as a touring base for the surrounding dry tropical forest, but its most appealing feature is its large pool, surrounded by shady palms. At the outdoor disco you can dance till you drop, then hop into the pool. The indoor-outdoor restaurant ($–$$) specializes in pizza and Italian food. Modest but comfortable upstairs rooms have private terraces. ⊠ *Pan-American Hwy., about 6 km (4 mi) north of La Cruz* ✉ *Apdo. 1049.3–1000, San José* ☎☎ 679–9132 ↝ *24 rooms* ⚲ *Restaurant, miniature golf, tennis court, pool, horseback riding, dance club, laundry service; no room TVs* ☰ *AE, MC, V.*

$ ▦ **Amalia's Inn.** The late U.S. artist Lester Bounds and his Costa Rican wife, Amalia, created this breezy little inn on the cliff overlooking Bahía Salinas. Amalia now runs the inn. Bounds is also survived by his art—colorful modern paintings and prints that decorate the place and rooms. The inn is has spacious rooms with private baths and balconies. Amalia's is a fine budget alternative to the two pricier resorts on the bay's south shore. ⊠ *East of central park, on left (south) side of road heading into town* ☎☎ 679–9181 ↝ *7 rooms* ⚲ *Pool, laundry service; no a/c, no room phones, no room TVs* ☰ *AE, MC, V.*

Bahía Salinas

⓮ *7 km (4½ mi) west of La Cruz.*

Several dirt and rock roads dead-end on different beaches along Bahía Salinas, the pretty little half-moon bay that lies at the very top of Costa Rica's Pacific coast. Just turn right off the "main" road to the resorts, and you'll probably end up on or near the beach, or in the hamlet of Puerto Soley, a tiny town tucked in off the bay—look for the salt flats to find the town, which is roughly 5–6 very slow-going km (3–4 mi) from La Cruz. There's public beach access along the bay.

The wind usually blows year-round, except in September and October, the height of the rainy season, so windsurfing here is supreme. Winds are generally not as powerful as those at Laguna de Arenal, but they're strong enough to make this a viable alternative (stay on the south side for stronger winds), or accompaniment, to the Arenal experience.

Ranking among the most beautiful beaches in all of Costa Rica are a couple of secluded, wind-sheltered strands, including the gorgeous, pristine **Playa Rajada**, with fine swimming and snorkeling. Just offshore is **Isla Bolaños**, a bird refuge and nesting site for thousands of endangered frigate birds as well as brown pelicans. The **Bolaños Bay Resort** (☎ 679–9444) has a motor launch for Isla Bolaños tours, but don't try to land—it's against the law.

Where to Stay

$$$ ⊞ **Ecoplaya Beach Resort.** Although it's on the same stretch of Bahía Salinas as the Bolaños Bay Resort, about 1 km (½ mi) to the west, Ecoplaya has plenty of luxury amenities unusual for the area. Every room has a small but fully equipped kitchen, a phone, air-conditioning, hot water, and custom hardwood furniture. The nearly 1-km-long (½-mi-long) beach fronting the hotel is flanked by bird- and wildlife-filled estuaries. Be warned, nonsailors: the wind blows hard here much of the time. ✉ *La Coyotera Beach* 🕾 *679–9380* 🕾 *Plaza Colonial, Escazú, No. 4, San José* 🕾 *289–8920* 🕾 *289–4536 in San José* 🌐 *www.ecoplaya.com* ⇨ *36 suites* ⚑ *Restaurant, kitchens, pool, beach, windsurfing, horseback riding, bar, laundry service; no room TVs* ⊟ *AE, MC, V.*

$$ ⊞ **Bolaños Bay Resort.** The first thing you spot on your approach to this resort is the high double rancho (thatched roof) that shelters the reception area, bar, and restaurant. Closer up you see the modest rooms built into low-rise cabinas neatly arrayed across grassy lawns. Given the winds that rocket across the bay, the resort's emphasis on windsurfing comes as no surprise. For those left behind, a sheltered pool with a swim-up bar provides a diversion. ✉ *Take dirt road 3 km (2 mi) down steep hill from La Cruz and follow signs for about 15 km (9 mi)* 🕾 *679–9444* 🕾 *679–9654* 🕾 *Apdo. 1680–1250, San José* 🕾 *289–5561* 🕾 *228–4205* 🌐 *www.3cornersbolanosbay.com* ⇨ *72 rooms* ⚑ *Restaurant, pool, hot tub, beach, windsurfing, volleyball, 2 bars, laundry service; no room TVs* ⊟ *AE, MC, V* ⍾ *FAP.*

The Outdoors

WATER SPORTS The windsurfing **Pro Center** (✉ Bolaños Bay Resort ☎ 679–9444) is run by friendly, knowledgeable Bjorn Voigt. **Tico Wind** (☎ 679–9380) at Ecoplaya Resort will fix you up for all your windsurfing needs.

For snorkeling, fishing, and waterskiing trips to Playa Cuajiniquil, other spots in the Golfo de Santa Elena, and boat trips around Isla Bolaños, contact Charlie at **Iyok Trips** (✉ Bolaños Bay Resort ☎ 679–9444). Charlie promises sightings of Nurse Sharks, Manta Rays, and lots of large fish. Iyok's guides also lead horseback and mountain-biking tours of the area and know where the monkeys hang out in the woods.

NORTHERN GUANACASTE & ALAJUELA A TO Z

To research prices, get advice from other travelers, and book travel arrangements, visit www.fodors.com

AIR TRAVEL

Delta Airlines connects Atlanta with Liberia's Daniel Oduber International Airport (LIR) three times weekly. Various charters serve the airport on changing schedules as well. If your destination lies in Guanacaste, make sure your travel agent investigates the possibility of flying into Liberia instead of San José, which saves some serious hours on the road. Costa Rican domestic airlines SANSA and NatureAir fly to Liberia from San José daily.

✈ Airlines & Contacts **Delta** ✉ C. 32, Avdas. Central and 2 San José ☎ 257–4141, 800/ 221–1212 in the U.S. **NatureAir** ✉ Aeropuerto Internacional Tobías Bolaños ☎ 220–3054. **SANSA** ✉ C. 42 and Avda. 3, San José ☎ 296–0909.

✈ Airports **Aeropuerto Internacional Daniel Oduber** ✉ Hwy. 21, 5 km [3 mi] west of Liberia ☎ 668–1032.

BOAT TRAVEL

Desafío Expeditions in La Fortuna and Monteverde provides a fast, popular three-hour transfer between the communities. The taxi–boat–taxi service costs $25 one-way.

✈ Boat Information **Desafío Expeditions** ✉ 75 m [80 yards] west of Banco Nacional, La Fortuna ☎ 479–9464 ⊕ www.desafiocostarica.com.

BUS TRAVEL

Buses in this region are typically large, clean, and comfortable but often crowded Friday–Sunday. Don't expect air-conditioning, and even supposedly express buses marked *directo* often make some stops.

Auto Transportes San José–San Carlos buses leave San José for the three-hour trip to San Carlos from C. 12, between Avdas. 7 and 9, daily every hour 5 AM–7 PM. The company runs three buses daily from this same station in San José to La Fortuna, near Arenal, at 6:15, 8:40, and 11:30 AM. From San Carlos you can connect to Arenal and Tilarán. The company also has buses for Los Chiles (Caño Negro), which depart from C. 12 at Avda. 9, daily at 5:30 AM and 3:30 PM; the trip takes five hours.

Transportes La Cañera has service to Cañas, and the turnoff for Tilarán and Arenal, daily at 8:30 AM, 10:20 AM, 12:20 PM, 1:20 PM, and 2:30 PM from C. 16, between Avdas. 3 and 5 in San José. The trip to Cañas takes 3½ hours. Transportes Tilarán sends buses on the four-hour trip to Tilarán daily from C. 12, between Avdas. 7 and 9 in San José, at 7:30 AM, 9:30 AM, 12:45 PM, 3:45 PM, and 6:30 PM. From Tilarán you can continue to Nuevo Arenal and Volcán Arenal. Transmonteverde makes the five-hour trip to Monteverde, departing weekdays at 6:30 AM and 2:30 PM. This route is notorious for theft; watch your bags.

Pulmitan Liberia has four-hour buses to Liberia that leave San José daily from C. 24, between Avdas. 5 and 7, every hour between 6 AM and 8 PM, with direct buses at 3 and 5 PM. Friday buses leave every hour from 1 PM to 8 PM, and Saturday they leave at 6, 7, 9, 10, and 11:30 AM. Transportes Deldu goes to La Cruz and Peñas Blancas, normally a six-hour trip that passes through Liberia; daily departures are at 5 AM, 1:20 PM, and 4:10 PM. Express buses cut the trip to 4½ hours; they leave from C. 20 and Avda. 1 in San José, at 4:30 AM and 7 AM. The slower buses pass the entrance to Santa Rosa National Park after about five hours.

Buses don't serve Rincón de la Vieja and Guanacaste National Parks.

If you prefer a more private form of travel, consider taking a shuttle. Fantasy Bus has daily service between San José and Arenal. Comfortable, air-conditioned vans leave various San José hotels at 8 AM and return at 2 PM. Tickets cost $21 and must be reserved a day in advance. Fantasy Bus also connects Arenal to Tamarindo on the Nicoya Peninsula. Interbus connects San Jose with La Fortuna ($25) and Monteverde ($30), with connections from there to a few of the north Pacific-coast beaches.

🚌 Bus Information **Auto Transportes San José–San Carlos** ☎ 256–8914 or 460–5032.
Pulmitan Liberia ☎ 256–9552. **Transmonteverde** ☎ 222–3854. **Transportes Deldu**
☎ 256–9072. **Transportes La Cañera** ☎ 222–3006. **Transportes Tilarán** ☎ 222–3854.
🚌 Shuttle Information **Fantasy Bus** ☎ 232–3681. **Interbus** ☎ 283–5573.

CAR RENTAL

Car rental in San José is the easiest option for traveling in this region,
but you'll find a few branch offices up here as well. Alamo has an office in La Fortuna and near Liberia's Daniel Oduber International Airport. Budget maintains a branch near Liberia's airport. Local firm Sol
Rentacar has an office across from the Hotel Bramadero in Liberia.
🚌 Major Agencies **Alamo** ⊠ 100 yards west of church, La Fortuna ☎ 479–9090 ⊠ 2
km [1 mi] north of Daniel Oduber Airport, Liberia ☎ 668–1111. **Budget** ⊠ 6 km [4 mi]
southwest of Daniel Oduber Airport, Liberia ☎ 668–1024.
🚌 Local Agencies **Sol Rentacar** ⊠ Pan-American Hwy., across from Hotel Bramadero,
Liberia ☎ 666–2222.

CAR TRAVEL

Road access to the northwest is by way of the paved two-lane Pan-American Highway (Carretera Interamericana, or CA1), which starts from
the west end of Paseo Colón in San José and runs northwest through
Cañas and Liberia and to Peñas Blancas (Nicaraguan border). The drive
to Liberia takes about three to four hours. Turnoffs to Monteverde, Arenal, and other destinations are often poorly marked—drivers must keep
their eyes open. The Monteverde (Santa Elena) turnoff is at Río Lagarto,
about 125 km (78 mi) northwest of San José. From here, an unpaved
30-km (19-mi) track snakes dramatically up through hilly farming country; it takes 1½ to 2 hours to negotiate it, less by four-wheel-drive vehicle. At the junction for Santa Elena, bear right for the reserve.

The turnoff for Tilarán and the northwestern end of Laguna de Arenal
lies in the town of Cañas. At Liberia, Highway 21 west leads to the beaches
of the northern Nicoya Peninsula. To reach San Carlos, La Fortuna, and
Caño Negro from San José, a picturesque drive (Highway 35) takes you
up through the coffee plantations and over the Cordillera Central by
way of Sarchí and Zarcero.

On the Pan-American Highway (CA1) north of Liberia, the first turn
for Rincón de la Vieja is easy to miss. Look for the Guardia Rural station on the right around 5 km (3 mi) north of town; turn inland and
head for Curubandé. Turnoffs for Santa Rosa National Park and La Cruz
on CA1 are well marked. Because of the nearness of the border, you need
to stop at two police checkpoints on the Pan-American Highway south
of La Cruz.

From the easterly zone of Arenal and the Cordillera de Tilarán (La Fortuna), you can head west by way of the road, badly potholed in sections, around Laguna de Arenal. For the paved road (Highway 4) that
parallels the Nicaraguan border and loops west all the way to La Cruz,
follow the signs out of Tanque (east of La Fortuna) northwest to San
Rafael de Guatuso, Upala, and Santa Cecilia.

ROAD
CONDITIONS
Four-wheel-drive vehicles are recommended, but not essential, at least
not in the dry season, for most roads. If you don't rent a four-wheel-
drive vehicle, at least rent a car with high clearance—you'll be glad you
did. Many rental agencies insist you take a four-wheel-drive vehicle if
you mention Monteverde as part of your itinerary. The most important
thing to know is that short drives can take a long time when the road
is potholed or torn up. Plan accordingly. Most minor roads are unpaved
and either muddy in rainy season or dusty in dry season—the pavement

holds out only so far, and then dirt, dust, mud, potholes, and other impediments interfere with driving conditions and prolong hours spent behind the wheel.

The Pan-American Highway (CA1) and other paved roads run to the Nicaraguan border; paved roads run west to small towns like Filadelfia and La Cruz. The roads into Rincón de la Vieja are unpaved and very slow; figure on an hour from the highway, and be prepared to walk the last ½ mi to the Las Pailas entrance. The road into Santa Rosa National Park is smooth going as far as the ruins of La Casona. Beyond that, it gets dicey and very steep in places. The National Park Service encourages you to walk, rather than drive, to the beach. A couple of dirt roads lead into various sections of Guanacaste National Park.

EMERGENCIES
In case of any emergency, dial 911, or one of the numbers below.
🚩 Emergency Services Fire ☎ 118. Police ☎ 911. Traffic Police ☎ 227–8030.
🚩 Hospitals Hospital de Los Chiles ✉ Hwy. 35, Los Chiles ☎ 471–1045. Hospital de San Carlos ✉ 2 km [1 mi] north of Central Park, Ciudad Quesada ☎ 460–1176. Hospital Dr. Enrique Baltodano ✉ across from stadium, Liberia ☎ 666–0011.

ENGLISH-LANGUAGE MEDIA
Librería Chunches in Santa Elena maintains a good selection of books, magazines, and day-old U.S. newspapers in English.
🚩 English-Speaking Bookstores Librería Chunches ✉ 45 m [50 yards] south of Banco Nacional, Santa Elena ☎ 645–5147.

TAXIS
Official red taxis hang out at designated taxi stands in La Fortuna, Ciudad Quesada, and Tilarán. Monteverde's rugged vehicles always manage to navigate the rough roads. Catch one on the main street in Santa Elena. Elsewhere, taxi service is much less official, with private individuals providing rides. To be on the safe side, ask your hotel or restaurant to call one for you.

VISITOR INFORMATION
The ubiquitous TOURIST INFORMATION signs around La Fortuna and Monteverde are really storefront travel agencies hoping to sell you tours rather than provide unbiased sources of information.

The tourist office in San José has information covering the northwest, including maps, bus schedules, and brochures. It's next to the Museo de Oro, beneath the Plaza de la Cultura, and is open weekdays 9–12:30 and 1:30–5. In Santa Elena, the local chamber of commerce operates a Monteverde tourist office called CETAM, across from the hardware store, open daily 9–6.
🚩 Tourist Information CETAM ✉ 150 yards downhill from La Esperanza Supermarket, Santa Elena ☎ 645–5771. Instituto Costarricense de Turismo (ICT) ✉ C. 5 between Avdas. Central and 2, Barrio La Catedral, San José ☎ 222–1090.

THE NICOYA PENINSULA

4

FODOR'S CHOICE

El Camarón Dorado, *Brasilito*

Hotel Capitán Suizo, *Tamarindo*

Hotel Punta Islita, *Punta Islita*

Lazy Wave Food Company, *Tamarindo*

Sueño del Mar, *Playa Langosta*

HIGHLY RECOMMENDED

RESTAURANTS

Marie's Restaurant, *Playa Flamingo*

La Puesta del Sol, *Playa Junquillal*

El Sano Banano Restaurant, *Montezuma*

El Sol y La Luna, *Playa del Coco*

HOTELS

Cabinas El Sano Banano, *Montezuma*

Colores del Pacífico, *Playa Flamingo*

Guacamaya Lodge, *Santa Cruz*

Hotel Amor de Mar, *Montezuma*

Hotel Giada, *Sámara*

Hotel Playa Negra, *Playa Negra*

Hotel El Velero, *Hermosa*

Hotel Villa Casa Blanca, *Playa Ocotal*

Land Ho! at Hotel Villa Serena, *Playa Junquillal*

Milarepa, *Malpaís*

Nature Lodge Finca Los Caballos, *Montezuma*

Resort Florblanca, *Malpaís*

Tambor Tropical, *Tambor*

Tango Mar Resort, *Tambor*

Villa Alegre, *Playa Langosta*

Updated by
Dorothy
MacKinnon

MOST FAMOUS FOR ITS MILES of palm-flanked beaches, Nicoya is also ecologically rich with limestone caverns, bird-filled river deltas, and tracts of wet and dry forest. Watch surfers master the Pacific's white-and-blue waves or catch a glimpse of turtles laying their eggs at Playa Grande on a midnight tour and you'll know why you're in Nicoya. Separated from the mainland by the Gulf of Nicoya, the peninsula is a roughly thumb-shape spit of land comprising the southwestern section of the province of Guanacaste. Its southern end, including Playa Naranjo, Tambor, and Montezuma, contains part of the Puntarenas province.

The Guanacastecos, descendants of the Chorotegan Indians and early Spanish settlers, started many of the traditions now referred to as typically Costa Rican. Chief Nicoya welcomed the *conquistadores* in 1523, and the name lives on in his namesake town and peninsula. Centuries later, the dry forest was cleared to create vast cattle ranges, lending a *sabanero* (cowboy) flavor to the landscape and culture. A strong folk-loric character is still evident here. As you travel down the peninsula, you might encounter traditional costumes, folk dancing, and music during seasonal fiestas and rodeos, as well as meals made from recipes handed down from colonial times.

As a travel destination, Nicoya—especially the coastal areas—attracts earthy ecotourists and their younger, backpack- and surfboard-toting cousins in search of environmental enlightenment or good waves. But it also attracts sun- and golf seekers, lured by azure pools and mani-cured putting greens bathed in tropical sun and content to admire caged toucans in plush hotel lobbies. The area has received huge amounts of investment and is under immense development pressure—at this writing, a Four Seasons hotel with a golf course was under construction in the huge Papagayo Peninsula resort area. The endless miles of untracked beaches and thousands of acres of wilderness are occasionally interspersed with sprawling, all-inclusive resort behemoths.

Exploring the Nicoya Peninsula

Bear in mind that aside from the Carretera Interamericana (Pan-American Highway, or CA1), many of the roads in this region are of the pit-ted, pocked rock-and-dirt variety, with the occasional river rushing across. Covering seemingly short distances can require long hours be-hind the wheel, and four-wheel drive is often essential. If you can swing it, fly instead; some beach resorts, such as Tamarindo, Carrillo, and Tam-bor, have nearby airstrips. Many northern beach resorts are most eas-ily reached from the international airport at Liberia.

About the Restaurants
New restaurants with international flavors are sprouting up around the Pacific beach resorts. Dining prices are approaching North American heights, but so is the quality of food and service. Seafood is abundant, but be sure to ask the market price for lobster and shrimp, which can be surprisingly expensive.

About the Hotels
Nicoya has a good mix of quality hotels, nature lodges, and more basic *cabinas* (cottages). Plenty act like B&Bs and include breakfast in the rate. It's wise to reserve ahead for the dry season (December–April), espe-cially weekends, when Ticos can fill beach hotels to bursting. A num-ber of luxury hotels line the coast, catering to an upscale clientele.

	WHAT IT COSTS				
	$$$$	$$$	$$	$	¢
RESTAURANTS	over $25	$20–$25	$10–$20	$5–$10	under $5
HOTELS	over $200	$125–$200	$75–$125	$35–$75	under $35

Restaurant prices are per-person for a main course at dinner. Hotel prices are for two people in a standard double room in high season, excluding service and tax (16.4%).

Timing

Averaging just 65″ of rain per year, the Nicoya Peninsula and much of Guanacaste constitute Costa Rica's driest zone. The dry season, from December to April, is generally the best time to visit Costa Rica, but the northwest, especially the Nicoya Peninsula, is most appealing in the rainy season (barring only the *really* wet months of September and October, when the roads become quagmires of mud and potholes). The Guanacastecos call the rainy season the "green" season, and that it is: the countryside—tending toward brown and arid the rest of the year—blooms lush and green from a few hours of rain each day. It's warm and sunny before and after the rain. The roads may be muddy, but there are far fewer tourists in the rainy season, and prices are lower everywhere. If you're bent on turtle-watching, you have to come during the dry season, but for most other activities any time of year will do. A good bet would be to travel in November, April, or May, around the edges of the dry season.

THE NICOYA COAST

Strung along the coast of the Nicoya Peninsula are sparkling sand beaches lined with laid-back fishing communities, along with hotels and resorts in every price category. Don't be in a rush to get anywhere; take things one hour at a time and you'll soon be as mellow as the locals. Tourism is still relatively new here. Only 20 years ago, fishing and cattle ranching were the area's mainstays. Development is picking up speed, bringing with it the advantages of sophisticated restaurants, hotels, and shops selling international surf gear and beachwear. But roads are only starting to catch up, so you'll find the interesting anomaly of a fabulous, world-class restaurant or hotel plunked at the end of a tortuous dirt road. Open-air bars, beach barbecue parties, and some traditional marimba folk music can be found at night, as well as sports bars with satellite TVs offering Monday Night Football. But after watching one of Nicoya's magnificent sunsets, most visitors head to bed early in order to catch the early morning waves, fishing boats, and wildlife walks.

Liberia

❶ *234 km (145 mi) northwest of San José.*

North of San José on the Pan-American Highway, Liberia is a low-rise, grid-plan cattle-market town with a huge central square dominated by a not-so-pretty modern church. As the capital of Guanacaste province, it's the gateway to several spectacular and biologically important national parks and turtle-nesting sites on the Pacific coast. More importantly, it is also a gateway for the coastal beaches. The jet runway at Liberia's Daniel Oduber International Airport serves both national and international flights, with direct flights from Atlanta, making it the arrival point of choice for many travelers. Bus travelers also change buses here for onward travel to Nicoya's Pacific beaches. Pleasant and pros-

4

The ideal Nicoya Peninsula trip can be comfortably divided between lazy days on the beach, swims in the surf, and hikes and leisurely exploration of natural sights—caverns, forests, rivers, and estuaries. The beach towns and resorts can be clustered into three loose geographical groups: those on the south end of the peninsula, accessible by ferry from Puntarenas or by plane to Tambor; areas in the central peninsula, accessible by plane to Punta Islita, Carrillo, and Nosara or by car via the new Río Tempisque Bridge or via the roads through Carmona, Curime, and Nicoya; and towns on the northern part of the peninsula, accessible by plane to Tamarindo or Liberia or by car through Liberia and Comunidad.

Numbers in the text correspond to numbers in the margin and on the Nicoya Peninsula map.

If you have 3 days
Fly to 🖼 **Tamarindo** ❼, 🖼 **Nosara** ⓬, **Tambor** ⓲, 🖼 **Punta Islita** ⓯, or **Playa Carrillo** ⓮ for a three-night stay at a beach resort. If you stay in Tambor or 🖼 **Montezuma** ⓳, a short drive takes you to Cabo Blanco, where you can hike through the **Cabo Blanco Strict Nature Reserve** to deserted Playa Cabo Blanco, a diving and frolicking ground for hundreds of pelicans. You can also visit the 🖼 **Curú National Wildlife Refuge.** If you surf and are staying at the Florblanca Resort, hit the waves at **Malpaís** ⓴, just north of Cabo Blanco, reputed home of the largest surfing waves in Costa Rica.

Or spend three to five nights at a beach between 🖼 **Playa Hermosa** ❷ and 🖼 **Tamarindo** ❼. In season, you can also watch the leatherback turtles arrive by night at Las Baulas Marine National Park. For dedicated surfers, 🖼 **Playa Negra** ❿ and **Playa Avellanas** ❾ offer great access to excellent waves and plenty of other recreational pastimes. You can also shop for pottery in the nearby artisan towns of Guaitil and Santa Cruz.

If you have 5 days
Extend one of the three-day itineraries above into five days. Book a three-day sea-kayaking adventure that leaves from **Curú National Wildlife Refuge,** or just settle into a hotel in **Tambor** ⓲ for a couple of extra days of luxurious R&R.

If you have 7 days
Begin with some bird-watching in **Palo Verde National Park** ㉑ ⌐; then continue on through **Nicoya** ㉓ and Santa Cruz and overnight in 🖼 **Tamarindo** ❼ or at one of the beach resorts. Spend several days relaxing on the beach or exploring the Tamarindo and Río San Francisco estuaries north and south of Tamarindo, with nights watching turtles (in season) at **Las Baulas Marine National Park.** Fly to 🖼 **Tambor** ⓲, spending your nights here or in 🖼 **Montezuma** ⓳. Here you can hike to a seaside waterfall, bird- and animal-watch; swim in the lazy, sheltered waters of the southern Nicoya Peninsula; and book a sea-kayaking tour that leaves from **Curú National Wildlife Refuge.** You can spend three days exploring the ruggedly beautiful islands in the gulf before flying back to San José.

perous, Liberia is a good place to make a bank stop and do some shopping at the MegaSuper. Or, if you need a dose of American culture, you can drop in at the huge Burger King food court or catch a movie at the multiplex cinema, the only one in Guanacaste.

Where to Stay & Eat

¢–$ ✕ **Cafe Europa/The German Bakery.** Just south of the Liberia airport, you can stop in to fuel up on hearty German breads baked in a wood-fired oven or sample the strudels, bundt cakes, and flaky fruit pastries. Breakfast is served, along with robust bratwurst and sauerkraut lunches, in a rustic, shady café screened by greenery abloom with orchids. ⊠ *2 km (1 mi) south of Liberia Airport* ☎ *668–1081* ▤ *No credit cards.*

¢–$ ✕ **La Cocina de José.** Locals gather at this simple restaurant with an outdoor patio, gingham tablecloths, and upscale Tico fare. Fish is a specialty, with fresh tilapia served six different ways. A signature dish is sirloin steak tips in a spicy jalapeño sauce, unusual for Tico cuisine, which is generally mild. There's also tasty *comida rapida* (fast food), such as tacos, *chalupas* (crisp, flat tortillas topped with chicken or meat and salad), and hamburgers. ⊠ *C. 4, 100 m (110 yards) south and 25 m (13 ft) west of Farmacia Lux* ☎ *666–1202* ▤ *AE, D, MC, V.*

$ ▦ **Best Western Las Espuelas.** A smaller-scale alternative to El Sitio on the other side of town, this friendlier 44-room hotel is also shaded by a majestic guanacaste tree. Rooms face a landscaped courtyard and a large, sunny lap-size pool. The modern, fresh rooms have private terraces. The restaurant is off a cool, shady lobby with a fountain. ⊠ *2 km (1 mi) south of Liberia* ☎ *666–0144* 🖷 *666–2441* ⊕ *www.bestwestern.co.cr* ⇄ *44 rooms* ⟁ *Restaurant, cable TV, pool, outdoor hot tub, bar, conference center* ▤ *AE, D, MC, V* ⚏ *BP.*

$ ▦ **Best Western Hotel El Sitio.** If you're stopping for a night in Liberia, consider El Sitio for its spacious, modern rooms and extensive facilities: an Italian restaurant, a casino, two pools shaded by stately guanacaste trees, and a car-rental agency. It's basically a nondescript roadside motel, but the conveniences and free breakfast redeem it. ⊠ *South of Burger King complex on road heading west toward airport and beaches* ☎ *666–1211* 🖷 *666–2059* ⊕ *www.bestwestern.co.cr* ✉ *Apdo. 134–5000, Liberia* ⇄ *52 rooms* ⟁ *Restaurant, cable TV, 2 pools, spa, horseback riding, volleyball, casino, laundry service, meeting room, car rental* ▤ *AE, MC, V* ⚏ *BP.*

Playa Hermosa

❷ *35 km (22 mi) southwest of Liberia, 25 km (16 mi) southwest of airport.*

Playa Hermosa, not to be confused with the mainland beach of the same name south of Jacó, has a relaxed village atmosphere that recalls a Mexican beach town. The full length of the beach has long been occupied by hotels, restaurants, and homes, so the newer hotel behemoths and other developments have been forced to set up shop off the beach or on other beaches in the area. Playa Hermosa's crescent of grayish sand fronts a line of trees that provide a welcome respite from the heat of the sun. At the beach's north end, low tide creates wide, rock-lined tidal pools. Playa Panama, just to the north, is a dark-sand beach that is rapidly being developed with large all-inclusive resorts and luxury condominiums.

Where to Stay & Eat

$ ✕ **Aqua Sport.** You can shop for a beach picnic at the minimarket and liquor store, buy souvenirs in the gift shop, and rent equipment or a car or organize a water adventure here. Fish fillet stuffed with shrimp or oysters is one of the fresh seafood dishes served at this casual beach-

4

Beaches

Palms and tamarind trees line most Nicoya beaches, though the shrubby dry-forest vegetation of northwestern Guanacaste contrasts sharply with the tropical backdrops farther south, in Puntarenas province. Each beach along Nicoya's coast has its distinct merits. Playa Brasilito, for example, gives you a taste of life in a Costa Rican fishing village. Turtles nest at Playa Grande. Tamarindo, a long, white strand, shelters sailing fleets and has good beachfront bars. Playa Negra has some of Costa Rica's best surfing waves. Playa Santa Teresa has miles of tidal pools. Hemmed in by rocks, Playa Pelada is a gem, and a great spot for snorkeling. Nosara has a long beach backed by rich jungle, with tendrils of sea grape reaching to the water's edge. The long, clean Playa Guiones has a coral reef suitable for snorkeling. Perhaps the most beautiful beach in the country, Playa Carrillo fronts an idyllic half-moon bay. The peninsula's great advantage is its climate, which in the rainy season (May–December) is far drier than that of other areas. Beware of riptides while swimming in surfing waters.

Festivals

Santa Cruz celebrates its saint's day on January 15 with marimba music, folk dances, and bullfights. On July 16 Puntarenas honors its patron saint with a colorful regatta and carnival. The annexation of Guanacaste is celebrated July 17–25 in Liberia with folk dances, bullfights, and rodeos. Nicoya's December 12 festival of La Yeguita includes a solemn procession, dancing, fireworks, and bullfights. Almost every small town in Guanacaste has a rodeo fiesta once a year, with carnival rides and the Costa Rican rodeo version of bullfighting. It's wild! Before you go, be warned that men do torment the bulls to rile them up and riders get thrown violently and are occasionally gored.

Surfing

Costa Rica was "discovered" in the 1960s surf-film classic *The Endless Summer* and revisited in the sequel. But with its miles of coastline marked by innumerable points, rock reefs, river-mouth sandbars, and other wave-shaping geological configurations, the Nicoya Peninsula would have emerged as a surfer's paradise in any case. Tamarindo is a good base for some decent sandbar and rock-reef breaks, a superb low-tide river-mouth break, and the consistently high quality Playa Grande beach break. Sámara, Guiones, and Nosara all have decent beach breaks. Avellanas' surf spots range from beach breaks to rock-reef breaks to river-mouth sandbar breaks. Witches Rock, in Santa Rosa National Park, and Playa Langosta both have right river-mouths. Ollie's Point offers excellent right point-break waves. Playa Negra's right rock-reef break was showcased in *The Endless Summer II*. Malpaís, just above Cabo Blanco, is hit by some of the largest waves in Costa Rica. In all these places, beware of riptides.

Turtle-Watching

The Nicoya Peninsula provides ace opportunities to watch the nesting rituals of sea turtles. Olive Ridley Sea Turtles nest year-round, but the peak season runs July to October. Leatherbacks arrive between October and April, though nesting is largely over by mid-February. Occasionally you can see Pacific Green Sea Turtles. Playa Nancite in Santa Rosa National Park and the Ostional National Wildlife Refuge are prime areas for watching the mass *arribadas,* or nestings, of thousands of Olive Ridleys.

More accessible are Playas Langosta and Grande, which used to teem Leatherbacks. Sadly, numbers have dwindled in recent years. Word of mouth has it that locals at Junquillal and Langosta are still stealing turtle eggs as if there were an endless supply. To watch the turtles, go with a legitimate guide and follow the rules to ensure the turtles' safety. Playa Grande's turtle tours are very well organized.

---

front restaurant. For big appetites, there's a huge, grilled mixed-seafood platter. ⊠ *Beach road; heading south, take second entrance to Playa Hermosa and follow signs* ☎ 672–0050 ▭ *AE, MC, V.*

$$ ⌂ **Resort de Playa Villa Acacia.** Luxury arrives in Playa Hermosa with this lovely new resort. Spacious rooms and private octagonal villas with hardwood details reside in a tranquil garden with brick paths and a round pool. Particularly impressive are the large, tiled baths with tubs and bidets and the vanity sinks, sensibly separated from the bathrooms. Each room has a private terrace. The café makes espresso with professional Italian machines. The beach is a short walk away. ⊠ *Beach road; heading south, take second entrance to Playa Hermosa* ☎ 672–1000 🖨 672–0272 ⊕ *www.villaacacia.com* ⟿ *8 rooms, 8 villas* ⚐ *Restaurant, café, refrigerators, cable TV, pool, Internet, conference center; no room phones* ▭ *AE, MC, V* ⦿ *CP.*

★ $ ⌂ **Hotel El Velero.** Spacious, attractive white rooms with arched doorways, terra-cotta tiles, bamboo furniture, and large windows create an air of elegance at this two-story beachfront hotel. A satellite TV room keeps you in touch with the world, and the hotel runs daily snorkeling cruises on a handsome 38-ft sailboat. In the restaurant, sample the jumbo shrimp with rice and vegetables or the always fresh mahimahi. Or come for barbecue night with live music on Wednesday and Saturday. ⊠ *100 m (110 yards) north of Aqua Sport* ☎ 672–0036 🖨 672–0016 ⊕ *www.costaricahotel.net* ⟿ *22 rooms* ⚐ *Restaurant, in-room safes, pool, snorkeling, boating, jet skiing, volleyball, bar, laundry service; no room phones, no room TVs* ▭ *AE, MC, V.*

$ ⌂ **Hotel Cabinas Playa Hermosa.** Ocean breezes, the sound of waves lapping on the shore, and a garden shaded by immense trees are the main attractions at this budget hotel favored by backpackers. Rooms in the one-story, pink-brick units are not all in tip-top shape; each has a curious hodgepodge of very cheap and very good furniture and art. The funky restaurant has an intriguing retro look, reminiscent of a 1960s writers' colony in a South Pacific backwater. ⊠ *1 km (½ mi) south of first entrance to Playa Hermosa* ☎☎ 672–0046 ✉ *Apdo. 174, Playa del Coco* ⟿ *22 cabinas* ⚐ *Restaurant, beach, laundry service; no a/c, no room phones, no room TVs* ▭ *V.*

Nightlife

Hotel El Velero hosts beach barbecues, with live music, on Wednesday and Saturday nights in high season. The **Monkey Bar** (⊠ main road to Playa Hermosa ☎ 672–0267) is a rollicking, round bar on stilts hiding behind a magnificent strangler fig tree. There's big-screen TV, darts, a pool table, and music every night. A Belgian chef cooks up *steak frites*. Bring insect repellent or the mosquitoes will feast on you.

The Outdoors

SCUBA DIVING Just off the beach at Hotel Sol Playa Hermosa (at north end of Playa Hermosa), **Bill Beard's Diving Safaris** (☎ 672–0012, 800/779–0055 in the U.S. 🖨 672–0231; 954/351–9740 in the U.S. ⊕ www.costaricadiving. net) runs a complete range of scuba activities, from beginner training

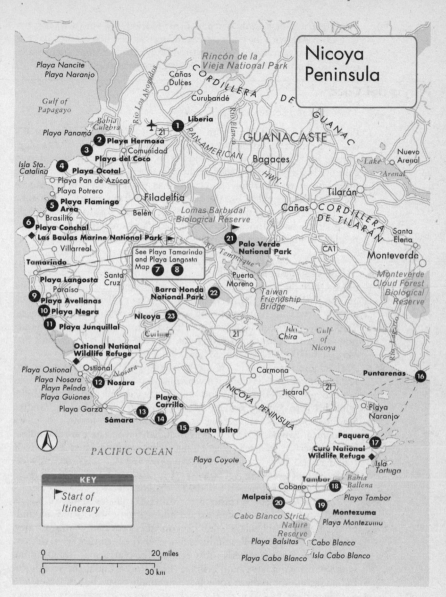

to open-water certification courses, and even multitank dives at more than 30 tantalizing sites off the Guanacaste coast. His guides and trainers know underwater Guanacaste—alive with rays, sharks, fish, and turtles. Prices range from $50 for a one-tank afternoon dive to $375 for a PADI (Professional Association of Diving Instructors) open-water certification course.

WATER SPORTS At the general store–cum–restaurant **Aqua Sport** (☎ 672–0050), you can rent water-sports equipment or organize a fishing or surfing trip. On the beach, below Bill Beard's dive shop, an independent **kiosk** rents boogie boards, plastic kayaks, Jet Skis, and other water toys.

Shopping
You can get any kind of souvenir you want at two shopping emporia conveniently located on the road between Liberia airport and the turnoff for

Playa Hermosa. **Kaltak Art and Craft Market** (⊠ south of airport ☎ 668–1048), with the giant parrot and toucan perched outside, has five rooms of quality crafts and gifts. **La Gran Nicoya** (⊠ just before small bridge over Río Tempisque ☎ 667–0062) has more souvenirs than crafts.

Playa del Coco

❸ *35 km (22 mi) southwest of Liberia.*

Playa del Coco has a reputation as a slightly seedy beachfront town. It's one of the most accessible beaches in Guanacaste, so it serves as a playground for Costa Rica's college kids, who, like students the world over, cannot always be trusted to clean up after themselves. The beaches are often littered with garbage, and Christmas and Semana Santa in March are impossibly crowded. But the quieter, north part of the beach has some lovely grown-up restaurants and hotels. Coco's scruffy pier, slightly down-at-the-heels appearance, and trinket and souvenir stands are appealing, though, if you like your resorts with some local color.

Where to Stay & Eat

$–$$ ✕ **Bob's Louisiana Bar & Grill.** This second-story restaurant is cool and breezy, but the Cajun cuisine is hot, with authentic jambalaya and gumbo. Fish is fresh, thanks to one of the owner's fleet of fishing boats, and it's served any way you like it, with a choice of 10 intriguing sauces. Save room for the moist, coconutty banana bread pudding with bourbon sauce. ⊠ *Main road through town, across street from Hotel Coco Verde* ☎ *670–0882* ▤ *AE, MC, V.*

★ **$** ✕ **El Sol y La Luna.** Finding haute-Italian cuisine in a romantic alfresco restaurant in Playa del Coco is a welcome surprise. Host Alessandro Tolo has brought his design ideas and superb jazz CD collection from Rome, while his wife, Silvia Casu, has brought culinary skills from her native Sardinia. Both food and service are memorable, with homemade pasta and homegrown basil lending authentic Italian flavor. There are also homebaked desserts, a wide selection of Italian wines, and two other distinctively Italian tastes: sparkling San Pellegrino mineral water and aromatic sambuca. ⊠ *La Puerta del Sol hotel, 180 m (200 yards) to right off main road to Playa del Coco* ☎ *670–0195* ▤ *AE, MC, V.*

$$$ ✕▦ **La Puerta del Sol.** A tranquil enclosure of stylish suites overlooks a formal garden with sculpted shrubs and a lovely pool. An aqua-and-tangerine color scheme in the modern guest rooms creates an airy, Mediterranean look. Filmy fabrics and even the furniture seem to float on a breeze. King-size beds roost atop adobe platforms, and gleaming white bathrooms have high ceilings. El Sol y La Luna, the wonderful Italian restaurant in the garden, has homemade pasta, Italian wines, and Sardinian flare. ⊠ *180 m (200 yards) right (north) off main road to Playa del Coco* ☎ *670–0195* 🖷 *670–0650* ⊕ *www.lapuertadelsol.com* ⇗ *10 suites ♨ Restaurant, in-room safes, cable TV, pool, gym, Ping-Pong* ▤ *AE, MC, V* ❡❍❘ *BP.*

$ ▦ **Villa Flores.** The American owners have prettied up this 10-room B&B with floral motifs inside and out. The gardens are replanted, and stenciled flowers border renovated bedroom walls. Rooms are spacious, with high ceilings. The pool is inviting, as are the hammocks slung between tall palm trees. A tiled terrace restaurant serves breakfast and, in high season, dinner, too. ⊠ *180 m (200 yards) east of main road* ☎ *670–0269* 🖷 *670–0787* ✆ *Apdo. 2, Playa del Coco* ⇗ *9 rooms, 3 suites ♨ Restaurant, fans, pool, gym, hot tub, laundry service; no room phones, no TV in some rooms* ▤ *V* ❡❍❘ *BP.*

$ ▦ **Villa del Sol.** The French-Canadian owners of this B&B offer seven quiet, spacious, light-filled rooms in a contemporary building with a pool out front. There are also open-plan studios, each with kitchen where you can cook your own breakfast, a queen-size bed, and a pull-out trundle bed that sleeps two. Well away from Coco's main drag, Villa del Sol is just 100 m (110 yards) from the quiet part of the beach. Views of the lush tropical garden and the ocean are best from the upstairs balconies. ✉ *1 km (½ mi) north of Villa Flores* 🏠 *670–0085* ⊕ *www.villadelsol. com* 🏠 *Apdo. 052–5019, Playa del Coco* 🛏 *7 rooms, 5 with bath; 6 studios* ⟁ *Some kitchens, pool, laundry service* 🚭 *AE, MC, V* ⵙ *BP.*

Nightlife

There's happy hour and gambling at the **Hotel Coco Verde** (✉ main road through town). **Banana Surf** (✉ across street from casino), a second-floor disco-restaurant, has dancing until 2 AM. Occasionally, there are dances down by the dock whenever a live band comes to town, but the dancing doesn't get under way until after 10 PM.

Playa Ocotal

④ *3 km (2 mi) west of Playa del Coco.*

Despite its proximity to student-thronged Coco, Playa Ocotal is a serene spot, with a lilliputian crescent of beach sheltered by rocks. Right at the entrance to the Gulf of Papagayo, it's a good place for sportfishing enthusiasts to hole up between excursions. There's good diving at Las Corridas, just 1 km (½ mi) away, as well as excellent snorkeling in nearby coves and islands.

Where to Stay

$$–$$$ 🏨 **El Ocotal Beach Resort.** High above secluded Ocotal Bay, this luxury hotel has a sportfishing fleet and a day spa. Rooms have huge French windows and unsurpassed views of verdant coast looking north to the Peninsula Santa Elena. The freestanding triangular bungalows down the hill are larger, with polished wood floors and private pools. ✉ *3 km (2 mi) south of Playa del Coco, down paved road* 🏠 *670–0321* 🏠 *670–0083* ⊕ *www.ocotalresort.com* 🏠 *Apdo. 1, Playa del Coco* 🛏 *59 rooms, 5 suites, 12 bungalows* ⟁ *Restaurant, fans, in-room safes, cable TV, tennis court, 3 pools, spa, dive shop, boating, horseback riding, bar, laundry service, Internet* 🚭 *AE, MC, V* ⵙ *BP.*

★ $$ 🏨 **Hotel Villa Casa Blanca.** Secluded and romantic, and surely one of the finest B&Bs in Costa Rica, the Casa Blanca occupies a hillside Mediterranean-style building buried in a bower of tropical plantings. The intimate, junglelike setting attracts numerous colorful birds (and talkative pet parrots are attracted by breakfast). Victorian-influenced rooms comfort you with pleasant wood details and artwork, canopy beds, and enormous bathrooms with mirrored walls. The pool is small but pretty, with a bridge and a sundeck. ✉ *Just inside gated entrance to El Ocotal Beach Resort, on paved road* 🏠 *670–0518* 🏠 *670–0448* ⊕ *www. informationcostarica.com* 🏠 *Apdo. 176–5019, Playa Ocotal* 🛏 *10 rooms, 5 suites* ⟁ *Pool, outdoor hot tub; no room phones, no room TVs, no smoking* 🚭 *AE, MC, V* ⵙ *BP.*

Nightlife

At sunset on the beach below El Ocotal, you can enjoy a quiet margarita with a view at **Father Rooster Sports Bar & Grill** (✉ El Ocotal Beach Resort 🏠 670–0321). The action heats up later in the evening with big-screen TV, music, pool, beach volleyball, and Tex-Mex bar food. During peak holiday weeks, huge crowds of partyers descend on the bar to dance by torchlight. For a sunset cruise, set sail on **Spanish Dancer** (🏠 395–6090 or 672–0012), a 36-ft MacGregor racing catamaran. The three-hour voyage includes appetizers and open bar and a chance to see dolphins, whales, and turtles. Tickets are $45, from December to May only, and cruises depart at 3 PM.

Playa Flamingo Area

⑤ *35 km (22 mi) west of Belén, 75 km (47 mi) south of Playa Ocotal*

Flamingo was one of the first of the northern Nicoya beaches to experience the wonders of overscale resort development, a fact immortalized in the huge Aurola Flamingo Marina Resort, which dominates the landscape. The beach, however, is still a welcome oasis, and a fleet of sportfishing boats is moored in the busy marina. To get to Playa Flamingo from Playa Ocotal, you drive northeast to Playa Coco, then east on the main road, south to Belén, and then west. If you have four-wheel drive and an excellent sense of direction, you can attempt to drive (dry season only) the 16-km (11-mi) Monkey Trail, which cuts through the mountains from Coco to Flamingo. But even some Ticos get lost on this route.

Playa Pan de Azúcar (Sugar Bread Beach) lends its only hotel a quality that can be hard to come by in this area: privacy. There are good islands for snorkeling just offshore. ⊠ *8 km (5 mi) north of Playa Flamingo, at end of hilly dirt road.*

With more development than Azúcar, and less than Flamingo, **Playa Potrero,** between the two is a wide, white-sand stretch. The road from Flamingo is dusty and bumpy, so this beach tends to be less crowded. You can rent boats from area hotels to go snorkeling. ⊠ *3 km (2 mi) north of Flamingo along rough road.*

There's excellent swimming as well as diving around **Isla Santa Catalina,** 10 km (6 mi) offshore from Playa Potrero. You can rent a boat from local hotels to make the trip. The island is also a bird-watching destination: it's one of the few places in Costa Rica where the bridled tern nests (March–September).

Where to Stay & Eat

★ $ ✕ **Marie's Restaurant.** At the north end of the beach, look for this veranda restaurant furnished with sliced-tree-trunk tables painted with sea creatures. Here you can settle back for generous helpings of fresh seafood at reasonable prices. Friendly Marie makes delightful ceviche and a delicious *plato de mariscos* (shrimp, lobster, and oysters served with garlic butter, potatoes, and salad). Save room for the dark and delicious banana-chocolate bread pudding. ⊠ *Main road, near north end of beach* ☎ 654–4136 ▭ V.

★ $$$ ▥ **Colores del Pacífico.** From high atop a commanding cliff, this small, exquisite hotel presides over Potrero Bay. It looks like a page out of *Architectural Digest.* The very modern, minimalist design incorporates terracotta walls, Mexican-tile floors, sculptural cactus plantings, and indirect lighting. Each room has a dramatic bed "treatment" by the Belgian interior designer–owner. Fresh flowers, fruit, and cookies greet you in your room, which has a private terrace with hammocks. Breakfast and lunch are served in a thatch-roof restaurant with a sweeping view of ocean and the infinity-edge pool, where there is aqua exercise everyday. Yoga is also available. ⊠ *At intersection of roads leading out of Flamingo and to Playa Potrero* ☎ 654–4769 ⎙ 654–4976 ⊕ *www.coloresdelpacifico. com* ⇆ *6 rooms* ⚭ *Dining room, minibars, pool, fitness classes, snorkeling, waterskiing, fishing, bar; no room TVs, no children under 12* ▭ *AE, MC, V* ☉ *Closed Sept.–Oct.* ▯◉▮ *BP.*

$$–$$$ ▥ **Hotel Sugar Beach.** A thin, curving white-sand beach is the view from this American-owned hotel, under renovation at this writing. Most of

the rooms have idyllic ocean views, and each room's wooden door has a hand-carved image of a local bird or animal. Bright yellow-and-blue fabrics along with watermelon, aqua, and yellow walls make the rooms feel fresh. The open-air rotunda restaurant serves good seafood dishes. The hotel offers surfing at Witches Rock and turtle-watching. Several golf courses are nearby. ⊠ *8 km (5 mi) north of Playa Flamingo, Playa Pan de Azúcar* ☎ *654–4242* ⊟ *654–4239* ⊕ *www.sugar-beach.com* ✉ *Apdo. 90, Santa Cruz* ↪ *22 rooms, 3 suites, 1 apartment, 2 houses* ♨ *Restaurant, bar, minibars, some kitchens, cable TV, pool, snorkeling, boating, horseback riding, bar, laundry service* ⊟ *AE, D, MC, V.*

$$ ▦ **Flamingo Marina Resort.** These hillside pink buildings with orange, yellow, and maroon tile roofs have more personality than most of the other large resorts in the area. The fashionably decorated rooms, wash-painted in a mango hue, have terra-cotta lamps, hand-carved wooden furniture, and shell-shape sinks. The luxurious condos have full modern kitchens and spacious sitting areas with leather couches. Nearly all rooms and condos have large verandas with excellent views of the sea below. ⊠ *On hill above Flamingo Bay* ☎ *654–4141* ⊟ *654–4035* ⊕ *www.flamingomarina.com* ✉ *Apdo. 321–1002, San José* ☎ *290–1858* ⊟ *231–1858* ↪ *75 condos, 22 rooms, 18 suites* ♨ *Restaurant, in-room safes, some kitchens, minibars, cable TV, tennis court, 4 pools, wading pool, dive shop, 2 bars, laundry service, meeting room* ⊟ *AE, DC, MC, V* ⦿ *CP.*

$ ▦ **Hotel Villaggio Flor de Pacífico.** Tuscany meets Costa Rica in an ambitious Italian-owned complex of red-roofed villas that will eventually include a shopping "village" and theater. Rooms have wooden ceilings and big screened windows that catch the breezes. The alfresco restaurant and pizzeria is elegant, with crisp tablecloths and a bountiful breakfast buffet. The property is very flat and not right on the beach, but the gardens are lovely and the curvaceous pool is enticing. There's a scuba-diving school on-site. ⊠ *200 m (220 yards) east of Playa Potrero and 1 km (½ mi) north of Flamingo* ☎ *654–4661* ⊟ *654–4663* ⊕ *www.hotelflordepacifico.com* ↪ *65 villas* ♨ *Restaurant, pool, piano bar; no a/c in some rooms, no room TVs* ⊟ *AE, MC, V* ⦿ *BP.*

$ ▦ **Mariner Inn.** Near the marina, this two-story white building is the cheapest hotel in Flamingo. The tiny, compact rooms, with firm beds and small TVs built into the dressers, feel like boat cabins. The upstairs bar is the main focus of the hotel with lots of sunburnt fishermen exchanging fish stories. The hotel happily arranges sportfishing trips. ⊠ *Near Flamingo Marina* ☎ *654–4081* ⊟ *654–4024* ↪ *11 rooms, 1 suite* ♨ *Restaurant, fans, cable TV, pool, bar, Internet, laundry service; no room phones.* ⊟ *AE, MC, V.*

Playa Conchal

❻ *35 km (22 mi) west of Belén; 1 km (½ mi) south of Playa Brasilito and 8 km (5 mi) south of Flamingo.*

Playa Conchal, one of Guanacaste's finest and most secluded beaches, is aptly named—it's sprinkled with shells. The sprawling Paradisus Playa Conchal resort looms large here, and the road leading to it is sprinkled with trendy new restaurants, shops, and small hotels.

A small fishing village just north of Conchal, charming **Brasilito** has a ramshackle row of houses that huddle around its main square, which doubles as the soccer field. Before high tide, boats line up just off a white-sand beach that is the equal of Flamingo minus the megahotels. ⊠ *1 km (½ mi) north of Playa Conchal.*

Where to Stay & Eat

$–$$ ✕ **El Camarón Dorado.** This bougainvillea-drenched bar-restaurant de-
Fodor'sChoice rives much of its appeal from its shaded setting on Brasilito's beautiful
★ beach. Some tables are right on the beach, with the surf lapping just yards
away, and a small-vessel fishing fleet anchored offshore assures you of
the freshness of the bountiful portions of seafood on the menu. Thanks
to its spectacular sunset views, this is a popular place for early evening
drinks. A van can pick up diners with reservations from Flamingo and
even Tamarindo hotels. ⊠ *200 m (220 yards) north of Brasilito Plaza,
Brasilito* ☎ *654–4028* ⊟ *AE, MC, V.*

$$$$ ▦ **Paradisus Playa Conchal Beach & Golf Resort.** The former Meliá Playa
Conchal has moved up a notch to become a deluxe, all-inclusive Paradisus resort, one of only four in the world. From the enormous, open-
air, marble-floored lobby, you can survey the massive grounds,
encompassing almost 4 square km (1½ square mi) of manicured golf
course, bungalows, tennis courts, the largest pool in Central America,
and a distant beach. Suites, set in low-slung, colonial-style houses, are
large and luxurious. The per-person rate is over $200 per night. The restau-
rants serve a range of à la carte international fare. ⊠ *Entrance less than
1 km (½ mi) south of Brasilito, Playa Conchal* ☎ *654–4123* ☎ *654–4181*
⊕ *www.solmelia.com* ⇱ *292 suites* ⟡ *5 restaurants, in-room safes, minibars, cable TV, 18-hole golf course, 4 tennis courts, pool, gym, hair salon,
beach, jet skiing, bicycles, Internet, children's programs (ages 0–12), casino,
dance club, laundry service, meeting room* ⊟ *AE, MC, V* ⦿ *AI.*

¢ ▦ **Hotel Brasilito.** This simple establishment is just off the beach. Fronting
the sea is the hotel's wooden, open-air restaurant, its tables and chairs
arrayed beneath lazily turning ceiling fans. The sparely furnished but
comfortable rooms occupy both floors of an old but freshly painted two-
story wooden building behind the restaurant; ask for one of the two rooms
with unobstructed sea views. There is no hot water. ⊠ *Next to square
and soccer field, Brasilito* ☎ *654–4237* ☎ *654–4247* ⊕ *www.brasilito.
com* ⇱ *15 rooms* ⟡ *Restaurant, fans, snorkeling, horseback riding, laundry service, Internet; no a/c, no room phones, no room TVs* ⊟ *V.*

Tamarindo

▸ ❼ *37 km (23 mi) west of Belén.*

Tamarindo is a vibrant beach community with a great variety of restaurants, cabins, bars, and hotels at all price levels. Surfing is the main attraction here for both the young crowd that parties hard at beachfront
bars after a day riding the waves and for the gray-haired veterans who
combine surfing with golfing at nearby golf courses, including Hacienda Pinilla, an 18-hole championship course with ocean views. The
older nonsurfing crowd is attracted by the upscale beachfront hotels away
from the bustling town center. Developmental hustle is everywhere, ev-
idenced by the presence of condo projects and mini–strip malls. Still,
Tamarindo remains appealing because it's virtually self-contained: its
beaches are great for snorkeling, boating, kayaking, diving, surfing, and
just plain swimming; there are estuaries north and south of town for
bird- and animal-watching; and there are two turtle-nesting beaches
nearby—Playa Langosta to the south, and Playa Grande to the north.
With an airstrip just outside town, Tamarindo is also a convenient base
for exploring all of Guanacaste. Except for some sections through the
middle of town, the very dusty road is in dire need of paving. The
sickly-sweet smell in the air is from the molasses mixture poured on the
roads to keep dust down in the dry season.

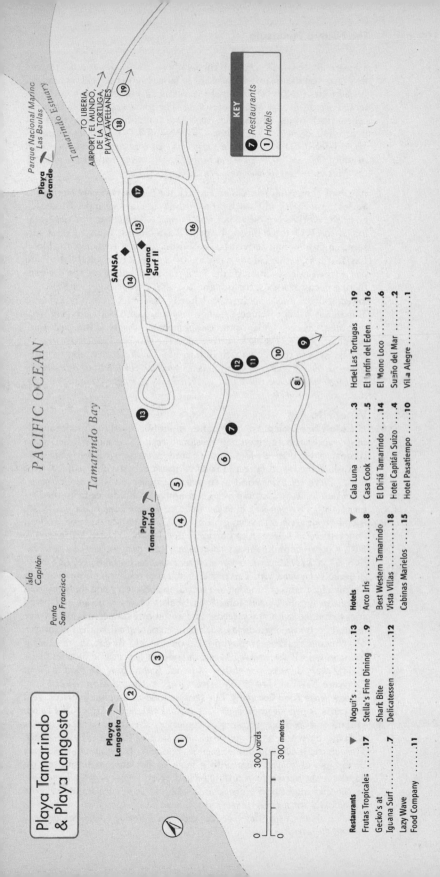

Playa Tamarindo & Playa Langosta

PACIFIC OCEAN

Isla Capitán

Punta San Francisco

Tamarindo Bay

Playa Langosta

Playa Tamarindo

Parque Nacional Marino Las Baulas

Playa Grande

Tamarindo Estuary

TO LIBERIA, AIRPORT, EL MUNDO, DE LA TORTUGA, PLAYA AVELLANES

SANSA

Iguana Surf II

KEY

7 *Restaurants*

1 *Hotels*

0 300 yards
0 300 meters

Restaurants

Frutas Tropicales	17
Gecko's at Iguana Surf	7
Lazy Wave Food Company	11
Nogui's	13
Stella's Fine Dining	9
Shark Bite Delicatessen	12

Hotels

Arco Iris	8
Best Western Tamarindo	18
Vista Villas	18
Cabinas Marielos	15
Cala Luna	3
Casa Cook	5
El Diriá Tamarindo	14
Hotel Capitán Suizo	4
Hotel Pasatiempo	10
Hotel Las Tortugas	19
El Jardín del Eden	16
El Mono Loco	6
Sueño del Mar	2
Villa Alegre	1

To learn about the life cycle of the Leatherback Turtles and the threats they face, visit the creative **El Mundo de la Tortuga** museum in Playa Grande. Audio tours (in English, Spanish, German, or French) through the interactive exhibits are 30 minutes long. The museum also conducts excellent turtle tours, which often occur late at night, sometimes till 3 AM, depending on turtle sightings. ⊠ *On road to Hotel Las Tortugas* ☎ *653–0471* ⊡ *$5* ☉ *Turtle tours daily during turtle nesting season (usually Oct.–Mar.) from 4* PM *onward, returning not earlier than 11* PM. *Museum 4* PM *until tours return. Closed June.*

North of Tamarindo, across an estuary, the **Parque Nacional Marino Las Baulas** marine park and beach protects the long **Playa Grande**. This beach hosts the world's largest visitation of nesting leatherback turtles (nesting season is October through April). Playa Grande is also a great surf spot. Environmental activist Lewis Wilson, also the owner of the Hotel Las Tortugas, struggled for a decade to get Las Baulas established and has a true understanding of the importance of balancing the oft-conflicting needs of locals, turtles, and tourists. An evening spent discussing ecotourism and ecopolitics with him is a real education. The adjacent **Tamarindo Wildlife Refuge,** a mangrove estuary with some excellent birdwatching, has been under some developmental pressure of late. Just south of Tamarindo, accessible by dirt road, is the **Río San Francisco,** with an estuary system that's also rich in bird life. Unlike Tamarindo, it's free of motorboats. ⊠ *Playa Grande is 33 km (20 mi) north of Tamarindo by rough road; most tours go by motorboat, a short ride across the estuary* ☎ *653–0470.*

Where to Eat

$$ ✕ **Stella's Fine Dining.** For a romantic night out, head to this elegant alfresco rancho restaurant with professional service. The sophisticated menu is equal to the relatively high prices. Standout starters include white marlin sushi served with sake and Pacific lobster cakes with a tropical fruit salsa. There are also wood-oven pizzas, fish served with any of seven sauces and classic German Wiener schnitzel, a holdover from the former German owner. Key lime pie and a chocolate cake made with Cafe Rico liqueur are worth saving room for. Along with Italian and Chilean wines, there's a selection of European and Japanese beers. You can take advantage of complimentary shuttle service when you make a reservation. ⊠ *90 m (100 yards) east of Hotel Pasatiempo* ☎ *653–0127* ▭ *V.*

$–$$ ✕ **Gecko's at Iguana Surf.** This rustic, thatch-roof restaurant brimming with trickling fountains is attached to a surf shop and is very popular with local American families. Chef John Szilasi bakes his own bread and bread sticks studded with spicy seeds. His ambitious dinner menus revolve around fresh local ingredients, such as tuna, plump calamari, and lobster. The chocolate cake is famous and sells out quickly. By day, the restaurant becomes Gil's Place, serving Mexican-style breakfasts and lunches, 8 AM to 3 PM every day except Sunday. ⊠ *Beside Iguana Surf, on road to Playa Langosta* ☎ *653–0334* ▭ *No credit cards* ☉ *Closed Mon.–Tues.*

$ ✕ **Lazy Wave Food Company.** For serious food at laughable prices, visit **Fodor's**Choice this casual, open-air restaurant built around a giant dead tree. Chef Derek ★ Furlani o Toronto entertains customers at the open-kitchen counter with his dry wit as he chops, swirls, and sautées fresh local ingredients. The eclectic lunch and dinner menus change daily. At lunch, there may be chunks of seared tuna with a heap of Furlani's signature crispy, hand-cut shoestring fries and blanched green beans swirled in sesame oil. Dinner might be a warm conch salad. Desserts are standouts, too. Come early for a glass of wine at the new, truly swinging lounge, with wooden chairs suspended from the ceiling. ⊠ *Beside Hotel Pasatiempo, behind storefronts* ☎ *653–0737* ▭ *V.*

$ ✕ **Shark Bite Delicatessen & Carnicería.** The young American owners deliver hearty sandwiches piled high on crusty French or sourdough bread. You can build your own from their wide selection of meats, cheeses, and roasted, marinated vegetables or try one of their special combinations. The bottomless cup of coffee and fudgy brownies, Internet access, and used-book exchange are good excuses to hang out inside the air-conditioned deli or outside at a picnic table. ✉ *Across street and south of Lazy Wave, next to Amnet office* ☎ *653–0453* ▤ *No credit cards.*

Where to Stay

$$ ✕▥ **El Jardín del Edén.** The only drawback to the "Garden of Eden" (this one, anyway) is that it's not right on the beach. Instead, the two-tier, Mediterranean-style, pink building resides amid lush hillside gardens. Air-conditioned rooms have carved hardwood furniture or oversize bamboo furniture and elegantly styled bathrooms. All rooms have ocean views, and two beautiful pools provide the missing water element. The thatch-roof restaurant ($–$$), romantically candlelit at dinner, prepares a variety of outstanding fresh seafood, pastas, and steaks. ✉ *From Hotel El Milagro on main road, turn left, go 180 m (200 yards), then right for 180 m (200 yards) uphill* ⬧ *Apdo. 1094–2050, San Pedro* ☎ *653–0137* ☒ *653–0111* ⊕ *www.jardindeleden.com* ⌦ *18 rooms, 2 apartments* ⟁ *Restaurant, fans, in-room safes, minibars, refrigerators, cable TV, 2 pools, hot tub, 2 bars, laundry service* ▤ *AE, MC, V* ⭘ *BP.*

$$$ ▥ **El Diriá Tamarindo.** A shady tropical garden right next to the beach eliminates the need to stray far from Tamarindo's first high-end hotel. Rooms in the contemporary three-story building with pre-Columbian design motifs have tile floors and modern furniture, and each has a spacious balcony. Try to avoid the rooms facing the noisy main road. The thatched rotunda bar and restaurant overlook a large rectangular pool. A newer pool in the residential condo development across the street is also made available to hotel guests. ✉ *¾ km (½ mi) before Tamarindo center* ☎ *653–0031* ☒ *653–0208* ⊕ *www.eldiria.com* ⬧ *Apdo. 476–1007, San José* ☎ *291–2881* ⌦ *123 rooms* ⟁ *Restaurant, in-room safes, minibars, cable TV, 2 pools, driving range, tennis court, bar, casino, laundry service* ▤ *AE, MC, V* ⭘ *BP.*

$$$ ▥ **Hotel Capitán Suizo.** Steps from a relatively quiet stretch of Tamarindo's
Fodor's Choice gorgeous beach, these elegant balconied bungalows surround a large,
★ shaded pool set in a lushly landscaped garden. The stunning, multilevel rooms have high, angled ceilings and amusing flourishes of colorful art on the walls. A beautifully decorated and subtly lit restaurant serves contemporary cuisine and hosts beach barbecues. Monkeys and birds visit the Swiss Captain's place, so the price of your room includes some wildlife. Diving and kayaking trips can be arranged. ✉ *Right side of road toward Playa Langosta (veer left before circle)* ☎ *653–0075 or 653–0353* ☒ *653–0292* ⊕ *www.hotelcapitansuizo.com* ⌦ *22 rooms, 8 bungalows* ⟁ *Restaurant, in-room safes, refrigerators, pool, boating, fishing, horseback riding, laundry service; no a/c in some rooms, no room TVs* ▤ *AE, MC, V* ⭘ *BP.*

$$–$$$ ▥ **Best Western Tamarindo Vista Villas.** A mecca for surfers, the comfortable rooms and villas in this sparkling-white garden resort overlook some of Tamarindo's best surf breaks. There's an on-site surf shop named for Robert Augustus, a veteran surfer of *Endless Summer* movie fame, with lessons and gear and lots of surfing talk during happy hour at the Monkey Bar. A pool with a waterfall and a swim-up bar give guests a chance to get wet without battling the waves. The hotel also leads diving trips. ✉ *On main road, entering Tamarindo* ☎ *653–0114* ☒ *653–0115* ⊕ *www.tamarindovistavillas.com* ⌦ *12 rooms, 17 villas* ⟁ *Restaurant, pool, snorkeling, cable TV, pool, minibars, fishing, bar* ▤ *AE, MC, V* ⭘ *CP.*

$$–$$$ ☒ **Casa Cook.** The one-bedroom, hardwood-detailed cabinas just off Tamarindo's beach are owned by a retired American couple. Each cabina has a full kitchen, its own water heater, a queen-size sofa bed in the living room, a queen bed in the bedroom, and screened doors and windows. The *casita* (literally, a small house)—a 550-square-ft, one-bedroom apartment—has a private bath, kitchen, living room, and outside eating area. Air-conditioning is $10 extra per night. ☒ *On road to Playa Langosta, north of the Hotel Capitán Suizo* ☎ *653–0125* 🖷 *653–0753* ⊕ *www.tamarindo.com/cook* ➪ *3 cabinas, 1 casita* ☼ *Fans, in-room safes, kitchens, cable TV, pool, beach; no smoking* ☰ *AE, MC, V.*

$–$$ ☒ **Hotel Pasatiempo.** One of the better bargains in Tamarindo, Pasatiempo is a friendly, laid-back hotel with updated cabinas, each named after a Guanacaste beach. They're scattered around the nicely landscaped grounds and the pool; each has a patio with a hammock and a unique hand-painted mural. Suites have one bedroom and day beds in the living room. Tuesday is open-mike night at the bar with local musicians. A wide-screen satellite TV provides sports fans with their periodic fix. Water sports, a sailing cruise, and other activities are easily arranged by the fun-loving American owners, who sometimes go along for the ride. ☒ *Off dirt road to Playa Langosta, 180 m (200 yards) from beach behind Tamarindo circle* ☎ *653–0096* 🖷 *653–0275* ⊕ *www.hotelpasatiempo.com* ➪ *11 cabinas, 2 suites* ☼ *Restaurant, some cable TV, pool, bar, laundry service* ☰ *AE, MC, V* ❘❍❘ *CP.*

$–$$ ☒ **Hotel Las Tortugas.** On a turtle-nesting beach, this hotel was built with turtles in mind. Room windows do not overlook the nesting beaches, since light interferes with the turtles' nighttime rituals. Rooms are otherwise quiet, with good beds, stone floors, and stucco walls. Long-term rentals are available in apartments with kitchenettes, as is basic housing for turtle volunteers. The surf is good but it sometimes has dangerous rip currents, at which times you can retreat to the pool with a turtle mosaic bottom. Local guides lead turtle tours at night, and the hotel also has canoe trips in the nearby Tamarindo Wildlife Refuge. ☒ *Las Baulas Marine National Park, 33 km (20 mi) north of Tamarindo, in Playa Grande* ☎ *653–0423* 🖷 *653–0458* ⊕ *www.cool.co.cr/usr/turtles* ⬠ *Apdo. 164, Santa Cruz de Guanacaste* ➪ *11 rooms, 7 apartments* ☼ *Restaurant, some kitchenettes, pool, boating, laundry service; no room phones, no room TVs* ☰ *V.*

$ ☒ **Arco Iris.** This arty, alternative hotel is on the hill behind the Tamarindo circle. The four cheery, wildly imaginative cabinas are painted in primary colors and decorated with distinct themes by the creative Italian owners. Aerobics, stretching, kick-boxing, and yoga sessions are taught on-site, and in case it all gets too strenuous, there's also a massage therapist and a tattoo artist. You can use the communal kitchen. ☒ *Follow signs past Hotel Pasatiempo and go up hill to right* ☎ *653–0330* ➪ *4 cabinas* ☼ *Restaurant, some kitchenettes, refrigerators, fitness classes, massage; no a/c, no room phones, no room TVs* ☰ *No credit cards* ❘❍❘ *BP.*

$ ☒ **Cabinas Marielos.** In high season Tamarindo presents few decent bargain rooms; among the best are these cabinas, which have a slightly alpine look. They're in two wings, flanking a colorful flower garden well back from the noise and dust of the road. Guests sometimes share their meals in the common kitchen. The atmosphere is surprisingly serene. Note that the water doesn't get terribly hot except in the three newest air-conditioned rooms. ☒ *Across main dirt road from beach, north of town center (follow signs)* 🖷 *653–0141* ➪ *20 rooms* ☼ *Fans; no a/c in some rooms, no room phones, no room TVs* ☰ *AE, MC, V.*

¢ ☒ **El Mono Loco.** Behind a sunny yellow wall you'll find eight spartan but fresh rooms arranged around a new small swimming pool in this recently renovated hotel close to the beach. All rooms are screened in and have fans only, but they have hot water and brand-new beds on tree-trunk frames. Up to six can fit into one room, making it a surfer-beach-goer's bargain. There's no restaurant, but there is a thatched picnic hut and communal kitchen. ⊠ *On road to Langosta, between Iguana Surf and Casa Cook* 🏠🏠 *653–0238* ➲ *8 rooms* ⌂ *Pool, fans; no a/c, no room phones, no room TVs* ▤ *No credit cards.*

Nightlife

During the week, you'll find musical entertainment at Tuesday open-mike sessions at **Hotel Pasatiempo** (⊠ off dirt road to Playa Langosta, 180 m (200 yards) from beach behind Tamarindo circle 🕾 653–0096). Wednesday night, the action is all at **Cantina Las Olas** (⊠ on road to Playa Langosta 🕾 no phone) near Iguana Surf, thanks to Ladies' Night, with free drinks for the ladies in town. Saturday night there is usually a big, noisy beach party thrown by **Big Bazar** (⊠ entrance just across from Iguana Surf 🕾 653–0307) with music, sometimes live, and a barbecue and bon-fire on the beach. For a more sedate evening, try barbecue on the beach at the **Capitán Suizo Hotel** (⊠ right side of road toward Playa Langosta; veer left before circle 🕾 653–0075 or 653–0353), starting at 6:30 with a welcome cocktail, lavish barbecue buffet, and live folk music and danc-ing ($25, reserve in advance). Sail off into the sunset aboard a 50-ft tra-ditional schooner with cruise company **Mandingo** (🕾 653–0623). Soft drinks, beer and wine, and *bocas* (snacks) are included. The boat leaves at 3 PM from the white tower on the beach ($45 per person).

The Outdoors

BOATING, SURFING & KAYAKING
Inquire about surfing conditions at Iguana Surf or the Robert August Surf Shop. At Playa Grande, the best waves usually break just south of the Hotel Las Tortugas.

Iguana Surf (⊠ on road to Playa Langosta 🏠🏠 653–0148 ⊕ www.iguanasurf.net) has information for surfers and visitors. **Iguana Surf 2** (⊠ at beach near Frutas Tropicales) rents surfboards, Boogie boards, and snorkeling equipment and gives motorboat-driven snorkeling tours. **Maresias Surf Shop** (⊠ next to Banco Nacional 🕾 653–0224) has equip-ment, lessons, and lots of local knowledge. Check out the **Robert August Surf Shop** (⊠ Tamarindo Vista Villas 🕾 653–0114) for boards to buy or rent, wax, surfing gear, swimsuits, and plenty of sunblock. **High Tide Surf Shop** (⊠ Tamarindo Aventuras 🕾 653–0108) has high-end surfing equipment and clothing and a large selection of beach wear; it also gives ATV tours.

SPORTFISHING
A number of fishing charters in Tamarindo cater to saltwater anglers. The best among them is probably **Tamarindo Sportfishing** (🕾 653–0090 🏠 653–0161 ⊕ www.tamarindosportfishing.com), run by Randy Wil-son, who has led the way in developing catch-and-release techniques that are easy on the fish. Wilson has roamed and fished the Guanacaste wa-ters since the 1970s, and he knows where the big ones lurk. His boat, the *Talking Fish,* is equipped with a marlin chair and a cabin with a shower. Full days run $975, half days $575.

Playa Langosta

❽ *2 km (1 mi) south of Tamarindo.*

Playa Langosta, a leatherback-turtle nesting beach, is less protected than the beach at Playa Grande. As a result, viewings are more infor-mal than the more organized Playa Grande turtle tours. Big, well-shaped river-mouth waves near the north end of the beach make it popular with surfers. But with its expensive, private villas and refined B&Bs, Playa Langosta is fast becoming an upscale, gentrified extension of Tamarindo.

Where to Stay & Eat

$$$ 🖼 **Sueño del Mar.** A garden gate opens onto a dreamy world of intimate
Fodor'sChoice gardens and patios adorned with frescoes and antique tiles. Seashells
★ are embedded in window frames and strung together in mobiles. The
adobe-style house, which descends down a stepped passageway, con-
tains three double rooms with high, queen-size beds, and Balinese show-
ers open to the sky. There's also a casita with its own kitchen and a breezy,
book-filled honeymoon suite upstairs. A lavish breakfast is served on
the patio looking onto a tiny garden pool. Or you can take your morn-
ing coffee a few steps down to the desert-island beach. ⊠ *130 m (140
yards) south of Capitán Suizo, turn right for 45 m (50 yards), then right
again for about 90 m (100 yards) to entrance gate, across from back of
Cala Luna Hotel* 🖼🖼 *653–0284* ⊕ *www.tamarindo.com/sdmar* ⇔ *3
rooms, 1 suite, 1 casita* ⟵ *Restaurant, dining room, some kitchens, pool,
snorkeling, boating, fishing, bicycles, horseback riding, laundry ser-
vice; no room phones, no room TVs* ⊟ *V* ⦿ *BP.*

★ **$$–$$$** 🖼 **Villa Alegre.** Owned by congenial and helpful Californians Barry and
Suzye Lawson, this homey but very sophisticated Spanish-style B&B has
a lovely location, close to a stand of trees and a somewhat rocky but
swimmable beach. The pool provides swimming and sunning with a beach
view. Rooms are furnished with souvenirs from the Lawsons' travels to
Japan, Russia, Guatemala, and other lands. Each well-appointed room
has a private patio, and the lavish gourmet breakfast is included in the
price. The hotel often plans and hosts weddings, with ceremonies tak-
ing place at a huge boulder on the beach dubbed Marriage Rock.
⊠ *Playa Langosta, south of Sueño del Mar* 🖀 *653–0270* 🖷 *653–0287*
⊕ *www.villaalegrecostarica.com* ⇔ *4 rooms, 2 villas, 1 casita* ⟵ *Fans,
pool; no-smoking rooms, no room phones, no room TVs* ⊟ *AE, MC,
V* ⦿ *BP.*

Playa Avellanas

❾ *17 km (10½ mi) south of Tamarindo.*

Geographically and atmospherically separate from Langosta, this beach
is a beautiful 1-km (½-mi) stretch of pale-gold sand with rocky out-
croppings, a river mouth, and a mangrove swamp estuary. You have to
drive inland from Tamarindo to Villa Real and then 13 km (8 mi) down
a very bumpy road to get from one to the other. Locals claim there are
eight surf spots when the swell is strong. There's a funky seasonal beach
café with no name where you can hang out at driftwood tables and stools
and exchange surfing stories.

Where to Stay

$ 🖼 **Cabinas Las Olas.** Frequented mainly by surfers, these spacious glass-
and-stone cabinas in an airy forest behind Playa Avellanas should also
appeal to bird-watchers, animal lovers, and naturalists. Monkeys and
other critters lurk around this isolated spot, which has expansive grounds
with trees galore. An elevated boardwalk leads from the cabinas to the
beach through a protected mangrove estuary. The restaurant, complete
with an adjacent outdoor video bar, serves reasonably priced breakfasts,
lunches, and dinners. ⊠ *Road to Avellanas; follow signs to Cabinas Las
Olas* 🖀 *233–4455 or 382–4366* 🖷 *222–8685* ⊕ *www.cabinaslasolas.
co.cr* 🖃 *Apdo. 1404–1250, Escazú* ⇔ *10 cabinas* ⟵ *Restaurant, dive
shop, boating, bicycles, bar, laundry service; no a/c, no room phones*
⊟ *AE, MC, V* ⊘ *Closed in Oct.*

Playa Negra

❿ *3 km (2 mi) south of Playa Avellanas, 4 km (2½ mi) northwest of Paraíso.*

Americans—surfers at least—got their first look at Playa Negra in *The Endless Summer II,* which featured some dynamite sessions at this spectacular rock-reef point break. Surfing cognoscenti will dig the waves, which are almost all rights and often beautifully shaped. Surfer culture is also apparent in the wave of casual restaurants, health-food bakeries, Internet cafés, and bikini shops springing up along the road. A roadside tent bazaar sells sarongs and crafts.

Where to Stay

★ $ 🏨 **Hotel Playa Negra.** Facing the ocean, this collection of round, brilliantly colored thatch-roof cabinas have sunny lawns strewn with lush plantings. The cabinas have built-in sofas and beautiful tile bathrooms. The ocean is good for swimming and snorkeling, with tidal pools, swimming holes, and rock reefs providing shelter. This is paradise found for surfers, with a good swell running. There is also a surfing school, as well as boogie-board classes. The restaurant serves deftly prepared Latin and European dishes. ✉ *Go northwest from Paraíso on dirt road 4 km (2½ mi) and follow signs carefully at forks in road* ☎ *658–8034* 🖶 *658–8035* ⊕ *www.playanegra.com* ⮎ *10 cabinas* ♿ *Restaurant, fans, in-room safes, pool, beach, horseback riding, volleyball, bar, laundry service; no a/c, no room phones, no room TVs* 🖃 *AE, MC, V.*

Playa Junquillal

⓫ *31 km (20 mi) south of Santa Cruz, or 4 km (2½ mi) south of Paraíso, along a rough road; 27 km (17 mi) south of Santa Cruz on mostly paved road.*

Junquillal (pronounced hoon-key-*yall*), to the south of Playa Negra, is a long swatch of uninterrupted beach stretching about 3 km (2 mi), with calm surf and only one hotel on the beach side of the road. This is one of the quieter beaches in Guanacaste and a real find for seekers of tranquility. But new restaurants—Peruvian, German, Italian, Swiss—are adding an international flavor; and away from the beach, Junquillal is definitely getting livelier. In rainy season, the beach road from Playa Negra to Playa Junquillal is not passable, and even in dry season it's challenging with four-wheel drive. Ask around about local conditions before attempting to take this route.

Where to Stay & Eat

★ $$ ✕ **La Puesta del Sol.** Food aficionado Alessandro Zangari and his wife, Silvana, have created what he modestly calls "a little restaurant in my home." But regulars drive all the way from San José just to enjoy the haute-Italian menu. Alessandro spares no expense or effort to secure the best ingredients. Each fall he travels to Italy to buy truffles in season. The softly lit patio restaurant, tinted in tangerine and deep blue, evokes a Moroccan courtyard. All the pasta is made from scratch, of course; the ravioli *boscaiolo* contains a woodsy trio of cremini, porcini, and Portobello mushrooms. ✉ *Just north of Playa Junquillal* ☎ *658–8442* 🖃 *No credit cards* ☉ *Closed May–June and Sept.–Oct.*

$–$$ 🏨 **Hotel Iguanazul.** Three kilometers (2 mi) of beach stretches south from this isolated resort on a bluff. Rooms are simply furnished, with two double beds. The hotel itself is looking a little tired, but the fabulous surf of Playa Negra is 10 minutes away, and there's often decent surfing in front of the hotel. Satellite TV is available in a recreation room.

⊠ *North end of Playa Junquillal* ☎ *658–8124* 🖷 *658–8123* ⊕ *www.iguanazul.com* ⅀ *Apdo. 130–5150, Santa Cruz* ➹ *24 rooms* ᗷ *Restaurant, fans, in-room safes, pool, beach, volleyball, bar, recreation room, laundry service; no a/c in some rooms, no room phones, no room TVs* ⊟ *AE, MC, V* ⅋Ol *BP.*

★ $–$$ 🏨 **Land Ho! at Hotel Villa Serena.** Cape Cod comes to Costa Rica. American owners Olive and John Murphy have created a tropical version of New England, with shell-motif quilts and wall stencils, and hooked rugs with palm trees. Rooms are spacious and comfortable; for the ultimate in romance, ask for No. 10, a round room with an ocean view. The lovely landscaped garden has a large pool, and there's a full-service day spa on the property. To reach the terrace restaurant overlooking the beach, you pass a collection of Costa Rican student art, some of it for sale. ⊠ *Across the dirt road from Playa Junquillal* ☎☎ *658–8430* ⊕ *www.land-ho.com* ➹ *12 rooms* ᗷ *Restaurant, pool, spa, tennis court, snorkeling, boating, fishing, horseback riding; no a/c in some rooms, no room phones, no room TVs* ⊟ *AE, MC, V* ⊙ *Closed in Oct.*

★ $ 🏨 **Guacamaya Lodge.** Secluded Guacamaya, on a breezy hill, has expansive views of surrounding rolling countryside and a river estuary below and is ideal for bird-watching. Swiss siblings Berni and Alice Iten have a delightful compound, where flocks of parrots visit each morning and cranes rise up from the estuary. The landscaping around the pool is exceptional, with chenille plants trailing velvety pink tails and tall gingers blazing vibrant red torches. The three-meal restaurant serves excellent, reasonably priced food. In addition to spacious cabinas, with lovely fabric curtains and bedspreads and lots of windows to let in the cooling breezes, there's an airy, well-equipped modern house with a full kitchen. ⊠ *275 m (300 yards) off Playa Junquillal* ☎ *658–8431* 🖷 *658–8164* ⊕ *www.guacamayalodge.com* ⅀ *Apdo. 6, Santa Cruz* ➹ *6 cabinas, 1 house* ᗷ *Restaurant, some kitchens, pool, volleyball, bar, playground, laundry service; no a/c, no room phones, no room TVs* ⊟ *AE, MC, V.*

Nosara

⑫ *23 km (14 mi) south of Paraíso along rough roads in dry season; 32 km (20 mi) south of Nicoya, with 22 km (14 mi) of bad road.*

Set a bit inland, Nosara itself is a minor and not very exciting town. The real attractions here are the surfing waves and wild stretches of neighboring beaches Playas Pelada and Guiones, as well as the nearby Ostional National Wildlife Refuge, a haven for nesting turtles. This whole area of Guanacaste is currently being subdivided and settled by Europeans and Americans at a fairly rapid pace, with a strong Swiss contingent, too. So far, Nosara has been kept as free as possible from really large-scale development. Local businesses have banded together to place wooden signs along the main road to help tourists find their way among the at-times-confusing side roads.

To approach from the north, you have to ford the Río Nosara, often impossible in the wet season; it's better to take the slightly longer but safer route from the Dulce Nombre turnoff, 10 km (6 mi) south of Nicoya. There's a sometimes passable 23-km (14-mi) beach road that connects Junquillal and Nosara during the dry season. Whichever way you go, the roads into Nosara are in really bad shape, and a four-wheel-drive vehicle is necessary.

Apart from sun and sand, the main reason to come to the central Nicoya is to visit the **Refugio Nacional de Fauna Silvestre Ostional** (Ostional National Wildlife Refuge), with its top-notch turtle-watching. During the rainy season you'll probably need a four-wheel-drive vehicle to cross the river just north of Nosara; a track then leads through shrubs to the reserve, which protects one of Costa Rica's major breeding grounds for Olive Ridley Turtles. Locals run the reserve on a cooperative basis, and during the first 36 hours of the arribadas they harvest the eggs, on the premise that eggs laid during this time would likely be destroyed by subsequent waves of mother turtles. These eggs, believed by some to be powerful aphrodisiacs, are sold to be eaten raw in bars. Members of the cooperative take turns guarding the beach from poachers, but they're happy to let you watch the turtles. Turtle arrivals at this and most other nesting sites depend on the moon and tides as well as the time of year; nesting peaks between October and April. Before you go, try to get a sense from the locals of when, if ever, the turtles will arrive. ⊠ *7 km (4½ mi) north of Nosara.*

Where to Stay & Eat

$ ✕ **Café de Paris.** High-spirited French-Swiss owners set a friendly tone at this popular open-air café, where colorful Peruvian tablecloths adorn the tables. The pastries and desserts are the main draw in the restaurant, the bakery, and the Internet café. Croissants, both sweet and savory, are excellent, as is the divine chocolate tart. You can also get pizza, nachos, casados, huge salads, and hearty sandwiches in the restaurant, where Spanish wines are available by the glass. ⊠ *Main road at Playa Guiones entrance* ☎ *682–0087* ▤ *AE, MC, V.*

$ ✕ **Pizzería Giardino Tropical.** You can get good pastas and grilled chicken here, but the pizzas are particularly delicious—they're loaded with mozzarella cheese and have a crispy crust. Gardens surround the dining area and service is fast, a novelty in these parts. Or you can have pizza delivered to your hotel. ⊠ *On main street, past entrance to Playa Guiones* ☎ *682–0258* ▤ *No credit cards.*

¢–$ ✕ **La Mariposa Panadería Café-Bar.** Swiss bakers Karin Lang and Roland Locher started out selling their baked goods door to door. Now they sell their multigrain breads, baguettes, carrot cake, and brownies from a garden café just a stone's throw from Playa Pelada. Savory empanadas, quiches, sandwiches, daily hot specials, and a chicken salad plate that is an edible work of art are other menu items. You can get takeout or counter service or sit down and enjoy a healthful meal at candlelit cedar tables under the sloping roof. ⊠ *Across from Los Condominios las Flores, Playa Pelada* ☎ *682–0545* ▤ *No credit cards.*

$–$$ ✕▥ **Harbor Reef Lodge.** Lose yourself in 3½ acres of jungly garden centered on a small pool presided over by a concrete crocodile. The rooms and suites cater to surfers of every age, with plenty of room to store both boards and families inside the large but sparely furnished rooms. The surf breaks at Playa Guiones are a 300-m (330-yard) walk away. The rancho restaurant is noteworthy for its generous portions of fresh fish and local specialties, plus—a rarity in Costa Rica—tasty heart-smart options. There's also a great shop here selling Costa Rican–made resort wear for North American–size women's bodies, also a rarity. ⊠ *Follow signs from Café de Paris turning, Playa Guiones* ☎ *682–0059* 🖷 *682–0060* ⊕ *www.harborreef.com* ⇨ *9 rooms, 7 suites* ⊛ *Restaurant, pool, some kitchens, refrigerators, fishing, bar* ▤ *AE, MC, V.*

$ ▥ **Hotel Rancho Suizo Lodge.** The lodge is linked to tiny Playa Pelada, just 275 m (300 yards) away by a forest trail. The Swiss operators aren't superfriendly but are renowned for their hearty breakfasts. The comfortable rooms are in five bungalows around the shady property. Two casitas come with their own kitchens. Monkeys are partial to the property's shady environs, and an aviary contains Scarlet Macaws imported from Switzerland; it's illegal to capture these birds in Costa

Rica. Turtle tours are run during the arribadas. ✉ *Follow signs from north end of Nosara, leading up a steep hill* ☎ *682–0057* 🖷 *682–0055* ⊕ *www.nosara.ch* 🖅 *Apdo. 14, Bocas de Nosara 5233* 🛌 *12 bungalows* ⚲ *Restaurant, some kitchens, pool, hot tub, 2 bars, laundry service, airport shuttle; no a/c, no room phones* 🖃 *V* ❙⦿❙ *BP.*

$ 🖭 **Lagarta Lodge.** This magnificent property on a promontory has the best views of Ostional National Wildlife Refuge. The private Nosara Biological Reserve is directly below, laced with trails running through mangroves. A 10-minute steep walk down takes you through a monkey-filled forest to beautiful Playa Guiones and surfing waves. The eagle's-nest lobby-restaurant is famous for its views and Sunday barbecues. Seven comfortable rooms are in a separate building, each with a balcony and a view. At meals, served at a communal table, birders and naturalists share sightings with friendly Swiss host Marcel Schaerer. ✉ *At top of hill, north end of Nosara* ☎ *682–0035* 🖷 *682–0135* ⊕ *www. lagarta.com* 🖅 *Apdo. 18–5233, Nosara* 🛌 *7 rooms* ⚲ *Restaurant, pool, boating, hiking, laundry service; no a/c, no room phones, no room TVs* 🖃 *MC, V.*

$–$$ 🖭 **Casa Romántica.** The name ("romantic house") says it all: the Spanish colonial–style house has a veranda upstairs and a graceful arcade below. Six older rooms are lined up under the shady arcade, with views of the large pool and huge, thatched cabana. But the real finds here are in the terra-cotta Casita Romántica house, with three exquisite suites complete with kitchens and another pool. Each suite has a wonderful wall mural, loads of light, and stylish furnishings. An alfresco restaurant serves Swiss specialties, and there are water aerobic classes every morning to work off the Swiss delights. The short path to the beach is lined with aloe, cactus, and costus. ✉ *Turn down road at Il Giardino Pizzería, Playa Guiones* 🖷🖷 *682–0019* ⊕ *www.hotelcasaromantica.com* 🛌 *6 rooms, 3 suites* ⚲ *Restaurant, some kitchens, 2 pools, outdoor hot tub, fitness classes, massage, beach; no a/c in some rooms, no room phones, no room TVs* 🖃 *V* ❙⦿❙ *BP.*

$–$$ 🖭 **Hotel Villa Taype.** Bordering long, lovely Playa Guiones and its good surf breaks, the standard rooms here are in a low-rise building that forms a U shape around a pair of garden swimming pools. More private and luxurious bungalows are down palm-lined paths. At the other end of the scale, there are seven cheap rooms with fans only. The hotel rents surfboards, Boogie boards, and snorkeling gear, as well as tennis rackets for the day-and-night tennis court. All local tours can be arranged through the hotel. ✉ *Turn down road at Il Giardino Pizzería Playa Guiones* 🖅 *Apdo. 8–5233, Nosara* ☎ *682–0333* 🖷 *682–0187* ⊕ *www. villataype.com* 🛌 *19 rooms, 13 bungalows, 2 suites* ⚲ *Restaurant, fans, some refrigerators, cable TV, tennis court, 2 pools, beach, bicycles, Ping-Pong, 2 bars, dance club, laundry service; no a/c in some rooms* 🖃 *AE, MC, V* ❙⦿❙ *BP.*

The Outdoors

SURFING If you ever wanted to learn to surf, this is the place; try **Corky Carroll's Surf School** (☎ 682–0385). The **Safari Surf School** (☎ 682–0573 ⊕ www. safarisurfschool.com) is run by two surfing brothers from Hawai'i. It's closed from September through October.

HORSEBACK RIDING **Boca Nosara Tours** (☎ 682–0610) takes small groups of two to four people on horseback nature tours through jungle and along beach ($35 per person for a 2½-hour ride). The experienced German-equestrian owner also offers introductory riding lessons.

Sámara

⑬ *36 km (23 mi) south of Nicoya by paved road, 26 km (16½ mi) south of Nosara by rough road in dry season.*

The drive to Sámara from Nicoya may be one of the most scenic in Costa Rica, and it is now one of the most comfortable, too, thanks to paving that extends all the way to Playa Carillo. Sámara's clean, white sweep of beach is framed by two forest-covered hills jutting out on either side. This giant protected cove is ideal for swimming, and there's a fantastic coral reef 1½ km (1 mi) from the shore, the site of many diving and snorkeling excursions. Long a favorite with Ticos, many of whom built summer houses on the beach, Sámara is flourishing these days and attracting a lot of improvement-bent Europeans—there's even a sidewalk. The town has a distinctively Italian flavor, but with a school, soccer field, and church right in the center of town, Tico spirit still predominates.

Where to Stay & Eat

$ ✕ **El Dorado di Dolcetti.** After one visit to Costa Rica, Andrea Dolcetti and his wife, Luigina Sivieri, sold their restaurant in Ferrara, Italy, and opened one here. Their open-air *palenque* (wood-and-thatch building) specializes in seafood, pasta, and, at dinner, wood oven–baked pizzas. Andrea brings home the fish and Luigina supervises the kitchen. Pasta is made from scratch, and real Parmesan cheese and salami are imported to help create authentic Italian flavors. The spaghetti *al mare* is an inspired marriage of local shellfish and Italian cooking. For dessert, there are fruit *crostatas* (tarts) and chocolate "salami." ⊠ *West off main road, just past church in Sámara* ☎ *656–0145* ▭ *MC, V.*

$ ✕ **Restaurante Las Brasas.** Seafood and meat grilled over hot *brasas* (coals) are the specialties at this Spanish restaurant, along with paella, gazpacho, and a variety of *tortillas* (hearty omelets). Avocado stuffed with shrimp salad makes an excellent shared starter or a light lunch. An upstairs balcony is perfect for sipping Spanish or Italian wines. Downstairs, enormous green elephant-ear leaves frame the rustic wooden-railed restaurant, decorated with oxen horns and yokes. Hungry groups can feast on an entire roast suckling pig with a three-day advance reservation. ⊠ *Main road to beach, beside soccer field* ☎ *656–0546* ▭ *DC, V.*

$$ ▦ **Villas Playa Sámara.** The white-stucco villas in this timeshare tourist village have a dreamy location on a long stretch of beach. The water is shallow and safe enough for swimming, though there's also a large pool. Families abound, with a regular clientele of Europeans and North Americans. The one-, two- and three-bedroom villas are comfortable and pretty. The restaurant food is not terrific; it's best to cook for yourself or dine in Sámara. ⊠ *Off main road, south of Playa Sámara* ☎ *656–0372; 220–3348 San José* ✐ *htlvilla@racsa.co.cr* ⬧ *58 villas* ⚭ *Restaurant, fans, kitchens, pool, outdoor hot tub, beach, boating, fishing, bicycles, mountain bikes, badminton, horseback riding, volleyball, bar; no room phones, no room TVs* ▭ *AE, MC, V.*

$–$$ ▦ **Las Brisas del Pacífico.** At one of the few beachfront hotels in Sámara, white, Spanish-style bungalows climb a steep, landscaped hill. Some of the bungalows face a gorgeous pool and thatch-roof restaurant. "Sky rooms," in a two-story building at the top of the hill, have ocean-view balconies and a pool topside, as well as a separate parking lot, so you don't have to climb up and down the hill except for meals and beach walks. The hotel can arrange diving trips. ⊠ *South end of beach, Sámara* ☎ *656–0250* 🖷 *656–0076* ⊕ *www.brisas.net* ⬧ *20 bungalows, 14 rooms* ⚭ *Restaurant, 2 pools, 2 outdoor hot tubs, in-room safes, massages, beach, snorkeling, bar, tours; no a/c in some rooms, no room phones, no room TVs* ▭ *AE, D, MC, V.*

★ $ ⊞ **Hotel Giada.** Giada, which means "jade," is truly a gem of a hotel. The artistic Italian owners have used washes in watermelon, terra-cotta, and yellow to give the walls an antique Mediterranean look. In contrast, tropical thatch roofs overhang private terraces, which overlook a tropical garden and curvaceous blue pool. The large rooms have elegant bamboo furniture, and whimsical sea creatures are hand-painted on the bathroom tiles. Other arty and clever details make this affordable hotel a delight to visit. ✉ *Main strip, 150 m (165 yards) from beach* ☎ *656–0132* 🖷 *656–0131* ⊕ *www.hotelgiada.net* ✆ *Apdo. 5235–67, Sámara* ⇩ *13 rooms* ⚭ *Restaurant, pizzeria, pool, snorkeling, boating, fishing, horseback riding, laundry service; no a/c, no room phones, no room TVs* ▭ *AE, MC, V* ⧈ *BP.*

Playa Carrillo

⑭ *7 km (4 mi) south of Sámara.*

With its long, reef-protected beach backed by an elegant line of swaying palms and sheltering cliffs, Playa Carrillo is a candidate for most picturesque beach in Costa Rica. Totally unmarred by even a single building, it's ideal for swimming, snorkeling, walking, and lounging—just remember not to sit under a loaded coconut palm. You can fly in and land at the airstrip, or head south on the newly paved road from Sámara.

Where to Stay & Eat

$–$$ ✕ **El Mirador.** A fabulous view of yachts moored in Carrillo Bay makes the fresh seafood taste even better at this open-air restaurant perched on a cliff. There is no decor to speak of, just a fabulous view and the natural air-conditioning of the breeze off the bay. Try the whole fried *pargo* (red snapper)—it's moist and crispy and comes with a salad and fries. Specialties include lobster (a good value here), jumbo shrimp, and mahimahi. ✉ *Beachfront, at bend in main road* ☎ *656–0307* ▭ *AE, MC, V.*

$$ ⊞ **Hotel Guanamar.** Formerly a private fishing club, this hotel was renovated in 2002 by new American owners who are putting emphasis on tourists as well as fishermen. With several levels connected by wooden terraces and steps, beautifully positioned high above the southern end of Playa Carrillo, this hotel brings to mind a luxury cruise liner. The large white bedrooms have amazing views. ✉ *On main road to beach, just before scenic overlook* ☎ *656–0054* 🖷 *656–0001* ⊕ *www.guanamar. com* ⇩ *41 rooms* ⚭ *Restaurant, in-room safes, cable TV, pool, fishing, horseback riding, bar, laundry service* ▭ *AE, MC, V* ⧈ *BP.*

$ ⊞ **Hotel Esperanza.** A young couple from Montréal designed and now run this attractive bed-and-breakfast hotel. They have given it an eclectic Mediterranean look, with columns seemingly from classical Greece and an arcade resembling one from Renaissance Italy. Rooms are stylishly simple with high ceilings, striking blue-and-yellow-tiled bathrooms, and handsome *pochote* hardwood headboards and furniture, made locally. Rooms have jacks and, on request, phones. A huge breakfast is served in a small garden, and fresh fish dinners can be ordered. ✉ *90 m (100 yards) west of Hotel Guanamar* ☎☎ *656–0564* ⊕ *www. hotelesperanza.com* ⇩ *7 rooms* ⚭ *Fans, in-room data ports; no a/c in some rooms, no room phones, no room TVs* ▭ *V* ⧈ *BP.*

Punta Islita

⑮ *12 km (7 mi) south of Carrillo when Río Oro is passable or 50 km (31 mi) by overland route on rough roads.*

Punta Islita is named for a tiny tuft of land that becomes an island at high tide. The beach is rather rocky, but there's some good snorkeling near the point. The draw here is the one and only hotel, a luxury destination perched high above the secluded beach. In rainy season, it's often impossible to cross the Río Oro, south of Carrillo, so you have to make a 50-km (31 mi) detour along dirt roads with spectacular mountain views but lots of potholes, too. Most people fly into the hotel's private airstrip.

Where to Stay

$$$$
Fodor'sChoice
★
▥ **Hotel Punta Islita.** Overlooking the Pacific from a forested ridge, this exquisite, secluded hotel is luxury incarnate. Hidden around the hillside are villas, casitas, suites, and spacious rooms, all with private porches, a view, and a hammock. If the view doesn't keep you mesmerized, some rooms also have VCRs and CD players. Beds have rough-hewn wooden bedposts, and bathrooms are tiled with deep tubs. Casitas have their own private plunge pools or outdoor hot tubs and private gardens, one of the main attractions for the myriad honeymooners here. A massive thatched dome covers the restaurant and opens onto an infinity-edge pool with a view and a swim-up bar. If you overdo with the many activities here, stop by the spa for unique massage treatments using local herbs. ⊠ *South of Playa Carrillo* ☎ *656–0470* 🖷 *656–0473* ⊕ *www. hotelpuntaislita.com* ✉ *Apdo. 242–1225, San José* ☎ *215–0303* 🖷 *215–2414* ➥ *15 bungalows, 7 casitas, 6 suites, 5 villas* ♨ *2 restaurants, minibars, cable TV, driving range, 2 tennis courts, 2 pools, gym, spa, beach, some in-room VCRs, snorkeling, boating, fishing, mountain bikes, horseback riding, 2 bars, laundry service, Internet, airstrip, heliport; no phones in some rooms* ☰ *AE, DC, MC, V* ⏸️ *BP.*

THE SOUTHERN TIP

PUNTARENAS TO MALPAÍS

Catch a ferry from Puntarenas to the southern tip of the Nicoya Peninsula and you'll be just a bus hop away from gorgeous beaches with waterfalls and tidal pools galore. Within the region are two quiet, well-preserved national parks where you can explore caves and pristine forests or travel by boat or sea kayak to remote islands and wildlife preserves for bird-watching, snorkeling, diving, and even camping. Not too remote, and thus at times overcrowded, is Isla Tortuga, ringed by some of Costa Rica's most beautiful beaches. If you like to mix nightlife with your outdoor adventures, the town of Montezuma and its nearby beaches are very often jammed with an international cast of surfers, eco-tourists, and misfits of all sorts, from practitioners of alternative lifestyles to expatriate American massage therapists living out their dreams.

Puntarenas

⑯ *110 km (69 mi) west of San José.*

The main reason to visit Puntarenas is to catch a ferry to the eastern coast of the Nicoya Peninsula and its beaches. But a millennial beautification campaign, plus a modern bus station and a major marine-life museum, make it worth an afternoon visit or a one-night stop before taking the ferry. This bustling commercial fishing center and docking point for international cruise ships sits on a narrow spit of sand—*punta de arenas* (literally, "point of sand")—protruding into the Gulf of Nicoya, with splendid views, especially at sunset, across to the peninsula. The locals, called Porteños, and tourist police scoot around on bicycles, enjoying what must be the smoothest stretch of paved road in Costa Rica, the Paseo de Los Turistas.

Sidewalk lamps, concrete benches, and a modern cruise-ship dock enliven this wide beachfront promenade. On days when cruise ships arrive, local artisans sell their wares at a market near the dock. The town's clean, tree-lined beach beckons to strollers and swimmers. Seafood restaurants, cafés, ice cream parlors, casinos, and an Internet café in an old restored building provide lots of diversions and places to people-watch.

Art exhibitions are shown in the grand entrance hall of the **Casa de la Cultura,** a former port headquarters. The **Museo Regional-Histórico Marino** (☎ 661–5036) shares the same august building. The free exhibits focus on the history of Puntarenas as Costa Rica's main coffee-shipping port. The museum is open Tuesday–Sunday 9:45–12:15 and 1–5:15. ⊠ *Three blocks from Parque Central* ☎ *661–1394.*

Ambitious **Parque Marino del Pacífico,** opened in 2002, is the new jewel in Puntarenas's slightly tarnished crown. The huge eye-level aquarium is full of Gulf of Nicoya sea life. ⊠ *300 m (330 yards) east of cruise-ship dock* ☎ 661–5272 ⊠ *$7* ☉ *Tues.–Sun. 9–5.*

off the beaten path

Isla Tortuga. Soft, bleached sand and casually leaning palms fringe Isla Tortuga, an island of tropical dry forest that makes a perfect day trip from Puntarenas, Montezuma, and other beach towns. Though state-owned, the island is leased and inhabited by a Costa Rican family who funded efforts to reintroduce such species as deer and wild pig to the island some years ago and now leads tours to the island from nearby Curú Wildlife Refuge in Paquera. A 40-minute hiking trail wanders past monkey ladders, strangler figs, bromeliads, orchids, and the fruit-bearing *guanabana* (soursop) and *marañón* (cashew) trees up to a lookout point with tantalizing vistas. You can take a short canopy tour on the beach. Transportation to the island and tours are arranged by tour operators in both Puntarenas and from San José, including Calypso Tours (⊠ Avda. 2 between Cs. 1 and 3 San José ☎ 256–2727 ☎ 256–6767 ⊕ www.calypsotours. com) for $99 per person in high season only, including transportation from San José. ⊠ *1 hr 15 mins by boat from Puntarenas* ⊠ *Hike $5, canopy tour $10.*

Where to Stay & Eat

$–$$ ✕ **La Caravelle.** The interior, dark blue walls adorned with antique musical instruments, is unexpectedly elegant—but then so is a French restaurant across the street from the ocean. True to the French manner, the service is somewhat insouciant and offhand. The cooking concentrates on sauces: try the corvina *ostendaise* (with a lemon and white-wine cream sauce smothered in tiny shrimp) or beef fillet *con salsa oporto y hongos* (with a port-and-mushroom sauce). Jumbo shrimp dishes can run as high as $22. Crispy fried chicken is a less-expensive choice. The wine selection is decent. ⊠ *Paseo de los Turistas, between Cs. 21 and 23* ☎ 661–2262 ⊟ *AE, MC, V* ☉ *Closed Mon. No lunch Tues.–Thurs.*

$ ⊡ **Hotel Las Brisas.** This white, two-story motel-style building wraps around its pool, where the views of the sun setting over the Nicoya Peninsula are terrific. The hotel is across the street from the beach and not far from the ferry docks. Three of the simple rooms have balconies with views of the ocean. The restaurant serves Greek-influenced seafood and meat and some Mexican dishes. ⊠ *West end of Paseo de los Turistas,* ☎661–4040 ☎ 661–2120 ⊕ *www.brisas.net* ⌨ *19 rooms* ♻ *Restaurant, cable TV, pool, laundry service, Internet; no room phones* ⊟ *AE, MC, V* ❚❙ *BP.*

$ ⊡ **Hotel Tioga.** The pastel green-and-yellow courtyard in this stately 40-year-old establishment has the look of an ocean liner. Your best bets are the seven guest rooms upstairs, with balconies overlooking the gulf.

They're handsomely decorated with colorful, tropical prints and heavy, varnished dark-wood furniture. The courtyard centers on a tiny pool with a *guachepelín* tree growing from the islet in its center. The second-floor restaurant is open to cool breezes off the gulf. ⊠ *Paseo de los Turistas, Apdo. 96–5400, Puntarenas* ☎ *661–0271* 🖷 *661–0127* ⊕ *www. hoteltioga.com* ⇕ *52 rooms* ₺ *Restaurant, cable TV, pool, bar, casino, laundry service* ▤ *AE, MC, V* ⎮◉⎮ *BP.*

Paquera

⑰ *1½ to 2 hrs southwest of Puntarenas by ferry.*

Most travelers heading south to the beach towns of Montezuma and Malpaís arrive in Paquera by car ferry or *lancha* (small passenger launch) from Puntarenas. Paquera itself is a growing small community about 5 km (3 mi) south of the ferry dock. You can pick up beach supplies at the many stores, supermarkets, and gas stations here. Since the roads around are rough on cars, it's better to fly into Tambor airstrip and take a taxi or bus to your destination. The trip overland by car from Nicoya via Playa Naranjo is grueling.

Refugio Nacional de Vida Silvestre Curú (Curú National Wildlife Refuge), established by former farmer and logger turned conservationist Federico Schutt in 1933, was given the indigenous name for the pochote and guanacaste trees that flourish here. Trails lead through the forest and high-salinity mangroves, where you see hordes of phantom crabs on the beach, howler and white-faced monkeys in the trees, and plenty of hummingbirds, kingfishers, woodpeckers, trogons, and manakins (including the coveted Long-tailed Manakin). The refuge is working to reintroduce spider monkeys and Scarlet Macaws into the wild. Some very basic accommodations, originally designed for students and researchers, are available by the beach ($25 per person, including three meals and park admission); call ahead to arrange for lodging, guides, and early morning bird-watching walks. Luis Schutt, son of the owner, arranges year-round **motorboat or kayak excursions** (⊠ main road, across from Esso station in Paquera ☎641–0673) to Isla Tortuga for $15; snorkeling equipment is $5 extra. Or you can take a horseback tour of the *finca* (property) or ride to a sparkling white beach. From Paquera, you can catch a bus to the refuge. ⊠ *7 km (4½ mi) south of Paquera* ☎ *641–0590* 🖷 *641–0004* ⓓ *Schutt family, Apdo. 14, Paquera 5357* ⊕ *refugiocuru@yahoo.com* ⊠ *$5* ⓧ *Daily 7–4.*

The Outdoors

SEA-KAYAKING   Respected San José–based adventure tour operator **Ríos Tropicales** (☎ 233–6455 ⊕ www.riostropicales.com) has three- and four-day sea-kayaking trips for a minimum of six people, which start from Curú National Wildlife Refuge and take you along the coast and among the barely inhabited islands of the Gulf of Nicoya. The professionally run camping and kayaking trips give kayakers at every level the opportunity to explore wild islands, wildlife reserves, and more. Expert natural guides explain the natural history of the region and teach kayak surfing.

Tambor

⑱ *20 km (12 mi) south of Curú National Wildlife Refuge, 27 km (17 mi) south of Paquera.*

Tucked into large half-moon Bahía Ballena, Tambor is undergoing a land-sale frenzy similar to that at Tamarindo—you can see a golf course and housing development from the road, and signs of further development all around them. The area's luxe resort hotels got a lot of press in 2001, thanks to the television series *Temptation Island,* which filmed episodes at Tango Mar Resort and Tambor Tropical. The resorts arrange plenty of activities, but you could break out on your own. The hike from Tambor around the Piedra Amarilla point to Tango Mar Resort is about 8 km (5 mi), and the trees along the way resound with the throaty utterings of male howler monkeys. You can fly directly to Tambor from San José.

Along the dusty road through town are interesting souvenir shops, a supermarket, a SANSA office, and an adventure-tour office as well as restaurants and hotels. **Cóbano,** 12 km (7½ mi) to the west of Tambor, is a bustling crossroads with supermarkets, a bank, restaurants, shops, a gas station, and even an ice cream parlor.

Where to Stay

★ **$$$–$$$$** 🏨 **Tango Mar Resort.** Tiki suites in palm-thatch cabins on stilts look rustic on the outside but are pure luxury inside. Rooms in the main hotel are luxurious, too, with private balconies right on the beach. The breezy Cristóbal restaurant serves international cuisine and has an ocean view. On the grounds are a lushly landscaped, spring-fed, two-tiered pool; a spectacular beachfront waterfall; and an immaculate golf course. ⊠ *2 km (1 mi) west of Tambor* ☎ *683–0001; 222–4657 San José* 🖷 *683–0003* ⊕ *www.tangomar.com* 🗗 *4 villas, 18 rooms, 17 suites* 🖧 *2 restaurants, in-room safes, some in-room hot tubs, some kitchenettes, refrigerators, cable TV, 9-hole golf course, 2 tennis courts, pool, beach, boating, jet skiing, fishing, hiking, horseback riding, 2 bars, Internet* 🖃 *AE, DC, MC, V* ⑪ *BP.*

★ **$$$** 🏨 **Tambor Tropical.** You may have seen this collection of five duplex cabinas, which surround a pool in the palm trees off Playa Tambor in Bahía Ballena, when it was featured on the TV series *Temptation Island.* The 1,000-square-ft cabinas are made from strips of local hardwoods arranged in attractive diagonal patterns. Each cabina has an upper and lower suite, and each suite has its own living room, bedroom, bathroom with hot water, and fully equipped kitchen. Friendly staff members go out of their way to be helpful. ⊠ *Follow main street of Tambor toward water (hotel fronts beach)* ☎ *683–0011* 🖷 *683–0013* ⊕ *www. tambortropical.com* 🗗 *10 suites* 🖧 *Restaurant, kitchens, pool, hot tub, beach, horseback riding, bar, Internet; no a/c, no room phones, no room TVs* 🖃 *AE, MC, V* ⑪ *BP.*

Montezuma

⑲ *7 km (4½ mi) southeast of Cóbano, 45 km (28 mi) south of Paquera, 18 km (11 mi) south of Tambor.*

Beautifully positioned on a sandy bay, Montezuma is hemmed in by a precipitous wooded shoreline. At the bottom of the hill, the funky town center is a pastel cluster of new-age health-food cafés, trendy beachwear shops, and jaunty tour kiosks mixed with older Tico *sodas* (casual eateries) and noisy open-air bars. Montezuma has been on the international vagabond circuit for years, attracting surfers and alternative-lifestyle types, and some unsavory characters as well. But the community, like its pioneers, is growing up, with Internet cafés and more sophisticated hotels and restaurants. Today you are as likely to meet older, outdoorsy European tourists as dreadlocked surfers. The main attraction for everybody is the beach that stretches across one national park and two nature preserves to the north, leading to a spectacular beachfront waterfall, a popular destination for hikers and horseback tours.

Just over a bridge, 10 minutes south of town, a slippery path patrolled by howler monkeys leads upstream to two waterfalls, the second one an impressive 108 ft high with a thrilling **swimming hole.** Do not jump or dive from the waterfalls. Despite signs posting the danger, some young people are still jumping to their deaths or serious injury.

Where to Stay & Eat

$-$$ ✕ **Playa Los Artistas.** This creative open-air Italian restaurant on the beach specializes in Mediterranean preparations of fresh seafood. Driftwood tables, lamps, and other rustic touches provide a romantic yet casual atmosphere at dinner. Try the carpaccio *de atun,* a raw tuna appetizer seasoned with oregano and garlic. The lunch menu emphasizes pasta. ⊠ *275 m (300 yards) south of town, just past Los Mangos Hotel* ☎ *no phone* ⊟ *No credit cards* ☉ *Closed Sun. and Oct.*

¢ ✕ **Cafe Iguana.** This funky café, subtitled La Esquina Dulce (The Sweet Corner), serves up real Italian espresso, fresh fruit juices, and baked goods from 6 AM on. Check out the impressive selection of huge muffins and dessert breads, including such exotic flavors as mango and pineapple. The overstuffed sandwiches, made on fresh, crusty home-baked bread, are big enough for two. Wooden stools on a terrace make perfect perches for watching the passing parade of *todo el mundo* Montezuma. ⊠ *Town center, Montezuma* ☎ *no phone* ⊟ *No credit cards.*

★ $ ✕▦ **El Sano Banano Restaurant and B&B.** Montezuma's original natural-food restaurant (¢–$) has grown more sophisticated and now includes fish and hormone-free chicken on its healthful but delicious menu. A new terrace café provides excellent people-watching, as well as tall glasses of sinfully delicious Mocha Chiller, made with frozen yogurt. A battalion of ceiling fans keeps the air moving in the spacious, adobe-style restaurant. It's open for breakfast from 7 AM; if you come for dinner around 7:30 PM, you can take in a nightly free movie. Attached to the restaurant is an Internet café, and above is a B&B annex built in 2002. The comfortable rooms have air-conditioning, a rare treat in Montezuma, and they're decorated in Mexican style. They are amazingly quiet for being in the center of town. ⊠ *Main road, Montezuma* ☎ *642–0638* 🖷 *642–0631* ⊕ *www.elbanano.com* ⇱ *12 rooms* ⌂ *Restaurant, Internet; no room phones, no room TVs* ⊟ *AE, MC, V* ⧍ *BP.*

★ $-$$ ▦ **Cabinas El Sano Banano.** This colony of eight tropical cabins is a fantasy island, huddled in the woods north of town close to the beach. Each geodesic-domed bungalow is a luxurious, cozy cave for two, perfect for honeymooners. A two-story building has three comfortable suites, with kitchenettes above, and three double rooms below. They're decorated with original watercolors of local birds. Adding to the romance is a garden-fringed pool with a series of waterfalls. The reception desk is at the El Sano Banano Restaurant, in town. ⊠ *Main road, on beach north of Montezuma* ☎ *642–0638* 🖷 *642–0631* ⊕ *www.elbanano.com* ⇱ *3 rooms, 3 suites, 8 bungalows* ⌂ *Some kitchenettes, refrigerators, pool, beach, hiking, laundry service; no a/c in some rooms, no room phones, no room TVs* ⊟ *AE, MC, V* ⧍ *BP.*

★ $ ▦ **Hotel Amor de Mar.** Take the time to walk the short trek south of town to find this ruggedly handsome, two-story natural-wood hotel surrounded by trees. A grassy lawn stretches to the rocky seashore, where you can cool off in a a natural tidal pool. Great breakfasts and immediate access to the waterfall hike make this one of the finest small hotels in Montezuma. The rooms, with wood paneling, are comfortable and simply furnished. The dining room serves breakfast and light lunches only. ⊠ *Beach road, south of town* ☎☎ *642–0262* ⊕ *www.amordemar. com* ⇱ *11 rooms, 9 with bath* ⌂ *Dining room, saltwater pool, beach, laundry service; no a/c, no room phones, no room TVs* ⊟ *V.*

$ ▦ **Hotel El Jardín.** Climbing the hill above town, this Italian-owned hotel has panoramic ocean views. True to its name, the cabins are scat-

tered around a garden lush with flowering gingers and populated by indigenous stone-sculpture people. Teak paneling and furniture, stained-
glass pictorial panels, and terraces with hammocks give this hotel style
as well as comfort. ⊠ *Main road, entering Montezuma* ☎ *642–0548*
🖷 *642–0074* ⊕ *www.hoteleljardin.com* ⟿ *15 rooms* ⚭ *Fans, pool, outdoor hot tub, some kitchens, refrigerators; no a/c in some rooms, no
room phones, no room TVs* ☱ *No credit cards.*

★ $ 🖼 **Nature Lodge Finca Los Caballos.** A spirited Canadian woman runs this
charming, small hotel high on a hill. The open-air restaurant and reception area both have bird's-eye views of ocean and valley below. Designed with a Southwestern U.S. motif, the rooms have pastel walls
decorated with stencils of lizards and frogs. A two-bedroom bungalow,
formerly the owner's house, is set apart from the hotel and accommo-
dates up to four. The owner leads wonderful horseback tours and often
invites guests to accompany her to rodeos. ⊠ *3 km (2 mi) north of Montezuma on main road* 🖷🖷 *642–0124* ⊕ *www.naturelodge.net* ⌕ *Apdo.
22, Cóbano de Puntarenas* ⟿ *7 rooms, 1 bungalow* ⚭ *Restaurant, fans,
pool, horseback riding; no a/c, no room phones, no room TVs* ☱ *AE,
MC, V* ☯ *Closed in Oct.*

The Outdoors

Surfing, diving, snorkeling, fishing, and horseback tours to the **El Choro
Beach Waterfall** are the most popular excursions. **Aventuras en Montezuma** (⊠ main road, at center of town 🖷🖷 642–0050) offers snorkeling, rafting, fishing, diving, and horseback tours.

Shopping

Beachwear and surfing gear abound, along with souvenirs and leather-
and-seed jewelry sold on street tables. For something special, visit **Ma-
condo** (☎ 642–0684) across from Chico's Bar. Subtitled Origen de la
Creación ("origin of creation"), the gallery-shop showcases local artists'
works and indigenous crafts. The mother-of-pearl silver jewelry made
by a local German artist is a standout.

Malpaís

⑳ *12 km (7½ mi) southwest of Cóbano, 52 km (33 mi) south of Paquera.*

Once considered a remote preserve, Malpaís was frequented only by
diehard surfers in search of some of the country's largest waves and by
naturalists en route to the nearby Cabo Blanco Nature Preserve. Since
the town and its miles of beach were only accessible down a steep gravel
road, it was likely that this reputation might have remained the case.
However, as in much of this coastal area, hotels and restaurants are now
springing up at both ends of the populated part of the beach, despite
the bad roads.

Surfing is best at Playa Santa Teresa, the sandy north end of this long
stretch of beach. The more southerly Malpaís end of the beach is rockier but interesting for its tidal pools and beachcombing. The crowd is
fairly young, with tanned-and-buff surfers walking or bicycling their
boards to wherever the surf is up. But increasingly, older, more upscale
visitors are drawn to the tranquility of luxury retreats that cater to mind
and body.

Conquistadors named this area Cabo Blanco on account of its white earth
and cliffs, but it was a more benevolent pair of foreigners—Nils Olof
Wessberg and his wife, Karen, arriving here from Sweden in 1950—who
made it the **Reserva Natural Absoluta Cabo Blanco** (Cabo Blanco Strict
Nature Preserve). Appalled by the first clear-cut in the Cabo Blanco area

in 1960, the couple launched a pioneering and international appeal to save the forest. In time, their efforts led not only to the creation of the 12-square-km (4½-square-mi) reserve but also to the founding of Costa Rica's national park service, the National Conservation Areas System (SINAC). Nils Olof Wessberg was murdered on the Osa Peninsula in 1975 while researching the area's potential as a national park. A reserve just outside Montezuma was named in his honor, and at this writing, a reserve was being created to honor his wife, who dedicated her life to conservation after her husband's death. The **Karen Mogensen Fischer Museum** (⌧ Internet Café, El Sano Banano Restaurant, Montezuma ☎ 650–0607) details her life and contributions.

The tropical moist forest in Cabo Blanco has a combination of evergreen species and lush greenery. Look for the sapodilla trees, which produce a white latex used to make gum; you can often see V-shape scars where the trees have been cut to allow the latex to run into containers placed at the base. Olof Wessberg cataloged a full array of animals here: porcupine, Hog-nosed Skunk, Spotted Skunk, Gray Fox, anteater, cougar, and jaguar. Resident birds include Brown Pelicans, White-throated Magpies, toucans, Cattle Egrets, Green Herons, parrots, and Turquoise-browed Motmots. A fairly strenuous 4-km (2½-mi) hike, which takes about two hours in each direction, follows a trail from the reserve entrance to **Playa Cabo Blanco**. The beach is magnificent, with hundreds of pelicans flying in formation and paddling in the calm waters offshore—you can wade right in and join them. Off the tip of the cape is the 7,511-square-ft **Isla Cabo Blanco**, with pelicans, frigate birds, Brown Boobies, and an abandoned lighthouse. As a strict reserve, Cabo Blanco has bathrooms and a visitor center but no other tourist facilities. Rangers and volunteers act as guides. Roads to the reserve are usually only passable in dry season. ⌧ *10 km (6 mi) southwest of Montezuma, about 11 km (7 mi) south of Malpaís* ☎ *642–0093* ⌧ *$8* ☉ *Wed.–Sun. 8–4.*

Where to Stay & Eat

¢–$ ✕ **Piedra Mar.** With all the new restaurants popping up along the beach road, the favorite standby is still this old shack down on the beach, part *pulpería* (grocery–juice bar), part restaurant. Plastic tables are set up under a corrugated tin roof and the only decor is the rocky seascape, about 3 m (10 ft) away. Your lobster (for less than $10) or grilled shrimp comes flavored with garlic and—on windy days—the sea spray crashing against the rocks. Sunset is popular with locals in the know, so come early. Or come for breakfast at 7 and watch the early morning sun lighting up the ocean. ⌧ *275 m (300 yards) south of Blue Jay Lodge* ☎ *No phone* ⊟ *No credit cards.*

★ $$$$ ✕⌧ **Resort Florblanca.** Named for the white flowers of the frangipani trees that shade the beachfront property, this collection of simply luxurious villas ministers to body and soul. Each handsome villa has an outdoor Balinese-inspired bathroom and a sunken tub. There's a dojo for karate and yoga, a massage therapist, a music room, cable TV in a comfortable lounge, and an art and pottery studio. Two pools flow into each other in front of Nectar, the excellent alfresco restaurant ($$–$$$), which serves four-course gourmet dinners with inventive menus. Multi-course breakfasts are lavish. Resident biologist guides lead horseback tours and nature walks into Cabo Blanco and snorkeling excursions in its surrounding waters. ⌧ *2 km (1 mi) north of Santa Teresa* ☎ *640–0232* ⊕ *www.florblanca.com* ⌧ *10 villas* ⌂ *Restaurant, refrigerators, 2 pools, gym, massage, beach, snorkeling, fishing, hiking, Internet; no room TVs* ⊟ *MC, V* ⦿ *BP.*

★ $$ ✕▣ **Milarepa.** Created by two Parisians searching for a tropical Shangri-la, Milarepa is a perfect place for renewal, whether romantic or spiritual. The four bamboo houses are spaced apart to ensure privacy and are furnished in ascetic but exquisite taste, with carved Indonesian wooden beds draped with mosquito netting, and bamboo armoires. Bathrooms are open to the sky, with alcoves for Buddhist deities. Each cottage has a veranda looking out onto the carefully raked white beach, shaded by a grove of palms. The restaurant is *très français*; try the salade niçoise. Twice a week, the restaurant is closed for meals to accommodate yoga classes. ⊠ *Playa Santa Teresa; at end of road from Cóbano, take a right and travel 4 km (2½ mi)* ☎ *640–0023* 🖷 *640–0168* ✍ *milarepa@mail.ticonet.co.cr* ⓓ *Apdo. 49-5361 Cóbano, Puntarenas* ⇆ *4 cottages* ☖ *Restaurant, fans, pool, snorkeling, fishing, hiking, horseback riding; no a/c, no room phones, no room TVs* ⊟ *V.*

$ ▣ **Blue Jay Lodge.** Here's your chance to live in a tree house. The wooden cabins, with only screens for walls (on three sides), are built on stilts. Steep stairs lead up the forested mountainside to the rustic aeries with hot-water showers, open to nature on one side. Ceiling fans keep the air moving, but warm blankets are on hand for cool, breezy nights. Breakfast is in the wooden-terrace restaurant at ground level. The beach is a short 220-yard walk, or you can climb the mountain to look for birds and howler monkeys. ⊠ *Turn left at main Malpaís crossroads at end of road from Cóbano* ☎ *640–0089* 🖷 *640–0141* ⊕ *www.bluejaylodgecostarica.com* ⇆ *7 cabins* ☖ *Restaurant, bar, laundry service; no a/c, no room phones, no room TVs* ⊟ *AE, D, MC, V* ⟊ *BP.*

THE TEMPISQUE RIVER BASIN

This northeastern section of the peninsula encompasses the parks in and around the Río Tempisque—prime places to watch birds and other wildlife—and Nicoya, the commercial and political hub of the northern Nicoya Peninsula. By road, Nicoya provides the best access to Sámara, Nosara, and points south and north and is also linked by a smooth, well-paved road to the artisan community of Guaitil and the northern Nicoya beach towns.

A $26.9 million bridge, built with funds from the Taiwanese government, was completed in 2003. The Taiwan Friendship Bridge, more commonly referred to as the Río Tempisque Bridge, crosses the Río Tempisque just above the present ferry crossing and Puerto Moreno and is expected to eliminate the long wait for the ferry and speed travelers to points west and south. The toll is 50¢ per car. For the bridge, head north from San José on the Pan-American Highway, turn left about 48 km (30 mi) north of the Puntarenas turnoff, and drive about 25 km (16 mi) farther.

Palo Verde National Park & Lomas Barbudal Reserve

▶ ㉑ *Palo Verde is 28 km (17 mi) southwest of Bagaces, which is 24 km (15 mi) south of Liberia; Lomas Barbudal is 20 km (12 mi) southwest of Bagaces.*

Bordered on the west by the Río Tempisque, these wildlife preserves protect a significant amount of deciduous dry forest. Palo Verde extends over 95 square km (37 square mi) of mainly flat terrain, and its main attraction is bird-watching. Its swampland is a temporary home for thousands of migratory birds toward the end of the rainy season. From December through March a raised platform near the ranger station, about 8 km (5 mi) past the park entrance, helps you to see dozens of species of aquatic birds, including herons, ducks, Wood Storks, and elegant Roseate Spoonbills.

Camping, rustic dormitory facilities ($10), and meals ($5 for lunch or dinner) can be arranged through the park headquarters. Or you can book a tour through the **Organization for Tropical Studies** (⊠ ½ km [¼ mi] west of Lincoln School in Moravia, San José ☎ 240–6696 ⊕ www.ots. ac.cr), which has double rooms with shared baths for $50 per person, including three meals, taxes, and a guided walk. Most people visit on a tour. The park headquarters is 8 km (5 mi) beyond the park entrance. *⊠ Pan-American Hwy.; drive 42 km (26 mi) north of Puntarenas turnoff to gas station in Bagaces, which is about 15 km (9 mi) north of Cañas, look for Palo Verde sign and drive 28 km (17 mi) along rough road to park* ☎ 671–1062 *⊠ $6 ⊙ Daily 8–4.*

From the Puerto Moreno area where the car ferry has traditionally crossed, you can hire a guided motorboat to take you north up the river into Palo Verde park for a closer look at the **Isla Pájaros** (Bird Island), home to thousands of migratory and local birds from January to March. Boats are to the right of the ferry dock as you disembark. The trip takes roughly 45 to 60 minutes; the price is negotiable, but expect to pay around $50. The hefty price is often worth it, since you might see alligators, howler monkeys, and other wildlife on the way to the birds themselves. Wear waterproof clothing—the river ride can be windy, bumpy, and wet.

The Outdoors

BOATING **CATA Tours** (☎ 674–0180; ⊕ www.catatours.com) runs wildlife and bird-watching boating adventures down the Río Bebedero into Palo Verde from a starting point on the Pan-American Highway north of Cañas. Calm adventure trips are led by **Safaris Corobicí** (☎☎ 669–6191 ⊕ www. nicoya.com) with guides rowing rafts down the Río Corobicí, covering some of the same wildlife-rich territory not far from Palo Verde and Lomas Barbudal. Follow signs from the highway to Km 193.

Barra Honda National Park

㉒ *21 km (13 mi) west of Puerto Moreno.*

The limestone ridge rising from the surrounding savanna was once thought to be a volcano but was later found to contain an intricate network of caves, formed as a result of erosion once the ridge had emerged from beneath the sea. Some caves on the almost 23 square km (14 square mi) park remain unexplored, and they're home to surprisingly abundant animal life, including bats, birds, blindfish, salamanders, and snails.

Every day in the dry season, from 8 AM to 1 PM, local guides can take you down a 67-ft flexible aluminum ladder to the **Terciopelo Cave,** which shelters unusual formations shaped like fried eggs, popcorn, and shark's teeth, as well as sonorous columns collectively known as "the organ." The guides have you wear a harness with a rope attached for safety. The tour costs $25, plus equipment rental and park admission. Travel companies no longer take tourists or speleologists deeper underground. Don't attempt to visit the caves unless accompanied by a guide authorized by the local community development association.

You can climb **Barra Honda peak,** 1,184 ft high, from the northwest (the southern wall is almost vertical), following the 3-km (2-mi) Los Laureles trail. From the summit you have fantastic views sweeping across the islet-filled Gulf of Nicoya. The surface is pocked with orifices and white rocks eroded into odd shapes, and some of the ground feels dangerously hollow. Surface wildlife includes howler monkeys, skunks, coatis, deer, parakeets, and iguanas. The relatively open, deciduous-forest vegetation makes viewing the fauna easy. Hikers must be accompanied by local guides. The park has camping facilities; a community tourism association provides guides and runs a simple, inexpensive restaurant and lodge by the park entrance. A park office in Nicoya, across from the colonial church, provides information and maps of the park. If you need food or lodging in the park, make reservations before the weekend. ☎ 686–6760 🖾 $6 ☼ *Park daily 8–4; Nicoya office weekdays 8–4.*

Nicoya

㉓ *30 km (19 mi) west of Puerto Moreno, 11 km (7 mi) southwest of Barra Honda National Park.*

Often referred to as Guanacaste's colonial capital, Nicoya is a prosperous provincial town, with a pleasant, shady central park where you can get a taste of everyday small-town life, including Sunday-night band concerts. With the promise of increased traffic from the Río Tempisque Bridge, the town has spruced up old buildings and added new ones, including three Internet cafés and an ATM that takes international cards.

The Chorotegan chief Nicoya greeted the Spanish conquistadors upon their arrival here in 1523, and many of his people were converted to Catholicism. A Chinese population, descendants of 19th-century railroad workers, gives the place a certain cosmopolitan air, manifested in part by numerous Chinese restaurants. If you're heading to Tamarindo, consider a stop in Santa Cruz, a small town known for its January folklore festival, or in Guaitil for pottery shopping.

Church of San Blas, Nicoya's only colonial landmark is an impressive, whitewashed 16th-century building in the central park. Inside, a museum displays silver, bronze, and copper objects from pre-Columbian times.

Where to Stay & Eat
¢–$ ✕ **Restaurant Nicoya.** There are many Chinese restaurants from which to choose in Nicoya. This one is the most elegant, with hanging lanterns, a colorful collection of international flags, and an enormous menu with 85 Asian dishes, such as stir-fried beef with vegetables, along with some familiar favorites, like fried chicken. The fresh sea bass sautéed with fresh pineapple, chayote, and red peppers is excellent. ⊠ *Main road, 70 m (75 yards) south of Coopmani building* ☎ 685–5113 ▤ *No credit cards.*

¢ ✕ **Café Daniela.** For baked goods and light lunches, including hamburgers and sandwiches, try this small, casual restaurant–art gallery, decorated in blue and yellow, with oil paintings on the walls. The pizzas are Costa Rican style, with very little tomato sauce, and there are typical Tico desserts, such as coconut flan and *tres leches* (three milks) cake. The television is usually tuned to a soccer game. ⊠ *Main road, 70 m (75 yards) south of Coopmani building* ☎ 686–6148 ▤ *No credit cards.*

$ 🏨 **Best Western Hotel Curime.** The old hotel underwent many modernizing improvements in 2002, but the tranquil, tree-shaded setting beside a stream can't be improved upon. The large, comfortable rooms are in citrus-color, adobe-style buildings arranged around a mango-bordered soccer field, a great place for kids to let off steam. The huge swimming pool allows for serious laps. The open-air restaurant is a little spare, but the view of the pool and the mature gardens makes up for it. ⊠ *On road to Sámara, ½ km (¼ mi) south of town* ☎ 685–5238 🖷 685–5530 ⇱ *27 rooms* ⚐ *Restaurant, in-room safes, some refrigerators, cable TV, pool, volleyball, playground, meeting room; no room phones* ▤ *AE, MC, V* ⦿ *CP.*

$ ⊡ **Cabinas Río Tempisque de Lujo.** These rooms are luxurious by any standards, but on the road to Santa Cruz they are a marvel. The owner is in the hardware business and the hotel has quality materials inside and out. Rooms have high wooden ceilings and big picture windows. The huge, white-tiled bathrooms have mirrored closets and showers big enough for two. The gardens and pool area are beautifully landscaped. There is no restaurant but room fridges are stocked with juice and soft drinks. ⊠ *On highway north to Santa Cruz, just outside Nicoya* ☎ *686–6650* ⤳ *30 rooms* ♻ *Refrigerators, cable TV, pool; no room phones* ⊟ *MC, V.*

¢ ⊡ **Las Tinajas.** The best of Nicoya's budget accommodations, this simple, clean hotel has a friendly staff and basic rooms with cold water. An outdoor café in back, from which you can watch strutting chickens in the neighbor's yard, serves breakfast. ⊠ *45 m (50 yards) east of Banco Central* ☎☎ *685–5081* ⤳ *28 rooms* ♻ *Fans; no a/c in some rooms, no room phones, no room TVs* ⊟ *V.*

Shopping

Nicoya has many trendy new stores, along with old-fashioned general stores that are fascinating to browse in. **Casa del Sol y La Luna** (⊠ 25 m [13 ft] west of the FujiFilm store ☎ 686–4646) sells sophisticated, locally made crafts and gifts in a wonderful old store with antique tiles on the floor and massive wooden doors.

In the country village of **Guaitil** (⊠ 24 km [15 mi] north of Nicoya) artists—most of them women—have revived a vanishing tradition by producing clay pottery handmade in the manner of pre-Columbian Chorotegans. The town square is a soccer field, and almost every house facing it has a pottery shop out front and a round, wood-fired kiln in back. Pottery designs range from imitation Mexican to inspired Cubist abstractions. Every artisan's style is different, so take the time to wander from shop to shop. Prices are very reasonable, and although the pieces are rumored to crack rather too easily, they make wonderful keepsakes and gifts if you can get them home in one piece.

THE NICOYA PENINSULA A TO Z

To research prices, get advice from other travelers, and book travel arrangements, visit www.fodors.com

AIR TRAVEL

Liberia is a good gateway town to the coast with its international airport, Aeropuerto Internacional Daniel Oduber. Additionally, there are airstrips at Tamarindo, Playa Nosara, Playa Carrillo, Punta Islita, and Tambor. Flying in from San José is the best way to start your vacation right away.

CARRIERS SANSA flies daily from Juan Santamaría International Airport to Tamarindo, Tambor, Playa Carrillo, Punta Islita, and Nosara. NatureAir leaves from Aeropuerto Internacional Tobías Bolaños in Tibás, a northern suburb of San José, to fly to Liberia, Tamarindo, Playa Carrillo, Punta Islita, and Tambor. International flights, mostly charters, arrive directly at Aeropuerto Internacional Daniel Oduber near Liberia; at this writing, Delta Airlines is the only regularly scheduled carrier to land here, with three flights per week from Atlanta.

🛪 Airlines & Contacts **Aeropuerto Internacional Daniel Oduber** ☎ 668-1032 or 296-0909. **NatureAir** ☎ 220-3054 🖶 220-0413 ⊕ www.natureair.com. **SANSA** ☎ 668-1047 Liberia; 656-0131 Sámara; 682-0168 Nosara; 653-0012 Tamarindo; 683-0015 Tambor 🖶 666-1017 ⊕ www.flysansa.com.

BOAT & FERRY TRAVEL

Car ferries run by Naviera Tambor and the Asociación de Desarrollo Integral Paquera (formerly Ferry Peninsula) connect Puntarenas with Paquera, with continuing bus service to Montezuma. The trip takes 1¼ hours, and the car ferries leave six times daily, between 5 AM and 8:15 PM, with an equal number of return trips. The Puntarenas–Playa Naranjo car ferry, run by Cooantramar, takes 1½ hours, departing daily at 3:15, 7, and 10:50 AM and 2:50 and 7 PM.

A passenger-only *lancha* (launch), run by the Asociación de Desarrollo Integral de Paquera, leaves Puntarenas for Paquera three times daily, at 6 and 11 AM and 3:15 PM, from a hard-to-find small dock just west of the Banco Nacional near the market. On the Paquera side, launches leave for Puntarenas on the same schedule. Bus links and cabs are available at the Nicoya end of the ferry lines.

These schedules are subject to change from weekdays to weekends, high to low season and during holidays. Expect long waits on all car ferries in high season and on weekends. Avoid Sunday crossings from Paquera at any time of the year. To avoid a longer-than-necessary wait and to get up-to-the-minute schedules, always call ahead.

At this writing, it is unclear how the Río Tempisque Bridge will affect the river's passenger-and-car ferry routes at Puerto Moreno.
🚤 Boat & Ferry Information **Asociación de Desarrollo Integral de Paquera** ☎ 641-0118 or 641-0515 **Coonatramar** ☎ 661-1069 **Naviera Tambor** ☎ 661-2084.

BUS TRAVEL TO & FROM THE NICOYA PENINSULA

Bus service connects the larger cities to each other and to the more popular beaches, but forget about catching a bus from beach to beach; you'll generally have to backtrack to the inland hubs of Nicoya and Liberia unless you take a minibus, which may take just as long as a bus, although they're usually more comfortable. Bus companies rarely answer their phones and the schedules are always changing, so if accurate information is important to you, it's best to ask at the stations in San José. Your hotel front desk should be able to confirm which station specific buses and lines depart from.

Buses range from plush coaches to dirty old rattletraps, and there is no way of knowing which will be your fate until you get on the bus. During busy times, they add the worst buses. Only some have air-conditioning.

With the forthcoming bridge across the Río Tempisque, bus routes and schedules to some Nicoya beach destinations may change radically. Check with the main ICT tourist office beneath the Plaza de la Cultura in San José; you can get a list of bus schedules there.

LIBERIA & NORTHERN COAST ROUTES From C. 24 between Avdas. 5 and 7, Pulmitan buses leave San José daily and hourly, 6 AM–8 PM for the four-hour trip to Liberia, and leave three times daily at 8 AM, 2 PM and 4 PM for the five-hour trip to Playa del Coco. Empresa Esquivel buses from Liberia leave daily for Playa Hermosa and Panamá at 4:45, 7:30, and 11:30 AM and 1, 3:30, and 5:30 PM. Five-hour buses for Brasilito and Playa Flamingo run by Tralapa leave San José daily from C. 20 between Avdas. 3 and 5 at 8 and 11 AM and 3 PM. For Tamarindo, a 5½-hour trip, buses run by Empresa Alfaro leave daily at 6 and 11 AM and 3:30 PM from C. 14 at Avda. 5.

CENTRAL & SOUTHERN COAST ROUTES Empresa Alfaro buses run from San José (C. 14 between Avdas. 3 and 5) to Nicoya daily, via Liberia, at 6:30 AM, 10 AM, 1:30 PM, 3 PM, and 5 PM, a five-hour trip; to Nosara daily at 6 AM, a six-hour trip; and to Sámara daily at 12:30 PM, a five-hour trip.

The Castillos company (no phone) runs a local bus to Junquillal from the central market in Santa Cruz, leaving at 10:15 AM, 2:30, and 5:30 PM. Buses leave Junquillal for Santa Cruz at 6 AM, noon, and 4 PM. Tralapa buses to Santa Cruz leave from Avda. 5, between Cs. 20 and 22, at 7 and 9 AM and then every hour on the hour until 6 PM. The trip to Santa Cruz takes five hours.

Empresa Rojas buses leave Nicoya for Nosara, Garza, and Guiones weekdays at 5 AM, 10 AM and 2 PM; the same line runs from Nicoya to Sámara, weekdays at 6 and 10 AM, noon, 3, and 4:15 PM, and to Carrillo from Nicoya at noon and 3 PM; weekends, buses leave at 10 AM and 3 PM for Nosara and Sámara.

Empresarios Unidos buses leave for the 2½-hour trip from San José (C. 16 between Avdas. 10 and 12) to Puntarenas daily every 40 minutes, from 6 AM to 7 PM. Buses run to Montezuma from Paquera, via Cóbano, six times daily between 6:15 AM and 6:15 PM, returning six times between 5:30 AM and 4:30 PM; but inquire about the latest schedule for this route before you set off. Buses to Malpaís run daily from Cóbano at 10:30 AM and 2:30 PM.

MINIBUS ROUTES For $21, you can ride on the comfortable, air-conditioned Gray Line Tours Fantasy Bus that connect San Jose, Liberia, Playa Flamingo, Playa Hermosa, Tamarindo, and other destinations in Guanacaste. The Fantasy Bus from San José to Tamarindo and Liberia begins picking up passengers from hotels daily around 6 AM. The return bus leaves Tamarindo around 2 PM and passes through Liberia around 3:30 PM. Gray Line has a weekly pass that lets you ride all over Costa Rica for $63.
🚍 Bus Information **Empresa Alfaro** ☎ 222-2666; 685-5032 in Nicoya. **Empresa Esquivel** ☎ 666-0042. **Empresarios Unidos** ☎ 222-1867. **Empresa Rojas** ☎ 685-5352. **Gray Line Tours Fantasy Bus** ☎ 223-4650 ⊕ www.graylinecostarica.com. **Pulmitan** ☎ 222-1650. **Tralapa** ☎ 223-5859 or 680-0392.

CAR RENTAL
It's best to stick with the main rental offices in San José, because they have more cars available and you're more likely to reach an English-speaking agent on the phone; some have local satellite offices. Alamo offers pickup and car delivery in Liberia. Budget has branches in San José and also 6 km (4 mi) west of Liberia's airport. Economy, Alamo, and Elegante rent cars in Tamarindo; Economy has a good supply of automatic four-wheel-drive vehicles.
🚗 International Agencies **Alamo** ✉ 2 km (1 mi)) north of Liberia airport, Liberia ☎ 668-1111, 800/462-5266 in the U.S. ✉ Hotel Diriá, Tamarindo ☎ 653-0727. **Budget** ✉ 6 km (4 mi) southwest of Liberia airport, Liberia ☎ 668-1024 or 668-1126 ✉ Tamarindo Vista Villas Hotel, Tamarindo ☎ 653-0829. **Economy** ✉ 3½ km (2 mi) south of Liberia airport, Liberia ☎ 666-2816 or 666-7560 ✉ on the main road entering Tamarindo, next to Restaurant Coconut, Tamarindo ☎ 653-0728.
🚗 Local Agencies **Elegante** ✉ 5 km (3mi) south of Liberia Airport, Liberia ☎ 668-1054. **Sol Rentacar** ✉ in front of Hotel El Bramadero, Liberia ☎ 666-2222 ✉ Playa Hermosa ☎ 356-9872.

CAR TRAVEL
The northwest is accessed via the paved two-lane Pan-American Highway (CA1), which begins at the top of Paseo Colón in San José. The bridge across the Río Tempisque, opened in 2003, should cut down travel time considerably to the Pacific beaches south of Liberia. Ferries continue to run from Puntarenas to Paquera and Playa Naranjo for access to destinations on the Gulf of Nicoya side of the peninsula.

Paved roads run down the spine of the Nicoya Peninsula all the way to Playa Naranjo, with many unpaved and potholed stretches. Once you get off the main highway, the pavement holds out only so far, and then dirt, dust, mud, potholes, and other factors come into play. The roads to Playa Sámara, Playa del Coco, and Ocotal are paved all the way; every other destination requires some dirt-road maneuvering. If you're headed down to the coast via unpaved roads, be sure to get advance information on road conditions. Take a four-wheel-drive vehicle if possible.

If you want to drive, be prepared to spend some serious time in the car. The road to Nicoya's southern tip is partly paved and partly just gravel, and it winds up and down and around various bays. Some roads leading from Liberia to the coast are intermittently paved. As you work your way toward the coast, pay close attention to the assorted hotel signs at intersections—they may be the only indicators of which roads to take to your lodging.

EMERGENCIES
In case of any emergency, dial 911 or one of the numbers below.
🛂 Emergency Services **Fire** ☎ 118. **Police** ☎ 118. **Red Cross Ambulance** ☎ 128.

TOURS
In addition to the following major agencies, most hotels can organize guided tours for you. Ríos Tropicales, a high-quality adventure tour company, runs excellent multiday sea-kayaking trips that leave from Curú National Wildlife Refuge and meander among the islands of the Gulf of Nicoya. The company also leads river-rafting trips throughout the country and a float trip for bird-watchers down Guanacaste's Río Corobicí. Day trips to the idyllic Isla Tortuga in the Gulf of Nicoya are very popular, and Calypso Tours has been leading them longer than anyone else. The excellent Horizontes specializes in more independent tours, with as few as eight people, that include four-wheel-drive transport, naturalist guides, and guest lecturers.

A boat service shuttles surfers between Montezuma and Jacó, another popular surfing town across the gulf. Tours can easily be arranged by your hotel or by any one of the tour agencies in town. Cocozuma organizes a boat shuttle service to Jacó and has some tours of the area.
🛂 Tour Companies **Calypso Tours** ⊠ Avda. 2 between Cs. 1 and 3, San José ☎ 256-2727 🖶 256-6767 ⊕ www.calypsotours.com. **Cocozuma** ⊠ next to El Sano Banano, Montezuma ☎ 642-0911 ⊕ www.cocozuma.com **Horizontes** ⊠ 130 m [140 yards] north of Pizza Hut Paseo Colón, San José ☎ 222-2022 🖶 255-4513 ⊕ www.horizontes.com. **Ríos Tropicales** ⊠ 45 m [50 yards] south of Centro Colón on C. 38, San José ☎ 233-6455 🖶 255-4354 ⊕ www.riostropicales.com.

VISITOR INFORMATION
The tourist office in San José has information on Guanacaste and the peninsula. As a cruise ship and ferry port, Puntarenas has two tourist offices. La Camera de Turismo is open weekdays 8–noon and 2–5, and weekends when cruise ships are in port. La Oficina de Información Turistica, near the Puntarenas car ferry terminal, provides information daily 8–7:30.
🛂 Tourist Information **La Camera de Turismo** ⊠ Plaza de las Artesanias, in front of Muelle de Cruceros, Puntarenas ☎ 661-2980. **La Oficina de Información Turistica** ⊠ near car ferry terminal, Puntarenas ☎ 661-9011.

THE CENTRAL PACIFIC COAST

FODOR'S CHOICE

Club del Mar, *Jacó*

El Gran Escape, *Quepos*

Makanda by the Sea, *Manuel Antonio*

HIGHLY RECOMMENDED

RESTAURANTS   Aparthotel Flamboyant, *Puntarenas*

Hotel Poseidon Restaurant, *Jacó*

Marisquería El Hicaco, *Jacó*

HOTELS   Aparthotel Flamboyant, *Puntarenas*

Costa Verde, *Manuel Antonio*

Hotel Vela Bar, *Manuel Antonio*

La Mariposa, *Manuel Antonio*

Villa Caletas, *Tárcoles*

Revised by
David
Dudenhoefer

WITH ITS LUSH TROPICAL FORESTS, palm-lined beaches, and excellent conditions for an array of outdoor activities, the Central Pacific region encompasses much of what draws people to Costa Rica—all within hours of San José. It's easy to understand why the area has become so popular: its verdant hills, vibrant sea, and soft-sand beaches provide a veritable cornucopia of vacation opportunities.

The region—Carara National Park in particular—is a transition zone between the tropical dry forests of the northwest and the wet forests of the Pacific coast farther to the south. Since most of its woodlands were cut decades ago, however, the Central Pacific landscape is dominated by steep coffee farms, vast oil-palm plantations, and bright green pastures populated by cows and Cattle Egrets. Manuel Antonio National Park, together with the private reserves of nearby hotels, protects one of the last patches of coastal rain forest in the region, as well as several idyllic, white-sand beaches.

Despite the fact that the region's protected areas are among the smallest in the country, they are rich habitats with an amazing variety of flora and fauna, including such endangered species as the Scarlet Macaw and the Central American Squirrel Monkey. The ocean here is equally diverse, which can be confirmed by a snorkeling session in Manuel Antonio or sportfishing off Playas Herradura, Jacó, or Quepos. Several of the region's beaches offer excellent surfing, and sea-kayaking is a great way to appreciate the rocky coastline between strands. The rain forest can be explored on horseback or foot, and the bird-watching is simply amazing. The area's forested mountains hold spectacular waterfalls, and several of the rivers flowing out of them are exciting white-water rafting routes; the meandering, muddy Río Tarcoles and Damas Estuary can be explored on boat trips that bring one eye to eye with crocodiles and other wild things.

Exploring Central Pacific Costa Rica

Attractions lie conveniently close to each other, making it easy to combine beach time with forest exploration or marine diversions. Every destination in this chapter is between two and four hours from San José by road. A winding mountain road passes through Atenas on the way to Orotina, from where the coastal highway, or Costanera, heads southeast to Tárcoles, Herradura, Jacó, Hermosa, and Quepos. The 30-minute flight from San José to Quepos is an excellent option for travelers who have little time or don't want to drive.

About the Restaurants

Restaurants in Manuel Antonio and Jacó serve some of Costa Rica's best meals, from upscale Pacific Rim flavors to traditional Tico fare. Thanks to world-class fishing, seafood—from fresh-caught dorado and yellowfin tuna to spiny lobster—is the forte of the area's best chefs. In Manuel Antonio, the ambience is often as exotic as the food, with tables set amid tropical foliage, overlooking the sea, or on the beach itself.

About the Hotels

This region has some of the priciest lodgings in the country—upwards of $150 for a double during high season—but it is not without its deals. Travelers on a budget can find plenty of doubles for under $100 and a few decent rooms for less than $50. As a rule, prices drop 20%–30% during the low season (May–mid-December). Though Playas Jacó and Hermosa have plenty of accommodations on the beach, most of Manuel Antonio's hotels are on a hill, a short drive from the beach, where they enjoy splendid views of the coast and jungle.

5

Numbers in the text correspond to numbers in the margin and on the Central Pacific Costa Rica map.

If you have 3 days
Head straight for ▦ **Quepos** ❼ ⌐, and hit the beach at ▦ **Manuel Antonio** ❽. If you're driving from San José, be sure to stop at **Carara National Park** ❷ on your way to Manuel Antonio. Rise early the next day to spend the morning exploring **Manuel Antonio National Park** ❾, and enjoy the afternoon horseback riding or relaxing on the beach. Dedicate the third morning to white-water rafting, sea-kayaking, skin diving, surfing, or exploring a private reserve, then catch an afternoon flight back to San José.

If you have 6 days
Spend your first night at one of the lodges near the ▦ **Carara National Park** ❷ ⌐ or ▦ **Tárcoles** ❸. Enjoy some bird-watching, hike to a waterfall, or take a canopy tour. On the second morning, visit the national park; then head to either ▦ **Jacó** ❺ or ▦ **Playa Hermosa** ❻ to get your beach fix. You may want to spend another night here to get into the rhythm of relaxation. On day three or four, go south to ▦ **Manuel Antonio** ❽ and spend the afternoon horseback riding, sea-kayaking, fishing, or lounging on the beach. Visit **Manuel Antonio National Park** ❾ early on day five; then drive back into the mountains to spend your last night in **Atenas** ❶, just 40 minutes from the international airport. Alternately, since Quepos and Manuel Antonio have so much to offer, fly straight there and stay put—you won't get bored.

WHAT IT COSTS				
	$$$$	$$$	$$	$	¢
RESTAURANTS	over $25	$20–$25	$10–$20	$5–$10	under $5
HOTELS	over $200	$125–$200	$75–$125	$35–$75	under $35

Restaurant prices are per-person for a main course at dinner. Hotel prices are for two people in a standard double room in high season, excluding service and tax (16.4%).

Timing

The weather in the central Pacific region follows the same dry- and rainy-season weather patterns common to the rest of the Pacific slope, which means lots of sun from December to May and frequent rain from September to November. Since you'll have to share the area with other travelers in the dry season, consider touring the region at another time. The weather tends to be perfect in July and August, with lots of sunny days and occasional light rain.

THE CENTRAL PACIFIC HINTERLANDS

Beaches may be this region's biggest draw, but the countryside hides vast haciendas interspersed with patches of tropical wilderness where you might encounter any critter from the capuchin monkey to the Collared Aracari to crocodiles lurking amid the estuaries' mangroves. Because it's an ecological transition zone, the region is extremely diverse biologically, making it a boon for bird-watchers and other wildlife enthusiasts.

Atenas

● *42 km (26 mi) west of San José.*

National Geographic once listed Atenas as having one of the 12 best climates in the world, and that's pretty much this little town's only claim to fame. In addition to having spectacular weather, Atenas is a pleasantly quiet, traditional community that few foreigners visit, despite the fact that it's en route to the central Pacific beaches. Some well-kept wooden and adobe houses are scattered around a small church and central plaza, and surrounding the town are coffee farms, cattle ranches, and patches of forest. Just west of Atenas, the road to Orotina winds its way down the mountains past breathtaking views.

Where to Stay

$ 🏨 **El Cafetal Inn.** A friendly Salvadorean-Colombian couple owns this B&B; they go out of their way to make you comfortable and help with your travel plans. On a hill and a coffee farm, the two-story cement lodge has comfortable accommodations. The superior tower rooms are larger and have curved windows for panoramic views. Breakfast includes home-roasted coffee and is served on the back patio. ⊠ *Santa Eulalia de Atenas, 8 km (5 mi) north of Atenas; heading west from San José on highway to Puntarenas, turn left (south) just before bridge 5 km (3 mi) west of Grecia, then follow signs* ✆ *Apdo. 105, Atenas* ☎ *446–5785* 📠 *446–7028* ⊕ *www.cafetal.com* ⊲ *12 rooms* ⌂ *Restaurant, fans, pool, bar, laundry service, no-smoking rooms; no a/c, no room phones, no room TVs* ⊟ *AE, MC, V* ⏀ *BP.*

Carara National Park

▶ **❷** *21 km (13 mi) southwest of Orotina, 83 km (51 mi) southwest of San José.*

On the east side of the road between Puntarenas and Playa Jacó, Parque Nacional Carara protects one of the last remnants of an ecological transition zone between Costa Rica's drier northwest and the more humid southwest. It consequently holds a tremendous collection of plants and animals. Much of the 47-square-km (18-square-mi) park is covered with primary forest on steep slopes, where the massive trees are laden with vines and epiphytes. The sparse undergrowth makes wildlife easier to see here than in many other parks, but nothing is guaranteed. If you're lucky, you may glimpse armadillos, basilisk lizards, Blue-crowned Motmots, Chestnut-mandibled Toucans, trogons, coatis, and any of several monkey species. Carara is one of the few places in Costa Rica where you might see Scarlet Macaws.

The first trail on the left shortly after the bridge that spans the Río Tárcoles (a good place to spot crocodiles) leads to a horseshoe-shape lagoon, called *laguna meandrica* (ox-bow lake). The small lagoon covered with water hyacinths is home to turtles, crocodiles, and waterfowl such as the northern jacana, roseate spoonbill, and boat-billed heron. It is a two- to four-hour hike from the trailhead to the lagoon. Cars parked at the trailhead have been broken into, so ask at the main ranger station (several miles south of the trailhead) if there is a ranger on duty at the *sendero laguna meandrica* lagoon. If there isn't, you may be able to leave your belongings at the main ranger station, where you can also buy drinks and souvenirs and use the rest room.

Two trails lead into the forest from the parking lot. At this writing, park officials are planning to make one short stretch wheelchair-accessible by mid-2003. A longer trail connects with the Quebrada Bonita loop,

Fishing

The sportfishing of Herradura, Jacó, and Quepos is among the best in the world. Year-round billfish makes Quepos a favorite flyfishing spot. But marlin, sailfish, dorado, Black and Yellowfin Tuna, mackerel, Wahoo, snook, and several kinds of snapper and jack can all be found in Central Pacific waters. Marlin fishing is best in October and November. Most species can be found year-round. Tuna are most abundant from May to September. Not a few world records have been broken off the Central Pacific coast. A number of hotels have excellent fishing packages.

Nightlife

Jacó has the region's most varied nightlife, especially on weekends, when Josefinos (residents of San José) roll into town. You'll also find plenty of after-dark options in Quepos and Manuel Antonio, the latter tending toward the upscale, with Quepos offering more for Costa Ricans and younger travelers.

Outdoor Adventures

Several white-water rivers—Ríos Naranjo, Savegre, and Parrita—flow northeast from the Cordillera de Talamanca chain, allowing for great Class III and IV rafting during and just after the rainy season. Other water-sport options include excellent surfing, sea-kayaking, and snorkeling. Prefer dry land? You can ride horseback through the forested hinterlands, hike through the area's national parks and private reserves, or explore the treetops on a skywalk or canopy tour.

---

which takes two to three hours to hike. The latter can be quite muddy during the rainy months, when you may want rubber boots. Carara's proximity to San José and Jacó means that tour buses arrive regularly in high season, scaring some animals deeper into the forest. Come very early or late in the day to avoid crowds. Bird-watchers can call the day before to arrange admission before the park opens. Camping is not permitted in Carara. ✢ *Turn left off CA1 for Atenas and follow signs for Jacó; reserve is on left after you cross Río Tárcoles* ☎ *383–9953* ✉ *$8* ☉ *Daily 7–4.*

Tárcoles

❸ *90 km (56 mi) southwest of San José.*

The town of Tárcoles doesn't warrant a stop, but it's the departure point for crocodile-watching boat tours up the Río Tárcoles. Two exceptional hotels are nearby, as is a spectacular waterfall in a private nature reserve. Bird-watchers have plenty to focus their binoculars on, because the combination of the transitional forest and adjacent river results in an inordinate diversity of birds within a small area.

If you pull over just after crossing the Río Tárcoles bridge, you can often spot massive crocodiles lounging on the banks (bring binoculars). Be sure to lock your car—vehicles have been stolen here. The entrance to the town of Tárcoles is on the west side of the road, just south of Carara National Park; across the highway is a dirt road that leads to the Hotel Villa Lapas and the waterfall reserve.

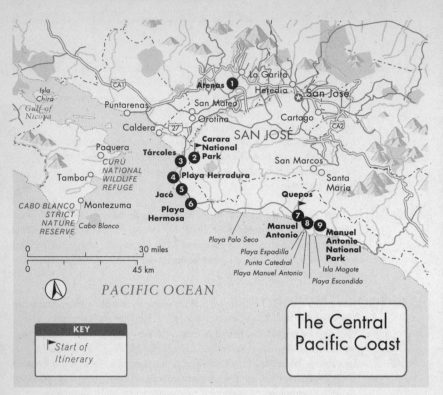

KEY

⮞ Start of
Itinerary

The Central
Pacific Coast

Manantial de Agua Viva, a 656-ft waterfall on a private reserve next to Carara National Park, flows into 10 natural pools, any of them perfect for a refreshing dip after the hike into the reserve. The forest surrounding the waterfall is home to parrots, monkeys, Scarlet Macaws, and most of the other animals found in the nearby park. A tough 2½-km (1½-mi) trail makes a loop through the woods, passing the waterfall and pools; it takes between 40 minutes and 2 hours to hike, depending on how much bird-watching you do—good physical condition and hiking shoes are needed. The entrance is 9 km (5 mi) from the coastal highway, up the same dirt road that leads to the Hotel Villa Lapas. ▨ *$10* ⊙ *Daily 8–5*.

Where to Stay

★ **$$$** ✕▥ **Villa Caletas.** Perched on a luxuriant promontory, this collection of elegant villas and suites sequestered in the jungle was designed with couples in mind. Views of surrounding verdure and the sea below are amazing. Standard rooms in the main buildings have less privacy; deluxe rooms are worth the extra expense for their ocean views. French and Caribbean motifs are combined throughout, with faux antiques, framed prints, and cane chairs. France is the predominant influence in the open-air restaurant ($$), which has a spectacular view, especially at sunset. Seafood and fresh beef are specialties. The infinity-edge pool is gorgeous but tiny, as is the hotel's private beach. ⊠ *Off coastal highway, 8 km (5 mi) south of Hotel Villa Lapas* ☎ *637–0606* 🖷 *637–0404* ⊕ *www.hotelvillacaletas.com* 🖃 *Apdo. 12358–1000, San José* ⇆ *15 rooms, 12 suites, 10 villas* 🖫 *Restaurant, fans, in-room safes, minibars, cable TV, pool, exercise equipment, spa, beach, bar, shop, laundry service, concierge* 🖃 *AE, DC, MC, V* �|⊙| *BP.*

$$ ▥ **Hotel Villa Lapas.** Tall trees and a stream flowing by make Villa Lapas a great place for nature lovers, as does the series of suspension bridges that wend through the canopy of the hotel's protected forest. Kids enjoy the ample lawns and games. For the adventurous, there is a canopy tour on the property. Rooms are in low cement buildings with porches and barrel-tile roofs. Though nothing special, they are pleasant enough, with terra-cotta floors, hardwood ceilings, and large baths. ⊠ *Off coastal highway, 4 km (2½ mi) after bridge over Tárcoles River* ⊕ *Apdo. 419-4005, Heredia* ☎ *637–0232* 🖷 *637–0227* ⊕ *www.villalapas.com* ⬐ *47 rooms* ⬧ *Restaurant, fans, in-room safes, miniature golf, pool, bar, recreation room, shop, laundry service, meeting room; no room TVs* ▭ *AE, DC, MC, V* ⦿ *FAP.*

The Outdoors

BOAT TRIPS One of the most popular activities in the area is the river trip on the muddy Río Tárcoles, which is home to massive crocodiles and colorful waterfowl. **Jungle Crocodile Safaris** (☎ 637–0338) runs a boat tour that guarantees close encounters of the crocodilian kind. **Fantasy Tours** (⊠ Best Western lobby, main road Jacó ☎ 777–0082 or 643–1000) leads a boat trip on the Río Tárcoles.

HIKING Hikers have enough options in this area to keep them afoot for a couple days. Carara National Park has four trails through its rain forest, and the Manantial de Agua Viva has a steeper trail to one of the country's highest waterfalls. Those who prefer an equestrian adventure can visit the Agua Viva waterfall on a horseback tour run by **Complejo Ecológico la Catarata** (☎ 661–8263), which is 9 km (5½ mi) up the dirt road to Hotel Villa Lapas.

THE COAST NEAR SAN JOSÉ

Along this short stretch of coast are patches of undeveloped jungle, the popular Manuel Antonio National Park, some of Costa Rica's most accessible beaches. The proximity of these strands to San José leads Costa Ricans and foreigners alike to pop down for quick beach vacations. Surfers have good reason to head for Playas Jacó and Hermosa, due to the consistency of their waves, and anglers and golfers should consider Playa Herradura's links and rocky strand. Other travelers may find these beaches overrated or overdeveloped. Manuel Antonio might be accused of the latter, but nobody can deny its natural beauty.

Playa Herradura

❹ *16 km (10 mi) south of Tárcoles.*

Large-scale development has put this long-neglected beach on the map for travelers and investors. The multimillion-dollar Los Sueños Resort is complemented by an 18-hole Ted Robinson–designed golf course, a modern marina, and an expanding supply of luxury condos, which make Herradura as much a real estate development as a tourist destination. The dark brown, rocky beach is one of Costa Rica's least attractive, but the hotel, while massive, is one of the country's loveliest. If sportfishing and golf are your priorities, this is a good option; if you're looking for a nice beach, nature, or seclusion, it isn't.

Where to Stay & Eat

$$$$ ✕⊡ **Marriott Los Sueños Beach and Golf Resort.** This palatial Spanish colonial–style masterpiece was built to resemble a Latin American village. Modern amenities are mixed with Nicaraguan barrel-tile roofing, traditional Guatemalan textiles and furniture, and Costa Rican hand-painted tiles. Rooms have large marble baths, watercolors of historic Costa Rica, and tiny "Juliet" balconies—request a room with an ocean view. The enormous pool has landscaped islands, bridges, and swim-

up bars and is the site of activities for all ages. The restaurant ($–$$$$) selection ranges from Italian to "Nuevo Latino," with such delicacies as saffron shrimp, grilled tenderloin, and plantain-crusted red snapper. A breakfast-and-dinner meal plan is available. ✉ *Playa Herradura* ☎ *630–9000, 800/228–9290 in the U.S.* 📠 *630–9090* 🌐 *www. marriotthotels.com* ↻ *191 rooms, 10 suites* ♿ *3 restaurants, café, in-room safes, minibars, cable TV, 18-hole golf course, pool, gym, massage, beach, boating, fishing, 2 bars, casino, shops, baby-sitting, children's programs, laundry services, concierge, business services, meeting rooms, travel services; no-smoking rooms* 🚭 *AE, DC, MC, V* ❢⃝❢ *BP.*

Jacó

⑤ *2 km (1 mi) south of Playa Herradura, 108 km (67 mi) southwest of San José.*

Its proximity to San José and wide, sandy bay resulted in Jacó's development as one of Costa Rica's first beach resorts decades ago. More than 50 hotels and cabinas back its long, gray-sand beach, and the mix of restaurants, shops, and hotels lining the town's main drag gives it a rather cluttered appearance. From the water, however, the development is mostly hidden behind the coconut palms that line the beach, and forest-covered hills rise in the distance. Jacó is primarily the destination of American surfers, Europeans on package tours, and Costa Ricans, who flock there on weekends and major holidays. In addition to sunbathing and surfing, you can take a kayak tour, go horseback riding or deep-sea fishing, hike through the nearby Carara National Park, or boat up the crocodile-infested Río Tárcoles.

Long, palm-lined **Playa Jacó** is a pleasant enough spot in the morning, but it can burn the soles of your feet on a sunny afternoon. Though the gray sand makes it less attractive than most other Costa Rican beaches, it's a good place to enjoy a sunset. Playa Jacó is popular with surfers for the consistency of its waves. Riptides can make the sea hazardous for swimmers, so don't go in deeper than your waist if the sea is rough.

Where to Stay & Eat

★ $$–$$$$ ✕ **Hotel Poseidon Restaurant.** One of Jacó's best restaurants, in front of the lobby at tiny Hotel Poseidon, has outdoor patio seating, friendly service, good music, and a small selection of inventive dishes that changes every few days. The half-dozen meat and seafood dishes are usually Pacific Rim innovations, such as mahimahi topped with toasted pecans, filet mignon with a balsamic demi-glace, or Thai-style prawns. ✉ *C. Bohío, 25 m (30 yards) west of main road* ☎ *643–1642* 🚭 *AE, MC, V.*

★ $$–$$$$ ✕ **Marisquería El Hicaco.** Set just back from the beach, El Hicaco is one of Jacó's only restaurants with an ocean view, and one of the best places for seafood. In fact you can get little else here. Tuna, mahimahi, squid, prawns, lobster, and other marine edibles are prepared in a half-dozen ways, with everything from garlic to shrimp sauce. A popular dinner buffet every Wednesday offers all of the above cooked to order, plus side dishes, beer, wine, and an impressive dessert selection. ✉ *100 m (110 yards) south and 90 m (100 yards) west of Mas X Menos supermarket* ☎ *643–3226* 🚭 *AE, DC, MC, V.*

¢–$ ✕ **Rioasis.** This colorful, open-air restaurant has an eclectic menu of burritos and other Tex-Mex treats, a few pastas, and salads, but the big draw is pizza—more than two dozen kinds are baked in a wood-burning oven. You eat on the front patio or under a high roof hung with ceiling fans, and there's a long bar in back. This is also a good place to shoot pool or play darts during happy hour (6 to 7). ⊠ *North of Banco Nacional, 6 m (20 ft) off the main road* ☎ 643–3354 ▤ V ◷ *Closed Tues.*

$$$ ✕⌨ **Club del Mar.** Nestled amid massive trees and gardens at the south-
Fodor'sChoice ern extreme of the beach, this friendly place has some of Costa Rica's
★ best accommodations. A dozen two-story buildings hold *casitas*: spacious one- and two-bedroom vacation apartments with abundant windows that take advantage of the ocean breeze and views of sea and foliage. Green-tile floors, carved hardwoods, and framed prints complement the natural surroundings, and the open design makes air-conditioning optional. Tasteful standard-size rooms with sea-view balconies are perched over the airy bar and restaurant ($$–$$$), which serves some of Jacó's best dinners—from chateaubriand to lobster thermidor. ⊠ *Costanera, 275 m (300 yards) south of gas station* ⌖ *Apdo. 107–4023, Jacó* ☎ 643–3194 ⊕ *www.clubdelmarcostarica.com* ⬐ *8 rooms, 22 casitas* ♨ *Restaurant, fans, in-room safes, kitchens, cable TV, pool, spa, bar, shop, laundry facilities, laundry service, travel services* ▤ *AE, MC, V.*

★ **$** ⌨ **Aparthotel Flamboyant.** This quiet oceanfront hotel is a good deal, especially if you take advantage of the cooking facilities. Most rooms have kitchenettes, though four on the second floor have cable TV, air-conditioning, and a refrigerator instead. Tiny terraces with chairs overlook a lush garden and pool area, where there's a grill for your use. It's all just a few steps from the beach and Jacó's busy main strip. ⊠ *Behind Wishbone Restaurant* ☎ 643–3146 ⧉ 643–1068 ⌖ *Apdo. 018–4023, Puntarenas* ⬐ *13 rooms* ♨ *Fans, in-room safes, some kitchenettes, some refrigerators, pool; no a/c in some rooms, no TV in some rooms* ▤ *AE, MC, V.*

$ ⌨ **Hotel Tangeri.** Spread over a verdant lot on the beach, the Tangeri offers various lodging options. Of the bright, spacious rooms in two-story cement buildings, six have ocean views (those with numbers ending in 1, 2, or 3); the rest overlook the palm-shaded lawn. All have white-tile floors and two double beds. Families and small groups can rent chalets, which have kitchenettes and either one bedroom and a sofa bed or three bedrooms; two lack air-conditioning but cost less. ⊠ *Main road north of river* ☎ 643–3001 ⧉ 643–3636 ⊕ *www.hoteltangeri.com* ⌖ *Apdo. 622–4050, Alajuela* ⬐ *14 rooms, 13 chalets* ♨ *2 restaurants, in-room safes, refrigerators, cable TV, 3 pools, volleyball, playground; no a/c in some rooms, no room phones* ▤ *AE, MC, V.*

$ ⌨ **Mar de Luz.** It may be a few blocks from the beach, and it doesn't look like much from the street, but Mar de Luz is a surprisingly pleasant, quiet place. The Dutch owners are dedicated to cleanliness and providing extra amenities, such as the poolside grill and plentiful lounges. The older, pastel-hue rooms have two queen-size beds and small porches; the newer, split-level rooms are a bit larger, with attractive stone walls, white-tile floors, and windows overlooking the gardens. ⊠ *45 m (50 yards) east of main road, across from Hotel Tangeri* ☎ 643–3259 ⊕ *www.mardeluz.com* ⬐ *29 rooms* ♨ *In-room safes, kitchenettes, cable TV, pool, Ping Pong, laundry service; no room phones* ▤ *V.*

¢ ⌨ **La Cometa.** If you want clean, convenient rooms without expensive frills, this place delivers. Across the street from Jacó's strip of souvenir shops and restaurants, La Cometa fills with budget travelers, who can usually be found reading or lazing on the long patio that overlooks a parking lot camouflaged by a simple tropical garden. Most rooms have ceiling fans; air-conditioning costs just a few dollars more. ⊠ *Across main road from Restaurante Colonial* ☎ 643–3615 ⌖ *Apdo. 116–4023, Jacó* ⬐ *10 rooms, 6 with bath* ♨ *Fans; no a/c in some rooms, no room phones* ▤ *No credit cards.*

Nightlife & the Arts

Jacó has a plethora of after-dinner options, from restaurants perfect for a quiet drink to bars with pool tables and/or rock music. There's also a dance club, a casino, and a strip bar. Jacó's only casino is in the **Hotel Amapola** (☎ 643–2255), about 130 m (140 yards) east of the Municipalidad. A mix of classic rock and sports on big-screen TVs makes the **Beatles Bar** (☎ 643–2211) a popular spot among resident expats and tourists alike. It is about 180 m (200 yards) north of Hotel Tangeri on the main road, For a funky, ghoulish ambience, try **La Bruja** (☎ 643-3493), The Witch, across the street from the Beatles Bar. There's live rock music from Thursday through Saturday. The club is closed Monday. The rather large **Club Ole** (☎ 643–3226), on the main road north of the Beatles Bar, has a dance floor, pool tables, darts, and other diversions. Dancing fools can cut loose on the floor of the air-conditioned **La Central** (☎ 643–3076), on the beach, at the end of the street across from Mas x Menos. Across from Club Ole and upstairs, **La Hacienda** (☎ 643–3191) caters to a younger crowd, with surf videos, pool tables, and darts.

The Outdoors

HORSEBACK RIDING **Jacó Beach Equestrian Center** (☎ 643–1569) leads three- to four-hour horseback rides with English or western equipment. To get there, follow the signs at the bridge.

KAYAKING **Kayak Jacó** (☎ 643–1233) runs river- and sea-kayaking tours for novices and seasoned adventurers. Owner Neil Kahn also arranges half-day outrigger-canoe trips to secluded Jacó area beaches.

SURFING Jacó has dozens of beach breaks, all of which are best around high tide. The waves are even better at nearby Playa Escondida, which is accessible only by boat. Surfboard-toting tourists abound in Jacó, but you don't need to be a bona fide surfer dude to enjoy the waves—there are several places that rent boards, and the swell is often small enough for beginners. However if the surf is big and you don't have much experience, stay on the beach: rip currents are common here, and they've drowned dozens of swimmers over the years.

Surfboard rentals are easy to arrange; one good outfitter is **Surf Shop Walter** (✉ main road, south of bridge ☎ 643–1056), which buys and sells boards. The shop also does ding repairs. If you plan to spend more than a week surfing it might be cheaper to buy a used board and sell it before you leave. **Mother of Fear** (✉ main road, south of Tangeri Chalets ☎ 643–2001) has the best selection of used surfboards in the country. The shop will usually buy the same board back for a fraction of the price you paid, which is still cheaper than renting one for a week or more.

Playa Hermosa

❻ *5 km (3 mi) south of Jacó, 113 km (70 mi) southwest of San José.*

Just over the rocky ridge that forms the southern edge of Jacó is Playa Hermosa, a swath of gray sand stretching southeast as far as the eye can see. Unlike its *tranquilo* northern neighbor of the same name, this southern belle has jaw-dropping surf breaks and caters to a much younger crowd. The beach's northern end is popular with surfers. Because of its angle, it often has waves when Jacó and other spots are flat. If you're not a surfer, Hermosa holds little charm: its gray sand gets extremely hot, and frequent rip currents make it unsafe to swim when the waves are big. Its only nonsurf attractions are horseback tours into the nearby hills and the olive ridley turtles that nest on the beach at night from August to December.

Where to Stay

$$ ⊞ **The Backyard.** Surfers are the main clientele at this two-story cement hotel overlooking the beach and a small pool. Rooms have high ceilings, tile floors, and sliding-glass doors that open onto small balconies furnished with plastic chairs and tables. The hotel owns a rustic eatery next door that serves burgers, Tex-Mex, and fresh fish dinners. The bar, with its pool and rockin' tunes, is a popular nightspot. ⊠ *West side of Costanera, Playa Hermosa* ⌂ *Apdo. 132–4023, Jacó* ☎ *643–1311* ⊕ *www. backyardhotel.com* ↪ *6 rooms* ⌂ *Restaurant, fans, in-room safes, cable TV, pool, bar, laundry service; no room phones* ⊟ *AE, MC, V.*

$ ⊞ **Ola Bonita.** Just steps from the surf break, this two-story building with a barrel-tile roof is a nicer alternative to Hermosa's other budget hotels. Rooms have red-tile floors, white stucco walls, simple kitchenettes, and one bunk and double bed each. They are a bit cramped, with low ceilings, but the common porch and tiny pool area in back are pleasant spots for loitering. ⊠ *West side of Costanera, Playa Hermosa* ☎ *643–3990* ⊕ *www.olabonita.com* ↪ *6 rooms* ⌂ *Fans, kitchenettes, cable TV, pool; no room phones* ⊟ *AE, MC, V.*

The Outdoors

HORSEBACK RIDING   For those who tire of surf and sand, **Discovery Horseback Safaris** (☎ 643–3808) leads two horseback tours into the mountains, stopping at waterfalls on the way, and sunset beach rides.

SURFING   Most people who bed down at Playa Hermosa are here for the same reason—the waves that break just a shell's toss away. One of the country's most consistent surf spots, Hermosa may have waves when all the other beaches are flat. There are dozens of beach breaks scattered along the beach, and the surf is always best at high tide. Because it is a beach break, though, it can close out when big. You can rent, repair, and purchase boards in nearby Jacó.

Quepos

▶ ❼ *23 km (14 mi) south of Parrita, 174 km (108 mi) southwest of San José.*

With a population of about 12,000, Quepos is the largest, most important town in this corner of Costa Rica. It owes its name to the tribe that inhabited the area when the first visiting Spaniard, Juan Vásquez de Coronado, rode through the region in the mid 1500s. It's not certain whether those Indians were called Quepos or Quepoa, but we do know that they lived by a combination of farming, hunting, and fishing until the violence and disease that accompanied the Spanish conquest wiped them out.

For centuries following the conquest, the town of Quepos barely existed, but in the 1930s the United Fruit Company put it on the map, building a banana port and populating the area with workers from other parts of Central America. The town thrived for a decade, until Panama disease decimated the banana plantations around 1945. The fruit company then switched to (less lucrative) oil palms, and the area slipped into a prolonged depression. Only since the early 1980s have tourism revenues lifted the town out of its slump, a renaissance owed to natural causes: the beauty of the nearby beach and of Manuel Antonio National Park. The town today, though still a bit seedy and down-at-the-heels due to the vestiges of its banana-port past, draws a number of expats for the world-class sportfishing. The nightlife moves along at a good clip, and some of the bars pace themselves just as well during the day. As Hemingway said of drinking in the morning, it must be noon somewhere in the world.

If you're traveling with children or have a keen interest in flora, you may want to visit the **Jardín Gaia,** an orchid garden and butterfly farm. Call in advance to set up a tour of the botanical project, which houses more than 1,000 orchid species. Admission is free for kids under 12. ☒ *Left side of road to Manuel Antonio, 2½ km (1½ mi) east of Quepos* ☎ *777–0535* ☒ *$5* ☉ *Daily 9–4.*

Where to Stay & Eat

$–$$$ ✕ **El Gran Escape.** A favorite with sportfishermen ("You hook 'em, we
Fodor'sChoice cook 'em"), the Great Escape is the best place for seafood in this area.
★ The menu is dominated by marine entrées, from shrimp scampi to blackened tuna, but you can also get hearty burgers and a small selection of Mexican food. Seating is scattered between an old wooden building and a large patio that is covered with a canopy during the rainy months. Next door is the popular Epicentro Bar, which draws young crowds late into the night. ☒ *Southwest corner of Quepos waterfront* ☎ *777–0395* ☒ *AE, MC, V* ☉ *Closed 2 wks in June.*

¢–$ ⊞ **Hotel Malinche.** This small hotel's older rooms, cooled by ceiling fans, are a bargain. The newer, air-conditioned, carpeted rooms in an annex have cable TV and large tile baths with hot-water showers, but they cost more than twice as much, and you can find a decent room in Manuel Antonio for a comparable price. Of the older rooms, those on the ground floor are nicer, with white-tile floors and baths; those on the second floor are older, smaller, and noisier. ☒ *½ block west of Quepos bus station* ☎ *777–0093* ✉ *hotelmalinche@racsa.co.cr* ⇌ *29 rooms* ⚐ *Fans, laundry service; no a/c in some rooms, no TV in some rooms* ☒ *AE, MC, V.*

Nightlife

The place for dancing is **El Arco Iris** (☎ 777–0449), built over the estuary just north of the bridge, which gets packed after midnight on weekends and holidays. The music is a mix of salsa, merengue, reggae, and pop. American expats gather beneath the ceiling fans of **El Banco Bar** (☒ Avda. Central ☎ 777–0478) to watch U.S. sports on TV or listen to live rock-and-roll. The hot spot with the young set is **Sargento García** (☎ 777–2960), at the southern end of Calle Central, where DJs spin reggae, Latin rock, and other popular sounds. The **Epicentro Bar** (☎ 777–0395), next to El Gran Escape restaurant, plays popular music and allows plenty of room to move. A popular watering hole with younger travelers is **El Tiburón** (☎ 777–3337), a.k.a. La Boquita, upstairs on Calle Central, behind the bus station. There is a small casino on the ground floor of the **Hotel Kamuk** (☎ 777–0811) across the street from the waterfront.

The Outdoors

HIKING A complement to exploring the forests of Manuel Antonio is the half-day tour to the 1,500-acre private reserve of **Rainmaker** (☒ across from Banco Nacional, Quepos ☎ 777–3565), in the mountains 22 km (13 mi) south of Quepos. The guided hike takes you through pristine rain forest and past waterfalls on well-maintained trails and narrow suspension bridges high in the forest canopy.

HORSEBACK **Lynch Travel** (☒ behind bus station, Quepos ☎ 777–1170) leads two horse-
RIDING back tours: a three-hour ride to a scenic overlook and an all-day trip to the Catarata de Nara, a waterfall that pours into a natural swimming pool.

SPORTFISHING The southwest has some of Costa Rica's finest deep-sea fishing, and Quepos is one of the best points of departure. Fewer boats troll these waters than off Guanacaste, and they usually catch plenty of sailfish, marlin, Wahoo, Mahimahi, Roosterfish, and Yellowfin Tuna. The fish-

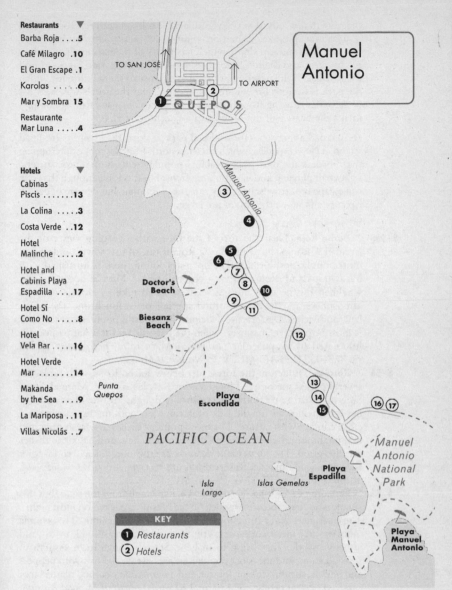

ing is better during the dry season, especially for sailfish and marlin. **Bluefin Tours** (☎ 777–2222) offers custom fishing charters from Quepos on its three boats. **Lynch Travel** (✉ behind bus station, Quepos ☎ 777–1170) arranges sportfishing excursions with various captains.

Manuel Antonio

❽ *3 km (2 mi) south of Quepos, 179 km (111 mi) southwest of San José.*

You need merely reach the top of the forested ridge that Manuel Antonio's hotels are perched upon to understand why it is one of Costa Rica's most popular destinations. The first glimpse of the sweeping view—beaches, jungle, and shimmering Pacific dotted with rocky islets—confirms its reputation. The unassuming town of Manuel Antonio sits atop the hill that separates Quepos from Manuel Antonio National Park, and the road that winds its way over that ridge is lined with restaurants and hotels that capitalize on their proximity to paradise. The best hotels are on the hill's southern slope, which has views of the national park's forest, beaches, and islands. Since there is nearly as much rain forest around the town as in the nearby national park, most of the wildlife for which the park is famous for can also be spotted near the area's hotels. A list of activities ranging from horseback riding to deep-sea fishing complements the beauty of the beach and adjacent jungle.

As the road approaches the national park, it skirts the lovely, palm-lined strand of **Playa Espadilla,** which stretches north from the rocky outcropping that borders the park. The beach is popular with sunbathers, surfers, volleyball players, and vacationing Ticos, but it is long enough that one can escape the crowds. It is often safe for swimming, but beware of deadly rip currents when the waves are large.

Where to Stay & Eat

$–$$$ ✕ **Barba Roja.** Near the top of the hill, with sweeping views of the Manuel Antonio shoreline, Barba Roja is one of this town's oldest and most popular restaurants. The open-air dining room is furnished with hardwoods and decorated with colorful prints, but the decor is overwhelmed by the surrounding scenery. Food takes a close second to atmosphere; try the daily seafood specials or, at lunchtime, the excellent sandwiches. Desserts are delicious. Breakfast is popular, but the view is most impressive at sunset, when the bar fills up for a happy hour illuminated by crepuscular colors. ⊠ *Main road, before top of hill* ☎ 777–0331 ⊟ *AE, MC, V* ⊘ *No lunch Mon.*

$–$$ ✕ **Karolas.** Hidden in the forest just below Barba Roja, with tables on several patios surrounded by greenery, Karolas is easily Manuel Antonio's most attractive, intimate restaurant at night. At breakfast and dinner it compensates for the lack of ocean view with quality cuisine and close contact with nature. The most popular dishes are fresh tuna and mahimahi, but the tenderloin, Caribbean chicken, and Mexican dishes are also good. The homemade desserts are top-notch: leave room for a slice of macadamia pie. Reservations are recommended. ⊠ *Main road, at top of hill* ☎ 777–1557 ⊟ *AE, MC, V.*

$–$$ ✕ **Restaurante Mar Luna.** It doesn't look like much from the road, but this simple wooden structure propped on the hillside is packed on most nights. The customers don't come for the ambience, which is limited to ceramic mobiles and a mediocre view; it's the fresh seafood, reasonable prices, and attentive service that bring them here. Starters range from sashimi to seafood soup, and the most popular entrées are grilled fish with peppers and onions, shrimp scampi, lobster, and a *mariscada* (seafood platter) that can feed several people. ⊠ *130 m (140 yards) north of Manuel Antonio Elementary School* ☎ 777–5107 ⊟ *AE, DC, MC, V.*

¢–$$ ✕ **Mar y Sombra.** You haven't been to Manuel Antonio unless you've contemplated the sea from one of the circular cement tables set in the beach at Mar y Sombra. The food may not win any awards, but you'd be hard-pressed to top the decor—a roof of Indian almond trees and thick lianas draped with moss, ferns, and orchids—and the view of sand and island-studded sea. You can get *gallo pinto* at breakfast and *casados* (plates of rice, beans, fried plantains, salad, cheese, and meat, chicken, or fish) for lunch, but the best bet is the fresh dorado and other seafood. Even if you don't eat, be sure have a drink, preferably at sunset. ⊠ *Playa Espadilla* ☎ 777–0003 ⊟ *AE, MC, V.*

¢ ✕ **Café Milagro.** The only place in town that serves home-roasted coffee, Café Milagro doubles as a souvenir shop and meeting place. Aside from the Cuban music, the atmosphere is decidedly North American, as is the menu of bagels, breakfast burritos, and banana bread. The consistently good breakfast food is available all day, but an inventive selection of sandwiches is also served. There's a sister locale in Quepos, just south of the bridge. ⊠ *Top of hill, across from Karolas* ☎ 777–0794 ☱ *AE, MC, V.*

$$$$
Fodor'sChoice
★
✕⊡ **Makanda by the Sea.** An idyllic, romantic retreat, this secluded collection of villas and studios is scattered through the rain forest. Ocean breezes waft through the spacious villas, which have stone floors, hardwoods, colorful fabrics that complement the natural surroundings, and hypnotic views of the jungle-framed Pacific. Nearby branches often sway with passing monkeys. Smaller studios have inferior views and ventilation, but the multicolored, infinity-edge pool and private beach are shared by all. Breakfast is delivered to the guest rooms, and the poolside restaurant ($–$$$) serves delicious, inventive lunches and dinners—a good meal option even if you stay elsewhere. ⊠ *1 km (½ mi) west of La Mariposa* ☎ 777–0442 ☐ 777–1032 ⊕ *www.makanda. com* ➴ *6 villas, 5 studios* ◊ *Restaurant, fans, in-room safes, kitchenettes, minibars, pool, spa, beach, laundry service, concierge; no a/c in some rooms, no room TVs, no kids* ☱ *AE, MC, V* ☉ *BP.*

★ **¢–$**
✕⊡ **Hotel Vela Bar.** Nestled against the jungle a mere hundred yards from Playa Espadilla, this small, low-key hotel has rooms of varying size and amenities at competitive rates. Though small, the rooms are attractive, with terra-cotta floors, white-stucco walls decorated with Guatemalan fabrics, and covered porches overlooking the hotel's gardens. A casita that sleeps four is a good value for a group. The open-air restaurant (¢–$), set beneath a conical, thatched roof, is popular for its ample selection of entrées that are rare on Manuel Antonio menus, such as chicken marsala, fish fillet in caper sauce, and various vegetarian dishes. ⊠ *Up side road from Soda Marlin* ☎ 777–0413 ☐ 777–1071 ⊕ *www.velabar. com* ➴ *8 rooms, 1 casita, 2 apartments* ◊ *Restaurant, fans, in-room safes, bar, laundry service, travel services; no a/c in some rooms, no room phones, no room TVs* ☱ *AE, MC, V.*

$$$
⊡ **Hotel Sí Como No.** Designed to damage as little of the forest as possible, this eco-friendly place uses partial solar power, energy-efficient airconditioning, and very little hardwood. Cement painted to resemble bamboo and palm trees may evoke Disneyland, but the forest and ocean views are 100% Costa Rica. Rooms are in two-story cement buildings of varying sizes; all have tile floors, colorful fabrics, wicker furniture, and balconies. Request a room away from the road, and ask for a deluxe room for a sea view. Two pools—one for adults only—have cascades, swim-up bars, and adjacent restaurants. Free shuttles head to the beach and park and to nightly movies. ⊠ *Top of hill, on right after Villas Nicolás* ☎ 777–0777 ☐ 777–1093 ⊕ *www.sicomono.com* ➴ *40 rooms, 18 suites* ◊ *Restaurant, grill, fans, in-room safes, some kitchenettes, minibars, 2 pools, exercise equipment, hot tub, spa, bar, cinema, shop, laundry service, concierge, Internet, meeting rooms; no room TVs* ☱ *AE, MC, V* ☉ *BP.*

★ **$$$**
⊡ **La Mariposa.** The best view in town is at La Mariposa: a sweeping panorama of verdant hills and aquamarine Pacific. The decor is Spanish colonial, and the gardens are ablaze with bougainvillea. Above the open-air lobby and restaurant tower four floors of junior suites with vertiginous views. More intimate are the six suites in bungalows along the hillside. Standard rooms have mediocre views, so spend a little more for a deluxe ocean, on the ground floor of a bungalow. Apartments have bright, spacious kitchenettes and long balconies and sleep six. A free beach shuttle is available. ⊠ *Top of hill, on right* ⊕ *www.hotelmariposa. com* ☎ 777–0355; 800/416–2747 *in U.S.* ☐ 777–0050 ➴ *37 rooms, 14 apartments* ◊ *Restaurant, some kitchenettes, cable TV, pool, 2 bars, laundry service, concierge* ☱ *AE, MC, V.*

★ **$$–$$$** 🏨 **Costa Verde.** You might spot monkeys from your window if you reserve one of the many rooms close to the forest. The hotel is spread over the lush hillside up the road from the beach. Studios in Building A are spacious, with large balconies, screened walls that let the breeze through, and ceiling fans for still moments. Those in other buildings are similar but can be closed and air-conditioned. Splurge for a "plus," which means you'll have an ocean view. Cheaper efficiencies vary, but those in Building D, set in the jungle overlooking the sea, are lovely. The open-air restaurant serves good seafood and grilled meats. ⊠ *South slope of hill, on left* ☎ *777–0584* 🖷 *777–0560* ⊕ *www.hotelcostaverde.com* ⏏ *44 rooms* ⚒ *2 restaurants, fans, kitchenettes, cable TV in some rooms, 2 pools, 2 bars, laundry service, Internet, travel services; no a/c in some rooms, no room phones* ⊟ *AE, DC, MC, V.*

$–$$ 🏨 **Hotel and Cabinas Playa Espadilla.** The simple but spacious rooms in the hotel have big windows and are across the lawn from a blue-tile pool, adjacent bar, and large restaurant with a tennis court behind it. The grounds are bordered by the national park, into which the hotel has a private trail. Across the street are the smaller cabinas, which lack TVs and phones, but are considerably cheaper. Those rooms open onto porches overlooking another pool and a lawn shaded by hammock-strung palm trees. Guests at the cabinas are welcome to use the hotel's restaurant, bar, and for a fee, its tennis court. ⊠ *1 block east of beach* ☎🖷 *777–0903* ⊕ *www.espadilla.com* ⚒ *Apdo. 195, Quepos* ⏏ *16 rooms, 16 cabinas* ⚒ *Restaurant, fans, in-room safes, some kitchenettes, cable TV in some rooms, tennis court, 2 pools, bar, laundry service, travel services; no phone in some rooms, no TVs in some rooms* ⊟ *AE, MC, V* ⏐⚒ *BP.*

$–$$ 🏨 **Hotel Verde Mar.** Also known as La Casa del Sol, this whimsical little hotel is set in the rain forest just a few steps from the beach. The rooms are in a long cement building, and, though a bit small, they have colorfully artistic interiors and large windows that overlook the ubiquitous tropical foliage. There's a small pool in back, from which a wooden catwalk leads through the woods and to the nearby beach. ⊠ *½ km (¼ mi) north of park* ⚒ *Apdo. 348–6350, Quepos* ☎ *777–1805* 🖷 *777–1311* ⊕ *www.verdemar.com* ⏏ *20 rooms* ⚒ *Fans, kitchenettes, pool, laundry service, travel services, no-smoking rooms; no room phones, no room TVs* ⊟ *AE, MC, V.*

$–$$ 🏨 **Villas Nicolás.** There's a certain serenity to the rooms in these Mediterranean-style villas. Narrow walkways between whitewashed, garden-lined villas lead to attractive split-level rooms built on a hillside. Rooms on the upper levels have Pacific views, lower-level rooms have jungle views, and those in the lower left corner overlook the hotel next door. Though each unit is decorated differently, all have terra-cotta floors and balconies, some of which are large enough to hold a table, chairs, and hammock. The small restaurant by the pool serves breakfast and dinner. ⊠ *Top of hill, after La Mariposa* ☎ *777–0481* 🖷 *777–0451* ⊕ *www.villasnicolas.com* ⏏ *18 rooms* ⚒ *Restaurant, fans, in-room safes, some kitchenettes, pool, laundry service, travel services; no a/c in some rooms, no room TVs* ⊟ *AE, DC, MC, V.*

¢–$ 🏨 **Cabinas Piscis.** Shaded by tall trees a short walk through the woods from the beach, this older hotel has some of Manuel Antonio's cheapest rooms. Half of them are in a cement building with a wide porch; they are spacious but timeworn, with basic bathrooms and lots of windows. Backpackers may opt for the tiny lower-price rooms that share a separate bathhouse. There are also a couple of cottages with more amenities. A small restaurant serves breakfast only. ⊠ *Bottom of hill, on right after Hotel Karahe* ☎🖷 *777–0046* ⏏ *15 rooms, 2 casitas* ⚒ *Restaurant, fans; no a/c, no room phones, no room TVs* ⊟ *No credit cards.*

Nightlife & the Arts

Barba Roja (✉ main road, top of hill ☎ 777–0331) has a popular sunset happy hour, and though it's primarily a restaurant, but the bar sometimes stays busy late. The **Billfish Bar** (✉ Byblos Hotel, across from Barba Roja ☎ 777–0411) is a sports bar with a casino next door. **Casino las Palmas** (✉ across from Barba Roja ☎ 777–0371), in the Hotel Divisamar, is one of Manuel Antonio's two gambling spots. **Cockatoo** (✉ north of Sí Como No hotel and shopping center ☎ no phone) plays danceable music in a gorgeous Spanish-style building. It has a gay bar on the second floor. The **Costa Verde** (✉ south slope of hill ☎ 777–0548) has live reggae nightly in the bar and restaurant across the road from the hotel. **Mar y Sombra** (✉ next to Cabinas Ramirez ☎ 777–0003), the most popular restaurant on the beach, becomes an open-air dance club Thursday through Saturday nights and is where many young locals end up on Saturday. The **Tutu** (✉ above Gato Negro, Casitas Eclipse ☎ no phone) is Manuel Antonio's late-night gay bar.

The Outdoors

HORSEBACK RIDING — **Equus** (☎ 777–0001) offers trail rides through Manuel Antonio's forest and on the beach. **Malboro Stables** (☎ 777–1108) rents horses for riding on the beach and leads guided tours through the surrounding forested hills of Manuel Antonio.

SEA-KAYAKING — **Iguana Tours** (☎ 777–1262) runs sea-kayaking trips to the islands of Manuel Antonio National Park, which requires some experience when the seas are high, and a mellower paddle to the mangrove estuary of Isla Damas, where you might see monkeys, crocodiles, and various birds.

SCUBA-DIVING — During high season, **Lynch Travel** (☎ 777–1170) in Quepos offers scuba diving for experienced divers only, around the islands in the national park. Playa Manuel Antonio, inside the national park, is a good snorkeling spot, as is **Playa Biesanz**, near the Hotel Parador and ½ km (¼ mi) south of Makanda by the Sea.

SWIMMING — When the surf is up, rip currents are a dangerous problem on **Playa Espadilla**, the long beach north of the park. Riptides are characterized by a strong current running out to sea; the important thing to remember if you get caught in one of these currents is not to struggle against it but instead to swim parallel to shore. If you can't swim out of it, the current will simply take you out just past the breakers, where its power dissipates. If you conserve your strength, you can then swim parallel to shore a bit, then back into the beach. Needless to say the best policy is not to go in deeper than your waist when the waves loom large. Manuel Antonio's safest swimming area is the sheltered second beach in the national park, **Playa Manuel Antonio**, which is also good for snorkeling.

WHITE-WATER RAFTING — The three white-water rivers in this area have limited seasons. The Savegre, which flows past patches of rain forest, has two navigable stretches: the lower section (Class II–III), which is a mellow trip perfect for neophytes, and the more rambunctious upper section (Class III–IV). It is usually navigable from June to March. The Naranjo (Class III–IV) offers a short but exciting run that requires some experience and can be done only from June to December. The Parrita (Class II–III) is a relatively mellow white-water route, and in the dry season it can be navigated only in two-person, inflatable duckies. **Amigos del Río** (✉ road to Manuel Antonio ☎ 777–0082) leads trips down the Savegre and Naranjo. **Iguana Tours** (✉ across from soccer field, Quepos

🖥 777–1262), the area's oldest rafting outfitter, offers trips down all three rivers, as well as sea-kayaking tours. **Rios Tropicales** (✉ road to Manuel Antonio 🖥 777–4092), the country's biggest outfitter, runs kayaking excursions, and rafting trips on the Savegre and Naranjo.

Manuel Antonio National Park

❾ *5 km (3 mi) south of Quepos, 181 km (112 mi) southwest of San José.*

Parque Nacional Manuel Antonio, though small (6½ square km [2½ square mi]), is one of the most popular protected areas in Costa Rica. This is no doubt because it protects such an impressive collection of natural attractions: three beaches; rain forest with massive ficus, cow, kapok, and gumbo-limbo trees; mangrove swamps; marshland; and coves that hold an abundance of marine life. Its forest is home to two- and three-toed sloths, Green and Black Iguanas, capuchin monkeys, agoutis, and nearly 200 species of birds. It is also one of the two places in Costa Rica where you can see squirrel monkeys.

The park entrance is at the southern end of Playa Espadilla, on the other side of a shallow estuary. Here you will find the ranger station and maps for the trails that take you through the rain forest. The first beach after the ranger station, **Playa Espadilla Sur,** is the longest and least crowded, since the water can be rough. At its southern end is a tombolo (and isthmus formed from sedimentation and accumulated debris) that connects a former island to the coast. The rocky hill draped with lush jungle is called **Punta Catedral,** and the steep path that makes a loop over it provides a wonderful perspective of the rain forest. The path also passes a lookout from which you can gaze over the blue Pacific at some of the park's 12 islands; among them is **Isla Mogote,** which was the site of pre-Columbian Quepos Indian burials.

The lovely strand of white sand east of the tombolo is **Playa Manuel Antonio,** a small, safe swimming beach tucked into a deep cove. At low tide you can see the remains of a Quepos Indian turtle trap on the right—the Quepos stuck poles in the semicircular rock formation, which trapped turtles as the tide receded. The bay, with coral formations on submerged volcanic rocks, is good for snorkeling. Walk even farther east, and you'll come to the rockier, more secluded **Playa Escondido.**

Beware of *manzanillo* trees (indicated by warning signs)—their leaves, bark, and apple-like fruit secrete a gooey substance that irritates the skin. And don't feed or touch the monkeys, who have seen so many tourists that they sometimes walk right up to them and have been known to bite over-friendly visitors. Because Manuel Antonio is so popular (the road between the park and the town of Quepos is lined with hotels), you should come as early as possible, especially on weekends, when it can get packed. 🕿 777–0654 ✉ $6 ☯ Tues.–Sun. 7–4.

CENTRAL PACIFIC COAST A TO Z

To research prices, get advice from other travelers, and book travel arrangements, visit www.fodors.com

AIR TRAVEL
The flight between San José and Quepos is 30 minutes and is more convenient than the 3½-hour drive or bus trip, which involves a steep mountain road.

CARRIERS   SANSA flies six times daily between San José and Quepos in the high season, four in the low season. NatureAir also has six daily flights between San José and Quepos year-round and once daily between Quepos and Palmar Sur, the gateway to Drake Bay.

🛫Airlines & Contacts **NatureAir** ☎777–1170 Quepos; 220–3054 San José ⊕www.natureair. com. **SANSA** ☎777–0683 in Quepos; 221–9414 in San José ⊕ www.flysansa.com.

BUS TRAVEL

The trip to Jacó from San José takes about three hours. From San José, Coopetransatenas buses leave for Atenas from the Coca-Cola bus station every 30 minutes from 6 AM to 10 PM. From Atenas, buses depart from the Banco Nacional. Transporte Jacó buses to Jacó leave San José's Coca-Cola station daily at 7:30 AM and 10:30 AM, 3:30 PM and 6 PM, returning from the Jacó bus terminal at 7:30 AM, 11 AM, 3 PM, and 5 PM. A more comfortable and quicker way to reach Jacó is on the hotel-to-hotel shuttle service offered by Interbus, which departs from San José at 9 AM and 2 PM, or the slightly more expensive Gray Line Tours Fantasy Bus, which departs at 8:30. Buses to Jacó can drop you off at the Carara National Park.

The trip to Quepos from San José takes about 3½ hours. Transportes Delio Morales runs express buses to Quepos and Manuel Antonio that depart San José's Coca-Cola bus station daily at 6 AM, noon, and 6 PM, returning at 6 AM, noon, and 5 PM. The buses drop passengers off and pick them up at the Quepos bus station and in front of most Manuel Antonio hotels. More comfortable shuttle service to Manuel Antonio hotels is offered by Interbus, with 8 AM and 1 PM departures from San José, and Gray Line Tours, which departs at 8:30 and is slightly cheaper. Direct buses to Quepos and Manuel Antonio can drop you off in front of Playa Hermosa's hotels. All buses heading *toward* San José can drop you off at the airport, but you need to ask the driver when you board, and then remind him again as you draw near to the stop.

Buses make the short trip from Quepos to Manuel Antonio every half hour daily from dawn to dusk then hourly until 10 PM. Buses leave Puntarenas for the three-hour trip to Quepos daily at 5 AM and 2:30 PM, returning at 10:30 AM and 3 PM, stopping at Playa Hermosa and on the outskirts of Jacó. For those moving on to the southern Pacific region, buses leave Quepos for Dominical (a 2½-hour trip) daily at 9 AM, 1:30 PM, 4:30 PM, and 6:30 PM, returning at 6 AM, 2 PM, and 2:45 PM.

🚌 Bus Information **Coca-Cola bus station** ✉ C. 16, between Avdas. 1 and 3, San José ☎no phone. **Coopetransatenas** ☎446–5767. **Gray Line Tours Fantasy Bus** ☎220–2126. **Interbus** ☎ 283–5573. **Transportes Delio Morales** ☎ 223–5567. **Transporte Jacó** ☎ 223–1109.

CAR RENTAL

There are several car-rental agencies in Jacó but only one in Quepos.
🚗 Major Agencies **Economy** ✉ Jacó ☎ 643–1719. **National** ✉ Jacó ☎ 643–1752.
🚗 Local Agency **Elegante/Payless** ☎ 643–3224 Jacó; 777–0115 Quepos.

CAR TRAVEL

The quickest way to get to this region from San José is to take the Carretera Inter-Americana (Pan-American Highway, CA1) west to the exit for Atenas, where you turn left (south). Once you leave the highway, the road is one lane in each direction for the rest of the route, and between Atenas and Orotina it is steep and full of curves. If you don't have experience in mountain driving, you're better off taking a bus or flight to the coast. The coastal highway, or *costanera,* heads southeast from Orotina to Tárcoles, Jacó, Hermosa, and Quepos. It is well marked and, except for a few stretches near bridges, well paved. An asphalt road winds its way over the hill between Quepos and Manuel Antonio National Park.

Driving times from San José are about 1 hour to Atenas, 2½ hours to Jacó, 3 hours to Quepos, and 3½ hours to Manuel Antonio.

EMERGENCIES

In an emergency, dial 911 or one of the numbers below.

🚘 Emergency Services **Ambulance** ☎ 777-0116. **Fire** ☎ 118. **Police** ☎ 117 in towns; 127 in rural areas. **Traffic Police** ☎ 222-9245.

TOURS

The *Okeanos Aggressor* makes all-inclusive 9- and 10-day guided dive trips to Cocos Island, one of the best dive spots in the world. Transfers to and from San José are provided from Puntarenas. Cruceros del Sur offers a seven-day natural-history cruise through Costa Rica's central and south Pacific regions and some islands off Panama aboard the *Temptress,* a 63-passenger ship. The *Undersea Hunter* also leads 10-day dive trips to Cocos Island.

A number of agencies can help you arrange land-bound tours. Costa Rica Expeditions and Horizontes, the country's two premier nature-tour operators, have expert guides and can arrange tours that visit Carara, Manuel Antonio, or both. Costa Tropical Expeditions is a small Jacó tour operator that specializes in trips to Carara but can arrange all kinds of personalized excursions. Book tours by phone or at Villa Caletas in Tárcoles or Club del Mar in Jacó. Fantasy Tours is the biggest operator in Jacó, but it deals primarily with large groups.

In Quepos, Lynch Travel offers a wildlife-watching boat trip to the Isla Damas Estuary, guided tours of the national park, several horseback trips, sportfishing, and more. Costa Rica Temptations has an office in Manuel Antonio from which it runs tours of the national park and other attractions. Iguana Tours specializes in sea-kayaking and river rafting, but it also druns trips on dry land. Fincas Naturales, in Manuel Antonio, runs hourly tours, Monday through Saturday, of its butterfly garden, private wildlife refuge, or both. Rainmaker leads daily hikes through a private reserve in the mountains south of Quepos that has canopy bridges through the treetops and waterfalls with swimming holes. Villas de la Colina, a hotel in Atenas, leads three eight- to nine-day motorcycle tours that include a trip from Volcán Arenal to the Monteverde Cloud Forest.

🚘 Tour Companies **Costa Rica Expeditions** ⊠ Avda. 3 and C. Central, San José ☎ 222-0333 🖷 257-1665. **Costa Rica Temptations** ⊠ Manuel Antonio ☎ 777-5130. **Costa Tropical Expeditions** ☎ 393-6622. **Cruceros del Sur** ⊠ across from Colegio Los Angeles, Sabana Norte, San José ☎ 232-6672 🖷 220-2103. **Fantasy Tours** ⊠ Best Western Jacó Beach Hotel ☎ 643-3032. **Fincas Naturales** ⊠ across from Hotel Sí Como No, Manuel Antonio ☎ 777-0850. **Horizontes** ⊠ 130 m [140 yards] north of Pizza Hut, Paseo Colón ☎ 222-2022 🖷 255-4513. **Iguana Tours** ⊠ across from soccer field, Quepos ☎ 777-1262. **Lynch Travel** ⊠ behind bus station, Quepos ☎ 777-1170. *Okeanos Aggressor* ⊠ 1-17 Plaza Colonial, Escazú ☎ 556-8317; 877/506-9738 in the U.S. 🖷 556-2825. **Rainmaker** ⊠ Quepos, ☎ 777-0850. *Undersea Hunter* ⊠ San Rafael de Escazú, ½ km [¼ mi] north and 45 m [50 yards] west of Rosti Pollos ☎ 228-6535 🖷 289-7334. **Villas de la Colina** ⊠ 6 km [4 mi] west of Coopeatenas on road to Orotina 🖅 Apdo. 165, Atenas ☎ 446-5015 🖷 446-8545 ⊕ www.motoscostarica.com.

VISITOR INFORMATION

The Instituto Costarricense de Turismo (ICT) office in San José has information on the central Pacific region and is open weekdays 9–12:30 and 1:30–5. Lynch Travel in Quepos can also give general advice.

🚘 Visitor Information **Instituto Costarricense de Turismo (ICT)** ⊠ C. 5 between Advas. Central and 2, Barrio La Catedral San José ⊠ C. 2 between Avdas. 1 and 3, Barrio La Merced San José ☎ 222-1090 **Lynch Travel** ⊠ behind bus station, Quepos ☎ 777-1170.

THE SOUTHERN PACIFIC COAST

6

FODOR'S CHOICE
Bosque del Cabo, *Puerto Jiménez*
Corcovado Lodge Tent Camp, *Corcovado National Park*
Lapa Ríos, *Puerto Jiménez*

HIGHLY RECOMMENDED
HOTELS Casa Corcovado, *Drake Bay*
Pacific Edge, *Dominical*
La Paloma Lodge, *Drake Bay*
Parrot Bay Village, *Puerto Jiménez*
Savegre Hotel de Montaña, *San Gerardo de Dota*
Trogon Lodge, *San Gerardo de Dota*
Villas Gaia, *Ballena Marine National Park*
Wilson Botanical Garden, *San Vito*

SIGHTS Cabo Matapalo
Casa Orquideas, *Golfito*
Hacienda Barú, *Dominical*
Wilson Botanical Garden, *San Vito*

SHOPPING Banana Bay Gallery & Gifts, *Dominical*

Updated by
Dorothy
MacKinnon

SOME OF COSTA RICA'S WILDEST COUNTRY is found in the southern Pacific coast, which makes it well worth the extra effort it takes to visit the remote area. A trip here reveals what most of the country looked like decades, or even centuries, ago. Because it was the last part of the country to be settled—a road into the region from San José wasn't completed until the 1950s—the southern Pacific zone retains a disproportionate percentage of its wilderness. Much of that nature lies within several of Costa Rica's largest national parks, and other patches are protected as private reserves. From the exhilarating highland scenery of the Cordillera de Talamanca, Costa Rica's highest mountain range, to the pristine beaches and coastal rain forest of the Osa Peninsula, the southern Pacific has some of the country's most dramatic scenery and wildlife.

In Chirripó National Park you can climb Costa Rica's highest mountain, Cerro Chirripó, and wander lands ranging from rugged forest to glacial lakes. On the Osa Peninsula, the creation of Corcovado National Park put a halt to the furious logging and gold mining that threatened the rain forest; the park now houses most of the country's endangered species in a wide range of habitats, including large areas of swamp, deserted beach, cloud forest, and luxuriant lowland rain forest.

Some of Costa Rica's best surfing breaks and diving areas are in the southern Pacific. Anglers can fish the renowned Pacific waters. Rafters can take on the rambunctious Río General. Trekkers can climb Cerro Chirripó. Bird-watchers who go to the right places are almost guaranteed glimpses of the country's two most spectacular birds: the Resplendent Quetzal and Scarlet Macaw. Botany lovers, too, will find their jaws dropping here, especially at the Wilson Botanical Garden near San Vito, with its spectacular displays of canopy plant life brought down to earth.

Timing
In the rainy season, it rains considerably more here than in the northwest, but in July and August you may catch a week without any serious precipitation. The Osa Peninsula and Talamanca highlands are especially susceptible to downpours, making this region the last place you want to visit during the October–November deluge, when many lodges are closed.

Exploring the Southern Pacific Coast

This area includes four very different landscapes: the clear rivers and cool forests of the western slope of the Cordillera de Talamanca; the hot, agricultural lowlands of the Valle de El General; the miles of uncrowded beaches running south from Dominical; and the wild, impenetrable—except on foot—Osa Peninsula with its two very different coastlines, the rugged Pacific and the gentler Golfo Dulce.

It's a lot of territory to cover on the ground. Although the driving is scenic, especially over the spectacular mountains of the Cordillera de Talamanca, it's tiring, especially if you are heading all the way down to the Osa and to Corcovado National Park. If you are Osa-bound, there are few drivable roads except on the Golfo Dulce side. It often makes more sense to fly into Puerto Jiménez, Golfito, or Drake Bay. If you fly into Palmar Norte, you can take a taxi to Sierpe and then a motorboat to destinations on the Pacific side of the Osa Peninsula.

If you're traveling by car, there are two routes into the region: the paved, heavily traveled Carretera Interamericana (Pan-American Highway, CA2), with lots of slow-moving trucks, and the Costanera (Route 34), or coastal highway, which is not paved between Quepos and Dominical. Heading south from San José, the two-lane Pan-American

Numbers in the text correspond to numbers in the margin and on The Southern Pacific Coast map.

If you have
3 days

Fly straight to the Golfo Dulce–Osa Peninsula area, where you can stay in a comfortable nature lodge in or near any of three pristine wilderness areas. You can fly direct to ⊞ **Playa Pavones** ⑩ ⌐ on a charter arranged by the Tiskita Jungle Lodge, or fly to ⊞ **Puerto Jiménez** ⑪, a short drive from the lodges of ⊞ **Cabo Matapalo** ⑬. A third option is to fly a charter to Carate and the Corcovado Lodge Tent Camp at the edge of ⊞ **Corcovado National Park** ⑫. Alternatively, you can fly to Palmar Sur, where the taxi and spectacular boat trip—complete with guide who points out iguanas, crabs, and birds—depart for ⊞ **Drake Bay** ⑭. Or you can fly directly to Drake on a daily scheduled flight.

If you have
5 days

In five days you can stretch out the three-day itinerary above or concentrate on inland areas. Drive south on the Pan-American Highway (CA2) into the cool mountain air and cloud forests of ⊞ **San Gerardo de Dota** ① ⌐, a perfect place to hike and bird-watch. The next day explore the Dota Valley. On day three, head down out of the mountains to the coastal enclave of ⊞ **Dominical** ④ or the nearby ⊞ **Ballena Marine National Park** ⑤. Spend day four and the morning of day five enjoying the area's waterfalls, nature reserves, and beaches.

Highway climbs up through the perennial fog at the top of Cerro de la Muerte, where you pass the turnoff for San Gerardo de Dota. The road then descends to San Isidro, the Valle de El General, and, eventually, to the Osa Peninsula and Panama.

About the Restaurants

Since the sun sets between 5 and 6 PM year-round, dinner is served relatively early down south, except in the Dominical area, where surfers keep restaurants and bars busy into the night. In the Osa Peninsula, don't count on finding many restaurants outside hotels, except in Puerto Jiménez.

About the Hotels

Nature lodges may be less expensive than they initially appear, as the price of a room usually includes three hearty meals a day, as well as tours and transportation to remote areas.

WHAT IT COSTS				
	$$$$	**$$$**	**$$**	**$**	**¢**
RESTAURANTS	over $25	$20–$25	$10–$20	$5–$10	under $5
HOTELS	over $200	$125–$200	$75–$125	$35–$75	under $35

Restaurant prices are per-person for a main course at dinner. Hotel prices are for two people in a standard double room in high season, excluding service and tax (16.4%).

VALLE DE EL GENERAL

The Valle de El General (General Valley) is bounded to the north by the massive Cordillera de Talamanca and to the south by the Golfo Dulce, or Sweet Gulf (the name connotes tranquil waters). This area includes vast expanses of highland wilderness, on the upper slopes of the Cordillera de Talamanca and the high-altitude *páramo* (shrubby ecosystem) of Chirripó National Park, as well as the isolated beaches and lowland rain forest of the Dominical and Golfito areas.

San Gerardo de Dota

▶ ❶ *89 km (55 mi) southeast of San José.*

Cloud forests, cool mountain air, pastoral imagery, and excellent bird-watching make San Gerardo de Dota one of Costa Rica's best-kept secrets. The town is in a narrow valley of the Río Savegre, 9 km (5½ mi) down a twisting, partially asphalted track that descends abruptly to the west from the Pan-American Highway. The peaceful surroundings look more like the Rocky Mountains than typical Central America, but hike down the waterfall trail and the vegetation quickly turns tropical again. Beyond hiking, activities include horseback riding and trout fishing, but you might well be content just to wander around the pastures and forests, marveling at the valley's avian inhabitants.

The damp, epiphyte-laden forest of giant oak trees is renowned for its high count of quetzals, for many the most beautiful bird in the Western world. Male quetzals are more spectacular than females, with metallic green feathers, bright crimson stomachs, helmetlike crests, and long tail streamers that look especially dramatic in flight. Quetzals commonly feed on *aguacatillos* (avocado-like fruits) in the tall trees scattered around the valley's forests and pastures. The staff in your hotel can usually point you in the direction of some quetzal hangouts; early morning is the best time to spot them. They are most easily seen here in their nesting season (March–May).

Where to Stay

★ $-$$$ 🗺 **Savegre Hotel de Montaña.** In the 1950s, Efrain Chacón and his brother bushwhacked through the mountains to homestead in San Gerardo. A staunch conservationist, Efrain now leads quetzal-spotting tours on his extensive property laced with forest trails. Cozy cabinas have heaters and plenty of hot water; newer, spacious cabinas are screened by a butterfly garden. The main lodge has a fireplace and a veranda famous for its hummingbird feeders. Home-grown trout is the restaurant's specialty; an all-inclusive meal plan is available. You can get a lift to the hotel from the Km 80 turnoff on the Pan-American Highway ($10). On the hotel grounds, the **Quetzal Education Research Center** (QERC; ☎ 740–1010) hosts students and researchers; many take their meals at the hotel and are a great source for natural lore. ✉ *Turn right at sign to San Gerardo de Dota on Pan-American Hwy., around 80 km (50 mi) from San José, and travel 9 km (5½ mi) down a steep, gravel road with some paving* ☎ *740–1028* 📠 *740–1027* 📠 *Apdo. 482, Cartago* 🌐 *www.savegre.co.cr* ☎ *31 cabinas* ⛄ *Restaurant, fishing, hiking, horseback riding, bar; no a/c, no room phones, no room TVs* ═ *AE, MC, V* 🍽 *BP.*

★ $ 🗺 **Trogon Lodge.** A collection of green cabins nestled in a secluded garden in an enchanting valley, the Trogon Lodge overlooks the cloud forest and boulder-strewn Río Savegre. Each cabin has two rooms with *almendro* (almond-wood) floors, big windows, white-tile baths with hot

6

Fresh Fruit

Apples, peaches, and plums are grown in profusion in the upper reaches of the Cordillera de Talamanca, and the lowlands are the source of those thirst-quenching pineapples. If you're here between June and August, try rambutans, locally called *mamones chinos;* their red, spiky shells protect a succulent white fruit very similar to a litchi. Even in the remote Osa Peninsula, where supply lines are difficult, you can eat surprisingly well at health-minded eco-resorts that don't stint on just-picked produce and imaginative cuisine.

Outdoor Adventures

Outdoors enthusiasts may never want to leave these parts. This is hiking territory, with treks ranging from one-day jaunts through private reserves to more demanding multiday treks up Chirripó or into the Corcovado jungles. Simple horseback rides take you along spectacular beaches and forest trails. The lively water habitat surrounding Isla del Caño offers some of Costa Rica's best scuba diving, and there's prime sportfishing off the entire southern Pacific coast. The surf whips up into a half dozen breaks, and you can navigate in the quieter waters of Golfo Dulce in a sea kayak.

Private Nature Preserves

In addition to celebrated national parks, this region has a growing number of private nature preserves, some of which run their own lodges. Dominical's Hacienda Barú, a 700-acre reserve, offers innovative ways to experience the rain forest, as does Lapa Ríos, on the southern tip of the Osa Peninsula, with its extensive protected rain forest. Savegre Hotel de Montaña, in San Gerardo de Dota, has a large cloud-forest reserve crisscrossed with footpaths that lead to almost guaranteed quetzal sightings.

---

showers, and electric heaters and extra blankets for chilly mountain nights. Meals are served in a small dining hall. Quetzal-watching and waterfall tours are offered. ⊠ *Turn right at the sign to San Gerardo de Dota on the Pan-American Hwy., around 80 km (50 mi) from San José, and follow signs; lodge is 7½ km (4½ mi) down a decent dirt road* ☎740–1051 ⊕ *www.grupomawamba.com* ✆ *Apdo. 10980–1000, San José* ☎ *223–2421* 🖷 *222–5463* ❑ *16 rooms* ♨ *Restaurant, hiking, horseback riding, bar; no a/c, no room phones, no room TVs* ▭ *AE, MC, V.*

The Outdoors

HIKING   A long, guided hike is led by expert birder Marino Chacón at Savegre Hotel: you drive up to the *páramo* (high altitude, shrubby ecosystem) near **Cerro de la Muerte,** and spend the day hiking from there back down through the forest into the valley. The best trail in El General Valley is the one that follows the **Río Savegre** down to a waterfall. Follow the main road past Savegre Hotel to a fork, where you veer left, cross a bridge, and head over the hill to a pasture that narrows to a footpath. The hike is steep and vigorous, especially near the bottom, and takes about three hours each way. Above the **Trogon Lodge,** a short trail heads through the forest and ends in a pasture, and miles of trails wind through the forest reserve belonging to Cabinas Chacón.

San Isidro

❷ *54 km (34 mi) south of San Gerardo de Dota, 205 km (127 mi) north-west of Golfito.*

While San Isidro has no major attractions, it's a good place to have lunch and get cash, if you need it, at the ATH cash machine (in the Coopealianza west of the church), which accepts North American debit cards. East of the central park and a few blocks south of the modern church is the market, where buses depart for San Gerardo de Rivas, the starting point of the trail into Chirripó National Park. The **National Parks Service** (⊠ across from Camara de Cañeros ☎ 771–3155) office has information about Chirripó and help you reserve lodging in the park's cabins. Buses to Dominical leave from a stop 100 m (110 yards) east and 50 m (55 yards) south of the cathedral, near the main highway.

Las Quebradas Biological Center. In a lush valley 7 km (4½ mi) northeast of San Isidro, a community-managed nature reserve (*centro biológico*) protects 1,853 acres of dense forest in which elegant tree ferns grow in the shadows of massive trees and where colorful tanagers and euphonias flit about the foliage. A 3-km (2-mi) trail winds through the forest and along the Río Quebradas, which supplies water to San Isidro and surrounding communities. ⊠ *At the bottom of mountain as you approach San Isidro, take sharp left turning off Pan-American Hwy. marked Las Quebradas and travel 7 km (4½ mi) northeast; center is 2 km (1 mi) north of town, along unpaved road* ☎ *771–1500* ✉ *Apdo. 73–8257, Perez Zeledon, San Isidro* 🔒 *$5* ⊙ *Tues.–Sun. 8–3.*

Where to Stay & Eat

¢ ✕**El Trapiche de Nayo.** This restaurant with a panoramic valley view serves the kind of food Ticos eat at *turnos* (village fund-raising festivals) including hard-to-find *sopa de mondongo* (tripe soup) and *gallos,* tortillas filled with chopped-up heart of palm or other root vegetables. Come on a Tuesday or a Saturday and watch raw sugar cane pressed in an antique mill and boiled in huge iron cauldrons to make smooth *sobado,* a molasses-flavored fudge. ⊠ *Pan-American Hwy., 6 km (4 mi) north of San Isidro* ☎ *771–7267* ⊟ *No credit cards.*

$ ▦ **Hotel del Sur Country Club & Casino.** An extensive and rambling complex with well-tended gardens, this hotel doubles as a local country club. Weekday stays are tranquil, but the casino makes for lively weekends. Rooms are spacious, but spartanly furnished, and have large windows looking out onto a courtyard garden. Basic cabinas in back have kitchenettes, bunks, and separate bedrooms. ⊠ *6 km (4 mi) south of town on Pan-American Hwy.* ☎ *771–3033* 🖨 *771–0527* ⊕ *www.hoteldelsur. com* ✉ *Apdo. 4–8000, Perez Zeledon, San Isidro* 🛌 *57 rooms, 10 cabinas* ⚬ *Restaurant, some in-room safes, some kitchenettes, some minibars, cable TV, tennis court, pool, wading pool, basketball, bar, casino, playground; no a/c in some rooms* ⊟ *AE, MC, V* ⦿⊚ *BP.*

$ ▦ **Talari Mountain Lodge.** A 10-minute drive northeast from San Isidro on the road to San Gerardo de Rivas, this family-run lodge is on a small farm near the gurgling Río General. Very simple rooms with big windows, tile floors, and porches are in two cement buildings. The surrounding fruit trees and forest patches make for excellent bird-watching. A resident naturalist guide lead tours in high season and organizes trips to climb Chirripó. Meals are excellent; the dining room is closed Wednesday. ⊠ *Turn left off of Pan-American Hwy. after second bridge south of San Isidro* ☎☎ *771–0341* ✉ *Apdo. 517–8000, Perez Zeledon, San*

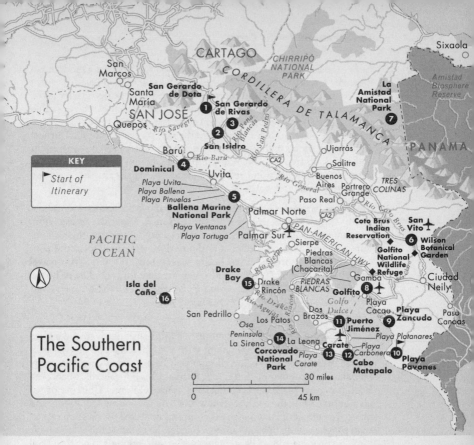

Isidro 🛏 8 rooms ⚂ Dining room, pool; no a/c, no room phones, no room TVs ▭ AE, MC, V ⧠ BP.

The Outdoors

WHITE-WATER RAFTING Experience the country's longest white-water run via raft or kayak on the **Rio General**. The white water flows through agricultural land and winds through a rocky canyon. Three-day camping expeditions on the Class III–IV river are offered by San José's major rafting companies from September to November. In San Isidro, **Selva Mar** (☎ 771–4582 ⊕ www.exploringcostarica.com) organizes rafting expeditions as well as hiking trips up Chirripó, bird-watching, and horseback tours.

San Gerardo de Rivas

③ *20 km (12½ mi) northeast of San Isidro.*

Chirripó National Park is the main reason to venture to San Gerardo de Rivas, but if you aren't up for this adventure, the town is still a great place to spend a day or two. Spread over steep terrain at the end of the narrow valley of the boulder-strewn Río Chirripó, San Gerardo de Rivas has a cool climate, good bird-watching, spectacular views reminiscent of Nepal, and an outdoor menu that includes hiking and horseback riding to waterfalls.

The trail up to **Parque Nacional Chirripó**, home of the highest mountain in Costa Rica, begins above the scenic agricultural community of San Gerardo de Rivas. Because it's so remote, there is no easy way in; hikers usually spend one night in San Gerardo de Rivas, which has several inexpensive lodges. It's a tough climb to the park—6 to 10 hours on the mountain road from town, depending on your physical condition—so try to head out of San Gerardo with the first light of day. You'll hike through pastures, then forests, and then the burnt remains of forest fires. There is a modern but unheated (and chilly) hostel near the top. This will be your base for a night or two if you want to continue your hike up to the peaks, glacier lakes, and *páramo*—a highland ecosystem common to the Andes with flora that includes shrubs and herbaceous plants. Trails lead to the top of Chirripó— the highest point in Costa Rica—and the nearby peak of Terbi. The hostel has small rooms with four bunks each, bathrooms with cold water only, and a cooking area. You can rent camp stoves, blankets, and sleeping bags here, but you should bring your own good-quality sleeping bag, and you must bring food and water. Pack plenty of warm clothes as well.

The **Aguas Termales** (Hot Springs), on a farm above the road to Herradura, about 1½ km (1 mi) after the ranger station, is a favorite tourist stop. To get here, you must cross a river on a rickety footbridge, then it's endure a steep climb on foot to a combination of natural rock and concrete pools in a forested area. In dry season only, the **Selva Mar travel agency** (☎ 771–4582) in San Isidro can arrange for a donkey or horse, as can local hotels. ⊠ *Above road to Herradura, about 1½ km (1 mi) past the ranger station* ☑ *$2* ⊙ *Daily 7–6.*

Where to Stay

$ ⊡ **Río Chirripó Retreat.** Crystal mountain air, a rushing river, and a huge conical-roofed adobe temple hung with a monastery bell and Tibetan prayer flags make you feel as though you have suddenly arrived in the Himalayas. A popular place for yoga retreats, this bougainvillea-bedecked B&B is a great place for acclimatizing before climbing Chirripó or for clambering along the river, strewn with Druidic-looking stone seats and altars. The two-storied wooden cabins are cantilevered over a steep ravine, with porches made of twig railings. Inside, the comfortable rooms have large bathrooms and walls stenciled with runic symbols. There's a pool by the river and great bird-watching all around. ⊠ *Down a steep road (4X4 required), just past cemetery* ☎ *771–7065; 707–937–3775 in the U.S.* ⊕ *www.riochirripo.com* ⊅ *8 rooms, 1 cabin* ⚭ *Dining room, pool, hiking, bar* ⊟ *No credit cards* ¡○¡ *BP.*

¢ ⊡ **El Pelícano.** Perched on a ridge south of town, this wooden lodge is named for a chunk of wood that resembles a pelican—and that's not its only oddity. The restaurant, which has a gorgeous view of the valley below San Gerardo, is also an art gallery, with dozens of idiosyncratic wooden sculptures carved out of tree roots by owner Rafael Elizondo. Above the restaurant-gallery are economical small rooms. There's a more private wooden cabin near the pool. The owners can arrange everything for a climb up Chirripó, including a free lift to the park entrance. ⊠ *260 m (270 yards) south of National Parks Office* ☎ *no phone* ☐ *Apdo. 942–8000, San Gerardo de Rivas* ☎ *390–4194* ⊟ *382–3000* ⊕ *www.ecotourism.co.cr/docs/elpelicano.com* ⊅ *10 rooms with shared bath, 1 cabin* ⚭ *Restaurant, pool, volleyball, horseback riding; no a/c, no room phones, no room TVs* ⊟ *No credit cards.*

Dominical

❹ *34 km (21 mi) southwest of San Isidro.*

Fifty minutes southwest of San Isidro, the small community of Dominical, once a sleepy fishing village, is now a slightly scruffy surfer town, with a smattering of interesting bars and restaurants that come and go with the waves of itinerant young people, though there are a few perennially popular places. Its real magic lies in the surrounding terrestrial and marine wonders: the rain forest grows right up to the beach in some places, and the sea offers world-class surfing. The beaches here are long, rarely crowded, and perfect for beachcombing among all the flotsam and jetsam that the surf washes up. Swimmers should beware of fatally dangerous rip currents. The local steep hillsides are covered with lush forest, much of it protected within private nature reserves. By leading hikes and horseback tours, several of these reserves are trying to finance preservation of the rain forest through ecotourism.

★ The **Hacienda Barú** nature reserve is a leader in both ecotourism and conservation, with a turtle protection project and nature education program in the local school. The bird-watching is spectacular, with excellent guides. You can stay at the hotel or just come for the day to walk the forest and mangrove trails, zip through the canopy on cables, or climb a tree to an observation platform. Tour prices range from $20 to $60 per person. ✉ *2 km (1 mi) north of bridge into Dominical* ☎ *787–0003* ☞ *Free* ☼ *Daily dawn–dusk.*

Two reserves border the **Cataratas de Nauyaca** (Nauyaca Waterfalls), a massive double cascade that is one of the most spectacular sights in Costa Rica. The waterfalls—also known as Barú Falls—are on private property, so the only way to reach them is to take a hiking or horseback tour. Don Lulo's and the Bella Vista Lodge both lead horseback tours to the falls. Don Lulo's tour departs 10 km (6 mi) northeast of Dominical, on the road to San Isidro. Bella Vista tours start at the lodge, 5 km (3 mi) south of Dominical, then left up the steep, rough Escaleras road. ☎ *771–3187 Don Lulo's, 388–0155 Bella Vista Lodge* ☞ *Don Lulo's tour $40, Bella Vista tour $45* ☼ *Tours daily at 8 AM.*

A considerably smaller waterfall than Cataratas de Nauyaca, **Pozo Azul** is in the jungle about 5 km (3 mi) south of town. It's accessible by foot or horseback. Head up road toward Bella Vista lodge; when it begins to climb hill, look for trail down to river on right.

Where to Stay & Eat

¢–$ ✕ **San Clemente Bar & Grill.** Signs you're in the local surfer hangout: dozens of broken surfboards affixed to the ceiling, photos of the sport's early years adorning the walls, and a big sound system and dance floor. Fresh seafood (grilled outdoors for dinner), sandwiches, and such Tex-Mex standards as burritos and nachos make up the menu. Owner Mike McGinnis is famous for making great hot sauces and for being a super source of information about the area. ✉ *Main road* ☎☎ *787–0055* ⊟ *AE, MC, V.*

$$ ✕ ◫ **Roca Verde.** A festive atmosphere pervades the huge thatched-roof open-air restaurant ($) festooned with arty, giant papier mâché fish. It's a good choice for drinks or a meal, even if you aren't staying here. If you are, the sunny, stylish rooms of the beachfront hotel have stucco walls painted with swirling wall flowers, luxurious bathrooms, and cane-balustraded verandas looking onto a garden. Late-night Saturday-night dances, sometimes with live music, draw *bailarinas* (dancers) from surrounding towns. ✉ *1 km (½ mi) south of Dominical* ☎ *787–0036* ◰ *787–0013* ☞ *10 rooms* ⌖ *Restaurant, pool, beach, fishing, laundry service; no room phones, no room TVs* ⊟ *AE, MC, V.*

$–$$ ◫ **The Necochea Inn.** The name sounds indigenous, but it's actually the Basque-origin last name of the young American owners, who have built a handsome B&B decorated with a sophisticated mix of safari-modern oversize furniture that is right at home in the huge rooms. Downstairs living and dining rooms face a wall of sliding glass doors looking onto a stone-decked pool. Two streams run through the forested property. A curved stone stairway leads up to two large rooms, which share a spacious bath, and two suites, each with private porch, decadent bathrooms with deep tubs or whirlpool tubs for two, antique armoires, and gleaming hardwood floors. ✉ *Marina Vista Dr., off main highway, Domini-*

calito; 4 km (2½ mi) south of Dominical ☎ *395–2984* ⊕ *www. thenecocheainn.com* ➪ *2 rooms with shared bath, 2 suites* ⚘ *Dining room, pool, some in-room hot tubs; no a/c, no room phones, no room TVs* ⊟ *MC, V.*

$ 🏠 **Hacienda Barú National Wildlife Refuge and Ecolodge.** These spacious but simple cabinas are an ideal base for exploring the rain forest. Newly tiled floors, sitting rooms with bamboo furniture, and two or three bedrooms make these cabins perfect for three or four people. Linger for an hour or two atop a lofty bird observation platform in the hotel's rainforest canopy, zip along the canopy tour, climb a 114-ft-high tree with ropes, or stay overnight at a shelter in the heart of the forest. Excellent local guides interpret the miles of forest and mangrove trails. ⊠ *2 km (1 mi) north of bridge into Dominical* ⌖ *Apdo. 215–8000, Perez Zeledon* ☎ *787–0003* 🖴 *787–0004* ⊕ *www.haciendabaru.com* ➪ *6 cabinas* ⚘ *Dining room, fans, kitchens, hiking, horseback riding; no a/c, no room phones, no room TVs* ⊟ *AE, MC, V* ⦾ *CP.*

★ $$ 🏠 **Pacific Edge.** The forest grows right up to this stylishly rustic lodge high on a mountain ridge south of town with an unbeatable Pacific view. Private wood cabinas—one sleeps six—have comfortable orthopedic mattresses and hammocks strung on wide porches. The lodge's bamboo-roof, pagoda-style dining room serves great breakfasts and dinners on request. Two lookout towers at each end of the tiny pool catch the spectacular sunsets. The road up to this lofty perch definitely requires a four-wheel-drive vehicle, but a hotel shuttle can pick you up in town with advance notice. The reception desk closes at 6 PM. ⊠ *Turn inland 4 km (2½ mi) south of Dominical on a rough road, follow road 2 km (1 mi)* ⌖ *Apdo. 531–8000, Dominical* ☎ *381–4369 or 771–4582* 🖴 *771–8841* ✉ *pacificedge@pocketmail.com* ➪ *4 cabinas* ⚘ *Dining room, pool, refrigerators, bar; no a/c, no room phones, no room TVs* ⊟ *AE, MC, V* ⦾ *BP.*

$ 🏠 **Villas Río Mar.** The fanciest hotel in town is upriver from the beach on exquisitely landscaped grounds adrift in clouds of orchids. The 10 adobe-style cabinas—each with four separate rooms—feel like private cottages, with thatched roofs, cane ceilings, and clean white bathrooms. Each room has a private porch screened with mosquito netting and furnished with bamboo chairs and hammocks. Plants and elegant table settings fill the restaurant, which is covered by a giant thatched roof. There is a luxurious, large pool, and the hotel spa offers yoga. ⊠ *1 km (½ mi) west of Dominical on riverfront road* ☎ *787–0052* 🖴 *787–0054* ⊕ *www.villasriomar.com* ⌖ *Apdo. 1645–2050, San José* ☎ *866/850–5260 in the U.S.* ➪ *40 rooms* ⚘ *Restaurant, refrigerators, tennis court, pool, fitness classes, gym, hot tub, massage, spa, beach, bar, convention center; no a/c, no room TVs* ⊟ *AE, MC, V.*

¢ 🏠 **Posada del Sol.** Going no-frills? Here you'll find simple, clean accommodations in a tranquil atmosphere. Rooms are on the ground floor of a cement building opening onto a narrow porch with chairs and tables. In back is a little garden with a cement table and an area for washing clothes (by hand). The Costa Rican owners are friendly and helpful. ⊠ *Main road, just south of San Clemente Bar & Grill* ☎☎ *787–0085 or 787–0082* ➪ *5 rooms* ⚘ *Fans; no a/c, no room phones, no room TVs* ⊟ *No credit cards.*

The Outdoors

ECOTOURISM **Hacienda Barú** (☎ 787–0003) is the best-organized ecotourism operation in Dominical. You can get hoisted to a platform in the crown of a giant tree on the rain forest canopy tour ($35); spend a night in a shelter in the woods ($60); or take a zip-line tour ($30).

HORSEBACK RIDING One way to get to Nauyaca Waterfalls is with **Don Lulo's Horseback Tours** (⊠ road to San Isidro, 12 km [8 mi] northeast of Dominical ☎ 787–0198). Lulo's trips to the falls ($40) include swimming in the natural pools below the cascades, a light breakfast, and a hearty Costa Rican lunch. Reserve a spot for Don Lulo's tour through your hotel or with **Dominical Adventures** (☎ 787–0191). You can travel to Nauyaca Falls via the private reserve of the **Bella Vista Lodge** (⊠ halfway between Dominical and Dominicalito, up a steep road ☎ 388–0155), on a high ridge with a truly magnificent view. It's a two-hour horseback ride through dense rain forest to get here ($45, including homemade picnic lunch). The lodge has 18 horses and more horseback tours.

KAYAKING **Southern Expeditions** (☎ 787–0100), at the entrance to town and in Hotel Villas Río Mar, arranges kayaking, rafting, surfing, snorkeling, and diving trips. **Dominical Adventures** (☎ 787–0191), in the San Clemente Bar & Grill, has a full range of watery adventures, including kayaking in mangroves and river tubing.

SPORTFISHING Angling options range from expensive sportfishing charters to a trip in a small boat with a local fisherman to catch red snapper and snook. **Steve Sandusky** (☎ 787–0230) has been fishing local waters since 1996 aboard a high-powered 28-ft boat. You can fish for sport and take some of your catch home to eat. The Roca Verde hotel and Dominical Adventures at the San Clemente Bar & Grill can also arrange trips.

SURFING Surfers have long flocked to Dominical for its consistent beach breaks. The surf shop near the San Clemente Cabinas and Surf Hostel rents, sells, and repairs surfboards.

Shopping

★ Shop in rare air-conditioned comfort at **Banana Bay Gallery & Gifts** in the Pacífica shopping center on the highway just above Dominical (☎ 787–0106). The shop is open 9–5 daily, and it's stocked with an always intriguing and amusing mix of arts and crafts and unusual items, along with indigenous crafts such as Boruca masks and colorful woven-cotton hats and bags.

Ballena Marine National Park

5 *20 km (12 mi) southeast of Dominical.*

One of Costa Rica's few marine parks, the Parque Nacional Marino Ballena (Whale Marine National Park) protects several beaches, a mangrove estuary, an important coral reef, and a vast swath of ocean with rocky isles and islets. There's some great snorkeling here. Humpback whales can be seen with their young from December to April, and frigate birds and Brown Boobies, a tropical seabird, nest on the park's rocky islands.

At the park's northern end, **Playa Uvita** stretches out into Punta Uvita, a long swath of sand, or *tombolo,* connecting a former island to the coast. At low tide, the sand bar resembles a whale's tail fanning out on either side of the point, hence the name of the bay: Bahía Ballena, or Whale Bay. **Playa Ballena,** to the southeast, is a lovely strand backed by lush vegetation. Tiny **Playa Piñuelas** is in a deep cove that serves as the local port. **Playa Ventanas,** south of Ballena Marine Park, is a beautiful beach that's popular for sea-kayaking. The mountains that rise up behind these beaches hold rain forests, waterfalls, and wildlife. For less than $1 admission, you'll receive a brochure and a plastic garbage bag to remind you to take your trash with you.

Where to Stay & Eat

$ ✕⊡ Balcón de Uvita. Food and view vie for attention at the hotel's excellent balcony restaurant ($), with just five tables. The sunset view of Bahía Ballena is spectacular, but it's the authentic Indonesian cuisine that wins out. The rijsttafel consists of seven exotic dishes that include sweetly spiced minced beef steamed in a banana leaf, succulent gingery chicken, and a toasted coconut and peanut condiment. The restaurant is closed Monday through Wednesday. Three stylishly modern, comfortable casitas with large tiled bathrooms sleep four to six, and one has a full kitchen. They share the bay view, plus a lovely pool and garden in which to soak up the mountain tranquility. ☒ *1 km (½ mi) north of gas station (4X4 vehicle required) Uvita* ☎ *743–8034* ⊕ *www. balcondeuvita.com* ⤺ *3 casitas* ⚬ *Restaurant, some kitchens, pool, bar; no a/c, no room phones, no room TVs* ⊟ *No credit cards.*

★ $ ✕⊡ Villas Gaia. This sophisticated lodge gives you access to beaches and wilderness that few foreigners see. The colorful villas are spread around the jungle on a ridge behind Playa Tortuga, south of Playa Ventanas. The villas have hardwood furnishings and balconies that overlook forested ravines. The poolside villas catch the best breezes. The restaurant ($) serves some of the region's best food, with an eclectic menu ranging from Greek salad to Thai-spiced fish, along with a tempting variety of banana desserts. Chandeliers are made of mangrove roots. Horseback, mangrove, and sea-kayaking tours can be arranged through the hotel. ☒ *15 km (9 mi) south of Uvita on coastal highway, Playa Tortuga* ☎ *382–8240* ☎ *256–9996* ⊕ *www.villasgaia.com* ⤺ *12 cabinas* ⚬ *Restaurant, pool, bar, laundry service; no a/c, no room phones, no room TVs* ⊟ *AE, MC, V.*

The Outdoors

Delfin Tours (☎ 743–8169), right on Punta Uvita beach, organizes snorkeling trips to the nearby reef as well as sportfishing excursions to Caño Island. For a different kind of boating experience, **Manglar Sur** (☎ 788–8351) offers day and sunset dinner cruises on an elegant paddle boat.

For a bird's-eye view of Bahía Ballena and the park, take off with aeronautical engineer Georg Kiechle in his ultralight flying machine for "the ultimate flying experience." Flights with **Skyline Fly Ultralight** (☒ on road into Uvita ☎ 743–8037 ⊕ www.flyultralight.com) cost $65–$150 for 20 minutes to 1½ hours.

San Vito

❻ *132 km (83 mi) southeast of San Isidro, 93 km (58 mi) northeast of Golfito.*

The little hilltop town of San Vito owes its 1952 founding to a government scheme whereby 200 Italian families were awarded grants to convert the rain forest into coffee, fruit, and cattle farms. Today this lively town retains a distinctive Italian flavor, with outdoor cafés serving ice cream and pastries, a Dante Alighieri Cultural Center, and lots of shoe stores. Because of its proximity to the Coto Brus Indian Reservation, San Vito is also one of the few towns in Costa Rica where you might see Ngwobe, or Guaymí, Indians, who are easy to recognize by the colorful dresses worn by the women. If you're short of cash, the Coopealianza near the church has an ATM machine that accepts foreign cards.

Twenty-five hillside acres were converted from a coffee plantation in 1961 by U.S. landscapers Robert and Catherine Wilson to create the extensive and enchanting **Wilson Botanical Garden.** The Wilsons planted a huge collection of tropical species, including palms (an amazing 700 species), orchids, aroids, ferns, bromeliads, heliconias, and marantas, all linked by a series of neat grass paths; the gardens now hold around 3,000 native and 4,000 exotic species. The property was transferred to the Organization for Tropical Studies (OTS) in 1973, and in 1983 it became part of Amistad Biosphere Reserve. Wilson functions mainly as a research and educational center, but visitors and overnight guests are welcome, and there's a resident botanist to lead tours. Spending the night in the garden is a pleasure, though considerably pricier than sleeping in San Vito. ⊠ *6 km (4 mi) south of San Vito on road to Ciudad Neily* ⌂ *Apdo. 73–8257, San Vito* ☎ *773–4004* 🖷 *773–3665* ⊕ *www.ots.duke.edu* ⊠ *$6* ⊗ *Daily 8–4.*

off the beaten path

Ciudad Neily. The 33-km (21-mi) road between San Vito and Ciudad Neily is twisting and spectacular, with views over the Coto Colorado plain to the Golfo Dulce and Osa Peninsula beyond. Much of this steep terrain is covered with tropical forest, making it an ideal route for bird-watching and picture-taking. The road from **San Vito to Paso Real** is equally scenic, traveling along a high ridge with sweeping valley views on either side. This road is well paved, so even the driver can enjoy the scenery.

Where to Stay & Eat

$ ✕ **Pizzeria Liliana.** Treat yourself to real Italian pizza at this large, friendly, family-run restaurant with a garden terrace out back. Pizzas have crispy olive-oil crusts and come in three generous sizes: even the small easily serves two. Or dig into the macaroni *sanviteña*-style, with white sauce, ham and mushrooms. The classics are here as well, and they're all homemade—lasagna, canneloni and ravioli. The vinaigrette salad dressing is a welcome change from more acidic Tico dressings. ⊠ *1½ blocks west of central square* ☎ *773–3080* ⊟ *V.*

★ $ 🏠 **Wilson Botanical Garden.** A must-see paradise for gardeners and bird lovers, this pretty garden has cabins of modern glass, steel, and wood that blend into a forested ridge. Private balconies cantilevered over a ravine make bird-watching a snap even from your room. Each room is named after a plant growing at the doorway. Room rates include either breakfast or three excellent home-style meals and 24-hour access to the garden. Staying overnight is the easiest way to see the garden at dusk and dawn, a highly recommended experience. It's also the only way to get a chance to walk the Sendero Río Java, teeming with streams, birds, and monkeys. ⊠ *6 km (4 mi) south of San Vito on road to Ciudad Neily* ⌂ *OTS, Apdo. 676–2050, San Pedro* ☎ *506/240–6696* 🖷 *506/240–6783* ⊕ *www.ots.duke.edu* ⊲ *12 cabinas* ⚖ *Restaurant, hiking; no a/c, no room TVs* ⊟ *AE, MC, V* ⦿ *BP.*

¢ 🏠 **Hotel El Ceibo.** Tucked in a quiet cul-de-sac behind Main Street, this well-maintained two-story hotel is reminiscent of Italy, with graceful arcades and white balconies. Rooms are compact but comfortable; many have views over a wooded ravine alive with birds. The restaurant serves homey Italian and Tico food at very reasonable prices. The curved 1950s-style wooden bar is a quaint spot to sit on a red stool and enjoy a drink. All in all, it's quite a deal. ⊠ *140 m (150 yards) east of San Vito's central park, behind Municipalidad* ☎ *773–3025* 🖷 *773–5025* ⊲ *40 rooms* ⚖ *Restaurant, cable TV, bar; no a/c, no room phones* ⊟ *MC.*

La Amistad National Park

7 *40 km (25 mi) northwest of San Vito.*

Covering more than 1,980 square km (765 square mi), Parque Nacional La Amistad is by far the largest park in Costa Rica, yet it's actually a mere portion of the vast **Reserva La Biósfera La Amistad** (Amistad Biosphere Reserve)—a collection of protected areas stretching from southern Costa Rica into western Panama. The national park covers altitudes ranging from 1,000 m (3,280 ft) to 3,500 m (11,480 ft) and has an array of ecosystems that hold two-thirds of the country's vertebrate species. The park is difficult to access, but it's a worthwhile excursion for the adventurous. The easiest part to visit is **Altamira**, 35 km (23 mi) north of Paso Real. There's a ranger station there, as well as a biodiversity office, picnic area, rest rooms, potable water, and trails. The road winding its bumpy way up into the mountains is suitable only for four-wheel-drive vehicles. Camping is allowed; reserve space at the **regional office** (✉ San Isidro ☎ 771–3155).

Golfito

8 *339 km (212 mi) southeast of San José.*

Overlooking a small gulf (hence its name) and hemmed in by a steep bank of forest, Golfito has a great location and little else—that is, unless you're an angler. Sport- and fly-fishing have taken off in this area, and many lodges here exclusively run these trips. Ecotourism is also on the rise; the **Camara Ecoturistica de Golfito** (CATUGOL; ☎ 775–1820) has an information office in front of the small ferry dock.

Golfito was a thriving banana port for several decades—United Fruit arrived in 1938—with a dock that could handle 4,000 boxes of bananas per hour and elegant housing for its plantation managers. United Fruit pulled out in 1985 in response to labor disputes and rising export taxes, and Golfito promptly slipped into a state of poverty and neglect from which it has yet to recover completely. In an effort to inject some life into the town, the government declared it a duty-free port to attract Costa Rican shoppers, but the proposed Latin free-trade zone may mean its demise. The town itself consists of a pleasant older section and a long, ugly strip of newer buildings, dilapidated former workers' quarters, and abundant seedy bars. Visiting U.S. Navy ships dock here, and small cruise ships moor in the harbor. The Costa Rica Coast Guard headquarters is also here.

The northwestern end of town is the so-called **American Zone,** full of stilted wooden houses where the expatriate managers of United Fruit lived amid flowering trees imported from all over the world. These houses were purchased by Costa Ricans when the company departed, and some now offer B&B rooms.

Golfito doesn't have a beach of its own, but **Playa Cacao** a mere five-minute boat ride across the bay. The beach has several restaurants and lodges, making it a convenient all-around option when the hotels in Golfito are full.

The hills behind Golfito are covered with the lush forest of the **Refugio Nacional de Vida Silvestre Golfito** (Golfito National Wildlife Refuge), known as Naranjal by the locals. At the entrance, just 550 yards along a dirt road that runs parallel to the airport, you find the botanical legacy of the United Fruit Company's experimental farm, with flora from all over the world. The forest paths have been rehabilitated by the local tourism chamber and University of Costa Rica students, with signs leading you to waterfalls.

Parque Nacional Piedras Blancas (White Stones National Park), adjacent to the Golfito National Wildlife Refuge, has some great birding. The park is covered in verdant forest and is home to many species of endemic plants and animals. It's an important wildlife corridor because it connects to Corcovado National Park, and it's one of the few places in Costa Rica where jaguars still live. Follow the main road northwest through the old American Zone, past the airstrip and a housing project: the place where a dirt road heads into the rain forest is ground zero for bird-watchers.

If you have four-wheel drive, you can follow the dirt track through the heart of Piedras Blancas National Park to the community of La Gamba and the comfortable Esquinas Rain Forest Lodge. In the dry season when it's passable, this back route can cut miles off a trip to or from the north, and it passes through some gorgeous wilderness.

★ A Garden of Eden with mass plantings of ornamental palms, bromeliads, heliconias, cycads, orchids, and flowering gingers, **Casa Orquideas** is accessible only by boat. It has been tended with care for more than 25 years by American owners Ron and Trudy MacAllister. A two-hour tour includes touching, tasting, and smelling, plus spotting toucans and hummingbirds. Tours are offered Saturday through Thursday at 8:30 AM and cost $5 per person, with a minimum of four per tour. The water taxi from Golfito to the garden (about $50 for two including the return trip) is a tour in itself. ⊠ *North of Golfito on the Golfo Dulce* ☎ *775–1614.*

Where to Stay & Eat

¢–$ ╳ **Restaurant Coconut.** Just across from the ferry dock, this popular diner is information central in Golfito, with tourist information and Internet access. Owner Dave Corella is a wealth of local lore. The diner serves the best breakfast in town, plus ceviche, burritos, *casados* (plates of rice, beans, fried plantains, salad, and meat, chicken, or fish), and vegetarian dishes. The homemade chocolate cake and whole wheat bread are standouts, and there are BLTs and tuna melts if you're looking for comfort food. ⊠ *Main road, facing city ferry dock, Golfito* ☎ *775–0518 or 775–1742* ▤ *No credit cards.*

$$$$ ▥ **Golfito Sailfish Rancho.** Wedged between *golfo* and jungle, this comfortable, white-stucco lodge has all-inclusive, first-rate fishing packages. Two wings of rooms with tiled verandas look onto a narrow strip of beach. The convivial rancho restaurant serves buffet meals. Spacious rooms are meant for sharing, and have racks for storing fishing rods. The Rancho's fleet includes 10 up-to-date fishing boats, where you spend the majority of your days. Non-fishing rates are also available. ⊠ *15-min boat ride north of Golfito* ☎ *380–4262* ✧ *5700 Memorial Hwy., Tampa, FL 33615* ☎ *800/450–9908 in the U.S.* ➠ *813/889–9189* ⊕ *www.golfitosailfish.com* ➳ *10 rooms* ⌂ *Restaurant, fans, beach, bar; no a/c, no kids under 12, no room phones, no room TVs* ▤ *AE, MC, V* ⦿ *FAP.*

$$$$ ▥ **Rainbow Adventures Lodge.** Handsome tropical hardwoods blend with Art Nouveau antiques and Tiffany glass in this three-story pagoda-style lodge. Spacious, flower-filled rooms and private cabins are open to the air: no screens, no shutters, just suspended panels of decorative stained glass and mosquito nets around the beds. Fruits from the surrounding orchards and sea make for mouthwatering meals. Trails lead to waterfalls, estuary forests, and excellent birding. Be sure to paddle a kayak at sunset and join the arcing dolphins. There's a superb natural history library. ⊠ *Playa Cativo, 35 min by boat, north of Golfito* ☎ *775–0220*

5875 N.W. Kaiser Rd., Portland, OR 97229 ☎ *503/690–7750, 800/565–0722 in the U.S.* ⊞ *503/690–7735* ⊕ *www.rainbowcostarica. com* ⤴ *4 rooms, 2 cabins* ⚭ *Dining room, pool, snorkeling, fishing, hiking, library; no a/c, no room phones, no room TVs* ¶Ol *AI.*

$$ ⊡ **Esquinas Rainforest Lodge.** The only nonprofit ecolodge in the country, this jungle lodge is financed by the Austrian government. A Teutonic sense of order prevails, with tidy gravel paths winding past five wooden cabins in manicured gardens. Rooms have tile floors, good reading lamps, and airy bathrooms with plenty of hot water. A spring-fed pool is delightful, and the candlelit dining room serves excellent food. Fragrant white ginger and ylang-ylang encircle a pond with a resident cayman, well fed on pond trout. Wild and thrilling trails head to the waterfalls and primary forest of Piedras Blancas park. Local guides lead river walks. ⊠ *Near La Gamba, 4 km (2½ mi) west of Villa Briceño turnoff* ☎⊞ *775–0901* ⊕ *www.esquinaslodge.com* ⤴ *10 rooms* ⚭ *Dining room, pool, hiking, horseback riding, bar; no a/c, no room TVs, no room phones* ☰ *AE, MC, V* ¶Ol *AI.*

$ ⊡ **Hotel Las Gaviotas.** Just south of town on the water's edge, this hotel has wonderful views over the inner gulf. Rooms have terra-cotta floors, teak furniture, and a veranda with chairs overlooking the well-tended tropical gardens and the shimmering gulf beyond. An open-air restaurant looks onto the large pool, whose terrace is barely divided from the sea. The bar-restaurant has an extensive wine list. The hotel can book sportfishing trips for guests and nonguests. ⊠ *Playa Tortuga, south of Golfito* *Apdo. 12–8201, Golfito* ☎ *775–0062* ⊞ *775–0544* ⤴ *18 rooms, 3 cabinas* ⚭ *Restaurant, fans, cable TV, pool, bar, shop* ☰ *AE, MC, V.*

The Outdoors

SPORTFISHING Fishing is great in the waters off Golfito, either in the Golfo Dulce or out in the open ocean. The open ocean holds plenty of sailfish, marlin, and Roosterfish during the dry months, as well as dolphin, tuna, and wahoo during the rainy season; there's excellent bottom fishing any time of year. Relatively low-cost **Froylan López** (☎ 385–9074) takes you fishing the traditional Tico way, with rod and reel and a full ice chest. **Golfito Sailfish Rancho** (☎ 380–4262, 800/450–9908 in the U.S.) runs the biggest fishing charter operation in Golfito. Its huge marina is right in town. **Hotel Las Gaviotas** (☎ 775–0062) can arrange sportfishing trips. **Tierra Mar** (Land Sea Services; ⊠ on the waterfront next to Banana Bay Marina ☎⊞ 775–1614 ⊕ www.marinaservices-yachtdelivery.com) arranges day trips with independent captains in the area.

Shopping

Tierra Mar (⊠ waterfront next to Banana Bay Marina) has an excellent selection of painted Boruca wood masks. It also has one-of-a-kind local crafts, such as woven straw hats, cotton purses, and painted gourds. Ticos are drawn to Golfito's duty-free bargains on such imported items as TV sets, stereos, and tires. To shop at the **Depósito Libre** you have to spend the night, which means you register in the afternoon with your passport and shop the next morning. Shopping is sheer madness in December.

Playa Zancudo

❾ *51 km (32 mi) south of Golfito.*

Playa Zancudo, a 10-km (6-mi), palm-lined beach fronting the fishing village of Zancudo, is accessible by car or boat. You can hire a boat at the municipal dock in Golfito for the 25-minute ride ($25 for two). The rough road entails two hours of bone-shaking and a short ride on a cable river ferry. There's a flurry of new construction here, with Canadians and Americans building substantial beachfront homes. Zancudo has a good surf break, but it's nothing compared with Playa Pavones a little to the south. There are some good swimming areas, and if you get tired of playing in the surf and sand you can arrange a boat trip to the nearby mangrove estuary to see birds and crocodiles. Zancudo is also home to one of the area's best sportfishing operations, headquartered at Roy's Zancudo Lodge.

Where to Stay

$–$$ ▣ **Roy's Zancudo Lodge.** Most people who stay here are anglers on all-inclusive sportfishing packages, taking advantage of Roy's 10 fishing boats. But the comfortable, modern hotel is a good choice even if you've never caught anything but a cold. It's right on the beach—the ample, verdant grounds surround an inviting pool and an open-air restaurant serves buffet meals. The sea foam–green two-story hotel has huge rooms with hardwood floors, two firm double beds, and ocean views. Four suites are in cozy private cabinas, and three cheaper rooms don't have refrigerators. ☒ *Main road, 1 km (½ mi) west of Cabinas Sol y Mar, Playa Zancudo* ☏ *Apdo. 41, Zancudo* ☎ *776–0008* ☒ *776–0011* ⊕ *www.royszancudolodge.com* ☞ *15 rooms, 4 cabinas* ☖ *Restaurant, fans, some refrigerators, cable TV, pool, hot tub, beach, fishing, bar* ▭ *V* ⑩ *FAP.*

$ ▣ **Cabinas Los Cocos.** This little beachfront colony of four self-catering cabins is designed for people who want to kick back and enjoy the beach. Artist Susan England and her husband, Andrew Robertson, are Zancudo fixtures and can organize any activity, including river safaris and kayaking tours. There are two idyllic tropical cabins with thatched roof and hammock. The other two cabins are renovated 40-year-old banana company houses moved here from Palmar Norte. These charming white-and-green wooden cottages give visitors a rare chance to live a little bit of Costa Rican history. ☒ *Beach road* ☎☎ *776–0012* ⊕ *www.loscocos.com* ☞ *4 cabins* ☖ *Kitchens, beach; no a/c, no room phones, no room TVs* ▭ *No credit cards.*

$ ▣ **Cabinas Sol y Mar.** As its name implies, Cabinas Sol y Mar has sun and sea and a coconut-fringed beach. Rose-colored cabinas with tiled porches and high ceilings look onto the gulf and have views of the Osa Peninsula. Each cabina sleeps four. The alfresco restaurant serves excellent fish—try the mahimahi in coconut-ginger sauce. The popular U-shape bar is an easy place to meet new friends. A shop sells sarongs and other clothing from Thailand. The staff can arrange transportation from the Zancudo dock (a 20-minute walk) or from Golfito if you call ahead. ☒ *Main road, at entrance to Playa Zancudo* ☎ *776–0014* ☒ *776–0015* ☏ *Apdo. 87, Golfito* ⊕ *www.zancudo.com* ☞ *5 cabinas, 1 house* ☖ *Restaurant, fans, beach, bar, shop; no a/c, no room phones, no room TVs* ▭ *V* ☼ *Closed Sept.–Oct.*

The Outdoors

SPORTFISHING If you've got your own gear, you can do some good shore fishing from the beach or the mouth of the mangrove estuary, or hire one of the local boats to take you out into the gulf. **Arena Alta Sportfishing** (☎ 776–0044) arranges daily fishing trips, serving up some of the day's catch as sushi every night in its bar. It also provides boat taxis and rents golf carts for getting around Zancudo. **Roy Ventura** (☎ 776–0008) runs the best charter operation in the area, with 10 boats ranging in length from 22 ft to 32 ft. Packages include room, food, and drink, and you can arrange to be picked up in Golfito or Puerto Jiménez.

Playa Pavones

▶ ⑩ *53 km (33 mi) south of Golfito.*

On the southern edge of the mouth of Golfo Dulce stands Pavones, a windswept beach town at the end of a dirt road. Famous among surfers for having one of the longest waves in the world, the town also has pristine black-sand beaches and virgin rain forest in its favor. It's not close to anything in particular, but its seclusion makes it a worthwhile destination for adventurous types. Most surfers here are serious about their sport and they bring their own boards, but you can rent surfboards, boogie boards, and bicycles at Cabinas La Ponderosa.

Where to Stay

$$$$ ▦ **Tiskita Jungle Lodge.** Monkeys, coatis, birds, and other wildlife are lured by the hundreds of exotic fruit trees from all over the world that have been planted on the grounds by the lodge owner, a passionate farmer. Guides lead tours of the grounds and day-long dolphin-watching trips. Screened wooden cabins on stilts are surrounded by lush vegetation and have rustic furniture and open-air bathrooms. Trails invite you to explore the jungle and a cascading waterfall with freshwater pools. Simple, buffet-style meals are speedy. Cabins are spread out, but many are joined. If you want privacy, ask when booking. Most guests arrive by air taxi at the hotel's private airstrip. There's no phone at the lodge. ⊠ *6 km (4 mi) south of Pavones* ⬧ *Apdo. 13411–1000, San José* ☎ *296–8125* 🖷 *296–8133* ⊕ *www.tiskita-lodge.co.cr* ⤴ *16 rooms* ⚖ *Dining room, fans, pool, beach, snorkeling, hiking, horseback riding, airstrip; no a/c, no room phones, no room TVs* ⊟ *MC, V* ⊙ *Closed Oct.* ⦿ *AI.*

$-$$ ▦ **Cabinas La Ponderosa.** The world-famous Playa Pavones surfing break is on the doorstep of this surfer-owned hotel. It's a cut above the usual surfer place, with high-ceiling rooms that sleep up to six and have hardwood furniture and walls. Screened porches overlook a lush garden, and nature trails wind through 14 acres. The house has two bedrooms and a screened balcony but no kitchen. You can rent surfboards, boogie boards, or bicycles here. ⊠ *On beach* ☎ *384–7430 for voice mail or 954/771–9166 in the U.S.* ⊕ *www.cabinaslaponderosa.com* ⤴ *5 rooms, 1 house* ⚖ *Dining room, some refrigerators, beach, bicycles; no a/c in some rooms, no room phones, no room TVs* ⊟ *No credit cards.*

THE OSA PENINSULA

Some of Costa Rica's most breathtaking scenery and wildlife thrive on the Osa Peninsula, one-third of which is covered by Corcovado National Park. It's a paradise for backpackers and upscale vacationers alike, who can hike into the park on any of three routes. Corcovado also works for day trips from nearby luxurious nature lodges, most of which lie within private preserves that are home for much of the same wildlife you might see in the park. And to complement the peninsula's lush forests and pristine beaches, the sea around it offers great sportfishing and diving.

Most visitors fly to Puerto Jiménez, Drake, or Carate, but there's also a 90-minute water-taxi ride from Golfito. A rickety-looking launch leaves at 11:30 AM every day from the *muellecito* (small municipal dock) in Golfito. It returns the next morning from Puerto Jiménez.

Puerto Jiménez

⑪ *127 km (79 mi) west of Golfito, 364 km (226 mi) southeast of San José.*

This sleepy and dusty town is the largest on the Osa Peninsula and is a convenient base for exploring some of the nearby wilderness. Main-street traffic consists mostly of bicycles and ancient pickup trucks. Be prepared for the humidity—Jiménez has plenty of it. You won't find relief in the Golfo Dulce, which borders the town, as its water is quite warm. New restaurants, hotels, Internet cafés, and "green" newcomers are lending this town an interesting, funky edge.

Most people spend a night here before or after visiting Corcovado National Park, as Puerto Jiménez has the best access to the park's two main trailheads and is the base for the *collectivo* (public transport via pickup truck) to Carate. The collectivo leaves for Carate from Autotransportes Blanco, 200 m (200 yards) west of the Super 96 in Puerto Jiménez, every day at 6 AM and 1:30 PM and returns from Carate at 8:30 AM and 4 PM. Reserve tickets in advance or at least show up early to get in line for the collectivo. If you're staying overnight in Puerto Jiménez, ask your hotel to reserve you a spot. The trip is 1½ hours along an extremely bumpy dirt road. Puerto Jiménez also lies just 40 minutes by car from spectacular Cabo Matapalo. The trip costs $40 by taxi. Buses leave from Autotransportes Blanco.

The only place to change money in Puerto Jiménez is Banco Nacional on the main street, 500 m (550 yards) south of Super 96, directly across from the church. The bank has an ATM but at this writing it accepts only Costa Rican bank cards. You can get an advance using your MasterCard or Visa at the teller windows. Bank hours are weekdays 8:30–3:45. There are no phones in Cabo Matapalo or Carate, so take care of calls in Jiménez.

Check in at the **National Parks Service Headquarters** (✉ Next to airstrip ☎ 735–5036 🖷 735–5276) to enter Corcovado or just to inquire about hiking routes and trail conditions. The Parks Service takes reservations for camping space, meals, or accommodations at **La Sirena ranger station** in Corcovado National Park.

Where to Stay & Eat

¢ ✗ **Soda Marisquería Morales.** Miriam Torres, a dried-flower artist, has created a charming rustic nook here, with tree-trunk tables and chairs, where she serves delicious shellfish soups and fresh fish ceviches. You'll also find local specialties such as cream of *ayote* (squash) soup and generous casados with fish, plus pasta dishes. The place is open daily 10–10. ✉ *Across from north end of soccer field Puerto Jiménez* ☎ *735–5746* 🚫 *No credit cards.*

★ $$ ✗🖷 **Parrot Bay Village.** A storybook collection of octagonal cottages in a tropical garden 20 minutes from town by foot, this hotel has caimans lurking in the nearby mangrove lagoon. Mahogany cabinas have four-poster beds, tile floors, hot-water showers, and intricately carved mahogany doors. They sleep up to eight; three cabinas have two stories. Some cabinas face the bar and restaurant, others face the gulf. The food at the attractive alfresco restaurant ($) is the best in town; the short dinner menu changes daily and full breakfasts are served. From the restaurant, you have a view of beach, gulf, fishing boats, and the distant hills of Piedras Blancas. Order dinner at least an hour in advance. ✉ *500 m (550 yards) southeast of airport, on beachfront* ☎ *735–5180* 🖷 *735–5568* ⊕ *www. parrotbayvillage.com* 🚤 *8 cabinas* ⚘ *Restaurant, in-room safes, beach,* *boating, fishing, volleyball, snorkeling, laundry service, bar, some pets allowed; no smoking* ⊟ *AE, D, MC, V* ⊙ *Closed 2 wks in Oct.*

¢ ✕⊞ **Restaurante y Cabinas Carolina.** This simple alfresco restaurant in the heart of Puerto Jiménez serves decent *comida típica* and reliably fresh seafood. It's also the central meeting place for every tourist and foreigner in town, ergo a good place to pick up information. The small guest rooms in back make it a good rest stop for backpackers entering or leaving Corcovado; rooms are basically cement boxes with cold running water, but they're clean and convenient. Don't count on using a credit card, as phone lines are not always working. ⊠ *Center of town, 2 blocks south of soccer field* ☎ *735–5185* ⟿ *7 rooms* ⟁ *No a/c in some rooms, no room phones, no room TVs* ⊟ *V.*

$$$$ ⊞ **Crocodile Bay Lodge.** This luxury fishing resort sits on 44 acres landscaped with a hot palette of scarlet, orange, and yellow flowers. Rooms are huge, some have whirlpool tubs for two. There's a large pool with waterfall and swim-up bar. Fishing boats moored at the private pier take you out into the gulf to fish for marlin and sailfish, or along the mangrove estuaries. There are lots of fish tales—and sushi—nightly at the lively bar, awash in a wall-size mural of underwater sea life. ⊠ *Just east of airport* ☎ *735–5632* ⊟ *735–5633* ⊕ *www.crocodilebay.com* ⟿ *28 rooms, 3 houses* ⟁ *Restaurant, some kitchens, pool, massage, snorkeling, fishing, bar* ⊟ *AE, MC, V* ۱◎۱ *AI.*

The Outdoors

HIKING If you have four-wheel drive, it's just a 30-minute ride west to **Dos Brazos** and the Tigre sector of the park, which few hikers explore. **Osa Aventura** (☎☎ 735–5670 ⊕ www.osaaventura.com) specializes in multiday Corcovado hiking adventures, led by Mike Boston, an ebullient tropical biologist who sounds like Sean Connery and looks like Crocodile Dundee.

RAFTING & SEA- Puerto Jiménez is a good base for boat or sea-kayaking trips on the Golfo
KAYAKING Dulce and the nearby mangrove rivers and estuaries. **Escondido Trex** (⊠ Restaurante Carolina ☎☎ 735–5210 ⊕ www.escondidotrex.com) arranges sea-kayaking, charter-fishing, and small-boat outings for watching wildlife (in addition to a number of land-based outings).

Cabo Matapalo

★ ⑫ *21 km (14 mi) south of Puerto Jiménez.*

The southern tip of the Osa Peninsula—where virgin rain forest meets the sea at a rocky point—retains the kind of natural beauty that people travel halfway across the world to experience. From its ridges you can look out on the blue Golfo Dulce and Pacific Ocean, sometimes spotting whales in the distance. The forest is tall and dense, with the highest and most diverse tree species in the country, usually draped with thick lianas. The name Cabo Matapalo means "cape strangler fig," a reference to the fig trees that germinate in the branches of other trees and extend their roots downward, eventually smothering the supporting tree by blocking the life-giving light with their roots and branches. Strangler figs are common in this area, as they are nearly everywhere else in the country, but Matapalo's greatest attractions are its rarer species, such as the *gallinazo* tree, which bursts into yellow blossom as the rainy season comes to a close. The brilliant Scarlet Macaw is another draw here.

A forested ridge extends east from Corcovado down to Matapalo, where the foliage clings to almost-vertical slopes and waves crash against the black rocks below. This continuous forest corridor is protected within a series of private preserves, which means that Cabo Matapalo has most of the same wildlife as the national park. Most of the point itself lies within the private reserves of the area's two main hotels, and that forest is crisscrossed by footpaths, some of which head to tranquil beaches or to waterfalls that pour into pools. The lodges in this area do not have phones, only radio contact.

Where to Stay

$$$$ **Bosque del Cabo.** On a cliff at the tip of Cabo Matapalo, this lodge **Fodor'sChoice** has unparalleled views of blue gulf waters meeting blue ocean. This is ★ the ultimate in romantic seclusion, with hundreds of acres of animal-rich primary forest and luxuriously rustic, thatched-roof, very private cabinas with outdoor (hot-water!) garden showers. From your private porch you can gaze at the stars or siesta in a hammock. Appetizing meals are served in a small rancho overlooking a garden alive by day with hummingbirds. Dinners are lit by lantern and accompanied by a chorus of frogs. Solar power provides enough light to read, and ocean breezes make air-conditioning superfluous. Resident guides are on hand to lead you along dense forest trails—on foot or along a canopy zip line—and down to the beach with its natural warm tidal whirlpools and river waterfalls. ⊠ *22 km (14 mi) south of Puerto Jiménez on rough dirt road to Carate* ☏ *735–5206* ⊕ *www.bosquedelcabo.com* ✉ *Apdo. 15, Puerto Jiménez* ⇋ *10 cabinas, 2 houses* ↻ *Restaurant, some kitchens, pool, beach, boating, fishing, hiking, horseback riding, bar; no a/c, no room phones, no room TVs* ⊟ *V* ⎍ *FAP.*

$$$$ **Lapa Ríos.** Spread along a jungle ridge, within its own nature reserve **Fodor'sChoice** teeming with wildlife, Lapa Ríos is the most luxurious eco-resort in Costa ★ Rica, winning awards worldwide for its mix of conservation and comfort. You can explore the pristine wilderness and nearby beaches on foot or on horseback, accompanied by resident naturalist guides. The spacious, airy cabins, built of gleaming hardwood with high, thatched roofs, have four-poster beds, showers with one screened wall open to nature, and private garden terraces from which you can view passing wildlife. Inspired meals are served in a dramatic rancho with a spiral staircase leading up to a crow's-nest viewing platform. The sophisticated menus include lots of seafood, exotic local fruits and vegetables, and mouthwatering desserts. The service here is exceptional. ⊠ *20 km (12 mi) south of Puerto Jiménez* ✉ *Apdo. 100, Puerto Jiménez* ✉ *Box 025216, SJO 706, Miami, FL 33102* ☏ *735–5130* ☏ *735–5179* ⊕ *www. laparios.com* ⇋ *14 cabinas* ↻ *Restaurant, pool, beach, fishing, hiking, horseback riding, bar, laundry service; no a/c, no room phones, no room TVs* ⊟ *AE, MC, V* ⎍ *FAP.*

$$$–$$$$ **El Remanso.** Find tranquility and elegance at this retreat in a forest brimming with birds and wildlife, 400 ft above a beach studded with tide pools. Luxurious cabinas have louvered screened windows, large verandas, and showers behind curving Gaudí-like walls. A two-story, hot-pink stucco-and-cane cabina has two rooms that sleep four to six each. Excellent meals use local produce and are served on a shaded deck restaurant. The property reflects the owners' conservationist ideals; they met as Greenpeace volunteers. Waterfall rappelling, zip-line access to a canopy platform, and biologist-guided nature walks are the highlights, apart from soaking in the serenity. ⊠ *Road to Carate, a few meters south of the entrance to Bosque del Cabo* ☏ *735–5569* ⊕ *www. elremanso.com* ⇋ *2 rooms, 3 cabinas* ↻ *Restaurant, outdoor hot tub, beach, hiking, bar; no a/c, no room phones, no room TVs* ⊟ *No credit cards* ⊙ *Closed Oct.–Nov.* ⎍ *FAP.*

The Outdoors

WATER SPORTS On the eastern side of the point, waves break over a platform that creates a perfect right, drawing surfers from far and wide. This area also has excellent sea-kayaking, and both Lapa Ríos and Bosque del Cabo can arrange horseback excursions, guided tours to Corcovado, or deep-sea fishing trips.

Cabo Matapalo Sportfishing (☎ 735–5773 🌐 www.cabo-matapalo.com), based in Puerto Jiménez, has excellent, experienced fishing captains and well-equipped boats, as well as surfing instruction.

Carate

13 *60 km (37 mi) west of Puerto Jiménez.*

A stretch of beach with a tiny store, Carate is literally the end of the road. There are no phones here and few lodgings. You can fly via charter plane to Carate's small airstrip and from here head into Corcovado National Park. Public transportation is available from Puerto Jiménez, via a collectivo that leaves twice daily (⇨ Puerto Jiménez, *above*).

From Carate, the La Leona ranger station in Corcovado National Park is a four-hour hike and the La Sirena station is about an eight-hour hike. The walk to the Corcovado Lodge Tent Camp is 2 km (30–45 minutes) along the beach. Vehicles are not permitted on the beach, but if you're staying at the tent camp, a horse and cart can pick up your luggage from the store. If you're driving to Carate and venturing on to the park or to Corcovado Tent Camp, you can park at the store for $5 per day. Carate has no phones; the store and lodges have radio contact.

Where to Stay

$$$$ **Luna Lodge.** Luna's charm lies in its remoteness and tranquility. Perched on a mountain overlooking the Pacific and the rain forest, it's a true retreat, with a huge hardwood pavilion for practicing yoga or contemplating magnificent sunsets. Round cabinas, spaced apart for privacy, have thatched roofs, garden showers, and decks for bird-watching or relaxing in wood-and-leather rocking chairs. Or you can semi-rough it in a well-ventilated, comfortable tent. Guided hikes to nearby waterfalls and swimming holes are precipitous and thrilling. Healthy meals have an imaginative vegetarian flare, tempered with servings of fish and chicken spiced with herbs from a hilltop organic garden. Host Lana Wedmore is a model of amiable helpfulness. ✉ *2 km (1 mi) up steep, rough track from Carate* ☎ *380–5036, 888/409–8448 in the U.S.* 🌐 *www.lunalodge.com* 📭 *Box 025216, Miami, FL 33102* *8 cabinas, 7 tents* *Restaurant, massage, boating, hiking, horseback riding, bar; no a/c, no room phones, no room TVs* 💳 *V* 🍽 *FAP.*

Corcovado National Park

14 *2¼ km (1½ mi) north of Carate.*

Comprising 435 square km (168 square mi) and covering one third of the Osa Peninsula, the Parque Nacional Corcovado is one of the largest and wildest protected areas in Costa Rica. Much of the park is covered with virgin rain forest, where massive *espavel* and *nazareno* trees tower over the trails, thick lianas hang from the branches, and animals such as toucans, spider monkeys, scarlet macaws, and poison dart frogs abound. Corcovado is also home to seldom-seen boa constrictors, jaguars, anteaters, and tapirs. In and around the park you will find some of Costa Rica's most luxurious jungle lodges and retreats.

The easiest way to visit remote Corcovado is on a day trip from one of the lodges in the nearby Drake Bay area, or from the Corcovado Tent Camp; but if you have a backpack and strong legs, you can spend days deep in its wilds. There are three entrances: La Leona (to the south),

San Pedrillo (to the north), and Los Patos (to the east). The park has no roads, however, and the roads that approach it are dirt tracks that require four-wheel drive most of the year. A very limited number of bunks are available at the La Leona and (more remote) Sirena ranger stations—you'll need sheets and a good mosquito net. Meals can be arranged at the La Sirena station if you reserve in advance, although this service may be ending soon. Check with the National Parks Service office in Puerto Jiménez before you go into the park without food supplies.

During the dry season, the park takes reservations for bunks and camping on the first day of each month for the following month. You may be asked to deposit money into the Environment Ministry's account in the Banco Nacional to reserve space. Be sure to reconfirm your reservation a few days before you enter the park. Camping is allowed at the Sirena, La Leona, Los Patos, and San Pedrillo stations, but only 35 people are allowed to camp at any given station, so reservations with the National Parks Service (➪ Puerto Jiménez, *above*) are essential in high season. ⊠ *La Leona, the southernmost entrance, is 43 km (27 mi) from Puerto Jiménez to Carate, then a 3-km (2-mi) hike. La Sirena entrance is another 13 km (8½ mi). Los Patos entrance is a 25-km (16-mi) drive from Puerto Jiménez to La Palma, then a 12-km (7-mi) hike. San Pedrillo entrance is accessible from Drake Bay by a 20-min boat ride or, in dry season only, via a 25-km (16-mi) hike along the Pacific-side beach.*

Where to Stay

¢ 🏕 **Corcovado Lodge Tent Camp.** Fall asleep to the surf pounding the
Fodor'sChoice beach in tents on wooden platforms at this rustic lodge. Ecotourist pi-
★ oneer Costa Rica Expeditions owns the lodge and its 400 acres of forest reserve 200 m (220 yards) from the La Leona entrace to Corcovado National Park. Side-by-side facing the ocean, tents have two single beds, no electricity, and share eight showers and toilets. Vegetables are plentiful at family-style meals served in an open-air hut overlooking the ocean. The "hammock house" has a bar, games, hammocks, and a deck. The mango tree outside is a good place to spot monkeys, as are the guided tours, one of which hoists you to a platform atop a 300-year-old tree; you can spend the night here, 90 ft off the ground. The proximity of the rain forest means you'll meet a mosquito or two (or twenty) and plenty of other creepy crawlers. You're roughing it in style, but you're still roughing it. Bring a flashlight (there's no electricity after 9 PM), insect repellent, and sandals for river hikes. Most guests opt for a package with all meals (there's nowhere to buy food nearby) and a charter flight to Carate, but you can also fly to Puerto Jiménez and take the collectivo—a rousing trip along bumpy dirt roads with beautiful scenery. Before you leave San José or Puerto Jiménez, call to arrange for a horse and cart to pick up your luggage from the store in Carate. Neither Carate nor the lodge has a phone; only radio contact. You can park at the store in Carate for $5 per day. ⊠ *On beach 2 km (1 mi) north of Carate; 30–45 minutes by foot* 🕾 *no phone* 🕾 *Apdo. 6941–1000, San José* 🕾 *222–0333, 800/886–2609 in the U.S.* 🖷 *257–1665* ⊕ *www. costaricaexpeditions.com* ➥ *20 tents with shared bath* ♿ *Dining room, beach, horseback riding, laundry service, bar; no a/c, no room phones, no room TVs* 🖃 *AE, MC, V.*

The Outdoors

HIKING There are three **hiking routes to Corcovado,** two beginning near Puerto Jiménez and the other beginning in Drake Bay, which follows the coast down to the San Pedrillo entrance to the park. You can hire a boat in Sierpe to take you to San Pedrillo or Drake Bay (from Drake it's a 25-km [16-mi] hike to San Pedrillo, but only in dry season). Alternately, hire

CloseUp
DIVING THE DEEP OFF COCOS ISLAND

RATED ONE OF THE TOP diving destinations in the world, Isla del Coco is uninhabited and remote, and its waters are teeming with marine life. It is no place for beginners, but serious divers enjoy 100-ft visibility and the underwater equivalent of a big-game park: Scalloped Hammerheads, White-tipped Reef Sharks, Galápagos Sharks, Bottlenose Dolphins, Billfish, and Manta Rays mix with huge schools of brilliantly colored fish.

Encompassing about 22½ square km (14 square mi), Isla del Coco is the largest uninhabited island on earth. Its isolation has led to the evolution of dozens of endemic plant and animal species. The rocky topography is draped in rain forest and cloud forest and includes more than 200 waterfalls. Because of Isla del Coco's distance from shore (300 mi) and its craggy topography, few visitors to Costa Rica—and even fewer Costa Ricans—have set foot on the island.

Costa Rica annexed Coco in 1869, and it became a national park in 1978. Today, only specialty-cruise ships, park rangers, scientists, and scuba divers visit the place Jacques Cousteau called "the most beautiful island in the world." The dry season (November–May) brings calmer seas and is the best time to see Silky Sharks. During the rainy season, large schools of hammerheads can be seen, but the ocean is rougher.

Most dive cruises to Isla del Coco are about 10 days, and include three days of travel time on the open ocean. The **Okeanos Aggressor** (☎ 222–5307, 800/348–2628 in the U.S. ⊕ www.aggressor.com) and the **Undersea Hunter** (☎ 228–6613, 800/203–2120 in the U.S. ⊕ www. underseahunter.com) run trips year-round at a cost of roughly $3,000.

---

a taxi in Puerto Jiménez for the inland Los Patos trailhead, or at least to the first crossing of the Río Rincón (from which you hike a few miles upriver to the trailhead). The beach route, via La Leona, starts in Carate.

Hiking is always tough in the tropical heat, but the forest route (from Los Patos) is easier than the two beach hikes (from La Leona and San Pedrillo), and the latter are accessible only at low tide. The hike between any two stations takes all day, and the longest hike is between San Pedrillo and Sirena. (Note that this trail is only passable in the dry season, as the rivers get too high to cross in the rainy months.) The Sirena ranger station has great trails around it. There is potable water at every station; don't drink stream water. Be sure to bring insect repellent, a sun hat and sunblock, and good boots.

Drake Bay

⑮ *10 km (6 mi) north of Corcovado, 40 km (25 mi) southwest of Palmar Sur.*

The rugged coast that stretches south from the mouth of the Río Sierpe to Corcovado probably doesn't look much different than it did in Sir Francis Drake's day (1540–96), when the British explorer anchored here. Small, picture-perfect beaches with surf crashing against dark, volcanic rocks, are backed by steaming, thick jungle. Nature lodges scattered along the coast are hemmed in by the rain forest, which is home to troops of monkeys, serene sloths, striking Scarlet Macaws, and hundreds of other bird species.

This is "Castaway" country, a real tropical adventure, with plenty of hiking and some rough but thrilling boat rides. Most people reach this isolated area by boat via the sometimes treacherous Río Sierpe, but direct flights to Drake are now available. At the height of the dry season you can reach the town via a treacherous road that requires a 4x4 vehicle.

Exceptionally fit backpackers can hike north out of Corcovado along a 25-km (16-mi) coastal path that follows the shoreline, cutting through shady forest when the coast gets too rocky. But it is impossible to walk during rainy season (September–December), when rivers flood and tides are too high. You can reach the Drake Bay area via small cruise ships sailing north from Panama or south from Jacó. The *Sea Voyager,* run by **Lindblad Expeditions** (☎ 212/765–7740, 800/425–2724 in the U.S. ⊕ www.lindblad.com), makes landings in the Drake Bay area. The *Pacific Explorer,* operated by **Cruise West** (☎ 206/441–8687, 800/580–0072 in the U.S. ⊕ www.cruisewest.com), brings passengers ashore for hikes, picnics, and horseback riding in Drake Bay and Corcovado.

The cheapest accommodations in the area can be found in the town of **Drake,** which is spread out along the bay. A trio of nature lodges—Drake Bay Wilderness Camp, Aguila de Osa Inn, and La Paloma Lodge—are also clumped near the Río Agujitas on the bay's southern end. They all offer comprehensive packages including trips to Corcovado and Isla del Caño, as well as horseback tours, scuba diving, and deep-sea fishing. Lodges farther south, such as Punta Marenco Lodge and Casa Corcovado, run the same excursions from even wilder settings.

Where to Stay

$$$$ 🏨 **Aguila de Osa Inn.** The spacious rooms here have gorgeous hardwood interiors, huge bamboo beds, and luxurious tile bathrooms. Stained glass with tropical themes and hand-carved doors add artistic flair. Be prepared for a steep climb up a concrete path to your room with a view of Drake Bay. Morning coffee arrives outside your room before 6 AM and the food is sophisticated and plentiful. The inn has two boats for sportfishing, its specialty. Scuba-diving, snorkeling, and other excursions are easily arranged. ⊠ *South end of Drake, at mouth of Río Agujitas* ☎296–2190, 291–0318, or 291–0319 🖷232–7722 ⊕*www.aguiladeosa. .com* ⊡ *Apdo. 10486–1000, San José* ⇌ *11 rooms* ⚘ *Restaurant, fans, massage, boating, fishing, horseback riding, diving, snorkeling, bar, laundry service; no a/c, no room phones, no room TVs* ⊟ *AE, MC, V* ☉ *Closed Oct.* ⧉ *FAP.*

★ $$$$ 🏨 **Casa Corcovado.** This hilltop jungle lodge has it all: a prime location on the edge of Corcovado National Park, resident naturalist guides, luxury accommodations, and first-class service and food. A trail leads right into the park from here, so you can explore its forests hours before anyone else arrives. Spanish colonial–style cabinas are spread around a garden for maximum privacy. The guest rooms have elegant Chinese furniture, four-poster beds, and huge tile bathrooms with separate vanity, shower, and toilet areas. There's a sunset bar near the top of the very steep hill that climbs up from the beach where you make a thrilling, very wet landing: a tractor-towed cart transports guests and luggage. The restaurant serves four-course gourmet dinners. Three-night packages include transportation, all meals, and a trip to Isla de Caño or Corcovado National Park. ⊠ *Northern border of Corcovado* 🕾 *no phone* ⊡ *Apdo. 1482-1250, Escazú* ☎ *256–3181 or 888/896–6097* 🖷 *256–7409* ⊕ *www. casacorcovado.com* ⇌ *14 rooms* ⚘ *Dining room, fans, pool, beach, snorkeling, boating, hiking, horseback riding, 2 bars; no a/c, no room phones, no room TVs* ⊟ *AE, MC, V* ☉ *Closed Sept.–mid-Nov.* ⧉ *AI.*

★ $$$$ 🏨 **La Paloma Lodge.** Sweeping views and a feeling of jungle seclusion make these deluxe cabinas the area's most romantic. Planted in a jungle garden on a high hill just south of Drake Bay, the elegant wooden villas have bedroom lofts and large porches with pretty green wicker furniture, huge wooden armoires, and hammocks. The tiled pool overlooks forest and ocean. The hotel runs a diving school and offers river kayaking, along with trips to Corcovado and Isla del Caño. The flower-filled restaurant serves delicious, fresh tropical fare. La Paloma is closest to Playa Cocolito, a gem of a beach just down the hill along the coastal path that eventually leads to Corcovado. ✉ *Apdo. 97–4005, Heredia, Heredia* ☎ *293–7502* 📠 *239–0954* ⊕ *www.lapalomalodge.com* 🛏 *4 rooms, 5 cabinas* ⚲ *Restaurant, pool, beach, snorkeling, fishing, horseback riding; no a/c, no room phones, no room TVs* ⊟ *AE, MC, V* ☽ *Closed Oct.* ¶⊙¶ *FAP.*

$$$ 🛏 **Drake Bay Wilderness Camp.** Spread over a grassy point between the Río Agujitas and the ocean, with the best views of Drake Bay, this camp has lots of open ground for kids to play and tidal pools to explore. The wooden cabins are camp-style with three to a building. But with hot-water, tiled bathrooms, wall murals, and carved animal bedposts supporting firm beds, this is very comfortable camping. Keep an eye out for the small troop of resident squirrel monkeys. Kayaks are at your disposal for paddles along the river. Most guests come here to see the rain forest, but you can also opt for scuba diving, sportfishing, and dolphin and whale-watching tours. ✉ *On peninsula just south of Río Agujitas, on southern end of bay* ☎☎ *770–8012* ⊕ *www.drakebay.com* ✇ *Apdo. 98–8150, Palmar Norte* ☎ *561/371–3437* 🛏 *20 rooms* ⚲ *Restaurant, fans, saltwater pool, boating, fishing, horseback riding, laundry facilities, bar; no a/c, no room phones, no room TVs* ⊟ *AE, MC, V* ¶⊙¶ *FAP.*

$$ 🛏 **Punta Marenco Lodge.** This small, rustic lodge has the best location on the Pacific side of the Osa, with idyllic, thatched-roof cabins along a ridge overlooking the sea. Private porches with two hammocks each are perfect for siestas, sunsets, and stargazing. Toucans and Scarlet Macaws are reliable visitors every morning. Trails lead down to the beach and coastal trail and deep into the Río Claro National Wildlife Refuge, and a resident guide is on hand to interpret the trails. The cozy rancho restaurant has a family feel, with communal tables and typical Tico food. There is electricity for only a few hours in the evening and no hot water. ✉ *Beachfront, directly east of Caño Island and north of Casa Corcovado* ☎ *no phone* ✇ *20 m (20 yards) north and 10 m (10 yards) west of Turrialba bus stop, near Plaza de la Democrazia, San José* ☎ *222–3305* ⊕ *www.puntamarenco.com* 🛏 *9 cabinas* ⚲ *Dining room, beach, hiking; no a/c, no room phones, no room TVs* ⊟ *No credit cards* ¶⊙¶ *FAP.*

The Outdoors

Jinetes de Osa (☎ 236–5637 ⊕ www.drakebayhotel.com), right in Drake village, has diving and snorkeling and dolphin-watching tours, as well as a canopy tour with some interesting bridge, ladder, and rope transitions between platforms. It also has a restaurant and reasonably priced comfortable rooms to rent.

Nightlife

When you're in the Osa Peninsula, the wildest nightlife is outdoors. Join entomologist Tracie Stice, also known as the Bug Lady, on the **Night Tour** (☎ 382–1619 ⊕ www.thenighttour.com) of insects, bats, reptiles, and anything else moving around at night. Tracie is a wealth of bug lore, with riveting stories from around the world. Special night-vision optics and infra-red flashlights help you see in the dark. Tours are $35 per person.

Isla del Caño

⑯ *19 km (12 mi) off Osa Peninsula, due west of Drake Bay.*

Most of this uninhabited isle (2½ square km [1 square mi]) and its biological reserve is covered in evergreen forest that includes fig, locust, and rubber trees. Coastal Indians used it as a burial ground, and the numerous bits and pieces unearthed here have prompted archaeologists to speculate about pre-Columbian long-distance maritime trade. Occasionally, mysterious stones that have been carved into perfect spheres of varying sizes are still found on the island. The uninhabited island's main attraction now is the ocean around it, which offers superb scuba diving and snorkeling. The snorkeling is excellent around the rocky points flanking the island's main beach; if you're a certified diver, you'll probably want to explore Bajo del Diablo and Paraíso, where you're guaranteed to encounter thousands of good-size fish. Lodges in Drake Bay run day trips here.

THE SOUTHERN PACIFIC COAST A TO Z

To research prices, get advice from other travelers, and book travel arrangements, visit www.fodors.com

AIR TRAVEL

Costa Rica's two domestic airlines offer regular flights from San José to Golfito, Palmar Sur, Puerto Jiménez, Coto 47 (near San Vito), and Drake Bay. Charter flights fly to more isolated spots. Because the drive from San José to this region takes six to eight hours, a one-hour flight is that much more attractive.

CARRIERS SANSA has several flights daily from San José to Golfito and some daily flights to Palmar Sur (for Drake Bay) and Puerto Jiménez. NatureAir has daily flights to Golfito, Palmar Sur, and Puerto Jiménez. Both airlines also have daily flights from Quepos to Palmar Sur. Costa Rica Expeditions runs several charter flights weekly to Carate. Drake Bay Wilderness Camp runs its own daily charter flights from Drake Bay, and both SANSA and NatureAir make daily scheduled flights to Drake Bay in small aircraft. Aerotaxi Alfa Romeo offers charter flights to Carate, Drake Bay, Puerto Jiménez, the Sirena ranger station in Corcovado National Park, the Tiskita Jungle Lodge in Playa Pavones, and anywhere else you want to go. You have to charter the whole plane, which is expensive, so it's best to fill it with the maximum capacity of five.

🚩 Airlines & Contacts **Aerotaxi Alfa Romeo** 🕾🖨 735-5178. **Costa Rica Expeditions** 🕾 222-0333 🖨 257-1665. **Drake Bay Wilderness Camp** 🕾🖨 770-8012. **NatureAir** ✉ Aeropuerto Tobias Bolaños, Pavas, San José 🕾 220-3054 🖨 220-0413. **SANSA** ✉ in front of Restaurante Uno, Golfito 🕾 775-0303 🖨 775-0021 ✉ 150 m [165 yards] south and 100 m [110 yards] east of the Caja Costarricense del Seguro Social offices, Palmar Sur 🕾 786-6353 ✉ 75 m [80 yards] west of Catholic church, Puerto Jiménez 🕾 735-5017 🖨 735-5495.

BOAT & FERRY TRAVEL

Drake Bay is usually connected by boat from Sierpe, south of Palmar Norte. Boat reservations are often part of your hotel package; otherwise, ask around at a supermarket or bar in Sierpe. Boats pick you up from your hotel on the return trip. Many local boatmen use open motorboats, so bring sun protection. The mouth of the river can have dangerous waves at low tide or during storms; make sure your boat has life jackets. The crossing takes about an hour and a half. Travel between the Drake Bay lodges, Corcovado, and Isla del Caño is most commonly accomplished in small boats owned by the major lodges, or call Corcovado Expediciones in Drake Bay to arrange boat transportation.

A ferry crosses the Golfo Dulce, leaving Puerto Jiménez daily at 6 AM and returning from Golfito at 11:30 AM. Boat transportation to Zancudo or the more distant Pavones can be arranged through the Coconut Restaurant in Golfito, which doubles as a general information center and Internet café, or through the Tierra Mar agency.

🛈 **Boat & Ferry Information Coconut Restaurant** ⊠ Golfito 🕾 775–1742. **Corcovado Expediciones** ⊠ Drake Bay 🕾 396–7774. **Tierra Mar** 🕾 775–1614.

BUS TRAVEL

Musoc buses from San José to San Isidro, a three-hour trip, depart almost every hour between 5:30 AM and 5 PM, returning at the same times. Tracopa-Alfaro buses leave San José for the eight-hour trip to Golfito daily at 7 AM and 3 PM, returning at 5 AM and 1 PM. Tracopa-Alfaro buses from San José to San Vito, a seven-hour trip, leave daily at 5:45 AM, 8:15 AM, 11:30 AM, and 2:45 PM.

Transportes Blanco-Lobo buses from San José to Puerto Jiménez, a nine-hour trip, leave at 6 AM and noon and return at 5 AM and 11 AM. Tracopa-Alfaro buses from San José to Palmar Norte, a six-hour trip, depart daily at 5, 7, 8:30, 10 AM and 1, 2:30, and 6 PM; buses to Golfito, Puerto Jiménez, and San Vito also stop in Palmar Norte. In Palmar Norte, you can hire a taxi to Sierpe, the river port for boats to Drake Bay.

Buses run by Transportes Blanco (not to be confused with Transportes Blanco-Lobo in San José) leave San Isidro for the one-hour trip to Dominical daily at 5:30 and 7 AM and 1:30 and 3 PM. Take a bus from San Isidro to San Gerardo de Rivas, the starting point of the trail into Chirripó National Park, at the terminal near the central market at 5 AM and 2 PM. From San Isidro, Transportes Blanco buses make the five-hour trip to Puerto Jiménez at 6:30 AM, 9 AM and 3 PM. A truck for hikers leaves Puerto Jiménez daily at 6 AM and 1:30 PM for Carate, returning from Carate at 8:30 AM and 4 PM.

🛈 **Bus Information Musoc** ⊠ C. Central, between Avdas. 22 and 24 San José 🕾 222–2422. **Tracopa-Alfaro** ⊠ C. 14 at Avda. 5, San José 🕾 222–2666. **Transportes Blanco** ⊠ 125 yards south of church San Isidro 🕾 771–4744 or 771–2550. **Transportes Blanco-Lobo** ⊠ C. 14 between Avdas. 9 and 11 San José 🕾 257–4121.

CAR RENTAL

There are no area car-rental agencies in the south, which is quite appropriate given the roads or lack thereof. You may rent in San José, or arrange to have a car delivered to or dropped off at a southern location for an extra fee. The Selva Mar travel agency in San Isidro can arrange for a rental car to be delivered within three hours.

🛈 **Car Rental Information Selva Mar** 🕾 771–4582 ⊕ www.exploringcostarica.com.

CAR TRAVEL

The quickest way to reach the Costanera, or coastal highway, which leads past Jacó and Quepos to Dominical and the rest of the southern Pacific zone, is to take the Carretera Interamericana (Pan-American Highway, or CA2) west past the airport to the turnoff for Atenas, turn left, and drive through Atenas to Orotina, where you head south. Between Quepos and Dominical the highway is still not paved, but heading south of Dominical, the paved road offers relatively smooth sailing.

To reach the Southern Zone from the Central Valley via the Pan-American Highway, drive east out of San José and turn south before Cartago. Be sure to leave in the morning, because dense clouds and fog often reduce visibility in the mountains to zero in the afternoons during both dry and wet seasons. The Costanera runs into the Pan-American Highway at Palmar Norte, 33 km (21 mi) south of which is the turnoff for Puerto Jiménez. Though a faithful translation of the Spanish, "highway" is really a misnomer for these neglected two-lane roads.

EMERGENCIES

In an emergency, dial 911 or one of the numbers below.

Emergency Services **Ambulance** ☎ 128. **Fire** ☎ 118. **Police** ☎ 295–3311. **Traffic Police** ☎ 222–9330.

TOURS

Horizontes designs customized tours led by naturalist guides to many remote jungle lodges. Costa Rica Expeditions, one of Costa Rica's oldest and best tour companies, runs guided tours to its Corcovado Tent Camp.

Tour Operator Recommendations **Costa Rica Expeditions** ✉ Avda. 3 at C. Central, San José ☎ 222–0333 📠 257–1665. **Horizontes** ✉ 140 m [150 yards] north of Pizza Hut on Paseo Colón, San José ☎ 222–2022 📠 255–4513.

BOAT TOURS Cruise West runs seven- and eight-day cruises on the 100-passenger *Pacific Explorer,* visiting Corcovado National Park, Drake Bay, Isla del Caño, and Manuel Antonio National Park. Guests are generally those drawn to "soft-adventure trips" and senior citizens; activities include hiking through national parks and refuges, bird-watching, nature walks, snorkeling, horseback riding, fishing, and diving accompanied by excellent naturalist guides. The ship sails from Los Sueños near Jacó with transport to and from the airport in San José. Lindblad Expeditions cruises the Pacific coast on nine-day trips aboard the *Sea Voyager,* which has 50 cabins. The ship sails from Los Sueños, and passengers can opt for extra days exploring by land on tours organized by Horizontes. For serious scuba divers in search of a thrill, there are 10-day scuba-diving expeditions to distant Cocos Island on the *Okeanos Aggressor.* A smaller vessel, the *Undersea Hunter,* makes similar dive trips to Cocos Island.

From a sunset paddle to a one-week trip around the entire Golfo Dulce, Escondido Trex, in Puerto Jiménez, can arrange any type of sea-kayaking adventure. Other adventures include rappelling down waterfalls.

Fees & Schedules **Cruise West** ✉ 2401 4th Ave., Ste. 700, Seattle WA 98121 ☎ 206/441–8687, 800/580–0072 in the U.S. 🌐 www.cruisewest.com. **Escondido Trex** ✉ Restaurante Carolina, Apdo. 9, Puerto Jiménez ☎ 735–5210. **Lindblad Expeditions** ✉ 720 5th Ave., New York NY 10019 ☎ 212/765–7740, 800/425–2724 in the U.S. 🌐 www.lindblad.com. ***Okeanos Aggressor*** 📫 2011 N.W. 79th Ave. Miami, FL 33122 ☎ 222–5307, 800/348–2628 in the U.S. 📠 222–5307 🌐 www.okeanosaggressor.com. ***Undersea Hunter*** 📫 Box 025216, Miami, FL 33102 ☎ 228–6613, 800/203–2120 in the U.S. 📠 289–7334 🌐 www.underseahunter.com.

HIKING TOURS Selva Mar leads hikes and nature tours to Chirripó and other areas. In Dominical, Hacienda Barú offers a number of guided hikes through the rain forest. Ecole Travel runs inexpensive guided hikes into Chirripó and Corcovado national parks. Osa Aventura specializes in multiday hikes into Corcovado.

Fees & Schedules **Ecole Travel** ✉ C. 7, between Avdas. Central and 1, San José ☎ 223–2240 📠 223–4128. **Hacienda Barú** ✉ 1 km [½ mi] north of Dominical ☎ 787–0003. **Osa Aventura** ☎📠 735–5670. **Selva Mar** ☎ 771–4582.

TRAVEL AGENCIES

In Puerto Jiménez, Osa Tropical has a visitor's center, sells domestic airline tickets, offers varied tours, and makes reservations at lodges on the Osa Peninsula. Selva Mar, in San Isidro, can make hotel reservations throughout the country but specializes in working with remote jungle lodges and tour operators in the Southern Zone.

🛈 **Local Agent Referrals Osa Tropical** ✉ 50 m [60 yards] south of Catholic church, Puerto Jiménez ☎ 735-5062 🖷 735-5043 ⊙ Mon.-Sat. 8-5. **Selva Mar** ✉ 45 m [50 yards] south of central park, San Isidro ☎ 771-4582 ⊕ www.exploringcostarica.com.

VISITOR INFORMATION

Official tourist offices in San José have information on the southern Pacific coast. In San Isidro, CIPROTUR is a helpful visitor information center, with an Internet café. Also in San Isidro, the travel agency Selva Mar doubles as a visitor information center. In Dominical, Dominical Adventures in the San Clemente Restaurant provides visitor's information and books tours. In Golfito, Land Sea Services offers traveler information, as does CATUGOL, the ecotourism board. In Puerto Jiménez, Osa Natural is a tourist chamber of commerce and visitor center with lots of information and Internet access.

🛈 **Tourist Information CATUGOL** ✉ ferry dock, Golfito ☎ 775-1820. **CIPROTUR** ✉ 70 m [80 yards] south of Instituto Costarricense de Electricidad, San Isidro ☎ 771-6096. **Dominical Adventures** ✉ in San Clemente restaurant, near soccer field, Dominical ☎ 787-0191. **Land Sea Services** ✉ next to Banana Bay Marina on left as you enter Golfito, Golfito ☎ 775-1614. **Osa Natural** ✉ near post office, on north side of town ☎ 735-5440 ⊕ www.osanatural.com. **San José Tourist Office** ✉ Central Post Office, Avda. 1 at C. 2 ☎ 258-8762. **Selva Mar** ✉ 45 m [50 yards] south of central park, San Isidro ☎ 771-4582 ⊕ www.exploringcostarica.com.

THE ATLANTIC LOWLANDS & CARIBBEAN COAST

FODOR'S CHOICE

Aviarios del Caribe, *Limón*

Cariblue Bungalows, *Puerto Viejo de Talamanca*

Cha Cha Cha, *Cahuita*

El Encanto Bed & Breakfast, *Cahuita*

Rain Forest Aerial Tram, *near Braulio Carrillo Park*

HIGHLY RECOMMENDED

RESTAURANTS Cha Cha Cha, *Cahuita*

La Pecora Nera, *Puerto Viejo de Talamanca*

HOTELS Gavilán Sarapiquí River Lodge, *Puerto Viejo de Sarapiquí*

Hotel Maribú Caribe, *Limón*

Magellan Inn, *Limón*

Mawamba Lodge, *Tortuguero*

Pachira Lodge, *Tortuguero*

Shawandha Lodge, *Puerto Viejo de Talamanca*

SIGHTS Tortuguero National Park

Updated by
Jeffrey Van
Fleet

CLOUD FORESTS, SPRAWLING BANANA PLANTATIONS, and thick tropical jungle characterize the Atlantic lowlands, in the provinces of Heredia and Limón on the Caribbean Sea. This expansive, largely untamed region stretches from the eastern slope of the Cordillera Central up to the Sarapiquí area northeast of San José (home to the private Rara Avis and La Selva reserves), east through banana-growing country, and down to the pristine beaches at Cahuita and Puerto Viejo de Talamanca on the southern Caribbean coast. The region also stretches north to the Nicaraguan border, encompassing the coastal jungles and canals of Tortuguero National Park and Barra del Colorado Wildlife Refuge, on whose beaches turtles arrive by the thousands to lay their eggs. The occasional caiman can be spotted here, sunning on a bank or drifting like a log down a jungle waterway; and farther north still, sportfishing fans find tarpon and snook to detain them off the shores of Barra del Colorado.

Roughly a third of the people in Limón province are Afro-Caribbeans, descendants of early 19th-century turtle fishermen and the West Indians who arrived in the late 19th century to build the Atlantic Railroad and remained to work on banana and cacao plantations. Some 4,000 Jamaicans are reputed to have died of yellow fever, malaria, and snakebites during construction of the first 40 km (25 mi) of railroad to San José. They were paid relatively well, however, and gradually their lot improved: by the 1930s many had obtained their own small plots of land, and when the price of cacao rose in the 1950s they emerged as comfortable landowners employing landless, migrant Hispanics. Until the Civil War of 1948, Afro-Caribbeans were forbidden from crossing into the Central Valley lest they upset the country's racial balance, and they were thus prevented from following work when United Fruit abandoned many of its northern Caribbean blight-ridden plantations in the 1930s for green-field sites on the Pacific plain. Although Jamaicans brought some aspects of British colonial culture with them, such as cricket and the maypole dance, these habits have long since given way to reggae, salsa, and soccer, much to the chagrin of the older generation. Many Atlantic-coast Ticos are bilingual, speaking fluent Spanish and Caribbean English, and around Puerto Viejo de Talamanca you may even hear some phrases derived from the language of the indigenous peoples, among them the Kekoldi, the Bribri, and the Cabecar.

With some justification, Caribbean residents bemoan the lack of attention their region gets from the government in San José and the tourism industry. Development has been slower to reach this part of the country. (Telephones and electricity are still newfangled inventions in some smaller communities here.) The Instituto Costarricense de Turismo, eager to tout Costa Rica to northerners as a fun-in-the-sun destination, devotes less space to the rainier Atlantic coast in its glossy tourist literature. The attention the region does get usually comes in the form of crime stories splashed across the front pages of San José newspapers. Many Ticos will advise you to avoid Limón province, but few have ever visited the area themselves. Communities are working hard to combat the problem with visibly beefed up security, and crime is really no worse here than elsewhere in Costa Rica. If you stick to well-trodden tourist routes, you ought to be fine.

You will likely receive a warm welcome when you visit this "other" Costa Rica, a section of the country long ago discovered by European visitors but little known in North American circles. Venture here and you might be pleasantly surprised to discover the personalized atten-

7

You need at least a week to cover this territory, but three days are enough to sample its charms if you plan your time judiciously. In addition to keeping in mind the difficulties of getting around, remember that the Atlantic lowlands offer various activities requiring different levels of physical endurance and commitment, ranging from seaside lounging to rain-forest trekking. If your time, energy, and stomach for discomfort—mud, mosquitoes, and rain, for starters—are limited, you'll have to make choices. Another consideration is travel time. The Rara Avis preserve, for example, is a great place to visit, but because it's so hard to reach—via two- to four-hour tractor haul into the park—the lodge obliges you to stay for at least two nights.

Numbers in the text correspond to numbers in the margin and on the Atlantic Lowlands and Caribbean Coast map.

If you have 3 or 4 days

Hop on an early flight from San José to ✈ **Tortuguero** ❼ ► or ✈ **Barra del Colorado** ❽ for a jungle-boat tour, turtle-watching session, or fishing trip. The next morning take the boat down to **Moín** ❿ and then head to ✈ **Limón** ❾. Drive or take a bus south to ✈ **Cahuita** ⓫ and/or ✈ **Puerto Viejo de Talamanca** ⓭, where you can relax on the beach, play in the surf, snorkel, or hike in **Cahuita National Park** ⓬. Camp at Puerto Vargas or stay a couple of nights in Cahuita, Puerto Viejo de Talamanca, Punta Uva, or farther south along the beach road that terminates at the bird-filled jungles and deserted beaches of the **Gandoca-Manzanillo National Wildlife Refuge** ⓮.

If you have 3 or 4 days

Set out early from San José and drive or take a bus over the Guápiles Highway to hike in **Braulio Carrillo National Park** ❶ ► or ride the Rain Forest Aerial Tram. Drive to ✈ **La Selva Biological Station** ❸ and hike its trails in the afternoon. Spend a night here or in one of the lodges in the ✈ **Puerto Viejo de Sarapiquí** ❹ area. Drive south to ✈ **Cahuita** ⓫ and/or ✈ **Puerto Viejo de Talamanca** ⓭, where you can relax on the beach, play in the surf, snorkel, or hike in **Cahuita National Park** ⓬. Stay a night or two in Cahuita, Puerto Viejo de Talamanca, Punta Uva, or farther south along the beach road that terminates at the bird-filled jungles and deserted beaches of the **Gandoca-Manzanillo National Wildlife Refuge** ⓮. Head back to San José, about a four-hour drive.

If you have 7 days

Throw in some variations on the above two themes: add an overnight rafting trip down the Río Pacuare, near Turrialba, or take a multiday fishing trip out of **Tortuguero** ❼ or **Barra del Colorado** ❽. Arrange to visit Bribri, Cabecar, or Kekoldi indigenous reservation in the hills west of **Puerto Viejo de Talamanca** ⓭; hike into the remote Hitoy Cerere Biological Reserve.

---

tion and quality you get for your colones. The flashy resorts so common on the Pacific are nowhere to be found here. Though they sometimes look with envy at their west-coast counterparts, most folks here on the Caribbean remain content to keep their tourism offerings smaller scale.

Exploring the Atlantic Lowlands & Caribbean Coast

Below the cloud- and rain-forested mountains and foothills of the Central and Talamanca ranges lie fertile plains and dense tracts of primary tropical jungle. Much of this land has been cleared and given over to farming and ranching, but vast expanses are still inaccessible by car. No roads lead to Barra del Colorado or Tortuguero; you have to fly from San José, take a jungle boat from Moín, or join one of the many organized tours from San José, an alluring prospect if it's solitude you crave. Coastal Talamanca, the region to the south, however, is accessible by car via the Carretera Guápiles.

There are two towns called Puerto Viejo in this region. One, Puerto Viejo de Sarapiquí, is a former river port in the northern, inland section of the lowlands; the other, Puerto Viejo de Talamanca, is on the southern coast not far from the Panamanian border. Keeping the two straight can be confusing, as locals often call both of them Puerto Viejo.

About the Restaurants

Dining is an informal, open-air affair, even at the nicest restaurants in the Caribbean region. Dinner is usually served from 7 to 10, and service is attentive but leisurely. Budget places serve their big meal of the day at noon and may not be open at all for dinner. Lunch comes Costa Rican *casado*-style—a "marriage" of rice, beans, fried plantains, salad, and meat, chicken, or fish, all on one plate—and is one of the best bargains around.

About the Hotels

The Atlantic lowlands have little in the way of luxury hotels, though a number of relatively upscale, self-proclaimed ecotourist lodges and some other, pricier accommodations exist along the highway south of Limón and (especially) on the beach road south of Puerto Viejo de Talamanca. The region's lower number of visitors compared to that of the Pacific coast means you can usually find vacancies at reasonable prices. Surprisingly few places on the coast have air-conditioning, but sea breezes and ceiling fans provide ventilation enough that you probably won't miss it. Most lodgings along the north Caribbean coast are rustic *cabinas* (cottages) or nature lodges. Often isolated in the jungle—accessible only by boat or strenuous hike—the lodges can be rough, no-frills places or can verge on the luxurious. Because it's hard to haul supplies to these places, indulgences like hot showers and cold beers come with a hefty price tag.

WHAT IT COSTS					
	$$$$	**$$$**	**$$**	**$**	**¢**
RESTAURANTS	over $25	$20–$25	$10–$20	$5–$10	under $5
HOTELS	over $200	$125–$200	$75–$125	$35–$75	under $35

Restaurant prices are per-person for a main course at dinner. Hotel prices are for two people in a standard double room in high season, excluding service and tax (16.4%).

Timing

This coastal area absorbs up to 200″ of annual rainfall, so unless you want to watch turtles lay their eggs on the beach (each species has its own schedule), you should try to avoid the worst of it. Chances are you'll be rained on no matter when you go, but the Atlantic coast has two short "dry" seasons: September–October, which unfortunately does not correspond to the dry season in the rest of the country, and March–April, which does. During the rainy season, you pay lower prices and see fewer tourists in exchange for being waterlogged.

7

Caribbean Flavors

Much of the cooking along the Caribbean has its roots in old Jamaican recipes. *Rondón,* for example, is a traditional Jamaican meat or fish stew cooked in coconut milk, along with cabbage, tomatoes, onions, green peppers, and/or other vegetables that requires hours of preparation. Equally labor-intensive, rice and beans—not at all the *gallo pinto* you've been eating elsewhere in Costa Rica— is flavored with coconut; meat is fried with hot spices to make *paties* (pies); and fish or meat is boiled in coconut milk along with yams, plantains, breadfruit, peppers, and spices. Johnnycakes and *panbón* (a heavy, spicy dried-fruit bread) are popular baked goods. Seafood is, of course, readily available, as is a wide variety of fresh fruit.

Jungle Exploration

From the beach hikes of Cahuita National Park to the more leisurely jungle-boat cruises arranged by the lodges near Tortuguero National Park, opportunities for plunging into tropical jungle and rain forest abound in the Atlantic lowlands. Farther inland, on the eastern slope of the mountains, Braulio Carrillo's cloud- and rain-forested mountains have scenic trails, and the private lowland reserves of La Selva and Rara Avis beckon with excellent jungle terrain. To the southeast, the jungle climbs into the hills of the Talamanca range, where the remote Hitoy Cerere Biological Reserve has both easy and difficult hiking trails. Look for waterfalls, swimming holes, and an encyclopedic variety of Costa Rican flora and fauna.

Snorkeling & Scuba Diving

Costa Rica's largest coral reef is off the coast of Cahuita National Park, and although it has been severely damaged by pollution, there's still plenty to admire. Other dive spots include the coral reef at Isla Uvita, off Limón, the many reefs off the beaches of the Gandoca-Manzanillo Wildlife Refuge, and the sea caverns off Puerto Viejo de Talamanca. The water is clearest during the dry season (September–October and March–April).

Sportfishing

World-class tarpon and snook attract serious sportfishing enthusiasts to the northern Caribbean shore in and off the Tortuguero and Barra del Colorado national parks. The months between January and May are best for tarpon, August through November for snook. The area's lodges offer all-inclusive, multiday packages if you want an angling angle to your Costa Rican vacation.

Surfing

Some point breaks were badly affected by coastal uplift during the 1991 earthquake, but others were created—a left at Punta Cocles and a right at Punta Uva. You can still ride Puerto Viejo de Talamanca's famous and formidable Salsa Brava, but its spectacular waves are really only for the experienced and fearless surfer. Less hairy spots include Playa Negra, Cahuita, the beach break just south of Puerto Viejo, Playa Bonita north of Limón, and Isla Uvita, 20 minutes from Limón by boat. Beware of riptides. This coast is best surfed from December to March and June to August.

Turtle-Watching Costa Rica's northern Caribbean shore is one of the few places in the world where the Green Sea Turtle nests: great groups of them descend on Tortuguero National Park from July to October each year. Three other turtle species—the Hawksbill, Loggerhead, and Giant Leatherback—also nest here. Leatherbacks nest on the beaches of the Gandoca-Manzanillo Wildlife Refuge on the southern Caribbean coast.

THE NORTHERN LOWLANDS
WITH BRAULIO CARRILLO NATIONAL PARK

The immense Braulio Carrillo National Park, looming northeast of San José, protects virgin rain forest on either side of the highway to Guápiles. You can get a feel for it as you pass through on the highway, but inside it's another world: everywhere you look green things sprout, twist, and bloom. Bromeliads and orchids cling to arching trees while white-faced monkeys climb and swing and blue morpho butterflies dance and flutter. Adjacent to the park is a private reserve where you can explore the flora and fauna of the rain-forest canopy from a Rain Forest Aerial Tram.

After threading through Braulio Carrillo, the Guápiles Highway branches at Santa Clara, having completed its descent onto the Caribbean plain, and continues southeast to Limón and the Caribbean coast. If you turn left and head north, the smoothly paved road (Highway 4) leads through flat, deforested pasture and pockets of old-growth forest toward two preserves, Rara Avis and La Selva. Just north are the old river-port town of Puerto Viejo de Sarapiquí and the forest-clad hills of the eastern slope of the Cordillera Central.

Continuing due east from Santa Clara, the well-maintained highway takes you through sultry lowlands to the growing community of Guápiles and the tropical agriculture research institution EARTH and, farther on, to Limón, the region's largest city.

Braulio Carrillo National Park

▶ ❶ *30 km (19 mi) north of San José.*

In a country where deforestation is still rife, Parque Nacional Braulio Carrillo provides a rare opportunity to witness dense, primary tropical cloud forest. The park owes its foundation to the public outcry provoked by the construction of the highway of the same name through this region in the late 1970s—the government bowed to pressure from environmentalists, and, somewhat ironically, the park is the most accessible one from the capital thanks to the highway. Covering 443 square km (171 square mi), Braulio Carrillo's extremely diverse terrain ranges from 108 ft to more than 10,384 ft above sea level and extends from the central volcanic range down the Atlantic slope to La Selva research station near Puerto Viejo de Sarapiquí. The park protects a series of ecosystems ranging from the cloud forests on the upper slopes to the tropical wet forest of the Magsasay sector; it is home to 6,000 tree species, 500 bird species, and 135 mammal species.

The **Zurquí ranger station** is to the right of the highway, ½ km (¼ mi) before the Zurquí Tunnel. Here a short trail loops through the cloud forest. Hikes are steep; wear hiking boots to protect yourself from mud, slippage, and snakes. The main trail through primary forest, 1½ km (1 mi) long, culminates in a *mirador* (lookout point), but alas, the highway mars the view. Monkeys, tapirs, jaguars, kinkajous, sloths, raccoons, margays, and porcupines all live in this forest, and resident birds include the quetzal and the eagle. Orchids, bromeliads, heliconias, fungi, and mushrooms live closer to the floor. Another trail leads into the forest to the right, beginning about 17 km (11 mi) after the tunnel, where it follows the Quebrada González, a stream with a cascade and swimming hole. There are no campsites in this part of the park.

The **Carrillo ranger station**, 22 km (14 mi) northeast along the highway from Zurquí, marks the beginning of trails that are less steep. For access to the 10,384-ft **Volcán Barva**, start from Sacramento, north of Heredia. The walk through the cloud forest to the crater's two lakes takes two to three hours, but your efforts should be rewarded by great views (as long as you start early, preferably before 8 AM, to avoid the mist). You can camp at the **Barva ranger station**, which is far from any traffic. Stay on the trail when hiking anywhere in Braulio; it's easy to get lost in the cloud forest, and the rugged terrain makes wandering through the woods very dangerous. In addition, muggings of hikers have been reported in the park. Go with a ranger if possible. ☎ *283–8004 Sistemas de Areas de Conservación, 192 in Costa Rica* ✉ *$6* ☉ *Daily 7–4.*

Where to Stay

$ 🍴 **CheTica Ranch.** A worldly Argentine and his Tica wife own this ranch, a good jumping-off point for those wanting to explore Braulio Carrillo National Park. Uniquely styled cabins follow an international theme: Old Tucson evokes the southwestern U.S., while the two-storied Interlochen looks like a genuine Swiss chalet. Cabins have kitchens, living rooms, and a large collection of videos and books. During the day there are horseback trips into the park. The ranch also serves as a medical recovery center. ✉ *Guápiles Hwy., ½ km (¼ ft) northeast of tollgate* ☎🖨 *268–6133* 🖃 *SJO 2989, Box 025216, Miami, FL 33102–5216* 🌐 *www.cresi-usa.com/chetica.htm* 🛏 *5 cabins, 2 rooms* ⚙ *Fans, some kitchens, cable TV, in-room VCRs, horseback riding, airport shuttle; no a/c, no room phones, no-smoking rooms* 🍴 *AE, DC, MC, V* 🍴 *BP.*

Rain Forest Aerial Tram

Fodor'sChoice   *15 km (9 mi) east of Braulio Carrillo National Park.*
★

Just beyond the eastern boundary of Braulio Carrillo, a 4-square-km (2½-square-mi) preserve houses privately owned and operated engineering marvel: a series of gondolas strung together in a modified ski-lift pulley system. (To lessen the impact on the jungle, the support pylons were lowered into place by helicopter.) The tram gives students, researchers, and travelers a way of seeing the rain-forest canopy and its spectacular array of epiphyte plant life and birds from just above, a feat you could otherwise accomplish only by climbing the trees yourself. The founder, Dr. Donald Perry, also developed a less elaborate system of canopy touring at nearby Rara Avis; of the two, this is more user-friendly. Though purists might complain that it treats the rain forest like an amusement park, it's an entertaining way to learn the value and beauty of rain-forest ecology.

The 21 gondolas hold five people each, plus a bilingual biologist-guide equipped with a walkie-talkie to request brief stops for gaping or snapping pictures. The ride covers 2½ km (1½ mi) in 1½ hours. The price includes a biologist-guided walk through the area for ground-level orientation before or after the tram ride. You can arrange a personal pickup in San José for a fee; alternately, there are public buses (on the Guápiles line)

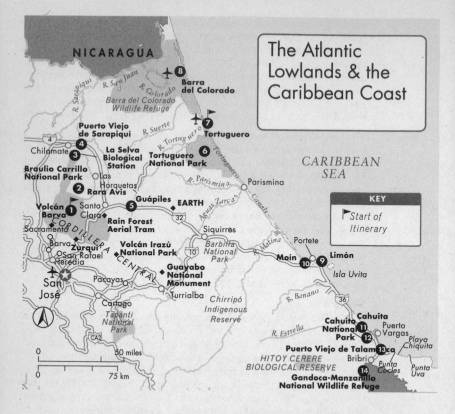

every half hour. Drivers know the tram as the *teleférico*. Ten rustic (no a/c or TV) but cozy cabinas are available on-site for $80 per person. (The facility only operates the lodging if at least two cabins are being rented at the same time.) Cabin rates include meals and tram tours. A café is open to all for lunch and dinner. ⊠ *Reservations: Avda. 7 at C. 7 San José* ☎ *257–5961* 🖷 *257–6053* ⊕ *www.rainforestram.com* 🖃 *$49.50* ▭ *AE, MC, V* ☉ *Tours Mon. 9–4, Tues.–Sun. 6:30–4. Call for reservations 6 AM–9:30 PM.*

Rara Avis

② *Las Horquetas is 17 km (11 mi) north of Santa Clara, 100 km (62 mi) north of San José.*

Toucans, sloths, Great Green Macaws, howler and spider monkeys, Vested Anteaters, and tapirs may be on hand to greet you when you arrive at Rara Avis, one of Costa Rica's most popular private reserves and open only to overnight guests. Ecologist Amos Bien founded Rara Avis with the intent of combining research, tourism, and the sustainable extraction of forest products. Bilingual guides take you along the muddy trails—boots are provided—and canopy observation platforms and help point out wildlife. Or go on your own to the orchid house and butterfly garden. Bring a camera: the reserve's lacy double waterfall is one of Costa Rica's most photogenic sights.

The town of **Las Horquetas** is the jumping-off point for the 13-square-km (8-square-mi) private reserve. The 16-km (10-mi) trip from Las Horquetas to the reserve can be accomplished in three hours on horseback, two to three hours by tractor (leaves daily at 8:30 AM), or one hour by four-wheel-drive vehicle, plus a rough 3-km (2-mi) hike up to the lodge proper. The trails are steep and rugged, but the flora and fauna en route are remarkable. Note: there have been some complaints that, although the reserve itself is lovely, the guides and services are considerably less impressive. ⊠ *From Braulio Carrillo, turn left at signs for Puerto Viejo de Sarapiquí and go 17 km (11 mi) to Las Horquetas.*

Where to Stay

$$–$$$ 🏨 **Rara Avis.** Three lodging options exist here. The Waterfall Lodge, near a 197-ft waterfall, has hardwood-paneled rooms with chairs, firm beds, balconies, and hammocks. Despite the prices, accommodation is rustic, with minimal amenities and no electricity. More basic, Las Casitas are three two-room cabins with shared bath. On the high end, ideal for a rustic honeymoon, is the River Edge Cabin, a 10-minute walk through the forest (it's dark at night, but you're given a flashlight), with private bath and balcony and solar panel–generated electricity. Rates include guides and transport from Las Horquetas. Minimum stay is two nights. ⊠ *Las Horquetas* ☎ 710–3131 🖷 764–4187 ⊕ *www.rara-avis.com* 🛏 *16 rooms, 10 with bath* ⚒ *Restaurant* ⊟ *AE, MC, V* ⊚⊫ *AI.*

La Selva Biological Station

❸ *14 km (9 mi) north of Rara Avis, 79 km (49 mi) northeast of San José.*

At the confluence of the Puerto Viejo and Sarapiquí Rivers, La Selva is a biologist's paradise. Its 15 square km (6 square mi) pack about 420 bird species, 460 tree species, and 500 butterfly species. Spottings might include the spider monkey, poison dart frog, agouti, Collared Peccary, and dozens of other rare creatures. If you want to see wildlife without having to rough it, La Selva is much more agreeable than Rara Avis. Run by the **OTS (Organization for Tropical Studies)**, a consortium of 65 Latin and North American and Australian universities, the research station is designed for scientists but welcomes visitors in the daytime and offers basic lodging. Extensive, well-marked trails and swing bridges connect habitats as varied as tropical wet forest, swamps, creeks, rivers, secondary regenerating forest, and pasture. To see the place, take an informative 3½-hour morning or afternoon nature walk with one of La Selva's guides, who are some of the country's best. Schedule a walk and lunch ($7) in advance. Or get a group of at least five together and enroll in the Saturday-morning Birdwatching 101 course—a bargain at $10 per person. Advance reservations are required. To get here, take a public bus to Puerto Viejo de Sarapiquí—La Selva is a $4 taxi ride from town—or use the OTS van ($10), which leaves San José on Monday at 7 AM and returns on Monday at 3 PM. ⊠ *6 km (3½ mi) south of Puerto Viejo de Sarapiquí; look for sign on west side of road* ☎ 766–6565 🖷 766–6535 ⊕ *www.ots.ac.cr* ⊕ *OTS, Apdo. 676–2050, San Pedro* ☎ 240–6696 ⊠ *Nature walk $25, morning and afternoon walks $40* ⊙ *Walks daily at 8 AM and 1:30 PM.*

Where to Stay

$$ 🏨 **La Selva.** Other lodges provide more comfort for the money, but none can match La Selva's tropical nature experience. The dorm-style rooms have large bunk beds, tile floors, and lots of screened windows. The restaurant, something like a school cafeteria, serves decent food but has a very limited schedule (reserve ahead). It's a good idea to pay an additional fee, which includes a guided nature walk and three meals a day with your room rate, since there's nowhere else to eat in town. Priority is given to researchers, so advance reservations are essential. ⊠ *6 km (3½ mi) south of Puerto Viejo de Sarapiquí* ☎ 766–6565 ⊕ *OTS, Apdo. 676–2050, San Pedro* ☎ 240–6696 🖷 240–6783 🛏 *60 bunk beds share 12 baths, 3 cabins.* ⚒ *Restaurant, fans, hiking, laundry facilities; no a/c, no room phone, no room TVs* ⊟ *AE, MC, V.*

Puerto Viejo de Sarapiquí

④ *6½ km (4 mi) north of La Selva.*

In the 19th century, Puerto Viejo de Sarapiquí was a thriving river port and the only link with the coastal lands straight east, now Barra del Colorado National Wildlife Refuge and Tortuguero National Park. Fortunes nose-dived with the construction of the coastal canal from the town of Moín, and today Puerto Viejo has a slightly run-down air. The activities of the Nicaraguan Contras made this a danger zone in the 1980s, but now that the political situation has improved, boats once again ply the old route up the Río Sarapiquí to the Río San Juan on the Nicaraguan frontier, from where you can travel downstream to Barra del Colorado or Tortuguero. Passports are required for the trip: the San Juan lies entirely within Nicaraguan territory.

A few tour companies, such as Costa Rica Expeditions and Ríos Tropicales (⇨ The Atlantic Lowlands and Caribbean Coast A to Z), have Sarapiquí River tours with up to Class III rapids and plenty of wildlife around. If you don't have much time to spend in this region, **Ecoscape Nature Tours** (☎ 297–0664 ⊕ www.costaricasbesttour.com) has an excellent daylong Highlights Tour of the Sarapiquí loop for $79. In addition to a boat ride on the river, and a stop at a banana processing plant, the day includes a visit to a coffee plantation and the Poás volcano. A two-day option includes an overnight at the Selva Verde Lodge and a white-water rafting excursion or rain-forest tour.

Heliconias abound at the aptly named **Heliconia Island** in the Sarapiquí River. Some 70 species of the flowering plant, a relative of the banana, are among the collections that populate 5 acres of botanical gardens here. Expect to see ample bird and butterfly life, too. ⊠ *La Chaves, 8 km (5 mi) south of Puerto Viejo de Sarapiquí* ☎ 766–6247 ☞ *$7.50* ☉ *Daily 9–5.*

Curious about the life and times of Costa Rica's most famous yellow fruit? The **Standard Fruit Company,** known as Dole in North America, has two-hour Banana Tours to guide you through the process from plantation to processing to packing. Visits are best arranged through several San José travel agencies, who will transport you to any of the three sites. Options include a plantation in Sarapiquí or sites in Siquirres or south of Limón. ☎ *768–8683 or 383–4596* ☞ *$10* ☉ *Tours daily at 10 AM.*

Where to Stay & Eat

¢ ✕🏠 **Rancho Leona.** Built largely with kayaking tours in mind by owners Ken Upcraft and Leona Wellington, this roadside ranch has rustic dormitories with shared bath facilities. The restaurant (¢–$) serves tasty, reasonably priced food including numerous vegetarian dishes and Italian classics like eggplant parmigiana and chicken cacciatore. Dazzling works of stained glass, all Ken and Leona's creations, are crafted in the adjacent studio. Activities include kayaking on the Sarapiquí, hiking to a 33-ft waterfall, and swimming in the river. ⊠ *La Virgen de Sarapiquí, 17 km (11 mi) southwest of Puerto Viejo* ☎ 761–1019 ⊕ *www.rancholeona.com* ➴ *5 rooms without bath* ♻ *Restaurant, sauna, boating, hiking, library; no a/c, no room phones, no room TVs* ⊟ *V.*

$$ 🏠 **Selva Verde Lodge.** Built on stilts over the Río Sarapiquí, this expansive complex stands on the edge of a 2-square-km (1-square-mi) private reserve of tropical rain forest and caters primarily to natural-history tours.

The buildings have wide verandas strung with hammocks, and the rooms come with polished wood paneling and mosquito blinds. Activities include guided walks, boat trips, canoeing, rafting, and mountain biking. Room prices include a bird-watching tour. ⊠ *7 km (4 mi) west of Puerto Viejo de Sarapiquí* ✆ *Apdo. 55, Chilamate* ☎ *766–6800* 🖶 *766–6011* ⊕ *www.selvaverde.com* ⇋ *40 rooms, 5 bungalows* ⚭ *Restaurant, fans, boating, fishing, hiking, horseback riding, library, laundry service; no a/c, no room phones, no room TVs* ⊟ *AE, MC, V* ❍| *FAP.*

$ 🖭 **Hotel Bambú.** Unlike the many isolated properties in this region, Bambú is in the heart of Puerto Viejo de Sarapiquí. The rooms are simple but comfortable. A dense cluster of tall bamboo stalks climbs like Jack's bean stalk out of the garden, lending shade for the bar and restaurant, the latter of which serves Costa Rican–influenced Chinese food at reasonable prices. ⊠ *Main street across from town square–soccer field* ☎ *766–6359* 🖶 *766–6132* ⊕ *www.elbambu.com* ✆ *Apdo. 1518–2100, Guadalupe* ⇋ *16 rooms* ⚭ *Restaurant, pool, bar, laundry service* ⊟ *AE, MC, V* ❍| *BP.*

★ $ 🖭 **Gavilán Sarapiquí River Lodge.** Beautiful gardens run down to the river, and colorful tanagers and three types of toucan feast in the citrus trees. Not bad for an erstwhile hub of a fruit and cattle farm. The two-story lodge has comfortable rooms with white walls, terra-cotta floors, and decorative crafts. The food, Costa Rican *comida típica* (typical fare), has earned its good reputation. Prime activities are horseback jungle treks and boat trips up the Río Sarapiquí. ⊠ *1 km (½ mi) southeast of Comando Atlántico (naval command)* ⊕ *www.gavilanlodge.com* ✆ *Apdo. 445–2010, San José* ☎ *766–6743* 🖶 *253–6556* ⇋ *13 rooms* ⚭ *Restaurant, fans, hot tub, fishing, horseback riding; no a/c, no room phones, no room TVs* ⊟ *AE, MC, V* ❍| *BP.*

Guápiles

⑤ *60 km (38 mi) northeast of San José.*

You may not see any reason to stop in Guápiles, off the main road, other than weariness or the need for a fuel fix, automotive or gastronomic. But because this farm and forest area is a crossroads of a sort—more or less equidistant to the palm beaches of the Caribbean shore, the jungles to the north, and the rain-forested mountains looming in the west—it's not a bad place to linger for a day or two, day-tripping in any of three directions. Guápiles is home to several major biological-research facilities as well as commercial producers of tropical plants.

Where to Stay

$ 🖭 **Hotel Río Palmas.** Think of it as a hacienda motel. Proximate to EARTH, near the town of Guácimo, the Río Palmas's red-tile-roof open-air restaurant grabs your eye as you're speeding by on the Guápiles Highway. Behind an arched, whitewashed entry gate, one-story, tile-roof whitewashed cabinas wrap around a central courtyard with a fountain and plants. Exotic plantings abound (the hotel is actually on an ornamental-plant farm), and the staff can arrange hikes, farm and jungle tours, and horseback rides to private waterfalls. ⊠ *Guápiles Hwy., Pocora de Guácimo* ☎ *760–0330* 🖶 *760–0296* ✉ *riopalma@racsa.co.cr* ⇋ *32 rooms, 24 with bath* ⚭ *Restaurant, fans, pool, hiking, horseback riding, laundry service; no a/c in some rooms, no room phones, no room TVs* ⊟ *AE, MC, V.*

EARTH

15 km (9 mi) east of Guápiles on Guápiles Hwy.

The nonprofit organization EARTH (Escuela de Agricultura de la Región Tropical Húmeda) researches the production of less pesticide-dependent bananas and other forms of sustainable agriculture, as well as medicinal plants. EARTH's elegant stationery and other paper products made from banana stems are for sale at the on-site Oropéndola store, as well as in many tourist shops. The property encompasses a banana plantation and a forest reserve with nature trails. Though priority is given to researchers and conference groups, you're welcome to stay in the school's 50-person lodging facility, with private bathrooms, hot water, and ceiling fans, for $55 a night, which includes the use of a swimming pool and exercise equipment. Advance reservations are required. ☎ *713–0000* 📠 *713–0001* ⊕ *www.earth.ac.cr.*

en route If you're bypassing Limón entirely en route south to Cahuita and Puerto Viejo de Talamanca, a right turn via Moín, 3 km (2 mi) shy of Limón, will give you an alternate route—a smooth road that weaves through the hills. Look for the green road sign indicating a right turn to Sixaola (the Panamanian border) and other points south.

TORTUGUERO & BARRA DEL COLORADO

Tortuguero means "turtle region," and, indeed, this northeastern sector remains one of the world's prime places to watch the life cycle of sea turtles. It also remains one of Costa Rica's most popular destinations, surprising given its remoteness and difficult access. The stretch of beach between the Colorado and Matina rivers was first mentioned as a nesting ground for sea turtles in a 1592 Dutch chronicle, and because the area is so isolated—there's no road here to this day—the turtles nested undisturbed for centuries. By the mid-1900s, however, the harvesting of eggs and catching of turtles had reached such a level that these creatures faced extinction. In 1963 an executive decree regulated the hunting of turtles and the gathering of eggs, and in 1970 the government established Tortuguero National Park. You can continue up the canals that begin in Moín and run parallel to the coast, to the less-visited Barra del Colorado Wildlife Refuge, an immense protected area that's connected to the park.

Tortuguero National Park

★ ❻ *50 km (31 mi) northwest (3 hrs by boat) of Moín.*

The palm-lined beaches of Parque Nacional Tortuguero stretch off as far as the eye can see, and its additional ecosystems include lowland rain forest, estuaries, and swampy areas covered with *jolillo* palms. You can wander the beach independently, but riptides make swimming dangerous, and shark rumors persist. At various times of the year, Green, Hawksbill, Loggerhead, and Giant Leatherback Turtles lumber up the beaches and deposit their eggs for safekeeping—a fascinating natural ritual. If you want to watch the *deshove* (the egg laying), contact your hotel or the parks office to hire a certified local guide. You won't be allowed to use a camera on the beach and must cover your flashlight with red plastic, as lights can deter the turtles from nesting.

Tortuguero

Inset (left map):

Boca del
Río San Juan

San Juan
del Norte

Laguna
Ciega

NICARAGUA

CARIBBEAN
SEA

Río San Juan

Laguna Agua Dulce

Laguna de Atras

Lac de Enascilo

Laguna Pereira

Isla
Machura

Isla Calero

Isla
Chapudero

Barra del Colorado
Norte

Barra del
Colorado Sur

Caño Bravo

Isla
Maria

Río Colorado

Isla Brava

Puerto
Lindo

Laguna
Danto

Cerro
Coronel

Laguna
Nueve

Islas
Buena
Vistas

Río Zapote

**Barra del Colorado
National Wildlife
Refuge**

Caño Moreno

Río Penitencia

Caño Suerte

Canal

Caño la Palma

Río Suerte

Caño Chiquero

*Parque
Nacional
Tortuguero*

TO LIMÓN

0   2 miles

0   3 km

Inset (right map):

▲ Cerro
Tortuguero
(119m)

Isla
Chica

Lagunas del Tortuguero

Tortuga Lodge

CARIBBEAN SEA

Lagunas Penitencia

◆ **El Manatí
Lodge**

◆ **Jungle
Lodge**

◆ **Mawamba
Lodge**

◆ **Caribbean
Conservation/Corporation
Visitor Center**

◆ **Pachira
Lodge**

Tortuguero
Village

TO JUNGLE
TARPON
LODGE

Park Entrance ℹ

Caño Chiquero

Isla Cuatro
Esquinas

*Parque
Nacional
Tortuguero*

0   1 mile

0   1 km

Freshwater turtles inhabit Tortuguero's rivers, as do crocodiles—most populous in the Río Agua Frío—and the endangered *vacas marinas,* or manatees. Manatees consume huge quantities of aquatic plants and are endangered mainly because their lack of speed makes them easy prey. You might also glimpse tapirs (watch for these in jolillo groves), jaguars, anteaters, ocelots, howler monkeys, Collared and White-lipped Peccaries, raccoons, otters, skunks, and coatis. Some 350 species of birds and countless butterflies, including the iridescent Blue Morpho, also call this area home. At a station deep in the Tortuguero jungle, volunteers from the Canadian Organization for Tropical Education and Rainforest Conservation manage a butterfly farm, catalog plants and animals, and explore sustainable forest practices. ▧ *$6* ⊙ *Daily* 6 AM–6 PM.

Tortuguero

▶ ❼ *There are officially no roads to Tortuguero, though illegal attempts have been made to cut one through the jungle. Travel time is 30 mins by plane from San José, 3 hrs by boat from Moín.*

North of the national park, the hamlet of Tortuguero is a pleasant little place to spend an hour or two, with its 600 inhabitants, two churches, three bars, and two souvenir shops. Pick up information on the park, turtles, and other wildlife at the kiosk in the town center. You can also take a stroll on the 32-km (20-mi) beach, but swimming is not recommended due to strong riptides and the presence of large numbers of bull sharks and barracuda (not threatening, say the locals). Visitors who have more than a week's time in Costa Rica typically spend a couple of nights here.

Tortuguero is one of those "everybody's a guide" places; the quality of guides varies, but most are quite knowledgeable. The **Caribbean Conservation Corporation** (☎ 710–0547) can recommend good local guides. If you stay at one of the lodges, guided tours are included in your package price.

At this writing, Tortuguero is slated to get new phone numbers by late 2003, though Costa Rica being Costa Rica, the changeover may or may not be in effect by that time. If you can't get through, call in-country telephone information or stick with e-mail.

The **Caribbean Conservation Corporation** (CCC) runs a visitor center and a museum with excellent animal photos, a video narrating local history, and detailed discussions of the latest ecological goings-on and what you can do to help. There's a souvenir shop next door. ⊠ *From beach, walk north along path and watch for sign* ☎ *710–0547; 224–9215 in San José; 352/373–6441 or 800/678–7853 in the U.S.* ⊕ *www.cccturtle.org* ⊡ *Apdo. 246–2050, San Pedro* ▧ *Donations accepted* ⊙ *Mon.–Sat. 10–noon and 2–5, Sun. 2–5.*

For the committed ecotourist, the **John H. Phipps Biological Field Station** has camping areas as well as dorm-style quarters with a communal kitchen. If you want to get involved in the life of the turtles or help catalog the population of neotropical migrant birds, arrange a stay in advance through the CCC. ⊠ *Near airport, across canal from Tortuga Lodge* ☎ *352/373–6441 in the U.S.*

off the beaten path

Coastal Canals. The jungle life that you see on a three-hour boat trip through the combination of natural and man-made canals between Tortuguero and Moín is awesome, providing a kind of real-life Indiana Jones adventure. Running parallel to the coast a couple of miles inland, the waterway provides a safer alternative to making the

TICO TURTLES

COSTA RICA'S TURTLE VISITATIONS are renowned among devoted ecotourists. An array of species makes predictable yet astonishing annual visits to beaches on both the Pacific and the Atlantic-Caribbean coasts, many set aside to protect them. Nesting turtles come ashore at night, plowing an uneven furrow with their flippers to propel themselves past the high-tide line, then using their hind flippers to scoop out a hole in which to lay their eggs. A few months later, hatchlings struggle out of the nests and make their perilous journey back, in effect, to the sea.

In spite of this protection, their "endangered" classifications, and the earnest ecologists and well-meaning animal lovers looking after them, turtle populations remain seriously threatened. Poachers have for generations harvested the eggs—a rumored aphrodisiac—and the meat and shells. Beachfront development, with its bright lights, can disorient the turtles; and long-line fishermen's hooks and lines entangle and drown them.

On Costa Rica's east coast, four species of turtles nest at Tortuguero National Park: the Green Turtle, Hawksbill, Loggerhead, and Giant Leatherback. Green Turtles reproduce in large groups from July to October. A Green Turtle lays eggs on average every two to three years and produces two or three clutches each time; between those times, the turtles feed as far afield as Florida and Venezuela. Small in comparison with their peers, Hawksbills are threatened by hunters because of their shells, a transparent brown hide much sought-after for jewelry making in, among other countries, Japan. Loggerheads, as their name implies, have outsize heads and shorter fins and make rare appearances at Tortuguero. Giant Leatherbacks are the largest of all turtles— they grow up to 6½ ft long and can weigh in at up to 1,000 pounds—and have a tough outer skin rather than a shell, hence the name. From mid-February through April, Leatherbacks nest mainly in Tortuguero's southern sector.

Olive Ridleys are the smallest sea turtles— the average carapace, or hardback shell, is 21" to 29" long—and the least shy. During mass nestings, or arribadas, thousands of Olive Ridley Turtles take to the Pacific shores at night, plowing the sand as they move up the beach sniffing for the high-tide line. An estimated 200,000 of the 500,000 turtles that nest in Costa Rica each year choose Playa Nancite, a gray-sand beach in Guanacaste's Santa Rosa National Park, backed by dense hibiscus and button mangroves. This is the world's only totally protected Olive Ridley arribada.

Easier to reach is the Ostional National Wildlife Refuge, near Nosara on the Nicoya Peninsula. Locals harvest the eggs in the early stages of the arribada—turtle visits run from August to December and peak in September and October— because later waves of mother turtles invariably destroy the earlier nests. Another more accessible spot is Playa Grande, also on Nicoya, stomping ground of the mammoth, ponderous, exquisitely dignified Leatherback Turtles from November to April. Las Baulas National Marine Park was created specifically to protect the Leatherbacks, who also show up in smaller numbers at Playas Langosta and Junquillal.

*To help save these gentle giants, you can volunteer with turtle research and protection at such organizations as the **National Association for Indigenous Affairs** (ANAI; ☎ 224-3570 in San José ⊕ www.anaicr.org), working in conjunction with locals to protect the turtles.*

journey up the coast via the ocean. Most San José tour operators will not take you all the way to Moín to board canal boats but instead access them via the Parismina or Aguas Zarcas River. As you swoop through the sinuous turns of the natural waterways, your captain-guide may spot monkeys, snakes, caimans, mud turtles, sloths, and dozens of bird species, including flocks of bright and noisy parrots, kingfishers, aracaris, and assorted herons. The densely layered greenery is highlighted by brilliantly colored flowers, and the visual impact is doubled by the jungle's reflection in the mirror-smooth surface of the water. Consider hiring a dugout canoe and a guide to explore some of the rivers flowing into the canal; these waterways bear less boat traffic and often have more wildlife.

Where to Stay & Eat

The big lodges here offer one- or two-night excursion packages. The rates are expensive, but prices include everything from guides, tours, meals, and snacks to minivan and boat transport, and in some cases air transport to and from San José. If you stop and calculate what you get, the price may not be as bad as it first seemed.

$ ✕ **Miss Junie.** Most Tortuguero travelers take meals at their lodges, but this restaurant is worth a special trip. Miss Junie, the village's most well-known cook, serves cheap, filling, tasty food. Selection is limited, and it's best to call ahead, but you can usually count on a chicken, beef, or fish platter with rice and beans simmered in coconut milk. Your meal includes a beverage and dessert. ⊠ *Tortuguero Village* ☎ *710–0523* ⊟ *No credit cards.*

$$$$ ▦ **Jungle Lodge.** The Jungle Lodge experience begins with your hotel pickup in San Jose and continues via a minivan trip to the docks north of Siquirres where you board the lodge's *Miss Caribe* or *Miss America* barges for the last leg of the canal trip. The luxuriously rustic hardwood cabins are well-ventilated and have huge bathrooms. Everything is included, save for a few small tours. Per-person rates begin at around $170 a night. The restaurant serves buffet-style meals. ⊠ *1 km (½ mi) south of airstrip* ☎ *233–0133* 🖷 *233–0778* ⊕ *www.grupopapagayo.com* 🗬 *50 rooms* ⚬ *Dining room, fans, bar, pool, hot tub, laundry service, shop; no a/c, no room phones, no room TVs* ⊟ *AE, MC, V* ⦿❘ *AI.*

$$$$ ▦ **Jungle Tarpon Lodge.** On 100 acres at the Parsimina River lagoon at the southern end of the park, this intimate lodge specializes in sport-fishing packages, but there's plenty to do here if you don't fish. Eco-adventure activities, turtle-watching, and custom tours are arranged here. Though small, the lodge is a deluxe affair, crafted in fine wood with large rooms, modern tiled bathrooms, and beamed ceilings. Savory local cuisine—heavy on fish, of course—is served in the dining room; some meals are enjoyed riverside. Transfers to San José, meals, and charters are included in the four- to nine-day packages. Packages begin at close to $1,100 per person. ⊙ *May–mid-Oct.: Great Alaska, 33881 Sterling Hwy., Sterling, AK 99672* ☎ *907/262–4515, 800/544–2261 in the U. S.* 🖷 *907/262–8797* ⊙ *Mid-Oct.–Apr.: Great Alaska, Box 2670, Poulsbo, WA 98370* ☎ *360/697–6454, 800/544–2261 in the U.S.* 🖷 *360/697–7850* ⊕ *www.jungletarpon.com* 🗬 *4 rooms* ⚬ *Restaurant, dining room, fans, bar, boating, fishing, hiking; no a/c, no room phones, no room TVs* ⊟ *AE, MC, V* ⦿❘ *AI.*

★ **$$$$** ▦ **Mawamba Lodge.** Nestled between the river and the ocean, Mawamba is the perfect place to kick back and relax. You're whisked from the put-in at the river town of Matina in a 2½-hour launch ride, to stay in comfortable rustic cabins with hot water and garden views and take meals in the spacious dining room, all on a 15-acre site. Meals, transfers, and guided tours of the jungle and canals are included; trips to turtle-heavy beaches cost $10 extra. Packages begin at about $210 per person. ⊠ ½ km (¼ mi) north of Tortuguero on ocean side of canal ☎ 710–7282 ⊕ www.grupomawamba.com ⌖ Apdo. 10980–1000, San José ☎ 223–2421 ⊟ 222–5463 ⊋ 54 cabinas ⚘ Restaurant, dining room, fans, pool, hot tub, beach, billiards, volleyball, bar, laundry service, meeting room, shop; no a/c, no room phones, no room TVs ⊟ AE, MC, V ⊙ AI.

★ **$$$$** ▦ **Pachira Lodge.** Here is the prettiest and most luxurious of Tortuguero's lodges—although not the costliest. Each almond-wood cabina in the lush, well-manicured gardens contains four guest rooms with high ceilings, king-size beds, and bamboo furniture. The stunning pool is shaped like a giant sea turtle: the head is a hot tub, the left paw is a wading pool, and the right paw is equipped for swimmers with disabilities. The only drawback here is that you have few options at night, as there is no cross-river transportation into town. Package deals include transport from San José, a jungle tour, and all meals; rates begin at about $165 per person. ⊠ Across river from Mawamba Lodge ☎ 382–2239 ⊕ www.pachiralodge.com ⌖ Apdo. 1818–1002, San José ☎ 256–7080 ⊟ 223–1119 ⊋ 44 rooms ⚘ Restaurant, fans, pool, wading pool, bar, laundry service; no a/c, no room phones, no room TVs ⊟ AE, MC, V ⊙ AI.

$$$$ ▦ **Tortuga Lodge.** Lush lawns, orchids, and tropical trees surround this thatched riverside lodge owned by Costa Rica Expeditions and renowned for its nature packages. Guest rooms are comfortable, with much-needed mosquito blinds—the mosquitoes can be voracious. Considering that most of the restaurant ingredients are flown in, the chefs do an excellent job of preparing hearty food. The lodge is across the river from the airstrip, 2 km (1 mi) from Tortuguero. Rates begin at around $230 per room, with double occupancy. An all-inclusive rate is available. ⊠ 20 min north by boat from Tortuguero National Park or 35 min by plane from San José ☎ 710–8016 ⊕ www.costaricaexpeditions.com ⌖ Apdo. 6941–1000, San José ☎ 222–0333 or 257–0766 ⊟ 257–1665 ⊋ 24 rooms ⚘ Dining room, fans, pool, fishing, hiking, bar, laundry service; no a/c, no room phones, no room TVs ⊟ AE, MC, V.

$ ▦ **El Manatí.** Simple and reasonably priced, El Manatí is popular with budget travelers and researchers, some of whom study the lodge's namesake—the endangered manatee. The comfortable but slightly run-down rooms have firm beds and mosquito screens. The contiguous terraces look across a narrow lawn to the river, where you can kayak and canoe. Chestnut-beaked toucans, poison dart frogs, and three types of monkey hang out in the surrounding jungle. ⊠ Across river, about 1 km (½ mi) north of Tortuguero ☎☎ 383–0330 ⊋ 8 rooms ⚘ Restaurant, fans, boating, Ping-Pong; no a/c, no room phones, no room TVs ⊟ No credit cards ⊙ BP.

Barra del Colorado

❽ 25 km (16 mi) northwest of Tortuguero, 30 minutes by plane from San José.

Farther up the coast from Tortuguero is the ramshackle hamlet of Barra del Colorado, a popular sportfishing hub characterized by plain stilted wooden houses, dirt paths, and a complete absence of motorized land vehicles (though some locals have added outboard motors to their hand-hewn canoes). Bordered to the north by the Río San Juan and the frontier with Nicaragua is the vast, 905-square-km (350-square-mi) **Refugio Nacional de Fauna Silvestre Barra del Colorado** (Barra del Colorado Wildlife Refuge), really the only local attraction for nonanglers. Most people approach by air or boat (via the canals) from San José or Tortuguero; you can also come from Puerto Viejo de Sarapiquí up the Sarapiquí and San Juan rivers. Transportation once you get here is almost exclusively waterborne, as there are virtually no paths in this swampy terrain. The list of species that you're likely to see from your boat is almost the same as that for Tortuguero; the main difference here is the feeling of being farther off the beaten track.

Where to Stay

$$$$ ⊞ **Río Colorado Lodge.** This jungle lodge caters almost exclusively to sportfishing folk and tours, complete with a modern fleet of 10- and 26-ft sportfishing vessels. Guest rooms have twin beds with patterned bedspreads, paneled ceilings, white curtains, and basket lamp shades. The all-inclusive tours include airport pickup, all meals, and fishing trips; rates begin at about $1,400 per person. Alternately, there are some fly-in, boat-out nature-tour packages that include Tortuguero National Park and are considerably cheaper. ⊠ *35-min flight from San José via NatureAir* ☎ *710–6879* 🖷 *231–5987* ⊕ *www.riocoloradolodge.com* ✉ *Apdo. 5094–1000, San José* ☎ *232–4063, 800/243–9777 in the U.S.* 🖷 *813/ 933–3280 in the U.S.* 🗪 *18 rooms* ♿ *Restaurant, fans, fishing, bar, laundry service; no room phone, no room TVs* 🖃 *AE, MC, V* ⦿*I AI.*

COASTAL TALAMANCA

The quickest route from San José to the Atlantic coast runs through the magnificent cloud forest of Braulio Carrillo National Park on its way to the Caribbean Sea and the lively and sometimes dangerous port town of Limón. The 160-km (100-mi) trip along the Guápiles Highway to the coast takes about 2½ hours if all goes well; the highway is carved out of mountainous jungle and is susceptible to landslides. Make sure it's not blocked before you set off. (The alternate route is a long, painfully slow journey via Turrialba and Siquirres—it's doable, but best avoided.) As the highway descends and straightens toward Guápiles, you'll enter the province of Limón, where cloud forest gives way to banana plantations and partially deforested pastureland. (Note well that the highway gives way to potholes, some big enough to swallow an entire wheel and ruin your car's suspension.) Local farms produce cacao, exotic export plants, and macadamia nuts. After passing through villages with names like Bristol, Stratford, and Liverpool, you arrive in the provincial capital, Limón.

Limón

❾ *130 km (81 mi) southeast of Braulio Carrillo National Park, 100 km (62 mi) southeast of Guápiles.*

Limón inherited its promontory setting, overlooking the Caribbean, from the ancient Indian village of Cariari, which lay close to Uvita Island, where Christopher Columbus dropped anchor on his final voyage in 1502. The colorful Afro-Caribbean flavor of Costa Rica's most important port (population 50,000) is the first sign of life for seafaring visitors to Costa Rica's east coast. Limón is a lively, if shabby, town with a 24-hour street life. The wooden houses are brightly painted, but the grid-plan streets look rather worn, due largely to the damage caused by a 1991 earthquake. Street crime, including pickpocketing and nighttime mugging, is not uncommon here. But "*Limón cambia,*" (Limón is changing) say residents. Long charged with neglecting the city, the national government has turned attention to Limón. New businesses are coming in, providing hopeful signs of urban renewal, and the town has beefed up security with a more visible police presence. Staying overnight in the city center may still be somewhat dicey, but there are several appealing hotels at Portete, just north of Limón town, with easy access to the docks at Moín.

On the left side of the highway as you enter Limón is a large **Chinese cemetery,** Chinese workers having made up a large part of the 1880s railroad-construction team that worked here. Thousands died of malaria and yellow fever. Follow the railroad as far as the palm-lined promenade that runs around the **Parque Vargas.** From the promenade you can see the raised dead coral left stranded by the quake. Nine or so Hoffman's two-toed sloths live in the trees of Parque Vargas; ask a passerby to point them out, as spotting them requires a trained eye. From the park, find the lively enclosed market on Avda. 2—a pedestrian mall—between Cs. 3 and 4, where you can buy fruit for the road ahead.

Where to Stay & Eat

¢–$ ✕ **Springfield.** Protected from the street by a leafy conservatory, this Caribbean kitchen whips up tasty rice-and-bean dishes. Decor consists of wood paneling, red tablecloths, and a white-tile floor. Bring your dancing shoes: the huge dance floor out back creaks to the beat of soca, salsa, and reggae on weekends ⊠ *On road north from Limón to Portete, left opposite hospital* ☎ 758–1203 ☐ *AE, MC, V.*

$ ⊞ **Hotel Matama.** If you're coming from San José and planning to catch an early boat north out of Moín, this is a great place to get your first taste of the Caribbean. Across the street from the beach, the property has a pool and bar in close proximity, and the grounds are gorgeously landscaped with botanical trails exhibiting 50 tropical plant species. The open-air restaurant dishes up seafood and Caribbean cuisine and has lovely garden views. ⊠ *4 km (2½ mi) west of Limón on road to Portete, Apdo.* 606–7300 ☎ 758–1123 *or* 758–4409 ⊟ 795–3399 ⊕ *www.matama.com* ⇆ *16 rooms* ♢ *Restaurant, pool, bar, dance club, laundry service, meeting room; no room TVs* ☐ *AE, MC, V.*

★ $ ⊞ **Hotel Maribú Caribe.** Perched on a cliff overlooking the Caribbean Sea between Limón and Portete, these white conical thatched huts have great views and hot water. The lovely grounds have green lawns, shrubs, palm trees, and a large, kidney-shape pool. The poolside bar discourages exertion. ⊠ *4 km (2 ½ mi) north on road to Portete, Apdo.* 623–7300 ☎ 795–2543 ⊟ 795–3541 ⇆ *52 rooms* ♢ *Restaurant, snack bar, pool, bar, laundry service; no a/c in some rooms, no room TVs* ☐ *AE, MC, V* ⊧◯⊧ *BP.*

$ ⊞ **Hotel Park.** The rooms are just a tad worn at the pastel-and-pink Park, but the prices can't be beat here at central Limón's business-class hotel. All rooms have modern furnishings and private balconies, so opt for one fronting the ocean. The air-conditioned dining room is a pleasant respite from the heat of the port city. ⊠ *Avda. 3, between Cs. 2 and 3* ☎ 798–0555 ⊟ 758–4364 ✑ *irlyxie@racsa.co.cr* ⇆ *32 rooms* ♢ *Restaurant, meeting room; no room TVs* ☐ *AE, MC, V.*

Moín

❿ *5 km (3 mi) north of Limón.*

The docks at Moín are a logical next stop after visiting neighboring Limón, especially if you want to take a boat north to explore the Caribbean coast. You'll probably be able to negotiate a waterway and national-park tour with a local guide, and if you call in advance, you can arrange a tour with the man considered the best guide on the Caribbean coast: Modesto Watson, a local Miskito Indian guide. He's legendary for his bird- and animal-spotting skills as well as his howler-monkey imitations (☎ 226–0986).

en route The proximity of the Panamanian border means added police vigilance on the coastal highway. Expect a passport inspection and cursory vehicle search at a checkpoint just north of Cahuita. The border itself lies at Sixaola, 44 km (26 mi) south of the turnoff to Puerto Viejo de Talamanca.

Cahuita

⓫ *44 km (27 mi) southeast of Limón.*

The Caribbean character of the Atlantic lowlands becomes powerfully evident in the surf rolling shoreward as you head south from Limón to Cahuita; the hot, humid stir of the Caribbean trade winds; and the laid-back pace of the people you meet. This is tropical Central America, and it feels like another country, its slow, somewhat sultry atmosphere far removed from the business and bustle of San José.

Dusty Cahuita, its main dirt street flanked by wooden-slat cabins, is a backpackers' vacation town with something of a seedy reputation—a hippie hangout with a dash of Afro-Caribbean spice tossed in. The town's image as a drug center is only partially deserved; like Puerto Viejo de Talamanca, Cahuita has a few junkies, but the locals don't see them as a threat. And after years of negative crime-related publicity, Cahuita has beefed up security and is making a small but well-deserved comeback on the tourist circuit. Tucked in among the backpackers' digs are a few surprisingly nice get-away-from-it-all lodgings, yours to have at surprisingly decent prices.

Lively reggae, soca, and samba blast weekend evenings from the turquoise **Coco's Bar** on the main road, and the assemblage of dogs dozing on its veranda illustrates the rhythm of local life. On the opposite corner from the bus stop, **Ricky's Bar** (☎ 755–0228) is more subdued, quiet, and touristed than Coco's. At **Cahuita Tours** (✉ 180 m [200 yards] north of the bus stop ☎ 755–0232), the friendly folks can set you up with any of a variety of adventures, including tours of the canals, indigenous reservations, and mountains; river rafting and kayaking; and bike rentals. They can also reconfirm flights and make lodging reservations. Across from Supermercado Safari, **Turística Cahuita** (☎ 755–0071) arranges personalized tours to nearby rain forests and indigenous reserves and rents snorkeling equipment.

Where to Stay & Eat

$–$$ ✕ **Sobre las Olas.** The name means "over the waves," and this is one of the few seaside restaurants around, at the black-sand beach heading just out of town. Octopus is a specialty here, but if you're not that adventurous, a variety of other seafood and pasta dishes await. Lunch includes sandwiches and lighter fare. Or stop by for the delicious all-afternoon *bocas* (appetizers) when those 3 PM hunger pangs hit you. ✉ *180 m (200 yards) west of police station at Playa Negra* ☎ 755–0109 ▤ *AE, MC, V* ⊘ *Closed Tues.*

$ ✕ **Cha Cha Cha.** You can order anything from Thai shrimp salad to Tex-Mex fajitas at this world-cuisine restaurant. A delectable specialty is *langosta cha cha cha,* lobster in a white-wine garlic sauce with fresh basil. Paintings by local artists hang on the light-blue walls of the candlelit outdoor dining area, separated from the street by miniature palm trees. ✉ *1 block north of bus stop on main strip* ☎ 755–0191 ▤ *MC, V* ⊘ *Closed Mon. No lunch.*

FodorśChoice ★

$ ✕ **Miss Edith.** Miss Edith is revered for her flavorful Caribbean cooking, vegetarian meals, and herbal teas for whatever ails you. You won't be fed in a hurry—most dishes are made to order—but the rondón (stew of vegetables and beef or fish) and spicy jerk chicken are worth the wait. Back in the day, Miss Edith used to serve on her own front porch; she's since moved to more ample surroundings on an easy-to-miss side street at the north end of town. ⊠ *From bus stop, follow main road north and turn right at police station* ☎ *755–0248* 🚫 *No credit cards* ⊘ *Closed Sun.*

¢–$ ✕ **Restaurante Relax.** You first notice the skewers of shrimp and chicken turning on the grill at this open-air restaurant in the center of town, but the Italian-Mexican owners also toss in pastas and fajitas to give their native cuisines sufficient representation. There are just three tables here. If they're full, take a seat at the bar and engage in some lively conversation with your fellow diners. ⊠ *45 m (50 yards) south of bus stop* ☎ *755–0322* 🚫 *AE, MC, V* ⊘ *Closed Tues.*

★ $ ✕🏠 **Magellan Inn.** This group of bungalows is arguably Cahuita's most elegant lodging. Graced with tile-floored terraces facing a pool and gardens growing on an ancient coral reef, the Magellan has carpeted rooms with original paintings and custom-made wooden furniture. Feast on intensely flavored French and creole seafood specialties in the Casa Creole ($–$$), a freestanding coral-pink structure with an outdoor dining room; don't miss the house pâté or the homemade ice cream. The hotel's enticing open-air bar rocks to great blues and jazz recordings in the evenings and mellows with classical music at breakfast. ⊠ *2 km (1 mi) north of Cahuita at far end of Playa Negra* 🏠 *Apdo. 1132–7300 Limón* ☎ *755–0035* 🛏 *6 rooms* ⚱ *Restaurant, fans, pool, bar; no room phones, no room TVs* 🚫 *AE, MC, V* 🍴 *BP.*

$ 🏠 **Atlántida Lodge.** Attractively landscaped grounds, the beach across the road, and a large pool are Atlántida's main assets. You're welcomed to your room with a lovely assortment of fresh and dried flowers; the rooms themselves have tile floors and pretty terraces. ⊠ *Next to soccer field at Playa Negra* ☎ *755–0115* 🏠 *755–0213* ⊕ *www.atlantida. co.cr* 🛏 *30 rooms* ⚱ *Restaurant, fans, pool, hot tub, massage, laundry service, meeting room; no a/c, no room phones, no room TVs* 🚫 *AE, MC, V.*

$$ 🏠 **Aviarios del Caribe.** It's a lodge, sloth rescue center, and bird-watch-
Fodor'sChoice ing sanctuary all rolled into one. More than 310 bird species have been
★ spotted here, many with the help of the telescope on the wide second-floor deck. Buttercup, the resident three-toed sloth, oversees the proceedings in the upstairs open-air dining room. The spacious guest rooms have white walls, blue-tile floors, and fresh flowers. For $5 you can hike the adjoining wildlife refuge, and $30 will get you an unforgettable 3½-hour riverboat tour guided by the owner, Luis, himself. ⊠ *9 km (5 mi) north of Cahuita, follow hotel signs on Río Estrella delta* 🏠 *Apdo. 569–7300, Limón* ☎ *200–5105 or 382–1335* ⊕ *www.ogphoto.com/ aviarios* 🛏 *6 rooms* ⚱ *Hiking, laundry service; no room phones, no room TVs* 🚫 *AE, MC, V.*

$ 🏠 **Alby Lodge.** You're right in town, but you'd never know it at this friendly lodging. Cabins with hardwood floors prop up on stilts and come complete with hot water baths, log tables, mosquito nets and a hammock on the front porch. Make use of the shared kitchen facilities and outdoor barbecue. The forested grounds and high thatched roof keep the temperature pleasantly bearable in otherwise balmy Cahuita. It's next to the park, so the howler monkeys will be your morning alarm clock. ⊠ *180 m (200 yards) west of national park entrance* ☎ *755–0031* ✉ *alby_lodge@racsa.co.cr* 🛏 *4 cabins* ⚱ *Fans; no a/c, no room phones, no room TVs* 🚫 *No credit cards.*

$ 🏠 **El Encanto Bed & Breakfast.** Zen Buddhists Pierre-Léon Tetreault and
Fodor'sChoice Patricia Kim Chiaw have cultivated a serene and beautiful environment
★ here, ideal for physical and spiritual relaxation. Lodgings are in an en-

chanting garden, with an extensive bromeliad collection and Buddha figures. There's a choice of comfortable rooms or bungalows, decorated with art from all over the globe. Amenities include queen-size beds, hot water, and secure parking. Breakfast comes complete with homemade breads and cakes, a rarity in Costa Rica. The beach is across the street, and massage and yoga classes are available weekends. ⊠ *West of police station* ☎☎ *755–0113* ⊕ *www.2000.co.cr/elencanto* ⌖ *Apdo. 7-7302, Cahuita* ⚐ *3 rooms, 3 bungalows* ♨ *Fans; no a/c in some rooms, no room phones, no TV in some rooms* ☰ *AE, MC, V* ⎟◎⎟ *BP.*

$ ⊞ **Kelly Creek Hotel–Restaurante.** Owners Andrés and Marie-Claude de Alcalá of Madrid have created a wonderful budget option in this handsome wooden hotel, on the creek bank across a short pedestrian bridge from the park entrance. Each of the four hardwood-finished guest rooms is big enough to sleep a small army and has two double beds. Señor de Alcalá barbecues meat and fresh fish on an open-air grill and also cooks paella and other Spanish specialties. Caiman come to the creek bank in search of snacks, and the monkeys, parrots, jungles, and beaches of the national park are just yards away, as is the lively center of Cahuita. ⊠ *Next to park entrance* ☎ *755–0007* ⊕ *www.hotelkellycreek.com* ⚐ *4 rooms* ♨ *Restaurant, fans, beach; no a/c, no room phones, no room TVs* ☰ *AE, MC, V.*

Cahuita National Park

⑫ *Puerto Vargas is 5 km (3 mi) south of Cahuita.*

The only Costa Rican park jointly administered by the National Parks Service and a community, Parque Nacional Cahuita starts at the southern edge of the town of Cahuita. The park's rain forest extends right to the edge of its curving, 3-km (2-mi) utterly undeveloped white-sand beach. Roughly parallel to the coastline, a 7-km (4-mi) trail passes through the forest to Cahuita Point, encircled by a 2½-square-km (1½-square-mi) coral reef. The hike takes only a few hours, but you have to ford several rivers on the way, so check conditions beforehand, as they can be prohibitive in the rainy season.

There's good snorkeling off Cahuita Point—watch for blue parrot fish and angelfish as they weave their way among equally colorful species of coral, sponges, and seaweeds. Sadly, the coral reef is slowly being killed by sediment, intensified by deforestation and the erosive effects of a 1991 earthquake. Use a local guide to find the best reefs (or to snorkel independently, swim out from the beach on the Puerto Vargas side), and don't snorkel for a few days after it rains, as the water is sure to be murky. You can take a ride in a glass-bottom boat from Cahuita (visibility is best in September and October). The road to the park headquarters at Puerto Vargas is 5 km (3 mi) south of Cahuita on the left. Here you find the ranger station as well as campsites that have been carved out of the jungle, scattered along the beachfront. ⊠ *Cahuita entrance at southern end of Cahuita's main street; Puerto Vargas entrance 5 km (3 mi) south of Cahuita* ☎ *755–0302* ▧ *Donation requested at Cahuita entrance; $6 at Puerto Vargas entrance* ☉ *Weekdays 8–4, weekends 7–5.*

The Outdoors

BICYCLING You can bike through Cahuita National Park, but the trail gets pretty muddy at times, and you run into logs, river estuaries, and other obstacles. Nevertheless, mountain bikes are a good way to get around on the dirt roads and trails surrounding Cahuita and Puerto Viejo de Talamanca. Cycling is easiest in the dry season, of course, though many hardy souls are out during the long rainy season. There are several area bike-rental outlets. **Caribbean Flavor** (☏ 755–0017), in the center of town, charges $8 a day for a mountain bike.

HIKING A serious hiking trail extends as far as Puerto Vargas. If you're staying in Cahuita, you can take a bus or catch a ride into Puerto Vargas and hike back around the point in the course of a day. If you camp at Puerto Vargas, you can also hike south along the beach to Puerto Viejo de Talamanca and bus or cab it back to the park. Be sure to bring plenty of water, food, and sunscreen. Along the trail you might spot howler and capuchin monkeys, coatis, armadillos, and raccoons. Swimming is prohibited here because of the extremely strong current.

SNORKELING & Cahuita's reefs are just one of several high-quality snorkeling spots
SURFING around here. You can rent snorkeling gear in Cahuita or Puerto Viejo de Talamanca or through your hotel; most hotels will also organize trips. It's wise to work with a guide, as the number of good snorkeling spots is limited and they're not always easily accessible. Cahuita established a community lifeguard team in 2002, a real rarity in Costa Rica. As elsewhere up and down the Caribbean coast, the undertow poses risks for even experienced swimmers. Use extreme caution and never swim alone.

The staff at the friendly storefront **Cahuita Tours**, 180 m (200 yards) north of the bus stop, can assist with tourist information, travel arrangements, snorkeling and surfing-equipment rental, horseback-riding, and other tours. Although it's not in town, **ATEC** (☏ 750–0398), an ecotourism organization in nearby Puerto Viejo de Talamanca, has tourism information and can help with travel arrangements, equipment rentals, and much more.

Puerto Viejo de Talamanca

🔞 *16 km (10 mi) south of Cahuita.*

Puerto Viejo de Talamanca was once quieter than Cahuita, but no more—it's one of the hottest spots on the international surf punk circuit. This muddy, colorful little town swarms with surfers, new-age hippies, beaded and spangled punks, would-be Rastafarians of all colors and descriptions, and wheelers and dealers both pleasant and otherwise. Time was when most kids came here with only one thing on their mind: surfing. Today, many seem to be looking only for a party, with or without surf.

But if alternative lifestyles aren't your bag, there are plenty of more "grown-up" offerings on the road heading southeast and northwest out of town. Some locals bemoan the loss of their town's innocence, as the ravages of crack cocaine and other evils have surfaced, but only in small doses: this is still a fun town to visit, with a great variety of hotels, cabinas, and restaurants in every price range.

You have access to the beach right in town, and the Salsa Brava, famed in surfers' circles for its pounding waves, is here off the coast as well. The surfing waves are at their best between December and April and again in June and July. The best strands of Caribbean sand outside the village. Play Negra, a black-sand beach, extends northwest from Puerto Viejo for about a kilometer. Heading southeast from town, Playa Cocles begins about 2 km (1 ¼ mi) from Puerto Viejo. A series of small beaches, collectively referred to as Playa Chiquita, runs from 4 to 7 km (2 ½ to 4 mi) out of town. Farther-flung Punta Uva extends for the next 2 km (1 mi) beyond Playa Chiquita. In these beach areas, you see some of the region's first luxury tourist developments, though still quite small-scale, and some interesting ecolodges. This is the place for those pre-

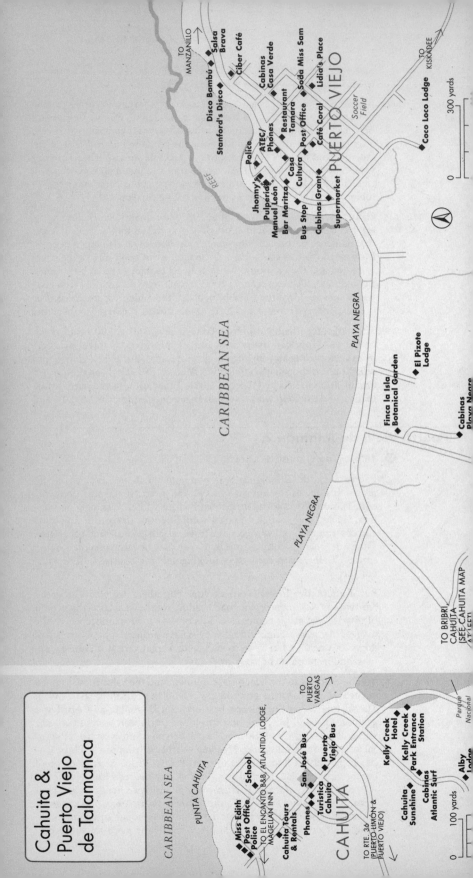

Cahuita & Puerto Viejo de Talamanca

CARIBBEAN SEA

CARIBBEAN SEA

REEF

PUERTO VIEJO

TO MANZANILLO

TO KISKADEE

Salsa Brava

Disco Bambú

Ciber Café

Stanford's Disco

Cabinas Casa Verde

Soda Miss Sam

Lidia's Place

Restaurant Tamara

Police

ATEC/ Phones

Post Office

Café Coral

Coco Loco Lodge

Soccer Field

Jhonny's

Pulpería

Manuel León

Casa Cultura

Cabinas Grant

Bar Maritza

Bus Stop

Supermarket

300 yards

0

PLAYA NEGRA

PLAYA NEGRA

PLAYA NEGRA

Finca la Isla Botanical Garden

El Pizote Lodge

Cabinas Playa Negra

TO BRIBRI, CAHUITA (SEE CAHUITA MAP AT LEFT)

PUNTA CAHUITA

TO EL ENCANTO B&B, ATLANTIDA LODGE, MAGELLAN INN

Miss Edith

Post Office

Police

School

Cahuita Tours & Rentals

Phones

Turística Cahuita

San José Bus

Puerto Viejo Bus

TO PUERTO VARGAS

CAHUITA

TO RTE. 36 (PUERTO LIMÓN & PUERTO VIEJO)

Cahuita Sunshine

Cabinas Atlantic Surf

Kelly Creek Hotel

Kelly Creek

Park Entrance Station

Alby Lodge

Parque Nacional

100 yards

0

ferring creature comforts who also wish to see this less-frequented part of the country.

Pulpería Manuel León (⊠ southeast of bus stop ☎ 750–0422), a local general store often called **El Chino**, changes cash or traveler's checks daily 9–8 if there is enough cash on hand. U.S. greenbacks fetch the best rates, but Manuel accepts Canadian dollars, pounds, and euros, too. During the December–May high season, most hotels will also change money. You can check e-mail at **Cíber Café** (☎ 750–0456), across from Stanford's Disco. Everyone gets around via bike here, and everyone has one for rent. Quality varies widely, but **Cabinas Grant** (⊠ 300 ft south of the bus stop ☎ 750–0292) rents quality bikes for a mere $3 a day. Rent snorkeling equipment and buy your official Puerto Viejo T-shirt at **Color Caribe** (⊠ 300 ft south of bus stop ☎ 750–0284).

In the middle of town, **ATEC** (the Association for Ecotourism and Conservation) plays an important role in the south coast's cultural and ecotourism movement. The agency's small office also serves as a fax and phone center and a general travel-information center for the town and the region. You can arrange walks focusing on Afro-Caribbean or indigenous culture—tours to the nearby Kekoldi indigenous reserve are especially popular; rain-forest hikes; coral-reef snorkeling or fishing trips; bird-watching; night walks; and adventure treks. ATEC is also an excellent source for information on volunteer vacations. Of the money collected for tours booked through the agency, 15%–20% goes to local organizations and wildlife refuges. ⊠ *Across from Restaurant Tamara* ☎ *750–0398* 🖷 *750–0191* ⊕ *www.greencoast.com/atec.htm* ☯ *Mon.–Tues. and Thurs.–Fri. 8 AM–9 PM; Wed. 8–noon and 2–9; Sat. 8–noon and 1–9; Sun. 8–noon and 4–8.*

West of town lies the **Finca La Isla Botanical Garden,** where you can wander around a working tropical fruit, spice, and ornamental plant farm, as well as view bird and animal life. Sloths abound, as well as a few poison dart frogs. An $8 guided tour includes admission and a glass of the farm's homemade fruit juice. ⊠ *½ km (¼ mi) west of Puerto Viejo at Playa Negra* ☎ *750–0046* ☯ *Fri.–Mon. 10–4* 💰 *$3.*

Where to Eat

★ **$–$$** ✕ **La Pecora Nera.** Though the name means "black sheep" in Italian, there's nothing shameful about this thatch-roof roadside restaurant. There's always a lot more to choose from than what appears on the sparse-looking menu; the owners come out of the kitchen and triumphantly announce which additional light Tuscan entrées, appetizers, and desserts they've decided to concoct that day. Be prepared for a pleasantly long, leisurely dining experience with all the attentive, fussed-over service. ⊠ *3 km (2 mi) south of Puerto Viejo on road to Manzanillo* ☎ *750–0490* ▭ *No credit cards* ☯ *Closed Mon. Apr.–Nov.*

$–$$ ✕ **Salsa Brava.** The restaurant at Salsa Brava—with sublime surf vistas—has taken the name of this famed surfing locale. Opt for casual counter service or grab a seat at one of the colorful roadside tables. Lunch and dinner center on grilled fish and meat. ⊠ *300 ft south of Stanford's Disco* ☎ *750–0241* ▭ *No credit cards* ☯ *Closed Mon.*

¢–$ ✕ **Café Coral.** It's a quaint but true tale that Café Coral shocked Puerto Viejo with the introduction of pizza in 1989—those were pre-telephone days here after all. These folks still do a bang-up job out of their open-air, thatch-roof restaurant. The Smoky, with sausage, mushroom, pineapple, chile dulce (red peppers), and more, is the most requested dish. Mornings, Coral transforms itself into the town's quintessential American-style breakfast joint. Feast on pancakes before heading out for the day. ✉ *45 m (50 yards) south of Adventist church* ☎ *750–0051* ▤ *No credit cards* ◷ *Closed Mon. No lunch.*

¢–$ ✕ **Restaurant Tamara.** In the nondescript indoor seating area you're cooled by a fan and entertained by TV; the outdoor seating area—with a large image of Bob Marley on red, yellow, and green walls—has a palpable Jamaican motif. The Caribbean food at this two-story unpretentious place is tasty and authentic: You can't lose with the chicken in Caribbean sauce or virtually any of the fresh fish dishes. And it's near the beach. ✉ *Across from ATEC* ☎ *750–0148* ▤ *AE, MC, V.*

¢ ✕ **Soda Miss Sam.** Older women in Caribbean communities here are often addressed as "Miss" regardless of marital status. Miss Sam has been dishing up hearty Caribbean cuisine for years, though she prefers not to divulge how many. She usually has rice and beans going, or can fix a casado with chicken, beef, pork, or fish and freshly squeezed fruit juices as accompaniment. ✉ *900 ft south, 600 ft east of bus stop* ☎ *750–0108* ▤ *No credit cards* ◷ *Closed Sun.*

Where to Stay

★ $$ ▥ **Shawandha Lodge.** The service is personalized and friendly at Shawandha, whose spacious, beautifully designed bungalows are well back from the road at Playa Chiquita. The thatch-roof bungalows have elegant hardwoods, four-poster beds, and verandas with hammocks. Each bathroom has a unique and gorgeous tile mosaic. Well-known local chef Madame Oui Oui crafts her distinctive French-Caribbean cuisine in the open-air restaurant. The hearty breakfast starts off with an impressive fruit plate. A white-sand beach lies 180 m (200 yards) away, across the road. ✉ *6 km (4 mi) south of Puerto Viejo, at Playa Chiquita* ☎ *750–0018* 🖷 *750–0037* ⊕ *www.shawandhalodge.com* ⇄ *12 bungalows* ⚭ *Restaurant, fans, in-room safes, bar, laundry service; no a/c, no room phones, no room TVs, no smoking* ▤ *AE, MC, V* ꪱꪮꪱ *BP.*

$$ ▥ **Villas del Caribe.** Right on the beach north of Punta Uva, these multiroom villas are commodious and comfortable, if somewhat pedestrian in design. Each has a blue-tile kitchen, a small sitting room with low-slung couches, a plant-filled bathroom, and a patio with excellent views of the beach. Upstairs are one or two spacious bedrooms with a wooden deck. ✉ *4 km (2½ mi) southeast of Puerto Viejo* ☎ *750–0202; 233–2200 in San José* 🖷 *750–0203; 221–2801 in San José* ⊕ *www.villascaribe. net* ⇄ *12 villas* ⚭ *Restaurant, kitchenettes, beach; no room phones, no room TVs* ▤ *AE, MC, V* ꪱꪮꪱ *BP.*

$–$$ ▥ **El Pizote Lodge.** El Pizote observes local architectural mores while offering more than most in the way of amenities. All standard rooms have polished wood paneling, reading lamps, mirrors, and firm beds. Each of the two-room bungalows sleeps six. The restaurant serves breakfast, dinner, and drinks all day. Guanábana and papaya grow on the grounds, and hiking trails lead off into the jungle. ✉ *Right side of road into Puerto Viejo, 180 m (200 yards) before town* ☎ *750–0088* 🖷 *750–0226* ✉ *pizotelg@sol.racsa.co.cr* ⇄ *8 rooms, 4 with bath; 9 bungalows* ⚭ *Restaurant, fans, pool, volleyball, bar, laundry service; no a/c in some rooms, no room phones, no room TVs* ▤ *AE, MC, V.*

$ ▥ **Cariblue Bungalows.** Cariblue's finely crafted all-wooden bungalows are spaciously arrayed on the edge of the jungle, across the road from the splendid white-sand beaches of Punta Cocles. Cabinas are linked to the main ranch-style building by paths that meander through a gently sloping lawn shaded with enormous trees. Expansive verandas and beautiful bathroom-tile mosaics add an air of refinement; hammocks add an air of relaxation. The youthful Italian owners serve a huge breakfast. ✉ *2 km (1 mi) south of Puerto Viejo on road to Manzanillo, across road from*

Fodor'sChoice
★

Playa Cocles ☎ *750–0035* 📠 *750–0057* ⊕ *www.cariblue.com* ⇗ *15 bungalows* ⌂ *Restaurant, fans, pool, billiards, laundry service, shop; no room phones, no room TVs* ▤ *AE, MC, V* ⏀ *BP.*

$ 🏨 **Escape Caribeño.** Wonderfully friendly Italian owners Gloria and Mauro Marchiori treat you like family at their lodging just outside of town. A dozen immaculate hardwood bungalows line a pleasant garden area amply populated with hummingbirds. All units come complete with hammocks, mosquito nets, double beds, and even a bunk bed or two for larger groups. Across the road lie two stucco cabins in a wooded area on the beach, both with kitchenette. Breakfast is served at a rancho in the center of the garden. ✉ *370 m (400 yards) southeast of Puerto Viejo* ☎📠 *750–0103* ⊕ *www.escapecaribeno.com* ⇗ *14 cabins* ⌂ *Fans, minibar, some kitchenettes; no a/c, no room phones, no room TVs* ▤ *AE, MC, V.*

$ 🏨 **Hotel La Perla Negra.** The original owners' previous experience as designers is evident in the fine construction of this handsome, two-story wooden structure across a tiny dirt road from Playa Negra. All rooms have balconies, half with ocean views, half with jungle views. The three-meal restaurant features grilled meats and fish. Between the building and the beach is a spacious, inviting pool. ✉ *Playa Negra, 1 km (½ mi) north of Puerto Viejo* ☎ *750–0111, 800/221–4713 in the U.S.* 📠 *750–0114* ⊕ *www.perlanegra-beachresort.com* ⇗ *24 rooms, 1 apartment* ⌂ *Restaurant, fans, tennis court, pool, laundry service; no a/c, no room phones, no room TVs* ▤ *AE, MC, V* ⏀ *BP.*

$ 🏨 **Agapi.** Agapi means "love" in Greek, and Costa Rican–Greek owners Cecilia and Tasso lovingly watch over their guests with some of the most attentive service around. Six furnished apartments overlook the beach and come complete with fully equipped kitchen, hot-water bath, hammock, and mosquito nets over the beds. A common area in the back contains a beachside barbecue. ✉ *1 km (½ mi) southeast of Puerto Viejo* ☎ *750–0446* 📠 *750–0418* ⊕ *www.agapisite.com* ⇗ *6 apartments* ⌂ *Fans, kitchens; no a/c, no room phones, no room TVs* ▤ *AE, MC, V.*

¢–$ 🏨 **Cabinas Casa Verde.** Set back a few blocks from the waterfront hustle, the comfortable cabinas at this Swiss Costa Rican–run hotel in town are decorated with an interesting variety of items such as shell mobiles, watercolor frescoes, and indigenous tapestries. And yet, overall, rooms have a neat-as-a-pin quality. Exotic birds flutter constantly through the lush plantings that screen the cabinas from the street. The place is immensely popular, since the price is low and it's clean and well run; reserve ahead. ✉ *200 m (220 yards) south and 200 m east (220 yards) of bus stop* ☎ *750–0015* 📠 *750–0047* ⊕ *www.cabinascasaverde. com* ✉ *Apdo. 37–7304 Puerto Viejo de Talamanca* ⇗ *17 rooms, 9 with bath* ⌂ *Cafeteria, fans, some refrigerators, laundry service; no room phones, no room TVs* ▤ *AE, MC, V.*

¢ 🏨 **Bungalows Calalú.** A French couple operates this budget option on a quiet lane off the main road just outside of town. Five wooden bungalows are scattered around the wooded grounds. Each comes with a porch equipped with a hammock, perfect for relaxing at the end of the day. Breakfast is served overlooking a small butterfly garden. ✉ *180 m (200 yards) southeast and 75 m (80 yards) west of Stanford's* ☎ *750–0042* ⊕ *www.puertoviejo.net/calalu* ⇗ *5 cabins* ⌂ *Fans, some kitchens; no a/c, no room phones, no room TVs* ▤ *AE, MC, V.*

¢ 🏨 **Coco Loco Lodge.** The cool, forested grounds here lie close to the center of town but seem so far away. The Austrian owners lavish you with lots of personal attention. The bungalows on stilts are simply furnished but contain hot-water baths, mosquito nets over the beds, and hammocks on the porch. There's also one fully furnished house available for short- or long-term rental. Great coffee is included in the room rate; a huge buffet breakfast is extra. ✉ *180 m (200 yards) south of bridge at entrance to town* 🏨 *750–0281* ⊕ *www.cocolocolodge.de* ⇨ *5 cabins, 1 house* ♨ *Fans; no a/c, no room phones, no room TVs* ☰ *MC, V.*

¢ 🖃 **Hotel Pura Vida.** The friendly owners help make this the nicest of the lowest-end budget lodgings in the center of town. Rooms are basic, but clean, bright, and well ventilated and arranged around a center patio. Guests have use of the shared kitchen. ✉ *270 m (300 yards) south of bus stop* ☎ *750–0002* 📠 *750–0296* ⇨ *10 rooms, 3 with bath* ♨ *Fans; no a/c, no room phones, no room TVs* ☰ *AE, MC, V.*

The Outdoors

SURFING   Surfing is the name of the game in Puerto Viejo. There are a number of breaks here, most famously Salsa Brava, which breaks rather far offshore and requires maneuvering past some tricky currents and a shallow reef. Hollow and primarily right-breaking, Salsa Brava is one gnarly wave when it gets big. If it gets *too* big, or not big enough, check out the breaks at Punta Uva, Punta Cocles, or Playa Chiquita. Boogie-boarders and body-surfers will also dig the beach-break waves at various points along this tantalizingly beautiful coast. But a surfer's paradise makes for dangerous swimming here. Undertows can carry you far from shore before you realize what's happening; exercise extreme caution.

NIGHTLIFE   Ticos come from miles around for the Friday and Monday reggae nights at **Disco Bambú** (✉ next to Jhonny's).Play backgammon or billiards, and chow down on pizza or sandwiches at **El Dorado** (✉ across from ATEC ☎ 750–0604). **Jhonny's Place** (✉ 230 m [250 yards] east of bus stop ☎ 750–0623) has nights variously devoted to reggae, jazz, R&B, and hip-hop. **Maritza Bar** (✉ 50 m [55 yards] east of bus stop) is a local favorite, and has karaoke on Saturday night. **Stanford's Disco** (✉ 100 m [325 ft] from the town center on the road to Manzanillo) is the place to merengue or salsa the weekend night away.

Gandoca-Manzanillo National Wildlife Refuge

⑭ *15 km (9 mi) south of Puerto Viejo de Talamanca.*

The Refugio Nacional de Vida Silvestre Gandoca-Manzanillo stretches along the southeastern coast from the town of Manzanillo to the Panamanian border. Because of weak laws governing the conservation of refuges and the value of coastal land in this area, Gandoca-Manzanillo is less pristine than Cahuita National Park and continues to be developed. However, the refuge still bears plenty of rain forest, orey and jolillo swamps, 10 km (6 mi) of beach where four species of turtles lay their eggs, and almost 3 square km (2 square mi) of cativo forest and coral reef. The Gandoca estuary is a nursery for tarpon and a wallowing spot for crocodiles and caimans.

The easiest way to explore the refuge is to hike along the coast south of Manzanillo. You can hike back out the way you came in, or arrange (in Puerto Viejo de Talamanca) to have a boat pick you up at Monkey Point (a three- to four-hour walk from Manzanillo) or Gandoca (six to eight hours). The park administrators, Benson and Florentino Grenald, can tell you more and recommend a local guide; inquire when you enter Manzanillo village and the locals will point you toward them. You can also arrange boat trips to dive spots and beaches in the refuge in Puerto Viejo de Talamanca and Manzanillo. ✉ *10 km (6 mi) southeast of Puerto Viejo* ☎ *750–0398 ATEC* ☉ *Daily 7–4.*

The nearby village of **Manzanillo** maintains that "end of the world" feel. Tourism is still in its infancy this far down the coast. **Aquamor Adventures** (⊠ main road, Manzanillo ☎ 759–0612) tends to all your water-sporting needs in these parts, with guided kayaking, snorkeling, and scuba-diving tours, as well as equipment rental. It also offers the complete sequence of PADI-certified diving courses. Aquamor is affiliated with the **Talamanca Dolphin Foundation**; its 2½-hour dolphin observation tours are excellent opportunities to see bottlenose, tucuxi, and Atlantic spotted dolphins swimming this section of the coast.

Where to Stay & Eat

¢–$$ ✕ **Restaurant Maxi's.** Cooled by sea breezes and shaded by tall, stately palms, this two-story, brightly painted wooden building offers weary travelers cold beer, potent cocktails, and great seafood at unbeatable prices after a day's hike in the refuge. Locals and expatriates alike—and even chefs from Puerto Viejo's fancier restaurants—come here for their lobster fix, and the fresh fish is wonderful, too. Locals tend to congregate in the rowdy but pleasant downstairs bar, where reggae beats into the wee hours. ⊠ *Main road, Manzanillo* ☎ *759–0673* ▭ *No credit cards.*

$$ ▥ **Almonds & Corals Tent Lodge Camp.** Buried in a dark, densely atmospheric beachfront jungle within the Gandoca-Manzanillo Wildlife Refuge, Almonds & Corals takes tent camping to a new level. The "campsites" are freestanding platforms raised on stilts and linked by boardwalks lit by kerosene lamps. Each safari-style tent is protected by a peaked roof, enclosed in mosquito netting, and has beds, electric lamps, hammocks, and hot water. A fine three-meal restaurant is tucked into the greenery halfway down to the property's exquisite, secluded beach. Your wake-up call is provided by howler monkeys and gossiping parrots. ⊠ *Near end of road to Manzanillo* ☎ *759–0656 or 272–2024* 🖷 *272–2220* ⊕ *www.almondsandcorals.com* ✉ *Apdo. 681–2300, San José* ⇝ *24 tent cabins* ⚴ *Restaurant, fans, hot tub, beach, snorkeling, laundry service, airport shuttle (fee); no a/c, no room phones, no room TVs* ▭ *AE, MC, V.*

¢ ▥ **Cabinas Something Different.** On a quiet street, these shiny, spic-and-span motel-style cabinas are the nicest option in the village of Manzanillo. Each bright tile-floor unit comes with TV—quite a rarity in these parts—a table, and small porch and sleeps up to four people. ⊠ *180 m (200 yards) south of Aquamor Manzanillo* ☎🖷 *759–0614* ⇝ *10 cabins* ⚴ *Fans, refrigerator; no a/c in some rooms, no room phones* ▭ *AE, MC, V.*

off the beaten path

Hitoy Cerere National Park. The remote, 90-square-km (56-square-mi) Reserva Biológica Hitoy Cerere occupies the head of Valle de la Estrella (Star Valley). The park's limited infrastructure was badly damaged by the 1991 quake, since the epicenter was precisely here. Paths that do exist are very much overgrown due to limited use—travelers scarcely come here. Jaguars, tapirs, peccaries, porcupines, anteaters, and armadillos all carry on, however, along with more than 115 species of birds. Watch for the Common Basilisk Lizard, also called the Jesus Christ Lizard because it walks on water. The moss-flanked rivers have clear bathing pools and spectacular waterfalls. Check with the park service in San José if you want to stay overnight. ⊠ *Catch a bus in Limón for Valle de la Estrella and get off at Finca Seis; then rent a four-wheel-drive vehicle; you can drive to within 1 km (½ mi) of the reserve* ☎ *283–8004.*

THE ATLANTIC LOWLANDS & CARIBBEAN COAST A TO Z

To research prices, get advice from other travelers, and book travel arrangements, visit www.fodors.com

AIR TRAVEL

You can fly from San José to the airstrip in either Tortuguero (TTQ) or Barra del Colorado (BCL). Though Limón has an airport, no airline flies here on a regular basis.

CARRIERS NatureAir flies from San José to Tortuguero daily at 6:15 AM and to Barra del Colorado daily at 6:15 AM. SANSA flies to Barra del Colorado daily at 6 AM with connections to Tortuguero.

🚩 **Airlines & Contacts NatureAir** ✉ Aeropuerto Internacional Tobías Bolaños, Pavas, San José ☎ 220-3054 🖷 220-0413. **SANSA** ✉ C. 42 at Avda. 3, San José ☎ 296-0909 🖷 255-2176.

BIKE TRAVEL

Bicycles are a popular means of utilitarian transport in Puerto Viejo de Talamanca and Cahuita. Seemingly everyone rents basic touring bikes for $4–$8 per day, but quality varies widely. Count on Cabinas Grant and Caribbean Flavor for decent equipment.

🚩 **Bike Rentals Cabinas Grant** ✉ Puerto Viejo de Talamanca ☎ 750-0292. **Caribbean Flavor** ✉ Cahuita ☎ 755-0017.

BOAT & FERRY TRAVEL

From Puerto Viejo de Sarapiquí, boats ply the old route up the Río Sarapiquí to the Río San Juan on the Nicaraguan border. From here you can travel downstream to Barra del Colorado or Tortuguero, but departure times vary—contact Gavilán Sarapiquí River Lodge or negotiate your own deal dockside. Passports are a must: the San Juan forms the boundary between the two countries, but Nicaragua has sovereignty over the river. Many private operators can take you from the docks at Moín, just outside of Limón, up the canals to Tortuguero, but there is no scheduled public transportation. Show up to the docks early and expect to pay around $100 round-trip for up to four people. Modesto Watson, an eagle-eyed Miskito Indian guide, will take you upstream if he has room on his boat. You can also hire boats to travel between Tortuguero and Barra del Colorado, but prices are quite high.

🚩 **Gavilán Sarapiquí River Lodge** ✉ 1 km (½ mi) southeast of Comando Atlántico [naval command] ☎ 766-6743 🖷 253-6556 🌐 www.gavilanlodge.com. **Fran and Modesto Watson** 🖷🖷 226-0986 🌐 www.tortuguerocanals.com.

BUS TRAVEL

If you prefer a more private form of travel, consider taking a shuttle.

Empresarios Guapileños buses from San José to Guápiles can drop you off in Braulio Carrillo National Park or at the Rain Forest Aerial Tram, a one-hour trip; they leave every half hour between 5 AM and 9 PM daily from the Gran Terminal del Caribe on C. Central and Avda. 13.

Autotransportes Sarapiquí buses also go to Río Frío and Puerto Viejo de Sarapiquí (a two-hour trip, with stops at Las Horquetas and La Selva en route) via Braulio Carrillo from the Gran Terminal del Caribe on C. Central; they depart daily at 6:30, 8, 10, and 11:30 AM and 1:30, 2:30, 3:30, 4:30, and 6 PM. Buses also travel from San José to Puerto Viejo de Sarapiquí via Vara Blanca—a four-hour trip that does *not* pass through Braulio Carrillo—daily at 6:30 AM, 1, and 5:30 PM. Though beautifully scenic, the Vara Blanca route is not one to take if you're prone to motion sickness.

Autotransportes Caribeños offers daily direct service from San José to Limón, a 2½-hour trip, departing the Gran Terminal del Caribe on C. Central hourly from 5 AM to 6:30 PM. Limón's bus terminal, also called the Gran Terminal del Caribe, is at Avda. 2 and C. 8, across from the soccer stadium.

Linaco has daily service to Siquirres with a stop at the entrance to EARTH. Buses depart hourly from 9 AM to 5 PM from the Gran Terminal del Caribe. Transportes Mepe runs daily service to Cahuita and Puerto Viejo de Talamanca, about a four-hour trip, from San José's Gran Terminal del Caribe at 6 and 10 AM and 1:30 and 3:30 PM. Transportes Mepe buses depart Limón for Cahuita (1 hour), Puerto Vargas (1¼ hours), and Puerto Viejo de Talamanca (1½ hours) in front of Radio Casino daily at 5, 8, and 10 AM and 1, 4, and 6 PM.

As an alternative to public buses, Fantasy Bus has a shuttle service that stops in Cahuita on its daily service between San José and Puerto Viejo de Talamanca. The comfortable, air-conditioned vans leave San José from many hotels at 7 AM and return at noon. Reserve tickets ($21) a day in advance.

🚌 Bus Information **Autotransportes Caribeños** ☎ 221-2596. **Autotransportes Sarapiquí** ☎ 257-6859. **Empresarios Guapileños** ☎ 222-0610. **Linaco** ☎ 222-0610. **Transportes Mepe** ☎ 257-8129.

🚌 Shuttle Van Information **Fantasy Bus** ☎ 232-3681.

CAR TRAVEL

There are no rental agencies in the area. Rent in San José.

The Carretera Braulio Carrillo (Braulio Carrillo Highway) runs from C. 3 in San José and passes the Zurquí and Quebrada González sectors of Braulio Carrillo National Park. It branches at Santa Clara, north of the park, with the paved Highway 4 continuing north to Puerto Viejo de Sarapiquí. Alternatively, an older winding road connects San José with Puerto Viejo de Sarapiquí, passing through Heredia and Vara Blanca. The roads in the Sarapiquí part of the Atlantic lowlands are mostly paved, with the usual rained-out dirt and rock sections; road quality depends on the time of year, the length of time since the last visit by a road crew, and/or the amount of rain dumped by the latest tropical storm.

The paved two-lane Guápiles Highway continues from Santa Clara southeast to Guápiles, EARTH, and Limón, a total distance from San José to the coast of about 160 km (100 mi).

You cannot drive to Tortuguero or Barra del Colorado. To get there, you must fly or take a boat. South of Limón, a paved road, badly potholed in sections, covers the roughly 40 km (25 mi) to Cahuita, then passes the Cahuita turnoff and proceeds for roughly 16 km (10 mi) toward Puerto Viejo de Talamanca. It is paved as far as Punta Uva (and, until paving is completed, navigable as far as Manzanillo in the dry season). Four-wheel drive is always preferable, but the major roads in this region are generally passable by any car. Just watch for potholes and unpaved sections—they can appear on any road at any time, without marking or warning.

Several gas stations flank the highway between Guápiles and Limón, and just outside Puerto Viejo de Sarapiquí. South of Limón, you'll find just one, north of Cahuita. Fill the tank when you get the chance.

EMERGENCIES

In an emergency, dial 911, or one of the numbers below.

🆘 Emergency Services Ambulance ☏ 128. **Fire** ☏ 118. **Police** ☏ 911. **Traffic Police** ☏ 227-8030.

🆘 Hospitals Hospital de Guápiles ✉ 90 m (100 yards) south of fire station Guápiles ☏ 710-6801 **Hospital Dr. Tony Facio** ✉ highway to Portete Limón ☏ 758-2222.

TAXIS

Official red taxis ply the streets in Limón, Guápiles, and Puerto Viejo de Sarapiquí or hang out at designated taxi stands. Elsewhere, taxi service is much less official, with private individuals providing rides. To be on the safe side, ask your hotel or restaurant to call one for you.

TOURS

Tortuguero tours are usually packaged with one- or two-night stays in local lodges. Grupo Papagayo offers three-day, two-night tours, including bus and boat transport from San José to the Jungle Lodge in Tortuguero, for about $240. Mawamba leads a slightly more expensive version of the same tour, with nights at the Mawamba Lodge. Costa Rica Expeditions flies you straight to its rustically charming Tortuga Lodge for three days and two nights, for about $380 a head. Ecole Travel offers a less expensive $95 excursion beginning and ending at the Moín docks and offering lodging at El Manatí, meals not included. Fran and Modesto Watson are experts on the history and ecology of the area; among other tours, they offer a two-day tour on their *Riverboat Francesca,* with the overnight at a nature lodge. The cost is about $190 per person, including meals and transfers. The Watsons can put together made-to-order packages for fishing as well.

ATEC conducts such special-interest tours as "Sustainable Logging," "Yorkin Indigenous Tour," and assorted bird-watching, turtle-watching, indigenous culture, and ecologically oriented excursions on the southern coast. Terraventuras leads you around Tortuguero and Gandoca-Manzanillo Wildlife Refuge as well as renting the best-quality surfboards, bicycles, Boogie boards, and snorkeling gear.

The excellent Horizontes specializes in more independent tours with as few as eight people, including transport by four-wheel-drive vehicle, naturalist guides, and guest lectures. The Caribbean Conservation Corporation can also recommend good local guides. Costa Rica Expeditions and Ríos Tropicales lead tours on the Sarapiquí River.

🆘 Tour Operator Recommendations ATEC ✉ across from Soda Tamara, Puerto Viejo de Talamanca ☏ 750-0191 ⊕ www.greencoast.com/atec.htm. **Caribbean Conservation Corporation** ☏ 710-0547 in Tortuguero; 224-9215 in San José ⊕ www.cccturtle. org. **Costa Rica Expeditions** ✉ C. Central and Avda. 3, Barrio Amón, San José ☏ 222-0333 ⎗ 257-1665 ⊕ www.costaricaexpeditions.com. **Ecole Travel** ✉ C. 7 and Avdas. Central and 1, San José ☏ 223-2240 ⎗ 223-4128. **Fran and Modesto Watson** ☏☏ 226-0986 ⊕ www.tortuguerocanals.com. **Grupo Papagayo** ✉ Paseo Colón and C. 38, Paseo Colón, San José ☏ 233-0133. **Horizontes** ✉ 450 ft north of Pizza Hut, Paseo Colón, San José ☏ 222-2022. **Mawamba** ☏ 710-7280 in Tortuguero; 223-2421 in San José. **Ríos Tropicales** ☏ 233-6455 ⊕ www.riostropicales.com. **Terraventuras** ✉ next to Manuel León Puerto Viejo de Talamanca ☏ 750-0426.

VISITOR INFORMATION

The tourist office in San José has information on the Atlantic lowlands. The ATEC office in Puerto Viejo de Talamanca is a great source of information on local tours, guides, and interesting activities.

🆘 Tourist Information ATEC ✉ across from Soda Tamara, Puerto Viejo de Talamanca ☏ 750-0191 ⊕ www.greencoast.com/atec.htm. **Instituto Costarricense de Turismo (ICT)** ✉ C. 5 between Avdas. Central and 2, Barrio La Catedral, San José ☏ 222-1090.

UNDERSTANDING
COSTA RICA

A BIOLOGICAL SUPERPOWER

COSTA RICA MAY LACK OIL FIELDS and coal deposits, but it's not without natural assets. The country's ecological wealth includes fertile volcanic soil, sun-swathed beaches, hundreds of colorful bird species, and massive trees whose branches support elevated gardens of orchids and bromeliads—the kind of priceless commodities that economists have long ignored. Investment bankers may wonder how this tiny nation ended up with so pretentious a name as "Rich Coast," but many a biologist, Bri Bri Indian, and binocular-toting traveler understands where the republic's wealth lies hidden.

Costa Rica's forests hold an array of flora and fauna so vast and diverse that scientists haven't even named some of the plant and insect species found here; and of the species that have been identified, few have been thoroughly studied. These forests are among the most diverse and productive ecosystems in the world—although tropical forests cover a mere 7% of the earth's surface area, they hold more than half the planet's plant and animal species—and few countries offer better exposure to tropical nature than Costa Rica.

About half the size of the U.S. state of Kentucky, Costa Rica covers less than .03% of the earth's surface, yet it contains nearly 5% of the planet's plant and animal species. The variety of native flora and fauna is astonishing: Costa Rica contains at least 9,000 plant species, including more than 1,200 types of orchids, some 2,000 kinds of butterflies, and more than 870 bird species (more than are found in the United States and Canada combined). But such numbers don't begin to convey the awe you feel when you stare up the convoluted trunk of a centennial strangler fig, listen to the roar of a howler monkey reverberate through the jungle, or watch a delicate hummingbird drink nectar from a multicolored heliconia flower.

Many of Costa Rica's plants and animals are beautiful, others are bizarre, and the ecological web that ties them all together is both complex and fascinating. It may be hard to recognize the richness of a Costa Rican forest at first glance—the overwhelming verdure of the rain forest can give the false impression of uniformity—but if you spend some time exploring one with a qualified nature guide, you come to understand why scientists have dubbed Costa Rica a "biological superpower."

Costa Rica's biological diversity is the result of its tropical location (on a slip of land connecting North and South America), its varied topography, and the many microclimates resulting from the combination of mountains, valleys, and lowlands. But to understand why Costa Rica is so biologically important today, we need to look back to prehistoric times, to a world that human eyes never saw but that scientists have at least partially reconstructed.

Just a Few Dozen Millennia Ago

In geological terms, Costa Rica is relatively young, which explains why there are precious few valuable minerals beneath its soil. Five million years ago, this patch of land didn't even exist: North and South America were separated by a canal the likes of which Teddy Roosevelt—father of the Panama Canal—couldn't have conjured up in his wildest dreams. In the area now occupied by Panama and Costa Rica, the waters of the Pacific and Atlantic oceans flowed freely together. Geologists have named that former canal the Straits of Bolívar, after the Venezuelan revolutionary who wrested much of South America from Spain.

Far beneath the Straits of Bolívar, the incremental movement of tectonic plates slowly created the Central American isthmus. Geologists speculate that a chain of volcanic islands appeared in the gap around 30 million years ago; a combination of volcanic activity and plate movement caused the islands to grow and rise from the water, eventually forming a connected ridge. The land bridge was completed around 3 million years ago, closing the interoceanic canal and connecting North and South America for the first time.

Because several tectonic plates meet beneath Central America, the region has long been geologically unstable, experiencing occasional earthquakes, frequent tremors, and regular volcanic eruptions. While it seems a curse to be hit by one of these natural disasters, there actually wouldn't be a Costa Rica were it not for such frightening phenomena. What is now the country's best soil was once spewed from the bowels of the volcanoes that dominate its landscape, and the jarring adjustments of adjacent tectonic plates actually pushed most of today's Costa Rica up out of the sea.

The intercontinental connection completed 3 million years ago had profound biological consequences: it separated the marine life of the Pacific and Atlantic oceans, and it created a pathway for interchange for the flora and fauna of North and South America. Though hardly the kind of lapse that excites a geologist, three million years is a long time by biological standards, and the region's plants and animals have changed considerably since the inter-American gap was spanned. Whereas evolution took different paths in the waters that flank the isthmus, organisms that had evolved on separate continents were able to make their way into the opposite hemisphere, and the resulting interaction determined what lives in the Americas today.

Mind-Boggling Biodiversity

Costa Rica's abundant natural diversity is in many ways the result of the intercontinental exchange, but the country's flora and fauna actually add up to more than what has passed between the continents. Although it is a biological corridor, the isthmus also acts as a filter, a hospitable haven to many species that couldn't complete the journey from one hemisphere to the other. The rain forests of Costa Rica's Atlantic and southwestern lowlands, for example, are the most northerly home of such southern species as the Crab-eating Raccoon and a dreaded jungle pit viper known as the Bushmaster. The tropical dry forests of the northern Pacific slope, on the other hand, are the southern limit for such North American species as the White-throated Magpie-Jay and the Virginia Opossum. In addition to species whose range extends only as far as Costa Rica in one direction, and those whose range extends into both North and South America, such as the White-tailed Deer and the Gray Hawk, Costa Rica's many physical barriers and microclimates have fostered the development of indigenous plants and animals, such as the Mangrove Hummingbird and Mountain Salamander.

What all this biological babble means to travelers is that they might spot a North American Pale-billed Woodpecker and a howler monkey (of South American descent) in the branches of a Rain Tree, which is native to Central America. And then there are the tourists—migrants, that is—such as the dozens of northern bird species that spend their winter holidays in Costa Rica, among them the Tennessee Warbler, Western Tanager, and Yellow-bellied Sapsucker. In addition to recognizing some of the birds that migrate here, you'll no doubt be at home with some of the plants, such as the philodendrons and impatiens that grow wild in the country, but cost a pretty penny in the garden shop back home. Costa Rica does have plenty of oak trees, squirrels, and sparrows, but most of its flora and fauna look decidedly tropical. Not only are such common plants as orchids, palms, and ficuses unmistakably tropical, but many of the resident animals are distinctly neotropical—found only in the American tropics—including sloths, iguanas, toucans, and monkeys with prehensile tails.

The wildlife is spread through an array of ecosystems, which biologists have divided into a dozen "life zones," but which actually consist of a biological continuum almost too multifarious for classification. Though the existence of specific flora and fauna in any given life zone is determined by various physical conditions, the two most important are altitude and rainfall. Average temperatures in the tropics change very little from month to month, though the temperature does change a good bit during the course of a day, especially in the mountains. The Costa Rican highlands are consistently cooler than the lowlands, which means you can spend a morning sweating in a sultry coastal forest, then drive a few hours into the mountains and find yourself needing a warm jacket.

In more temperate parts of the world, cold weather hits the mountaintops a month or two before the lowlands, but old man winter eventually gets his icy grip on everything. In the tropics, however, only the tops of the highest mountains freeze, so the very highest-altitude flora tends to look completely different from that of even nearby valleys. Altitude also plays a substantial role in regulating humidity, since clouds accumulate around mountains and volcanoes, providing regular precipitation as well as shade, which in turn slows evaporation. These conditions lead to the formation of luxuriant cloud forests on the upper slopes of many mountains. In general, the higher you climb, the more lush the vegetation, except for the peaks of the highest mountains, which often protrude from the cloud cover and are thus fairly arid.

While you may associate the tropics with rain, precipitation in Costa Rica varies considerably depending on where you are and when you're there. This is a result of the mountainous terrain and regional weather patterns. A phenomenon called rain shadow—when one side of a mountain range receives much more rain than the other—plays an important ecological role in Costa Rica. Four mountain ranges combine to create an intercontinental divide that separates the country into Atlantic and Pacific slopes; and thanks to the trade winds, the Atlantic slope receives much more rain than the Pacific. The trade winds steadily pump moisture-laden clouds southwest over the isthmus, where they encounter warm air or mountains, which make them rise. As the clouds rise, they cool, lose their ability to hold moisture, and eventually dump most of their liquid luggage on the Caribbean side.

During the rainy season—mid-May to December—the role of the trade winds is diminished, as regular storms roll off the Pacific Ocean and soak the western side of the isthmus. Though it rains all over Costa Rica during these months, it often rains more on the Pacific side of the mountains than on the Atlantic. Come December, the trade winds take over again, and hardly a drop falls on the western side until May. The dry season is most intense in northwestern Costa Rica (the province of Guanacaste), where most trees drop their foliage and the forests take on a desert visage. That region quickly regains its verdure once the rains return in May, marking the beginning of a springlike season that Costa Ricans nonetheless refer to as *el invierno* (winter).

Climate variation within the country results in a mosaic of forests, from those that receive only a few feet of rain each year to those that soak up several yards of precipitation annually. The combination of humidity and temperature helps determine what grows where; but while some species have very restricted ranges, others seem to thrive just about anywhere. Plants such as strangler figs and bromeliads grow all over Costa Rica, and animals such as the Collared Peccary and coati—a long-nosed cousin of the raccoon—can pretty much live wherever human beings let them. Other species have extremely limited ranges, such as the Mangrove Hummingbird, restricted to the mangrove forests of the Pacific coast, and the Volcano Junco, a gray sparrow that lives only around the highest peaks of the Cordillera de Talamanca.

It's a Jungle Out There

Costa Rica's incredible natural spectrum is part of what makes it such an invigorating vacation spot, but the landscape that travelers most want to see is the tropical rain forest. The protected areas of the Atlantic and southern Pacific lowlands hold tracts of virgin rain forest where massive tropical trees tower more than 33 m (100 ft) over the forest floor. The thick branches of these jungle giants are covered with an abundance of epiphytes (plants that grow on other plants but are not parasites) such as ferns, orchids, bromeliads, mosses, vines, and aroids. Most of the rain forest's foliage and fauna is clustered in the arboreal garden of the canopy.

Although life flourishes in the canopy, the intense sunlight that quickly dries the treetops after downpours results in a recurrent water shortage. Consequently, plants that live up here have developed ways to cope with aridity: many orchids have thick leaves that resist evaporation and spongy roots that can quickly soak up large amounts of water when it rains. Tank bromeliads have a funnel shape that enables them to collect and hold water at the center of their leaves. Acting as miniature oases, these plants attract arboreal animals to drink from, hunt at, or—in the case of certain insect larvae and tree-frog tadpoles—live in their pools. In exchange for vital water, the waste and carcasses of these animals give the plants valuable nutrients, which are also scarce in the canopy.

The fact that so many animals spend so much of their time in the canopy can be frustrating for people who come to the rain forest in to see wildlife. But by peering through binoculars, you might glimpse the furry figure of a sloth, or the brilliant regalia of a scarlet macaw; and it's hard to miss the arboreal acrobatics of monkeys, who leap from tree to tree, hang from branches, and generally make spectacles of themselves. For a closer look at the canopy, you may want to take a ride on the Rain Forest Aerial Tram, near the Guápiles Highway, stroll down Monteverde's Sky Walk, or linger on a tree platform at Hacienda Barú, in Dominical, or at the Corcovado Lodge Tent Camp. For an adrenaline-pumping introduction to treetop ecology, you can take one of the canopy tours offered in various parts of the country, but don't expect to see much wildlife as you zip from tree to tree along steel cables.

Because little sunlight reaches the ground in a virgin rain forest, the jungle floor is a dim, quiet place, with not nearly as much undergrowth as in those old Tarzan movies. Still, an array of plants, from ferns to palm trees, have adapted to this shady world. The light level inside a rain forest is comparable to that of the average North American living room, or shopping mall, which is why some of the plant species that grow there have become popular houseplants up north. But the vegetation is not sparse everywhere: whenever an old tree falls, it creates a gap in the canopy, which leads to a riot of growth on the ground, as plants compete for the newfound sunlight.

Few travelers are disappointed by Costa Rica's forests, but some are discouraged by the difficulty of spotting animals. Hikers occasionally encounter such earthbound creatures as the coati or the agouti, a terrier-size rodent that resembles a giant guinea pig, and in most areas you're likely to see iridescent Blue Morpho butterflies, hyperactive hummingbirds, brightly colored poison dart frogs, and tiny lizards standing guard on tree trunks. Most forest critters, however, spend much of their time and energy trying *not* to be seen, and the foliage aids them in that endeavor. An untrained eye can miss the details, which is why a naturalist guide is invaluable: in addition to spotting and identifying plants

and animals, a good guide can explain some of relationships that weave them together in one of the planet's most complex ecosystems.

The rain forest is characterized by intense predation. Its inhabitants dedicate most of their resources to the essential tasks of finding their next meal and avoiding *becoming* a meal in the process. Whereas animals must often hide or flee when in danger, plants have developed such survival tactics as thorns, prickly hairs, and toxic substances that make their leaves unappetizing. Because of the relative toxicity of most rain-forest foliage, many insects eat only a small portion of a leaf before moving on to another plant, so as not to ingest a lethal dose of any one poison. You can see the results of this practice by looking up into the canopy—almost every leaf is full of little holes.

Camouflage is another popular animal defense. The tropical rain forest is full of insects that have evolved to resemble the leaves, bark, moss, and leaf litter around them. Some bugs have adopted the colors of certain flowers, or even the mold that grows on plants. Though they can be a chore to spot, those camouflaged critters are quite intriguing.

Some creatures go to the opposite extreme and advertise themselves with bright colors. Some hues are meant to help find a mate amid the mesh of green; others serve as a warning to potential predators. Some species of caterpillar, for example, are not only immune to the toxins of the plant on which they live, but they actually sequester that poison within their bodies, making themselves toxic as well. Native tribes have used the toxic secretions from aptly named poison dart frogs to poison the tips of their arrows and blowgun darts. These frogs' typical warning pattern mixes bright colors with black or dark blue, a coloration that conveys a simple message to predators: eat me and die.

As with any successful strategy, there are bound to be copycats. "Mimics" have warning coloration, but lack the poison to follow through with the threat—certain edible caterpillars look like venomous ones, and some harmless serpents have markings similar to those of the deadly coral snake. Such acts of deception often reach amazing levels of intrigue. The cocoons of certain butterflies not only resemble the head of a viper, but if disturbed, they begin to move back and forth just as a snake's head would. One large butterfly has spots on its wings that look like eyes, so that when it opens them it resembles an owl, whereas another butterfly species looks exactly like a wasp.

In addition to avoiding predators, plants and animals must compete with other species that have similar niches—the biological equivalents of jobs. This competition fosters cooperation between noncompetitive organisms. Plants need to get their pollen and seeds distributed as far as possible, and every animal requires a steady food supply, which brings us to everyone's favorite subject: the birds and the bees.

Although butterflies and bees do most of the pollinating up north, tropical plants are pollinated by everything from fruit flies and hummingbirds to beetles and bats. The flowers of such plants are often designed so that their nectar is readily available to pollinators but protected from freeloaders. The beautiful hibiscus flower is designed to dust a hummingbird's forehead with pollen and collect any pollen that's already there while the tiny bird drinks the nectar hidden deep in its base; the flower is too long for a butterfly, and the nectar is held too deep for a bee to reach. No system is perfect, though: you may see a Bananaquit—a tiny bird with a short beak—biting holes in the bases of a hibiscus flower in an effort to drink its nectar without getting anywhere near its pollen.

Intense competition for limited resources keeps the rain forest's trees growing taller, roots reaching farther, and everything mobile working on a way to get more for less. The battle for light sends most of the foliage sky high, and the battle for nutrients speeds to a breakneck pace the process of decay and recycling that follows every death in the forest. One result of this high-speed decomposition is that most of the nutrients in a rain forest are present in living things, while the soil beneath them retains few essential elements. Rain-forest soils consequently tend to be nutrient-poor, less than ideal for farming.

A Mosaic of Ecosystems

Though the rain forest is most iconic, Costa Rica has other types of forests that are equally rich in life and well worth exploring. The tropical dry forests of the northwestern lowlands are similar to rain forests during the rainy season, but once the daily deluges subside, the dry forest changes profoundly: most trees lose their leaves, and some burst simultaneously into full, colorful flower. The yellow-blossom buttercup tree and the pink tabebuia, among others, brighten up the arid northwestern landscape in the dry season. The dry forest contains many of the plants, animals, and exclusive relationships found in the rain forest, but it's also home to species often associated with the forests and deserts of Mexico and the southwestern United States, such as cacti, coyotes, and diamondback rattlesnakes. Because dry forests are less dense than rain forests, it can be easier to see animals in them; this is especially true in the dry season, when foliage is sparse and animals often congregate around scarce water sources and trees with fruit or flowers.

The cloud forests on the upper reaches of many Costa Rican mountains and volcanoes are even more luxuriant than rain forests, so deeply lush that it can be hard to find the bark on a cloud-forest tree for all the growth on its trunk and branches. Plants grow on plants that are growing on other plants: vines, orchids, ferns, aroids, and bromeliads are everywhere, and mosses and liverworts often cover the vines and leaves of other epiphytes. Because of the steep terrain, a cloud forest's trees grow on slightly different levels, and the canopy is less continuous than that of a lowland rain forest. Because more light reaches the ground, there is plenty of undergrowth, including prehistoric-looking tree ferns, a wealth of flowering plants, and "poor man's umbrellas"—made up of a few giant leaves.

Cloud forests are home to a multitude of animals, ranging from delicate glass frogs, whose undersides are so transparent that you can see many of their internal organs, to the Resplendent Quetzal, a bird considered sacred by the ancient Maya. The male quetzal has a crimson belly and iridescent green back, wings, and tail feathers that can grow longer than two feet in length. Those tail feathers float behind the quetzal when it flies, a splendid sight that no doubt inspired its ancient name, "the plumed serpent." Although the tangle of foliage and almost constant mist make it hard to see cloud-forest wildlife, you should still catch glimpses of such colorful birds as the Emerald Toucanet, Collared Redstart, and various species of hummingbird.

Humidity protects the cloud-forest canopy from the water shortages that often plague the upper reaches of lowland rain forests. In fact, the cloud forest's canopy is often soaking wet. During much of the year, a moisture-laden mist moves through the cloud forest, depositing condensation on the plants; this condensation causes a sort of secondary precipitation, with droplets forming on the epiphytic foliage and falling regularly from the branches to the forest floor. Cloud forests thus function like giant sponges, soaking up humidity from the clouds and sending it slowly downhill to feed the streams and rivers on which many regions and communities depend for water.

On top of high ridges, and near the summits of volcanoes, the cloud forest is transformed by strong, steady winds that topple tall trees and regularly break off branches. The resulting collection of small, twisted trees and bushes is known as an elfin forest. On the upper slopes of the Cordillera de Talamanca, Costa Rica's highest range, the cloud forest gives way to the *páramo*, a high-altitude ecosystem composed of shrubs, grasses, and hardy herbs. Most of these plants are common in the heights of South America's Andes; the Costa Rican páramo defines their most northerly distribution.

On the other extreme, along both coasts, are river mouths and estuaries with extensive mangrove forests. These primeval-looking, often flooded profusions grow in tidal zones all over the tropics. Many of the trees in mangrove forests grow on "stilt" roots, which prop their leaves up out of the saltwater and help them absorb carbon dioxide when the tide is high. The roots also lend protection to various small fish and crustaceans and are often covered with barnacles, mussels, and other shellfish.

Mangrove forests are fairly homogeneous, with stands of one species of tree stretching off as far as the eye can see. They are also extremely productive ecosystems that play an important role as estuaries: many marine animals, such as shrimp, spend the early stages of their lives in mangrove estuaries; other animals spend their entire lives there. Vital to the health of the ocean beyond them, mangroves are attractive sites for animals that feed on marine life, especially fish-eating birds like cormorants, herons, pelicans, and ospreys.

The forests that line the Caribbean canals, along Costa Rica's northeastern coast, are dominated by the water-resistant *jolillo* palm or *palma real*. This area is home to many of the same animals found in the rain forest monkeys, parrots, iguanas—as well as river dwellers such as turtles, crocodiles, and anhingas. A boat trip up the canals is thus a great opportunity to observe wildlife, as are similar excursions on jungle rivers such as the Río Frío and the Río Sarapiquí. Seasonal *lagunas* such as Caño Negro and the swamps of Palo Verde National Park, which disappear during the dry months, are excellent places to see birds when they have water.

In addition to its varied forests, Costa Rica has 1,224 km (760 mi) of coastline, which consists of beaches separated by rocky points. The points are home to a variety of marine life, but even more remarkable, many of the country's beaches are important nesting spots for endangered sea turtles. And submerged in the sea off both coasts are various reefs—some rocky, some covered with coral—that are home to hundreds of species of colorful fish, crustaceans, and other invertebrates. With their vertiginous biological variety, the coral reefs off the southern Caribbean coast could well be the marine equivalent of the rain forest.

Where Have All the Forests Gone?

All this natural diversity notwithstanding, as you travel through Costa Rica, you see that its predominant landscapes are not cloud and rain forests but the coffee and banana plantations that have replaced them. The country's pre-Columbian cultures may have revered the jaguar and the Harpy Eagle, but today's inhabitants are largely less-illustrious beasts: the cows and the Cattle Egrets that populate countless acres of pasture.

In the last half century, more than two-thirds of Costa Rica's original forests have been destroyed. Forests have traditionally been considered unproductive land, and their destruction was for a long time synonymous with development. In the 1970s and 1980s, international and domestic development policies fueled the destruction of large tracts of wilderness. Fortunately, Costa Rican conservationists grew alarmed by this deforestation, and in the 1970s they began creating what has since grown to become the best national park system in the region.

In addition to protecting vast natural expanses that make up nearly a quarter of Costa Rica's national territory, the Costa Rican government has made progress in curbing deforestation outside the national parks. The rate of destruction has dropped significantly, but poaching and illegal logging continue to be problems that, if left uncorrected, could eventually wipe out entire species or wilderness areas.

Deforestation not only spells disaster for the jaguar and the eagle, but it can have grave consequences for human beings. Forests absorb rain and release water slowly, playing an important role in regulating the flow of rivers—which is why severely deforested regions often suffer floods during the rainy season and drought during the dry months. Tree covers also prevent topsoil erosion, thus keeping the land fertile and productive; in many parts of the country, erosion has left once-productive farmland almost worthless. Finally, hidden within Costa Rica's endless living species are countless unknown or understudied substances that might eventually be extracted to cure diseases. The destruction of this country's forests is a loss for the entire world.

Travel Responsibly and Save a Few Trees

With each passing year, more and more Costa Ricans are coming to realize how valuable and imperiled their remaining wilderness is. Costa Ricans visit their national parks in significant numbers, and they consider those protected areas vital to the national economy, both for the natural resources they preserve and for their commercial role as tourist attractions. Local conservationists, however, are still a long way from achieving their goal of involving communities in the protection of the parks around them.

Costa Ricans who cut trees and hunt endangered animals usually do so out of economic necessity, and alas, the people who live near protected areas are often the last to benefit from the tourism that wilderness attracts. When you visit a park or reserve, your entrance fee helps pay for the preservation of Costa Rica's wildlife; but you can also make your visit beneficial to the people living nearby by hiring local guides, horses, or boats; eating in local restaurants; and buying things (other than wild-animal products, of course) in local shops.

You can go a few steps further by making donations to local conservation groups or to such international organizations as Conservation International, the Rainforest Alliance, the Nature Conservancy, and WWF, all of which support important conservation efforts in Costa Rica. It's also helpful to stray from the beaten path: explore private preserves, and stay at lodges that contribute to environmental efforts and to nearby communities. By planning your visit with an eye toward grassroots conservation efforts, you join the global effort to save the earth's tropical ecosystems and help ensure that the treasures you traveled so far to see remain intact for future generations.

David Dudenhoefer

A BRIEF HISTORY

First Encounters

In mid-September 1502, on his fourth and last voyage to the New World, Christopher Columbus was sailing along the Caribbean coast of Central America when his ships were caught in a violent tropical storm. Seeking shelter, he found sanctuary in a bay protected by a small island; ashore, he encountered native people wearing heavy gold disks and gold bird-shape figures who spoke of great amounts of gold in the area. Sailing farther south, Columbus encountered more natives, also wearing pendants and jewelry fashioned in gold. He was convinced that he had discovered a land of great wealth to be claimed for the Spanish empire. The land itself was a vision of lush greenery; popular legend has it that, on the basis of what he saw and encountered, Columbus named the land Costa Rica, the rich coast.

The Spanish Colonial Era

The first Spaniard to attempt conquest of Costa Rica was Diego de Nicuesa in 1506. But his sick and starving troops were not able to surmount the resistance of the indigenous population and the Spanish were unsuccessful. Similar hardships were encountered by other Spaniards who visited the region. The first "successful" expedition to the country was made by Gil González de Ávila in 1522. Exploring the Pacific coast, he converted more than 6,000 people of the Chorotega tribe to Catholicism. A year later he returned to his home port in Panama with the equivalent of $600,000 in gold, but more than 1,000 of his men had died on the exhausting journey. Of course, just as many native peoples, if not more, died due to disease and skirmishes with the Europeans. Many other Spanish expeditions were undertaken, and, fortunately for the people indigenous to the area, all were less than successful at colonization, often because of rivalries between various expeditions. By 1560, almost 60 years after its discovery, no permanent Spanish settlement existed in Costa Rica (this name was then in general use, although it incorporated an area far larger than its present-day boundaries), and the indigenous peoples had not been subdued.

Costa Rica remained the smallest and poorest of Spain's Central American colonies, producing little wealth for the empire. Unlike other countries around it, Costa Rica tended to be largely ignored in terms of conquest and instead began to receive a wholly different type of settler—hardy, self-sufficient individuals who had to work to maintain themselves. Costa Ricans, both settlers and native peoples, endured the difficult living conditions of an agriculture-based existence in exchange for Spain's lack of interest. The population stayed at fewer than 20,000 for centuries (even with considerable growth in the 18th century) and was mainly confined to small, isolated farms in the highland Central Valley and the Pacific lowlands.

By the end of the 18th century, however, Costa Rica began to emerge from isolation. Some trade with neighboring Spanish colonies was carried out—in spite of constant harassment by English pirates, both at sea and on land—and the population had begun to expand across the Central Valley.

Seeds of political discord, which were soon to affect the colony, had been planted in Spain when Napoléon defeated and removed King Charles IV in 1808 and installed his brother Joseph on the Spanish throne. Costa Rica pledged support for the old regime, even sending troops to Nicaragua in 1811 to help suppress a rebellion against Spain. By 1821, though, sentiment favoring independence from Spain was prevalent throughout Central America, and Costa Rica supported the declaration of independence issued in Guatemala on September 15 of that year. Costa Rica did not become a fully independent sovereign nation until 1836, after annexation to the Mexican empire and 14 years as part of the United Provinces of Central America. The only major threat to that sovereignty took place in 1856, when the mercenary army of U.S. adventurer William Walker invaded the country from Nicaragua, which it had conquered the year before. Walker's plan to turn the Central American nations into slave states was cut short by Costa Rican president Juan Rafael Mora, who raised a volunteer army and repelled the invaders, pursuing them into Nicaragua and joining troops from various Central American nations to defeat the mercenaries.

It was this conflict that produced national hero Juan Santamaría, a young drummer boy from a poor family who is immortalized today in a monument in the Central Valley city of Alajuela. When the Costa Ricans drove Walker's troops from their country in 1856, they chased the troops to Rivas, Nicaragua. The filibusters took refuge in a wooden fort and Juan Santamaría, with a militia from Alajuela, offered to burn it down to drive them out. Legend says that Santamaría ran toward the fort carrying a torch, and although he was shot repeatedly, he managed to throw it and to burn the fort down. His bravery wasn't recognized at the time, probably because of his modest origins, but in 1891 a statue depicting a strong and handsome soldier carrying a torch was placed in Alajuela, thus immortalizing Santamaría. For this occasion, Ruben Darío, the great Nicaraguan writer, dedicated a poem to him. April 11 is now a national holiday in Costa Rica, called Juan Santamaría Day, which celebrates the Costa Rican victory at the Battle of Rivas.

Foundations of Democracy

The 19th century saw dramatic economic and political changes in Costa Rica. For the major part of that century, the country was ruled by a succession of wealthy families whose grip was partially broken only toward the end of the century. The development of agriculture included the introduction of coffee in the 1820s and bananas in the 1870s, both of which became the country's major sources of foreign exchange. First head of state Governor Juan Mora Fernández gave away free land and coffee seeds to any farmer who agreed to cultivate the crop for export, and many citizens prospered thanks to the "grain of gold." The government spent profits from the coffee trade on improving roads and ports, and other projects that included San José's Teatro Nacional. Bananas arrived with U.S. entrepreneur Minor Keith, who the Costa Rican government hired to build a railroad. In exchange for his work, he was given a land grant on both sides of the track. Keith planted bananas, and

the crop has since displaced coffee as Costa Rica's top agricultural export.

In 1889 the first free popular election was held, characterized by full freedom of the press, frank debates by rival candidates, an honest tabulation of the vote, and the first peaceful transition of power from a ruling group to the opposition. This event provided the foundation of political stability that Costa Rica enjoys to this day. During the early 20th century each successive president fostered the growth of democratic liberties and continued to expand the free public school system, started during the presidency of Bernardo Soto in the late 1880s.

Booming exports were cut short by the arrival of World War I, followed by the Great Depression and World War II. Poverty skyrocketed and a social revolution threatened in the late 1930s, as the popular Communist Party threatened strikes and violence. Costa Rica's version of the New Deal came in 1940, when conservative president Rafael Angel Calderón Guardia—the son of aristocrats—allied with the Catholic Church and implemented many of the Communist Party's demands. This willingness to compromise led to an impressive system of socialized medicine, minimum wage laws, low-cost housing and many other laws and Constitutional reforms that protected workers.

The success of Calderón's social reforms was tainted by accusations of corruption. In 1944, Calderón left office, only to be replaced by his close associate, Teodoro Picado. Calderón and his United Social Christian Party were accused of rigging the election. Serious trouble flared when Calderón sought reelection in 1948, and lost to Otilio Ulate. Calderón refused to accept defeat and demanded a recount. Soon after, the local schoolhouse where the ballots were kept mysteriously caught fire. When Calderón's political allies in Congress appointed him president, the result was a civil uprising by outraged citizens, led by the still-revered José Figueres Ferrer, who had been exiled by Calderón. After a few months of armed conflict, a compromise was reached—Figueres and his "Army of National Liberation" would respect Calderón's social guarantees, and Figueres would preside over an interim government which would end after 18 months. In 1949, Figueres abolished Costa Rica's army and created a national police force, nationalized the banking system and public utilities, and implemented more health and education reforms. He stepped down after the 18-month period, only to be re-elected twice in free elections. Sons of both Calderón and Figueres served four year terms as president in the 1990s.

The Modern Era

Significant changes took place during the 1950s and 1960s, including greater involvement by the state in economic affairs. Insurance, telecommunications, the railroad system (now defunct), ports, and other industries were nationalized. The state-led economic model, although increasingly inefficient, led to a rising standard of living until the early 1970s, when an economic crisis introduced Costa Ricans to hyperinflation. By the mid-1980s, Costa Rica had begun pulling out of its economic slump, in part thanks to efforts to diversify the economy, which had long been dominated by coffee and bananas. Costa Rica made international headlines in 1987, when President Oscar Arias (1986–90) won the Nobel peace prize for his efforts to bring peace to other Central American countries. Arias remains a champion for peace and democracy through the Arias Foundation for Peace and Human Progress in San José. By the mid-1990s, tourism surpassed bananas as the country's largest earner of foreign exchange, and high-tech companies such as Intel, Dell Electronics, and Motorola opened plants and service centers in Costa Rica, providing relatively well-paying jobs for educated, bilingual Ticos.

Recent years have seen the continued growth of the tourism industry, and the establishment of a thriving but controversial Internet-based gambling industry tied to U.S. sporting events. Still, inflation hovers around 12% annually, the per capita income in Costa Rica is only $3,300 per year, and the country's currency continues to be devalued on a regular basis. Attempts to privatize state-owned industries have been unsuccessful, and many younger professional Ticos feel frustrated by their country's resistance to change.

Today the challenge facing Costa Rica is how to conserve its natural resources while still permitting modern development. The government has been unable or unwilling to control illegal logging, an industry that threatens to destroy the country's old-growth forests. Urban sprawl in the Central Valley and the development of megaresorts along both coasts threaten forests, wildlife, and the slow pace of life that makes Costa Rica so enjoyable for visitors. Although tourism provides a much-needed injection of foreign exchange into the economy, the government has not fully decided which direction it should take. The buzzwords now are "ecotourism" and "sustainable development," and it is hoped that Costa Rica will find it possible to continue down these roads rather than opt for something akin to the Acapulco or Cancún style of development.

MENU GUIDE

Rice and beans is the heart of Costa Rica's *comida típica* (typical food). It's possible to order everything from sushi to crêpes in Costa Rica, but most Ticos have a simple diet built around rice, beans, and the myriad fruits and vegetables that flourish here. Costa Rican food isn't spicy, and many dishes are seasoned with the same five ingredients—onion, salt, garlic, cilantro, and red bell pepper.

Two common rice-and-beans variations are *arroz con pollo* (chicken with rice) and *gallo pinto* (rice with black beans), which is often served for breakfast. One of the most important words to know is *casado,* a heaping plate of rice, beans, fried plantains, cabbage salad, tomatoes, *macarrones* (noodles), and fish, chicken, or meat—or any variation thereof. Casados are served for lunch and dinner at *sodas,* inexpensive casual restaurants.

Plentiful seafood on the coasts results in delicious *camarones* (shrimp), *langostinos* (langoustines), and a fine variety of fish—including dorado, mahimahi, and yellowfin tuna—at reasonable prices. A popular fish on Tico menus is *corvina,* a white flaky sea bass, which is usually breaded and panfried or sautéed with garlic. On the Caribbean, you can usually get your fish smothered in *caribeño* sauce, which is some combination of tomatoes, onions, and spices. Other popular dishes are ceviche, and *arroz con mariscos,* fried rice with fish, shrimp, octopus, and clams—or whatever's fresh that day.

Fresh fruit is one of Costa Rica's finest and most abundant culinary assets. Most restaurants have many flavors of *fresca natural* (fresh-squeezed juice) or *batidos* (fruit shakes made with milk or water). Common choices are mango, pineapple (*piña*), banana (*banano*), coconut (*coco*), canteloupe (*melon*), watermelon (*sandia*), strawberry (*fresca*), blackberry (*mora*), star fruit (*tiriguro*), papaya, and mango. Tart green mangoes cut into slivers and served with salt are a local favorite.

Stands along the highway have colorful displays of fruits that may be unfamiliar. *Mamones chinos* (rambutans) are red spiky balls protecting a white fruit similar to a litchi. *Guayabas* (guavas) are huge bean pods with large seeds covered in sweet pink pulp. A smaller version, *cas,* finds its way into juices and ice cream. The yellowish red, egg-size fruits are *granadillas* (passion fruit). *Anones* (sugar apples) have sweet white flesh and resemble artichokes with thick rinds. *Guanábana* (soursoup) is a large, spiky yellow fruit with white flesh and a musky taste. *Marañone* (cashew fruit), which has a meaty taste is used in juices. *Pipas,* green coconuts with sweet coconut water inside, are sold ready-to-drink at roadside stands with ends chopped off and straws stuck inside.

Savory fruits like avocado (*aguacate*) and palm heart (*palmitos*) are used in salads. *Bilimbi,* which looks like a mix between a miniature cucumber and star fruit, is ground into a savory relish to accompany rice and beans. Popular Costa Rican desserts are *flan* (a baked custard covered with caramel) and *tres leches* (three milks), a sinfully rich cake of condensed milk, evaporated milk, cream, and sugar.

Bocas are literally, "mouthfuls," and are served with drinks in the same tradition as Spanish tapas. *Empanadas* are savory or sweet pastry turnovers filled with fruit or meat and vegetables. (*Empanaditas* are small empanadas.) *Picadillo* is a uniquely Costa Rican way to prepare vegetables: water squash, potatoes, carrots, or other veggies are chopped into small cubes and combined with onions, garlic, and a small bit of ground beef for seasoning.

Costa Rica's national beverage, *café* (coffee) may come presweetened in the countryside. If you order it *con leche,* it is usually served with steamed milk. Costa Rican coffee is strong, and a few places in San José still serve it the old-fashioned way; hot milk in one pitcher and hot coffee in the other. Coffee is generally taken with bread or a sweet. Homemade tortillas accompany every traditional Costa Rican meal, and if you're lucky enough to be offered thick, warm corn tortillas made by hand, don't pass them up.

WILDLIFE GLOSSARY

Here is a rundown of some of the most common and attention-grabbing mammals, birds, reptiles, amphibians, and even a few insects that you might encounter. We give the common Costa Rican names, so you can understand the local lingo, as well as the latest scientific terms.

Agouti (*guatusa*; *Dasyprocta punctata*): A 20″ tail-less rodent with small ears and a large muzzle, the agouti is reddish-brown on the Pacific side, more of a tawny orange on the Caribbean slope. It sits on its haunches to eat large seeds and fruit.

Anteater (*oso hormiguero*): Three species of anteater inhabit Costa Rica—the Giant (*Myrmecophaga tridactyla*), Silky (*Cyclopes didactylus*), and Collared, or Vested (*Tamandua mexicana*). Only the last is commonly seen, and too often as roadkill. This medium-size anteater, 30″ long with an 18″ tail, laps up ants and termites with its long, sticky tongue and has long, sharp claws for ripping into insect nests.

Armadillo (*cusuco*; *Dasypus novemcinctus*): Widespread in Costa Rica and also found in the southern U.S., this nocturnal and solitary edentate roots in soil with a long muzzle for varied diet of insects, small animals, and plant material.

Caiman (*cocodrilo*): The Spectacled Caiman (*Caiman crocodilus*) is a small crocodilian (to 7 ft) inhabiting fresh water, subsisting mainly on fish. Most active at night (it has bright-red eye shine), it basks by day. It is distinguished from the American crocodile by a sloping brow and smooth back scales.

Coati (*pizote*; *Nasua narica*): This is a long-nose relative of the raccoon, its long tail often held straight up. Lone males or groups of females with young are active during the day, on the ground or in trees. Omnivorous coatis feed on fruit, invertebrates, and small vertebrates.

Cougar (*puma*; *Felis concolor*): Mountain lions are the largest unspotted cats (to 5 ft, with 3½″ tail) in Costa Rica. Widespread but rare, they live in essentially all-wild habitats and feed on vertebrates ranging from snakes to deer.

Crocodile (*lagarto*; *Crocodylus acutus*): The American Crocodile, up to 16 ft in length, is found in most major river systems, particularly the Tempisque and Tárcoles. It seldom attacks humans, preferring fish and birds. It's distinguished from the caiman by a flat head, narrow snout, and spiky scales.

Ctenosaur (*garrobo*; *Ctenosaura similis*): Also known as the Black, or Spiny-tailed Iguana, this is a large (up to 18″ long with 18″ tail), tan lizard with four dark bands on its body and a tail ringed with sharp, curved spines. Terrestrial and arboreal, it sleeps in burrows or tree hollows. It lives along the coast in the dry northwest and in wetter areas farther south.

Dolphin (*delfin*): Several species, including Bottlenose Dolphins (*Tursiops truncatus*), frolic in Costa Rican waters. Often seen off Pacific shores are Spotted Dolphins (*Stenella attenuata*), which are small (up to 6 ft), with pale spots on the posterior half of the body; they often travel in groups of 20 or more and play around vessels and in bow wakes.

Frigatebird (*tijereta del mar*; *Fregata magnificens*): A large, black soaring bird with slender wings and forked tail, this is one of the most effortless and agile fliers in the avian world. More common on the Pacific coast, it doesn't dive or swim but swoops to pluck its food.

Frog (*rana*): Some 120 species of frog exist in Costa Rica; most are nocturnal, except for the Strawberry Poison Dart Frog (*Dendrobates pumilio*) and Green-and-black Poison Dart Frog. The bright coloration of these two species, either red with blue or green hind legs or charcoal black with fluorescent green markings, warns potential predators of their toxicity. The Red-eyed Leaf Frog (*Agalychnis callidryas*) is among the showiest of nocturnal species. The large, brown Marine Toad (*Bufo marinus*), also called Cane Toad or Giant Toad, comes out at night.

Howler Monkey (*mono congo*; *Alouatta palliata*): These dark, chunky-bodied monkeys (to 22″ long with 24″ tail) with black faces travel in troops of up to 20. Lethargic mammals, they eat leaves, fruits, and flowers. The males' deep, resounding howls serve as communication among and between troops.

Iguana (*iguana*): Mostly arboreal but good at swimming, the iguana is Costa Rica's largest lizard: males can grow to 10 ft, including tail. Only young Green Iguanas (*Iguana iguana*) are bright green; adults are much duller, females dark-grayish, and males olive (with orange-ish heads in breeding season). All have round cheek scales and smooth tails.

Jacana (*gallito de agua*; *Jacana spinosa*): These birds are sometimes called "lily trotters" because their long toes allow them to walk on floating vegetation. Feeding on aquatic organisms and plants, they're found in almost any body of water. They expose yellow wing feathers in flight. The "liberated" females lay eggs in several nests tended by different males.

Jaguar (*tigre*; *Panthera onca*): The largest New World feline (to 6 ft, with 2-ft tail), this top-of-the-line predator is exceedingly rare but lives in a wide variety of habitats, from dry forest to cloud forest. It's most common in the vast Amistad Biosphere Reserve.

Jesus Christ Lizard (*gallego*): Flaps of skin on long toes enable this spectacular lizard to run across water. Costa Rica has three species: the Lineated Basilisk (*Basiliscus basiliscus*) on the Pacific side is brown with pale lateral stripe; in the Caribbean, the Emerald Basilisk (*Basiliscus plumifrons*) is marked with turquoise and black on a green body and the Striped Basilisk (*Basiliscus vittatus*), also on the Caribbean side, resembles the lineated basilisk. Adult males grow to 3 ft (mostly tail), with crests on head, back, and base of tail.

Leaf-Cutter Ant (*zompopas*; *Atta* spp.): Found in all lowland habitats, these are the most commonly noticed neotropical ants. Columns of ants carrying bits of leaves twice their size sometimes extend for several hundred yards from an underground nest to plants being harvested. The ants don't eat the leaves; their food is a fungus they cultivate on the leaves.

Macaw (*lapas*): Costa Rica's two species are the Scarlet Macaw (*Ara macao*), on the Pacific side (Osa Peninsula and Carara Biological Reserve), and the severely threatened Great Green Macaw (*Ara ambigua*), on the Caribbean side. These are huge, raucous parrots with long tails; their immense bills are used to rip fruit apart to reach the seeds. They nest in hollow trees and are victimized by pet-trade poachers and deforestation.

Magpie Jay (*urraca*; *Calocitta formosa*): This southern relative of the blue jay, with a long tail and distinctive topknot (crest of forward-curved feathers), is found in the dry northwest. Bold and inquisitive, with amazingly varied vocalizations, these birds travel in noisy groups of four or more.

Margay (*caucel*; *Felis wiedii*): Fairly small, this spotted nocturnal cat (22″ long, with 18″ tail) is similar to the ocelot but has a longer tail and is far more arboreal: mobile ankle joints allow it to climb down trunks headfirst. It eats small vertebrates.

Morpho (*morfo*): Three Costa Rican species of this spectacular large butterfly have a brilliant-blue upper wing surface, one of which, the Blue Morpho (*Morpho peleides*), is common in moister areas; one has an intense ultraviolet upper surface; one is white above and below; and one is brown and white. Adults feed on rotting fallen fruit; they never visit flowers.

Motmot (*pajaro bobo*): These handsome birds of the understory have racket-shaped tails. Nesting in burrows, they sit patiently while scanning for large insect prey or small vertebrates. Costa Rica has six species.

Ocelot (*manigordo*; *Felis pardalis*): Mostly terrestrial, this medium-size spotted cat (33″ long, with 16″ tail) is active night and day, and feeds on rodents and other vertebrates. Forepaws are rather large in relation to the body, hence the local name, which means "fat hand."

Oropéndola (*oropendola*; *Psarocolius* spp.): This crow-size bird in the oriole family has a bright-yellow tail and nests in colonies, in pendulous nests (up to 6 ft long) built by females in isolated trees. Males make an unmistakable, loud, gurgling liquid call. The bird is far more numerous on the Caribbean side.

Parakeet and Parrot (*pericos*, parakeets; *loros*, parrots): There are 15 species in Costa Rica (plus two macaws), all clad in green, most with a splash of a primary color or two on the head or wings. They travel in boisterous flocks, prey on immature seeds, and nest in cavities.

Peccary: Piglike animals with thin legs and thick necks, peccaries travel in small groups (larger where the population is still numerous); root in soil for fruit, seeds, and small creatures; and have a strong musk odor. Costa Rica has two species: the Collared Peccary (*saíno, Tayassu tajacu*) and the White-lipped Peccary (*chancho de monte, Tayassu pecari*). The latter is now nearly extinct.

Pelican (*pelícano*): Large size, a big bill, and a throat pouch make the Brown Pelican (*Pelecanus occidentalis*) unmistakable in coastal areas (it's far more abundant on the Pacific side). Pelicans often fly in V formations and dive for fish.

Quetzal: One of the world's most exquisite birds, the Resplendent Quetzal (*Pharomachrus mocinno*) was revered by the Maya. Glittering green plumage and the male's long tail coverts draw thousands of people to highland cloud forests for sightings from February to April.

Roseate Spoonbill (*garza rosada; Ajaia ajaja*): Pink plumage and a spatulate bill set this wader apart from all other wetland birds; it feeds by swishing its bill back and forth in water while using its feet to stir up bottom-dwelling creatures. Spoonbills are most common around Palo Verde and Caño Negro.

Sea Turtle. *See* Close-Up: Tico Turtles, *in* Chapter 7.

Sloth (*perezoso*): Costa Rica is home to the Brown-throated Three-toed Sloth (*Bradypus variegatus*) and Hoffmann's Two-toed Sloth (*Choloepus hoffmanni*). Both grow to 2 ft, but two-toed (check forelegs) sloths often look bigger due to longer fur and are the only species in the highlands. Sloths are herbivorous, accustomed to a low-energy diet, and well camouflaged.

Spider Monkey (*mono colorado, mono araña*): Lanky and long-tailed, the Black-handed Spider Monkey (*Ateles geoffroyi*) is the largest monkey in Costa Rica (to 24", with 32" tail). Moving in groups of two to four, they eat ripe fruit, leaves, and flowers. Incredible aerialists, they can swing effortlessly through branches using long arms and legs and prehensile tails. Caribbean and southern Pacific populations are dark reddish-brown; northwesterners are blond.

Squirrel Monkey (*mono tití*): The smallest of four Costa Rican monkeys (11", with 15" tail), the Red-backed Squirrel Monkey (*Saimiri oerstedii*) has a distinctive facial pattern (black cap and muzzle, white mask) and gold-orange coloration on its back. The species travels in noisy, active groups of 20 or more, feeding on fruit and insects. Numbers of this endangered species have been estimated between 2,000 and 4,000 individuals. Almost all *Saimiri oerstedii* in Costa Rica are found in Manuel Antonio National Park or in parts of the Osa Peninsula.

Tapir (*danta; Tapirus bairdii*): The largest land mammal in Costa Rica (to 6½ ft), the tapir is something like a small rhinoceros without armor. Adapted to a wide range of habitats, it's nocturnal, seldom seen, but said to defecate and sometimes sleep in water. Tapirs are herbivorous and use their prehensile snouts to harvest vegetation.

Toucan (*tucán, tucancillo*): This bird is familiar to anyone who's seen a box of Froot Loops cereal. The Aracaris is one, a slender toucan with the trademark bill. Keel-billed (*Ramphastos sulfuratus*) and Chestnut-mandibled Toucans (*Ramphastos swainsonii*) are the largest (18" and 22"); they are black with bright-yellow "bibs" and multihued bills. The smaller, stouter Emerald Toucanet (*Aulacorhynchus prasinus*) and Yellow-eared Toucanet (*Selenidera spectabilis*) are aptly named.

Whales (*ballena*): Humpback Whales (*Megaptera novaeanglia*) appear off the Pacific coast between November and February; they migrate from California and as far as Hawaii.

White-Faced Capuchin Monkey (*mono cariblanca; Cebus capuchinus*): Medium-size and omnivorous, this monkey (to 18", with 20" tail) has black fur and a pink face surrounded by a whitish bib. Extremely active foragers, they move singly or in groups of up to 20, examining the environment closely and even coming to the ground.

BOOKS & MOVIES

Books

Inside Costa Rica, by Tom Barry and Silvia Lara (Interhemispheric Resource Center), is an in-depth factual rundown of the country. For an analysis of Costa Rican culture and society, read *The Ticos* (Lynne Rienner Publishers), by Mavis Hiltunen Biesanz et al. David Rains Wallace's *The Quetzal and the Macaw: The Story of Costa Rica's National Parks* (Sierra Club Books) is an entertaining and informative account of Costa Rica's exemplary conservation efforts. *The Costa Rica Reader* (Grove Weidenfeld), by Marc Edelman and Joanne Kenen, is a critical anthology and comparison of traditional and progressive versions of the country's history.

Some of the most popular books on this country feature its rich natural history. *A Guide to the Birds of Costa Rica,* by F. Gary Stiles and Alexander F. Skutch (Cornell), is a first-rate field guide. Alexander Skutch has also written some entertaining chronicles combining natural history, philosophy, and anecdote, among them *A Naturalist in Costa Rica* (University Press of Florida).

The *Costa Rica: Eco-Traveller's Wildlife Guide,* by Les Beletsky (Academic Press), gives an overview of the most common fauna. For an in-depth look at local ecology, read *A Neotropical Companion,* by John Kricher (Princeton University Press); *Tropical Nature,* by Adrian Forsyth and Ken Miyata (Macmillan); or the encyclopedic *Costa Rican Natural History* (University of Chicago Press), compiled by tropical biology expert Daniel Janzen, Ph.D.

Costa Rica has a rich literary tradition, but few of its writers have been translated into English. Those who have can be hard to find in the United States. For insight on local culture, pick up *Costa Rica: A Traveler's Literary Companion,* edited by Barbara Ras (Consortium), a collection of translated short stories by the country's best writers. *Years Like Brief Days* (Dufour Editions) is one of the most popular novels of Fabián Dobles, famous for his humorous depiction of life in rural Costa Rica in the early 20th century. *The Lonely Men's Island* (Editorial Escritores Unidos, Mexico), the first novel of José León Sánchez, recounts the author's years on Isla San Lucas—the Costa Rican version of Alcatraz—where he was sent for stealing a statue of the country's patron saint, La Virgen de los Angeles.

Movies

Jurassic Park (1993) was set on Costa Rica's isolated Cocos Island, but the film was actually shot in Hawaii. Oddly enough, much of the film version of *Congo* (1995), another Michael Crichton novel, was shot in Costa Rica. Most of Ridley Scott's *1492: Conquest of Paradise* (1992) was filmed on Costa Rica's Pacific coast. If you're more interested in the waves that break off that coast, check out the surf classic *The Endless Summer* (1966); both the original and remake have Costa Rica footage. An excellent documentary on underwater life in Costa Rica (as well as in the Galápagos and Australia) is *Wonders of the Deep* (1998; Madacy Entertainment).

VOCABULARY

	English	Spanish	Pronunciation
Basics			
	Yes/no	Sí/no	see/no
	OK	De acuerdo	de a-**kwer**-doe
	Please	Por favor	pore fah-**vore**
	May I?	¿Me permite?	may pair-**mee**-tay
	Thank you (very much)	(Muchas) gracias	(**moo**-chas) **grah**-see-as
	You're welcome	Con mucho gusto	con **moo**-cho **goose**-toe
	Excuse me	Con permiso	con pair-**mee**-so
	Pardon me	¿Perdón?	pair-**dohn**
	Could you tell me?	¿Podría decirme?	po-dree-ah deh-**seer**-meh
	I'm sorry	Disculpe	Dee-**skool**-peh
	Good morning!	¡Buenos días!	**bway**-nohs **dee**-ahs
	Good afternoon!	¡Buenas tardes!	**bway**-nahs **tar**-dess
	Good evening!	¡Buenas noches!	**bway**-nahs **no**-chess
	Goodbye!	¡Adiós!/¡Hasta luego!	ah-dee-**ohss**/ah-stah-**lwe**-go
	Mr./Mrs.	Señor/Señora	sen-**yor**/sen-**yohr**-ah
	Miss	Señorita	sen-yo-**ree**-tah
	Pleased to meet you	Mucho gusto	**moo**-cho **goose**-toe
	How are you?	¿Cómo está usted?	**ko**-mo es-**tah** oo-**sted**
	Very well, thank you.	Muy bien, gracias.	**moo**-ee bee-**en**, **grah**-see-as
	And you?	¿Y usted?	ee oos-**ted**
	Hello (on the telephone)	Diga	**dee**-gah
Days of the Week			
	Sunday	domingo	doe-**meen**-goh
	Monday	lunes	**loo**-ness
	Tuesday	martes	**mahr**-tess
	Wednesday	miércoles	mc-**air**-koh-less
	Thursday	jueves	hoo-**ev**-ess
	Friday	viernes	vee-**air**-ness
	Saturday	sábado	**sah**-bah-doh

Months

January	enero	eh-**neh**-roh
February	febrero	feh-**breh**-roh
March	marzo	**mahr**-soh
April	abril	ah-**breel**
May	mayo	**my**-oh
June	junio	**hoo**-nee-oh
July	julio	**hoo**-lee-yoh
August	agosto	ah-**ghost**-toh
September	septiembre	sep-tee-**em**-breh
October	octubre	oak-**too**-breh
November	noviembre	no-vee-**em**-breh
December	diciembre	dee-see-**em**-breh

Useful Phrases

Do you speak English?	¿Habla usted inglés?	**ah**-blah oos-**ted** in-**glehs**
I don't speak Spanish	No hablo español	no **ah**-bloh es-pahn-**yol**
I don't understand (you)	No entiendo	no en-tee-**en**-doh
I understand (you)	Entiendo	en-tee-**en**-doh
I don't know	No sé	no seh
I am American/ British	Soy americano (americana)/ inglés(a)	soy ah-meh-ree-**kah**-no (ah-meh-ree-**kah**-nah)/ in-**glehs** (**ah**)
What's your name?	¿Cómo se llama usted?	koh-mo seh **yah**-mah oos-**ted**
My name is . . .	Me llamo . . .	may **yah**-moh
What time is it?	¿Qué hora es?	keh **o**-rah es
It is one, two, three . . . o'clock.	Es la una. . . . Son las dos, tres	es la **oo**-nah/sohn lahs dohs, tress
How?	¿Cómo?	**koh**-mo
When?	¿Cuándo?	**kwahn**-doh
This/Next week	Esta semana/ la semana que entra	**es**-teh seh-**mah**-nah/lah seh-**mah**-nah keh **en**-trah
This/Next month	Este mes/el próximo mes	**es**-teh mehs/el **proke**-see-mo mehs
This/Next year	Este año/el año que viene	**es**-teh **ahn**-yo/el **ahn**-yo keh vee-**yen**-ay
Yesterday/today/ tomorrow	Ayer/hoy/mañana	ah-**yehr**/oy/mahn-**yah**-nah
This morning/ afternoon	Esta mañana/ tarde	**es**-tah mahn-**yah**-nah/**tar**-deh
Tonight	Esta noche	**es**-tah **no**-cheh

What?	¿Qué?	keh
What is it?	¿Qué es esto?	keh es es-toh
Why?	¿Por qué?	pore keh
Who?	¿Quién?	kee-yen
Where is . . . ?	¿Dónde está . . . ?	dohn-deh es-tah
the bus stop?	la parada del autobus?	la pah-rah-dah del oh-toh-boos
the post office?	la oficina de correos?	la oh-fcc-see-nah deh koh-reh-os
the museum?	el museo?	el moo-seh-oh
the hospital?	el hospital?	el ohss-pee-tal
the bathroom?	el baño?	el bahn-yoh
Here/there	Aquí/allá	ah-key/ah-yah
Open/closed	Abierto/cerrado	ah-bee-er-toh/ ser-ah-doh
Left/right	Izquierda/derecha	iss-key-er-dah/ dare-eh-chah
Straight ahead	Derecho	dare-eh-choh
Is it near/far?	¿Está cerca/lejos?	es-tah sehr-kah/ leh-hoss
I'd like . . . a room	Quisiera . . . un cuarto/una habitación	kee-see-ehr-ah oon kwahr-toh/ oo-nah ah-bee-tah-see-on
the key	la llave	lah yah-veh
a newspaper	un periódico	oon pehr-ee-oh-dee-koh
a stamp	la estampilla	lah es-stahm-pee-yah
I'd like to buy . . .	Quisiera comprar . . .	kee-see-ehr-ah kohm-prahr
cigarettes	cigarrillos	ce-ga-ree-yohs
a dictionary	un diccionario	oon deek-see-oh-nah-ree-oh
soap	jabón	hah-bohn
suntan lotion	loción bronceadora	loh-see-ohn brohn-seh-ah-do-rah
a map	un mapa	oon mah-pah
a magazine	una revista	oon-ah reh-vess-tah
a postcard	una tarjeta postal	oon-ah tar-het-ah post-ahl
How much is it?	¿Cuánto cuesta?	kwahn-toh kwes-tah
Telephone	Teléfono	tel-ef-oh-no
I am ill	Estoy enfermo(a)	es-toy en-fehr-moh(mah)
Please call a doctor	Por favor llame a un medico	pohr fah-vor ya-meh ah oon med-ee-koh
Help!	¡Auxilio! ¡Ayuda! ¡Socorro!	owk-see-lee-oh/ ah-yoo-dah/ soh-kohr-roh
Fire!	¡Incendio!	en-sen-dee-oo
Caution!/Look out!	¡Cuidado!	kwee-dah-doh

INDEX